THE ART OF ANCIENT GREECE AND ROME

From the Rise of Greece to the Fall of Rome

THE ART

OF ANCIEN

GIOVANNI BECATTI

T GREECE
AND ROME

From the Rise of Greece to the Fall of Rome

PRENTICE-HALL, INC., Englewood Cliffs, N.J.

AND HARRY N. ABRAMS, INC., New York

Translated by John Ross

Contents

THE ART OF
ANCIENT GREECE
AND ROME

From the Rise of Greece to the Fall of Rome

I | From the Decline of the Art of the Mycenaeans to the Beginning of Greek Art in the Geometric Period

Before the birth of Greek art, fully developed civilizations had indeed existed for thousands of years in Mesopotamia, Egypt, and Crete; but from its earliest appearance Greek art quickly rose to dominate the entire Aegean and Mediterranean areas. Its underlying principles — which we call "Classical" — imposed themselves over the whole of the ancient world. While other civilizations, reaching the end of their development, became exhausted, Classical art injected new life into the Italo-Etruscan tradition, spread through the provinces of Alexander's great empire, gave form to the art of Imperial Rome, and remained the vital inheritance and basic premise for all European art.

The singular position of Classical art in the complex historical framework of the arts of the world can be explained by its humanity, its naturalism, and its organic conception.

The arts of the Sumerian, Akkadian, and Babylonian civilizations were closely bound to their religions, and drew their themes from the sacred and symbolic world of gods and monsters. The citizens lived in the service of the gods; the statues of rulers were votive objects, images to be adored by the faithful. As the religion of these peoples declined, so

did their art. Thus, the art of the neo-Assyrian period, which filled the friezes of the royal palaces with symbols of invincible power in the form of military campaigns and hunting expeditions of deceased dynasts, could not but end with the end of the dynasty itself.

Egyptian art followed fixed, immutable guide lines, determined either by the obligatory exaltation of the Pharaoh in his various undertakings, or by the rigid religious beliefs that dictated the scenes decorating tombs, and gave rise to a portrait style aimed at perpetuating life through the faithful reproduction of physical features, which the soul was to recognize. For these reasons Egyptian art remained somewhat cut off from outside influences, developing for thousands of years, yet always maintaining its fundamental characteristics of theme, iconography, and style. Just as the verdant banks of the Nile, narrowing progressively from the breadth of the delta to the rocks of Aswan and Abu Simbel, are separated from neighboring lands by desert wastes, so the art that flourished on the river's banks was largely separated from and insensible to foreign artistic currents. And this was true even though the deserts were constantly crossed by caravans and armies, and the sea was black with ships bound for the delta ports, which offered close contacts successively with Mesopotamian, Minoan, Greek, Hellenistic, and Roman art. Particular significance must therefore be attached to the few rare responses to these artistic influences that can be traced in the compact

This oinochoe *bears some of the typical* *[fig]urative repertory of the later Attic* *[Ge]ometric style: man, horse, deer, and bird.* *[75]0–710 B.C. Berlin, State Museums*

artistic tradition of Egypt. Indeed, we shall see that the creation in Alexandria of a lively Hellenistic center was a phenomenon that remained limited to that one cosmopolitan city, while traditional Egyptian culture was to linger on in its old formulas — by then empty and conventional — until the new Coptic artistic current, based on a totally different spiritual foundation, took shape.

By comparison with the great Mesopotamian, Assyrian, and Egyptian arts that preceded it, Greek art appears as a completely new and independent phenomenon. However, it is closely related to the other great current of the times, Minoan-Mycenaean art, which arose in Crete during the Bronze Age and soon spread through the Greek mainland and along all the shores of the Aegean and even the western Mediterranean. It is, in fact, from an understanding of the nature and limitations of this link that we can grasp the full significance of the beginnings of Classical art.

Minoan-Mycenaean art was an immediate predecessor and a high artistic manifestation that flourished on the very soil of Greece and, at least during the Mycenaean period, was the work of a people speaking a language related to Greek. The deciphering of the Mycenaean *Linear B* script and the recognition of its proto-Greek nature raises once again, and more forcefully than before, the question of whether or not the bases of Classical art can be sought in the art of the Minoans and Mycenaeans. The passage from Mycenaean to Classical artistic culture, by way of sub-Mycenaean and proto-Geometric phases, thus takes on considerable importance, and appears as one of the critical points in the history of humanity.

One would have to study every aspect of the phenomenon in order to draw historical conclusions, but here we must confine ourselves to outlining its artistic side. Apart from the language factor, at present the object of active research, we shall have to bear in mind some essential facts to be evaluated in terms of data yielded by stylistic analysis.

There can be no doubt that during the twelfth century B.C. a profound crisis shook the world that centered around the Aegean Sea: major population movements, the collapse of the Hittite Empire, and the Dorian invasion which, as we can see from the traces of fire and ruin, destroyed many Mycenaean centers. All these events accompanied the decline of Mycenaean civilization, but its disappearance was neither uniform nor simultaneous. While in some cases centers were totally destroyed, others survived intact, and although some regions were occupied by waves of migrants who imposed a new and alien cultural

outlook, in others the prevailing native traditions continued. Persistent late survivals of Mycenaean culture can be traced, particularly in peripheral areas and on the islands, where we find special mixtures and differing reactions. Thus the over-all picture of this change emerges as varied and many sided. Giving greater weight now to one, now to another of the many factors that contributed to this complex phenomenon, many conflicting theories have been proposed. Some explain the transformation in terms of an uninterrupted process, others as a clean break, interpreting the break sometimes in a cultural and spiritual sense, sometimes ethnically.

In the complex historical panorama of ethnic, linguistic, religious, and cultural relationships, art certainly constitutes the factor best suited to initiate us into the sensibility, the taste, the tendencies, characteristics, and ideals of these two civilizations.

Classical art was centered on religion and myth, and it cannot be forgotten that the names of the main deities of the Hellenic Olympus — Zeus, Hera, Athena, Poseidon, Dionysus, Artemis, Themis — have been found in Mycenaean documents. These divine figures, so important to Greek civilization, thus seem to have their roots in Mycenaean culture.

The other great source of inspiration for Greek art, represented by the heroic legends of the Homeric *epos*, is also indirectly connected with the bygone Mycenaean world. The first great poetry created by Greek genius drew its substance from the patrimony of legend taken from the Mycenaean courts, narrating the expedition against Troy. The songs of Mycenaean bards, transmitted orally in the form of antique strophes, survived the destruction of their world. Indeed, between the ninth and eighth centuries B.C., in the Ionian centers which were already deeply marked by Mycenaean influences, they found an organic re-elaboration through the efforts of a new creative spirit which was to be given the name of Homer. The repertory of figured scenes in the seventh century bears witness to a widespread knowledge of Homeric poems on the Greek continent, and a written version was to be completed during the sixth century in the Athens of the Pisistratids. In this way the names, epithets, and adventures of these heroes from a distant past became the living material for the youthful Greek culture, providing an inexhaustible source of artistic inspiration. The *Catalogue of Ships* in the second book of the *Iliad* shows us the vast ranks of these heroes, leaders of entire peoples; Mycenaean armor lives again in the memory of the historical age with the elements — no longer known to the

Greeks — of the boar's-tusk helmet and Ajax's great cowhide shield, protecting the body like a tower; even palace architecture with its *propylon*, *aule*, and *megaron*, buried under centuries of ruin, once more excited the Greek fancy, along with the scintillating wealth of the *polychrysos* Mycenae and its brilliant, luxurious, dynastic world.

When we consider the artistic aspects involved in this change from Mycenaean to Classical culture, the first point of departure for examination can only be Athens, for it was there that an artistic language first manifested itself in highly significant, elevated forms in the proto-Geometric period, thus marking the beginning of a new civilization. Furthermore, unlike Mycenae and the other Mycenaean fortresses, Athens was not destroyed by the Dorian invasion, nor did it languish in a marginal survival culture, as did other centers that escaped ruin. Its Mycenaean flowering may have been rather late and its heroes, such as Menestheus, are of little importance in the Homeric epic. But the strong citadel of Erechtheus, surrounded by the walls of the Pelargikon, accessible only through the complicated entry barred by nine gates, the Enneapylon, escaped the Dorian onslaught. It may have served as a refuge for Mycenaean fugitives from Pylos, as is suggested by the legend of the Neleids, attested by the cult of Neleus and Basile near the Acropolis. Continuous habitation, confirmed by excavations, and a series of finds from the late and sub-Mycenaean, proto-Geometric, and Geometric periods document the various phases of this change. The tombs, with four-sided chambers and *dromos* (entrance), from the late Mycenaean period, on the northernmost slopes of the Acropolis and the Areopagus, are found beside sub-Mycenaean, proto-Geometric, and Geometric tombs of the trench type where the Agora was later to rise. Similarly, we find sub-Mycenaean, proto-Geometric, and Geometric tombs stratified in the necropolis of the Kerameikos. The remains of the *anax* palace, with the two stone disk bases for the wooden columns of the Mycenaean *megaron*, were to disappear in the construction of the new temple, known as the Hekatompedon (name derived from its hundred-foot-long hall). Although the mythical Erechtheus gave way to Athena and Poseidon, he still lived on in the epithet "shaker of the sea," eventually assumed by Poseidon. Mycenaean myths and rites, such as the sacrifice of the bull and the unusual double-ax ceremonies that took place on the Acropolis, survived into the historical period, and the weighty Mycenaean walls continued to defend the citadel of the Archaic era.

The last phase of Mycenaean art showed all the signs of a progressive decline: its rich decorative repertory became impoverished and schematized, increasingly more abstract and linear. All motifs of naturalistic origin were distorted and decomposed into ornamental images, from the octopus with its tentacles treated as thread-like volutes and entwining lines, to the nautilus with its shell and tentacles reduced to a geometrical flourish; birds were no more than decorative networks of plumage, and the bodies of bulls, horses, and deer, inarticulate and inorganic, were transformed into expanses of ornate arabesques and patches of color; floral motifs were transmuted into abstract geometrical diagrams, and the repertory of curvilinear decoration lost its finesse and precision; even the human figure was deprived of its original dynamic tension and elastic curvature of the torso and stiffened into clumsy, angular outlines, with stringy limbs and pinheaded bodies. This degeneration, which was to be found everywhere during the twelfth century B.C., is a sure sign of the exhaustion of an artistic culture. In fact, new elements were never introduced; instead, traditional themes were continually rarefied and simplified. This approach, which leads to disorganized abstraction and geometric schematization, is the symptom not of a growing taste capable of transforming these elements into a new style, but rather of an inexorable separation from the vital energies that had formerly given naturalistic, dynamic form to a fabulous, fascinating world.

In fact, this process developed technically and stylistically toward an even more simplified and impoverished expression, culminating in the sub-Mycenaean period of the eleventh century B.C., which marked the end of this artistic culture of Cretan origin.

1. The Proto-Geometric Style

Pottery is the only form of art to be found in the sub-Mycenaean period. And in this epoch of decline we see that the types of vases, which had numbered over sixty globular forms in the thirteenth century, are by now reduced to ten or so, bearing witness to a profound technical regression, visible too in the quality of the clay and glazes used. Decoration became less and less important, leaving large areas of the vase in the natural light color, and limiting painting to the shoulders or base, where it took the form of irregularly executed freehand, wavy, or straight lines, groups of concentric circles, V-shaped motifs, or other sparse geometrical ornament such as volutes and crosshatched triangles.

2. In Crete, the cradle of Minoan civilizati[on] the proto-Geometric style took on a particul[ar] local accent: on this krater figurative element[s] appear in a heraldic composition. 950–900 B.C. Herakleion, Museum

In Athens the inhumation of the dead practiced in the sub-Mycenaean period gave way to cremation (except for infants, who were still buried), and this change, while it was not linked to ethnic differences, still constitutes a sign of a change in customs and tendencies that is far from unimportant. The proto-Geometric pottery that appeared in Athens at the beginning of the eleventh century and developed throughout the tenth was linked, in some forms, to Mycenaean types, but these had been transformed through a different structural approach. The potters limited themselves to a few basic forms which were clearly defined, organic, and functional. To the fanciful variety of Mycenaean work were contrasted the new, rigorous, typological selection of about fourteen shapes: the amphora with its clearly shaped neck and handles placed on the neck, shoulders,

or belly; the pitcher with its three-lobed mouth; the *lekythos*; the krater; the deep *skyphos* set on a conical foot; the cup on a similar foot with only one handle; the analogous *kantharos* with two handles; and in addition, some secondary forms such as the *kalathos*, the flat dish, the *pyxis*, which is a small covered jar, and the three-footed dish. Mycenaean vases had generous, swelling forms, and continuous, curving outlines; proto-Geometric vases showed a sharp articulation between the various parts of lip, neck, shoulders, body, foot, and handles, with clear-cut, organic divisions. The original globular forms tended toward an ovoid shape that became progressively slimmer.

Decoration, too, showed traditional sub-Mycenaean motifs, but the execution of the individual elements and the syntax according to which they were arranged were different: the

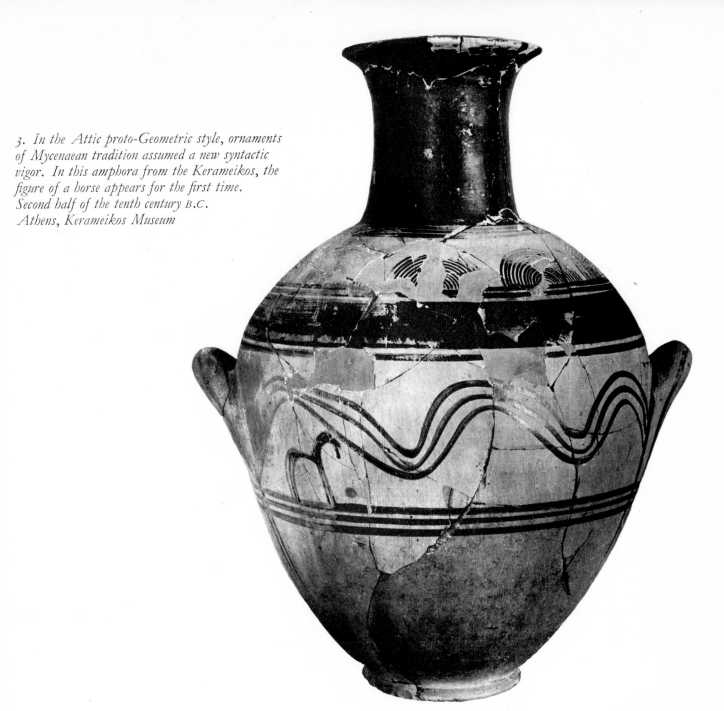

concentric circles and semicircles became perfectly regular and were precisely drawn with a compass; lines and bands were parallel and their breadth was constant. Mycenaean ornament was arranged freely over the entire surface with a certain tendency in the later phase to limit decoration to the faces of the vase. Proto-Geometric ornament, on the other hand, was immediately coordinated in precise arrangements following the structure of the vase in question, whether accenting the lip, the neck, or the foot with a black glaze, using bands of black to distinguish the zones of the neck and body, outlining the handles, or composing the simple decorative motifs in order to underline with concentric semicircles the shoulders of the amphorae and *oinochoai* (jugs). Circles marked the bodies of *oinochoai* and the faces of *skyphoi*, using the geometric repertory of cross-hatch-

ing, checkerboard pattern, rhomboids, and triangles within the precise limits of the upper metopal spaces (the zone running around the vase at the level of the handles). Circular series of rhomboids, dog-tooth patterns, and zigzags were used around the lower parts of the vase.

In the mature phase of proto-Geometric pottery the broad light areas tended progressively to disappear, covered by a black glaze and interrupted only by the decorated zones and narrow groups of parallel bands. The vase acquired a greater preciosity with this gleaming cover, which threw into even greater relief the calligraphic rigor of the ornament set on this monochrome surface. Whereas the first proto-Geometric vases with light grounds could be considered close to the sub-Mycenaean taste, these late black-glazed examples, the conclusive formulation of a style, show a totally different syntactical taste. Circular motifs and wavy lines tended to disappear, while the meander pattern began to assert itself in the transition to the Geometric style; the curvilinear ornament so dear to the Mycenaeans, was replaced by rectilinear motifs, which lie at the very foundation of Greek Geometric syntax.

Athens occupied a place of first importance in the birth of proto-Geometric and Geometric art because of its chronological priority and the spread of its decorative heritage.

Attic proto-Geometric pottery was widely exported and imitated during its mature phase, influencing the production of Boeotia, Phocis, Thessaly, the northern Cyclades, Corinth, Argolis, and in part that of Crete. Indeed, its influence can be seen in the pottery of Assarlik in far-off Caria. Relationships have been traced between the style of Argos and that of the Dodecanese, and it seems also that Corinth exercised an influence on the style of the Ionian islands. But none of these local styles reached the logic and rigor of Attic work. Decoration was limited to pendulous circles in Thessaly, Macedonia, the Cyclades, Cyprus, and the eastern centers, while in Knossos we find persistent Mycenaean forms and ornament, imitations of Athenian work, Cypriot influences, as well as the prevalence of light backgrounds.

A late krater from Crete (fig. 2) shows two goats flanking a vertical ornament, and on the other side, two ships, the whole carried out with stylized but lively forms. It is significant that the first figures represented were those of goats, so typical of Crete and all the island world, where during the Orientalizing period the so-called Wild Goat style developed. As for the ships, they were the basic means of maritime living for the island-dwellers.

On the other hand, in the Athenian proto-Geometric vases the first figure timidly introduced into this decorative style was the horse, the inseparable companion of the warrior in the Hellenic heroic ideal. On the body of an amphora from the Kerameikos (fig. 3), the animal is reduced almost to an ideogram, with long, slender legs and a thick, arched neck, and he is placed below the wavy, decorative lines, which are still inspired by Mycenaean tradition. It is as if the animal had fled to one side, unable to find a place among the continuous distribution of the exclusively geometric ornament that covers the surface of the vase. Only the exceptionally wide neck of a mature amphora from the Kerameikos will allow a later potter to repeat there two small, stylized horses, as if in two metopes divided by a triglyph.

2. The Geometric Style

Attic art developed these rich premises with organic logic and coherency throughout the ninth and eighth centuries B.C., during which time the Geometric style was enriched with new forms and motifs. The structure of the vases became more and more articulated, graceful, and harmonious, and alongside a variety of small forms we find the larger amphorae and kraters. These sometimes reached a height of five feet and were used as markers on the tombs of the cremated, just like true funerary monuments. They attest to the technical skill of Athenian potters and the refined taste of the pottery painters.

This more mature decorative sense progressively broke up the severe chromatic unity of the simple black glaze with increasingly numerous bands of decoration, in which the various forms of hatched meander (fret or key pattern) spread and dominated and, by comparison with the other traditional motifs, became the favorite and most typical expression of this Geometric language. In the mature phase of the style, the entire surface of the vase became an uninterrupted succession of decorative bands, rhythmically encompassing the architecture of the form, filled with chains of rhomboids, meanders, zigzags, dog-tooth patterns, and dots. In the major zones on the shoulder and neck we find inset panels and frieze-like compositions filled with checkerboard patterns, cross-hatching, swastikas, circles and wheels, geometric and striated quatrefoil rosettes, and meander elements, assembled in a compact, rigorous composition, in which can be detected an inspiration from the art of weaving, and which is the fruit of the austere concentration of the Greek spirit.

The growing importance of ornament led to its enrichment with figurative images, and in the Attic style known as the Dipylon style, after the principal necropolis of the Kerameikos outside the Dipylon (double gate), the first figures used were the man and horse, which appeared in the first half of the eighth century B.C. Toward the middle of the century this style reached its full expression, exemplified in the imposing funerary amphora decorated with the *prothesis* (lying-in-state of the dead). This vase (fig. 4) is the work of the head of a school, a master known as the Dipylon Painter, to whom are attributed ten or so other vases, amphorae, kraters, and *oinochoai*.

This style marked a whole series of contemporary works, so closely linked by a similar taste that we can talk of a Dipylon style, which developed during the second half of the eighth century. In this corpus of about a thousand vases it is possible to distinguish different hands among the vase painters, to assign some groups of work to specific workshops, and to group together vases with a typical, prevalent decorative motif. But more significant than the differences is the substantial stylistic unity of the whole series, which is characterized by a sense of controlled discipline, and absolute adherence to the canons of the geometric approach applied to a very elevated artistic craft.

We can recognize five large kraters as the work of one man, known as the Kunze Painter, very close to the Dipylon Painter in tone and quality. A group of amphorae is also closely linked to the Dipylon Workshop. A series of *oinochoai* from this circle is grouped together because of the common features of striations of the body and a grazing deer on the neck. In addition, a group of vases show a characteristic motif of four broad bands of lozenge shapes filled alternately with cross-hatching and minute lozenges, inspired by textile work and imitated in other workshops, so that some authors refer these works to the so-called "Tapestry Hand." A series of five kraters from one workshop, known as the Villard series, shows horses with long bodies, full cheeks, and broad muzzles, drawing chariots adorned with sigma motifs or cross-hatching. Another group, referred to as the Hirschfeld series, shows oval-headed horses, wheels completely detached from the chariots, figures with legs set very wide apart, and beak-like heads with a dot for the eye.

The prevailing funerary function dictated the themes of *prothesis*; the transportation of the dead man on a chariot; processions of chariots and horsemen accompanying the funeral cortege; or contests and duels recalling war, the source of death. War and death are further evoked in scenes of naval battles and shipwrecks, observed with lively attentiveness in the precise structure of the vessels, in the tense efforts of the rowers, in the layers of floating corpses, and the confusion of survivors swimming away from the wrecks. On an *oinochoe* of the mature period, now in Munich (fig. 5), the shipwreck scene seems to assume epic stature, dominated by one survivor who could almost be Odysseus sitting astride the capsized boat.

Funerary scenes, with their solemn tone, seem conceived as heroic elevations of the deceased in the spirit of the *epos*, and treated with a conscious archaizing in order to project these processions of warriors into the distant, fabled world of Homer.

Only in this way can we explain the shield, drawn by the Dipylon painters: an absurd and abstract outline like a double ax with a thin stroke joining the two half-moons. It is definitely not a real, contemporary shield, but one which, in the minds of these distant descendants in the Geometric period, was intended to evoke the great Mycenaean figure-eight shield, with its sharp lateral outlines calculated to facilitate the handling of the spear and sword. Moreover, it is conveyed in an exaggerated, symbolic geometrical formulation which is radically different from the functional structure of the Boeotian two-lobed shield. This Mycenaean-inspired shield tended to disappear on vases at the end of the eighth century, and was replaced by the then actually existing round shield. This fact indicates the growing affirmation and development of the Greek spirit.

In the world of the *epos* even the Siamese twins, called Actoriones or Moliones, who had defeated Nestor in the chariot race during the funerary games of Amarynceus and who had appeared with Augeas, as the adversaries of Heracles, seem to have appealed to the fantastic sense of the Dipylon painters. This unusual group can be recognized with certainty in the two warriors with bodies joined behind a single shield, which significantly takes on a rectangular form, the better to cover this strange fusion of two torsos. They appear in scenes of chariot-driving and combats that have no precise reference to Homer, and constitute only a motif evoking a heroic atmosphere.

Considering the fundamental role played by the *epos* in Greek culture during this period, it is tempting to assume that the Theban krater in London, dating from the end of the eighth century B.C., which depicts a hero and a woman about to step aboard a long ship well supplied with rowers (symbolizing a long journey) was intended as an allusion to the departure of Helen with Paris, rather than to Theseus and Ariadne, whose adventures came into favor only later, or to the general themes of abduction or departing warrior. The crown the woman carries in her hand seems a worthy attribute of Helen's legendary beauty.

These figurative panels are set into the compact texture of ornament according to a rigid order that stretches the scenes of funerary ceremonies into broader panels on the shoulders of the vase, and underlines the roundness of the container with continuous processions of chariots and soldiers. Similarly, on the necks of amphorae and *hydriai* (water jars) or the bodies of *oinochoai* there is the cadenced chain of the *choros*, composed of male and female figures that move forward, dancing and holding each other by the hand, in a composed, circular rhythm. The human figure is treated as a solid black silhouette, reduced to a schematized, abstract type that does away with drapery and renders the torso as a triangle to which are attached the stick-like arms bent at right angles to hold reins, spears, oars, or musical instruments, or to beat heads and tear hair in attitudes of collective mourning. Legs are shown in profile, attached to the lowest point of the triangle, as to a wasp-waist. Heads are either dark spots with the occasional pointed excrescence for nose or chin, or surmounted with helmet plumes, as in the case of warriors, who are often entirely covered by their great shields with inward-curving sides, out from which come their arms and legs. An absolute symmetry arranges these figures around the deathbed or funeral chariot, marshals the processions and the dances with perfectly regular alignment of the heads, and builds up the composition mainly from horizontal and vertical lines. The various elements from the ornamental repertory — spoked disks, zigzags, rhomboids, and hourglass shapes — fill all the empty space left between the figures. Like a connective tissue they link them to the decorative context, so that the schematization of the images themselves, the geometrical syntax, the pattern that fills in the surplus space, all give to these scenes a compact, abstract, geometrical scansion, which merges organically with the thickly packed ornamental complex. Without disturbing its unity, this gives richness and life to the whole composition.

In addition to horses, we also find birds, most often composed of sinuous segments in an erect, stylized pose, arranged in tightly packed rows of Corinthian inspiration, and having the abstract quality of geometrical ornament. The Dipylon Painter had a predilection for bands with processions of deer and goats shown either grazing or lying down and looking backward (fig. 4). Reduced to elegant ciphers in a geometrical sequence that destroys any illustrative or naturalistic quality, they are assimilated in the general ornamental treatment. These animals represent the first acceptance of Oriental motifs by the Athenian world; the softer forms of their distant models were however not merely copied, but actively transformed into structures that were pared down to their essentials, so as to harmonize with the geometrical decoration on painted vases, on the diadems of thin embossed sheets of gold that bound the brows of the dead during funeral ceremonies and were then deposited in the tomb (fig. 6), or on the thin sheets of gold covering the wooden caskets that held the ashes. After Mycenaean luxury, followed by the poorness of the sub-Mycenaean

4. *Funerary amphora, masterpiece of the Dipylon Painter, with* *of the* prothesis *harmoniously set into the rigorous calligraphic s* *of the Geometric style.* Circa 750 B.C. *Athens, National Muse*

and proto-Geometric periods, gold appears once more in richer funerary decorations that bear witness to the economic resurgence of Athens. From the East, too, came the lion, which was often shown striking down and devouring a timid, helpless deer, or sometimes a man, in an allegorical, symbolic scene which often appears on funerary diadems and painted vases.

In the last quarter of the eighth century, in the most mature phase of the Geometric style, the lion appears in a crouching position, with a tight-waisted, hourglass-shaped body, as seen on vases by the so-called Lion Painter.

16

Birds become less stylized, and are used as isolated motifs in friezes or in antithetical arrangements, as was the figure of the swan with its striated body that characterized, among other works, the *olpai* (pitchers) of the so-called Swan Workshop. A bird motif widely used in approximately forty vases that are grouped as products of the Birdseed Workshop is composed of lines of water birds connected by oblique rows of dots. Grazing horses and running dogs with pointed muzzles become more widespread. We find the first appearance

exhibits a sampling of this later Geometric figurative repertory.

But the Dipylon style had its logical, rigorous foundation in geometrical abstraction, in *akribeia* (precision) and the calligraphic approach, which could not be discarded without destroying the style. These products of the painters of the late eighth century, of the Philadelphia Painter and the Workshop of Athens 894 (so called after the catalogue number of a particular vase in the Athens National Museum), show a slackening of the wonderful

5. The Attic Geometric style assumes a narrative and epic tone in this shipwreck scene from an oinochoe. *Circa 725 B.C. Munich, Antikensammlungen*

of the centaur, whose front legs are human, also appearing on golden diadems. Human figures become more solid, exhibiting more articulated outlines in their limbs; heads are more detailed, with flowing streaks of hair and eyes that stand out against the light ground color of the vase; women's skirts are outlined on the light ground and filled in with stripes or cross-hatching. At this time the charioteer appears, clad in a long chiton. Amphorae and *hydriai* are enriched with a plastic serpentine decoration around the neck, on the lip, shoulders, and handles. Colorplate, figure 1,

stylistic cohesion of the middle of the eighth century: the *prothesis* scenes are reduced to abbreviated, discomposed vignettes; the chariot races become confused; the processions of warriors with round shields, sometimes decorated with *episemata* (insignia) painted in white, now become heavy; the chorus of draped women becomes ostentatious and untidy. The running, cursive style that characterizes these late works in the iconographic tradition of the Dipylon painters represents a crisis symptomatic of an impatience with the severe rules of the Geometric style. It also indicates the need

17

for renewal, for new expressive and narrative experiments, accomplished by breaking up the abstract black silhouette with elements left in outline on the light ground. This permitted the use of additional details, giving individual bodily presence to the figures and making possible the introduction of new themes.

The attempts at perspective in the traditional quadriga, by progressively diminishing the proportions of the horses' necks, seen on an amphora in the Carlsberg Glyptothek, seem naïve, while the newly full-bodied grazing horses, with their stiff, bristling, comb-like manes, appear clumsy and badly articulated. The bold rearing of a prancing horse held by a warrior on the conical base of an urn from the Workshop of Athens 810 is nonetheless a daring, original infraction of one of the canons of the Geometric style, and a decisive leap forward toward the new expressive world that was to be laid open at the end of the century under the influence of the East.

During the Geometric phase of the eighth century there was still no monumental architecture, no statuary. The small sculptures of a votive or funerary nature were limited, significantly enough, to images of men, mostly shown as warriors with spears and helmets, and to horses. In the series of small, solid-cast bronzes the male figure developed slowly from

legs and the arched neck on which the mane was later indicated, and with a very slim, tubular body, in a stylized but expressive conception corresponding to that favored by vase painters (fig. 8). Modeled in clay and then painted, it also formed the knob on the lids of *pyxides* and handles of vases.

In this eighth-century, small-scale plastic work, Oriental influences are responsible for the type of the ivory statuette of a naked goddess found in the Dipylon tombs, which takes the form of a stiff idol, her arms pinned to her sides, but with fuller, rounded modeling in the body (fig. 9). The large oval face is crowned with the *polos* (high, cylindrical headdress) decorated with the Geometric meander motif, while the twisted braids of hair flowing down to the shoulders are stylized into fish-spine forms.

From the extreme decadence and collapse of the artistic world of the Mycenaeans, through the proto-Geometric remodeling of certain sub-Mycenaean decorative elements, a concentration of new vital energies had given rise to this Greek Geometric style, which, with its rectilinear, rigorous, controlled, intellectualized, abstract, stylizing taste, was completely opposed to the disorganized, impressionistic, curvilinear, decorative inheritance of the Mycenaeans. The new style represented the solid basis on which Classical art was to be built.

6. *The meander pattern, deer, and lions, which appear on vases, were also embossed on gold diadems found in the Dipylon graves. Second half of the eighth century* B.C. *Paris, Louvre*

a stylized, stick-like, unorganic structure into a more articulated, though still spindly, modeled form (fig. 7). A certain rhythmic vivacity appears in the right arm, which was raised to grasp the spear, while the left was bent to hold the shield (both these implements are usually missing). A similar animation marks the twisted heads and outstretched arms of other figures that were fixed to either side of the rim of bronze caldrons, where they held the tall, ring-shaped handles, decorated with geometrical motifs and sometimes crowned with a small horse nailed on by the hooves. The horse reappeared with the long, slender

It was the art of the new *polis*, born from the ruins of the Mycenaean dynastic citadels.

Athens, which did not waste its energies in colonial expansion, developed as a unit and reached a very high level of expression, so that Attic Geometric vases were imitated and exported throughout the Aegean as far as Cyprus.

In this period, Corinth, the center of a vast network of trade routes, was economically more active than Athens, and Corinthian Geometric pottery spread everywhere from Syria to Etruria, and was also widely imitated. Technically refined and marked by a sure

graphic sense, its decoration was mnch more sober and simple than that found on Attic work; the surface of the vase was covered with numerous very slender parallel lines, setting off the shoulders by a linear frieze ornament of zigzags or vertical strokes (fig. 10). Unlike Athenian potters, the Corinthians preferred small forms, among which the characteristic *kotyle*, a small *skyphos*, universally exported and imitated, was the dominant form.

Although Corinthian pottery imposed itself by virtue of its technical quality and its elegant simplicity, no other Greek center reached the same high level of decorative richness as Athens. Argive geometrical pottery, with large panels, diagonal meanders, horses, and fish, was heavier and less correct; Laconian work showed human figures, quatrefoils, birds, and checkerboard patterns with Argive and Corinthian influences; Boeotian pottery with human figures was coarsely drawn and its composition tended to be confused; Cycladic decoration was limited to concentric circles and rings of dots; Rhodes used only triangles, circles, hooked squares, and hatching; in Samos scenes of funeral lamentation were attempted; and Cretan pottery appeared less pure and organic, due to survivals of Mycenaean tradition and Oriental influences.

In more distant environments we find original elements in the Phrygian Geometric style practiced in Alisar, Boghazöy, Konya, Masat, and Malatya, with kraters on which animal figures in the Oriental vein — deer and goats and, more rarely, horses, fish, and birds — underwent a typical angular stylization with feet rendered as oblique segments in representations of movement. Bristling trees were set in a geometrical repertory of small circles, and later, in the phase of transition to the Orientalizing style, meanders and cross-hatched triangles, which seem to echo the far-removed motifs of the Greek Geometric style (fig. 12).

3. The Italic Geometric Style

In Italy, in the Iron Age cultures of the Villanovans and of Latium, biconical and hut-shaped clay ossuaries, *ollae*, and *askoi* show an engraved Geometric decorative repertory of dog-tooth, herringbone, and zigzag designs,

7. In the small bronzes of the Geometric period, organic form was progressively developed in figures of warriors, such as this one from the Acropolis. Second half of the eighth century B.C. Athens, National Museum

8. *The figures of horses in bronze or clay, such as this one from the Kerameikos, are analogous in form to those painted on Geometric vases. Second half of the eighth century* B.C. *Athens, Kerameikos Museum*

and later, meanders and swastikas, proving the common possession of elements of the various components of Geometric style, which were indeed characteristically expressed even in the Balkan area. Although the Italic Geometric style lacked Greek rigor, a happy inspiration, characteristic of the native spirit, showed itself in the structure of the hut, the modeling of the *askoi* in the form of animals, the little human figurines used as idols or vase decorations, and in the bronze work of the various types of fibulae, belt buckles, helmets, and capricious, stylized vase handles.

Painted pottery began in this area in the mature phase of the Greek Geometric style, when the Hellenic colonizing movement was established in Sicily and Magna Graecia, and commercial contacts between Etruria and Greece became closer. A few rare fragments of Athenian Geometric pottery have been found in Syracuse and an *oinochoe* decorated with the running-dog pattern analogous to that on Athenian vases has been found in the necropolis of Canale, but Corinthian pottery was far more widespread. There are many evident influences from the Cyclades, Rhodes, and Cyprus, but it is difficult to establish precise classifications because Italic Geometric work remains

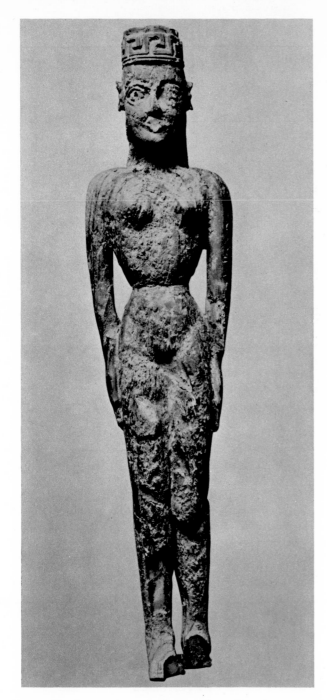

9. The Oriental motif of the nude goddess was taken up according to an Attic Geometric conception in this ivory statuette from the Dipylon. Second half of the eighth century B.C. Athens, National Museum

on a modest level, uncultivated and provincial. On amphorae, kraters, and pitchers in Sicily we find a poor repertory of straight and wavy lines, circles, meanders, and zigzags, and even a few examples of metopal compositions. In southern Italy amphorae and pitchers show possible Athenian and Cycladic influences with dots linked by dashes, crouching deer, quatrefoil and rhomboidal motifs, and metopal panels. Etruria has left a series of Geometric amphorae from Vulci, footed kraters, footless and footed cups, cask-shaped vases along Cypriot lines, and at Bisenzio, characteristic *askoi* with birds, based on the Cypriot model. A sort of sub-

Geometric *koine*, or common language, runs through the pottery of Tarquinia, Vulci, Sovana, Chiusi, Bisenzio, and Vetralla.

Simplicity and roughness set this Italic painted pottery well apart from the corresponding Athenian and Corinthian work. Even the exceptional *olla* from Bucacce near Bolsena (fig. 11), with its more symmetrical composition, reveals in its female chorus the childish stylization of hourglass figures which seem to have been cut out in paper-doll fashion, an expression far removed from the cadenced, articulated, dancing figures of the Dipylon style. In some late products, such as the

21

10. The theme of the ship, on this Corinthian Geometric krater from Thebes, assumes an extreme elongation by extending the vessel as a frieze between the two handles of the vase. Second half of the eighth century B.C. Toronto, Royal Ontario Museum

curious painted clay sphere from Sala Consilina (fig. 13), an unusual, ingenuous effect is obtained in an attempt to animate these fully geometric figures with gesticulating movements.

This Geometric decoration persisted in Italy during the seventh and even the sixth centuries, and we shall see how, in particular areas, for instance in Apulia, a peculiar Geometric style, free from figurative elements, was to develop and remain until the Hellenistic period. Corinthian Geometric was also imitated for a long time in the so-called Italo-Geometric production, and its simple repertory sufficed

to satisfy the modest local artisans' needs.

The particular position of Ischia, the ancient Pithecusae, colonized by the Chalcidians, perhaps even before Cumae, can explain the diverse character shown by some late Geometric vases from the end of the eighth century. It is significant to find there a locally produced krater with a shipwreck scene (fig. 14), similar to Attic Geometric scenes, but revived by a narrative and dramatic animation, in the victims swallowed up by fish, that is closer to the spirit of Corinth.

In Italy, while the Etruscans were acquiring an identity of their own and emerging as the

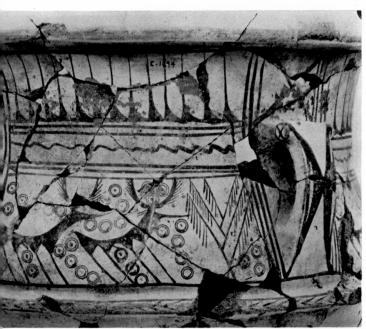

11. The rather infantile paper-doll forms of
the female chorus and the garish ornament on this
olla *from Bucacce characterize the Italic style.
Beginning of the seventh century* B.C.
Florence, Archaeological Museum

12. Among the peripheral Geometric styles, peculiar
decorative aspects are presented by Phrygian pottery,
as in this vase from Alisar.
Middle of the eighth century B.C. *Ankara, Museum*

13. *A curious attempt at a gesticulating movement within the Geometric idiom is seen in this clay sphere from Sala Consilina, showing fighters and referee in the ring. Second half of the sixth century* B.C. *Certosa di Padula, Museum*

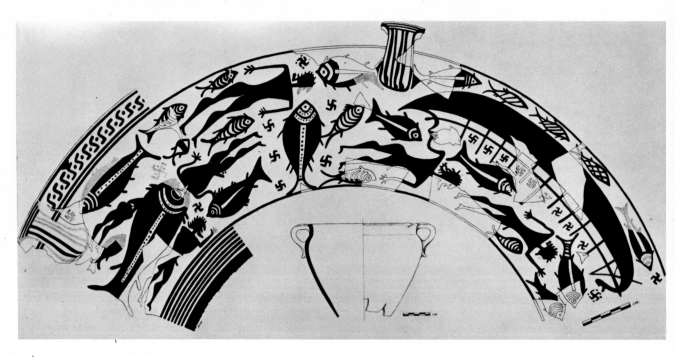

14. *In the Hellenizing community of Ischia, the shipwreck theme of the Geometric style is revived with dramatic vivacity on this krater. End of the eighth century* B.C. *Ischia, Museum*

most lively cultural force in the peninsula, the founding of Rome toward the middle of the eighth century marked a historical event that was later to have fundamentally important consequences for the whole Classical world.

Varronian tradition fixes the founding of Rome on the Palatine hill, in a commanding position overlooking the Tiber, around 754–753 B.C., and excavations reveal that it was a simple shepherds' settlement, part of the first Iron Age civilization of Latium. "Divine wisdom," says Vitruvius, "placed the city of Rome in an outstanding and temperate region

so that the Roman people could conquer and rule over the world." But although Roman power was not long in developing, Roman art was to appear only with the decline of Greek art. While the illustrious *polis* of the Athenians, along with the Dipylon Painter, was carrying the Geometric style to its zenith, the Roman village of huts, and the cemetery in the valley below where the Forum was later to rise, yielded only pottery with a little sparsely engraved geometrical decoration, and simple fibulae, remaining within the limits of a modest local craft.

II | The Orientalizing Trend and Its Diffusion

During the last decades of the eighth century B.C., there was an intensification of contact with the East. Phoenician traders, after the fall of the Mycenaeans, dominated many trade routes and played a major role in linking East and West. It was they who introduced the alphabet into Greece. The Greeks themselves were settling in Al-Mina, at the mouth of the Orontes in Syria, while the traffic along the caravan routes made its final stops at the Greek cities on the coast of Anatolia. The general colonial expansion of Greece continually increased exchange and influence over an area that stretched from the Black Sea to the Nile Delta, Sicily, and Magna Graecia.

1. Proto-Corinthian Miniaturism

Rather than Athens, which was enclosed in its own secure, prosperous world, at this historical moment Corinth was the city that made its way into this commercial network with its ceramic production, which reached the highest level in technique and style, and was adopted everywhere.

Already toward the middle of the eighth century, Corinthian Geometric vases — such as the characteristic *kotyle* — soberly decorated with a sure calligraphic taste, scored with innumerable parallel lines, simpler, but also more refined and elegant than Athenian work, were to be found everywhere from Syria to Etruria, and were widely imitated. Between 725 and 700 B.C., Corinth dominated the market with its proto-Corinthian production, exporting *oinochoai* and the typical round *aryballoi*, which during the seventh century bore decoration composed of radial motifs around the base: birds, chickens, grazing deer, fish, winged horses, rosettes, ribbons, volutes, and palmettes. At the beginning of the seventh century, figures in full silhouette were introduced, executed in solid black retouched in purple, then in white, with incised lines to indicate details. During the first half of the seventh century, the middle proto-Corinthian style was enriched with an interlaced ornament, lotus flowers, palmettes, and elegantly interwoven volutes, buds, and tendrils (as in the group of vases from Cumae), and dotted rosettes on stems. Animals appeared more frequently and in greater variety, and included the stag, the goat, the lion — first in the square-headed Hittite type, then in the long-maned Assyrian version — scenes of dog races, and hunting scenes with lions, hares, and boars, favored by the Aetos Painter.

Floral ornament and animal friezes were well suited to the decorative requirements of these little vases made for export, which reached an outstanding level of sureness and refinement in their technique and composition. On the other hand, the first attempts at a narrative style were less organic, more ingenuous, as in the suicide of Ajax, the rape of Helen, and the centauromachy of the Ajax Painter. The Bellerophon Painter, however, treated the myth of Bellerophon and the Chimaera with vigorous drawing, elegant line, accurate incising, and lively color. At this time, also, were introduced the battle scenes with duels and opposing ranks of infantrymen, and with processions of horsemen, which developed toward the middle of the seventh century, culminating in the masterpiece of this theme, the famous Chigi vase (colorplate, fig. 15) by the so-called Chigi Painter, who was active between 650 and 630 B.C. In this *olpe* the painter took the refined elegance of the miniaturist style and added a very lively narrative spirit both ingenious and dynamic, and further sustained by the rich, precious polychromy that distinguishes a certain group of works from the most mature and important phase of the middle proto-Corinthian period.

It is indeed a very fine polychrome style, playing on flesh-pinks, orange, black, crimson, and white, with a pictorial sense that was probably inspired by the full-scale paintings of contemporary Corinthian masters. It is by no means insignificant that Corinth is classed with Sicyon as the cradle of the earliest painting, which was done in outlined silhouette, and according to the tradition recorded by Pliny, was "invented" by the Corinthian Kleanthes, or else by the Egyptian Philokles, which perhaps suggests contacts with ancient Egyptian painting transmitted through the Greek port of Naucratis in Egypt. Arideikes, another Corinthian, and Telephanes of Sicyon supposedly added linear details within the silhouette, corresponding to the incisions on pottery. And finally a Corinthian, Ekphantos, was the first to introduce color, using ground potsherds, equivalent to the pinks of flesh tones in vase painting.

New weapons and the introduction of the phalanx seem to have inspired these Corinthian painters to breathe intense life into the vigorous, muscular little figures of infantrymen. The older, heavy, archaic shields which hung from the belt were discarded. These were replaced with the new, round ones, which the vase painters obviously enjoyed decorating, tirelessly searching for new emblematic motifs for their external ornament and their internal geometrical structure. They were all lovingly painted with overlapping forms so as to suggest the depth of formations of men.

Corinthian taste was refined and miniaturistic, vivid and calligraphic, and the elaborate little perfume vases which were modeled into a variety of animal forms and human heads and enlivened with painting are little masterpieces of clay-modeling.

2.   The Grandiose Proto-Attic Style

Athenian work exhibited a tendency opposed to the Corinthian. The Attic style aimed at the grandiose and monumental and the severe effect of a black glaze, and the Athenians persevered and developed along those lines during the period of Oriental influence in the seventh century. Attic vases may have been less attractive in appearance than Corinthian work, and few were exported, since they were predominantly destined for funerary use. Yet, Athens' very fidelity to its own ideals, the tenacious and constant elaboration of its own themes, and the organic development of a style using black figures, laid the solid foundation for the Classical flowering that was to give Attic art its uncontested primacy.

The forms of these vases kept their large dimensions. Amphorae with very elongated bodies tended to swell out into ovoidal shapes like *hydriai*, and the most noteworthy pieces reached over 3 feet in height. Kraters also were grandiose, with their deep, elongated, semiovoidal bodies placed on a tall conical foot in imitation of metalwork, like the bronze caldrons with large disk-handles and tall stands. The stands were at times decorated with openwork, which was also to be found in the diaphragms that connected the long handles to the necks of large monumental amphorae (fig. 16). These long handles were still decorated with modeled serpents in the first phase of the proto-Attic style. Naturally, the output was not limited to these larger vases, but also included *oinochoai*, *kantharoi*, *pyxides*, cups, and other minor forms.

Whereas the bands of thick geometrical ornament faithfully followed the clear-cut articulation of the vase, the broad, unbroken surfaces of the large-scale ovoid pots offered a more generous field for complicated scenes and figured panels, paralleling the development of a narrative and mythological pictorial language. The surface of the vase was still viewed as a unit, and the break between the various parts was reduced by the development of a more continuous profile. A broad, figured zone was thus created on amphorae and *hydriai*, covering the entire wider part of the body of the vessel, while another minor frieze appeared on the neck in the form of a metope, with only a secondary zone on the shoulders, quite unlike the Cycladic treatment, which gave greater prominence to the shoulder zone. Similarly, a broad, figured frieze was developed on the bodies of kraters.

At the end of the eighth century and the beginning of the seventh the personalities of a few innovating vase painters emerged beside the late and by now careless practitioners of the Dipylon style. They modified existing techniques with the more generous use of drawing on the unpainted ground, as opposed to forms created of a solid black silhouette. They also timidly introduced incised details inside the black silhouette, and used white and

15. The Chigi vase, masterpiece of the proto-Corinthian style. Mid-seventh century B Rome, Villa Giulia

26

16. On this amphora from Mykonos, with relief decoration and openwork, the lively narrative spirit of the Orientalizing period can be seen in a colorful rendering of the story of the Trojan horse. Circa 670–660 B.C. Mykonos, Museum

sometimes red pigments. They adopted new themes and ornamental motifs under the stimulus of Orientalizing influences, thus opening a stylistic phase rich in new developments.

A key figure was the Analatos Painter, who gave new life to traditional funerary themes and pioneered the use of floral decoration — stylized into palmettes outlined on the unpainted ground and filled with dots, curvilinear leaves, and lyre-shaped tendrils — alongside the increasingly limited repertory of the rectilinear Geometric style. The heads of his human figures, his sharp-nosed sphinxes, and his full-bodied lions are in part sketched directly on the pale ground rather than appearing in solid silhouette; his horses' manes are no longer bristly combs, but are either drawn in groups of semicircular curls, as on the krater seen in figure 17, or straightforwardly engraved in flowing waves on the necks of the horses on the amphora in the Louvre.

The contemporary Mesogheia Painter richly

developed the theme of the sphinx. A new interest in drapery is to be seen in the work of the Passas Painter, who draws solemn warriors on parade, in stole-like mantles decorated with tassels and braid (fig. 18). On funerary kraters he contrives to evoke the macabre battlefield strewn with unburied corpses, and shows whole regiments of starving dogs with tongues hanging out — sometimes with their ribs deeply etched to accentuate their thinness — while waiting vultures, sketched in with effortless effectiveness, wheel overhead, like symbols of some revolting death-banquet. The cock, which appears on vases by the Passas Painter, reappears, with the dogs, in a London *oinochoe* attributed to the "N" Painter (who takes his name from his characteristic fill-in motif), and presents a lively physical presence, very different from the earlier, mannered proto-Corinthian versions. The lion that stalks and seizes the timid little deer takes on a fable-like quality in the images of the "N"

The outlining of the heads on the light ground, the new solidity of forms, and the dotted palmettes on this krater by the
alatos Painter, all announce the beginnings of the proto-Attic style. Circa 690 B.C. Munich, Antikensammlungen

Painter. The lion became the dominating motif in the middle proto-Attic period, acquiring structural solidity and vigor, and rich detailing on the muzzle and outlined mane in the vivid works of the Checkerboard Painter. This painter also had a weakness for full-bodied water birds, bullocks, and spotted deer. The theme of the lion culminated toward the middle of the century in the lion masks drawn by the Ram Jug Painter.

Besides the world of animals and monsters, proto-Attic painters also turned to myth, showing themselves masters of a narrative language that articulated the figures in solid, monumental forms. An epic content may have been intended in the traditional fighting scenes, which now became series of duels with groups of antagonists drawn up face to face in loose, angular rhythms. The whole design was accented with a white pigment, and the widespread use of this technique was to lead to the development of a black-and-white style in

this middle proto-Attic period. It was from the *epos* that vase painters drew the inspiration for their first mythological subjects. In the amphora in the Schliemann Collection in Athens, the Checkerboard Painter shows the famous farewell of Hector and Andromache, with the hero in his chariot and his wife holding out their infant son. The highly dramatic episode of the blinding of Polyphemus in the ninth book of the *Odyssey* is relived in monumental pictorial form around the neck of a large amphora from Eleusis by the so-called Polyphemus Painter (fig. 19), the most important artistic personality of the mid-seventh century. The rich, dramatic, and fabulous content of the myth of the Cyclops Polyphemus attracted and excited the archaic sense of the fantastic, giving life to other contemporary versions by an Argive painter and by the Siceliot Aristonothos or Aristono-phos, in the lively krater found at Cerveteri, in the Museo dei Conservatori in Rome. The

29

18. In the still abstract, geometric style of this early proto-Attic amphora, the Passas Painter introduces the peculiar representation of richly decorated mantles. Circa 700 B.C. New York, Metropolitan Museum

originality of the Polyphemus Painter is shown again in his treatment of the beheading of the Medusa and the pursuit of Perseus by the Gorgons on the same amphora from Eleusis, the latter scene with a fantastic caldron-shaped gorgon mask, which is independent of the type created by Corinthian vase painters that was to impose itself universally by virtue of its high decorative quality and its compositional logic. The use of diluted glazes to render anatomical details and the superimposed white pigment confer a new plastic nature on the figures, but they still remain unorganic, with spindly arms and stiff, decorated costumes.

Another episode that interests these artists,

no doubt because of its dramatic content and pathos, is the slaying of Nessus by Heracles, in revenge for the centaur's violence in carrying off his wife, Deianira, across the river Euenus. The two versions of the killing, with bow and arrow or with a club, which were to live again in Bacchylides' dithyrambs, were apparently already known to the painter of a stand in the Argos Heraion and to the master of the imposing amphora in New York, with its full-bodied forms, polychromy, and showy decorative elements. The close fighting of Heracles and Nessus, adapted to vase painting composition, was to appear frequently throughout all sixth- and fifth-century pottery.

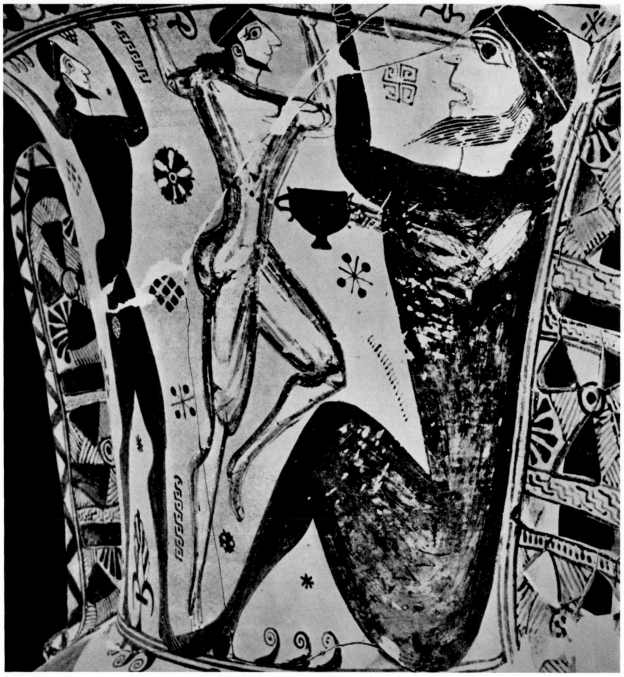

19. The conquest of a lively narrative style led the proto-Attic Polyphemus Painter to use the whole neck of this amphora from Eleusis for the blinding of the Cyclops Polyphemus. Circa 650 B.C. Eleusis, Museum

The polychrome technique, which by this time also used red in large expanses to indicate drapery, animals' necks and bellies, and other figured elements, triumphed in the third quarter of the seventh century. A typical example is provided by the so-called Painter of Women, with his composed processions of draped figures and elegant, accurately incised swans. Cycladic influences are revealed by a taste for ornamental spiral forms arranged in grandiose arabesques in the work of the Protome Painter, who employs pairs of bulls and horses on the necks and bodies of his modest, measured amphorae. On the other hand, the influence of Corinthian pottery is increasingly strong in palmettes, flowers, and tendrils, assuming more elaborate and disciplined forms in rosettes and animals; it is also obvious in the use of crimson pigment and incising, as well as in the type of the gorgon.

Black-figure technique, supported by increasingly surehanded, delicate incising, triumphed in the last quarter of the seventh century in an original Attic conception, profoundly different from Corinthian work, though nonetheless influenced by it to a certain extent. These images are clear, tense, and robust, bursting with life so that they seem to strain against the limits imposed by the forms of *lekanides* (basin-shaped bowls, often with lids),

20. On this grandiose amphora, from which the Nessus Painter takes his name, he depicts with vigorous expression and harmonious form Heracles' slaying of Nessus. Circa 615 B.C. Athens, National Museum

kraters, and amphorae. Lack of discipline, disorganized composition, and the unsophisticated nature of some aspects of the middle proto-Attic style disappear in the vigorous monumental language of the last phase of proto-Attic, which represents the happy fulfillment of premises laid down at the beginning of the century.

The Nessus Painter revives the themes of Heracles and Nessus, and the beheading of the Medusa, with new vigor in his masterpiece, the amphora partially shown here in figure 20, which can be dated around 615 B.C. The weighty but compact group of Prometheus enchained and Heracles, on a monumental krater in Athens, is evidence of the high level and strength achieved by this mature proto-Attic style. Through the works of these seventh-century painters we can form an understanding of the energies that were

fermenting in the Athenian world, and why it was there that Classicism was to find its highest expression.

3.   The Corinthian Animal and Narrative Styles

In the second half of the seventh century Corinth continued to dominate the markets with its production of pottery, notwithstanding the fact that the decorative delicacy of the proto-Corinthian style had given way to a more flowing, showy effect, with the formation of the Corinthian style in the last two decades of the century. The characteristic *alabastra* with animals, round *aryballoi* with warriors and lions, *olpai* and three-lobed *oinochoai* with animal friezes, and globular kraters

21. The pictorial, graphic, and narrative refinements of the Corinthian style culminate in this krater with the scene of the banquet of Heracles and Eurytus. Last quarter of the seventh century B.C. Paris, Louvre

with figured scenes, were widely distributed. Orientalizing influences can be traced in the rosettes with incised petals of Assyrian origin, which became more and more bulky and monotonous when used for filling spaces. Oriental sources are also responsible for the polychrome scale pattern that covers large expanses of vases, the Assyrian type of lion and four-winged monster, and the fourfold lotus with radiating buds.

Animals became increasingly massive and angular, their structures more elongated, and incised details of stylized anatomical segments more prevalent. In addition, painted areas of unbroken red or white began to stretch over the vases. The syntax of this style created fixed groupings of animals, such as the lion, bull, and panther, and heraldic compositions with lions, panthers, cocks, or sphinxes around a central motif, particularly

on *alabastra*. Other vases retained their bands of animals: placing panthers face to face with ibexes; inventing new monsters by giving birds human heads or heads of griffins, lions, panthers, or gorgons; mingling the bodies of two animals in one; transforming the typical sirens and sphinxes; and creating the serpent-bodied Typhon.

The lively Corinthian spirit also shows itself in the elaboration of the figure of the reveler, with his padded costume grotesquely exaggerating the roundness of his buttocks and paunch. He is represented in orgiastic dances in positions of expressive mimicry, and is later imitated widely by Attic, Chalcidian, and Ionian vase painters. A krater from the end of the seventh century, on which a painter has depicted Heracles in the house of Eurytus above a band with a lively cavalcade of riders (fig. 21), clearly illustrates the profound difference between the witty elegance of the rhythmic Corinthian narrations and the exuberant monumentality of contemporary proto-Attic images. The large panel shown here depicts the banquet given for Heracles by Eurytus and his four sons: Iole gracefully entertains the guest, and the dogs strain at their leashes under the couches.

4. Orientalizing Influences in the Various Greek Centers

Orientalizing influences, which had found their first and most welcome reception in Corinth in the second half of the eighth century, and then in Athens, began to enrich the ornament of

Aristocratic Sparta, with its rigid political organization, developed a ceramic style with predominantly abstract decoration and summary animal figures whose heads were barely sketched in on the light ground. Toward the middle of the seventh century, however, under Corinthian influence, Laconian vase painters adopted the black-figure technique. Nevertheless, they still preferred the repetition of a single animal, fish, or bird, arranged in neat lines without fill-in ornament, which produced an effect of sober elegance in cups dating from the late seventh and early sixth centuries. Contacts with the East are well attested by the arrival in Sparta of the artist Bathykles, who had come from Magnesia to decorate the monumental throne of the statue of Apollo

22. A sober and measured ornamental elegance characterizes a type of cup decorated with birds in the Orientalizing style of the islands and Asia Minor, as seen in this example from Camirus. Beginning of the seventh century B.C. London, British Museum

other centers during the seventh century.

Though importing a large amount of Corinthian pottery, conservative Boeotia nonetheless remained faithful to the Geometric tradition, lightening it with Oriental-inspired motifs in its large amphorae.

at Amyclae, and also by ivories imported from Syria and Phoenicia, but these did not stimulate a native taste for fanciful ornament.

Throughout the Graeco-Oriental regions was found the characteristic cup, decorated with the traditional metope and lozenge ornament

34

23. The characteristic elements of the Wild Goat style are composed in a zonal rhythm in this oinochoe *from Rhodes.* Circa *630–615 B.C. Munich, Antikensammlungen*

of the Geometric style mingled with the Oriental motif of the bird, its cross-hatched body set in the central metope with simple, mannered elegance (fig. 22). These works found a ready export market during the seventh century, before declining into a decoration with rosettes, eye motifs, and lotus flowers in the sixth century.

5. The Decorative Nature of the Wild Goat Style

Toward the middle of the seventh century another typical Orientalizing style appeared, and embraced a vast area of Asia Minor and the islands, from the Ionian cities with their center at Miletus, to those of Aeolia, to Rhodes, Chios, and Samos. This was evidence not only of the close links between these centers, but also of the importance of the commercial routes to Syria, Egypt, and the Black Sea, as can be seen from the presence of this pottery as far afield as Naucratis, Al-Mina, and in the easternmost colonies. This was the so-called Wild Goat style, which takes its name from the grazing goats that appeared most frequently and came to characterize the style's repertory of animals, which also included deer, lions, bulls, boars, swans, griffins, and sphinxes. The animals' heads, and sometimes their bellies, too, were only outlined and left in the original, cream-colored ground, and the figures were neatly lined up within their compositional zones, which were filled in with rosettes, curled swastikas, and broad bands of lotus flowers and buds (figs. 23, 24).

This type of composition was well adapted to the form of the *oinochoe*, which was first squat and fat, then tall and trefoil-mouthed, the latter form dominating for a long time, alongside kraters, the round *deinoi*, and plates. The repertory and general effect suggest an inspiration from Oriental embroidered textiles. The common stylistic denominator then became differentiated into local inflections indicating various centers of production: rougher, more angular forms of vases appeared in the Aeolian area, chalice shapes in Chios (fig. 25), and more unified profiles in Rhodes. Corinthian influences appeared in the fill-in patterns and closer groupings of animals toward the end of the seventh century, and in the late production of the first half of the sixth century.

6. The Ornamental Taste of the Islands and Asia Minor

A certain artistic common denominator in the Ionian islands and the corresponding region of Asia Minor is also shown in goldsmith's work which, along with pottery, satisfied and gave concrete form to the decorative leanings of the Orientalizing period. One of the main areas of production seems to have been Rhodes, a rich center of commercial exchange and colonial power. In embossed diadems from Rhodes we find the Orientalizing motifs of

24. As seen in this detail from a Rhodian oinochoe, the light ground gives an attractive relief to the motifs of the Orientalizing Wild Goat style. Circa 630–615 B.C. Berlin, State Museums

heraldic lions, pairs of sphinxes, *peplophoroi*, birds, and the typical elegant rosettes that provide plastic decoration for the characteristic gold pendants with metopes showing the *Potnia Theron* (mistress of the beasts), the *Melissa* (the bee), the sphinx, and the centaur, rendered in strong relief and enhanced with granular decoration. In the triangularly constructed heads and flowing, segmented coiffures one can see the traces of Daedalic sculptural models. Typical spiral or anchor-shaped earrings, with leonine or griffin-like masks or rosettes on the ends, are found in Rhodes, Melos, Delos, and Ephesus.

The same dominantly decorative approach runs through the pottery styles that flourished during the seventh century in the Cyclades, with decorative effects reminiscent of embroidered textiles, and a style that remained foreign to narrative or mythological compositions.

This particular vision included a variety of styles. In the first quarter of the seventh century appeared a style of strong black-and-white contrasts, wholly in the Geometric tradition, with thickly packed background patterns, and winged horses, deer, griffins, and lions. In the first half of the seventh century a simple, elegant, linear style can be seen on amphorae and kraters from Thera, Delos, and Paros. This style harmoniously blended Geometric ornament and floral, curvilinear decoration borrowed from the East with carefully composed arrangements of lions and birds. In the first quarter of the seventh century can also be found an elegant and measured style which set lions in abstract, heraldic groups, and isolated horses or sphinxes on narrow bands around the necks of slim amphorae decorated with the rich repertory of geometrical and floral ornament divided by plaited bands. Lastly, there was a style that placed the single protome of a horse, a lion, or a man on the necks and shoulders of amphorae and *hydriai*.

Spirals and protomes influenced proto-Attic pottery of the first half of the seventh century, while some proto-Attic figurative elements, like the grazing horse created by the Ram Jug Painter, clearly inspired the figures on the elegant Cycladic jug from Paros, with the modeled griffin's head (fig. 26). The superior

Cycladic ornamental repertory. But the proto-Attic image always reveals a conscious effort to construct and articulate the human and animal figures organically within the general structure, even in the case of the least gifted painters. In the Cycladic style, on the other hand, lions or horses have a flowing, elusive outline that draws the image in terms of surfaces, not of volumes, and detail is thought of as abstract ornament, as can be seen from the Cycladic attachment to the Oriental-inspired animal style.

It is significant that even when the human figure is developed — above all in the production of Delos and Melos — and we meet mythological figures such as Ares and Aphrodite, *Potnia Theron*, Thetis and Achilles, Apollo and Artemis, Heracles and Deianira in abun-

The Orientalizing repertory is brought together in a purely ornamental manner with pleasing clarity and elegance ...his typical chalice from Chios, found at Vulci. Last quarter of the seventh century B.C. Würzburg, University Museum

decorative sense and compositional style of the Cyclades affected the less disciplined proto-Attic work, and the lively Athenian figurative sense did not fail in its turn to influence the

dantly decorated costumes with a profusion of detail, as well as large animals like sphinxes or horses — themes found into the first decades of the sixth century — the prevalent ornamental approach to the subject remains unchanged. The extensive surface of large *hydriai* or wide-necked amphorae set on high conical feet continues to be conceived as a tapestry, with a luxurious employment of eye-catching background patterns of large spirals, palmettes, swastikas, meanders, radial motifs, and flowers.

In addition to Attic influences, Corinthian influences are clearly noticeable in late seventh-century production of the Cyclades. Yet nothing could be more different in its underlying spirit than the play of multicolored ornament creating abstract and figured repertories in a tapestry-like composition in the Cycladic style, as opposed to either the plastic, concentrated power of proto-Attic mythological figures or the interpretation of great narrative painting by Corinthian vase painters.

Crete occupied a place of its own in the vast framework of this Orientalizing period, and it is interesting to note, in tracing cultural and commercial currents, that it shows prevalent relationships with Cyprus, from which it assimilated characteristics such as the lotus motif, concentric circles on flasks, and a polychrome technique. The Orientalizing current was early received in Crete, and even if the Geometric approach and repertory survived for quite a time, it was combined with the new floral and plaited motifs, figures of birds and sphinxes, and human figures which were often crude and unorganic in form. Techniques included incised lines, outlined areas, and white pigment, on *pithoi* (large earthenware jars), *deinoi*, *alabastra*, *aryballoi* — round and ovoid in imitation of their Corinthian counterparts — cups, and dishes. This Cretan style did not reach an organic and rigorous unity, and is indicative of a society dominated by survivals and influences from various sources.

Strong links with Assyria and the Oriental world, reinforced by the active intermediary role of the Phoenicians, are better documented in Crete by the important series of votive bronzes from the Mount Ida cave, the mythical grotto of Zeus. These include, apart from three imported Phoenician cups, sixty-nine shields, one tympanum or bronze disk, and five cups, dating from the first half of the seventh century.

Some leather-mounted shields were made for actual use, whereas others were purely votive objects, particularly the type with a central boss modeled in the form of a lion's head, clearly derived from Assyrian art. Another imitation of Assyrian models in Crete was the division of the shield into zones of alternating figured and ornamental bands, the latter with palmettes, rosettes, and lotus flowers of the Oriental type. But even the figurative motifs

26. *Proto-Attic themes translated into the decorative Orientalizing style of the Cyclades are seen on this refined jug from Paros. Mid-seventh century B.C. London, British Museum*

recall the Orient: the hero, similar to the Babylonian-Hittite Gilgamesh, flanked by two winged demons, who constitutes the decoration of the tympanum; the typical naked goddess, similar to *Potnia Theron*, who appears between two lions which she leads by the ears, or is reduced to a simple bust between grazing ibexes; the solid sphinxes who face each other between scorpions or floral elements; the motif of the warrior whose head is seized by a lion; and the hunting figures, archers, and processions of deer, rams, winged lions, and griffins. The analogies that do exist between this Oriental repertory and the Orientalizing decoration of the Attic world — seen in golden diadems, painted vases, hunting scenes, and female chorus motifs — only render all the more evident the profound difference between the Assyrian and Phoenician tendencies of these Cretan bronzes and the transformation that these same motifs underwent in their active assimilation by Athenian artists.

The particularly fine goldsmith's work to be found in Crete also shows Phoenician influences in its use of falcons and palmettes. There are also analogies with the jewelry of Tralles in Asia Minor in the half-moon shapes of pendants; with that of Ephesus in the type of the bee; and links with Rhodes in the metopal decoration with plastically treated figures of Daedalic *peplophoroi*, heightened with a minute granular work.

In Cyprus the Aegean-Cypriot element, already mingled with Assyrian and Anatolian influences, underwent Phoenician colonization in the region of Citium and the island became one of the centers in which Phoenician art was most profoundly active, manifesting itself in characteristic metalwork, in cups of gold, silver, and bronze, eclectic in style, with Assyrian, Phoenician, and Egyptian motifs. After the forty years of Assyrian domination, the period of independence from the mid-seventh to the mid-sixth century under an Orientalized autocracy seems to have been a flourishing epoch in Cyprus, as evidenced by the island's dynastic palaces and rich tombs. It was at this time that the poet Stasinus wrote his *Cypria*, and the local metal-workers, weavers, and ivory carvers became famous. In this provincial setting the taste for the magnificent took concrete form in metalwork and the art of the goldsmith rather than in pottery, and when the art of statuary came into being, the jewels worn by the sitter were reproduced — jewels with which the figures seem overloaded, in a taste similar to that of the Etruscans or the Iberians. The nude Oriental goddess with her arms raised or clasping her breasts; masks with Syrian coiffures; Hathoric heads; the god Bes in Assyrian costume tethering lions or wild goats; and sphinxes: all these themes appearing in Cypriot gold work clearly indicate the convergence of artistic currents in this important part of the Mediterranean.

7. Orientalizing Influences in Etruscan Art

In the West the most fertile field for these currents was certainly Etruria, which in the seventh century could boast a number of rich cities, particularly those on the Tyrrhenian coast: the most important were Caere (Cerveteri) and Tarquinia. These cities became ports for Phoenician trade, perhaps through the intermediary of the Phocaeans and Ionians. Eastern products and influence spread from here to the most inland centers, from Praeneste (Palestrina) to Chiusi and to Bologna. These eye-catching objects, including gold and silver cups in an Egyptianizing style, bronze-relief vases, bronze appliqués from as far afield as Urartu, carved ivories, goldsmith's work, faïence, and scarabs, must have appeared very attractive to the country-dwelling Etruscans, who were just then breaking away from the sober tradition of the Villanovan culture and were acquiring power and wealth. Thus these products found particular acceptance with the local taste for splendor and color.

In Etruria the transformation of Villanovan Italic customs under Orientalizing influences can be compared with the middle-Helladic basis of Mycenaean culture undergoing the powerful Minoan influence. Making allowances for the difference in spirit that distinguished the Hellenic from the Italic world, an analogous vision of dazzling splendor is offered by the furnishings from the shaft graves of the first Mycenaean dynasty and those of the monumental tumuli of the Etruscan chiefs at Caere. On the other hand, the profusion of gold, bronze, and ivory in the Regolini-Galassi Tomb at Caere, the Barberini and Bernardini tombs at Praeneste, and the circular tombs at Marsigliana exhibit a wealth that contrasts with the far more sober picture presented by the contemporary Hellenic culture. Etruscan civilization insisted on monumental tombs: burial chambers hollowed out in the rock; underground rooms with corridors; enormous tumuli on stone bases which, as at Caere, sometimes reached a diameter of 150 feet; and finally the *tholos*, a circular tomb in the shape of a beehive, constructed with corbeled courses of stone.

But more strikingly than anything else, goldsmith's work gives the true measure of the Etruscan taste for splendor (fig. 27). While the techniques used could hardly have been more refined, the forms are often ostentatiously ornate. The modest, reserved note struck by

27. Orientalizing motifs are evident in the elaborate and technically refined Etruscan gold work of this grandiose fibula from the Regolini-Galassi Tomb at Caere (Cerveteri). Mid-seventh century B.C. Vatican, Museo Gregoriano

the thin gold funerary diadems of Attica contrasts significantly with the exuberant, showy fanfare of Etruscan work: such as the gigantic, disk-shaped fibulae about a foot wide; the Egyptian-inspired pectorals; plaques and brooches; large buckles with long bars; wide bracelets; enormous earrings of curved shapes, or earrings with ornament intended to be hung by a little chain at the sides of the ears, as in Iberia. All these works are covered

28. In the rustic and vigorous Etruscan style, the essential elements of the human image are summarized on this "canopic" vase from Chiusi. Sixth century B.C. Florence, Archaeological Museum

with sphinxes, lions, chimaeras, die-modeled in full relief, or embossed, then heightened with granular decoration. This granular technique, Eastern in origin, assumes virtuoso refinements, becoming almost a fine dust used to draw solid silhouettes of animals and geometrical figures on fibulae, stick-pins, and pendants. A more exuberant, sculptural, plastic approach distinguishes work from the south of Etruria, as far as Caere, from the finer, more linear work of the north, centered at Vetulonia, with delicate, lacy openwork and miniature-like decorative figures.

The naked goddess, the *Potnia Theron*, the Assyrian lions, along with the procession of winged animals, bring us back to the influence that stems from the Orient but, whereas in Crete and in Cyprus these themes retained notable stylistic resemblance to their original models, in Etruria we see a more free and fanciful development. The string of animals which provided one of the favorite ornamental devices used for the surfaces of jewelry, ivory, beaten bronze, and painted vases is Etruscanized and takes on hybrid form: one characteristic touch is the lion with a human leg hanging from its jaws, while volutes and stylized filiform elements flow in arabesques from the mouths of other monsters.

Imitation of Oriental sources is clear in the great bronze caldrons topped with hollow masks of lions and griffins, always showing the Etruscan stylization that distinguishes them from the originals; these masks are also repeated on Etruscan vases of the black so-called *bucchero* ware. The tall, conical bronze stands of the caldrons decorated with figures in relief, or those of the Faliscan region in clay decorated with painted wild animals, evidence the striking ornamental taste of the Etruscans.

In addition to Oriental influences, Etruria became increasingly affected by Corinthian work, which also predominated in Sicily and Magna Graecia during the seventh century. This Corinthian influence was the result of large-scale importation of proto-Corinthian and then Corinthian vases, which led to a considerable series of imitations, more or less provincial in tone, which reached greatest coherency in the Etruscan style known as Italo-Corinthian. This begins with typical *oinochoai*, and in the second half of the seventh century continues with the characteristic *olpai* decorated with zones of animals and Phoenician palmettes, and *aryballoi* and *alabastra*, often with linear decoration. This imitation shows some incongruencies — disproportion in the animal figures and Etruscanized types — though products faithfully adhering to the Corinthian models are by no means lacking.

The originality of the Etruscan spirit, however, manifests itself best toward the mid-seventh century in the creation of vases in a fine black clay which gives them the name of *bucchero* ware. It is not certain whether this color was achieved by using powdered charcoal, or through firing over a smoky flame with the reduction of ferric oxide to ferrous oxide. In the second half of the century this production, which had one of its most important centers at Caere, reached considerable elegance and variety of form, with thin-walled vases inspired by metal models and ivory work, and also by Corinthian pottery. Yet the vases were always marked by a lively sense of the fantastic, which resulted in the creation of original shapes, such as the star-shaped chalice decorated with monsters, *askoi* (small vases or jugs shaped like wineskins), and an ampulla from Caere modeled with a charioteer standing on two plumed protomes of horses, a technically skillful, highly inventive work.

The Orientalizing repertory of monsters, which lasted throughout the sixth century in Etruria, reappeared in stamped decoration, in which an engraved cylinder was rolled over the wet clay to obtain relief ornament. The same technique was also used for the reddish ceramics of polished clay from the Faliscan region and from Latium.

The oldest painted tomb in Etruria, the Campana Tomb at Veii, forms part of the late Orientalizing tradition. Its decoration is characterized by a fantastic repertory of sphinxes, lions, deer, floral volutes, and tendrils, through which move horsemen and hunters, conceived in an abstract polychromy, and exhibiting no dimensional relationships even though the work is to be dated in the sixth century.

A typical manifestation of the Etruscan expressive imagination is also to be found in the schematic modeling of facial features, first in the bronze masks which were applied to the covers of clay cinerary urns from the Chiusi area, and later in the heads that were modeled directly in the clay of the urn itself. These urns are known as Canopic vases through a false association with those of Egypt. In these works the whole urn takes on a human appearance, conveyed by a few prominent features conceived with refreshing freedom (colorplate, fig. 28), thus conferring an impression of life on this common, popular form of plastic art. Although some schematically vigorous specimens go back to the seventh century, and the taste for Oriental forms and motifs is affirmed by the type and the animal decoration of the bronze or clay thrones on which these "Canopic" vases were placed, the greater part of them date from the sixth century.

The Birth of Monumental Sculpture and the Arts of the Archaic Period

While the varied range of accents in Orientalizing art, from the mainland of Greece to the islands, Asia Minor, and Italy, was most prominently characterized by a decorative, ornamental sense, this same period also saw the beginnings of a monumental Hellenic sculpture.

1. The Daedalic Tradition and the Creation of the Kouros and the Kore

Ancient tradition sums up the creative process of the first statuary in the symbolical name of the mythical Daedalus, who was thought of as the inventor of the first life-like images of men. But it is significant that various aspects of the Daedalic legend link this demiurge with the Mycenaean world, as the creator of the *choros* for Ariadne and the labyrinth of Knossos for King Minos, and as an expert bronze-worker and unrivaled goldsmith in the refined technique called *daidallein*, after his name.

Daedalus' contacts with the Sicilian King Kokalus make him a symbol of the links forged by the first Mycenaean trade routes between the Aegean and the West, while *daidallein* art places him in the Orientalizing current, in terms of which he is supposed to have conceived his altar to Poseidon, adorned with figures, lions, and dolphins.

But Daedalus is remembered above all as the first *agalmatopoios* (creator of images of the gods), that is, for his statues in wood and in marble, in which human images gained life in space, freed from their primitive rigidity, their legs placed apart and their eyes open so that it seemed that they were really walking or looking. This led to the rhetorical declaration that his statues had to be tied down so that they would not run away. Daedalus thus embodies all the experiments that lie at the roots of Greek art, and antiquity attributed to his hand many works in different places, calling them wonder-working — *thaumazomena*, to use the word of the historian Diodorus Siculus. Although, as Pausanias says, the primitive appearance of these statues may have seemed rather strange (*atopotera*), nonetheless they appeared to be endowed with a touch of the divine (*entheon*). This aptly describes the most ancient statuary, in the fascination and suggestive power that emanate from its monumentality and abstract qualities and transport the human image onto a transcendental, ideal plane.

As the ancients gave the label "Daedalic" to primitive statues, today the term is used to denote all sculptural work dating from the Orientalizing period. During this time the structure of the figure became progressively more articulate; heads assumed a triangular shape, with the top of the cranium flat; low forehead and protruding ears framed bulging eyes in the flattened face; and hair came to resemble the Egyptian *klaft* style, with waves modeled in horizontal, parallel grooves, like a stiff, tiered wig. This conception was firmly rooted in Crete, considered the cradle of Daedalic art, as well as in Rhodes, the other islands, Asia Minor, the Greek mainland, and Magna Graecia. Daedalic art was expressed in terracottas, ivories, small bronzes, modeled bronze appliqués, small heads modeled on proto-Corinthian vases, heads of sphinxes and centaurs, goldsmith's work, reliefs, and, finally, in statuary, which represents the new aspect of this style.

Already in the small bronze figures of the Geometric period with their spindly and in-

29. This bronze warrior from Olympia shows that the human image began to acquire a greater volumetric articulation, while still maintaining the triangular form of the torso and a tubular structure of the limbs. Beginning of the seventh century B.C. Olympia, Museum

long striated hair, and the lively forward movement of the arm.

Even in its infancy this art surpassed the miniaturist models offered by the Mycenaean and Geometric styles, and for the first time free-standing figures were hewn directly out of solid blocks of marble found in the many quarries of the Aegean islands. These early sculptors had grandiose visions, which not only gave tiny bronzes a monumental quality, but aimed, toward the end of the seventh century, at works on an increasingly colossal scale, as if motivated by the first joy of having broken free from ancient limitations. The Apollo *kriophoros*, from the island of Thasos, executed in the local marble, measures 11 feet in height although unfinished; the torso of the Naxian Apollo of Delos is a fragment measuring 7 feet in height; the gigantic bearded statue left rough-hewn in the quarries at Naxos measures 35 feet. All these examples bear witness to the striving for monumentality.

The colossal dimensions, the basic model of a male figure standing with one leg advanced, and the hairstyle which recalls the Egyptian *klaft*, have led to a theory that traces this Archaic statuary to Egyptian work; and the busy Greek commercial colony of Naucratis on the Nile Delta has been considered one of the intermediaries for this artistic influence. It may have been that Daedalic sculptors also felt the need to emulate Egyptian monumentality and models, and Diodorus admits that Daedalic statues had the same *rhythmos* as Egyptian work, which the Apollo of Samos also resembles. However, these factors remain completely contingent and extraneous, for the actual creative process was determined by new forces on new, original bases, and with a conception and approach profoundly different from those of the Egyptians. Guided by a fundamentally different spirit, the Egyptian sculptor was acutely aware of the problem of portraiture, and sought to record individual facial characteristics, while he reduced the body to a stereotyped formula. The Archaic Greek sculptor saw the human image as a unified sculptural problem; uninterested in facial details, he searched for a type of universal, ideal beauty, constructing the figure rationally in space with an organic exploration of volumes.

Furthermore, there had always been contact with Egypt, and Greek statuary did not develop because of an occasional resurgence of these ties, but on the contrary, stemmed directly from the emergence of a new spiritual, religious, social, and political climate that was born in the setting of the *polis*.

Unlike Egyptian and all the other Oriental arts, the Greeks affirmed the human image in

distinct forms there began to emerge virile nude figures of warriors (fig. 29) and offering bearers with clearly articulated volumes and architectonically composed structures. We feel that a new world is already born in the aggressive impact of the Apollo, dedicated by Mantiklos (fig. 30), with its abstract monumentality and compact, articulate structure, implied by the incisions marking the collarbone, ribs, and crease along the stomach, the expressive elongation of the neck framed by the

30. *A clearly articulated structure characterizes this bronze Apollo from Boeotia, which bears on its thighs a dedicatory inscription of the donor, Mantiklos.* Circa 690 B.C. *Boston, Museum of Fine Arts*

its complete nakedness, as the type of both man and male divinity. The heroic nude was to be one of the basic elements distinguishing Greek art from all its predecessors and contemporaries, one of the traits that separated Hellenic art from that of the barbarian world. A sense of modesty still wrapped human nudity with high poetry in the Homeric poems, echoing Mycenaean conceptions; but the images of the Geometric period were already nude, reflecting the new Classical mentality.

In the actual practice of the *palaestra* (gymnasium), from which art was to draw endless inspiration, nakedness in the Olympic games is fixed by various traditions around 720 B.C.

and attributed either to the Megarian athlete Orsippus or Orrhippus, or to the Spartan Acathus. However, the war-like and austere atmosphere of Laconia was considered the first center of this Hellenic custom. But it is more by virtue of the essential underlying spirit of Archaic art itself that when the male figure appeared, it appeared nude.

Unlike Mycenaean art, Greek art did not range over the whole vast picture of nature, but concentrated on man, conceived as the measure of all things, as the concrete image of universal order. It examined man in a search for a human type and, at the same time, a formal canon with which to clothe the figure

45

31. Sculptures in clay also affirm the
Archaic principles of rigidity, frontality, and
construction in parallel planes, as in these
female deities from Gortyn. First half of the
seventh century B.C. Herakleion, Museum

32. A rare example of Archaic wooden sculpture
is preserved in this female xoanon from Palma di
Montechiaro. Second half of the seventh
century B.C. Syracuse, National Museum

46

of the divine made in the image of man. In this idealization of man and its corollary, the humanization of deities, the demarcation between human and divine became blurred. Thus, in monumental Archaic sculpture the nude male figure (*kouros*) and the clothed female figure (*kore*), which were the fundamental themes, remain indistinguishable in their ideal abstraction and could be the material form of either the human or divine, since we cannot know whether the donor wanted to represent the divinity invoked, or himself, so as to place himself under divine protection. The kouroi are usually designated as Apollos, but it would be strange if Apollo had been the only god represented. Moreover, we know that the type was used to portray donors, as well as victorious athletes, as in the case of Arrhachion, winner of the Olympic pancratium, which was seen by Pausanias. The korai have no attributes to distinguish them as figures of Artemis, Hera, or Athena. Kouroi and korai therefore appear more as ideal images of humanity in timeless, flourishing, unimpaired youth, and it is indeed significant that the statues of deities (*agalmata*), clearly distinguished as such by inscriptions or attributes, differ from the statues of their donors only in that they bear such inscriptions or attributes. Apollo is sung as a strong, healthy, powerful man, in the first flower of his youth, in the *Hymn to Apollo Pythius* (lines 449–450), and this is the conception that lies at the foundation of the Classical spirit.

The kouros and kore first appear in rigid, static poses with clenched fists and arms rigidly at their sides (fig. 31), but during the sixth century we see the progressive disengagement of the arms, which begin to bend forward in the gesture of giving. Anticipations of this trend are more easily found in small bronze figures. This rigid pose is intimately linked with the abstract, monumental conception that sums up the human image in its essential volumes, constructing it in space in parallel planes.

Already in the very first statuary from the area of Crete and the Peloponnesus and the rest of the Greek mainland one notes a robustness and vigor in the figures; subtlety and energy in the structure of works from the Cyclades; and a rounding of planes, subtle carving of surfaces, and fluidity of outlines in Asia Minor and on a few of the islands, such as Samos. This diversity of approach was also reflected in the different tastes and styles of vase painting in the same cultural areas. But whereas in vase painting stylistic influences and interchanges were easier and more marked, in sculpture the artists tended to affirm their own particular character.

33. Clay torso of a goddess from Gortyn, which in the rigorous modeling of the breasts recalls Minoan forms; it exemplifies the Daedalic style in Crete. First half of the seventh century B.C. Herakleion, Museum

In this varied stylistic scale a difference of spirit creates a major separation between the Dorian and Ionian areas.

At the end of the nineteenth century the squareness of sculptures from Crete and the Greek mainland and the roundness of work from Asia Minor were interpreted by scholars simply as forms derived from the woodworking technique of the primitive sculptures in wood, *xoana* (fig. 32), hacked out of the tree trunk, which had been either square-cut like a beam, or left in the natural cylindrical form and

then smoothed down. Ancient authors sometimes refer to *xoana* as beams (*sanis*): an example of this is the *xoanon* of Hera at Samos, which was the work of Smilis of Aegina. But it is obvious that only the artist's individual outlook, and not technical considerations, could have been responsible for so important a part of the creation and final appearance of the work. Squared or rounded structures are also to be found not only in marble, but also in work executed in other media and using other techniques: modeled in clay, hammered or cast in bronze, carved in ivory, or embossed in gold. These common results stemmed from a single Archaic conception, according to which the figure was either broken down into the four principal views and planes — front, back, and both profiles — or created in the round, fusing the many successive, continual views obtained by moving around the model. In the first case, the joining of the four planes forms sharply defined corners which give the work a squared appearance; in the second, the transitions between planes are eliminated, and every articulation of structural volumes is smoothed down so as to give a cylindrical aspect.

Heads, too, developed a different structure. In the Dorian area sharply distinct planes and a cubic form predominated, and the dome of the skull was flattened, whereas in the Ionian region receding, rounded planes and a high, curving cranial dome were the rule.

In the most Archaic statues and reliefs of the Daedalic style the sculptors were often content to accentuate facial features by thickening the horizontal, tightly closed lips, and opening wide the big eyes that bulged out beneath the flattened forehead. But soon attempts were made to give the mouth a three-dimensional appearance, curving the lines of the lips as though to follow the curve of the face, but actually placing them on a single, frontal plane. This gave the lips the half-moon shape that has generally been interpreted as the "Archaic smile."

This "smile" has been considered an expressive element, whether denoting serene benevolence in images of deities, serving as a conventional aulic mask for hiding inner feelings, or reflecting the inner pleasure and satisfaction of a healthy body or a magical inner vitality. It has even been claimed, not too convincingly, that the smile was an optical

34. Dedicated by Nikandre of Naxos to Artemis, this work exhibits the smooth, unified planes of the monumental Daedalic style.
Circa *660 B.C. Athens, National Museum*

correction for statues placed on high plinths and viewed from below to prevent the lips from appearing "Mongoloid," that is, to prevent them from having a sad expression with the corners turned down. But it must be remembered that this half-moon shape also appears in statuettes and on objects that were never intended to be placed above the viewer. Furthermore, it would be impossible to justify the disappearance of this trait in the first decade of the fifth century, when statues were still viewed from below, indeed, placed high up on the pediments of buildings.

The Archaic smile was actually the result of an image constructed in parallel planes before organic construction, the third dimension, or foreshortening were understood. Thus, the eyes were also brought onto a single frontal plane and, in the artist's inability to make the outer corners of the eyes recede, the deep curves of the eye were conveyed by placing the main axis of the eye along an oblique line on this frontal plane. The effect of this procedure has been taken as another expressive element which, interpreted in accordance with the putative smile, is considered almost a happy wink.

The principles governing the composition of the image in terms of views of parallel planes characterize all the sculptural work of the sixth century, and are increasingly accentuated as the artist becomes more engrossed in studying the ways of interpreting the various elements of the face, culminating in the refined series of korai from the Acropolis.

The Daedalic circle in Crete can be illustrated by a series of terracotta works (fig. 33) and by statuettes modeled in hammered sheets of bronze found in a shrine at Dreros. The latter, representing two *peplophoroi* and a kouros, date from the mid-seventh century, and are interesting relics of the primitive *sphyrelaton* technique (hammered plates of bronze nailed to a wooden core), with clearly constructed forms recalling *peplophoroi* in contemporary goldsmith's work.

Daedalic sculpture on Crete gives us the heavy female torso in limestone from Eleutherna and similar works from Prinias and Gortyn. In the primitive, flat-roofed temple *in antis* at Prinias, dating from 640–630 B.C., the architrave of the door has an Orientalizing

35. This statue, known as the "Hera" of Samos, was dedicated by Cheramyes. It is conceived as a continuous cylindrical surface with a refined fluidity of profile and modeling.
Circa 565 B.C. Paris, Louvre

*36. Stylistically related to the "Hera"
of Samos, this female figure with a hare was
dedicated by the same Cheramyes. It exemplifies
the structural coherence and delicate calligraphy
of Ionian sculpture.*
Circa *560 B.C. Berlin, State Museums*

*37. Statue of Ornithe by the Samian sculptor
Geneleos. The work shows a marvelous
structural unity of body and drapery and a
development beyond the enclosed cylindrical
profile of previous Samian works.*
Circa *555–550 B.C. Berlin, State Museums*

sculptured frieze of converging panthers. This architrave is surmounted at either end by two hieratic figures of goddesses, each wearing a *polos* (high, cylindrical headdress), modeled in limestone with soft, unified planes. The façade frieze depicts a procession of horsemen, like those on Dipylon vases, but the rule of iso-cephaly (having all the heads arranged on one horizontal line) and the need for filling the full height of the available surface make the warriors minute, while by comparison the horses are gigantic and elongated. Close to the

modeling and plastic sense of the two goddesses of Prinias is the accurately carved limestone "Lady from Auxerre" in the Louvre. This statuette of a female offering bearer wearing a peplos decorated with a rich, incised border, and with long volumetric hair, can be attributed to a Cretan sculptor of the mid-seventh century.

On the islands, more contained volumes and slenderer forms characterize, besides the kouroi of Delos, the life-size marble statue dedicated to Artemis in Delos by Nikandre of Naxos about 660 B.C. (fig. 34). Entirely sheathed in

38. Solidity of structure and architectonic rhythm of drapery characterize this goddess with polos and a pomegranate. Probably an Attic work, this figure contrasts in style and conception with the Samian sculptures shown on opposite page. Circa 580–570 B.C. Berlin, State Museums

a peplos, this statue consists basically of four parallel surfaces, barely interrupted by the slight projection of the breasts and the narrowing of the waist.

From small bronzes, terracottas, ivories, and goldsmith's work we know the type of sculpture from Asia Minor and Samos of this period of the seventh century, with cylindrical statuettes of continuous curving planes, and a type of Daedalic kouros dressed in a chiton, known from a *xoanon* from Samos. These basic characteristics of style and type persist in the later sculpture of Samos illustrated here in

figures 35, 36, 37, and 40, which we shall discuss farther on.

The work of the Peloponnesus shows close contact with the Daedalic sculpture of Crete, in a heavy seated female figure of limestone from Hagiorgitica in Arcadia. The same contact is evidenced in the statues from the Ptoan sanctuary in Boeotia.

Although Crete and the islands preceded Attica in the creation of Archaic statuary, Athens soon came to a front-ranking position at the end of the seventh and the beginning of the sixth century. This new prominence is

51

39. *Characteristic Ionian fluidity and soft, delicate surface modeling animate this veiled female head from Miletus (two views). Circa 540 B.C. Berlin, State Museums*

40. *Ionic bronze statuettes from the Samos-Asia Minor region, such as this example found at Olympia, have the typical cylindrical structure and fluidity of line. Circa 550 B.C. Athens, National Museum*

attested by some monumental kouroi, the grandiose conception of which bears similarities to the spirit that animated proto-Attic pottery, where flamboyant images were often too large for the surface of the vase. The larger of the two kouroi from Sounion (figs. 41, 42) is about ten feet high, and is the most organic, controlled, and significant version of the male nude produced in this first phase of the Archaic style. Here vigor is expressed in the heavy, strong modeling of the kneecaps attached to the powerful, prominently displayed thigh muscles, the generous volume of the chest, and the solidity of the limbs. The compactness of the neat, squared-off surfaces of the torso is not broken but rather heightened by the sparsely incised anatomical details: the arched line over the stomach, whose acute angle is re-echoed in the groin line; the plastic furrow running down the chest; the linear design of the abdominal muscle on the stomach and shoulder blades on the back. The Archaic over-elaboration is affirmed in the details on the wreath of tendrils and rosettes that binds the figure's brow and is tied in a subtle knot at the back of the head, where the falling ribbons are superimposed on the long, curly hair with perfect compositional balance. The clear volumetric treatment of the head shows its construction in terms of four viewpoints: the large horizontal eyes stretch over the frontal plane, and each of the lateral planes carries an ear, abstractly reduced into elegant volutes.

The squarish structure used by the Sounion master contrasts with the rounded, more fluid approach of the artist responsible for the colossal Dipylon head (fig. 43). The resemblances to the Sounion kouros only places the difference in conception in greater relief. The Dipylon head is modeled in generous, crystalline, rounded surfaces and an attempt has been made at smoothing down the junctions of planes in the unbroken oval of the face. Due to this merging of planes, the eyes are already almond-shaped instead of semi-circular, and are placed in a slightly oblique position, so as to give the impression of a continuous surface. The squarish schematization of the curls of the Sounion kouros is replaced in the Dipylon head with perfectly oval modeling that harmonizes with the curvi-

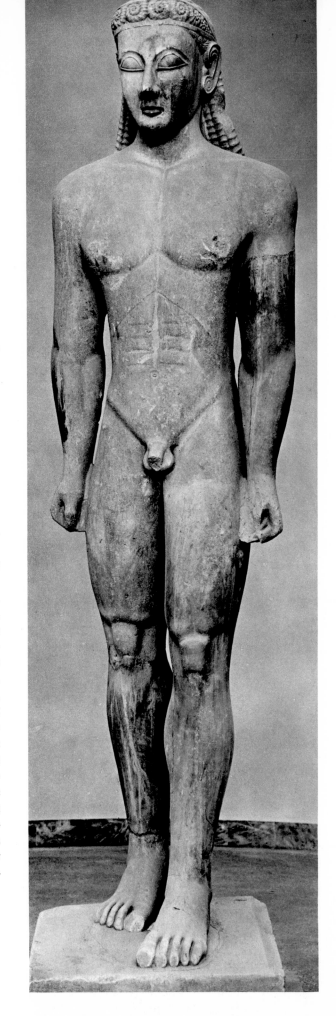

41. *Attic sculpture affirmed characteristics of grandeur and monumentality in the earliest formulations of the kouros figure, such as this colossal example from Sounion.*
Circa 600 B.C. Athens, National Museum

53

linear cut of the hair, over which the ends of the ribbon curve at the back of the head.

No other work of this phase reaches the refinement of these particular Attic creations; even the seven-foot statues of the twins Cleobis and Biton (fig. 44) by Polymedes of Argos, executed at the beginning of the sixth century for Delphi, appear more massive and more archaic in conception, with their flat faces, hair falling over their shoulders, and anatomical details limited to the incised arch over the stomach. This expression of vigor, which is the essential significance of the work, is well adapted here to the theme of the twin brothers who dragged the chariot of their priestess-mother for forty-five stadia (more than five miles). The same basic strength and massive

43. In comparison with the squarish structure of the kouros of Sounion is the rounded continuity of form in this kouros head from the Dipylon. Circa 610 B.C. Athens, National Museum

44. Exemplifying the Doric, Peloponnesian style is this figure of one of the twins, Cleobis and Biton, sculpted by Polymedes of Argos. Circa 590 B.C. Delphi, Museum

*. In this detail of the head of the kouros
m Sounion seen in figure 41, the structural
rity of the broad planes of the face are
rmoniously united with the decorative
ception of the diadem, hair, and ears.*

*45. The influence of Doric sculpture is
seen in this massive stone centaur from Vulci
by an Etruscan master.
Circa 575 B.C. Rome, Villa Giulia*

Daedalic forms survived in Etruria through the sixth century in sculptures with massive structures and clear-cut, square planes, like the stone centaur from Vulci (fig. 45), whose body resembles an Etruscan version of the Greek kouros. The alabaster statuette of a woman from the Isis Tomb in Vulci, and the sepulchral pillar with female bust from Chiusi, both from the first half of the sixth century, also bear the characteristics of the Daedalic style.

2. The Archaic Greek Temple and the Creation of the Doric and Ionic Orders

The slow, progressive elaboration of the temple structure, which represents one of the fundamental creations of the Greek spirit, paralleled the rise of monumental statuary in the seventh and sixth centuries B.C. The Minoan-Mycenaean civilization had only small cult shrines with simple podia for modest idols, and the most monumental architectonic undertaking, the *megaron*, or main hall, was intended for the *anax*, not for the divinity. Greek civilization, in contrast, reserved its finest, most splendid house for its anthropomorphized deities, thus creating the temple which, after various structural and technical experiments of the eighth and seventh centuries, was to take on a standard form in the sixth century. The stratified excavations of such famous sanctuaries as the Heraion on Samos, the Artemision at Ephesus, the Temple of Apollo at Thermos, the Heraion at Olympia, the Temple of Apollo at Cyrene, the Temple of Artemis Ortia in Sparta, the temple at Neandria in Asia Minor, and the temple at Locri Epizephyri in southern Italy, together with some clay models of shrines, enable us to follow the development of temple architecture. The Greeks, however, wrapped the origins of the temple in myth when they told of how the Temple of Apollo at Delphi was built first out of laurel branches, then wax and feathers, and then bronze.

From the primitive technique of a stone plinth with a superstructure of crude bricks the Greeks progressed to complete stone construction; from the simple room they passed to the cella, first with a vestibule and then with a portico; from the first pilasters and supports in wood and stone they developed the column; and from the traditional Mycenaean flat roof they moved to the pitched roof. The roof later took on the fixed form of two slopes with a central ridge along the main axis, thus creating the triangular spaces of the pediments at each end. The expanse of the roof was originally upheld by a central row of supports

vigor run through other works of this Dorian current, an example of which is the kouros of Orchomenos with its exaltation of muscular volumes. Yet even more simple and stylized by comparison with Attic work is the conception of the stele with the angular embracing figures of Dermis and Citylus, from the backward Boeotia. And the first attempts at a Daedalic sculpture found in the retarded area of Sicily appear quite provincial.

and columns. This divided the cella in two and made it necessary to place the cult statue at one side. This arrangement was replaced either by a cella without columns, or by a cella with columns near the walls to which they were joined by spur walls, as in the Heraion at Olympia. In other temples two sets of columns divided the space into three naves. The proportions of the very elongated seventh-century buildings were also improved during the sixth century. During the seventh century the entablature was predominantly of wood, faced and decorated with painted terracotta — interesting examples of which have been found in Calydon and Thermos (colorplate, fig. 53). But we can witness a progressive translation into stone of architectonic and ornamental forms originally constructed in wood. The creation of the column led to definition of the forms of the shaft, capital, and entablature, which became organized and fixed in architectural orders, eloquently testifying to the rational qualities of the Classical spirit. These orders constituted the foundation on which all European architecture was to be based for centuries.

The Doric order took root in mainland Greece, Crete, and the colonies of Sicily and Magna Graecia, while the Ionic order flourished in some of the islands and in Asia Minor. In the case of the Doric, the column and the capital with its echinus may have been derived from the Mycenaean column, but there are substantial differences in the tapering of the shaft: this proceeds from foot to top in the Doric column, but from top to foot in the Mycenaean models. Moreover, the abstract ornamentation of the Mycenaean shaft, which was placed on a circular base, contrasts with the functional vertical ribbing of the Doric column, which rises directly from the stylobate. While the Mycenaean column was considered an element in its own right, so that it was often reproduced as an isolated motif, the Doric column was an integral part of an organic architectural structure, supported by the stylobate and serving as an elastic support for the entablature. The column was topped by the expansive curve of the echinus, upon which rested the quadrangular surface of the abacus, which in turn supported the beams of the architrave. Greek architecture followed the organic logic of this structure by making the shaft swell out slightly, almost as to convey the tension to which the load-bearing column was subjected. In the same logical way, the structural framework of the original wooden building gave rise to the various elements of the Doric entablature: the ends of the main beams now appeared in stylized form as triglyphs with two vertical grooves and beveled lateral edges, and the empty spaces between them were filled with tablets (metopes) inserted between the triglyphs. The metopes were originally of wood, later of terracotta, and finally of stone and marble decorated in high relief. Beneath the triglyphs the regulae, and below them the guttae, were simply the translation into stone of the plain wooden strips with their rows of pegs. In the same way, the mutules and guttae just below the cornice were a translation of originally wooden pieces into their stone form. The ends of the roof tiles were concealed and decorated with semicircular or semiovoidal elements called antefixes. These were at first of clay and later of stone. The rain spouts of the roof were fancifully modeled with openmouthed lion masks. The pediment was crowned with an akroterion, at first a disk-shaped or semicircular element of painted clay, and later of stone variously decorated with figured or floral motifs. The akroterion harmoniously concluded the whole construction, while minor akroteria of figured or floral decoration were placed at the two extreme ends of the pediment triangle.

The logical relationships seen in the elevations of the Doric temple are also to be found in its ground plan which through various experiments reached, in the sixth century, its most organic and harmonious formulation in the peripteral plan. This led to the perfection of the hexastyle plan, in which the use of six columns at either end permitted the exact alignment of the antae of the cella with the next to outermost, or penultimate, columns of the pronaos in the front of the temple and the opisthodomos in the rear. This still left a suitably spacious colonnade around the outside of the temple, which, in the plan with thirteen columns along either side, was to achieve its most balanced proportions.

The Ionic order was developed from proto-Ionic — also called Aeolic — forms, known from specimens of capitals found at Neandria in the Troad, at Napis and Mytilene in Lesbos, and Larisa near Smyrna (fig. 46). In these examples a girdle of leaves at the top of the shaft makes the transition from shaft to capital and provides a starting point for the two volutes which rise and spread to either side, a palmette filling the space between them, thus creating a continuous surface supporting the abacus. Leaves and volutes, which recall a stylized lily, and the palmette are all elements that mark the vegetal and ornamental conception of the Ionic capital, very different from the abstract, solid geometry of the Doric and more in keeping with the refined, fanciful Ionian atmosphere. This proto-Ionic capital

57

46. In this Aeolic limestone capital from Larisa, near Smyrna, we see the vegetal-inspired decoration of Orientalizing taste, for which Classical architectonic sense will substitute the abstract volutes of the Ionic capital. Seventh century B.C. Istanbul, Archaeological Museum

certainly drew inspiration from Oriental types of capitals and ornaments, elements of which can be traced in Hittite, Assyrian, and Egyptian art, subsequently remodeled and disseminated mainly through the intermediary of the Phoenicians. The area in which these first voluted capitals were found has led to their being called "Aeolic," but they appear to be the direct antecedents of columns of the Ionic order as it was to become fixed toward the middle of the sixth century.

The Ionic capital progressively subdued and transformed the vegetal elements, stylizing them in terms of an abstract, structural conception more in tune with the unified architectural treatment. The girdle of hanging leaves was suppressed and replaced by a band of ovoli, while the volutes, instead of springing vertically from the shaft, were joined together horizontally forming a cushion-like member.

It is significant that in Cyprus, strongly within the Phoenician and Oriental spheres, the proto-Ionic capital survived longer than elsewhere.

Moreover, it was used as an isolated support for votive objects, extracted from the architectural system because of its prevalently ornamental function. This capital was also imitated by the sumptuous architecture of the Achaemenids.

By comparison with its Doric counterpart, the character of the Ionic capital was more refined and decorative. An equivalent difference can also be seen in the column shafts of the two orders. The Ionic shaft is slimmer, enlivened with a greater number of grooves and enriched with a base of convex and concave moldings, often decorated with a braided pattern or with *kymatia* (a wave molding of double curvature). The Ionic entablature was also less massive in character than the Doric. The Ionic architrave, unlike the smooth, full volume of the Doric structure, was accented by three successive projecting bands which divided the mass with lines of shadow. The Ionic frieze, accompanied by ovolo moldings, made a dainty denticulation which translated into stone, in a sustained architectural rhythm, the originally wooden projections of the smaller joists. Leaf-and-dart moldings embellished the cornice and entablature which, in the remarkable flowering of the Ionic order on the Greek mainland during the sixth century, was to be further enriched with a continuous figured frieze above the architrave, more refined than the plastic decoration of the metopes of the Doric order.

The treasury (*thesauros*), a building erected in the sanctuaries to house the precious votive offerings of the various peoples, repeated the temple structure on a reduced scale, with either a prostyle plan or a plan *in antis*. The latter had columns between the pilasters which terminated the extended side walls of the cella.

Ionic splendor gave gigantic proportions to some Archaic temples, like the Artemision at Ephesus, measuring roughly 180 by 377 feet, or the Heraion of Samos, about 197 by 380 feet. The Greek mainland, however, proceeded with greater control and elegance.

The Doric order tended to grow in sheer size when it moved from the Greek mainland to the colonies of Sicily and Magna Graecia. It was as if the exuberant taste of the provinces aimed at surpassing the motherland. This region also took liberties with the Doric

ornamentation, inserting *kymatia* in the capitals and using lively polychromed clay revetments on the entablature.

The development of the temple and the definition of the orders, which represent the great achievement of Archaic Greek architecture, posed precise decorative problems for sculptors: in the metopes of the Doric order; in the continuous figured frieze of Attic Ionic; and in both orders, the pediments, akroteria, and decorations of the rain spouts. Thus in architectural decoration, just as in cult, votive, and funerary statuary, there was a rigorous concentration on limited, well-defined problems of composition, confined to a restricted corpus of themes and linked with the celebration of the deity. And, as in sculpture, this approach gave rise to an organic, systematic, and intense development which, through constant perfecting, ultimately arrived at solutions of universal validity.

3. The Problem of the Pediment Decoration

A great problem was represented by the decoration of the pediment with its low, elongated, triangular space in which it is difficult to arrange an organic composition of figures without making one conscious of a solution imposed by the spatial limitations. Greek artists worked incessantly on the composition of pediments and finally arrived at the perfect solution with Phidias' work on the Parthenon. After painted clay facings, which have not survived, the Greeks began in the early sixth century to carve low reliefs in soft limestone (*poros*) or stone, passing first to high relief, and then in the second half of the sixth century, to sculpture in the round, first in *poros* and eventually in marble. This constant technical evolution was accompanied by developments in thematic unity and syntax. From the most archaic works, which bear Orientalizing figures of animals, serpents, and fish-tailed monsters, whose bodies were more convenient for filling the awkward, long, low angles of the gable, sculptors moved to unified mythological scenes, increasingly related to the celebration

47. The head of this heraldic feline from the pediment of Corfu translates into sculpture the decorative play of pictorial Corinthian models.
Circa *585 B.C. Corfu, Museum*

59

of the deity worshiped in the temple. The apotropaic purpose was progressively replaced by more illustrative interests and the fabulous world of monsters gave way to the narrative world of myth.

One of the earliest stages of this fundamental process in Greek architectural sculpture is shown by the vigorous high-relief pediment of the great limestone Doric temple in the Corinthian colony of Corfu. The temple has a perip-

48. The compositional and ornamental refinement of the unknown Archaic sculptor of the pediment of Corfu culminates in this knot of serpents tied at the waist of the Gorgon. Circa 585 B.C. Corfu, Museum

49. Detail of the three-bodied monster from a poros *pediment of the Acropolis. The marked structural deformations of these vigorous figures show the interest of the Archaic artist in the problem of optical corrections. Circa 565 B.C. Athens, National Museum*

50. In the pediment of the Siphnian Treasury at Delphi, the modest sculptor does not succeed in giving plastic life to the narrative theme of the contest for the tripod. Circa 525 B.C. Delphi, Museum

teral octastyle plan and can be dated around 585 B.C. The artist did not yet know how to conceive a single scene to fill the generous expanse of the pediment. Without attaining thematic unity, he placed the gigantic Gorgon in the center, and transformed the simple, apotropaic *gorgoneion* of the primitive pediments found in the West at Selinus, Gela, Hipponium, and Locri, into a mythical figure shown with her sons Pegasus and Chrysaor. Two large heraldic felines serve as enframement for the figure of Gorgon and her sons and separate this central group from the mythological groups on either side. In these side groups are shown, on the right, Zeus fighting a giant, and on the left, Neoptolemus slaying Priam. These scenes afford the possibility of filling the angles with two fallen figures symbolizing the massacres of the giants and the Trojans, and the knees of these fallen figures are conveniently bent to make them fit better into the extreme angles of the pediment. A Corinthian influence is visible in the types of the Gorgon and her sons; a conception in parallel planes places full-face heads and torsos on legs seen in profile, conveying the Gorgon's flight with one knee resting on the ground and the other bent at right

angles — the Archaic symbol for a rapid running motion known as " running on bent knees." Yet, a strong plastic sense breathes a magical vitality into the images and is accompanied by a decorative preciosity in engraved details, such as the small circles of the heraldic felines' spotted skins (fig. 47), the hair of the figures, and the decoration on their draperies, and the scales of the remarkable knot of serpents tied around the Gorgon's waist (fig. 48).

Other significant steps in architectural sculpture are marked by the series of *poros* pediments from unknown buildings once on the Acropolis in Athens. These buildings were destroyed during the ferocious Persian sack of the city in 480 B.C., and the Athenians piously deposited the broken statues in trenches, so that excavations have laid bare one of the most stimulating pages in the history of Archaic Athenian sculpture.

With the reforms of Solon, the advent of the Pisistratids in 560 B.C., and the foundation of important religious festivals like the Panathenaic and Dionysiac rites, Athens developed an intense building activity. The heavy pediments — often with groups of lions and lionesses seizing and mauling a bull in a heraldic arrangement that suits the center of the triangle — find parallels with similar subjects on proto-Attic pottery, and express in three dimensions the same grandiose, intensely dynamic vision, the same overflowing exuberance of volume, the same love for incised and polychromed calligraphic detail. Accurately drawn serpents with painted scales fill with their sinuous spirals the corners of these pediments having ornamental and monster themes. When, toward 570 B.C., a sculptor working on a minor pediment attempted a mythological narration in a single, unified composition, he fell back on a relief composition derived from painting. In the right-hand section the Hydra of Lerna — being fought and slain by Heracles, who stands in the center — is well suited to fill the angle with its multiple spirals, but on the left, the horses drawing Iolaus in his chariot are forced by the slope of the pediment to lower their heads as if grazing, and the large crab symbolizing the marshes must serve as a space-filling device for the angle.

The monumental quality and overflowing vitality of Attic sculpture were better expressed in the pediment sculptures carved in the round, which may have adorned the Hekatompedon of Athena and Poseidon at the time of the institution of the great Panathenaic Festival of 566 B.C. Here, Heracles throws himself into the struggle against the fleeing, snake-tailed Triton on one side, while on the other a three-bodied monster with demoniacal long hair and curved, pointed beards emerges colorfully and solidly from among the tangle of its writhing tails (fig. 49). In the prominent muscles, strong facial asymmetries calculated for the necessary optical correction when seen from below, as well as the vigorous structure and the vivid, abstract polychromy, this work contains all the Athenian spirit of the first half of the sixth century; it burst forth with a sure, though still undisciplined energy, before beginning to coordinate and refine itself toward the middle of the century.

In another of these *poros* pediments a sculptor, dealing with the more composed unified subject of the admission of Heracles to Olympus, was obliged to progressively reduce the size of his figures towards the angles, although the larger size of Zeus and Hera in the center could, of course, be justified iconographically. In the so-called "Olive Tree Pediment" another artist worked in a narrative vein to illustrate the ambush of Troilus by Achilles, contriving to avoid disproportion by reducing the dimensions of the central section. He showed great originality in the way he incorporated the spring around which the tragic myth took place, thus partially linking his figures with the background, in a thematic and compositional unity derived from painting.

The marble pediment of the Siphnian Treasury at Delphi, which dates from about 525 B.C., develops a single theme, the contest between Heracles and Apollo for the tripod (fig. 50). A centralized composition is achieved with the median axis occupied by the figure generally called Athena, but now more correctly identified as Zeus, who is placed between the two contenders, but the modest sculptor was once more forced to fall back on the progressive scaling down of the side figures without any compositional or structural links. The artist's aim was to work in the round, but he only succeeded in partially deepening the background plane of a high relief, obviously conceived in two-dimensional terms; the task of transforming the linear motifs of his original design into volumes proved too much for him. Greater compositional coordination was more easily achieved in the small, polychromed stone pediment of the Megarian Treasury at Olympia. Here the motif of the gigantomachy, the battle of the gods and giants, was translated into a vigorous high relief, in which the various positions taken by the combatants were well adapted to the form of the pediment, yielding an effect of movement and a unity of composition and theme.

The gigantomachy is also the theme of the west pediment of the Temple of Apollo at Delphi, rebuilt by the Alcmaeonids about 510 B.C., with the participation of the sculptor Antenor. The pediment of the west end is of stuccoed and painted tufa, while the east pediment is of marble. On the west pediment there are signs of an original personality in the way the sculptor has broken free from the arrangements of the traditional gigantomachy: he models figures conceived in a truly three-dimensional sculptural isolation, and places the frontal quadriga of Zeus and Hera so that it daringly fills the center of the pediment. Around the quadriga he groups the two diverging ranks of gods, whose progressively bent poses are justified by their increasing closeness to the enemies grouped at either end. The filling of the corners is achieved with the fortunate compositional devices of Athena's snake and Cybele's lion, who assault the giants. While the

51. Full corporeality and a rhythmic, harmonic articulation compose this figure of an archer from the west pediment of the Temple of Aph. at Aegina. Beginning of the fifth century B.C. Munich, Glyptothek

iconographic tradition of the gigantomachy offered various solutions for the west pediment,
the new theme of the glorification of Apollo,
taken as the single subject for the east pediment, left fewer narrative possibilities. The
sculptor here revealed more of his imaginative
sculptural sense by lining up three kouroi and
three korai beside the central quadriga, and
placed them frontally on the same plane with
the god. These figures constituted a row of
independent, separate figures, with a mechanical, progressive decrease in their size. To fill
the end angles the sculptor used unrelated
groups of a lion attacking a bull on one side
and a lion attacking a deer on the other, recalling the breaking up of the thematic unity
of the composition in Attic pediments. But
in spite of the compromise between subject
and composition in this pediment, there nevertheless emerges a determination to conceive a
decoration composed of figures inhabiting space
fully as statues, no longer stuck against the
background plane, but exhibiting their full
volumes in the shadowy recess of the pediment.

In Athens we find ponderous figures completely modeled in the round from a block of
marble, in the gigantomachy created by an
Athenian sculptor for the east pediment of the
Hekatompedon on the Acropolis, renovated by
the Pisistratids. This work corresponds significantly to the contemporary temple of the
exiled Alcmaeonids at Delphi. The divine combat, limited to a few figures conceived as autonomous statues, finds its focus in Athena, who
occupies the central axis and is in the process
of striking down Enceladus. The action then
develops in two counterpoised groups, ter-
minating in groups of kneeling giants stretched
out obliquely so as to fill the outer angles.
Once again, a conception in parallel planes
determines combinations of legs seen in profile
and frontal bodies, though there are obvious attempts at optical correction and foreshortening.
The elaborate sculptural conception which
animated the earlier *poros* pediments is developed further in the more refined modeling of
these marbles and acquires a delicate sense of
chiaroscuro in the treatment of flesh.

The culmination of the statuary conception
of pedimental decoration appeared on the peripteral, hexastyle Doric Temple of Aphaia in
Aegina at the beginning of the fifth century.
A perfect architectural balance was also achieved
in this temple in the ground plan and elevation. Although the east pediment is about
ten years later than that of the west side, both
pediments bear thematically unified scenes of
epic combats of Homeric heroes before Troy,
both using the figure of Athena as the central
axis. The three-dimensional figures, completely

*52. The master of the later, east pediment of
the Temple at Aegina shows still more mature
powers, as in this archer with a lion helmet.
Beginning of the fifth century B.C.
Munich, Glyptothek*

free in space, are articulated with studied
rhythmic cadences in various falling positions
as they move toward the end angles: the
forward-stretching attacker, the kneeling archer
(figs. 51, 52), and the fallen, wounded warrior.
In fact, they are so independently balanced in
their plastic isolation that it is difficult to
reconstruct their original compositional grouping with any certainty. As a result, the solutions proposed up to the present have been as
varied as they are unsatisfactory.

*53. The painted clay metopes from Thermos a
precious documents of painting in the Corinthi
style. Depicted here is a hunter returning with
two fawns.
Circa 630 B.C. Athens, National Museum*

54. Metope from Temple C at Selinus, with Heracles and the Cercopes. Massive figures in symmetrical and frontal composition characterize this Sicilian work. 520–510 B.C. Palermo, National Museum

4. The Development of Metope Decoration

The metopes of the Doric frieze represent another of the basic problems that faced Archaic sculptors. Painted terracotta metopes gave way to limestone and later to marble carved in relief. The relief became increasingly high until the metopes finally gave the impression of figures sculpted in the round and placed against a smooth background, which was presumably painted a single color. The painted clay metopes of Thermos and Calydon provide us with precious evidence from the

end of the seventh century (colorplate, fig. 53), showing strong reflections of Corinthian painting of the time. Brown was used for male flesh and white for female; red, yellow, and black were used for details and costumes.

The series of metopes in soft tufa from the Treasury of the Heraion of Sele, near Paestum, of about 560 B.C., enables us to trace the various stages of work, from the flat, linear relief carved into the background plane to the vigorous high relief with carefully finished modeling. Three low-relief metopes in limestone come from the oldest temple at Selinus, while those from Temple C at Selinus are in high relief with deep undercutting. The high relief

55. A vigorous, fluid narrative style is seen in this metope from the Treasury of the Heraion at Sele, depicting Heracles and the Cercopes. Circa *560 B.C. Paestum, Museum*

in marble from the metopes of the Sicyonian Treasury at Delphi, datable around 560 B.C., is softer and more delicate, while those of the Athenian Treasury, also in Delphi, are almost entirely worked in the round.

For the metope the artist had to compose a figured motif which harmoniously filled the whole of the quadrangular space, constituting a composition in its own right. Parallel developments of the problem are to be found in the contemporary metope vignettes on Attic painted vases, and on the arm pieces of Archaic bronze shields, found principally at Olympia, which have yielded rich examples of monsters and mythological groups.

When decoration was limited to a single figure, solutions were easily found: in the traditional gorgon and chimaera motifs, as in painted metopes from Thermos; in the sphinx, as on the Archaic metope from Selinus; or in the centaur who strikes various poses in the metopes from the Treasury at Sele. Since it was more difficult to fill the area of the metope with one human figure, the artist imaginatively depicted the figure in movement, with outstretched limbs forming a swastika pattern and thus occupying more space. Examples of this are seen in the metope from Thermos of Perseus fleeing with the head of Medusa in a bag, and in the metope from the Treasury at Sele de-

56. *Metope from Temple C at Selinus, showing Athena and Perseus decapitating the Gorgon. This Sicilian sculptor depicts static figures, with large, frontally placed heads. 520–510 B.C. Palermo, National Museum*

picting Iris, the messenger of Zeus, "running on bent knees" and carrying the discus, the curve of her arm in opposition to that of her arched wings.

Seated figures can fit more easily into a quadrangular space, as with the figure of Zeus, or the figure of Heracles Archer bent in the act of shooting an arrow, or the kneeling figure of Achilles lying in wait behind the palm tree. All these appear in the metopes from the Treasury at Sele where we also find the singular motifs of Odysseus astride the turtle, anxiously scanning the vastness of the sea during his long journey, and Sisyphus straining to reach the summit, while a demon drags him back by the shoulders.

The standing figure needed a compositional complement; this is provided in the Orestes metope from Sele by an Erinys who wraps the hero's body in her coils; in the painted metope from Thermos by the two fawns which hang from the ends of the stick balanced on the hunter's shoulders (colorplate, fig. 53); and similarly, in the metopes from Temple C at Selinus (fig. 54), and the Treasury at Sele (fig. 55), both representing Heracles and the Cercopes, these buccaneering sons of Oceanus, like the huntsman's fawns in the Thermos metope, fill the side spaces hanging head downward from the staff over the hero's shoulder.

Groups of two figures were more widely used, for they lent themselves to many dif-

57. In a metope from the Treasury of the Heraion of Sele, this Italic sculptor depicts with humor and energy the episode of Heracles carrying the Erymanthian boar to Eurystheus. Circa 560 B.C. Paestum, Museum

ferent arrangements — facing each other, side by side, or engaged in combat — and became a typical device for narrating the adventures of Theseus or Heracles. When three or more figures were represented, the artist simply assembled various triads: Apollo, Latona, and Artemis on the Archaic metope of Selinus; Athena, Perseus, and the Gorgon on the Selinus Temple C metope (fig. 56); and the Dioscuri and the sons of Aphareus as found on the metopes of the Sicyonian Treasury at Delphi.

Out of all the variety of apotropaic motifs and mythological subjects available, artists tried to arrive at a coordination of subject matter for the whole series of metopes of a given temple. Already in the richly decorated me-

topes of the Heraion of Sele several metopes were grouped together in a single narration of the *Oresteia* and the *Iliupersis*, with the unified cycle of the story of Heracles and the centaur Pholus developed on six metopes. A harmonious and unified coordination was achieved in the fifth century on the Athenian Treasury at Delphi, built to celebrate the battle of Marathon. Here, the Amazonomachy on the front exalted the victory over Oriental barbarians, and the adventures of Theseus and Heracles constituted homogeneous cycles in the metopes on the sides of the building. The theme of the twelve labors of Heracles lent itself to division into two parts with six scenes on each front. This solution was adopted in the Temple of

69

Zeus at Olympia, about 465 B.C. For the exceptional series of ninety-two metopes on the Parthenon, Phidias was to use the gigantomachy for the east side, the victory of Theseus over the Amazons for the west, and a long succession of scenes from the *Iliupersis* on the north, while on the south side he interrupted the centauromachy with an important interval of Attic myths, all precisely relevant to the celebration of Athena.

Besides the striving for unified subject matter, there was also a demand for coordinating the compositional rhythms of each metope in terms of the other members of the sequence along one side of the temple. These rhythms, like the feet of a line of poetry, with its shorts, longs, and stops, were exploited to achieve converging or diverging arrangements and particular accents — an intensive research that was to reach its culmination in the work of Phidias.

The series of metopes from Sele are immersed in the highly colorful Italic spirit, in which the Greek substance acquired a new feeling for flamboyant volumes and for the vivid representation of gestures. The capricious narrative *brio* gave new twists to the most traditional themes, as exemplified in the note of carefree humor in the scene of Heracles carrying the Erymanthian boar to the frightened Eurystheus, the latter shown in the act of closing himself inside the *pithos* (fig. 57).

The more refined spirit of the artists of Sele in comparison with those of Selinus can be seen in the confrontation of two metopes, both representing Heracles and the Cercopes, one from Sele and one from Temple C at Selinus (figs. 54, 55). In the Selinus metope the figures are rough and thickset, with large heads frontally placed. This has led some authorities to date the metopes of Temple C at Selinus even before 550 B.C., but instead this is really a case of a retarded Archaic style in a provincial

70

form, and these works can actually be dated at the end of the sixth century, 520–510 B.C.

When compared with reliefs from the mother country, the Sicilian character of this work at Selinus becomes even more pronounced, as can be seen from the treatment of two metopes, both depicting Europa astride the bull on the surface of the sea, one from the Sicyonian Treasury at Delphi and one from Selinus. The sculptor of the metope from the Sicyonian Treasury worked with flowing contours in the marble, modeling the structure of the bull with a fine sensibility and folding the soft body of Europa in dynamic curves. On the other hand, the sculptor responsible for this same subject in the Archaic metope from Selinus froze the scene in stiff, massive, angular forms. Thus, apart from chronological and technical differences, the over-all spirit and tone of the two works reveal two very separate artistic climates.

It is to Ionicizing models from the end of the sixth century that we must attach the two metopes from Temple F at Selinus, worked in high relief in tufa, in two halves, the lower of

which has survived. These represent the battle of Athena and Dionysus against the giants, and the lively plastic treatment could place them with the metopes of the Athenian Treasury at Delphi. However, when compared with the frieze on the Siphnian Treasury, where one finds the analogous theme of the gigantomachy, one notices in the Sicilian work the unorganic nature of the structure, the linearity, and the conventional, mannered fall of the Ionic draperies. Yet the head of the dying giant from Selinus (fig. 58) with closed eyes and half-open lips appears more expressive than similar heads of warriors from Aegina (fig. 59).

5. The Decoration of the Ionic Figured Frieze

The structural logic of the Ionic entablature with dentils in the frieze area did not originally include figured decoration, and in Asia Minor and the islands, where the Ionic style was first

60. In this frieze of banqueters from the Doric temple at Assos, the expressiveness of the Ionic idiom recalls analogous Etruscan interpretations. Circa 540 B.C. *Paris, Louvre*

61. Detail of the sharply profiled procession of quadrigas from the south frieze of the Siphnian Treasury at Delphi. Circa 525 B.C. Delphi, Museum

developed, we find no sculptured friezes. The *zoophoros* (a frieze having continuous relief sculptures of men or animals, or both) was found in Attica and Delphi during the sixth century, but was not canonized until the second century B.C. by the architect Hermogenes, in the Artemision at Magnesia. This concept of the Ionic order with a frieze will later appear in the treatise of Vitruvius. In the sixth century in Asia Minor, clay slabs, decorated principally with processions of chariots and warriors, were arranged in continuous series and applied to the wooden entablature. It is possibly this usage that accustomed one to the conception of a frieze. The taste for splendor characteristic of Asia Minor is seen in the Doric temple built at Assos in the Troad, about 540 B.C., where not only the metopes, but also the architrave beneath is decorated with a con-

tinuous relief frieze which has unity neither of theme nor composition. Here we see the adventures of Heracles with the sea monster and the centaurs, and banqueting scenes (fig. 60), all converging on the center, which is occupied by a heraldic group of sphinxes. The theme of Heracles and the monster recalls the analogous subject matter on the *poros* pediment from the Acropolis (fig. 49), and comparison makes evi-

62. The thick curls, the curve of the mouth and chin, and the brim turned back on his cap transform the Greek Hermes into a lively Etruscan Turms in this terracotta from Veii. Beginning of the fifth century B.C. Rome, Villa Giulia

dent the contrast between the styles of Attica and Asia Minor. This Assos temple demonstrates both the greater liberty acquired by the Doric order in the Ionian world, and the absence of friezes in the Asiatic Ionic order.

The Greek mainland — and in particular the Panhellenic sanctuaries, where many temples and treasuries were built side by side — was perhaps the first to feel the need to celebrate the gods in figured representations even within the Ionic order. In these Ionic buildings the function fulfilled by metopes in a Doric temple was taken over by a continuous frieze inserted between the dentils and the banded moldings of the architrave. Examples appeared in Delphi on the front of the Cnidian Treasury of about 545 B.C., and later on all the sides of the Siphnian Treasury of about 525 B.C.

The compositional problem of the Ionic frieze differed from that of the Doric metopes, since the frieze demanded a continuous, unified series of figures. The parade of panthers and horsemen on the Daedalic frieze at Prinias, similar to those on proto-Corinthian vases, was transformed into a mythological narrative in the sixth century, thus paralleling the change in the figured zones on Corinthian and Attic kraters and *deinoi*. On the east side of the frieze of the Siphnian Treasury the traditional Homeric duel takes place between two ranks of divinities vigorously participating in the action. The judgment of Paris appears on the west side, broadening the unified composition by placing the three goddesses on carefully spaced quadrigas. This quadriga motif also constitutes the fundamental decoration on the longer south side depicting the rape of the Leucippides. An animated gigantomachy stretches over the north side. The frieze was divided between two different sculptors; one, who worked in terms of volume and color, executed the east and north friezes, while the other, with a more two-dimensional approach that produced figures sharply outlined as silhouettes, was responsible for the friezes of the west and south sides (fig. 61). The precise rhythm of the spectator goddesses; the compact composition of the gigantomachy with its complex devices of fallen bodies, superimposed planes, and folds of drapery; the well-spaced quadrigas; the details added in bronze and polychromy — all make this frieze particularly exciting. The refined Ionic architecture of this treasury is further embellished by the two korai serving as caryatids in the pronaos — an idea already used in the Cnidian Treasury.

After these Archaic experiments at Delphi, the frieze underwent organic development in the creative climate of Pericles' Athens, and was used in the Ionic Temple of Athena Nike and the Erechtheion on the Acropolis. A frieze was also incorporated into the Doric order of the Parthenon to celebrate more fully the Athenians' magnificent offering to Athena. The frieze ran along the outer walls of the cella, depicting the long unfolding of Panathenaic pomp and ceremony. The same procedure was adopted for the Doric Hephaesteion, in order to heighten its resemblance to the Parthenon. Here the centauromachy, and mythical Attic battles against the Cyclops armed with gigantic boulders in the presence of gods, appeared on the two fronts of the cella. Iktinos, the architect of the Parthenon, later incorporated the figured frieze into the Ionic order in the cella of the composite Temple of Apollo at Bassae, reviving the themes of the centauromachy and Amazonomachy.

6. The Etruscan Temple and Its Decoration

Although the Doric order was prevalent in the Greek colonies of Sicily and Magna Graecia, Etruria developed a temple architecture that corresponded to its own cultural and ritual needs. We know from sources and monuments that Etruscan religion had evolved a complex of beliefs and rites regulated by a peculiarly Etruscan discipline. The aim was to interpret the will of the gods through the examination of the entrails and liver of sacrificed animals, through the observation of lightning and thunder, and of the flight of birds, all in accordance with norms regulating the orientation and subdivision of sacred space, and with a precise liturgical calendar. Thus, Arnobius was to call Etruria "the prime begetter and mother of superstitions," and Livy was to consider the Etruscan people particularly devoted to religious practices. Many aspects of this Etruscan religion may have stemmed from the Orient, but in the sixth century the assimilation of the anthropomorphic forms of Hellenic deities must already have been quite advanced. To the Hellenic gods were imparted aspects and concepts of Etruscan divinities (colorplate, fig. 62), but there were also persistent survivals of the native deities, of particular diads and triads and closely knit groups of gods, in addition to the vast world of demons that was faithfully mirrored in the cult of the dead. This complex, highly colorful religious sense explains the creation by the Etruscans of their own form of temple and tomb.

63. Clay revetment tile from the cornice of the pediment of an Etruscan temple at Arezzo. Circa 460–450 B.C. Arezzo, Archaeological M

The live tradition of clay-modeling and the lack of marble kept the Etruscan temple limited to a constant, prevailing wooden structure and a decoration of painted terracotta tile revetment (*antepagmenta*) on the entablature, friezes, hanging and pierced cornices, a plaque (*pinax*) decorating the end of the main beam (*columen*), antefixes, and statues used in the pediment and as akroteria.

The need for raising the wooden structure of the cella above ground level, so as to give it a solid support and provide a raised terrace for the rites of augury, resulted in the placing of the building on a stone podium finished with moldings. This podium sharply distinguished the Etruscan temple from the Greek, which rose directly from a low, stepped stylobate. Moreover, the Greek temple was designed to be viewed from all sides, a conception which culminated in the peripteral plan, whereas the Etruscan was built to be seen from the front. The entire plan was subordinated to this frontal point of view with a deep pronaos, a single staircase, and the rear chambers generally enclosed and placed against a back wall; this arrangement led to the creation of the cella with two lateral wings or of the rarer tripartite cella. The outline of the wooden structure remained low, rough, and heavy, with large spaces between the columns, and the dominant features of the elevation were the entablature with its splendid clay decoration and the heavy tiling of the roof. The stone foundations, podia, and terracottas that remain from excavated temples, the few clay or stone models, and the literary and Vitruvian sources are not sufficient to reconstruct the varied forms of the superstructure. We can only follow the stylistic development of the clay decoration through its various phases, which show traces of Greek motifs and the influence of Greek artists operating in various degrees within the local elaboration of the style.

The first phase of temple decoration bears the clear imprint of the Ionic current of the second half of the sixth century, and lasts into the first decade of the fifth century. The revetment tiles show a relationship with work in Asia Minor, while antefixes recall Campanian models. The antefixes with maenads' heads, from the first temple at Veii, of about 550 B.C., are in the late Daedalic tradition, whereas the decoration of the other temple at Veii from the end of the sixth or beginning of the fifth century — erroneously called Temple of Apollo, but really dedicated to Minerva — is fully influenced by the Ionian style.

The metopes of the Greek Doric temple contrast with the continuous frieze of the Etruscan, with its ornamental and figural motifs, processions of chariots and horsemen, donors and seated deities. Although the Greeks began to decorate temple pediments even in Archaic times, in Etruria pedimental decoration was undertaken for the first time only in the fifth century. We now have a fine example in the Etruscan pediment with a gigantomachy recently found at Pyrgi. From the earliest beginning a different structure was developed, with most of the triangle left empty, occupied only by the decorated plaque of the *columen* and by projecting the roof on the architrave bearing antefixes. Antefixes assumed much greater importance than in Greek temples, and were decorated with large gorgon heads, lively groups of maenads and satyrs, various monsters, and masks. Sculptural decoration also crowned the roof with clay statues at the outer corners of the pediment and on the akroteria, and even along the ridge of the roof, with a luxurious, baroque taste evidenced by the statues of Apollo, Hermes (colorplate, fig. 62), Latona, and Heracles found in the temple at Veii, from the beginning of the fifth century. The cornices of the pediment were also at times adorned with concave tiles with superimposed figures in high relief, as in examples from Arezzo from the first half of the fifth century (colorplate, fig. 63). These painted terracotta tiles bearing horsemen were lined up along the two slopes of the pediment, forming its cornice, in an architectural conception that would have been out of the question for any Greek architect.

The free, ornamental imagination of the Etruscans avoided the severe construction of the metope; and only much later did they adapt themselves to the compositional discipline of the pedimental field. And, although they emulated the important Greek decoration, the Etruscan artists preferred to expand their own, exuberantly rich decoration in friezes, antefixes, and akroterial statues, all of which provided ample field for clay-modelers to unleash their talents.

The Etruscan spirit remained foreign to the rigid canons of the Greek orders, and created a type of smooth-shafted, swelling column in wood or stone, with a simple base and a capital with semicircular molding. This column has been thought of as a survival of a proto-Doric column, but might rather be an Etruscanized adaptation of the Doric proper. Vitruvius calls these Etruscan architectural forms the "Tuscan order," though it was not an order in the sense of the fixed, rigorous canons of Greece. Moreover, the simultaneous varieties of columns and pilasters in tombs, of sepulchral pillars, figured monuments with faceted shafts, and capitals with floral volutes in which Phoenician, Cypriot, and Asian influences mingle and survive, are evidence both of the freedom from any fixed architectural order and of the prevailingly ornamental orientation of Etruscan architecture.

At the end of the sixth century architects

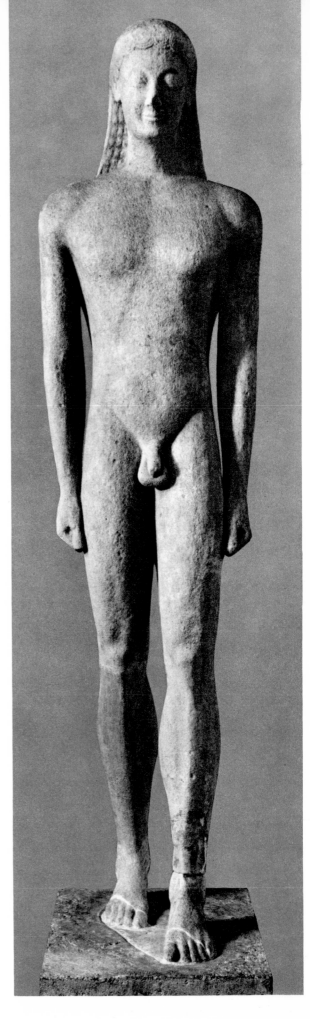

64. The Sphinx, dedicated by the people of Naxos, rises like an apotropaic sentinel on top of its high Ionic column in the sanctuary of Delphi. Circa 550 B.C. Delphi, Museum

65. The slim proportions and soft, sensitive modeling of this kouros from Melos characterize the Ionic style of the islands. Circa 540 B.C. Athens, National Museum

77

and terracotta modelers from all over Etruria were called to Rome to erect the Temple of Jupiter Capitolinus. The artist Vulca came from Veii to model the statue of Jupiter, a figure of Hercules, and perhaps the large akroterial quadriga. Rome, under the dynasty of the last three kings, had entered the orbit of Etruscan culture in the course of Etruscan expansion toward Campania and the plains of the Po. From a shepherds' village Rome had been turned into a city organized in four districts and surrounded by a tufa wall, with the Forum Romanum systematized, commercial quarters along the Tiber, the Forum Boarium, the Forum Olitorium, and with the monumental sacred area on the Capitoline Hill.

The Romans, however, were still simple in their customs. "They were not concerned with beauty," says the historian Strabo, "as they were all preoccupied with greater, more necessary things." Their houses were still as modest as their tombs, whereas in the surrounding area from Caere to Praeneste the sumptuous Orientalizing splendor had already flowered in the seventh century. Pottery from Corinth, Ionia, and Attica, first with black and then with red figures, arrived in Rome, but there were still no signs of an assimilation of the artistic and cultural currents from Etruria, Greece, and Campania. There were no examples of rich furnishings, but only the outward signs of a simple, rustic way of life. It is therefore all the more significant that the coarse Romans, with a religious fervor that was at the same time a uniting political force, should have seen fit to make their Capitolium rich and monumental, concentrating all their energies on the project and summoning the finest Etruscan artists of the time. The tufa foundations that have survived bear witness to the grandeur of the temple, measuring about 200 by 184 feet. The temple also served for Senate meetings, triumphal ceremonies, the dedication of *spolia opima*, and as an archive of treaties with foreign powers. The miraculous legends surrounding the clay statues convey the bewildered admiration of the Romans when faced with these artistic manifestations. During the sixth century other temples of the Etrusco-Italic type were certainly built in Rome, as is shown by the architectural slabs with Orientalizing heraldic felines found in the Forum, and those with Ionian processions of chariots found near the church of Sant'Omobono, where the temple of Fortuna and Mater Matuta stood. The same site yielded an akroterion with a figure of a warrior, while a female antefix of Ionic inspiration was found on the Capitoline Hill. These Roman temples were therefore similar to those of Veii, Velletri and the Faliscan area.

7. Greek Artists of the Archaic Period

During the seventh century anonymous primitive statuary was all grouped under the symbolic name of Daedalus, but by the sixth century both literary and epigraphic sources began to record the names of individual artists.

Cretan tradition mentions the sculptors Dipoinos and Skyllis, who are supposed to have been active around 580 B.C. They were pupils of Daedalus himself, and were supposed to have worked in Sicyon, Argos, Cleonae, and Ambracia, creating statues of gods in marble, ivory, and wood. Their pupils were the Spartans Dontas, Dorykleidas, and Theokles, who worked in Olympia, and Klearchos of Reggio, who worked in his home country and also in Sparta.

A true dynasty of sculptors is recorded in Chios with the founder, Melas, his son Mikkiades and grandson Archermos, who are referred to in two inscriptions at Delos and Athens; and later his great-grandsons Bupalos and Athenis, who were active around 540 B.C. and were supposed to have made a realistic portrait of the ugly Hipponattes and sculpted statues on Delos and Lesbos, and at Smyrna, Clazomenae, and Pergamon. An inscription on a base at Delos names Mikkiades and Archermos, and there has been much discussion concerning the identification of this base as that belonging to an Archaic marble Nike, datable about 550 B.C. This Nike of Delos, whose flight is transformed into a "running on bent knees" position in parallel planes at right angles to the spectator, is, in any case, a typical example of Archaic island sculpture, and we do know from sources that Archermos executed a winged Nike. On Delos, the primitive Temple of Apollo had held a grandiose image in gold and ivory made by the sculptors Tektaios and Angelion, pupils of the sculptors Dipoinos and Skyllis. On Naxos, which was rich in marble, Byzes, supposedly the first to make marble roof tiles for temples, and his son Euergos were active. The great sculptural activity on this island is evidenced by kouroi left in various stages of completion, and by the superb Sphinx at Delphi dedicated by the people of Naxos (fig. 64). The Sphinx stands vigilant upon the tall Ionic column, in a Hellenized interpretation of the apotropaic Oriental monster, its vibrant, bony body bursting

66. In comparison with the nudity of Attic, Doric, and Cycladic kouroi, the Ionic kouros of Samos and Asia Minor were fully clothed in this example from Cape Phoneas on Samos. Circa 550 B.C. Samos, Museum

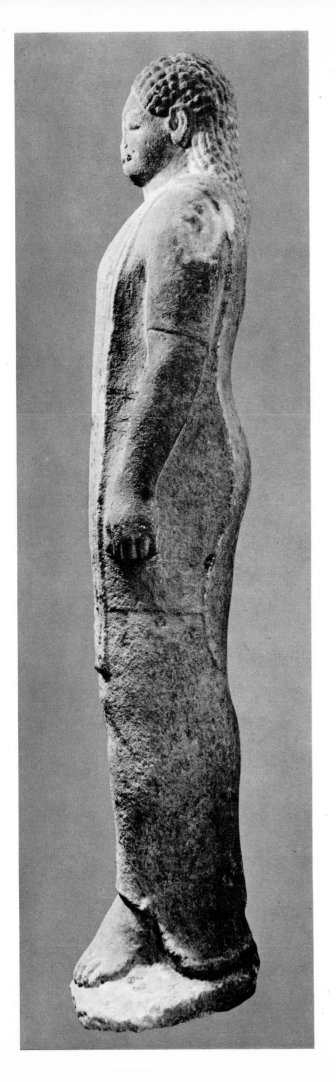

with vital strength. There is an elaborate calligraphic treatment of its wings and other details. This vigorous linear sense is also present in some marble korai from Naxos discovered on the Athenian Acropolis, which must be attributed to a sculptor from this island.

In the Cyclades the kouros takes on the delicate, slender structure typified by the slim figure from Melos (fig. 65), dating from about 540 B.C. On Thasos, beside influences from Chios and Paros to be seen in the kouroi, we find clearly discernible currents from Asia Minor in the full-blown reliefs on some gates,

67. This Ionic head from Ephesus is modeled with the softness of gently curving planes typical of the work of Asia Minor. Circa 530 B.C. London, British Museum

68. This Ionic lion (two views) from Miletus differs from Egyptian lions in its lively psychological interpretation; and in its languid fluidity of form it is also very different from the vigorous stalking felines of Archaic Doric sculpture. Circa 525–510 B.C. Berlin, State Museums

69. The aristocratic image of the Athens of the Pisistratids is seen in this figure of a horseman, recomposed from a torso found on the Acropolis, the so-called Rampin Head. Circa 550 B.C. Head: Paris, Louvre; torso: Athens, Acropolis Museum

like Heracles the Archer and the satyr with a *kantharos*. Samos seems to have been even more closely linked with the Ionic conceptions of Asia Minor. The celebrated sanctuary of Hera on that island attracted faithful pilgrims from all parts, so that discoveries have included Egyptian, Assyrian, and Oriental statuettes, testifying to the fervent artistic climate. The sources record two artists with the name of Theodoros, perhaps one older than the other, as well as Rhoikos, and Telekles. Theodoros appears to have been an original architect in Ephesus and Sparta, and along with Rhoikos at the Heraion of Samos. Theodoros was also an expert metal-worker, and engraver of the famous ring of Polycrates, a silver krater for Croesus in Delphi, and another for the King of Persia. He was credited with the invention of the lathe, the mason's level, the square rule, and, again with Rhoikos, the technique of using sand for casting bronzes hollow or in pieces.

Six statues from the Sacred Way at Samos, which were dedicated about 550 B.C., are the important documentation of the work of the sculptor Geneleos and the artistic style of this center. These works include: the seated figure of the priestess Phileia; three standing females, Philippe, Ornithe (fig. 37), and another; a kouros; and a reclining woman holding a dove. The full-bodied figures are modeled in generous, soft volumes. Their surfaces are enlivened by fine incising, which traces the folds of the chitons.

This fluidity of line and fine modeling is also typical of the slightly earlier *"Hera" of Samos* and the related figure of a kore holding a hare, both dedicated by Cheramyes (figs. 35, 36). And rounded forms and continuous lines can also be seen even in the small bronzes from

70. *Ionic charm finds a lively interpretation in this polychrome Acropolis Maiden (no. 675) of Cycladic style.*
Circa 530 B.C. *Athens, Acropolis Museum*

71. *Silver coin of Syracuse with a female head in pure Hellenic Archaic style, similar to a kore of the Acropolis; surrounded by leaping dolphins. Second half of the sixth century B.C.*

72. *To the Attic sculptor of the* Rampin H is attributed this kore. The work is sturdy in structure, with an articulated rhythm and delicate chiaroscuro effect in the modeling.
Circa 540 B.C. *Athens, Acropolis Museum*

the Samos-Asia Minor area (fig. 40). But if we compare the two cylindrical figures dedicated by Cheramyes with the Ornithe of Geneleos (figs. 35, 36, 37), we see that the work of Geneleos is no longer enclosed in a cylindrical structure, and indeed represents a further development of the Samian style.

Geneleos' seated figure of Phileia corresponds exactly to the seated figures of priests and priestesses of the family of the Branchidae at Miletus, with their volumetric structure defined by a solid block with rounded corners, and an immobile, hieratic quality that seems inspired by Oriental models. Over the incised folds of the chitons, the himatia fall in broad, flattened, soft ridges. The kouros wearing a mantle, from the Geneleos group, represents a type that was widespread in Asia Minor, where there was a continual reluctance to accept the nudity characteristic of Dorian and Attic art due to the influence of Eastern customs. Indeed, Herodotus tells us that it was considered extremely shameful among the Lydians and other barbaric peoples for a man to be seen naked. And it is significant that in the lists of contestants in the Olympic games, where nudity was prescribed, the percentage of athletes from Eastern countries was small.

A typical kouros, well wrapped in a long mantle that clings to the swelling structure of his body as he catches a corner of his garment with a lazy, feminine gesture that is Ionian in spirit (fig. 66), comes from Cape Phoneas on Samos and is similar to another dating from 530 B.C. from Pitane near Pergamon, and also to certain terracotta figures. The rounded, receding structure of the head relates these kouroi to similar kouroi heads from Miletus and Rhodes and to female figures, now in London, found near the Artemision of Ephesus. A fragment of a mid-sixth-century female head from Ephesus (fig. 67) attains a painterly, soft modeling, and a veiled head from Miletus, in Berlin (fig. 39), resembles the veiled figures decorating a carved column of the Temple of Apollo at Didyma, near Miletus. These heads, such as that shown in figure 67, sum up all the Ionian spirit in the subtle line of the elongated eyes, the flowing continuity of the surface, and their refined grace.

Animal figures from this region also reveal this same soft, fleshy structure, as illustrated

73. As the inscription tells us, this funerary stele with the Athenian warrior Aristion was made by Aristokles. The precisely carved relief is modeled with a fine chiaroscuro effect. Circa 520 B.C. Athens, National Museum

by the monumental statues of crouching lions from Miletus (fig. 68). Their heavy mass relaxes and spreads, merging with the base in unified surfaces, against which stands out the accurate, sharp drawing of the flamboyant mane. Comparison with the alert, vigorous, bony feline from Corfu (fig. 47), who crouches but is ready to leap forward, throws into relief the difference between Ionic and Doric conceptions.

Athens during the sixth century, in addition to sculptured decoration of temples, also developed statuary in marble. After the first monumental kouroi of the late seventh century there

74. *Small head of a kouros in Greek marble, from a statue not more than 3 feet high. This piece, found at Marzabotto, is a singular example of original Greek sculpture imported into Etruria. End of the sixth century* B.C. *Marzabotto, Museo Aria*

75. *The discus raised in the hand of this athlete was formerly painted blue, and provided a background for the crystalline modeling of the head. Attic funerary stele.* Circa *550–540* B.C. *Athens, National Museum*

followed an uninterrupted series of creations in which Doric vigor was combined with Ionic grace, and animated by a very sensitive, delicate chiaroscuro effect in the modeling that was governed by a superbly balanced taste.

Artists now generally signed their works, and we know the names of various sculptors. Among them stands out Endoios, who was alleged to have been a pupil of Daedalus. His favorite theme would appear to be the image of Athena, the patron goddess of his city. He sculpted Athena in wood as Athena Polias for the city of Eretria; in marble, Athena with Graces and Horai; in ivory as Athena Alea for Tegea; and he executed an enthroned Athena in marble for Athens itself. This last work, dedicated by Kallias on the Acropolis, has been identified with a mutilated, headless statue found in the slopes of the Acropolis. It is distinguished by a tense, energetic rhythm, very different from the stasis of the massive, enthroned figures of the Branchidae at Miletus. Since Endoios sculpted the effigy of Artemis at Ephesus, and was commissioned by the Ionian Lampito to make a funerary monument in Athens at the end of the sixth century, it has been thought that Endoios was educated in Ionia and later emigrated to Athens, perhaps as a result of Persian expansion. Yet the headless statue from Athens shows absolutely no relationship with the style of Asia Minor and is more easily related to the lively gods on the east frieze of the Siphnian Treasury. However, it may be that Endoios represents one of the artists who contributed to the spread of Ionic influence in Attica. In Athens he also executed a funerary monument for the Alcmaeonid Nelonides between 527 and 515 B.C.

We have the signatures of the sculptors Epistemon, Phaidimos, Philermos, Pollias, Bion, and Amphikrates, evidence of intense artistic activity in Athens. A certain structural exuberance that recalls contemporary pedimental sculpture in *poros*, but with an intense dramatic interplay of planes, is to be seen in the robust marble statuary of the *Moschophoros*, or Calf-Bearer, dedicated by Rhombos on the Acropolis around 565 B.C. The figure is architecturally constructed with a rhythmic crossing of his arms and the legs of the animal, and is fixed in a direct, compelling relationship with the viewer. A decade later, a similar vigor, though not yet entirely disciplined, created the strong limbs of the so-called "Aphrodite of Marseilles" (fragments conserved in the Museum at Lyons and the Acropolis Museum in Athens), who holds a dove in her right hand and does not yet wear the Ionic costume of the later figures. But by the middle of the century a great Athenian master had already attained the most exciting

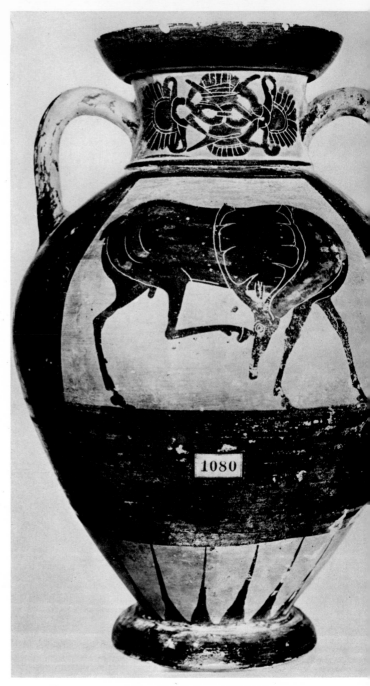

76. The deer licking itself, a favorite motif of Minoan-Mycenaean and Orientalizing artists, is here used by an Attic vase painter within the new monumentality of a single large metope. Mid-sixth century B.C. Athens, National Museum

results, with exceptional control and enormous grace, in two masterworks, one known as the *Rampin Horseman*, with the *Rampin Head* (fig. 69), the other a more mature kore wearing a peplos, from about 540 B.C. (colorplate, fig. 72). The remaining Archaic accents of the detailed, analytical calligraphy that indicates the short hair and beard of the *Rampin Head*, the delicate half-moons of his lips and the slightly slanted eyes that softly gaze out of both these statues, as well as the smooth, unbroken surface of the kore's peplos, are all transformed under

77. *As written in the inscription, the spectators seated as if in tiers of an arena are watching the funeral games in honor of Patroclus;* deinos *signed by Sophilos. Circa 570 B.C. Athens, National Museum*

this master's chisel into notes of intense poetry and magical vitality.

During this period Athens summoned artists from Ionia and the islands, and indeed imported marble for statues from these regions, for although Pentelic marble was being quarried in the mid-sixth century, it was used mainly for building. Pythis was Ionian, Bion came from Miletus, and Archermos and Bupalos came from Chios to work; Paros sent Aristion; and Archedamos came from Thera; Gorgias, who had come from Sparta, signed the bases of five statues on the Acropolis between 530 and 500 B.C., and seemingly preferred the subject of horses; and at the end

of the sixth century Kalon arrived from Aegina. The series of fifty-six korai dedicated in the second half of the sixth century on the Acropolis, known as the Acropolis Maidens (fig. 70), and generally placed on columns or pilasters, reveal Ionic and island influences in the varying quality and interpretations of the different sculptors. These influences are further seen in the graceful drapery of the thin tunics ruffled with tightly packed little pleats and the oblique mantles with their folds emphasized by the curving zigzag of the hem and the swallow-tail border, liberally sprinkled with ornament and edgings in bright polychromy. Archaic rigidity has been relaxed in the arms of these figures, whether outstretched in offering, or bent in the rather affected gesture of hitching up the garment to one side.

This Ionian influence has often been considered the effective cause of a "renaissance" in Attic art. However, the inherent Attic qualities had already been manifest for half a century in the rich opportunities offered by monumental statuary and pedimental carving, and with a vitality so great as to justify an autonomous, original, and enlightened development. On the other hand, the more Ionic works were the most mannered, whereas the authentic Attic spirit gave substance to works of a more elevated tone, with an organic development stretching from the "Aphrodite of Marseilles" to the great kore by the sculptor Antenor, the son of the painter Eumares. In this kore, dedicated by one Nearchos in about 520 B.C., Ionic accents have a solid Attic framework and take on a new, monumental quality. These qualities enabled Antenor to conceive the figures on the pediments of the Temple of Apollo at Delphi as statues, multiplying the types of korai and kouroi. After Athens was freed from the tyranny of the Pisistratids, Antenor created the first public monument in the city, which was erected in the Agora. It represented the tyrannicides, Harmodius and Aristogiton, idealized in heroic nudity and cast in bronze. During the sack of Athens Xerxes carried off the group, and it was remade by Kritios and Nesiotes about 477 B.C. Antenor's group is perhaps reflected in the summary sketch by a modest vase painter on a black-figured *lekythos* now in Vienna.

Sculptors also played creative roles in the area of funerary steles, which by now replaced the large vases that had been placed on tombs. During the time of Pisistratus the stele assumed imposing proportions, topped by a capital surmounted by a sphinx carved in the round, while on the long, narrow face of the stele the figure of the dead, and at times a frieze of chariots below, were either incised or carved in low relief. After about 530 B.C. the crowning capital was replaced by a simpler palmette. The finely carved stele by Aristokles of about 520 B.C. shows the warrior Aristion (fig. 73). Others bear the discus thrower (fig. 75), or the man leaning on a stick and offering a grasshopper to his dog, and are carved in low relief and heightened with polychromy.

The votive relief in marble appears at this time alongside the more modest votive tablets (*pinakes*) of painted terracotta. A relief dedicated by the potter Pamphaios shows him seated among his *kylixes*. The kore of Antenor was probably dedicated by the potter Nearchos, the father of the potters Ergoteles and Tleson,

and we also have ex-voto bases dedicated by Andokides, Mnesiades, Euphronios, Peikon, Archeneides, Brygos, Charinos, Onesimos, and Kriton, the son of Skythes. Generally these date from after the death of Pisistratus, and indicate that potters and vase painters were acquiring an important position in Athenian society with the affirmation of democracy.

8. Attic Vase Painters: The Black-Figure Technique

Toward the middle of the sixth century Corinthian painted pottery, which had dominated the markets for a long time, went into a rapid decline. As if to balance this phenomenon, Attic work triumphed and took first place, reaching a very high level of technical and stylistic perfection.

After the unbridled, exuberant flowering of the proto-Attic style in the seventh century, Attic vase painters seem to have coordinated their energies and concentrated on specific problems, developing a more controlled and accurate narrative language. Already at the end of the seventh century the type of amphora with a continuous profile appeared, still heavy and fat but with unbroken lines and an over-all coat of black paint, except for one large metope left in the light ground; in this space was sketched, in black, a horse protome or woman's head shown framed as if looking through an open window. The creation of this type of decoration seems to have been a conscious reaction against the very large figures that had overflowed the surface of the vase in the most characteristic proto-Attic style. This new decorative scheme imposed a well-defined space on the subject treated, just like that imposed by the metope of the Doric frieze. The sizable female head, which is an enlargement of Corinthian types, reveals an organic study of the human face which was also being realized at that time in sculpture in the monumental kouroi and korai. An amphora with a metope showing a deer licking itself seems to attempt to transpose an Orientalizing motif onto the structural monumentality of this new type of single-metope decoration (fig. 76).

The large dimensions of the animal and human protomes offered little scope for ornament, thus limiting the development of a narrative style. It is therefore significant that Attic vase painters now seemed to look on Corinthian pottery with interest. Indeed, Corinthian pottery possessed many qualities — refined decorative sense, compositional logic, minute detail, and narrative clarity — that pro-

78. Detail of the two zones on the neck of the François vase, the oldest Attic volute-krater, masterpiece of the potter Ergotimos and the painter Kleitias. Circa *570 B.C. Florence, Archaeological Museum*

vided Attic artists with exercises in discipline, as well as fertile teaching. The Athenians also at this time copied some Corinthian vase forms such as the deep *kotyle*, the cup with a flared lip, known as a Comast cup, the *hydria* (water jar), the *pyxis* (small box), the *lekythos*, the *alabastron* (small bottle), and the column-krater. They also imitated motifs such as the characteristic Corinthian animal friezes, which were to be remodeled continuously until the middle of the sixth century, and the dynamic types of padded dancers and revelers, common in the middle Corinthian style. A few vase painters, like the so-called Corinthianizing Painter, whose title needs no explanation, had a fondness for the long processions of warriors carrying round decorated shields, visibly derived from proto-Corinthian work. This type of scene was used by painters to fill out mythological exploits such as the slaying of Priam or the ambush of Troilus by Achilles. The latter theme was very widespread during the sixth century: it was carved on a *poros* pediment of the Acropolis, and also painted by the Corinthian Timonidas. Corinthian-style warriors also fight on the cover of a *kothon* (three-footed *pyxis*), in which the Corinthianizing Painter, showing a taste for narration, gives us the first formulation of a typically Attic subject treated often by later painters, the birth of Athena.

A current style that combined Attic and Corinthian traditions, lotus flowers, animal friezes, mythological scenes from the sacrifice of Polyxena to the departure of Amphiaraus, and monotonous Amazonomachies developed in the second quarter of the sixth century on a type of ovoid amphora, called Tyrrhenian, since it was found particularly in Etruria.

Perfecting the techniques of black glaze and incising, Attic vase painters studiously began composing complex scenes, reducing the dimensions and increasing the amount of incised detail. After the grandiosity of proto-Attic the trend was now toward a miniaturist style, not only in small vases like the conical-footed *kylixes* with wide, flared rims, but also in the large *deinoi*, in kraters, amphorae, and *hydriai*.

Vase painters, conscious of the diligence lavished on their work, now began to sign their names as the sculptors did. The first name known is that of Sophilos. This painter, particularly in his first works, is inspired by Corinthian principles, seen in his generous use of animal friezes, in the use of a white pigment for female nudes and for horses, and in the forms of his vases. A new spirit of mythological narration, however, appears in scenes on his *deinoi*: for example, the marriage of Peleus and Thetis, with the colorful procession of gods two by two, or the funeral games in

79. Skillfully composed and set into the metope field, the ponderous horses of the Attic vase painter Lydos file by in measured pace with solemn monumentality. Circa 545 B.C. Naples, National Museum

honor of Patroclus, with miniature-like spectators seated in tiers and gesticulating vivaciously (fig. 77). Though his drawing was not particularly rigorous, he tried to add minute animal friezes as decoration for the women's rich costumes, and to give expression to the action he depicted. He was the first to produce the image of the hairy, bearded satyr.

But the true measure of the level reached by Attic pottery at the end of the first half of the sixth century is shown by the masterwork of another painter, Kleitias, in the striking François vase in Florence (colorplate, fig. 78), the oldest and perhaps the finest volute-krater in existence, the work of the potter Ergotimos. Zonal composition is here remarkably well

adapted to the form of the vase. The most important frieze, with the picturesque parade of deities on their way to the marriage of Peleus and Thetis, is kept for the widest point of the vase, followed below by the ambush of Troilus by Achilles, two themes already treated by Sophilos and the Corinthianizing Painter. On the same band with the ambush of Troilus is the return of Hephaestus into Olympus which bears many witty touches, while the lowest frieze consists of the less important, more traditional animal theme. In the tapered lower part of the high neck, the painter placed the themes of the chariot race for the funeral games of Patroclus and the centauromachy, creating a circular rhythm that underlines the

80. *On this amphora by the Amasis Painter a vivacious and rhythmic pair of elaborately dressed maenads offer fawns to a sumptuously clad Dionysus. Circa 530 B.C. Paris, Bibliothèque Nationale*

ample girth of the large krater. The frieze directly above this, which decorates the part just below the rim, consists of two refined and lively compositions, the Calydonian boar hunt centered round the enormous boar, and an original scene of the ship of Theseus and his companions, with Theseus and Ariadne leading a dance of boys and girls to celebrate the slaying of the Minotaur. With the same sense of harmony, the painter chose to fill the restricted space on the foot with a theme whose protagonists are tiny pygmies in a furious battle with their enemies, the aggressive cranes. On the outer side of the broad ribbon-form handles is a hieratic Artemis shown as mistress of the beasts. Below her, as a tragic

epilogue to the adventures of the son born of the marriage of Peleus and Thetis, is the isolated group of Ajax carrying the inert body of Achilles. The inner face of the volute bears an apotropaic gorgon, like those seen by the drinker on the inside of a *kylix*.

This masterful handling of composition on the François vase corresponds with the accuracy and sureness of style, the narrative verve, and the subject matter which is as original in the treatment of traditional themes as in the development of less well-known material. There is, moreover, a richness of detail that culminates in the minute incising of the women's costumes, as well as a wide variety of vivid touches, from the figure of Dionysus who stares at the on-

81. The theme of the horse, dear to Exekias, finds a lively representation in a scene of the yoking of the horses to the chariot on this amphora, found at Tarquinia and attributed to Exekias. Circa 530 B.C. Boston, Museum of Fine Arts

looker as he carries the great amphora on his shoulders, to the gestures that give subtly varied characterization to the various figures in the nuptial procession. The entire vase is animated, from the changing rhythms of the hunt to the expressive intensity of the joy that moves and excites Theseus' sailors so that their spirits brim over at the sight of the dance announcing their liberation from the Minotaur.

Here Attic vase painting surpasses Corinthian work. Although Kleitias did not have the vivacity of Sophilos, he was well ahead of him in elegance, dignity, and expressive clarity. His refined taste shows even in a simple cup from Gordion, now in Berlin, decorated only

with three dolphins and a fish. The potter Ergotimos was the creator of this new type of *kylix*, known as the Gordion cup, set on a tall stem with a decorated medallion inside. The Gordion cup was preceded by a type known as the Siana cup, and was followed, after the middle of the century, by the Little Master cups. These were the culminating point of the miniaturist style, with minute friezes even smaller than those of the Siana cups.

The numerous class of *kylixes* by the Little Masters breaks up into three main types. The band-cup is entirely painted in black except for a single band running between the handles, in which complicated figures or animal friezes

82. *The epic and heroic character of the style of Exekias resounds in the complex group of Ajax carrying the inert body of Achilles on this amphora found at Chiusi. Circa 530 B.C. Berlin, State Museums*

extend in converging arrangements. The lip-cup is black only on the foot and the lower part of the basin, the rest being left its natural color and divided into two zones by a groove and a thin line running between the handles; the part above this line carries decoration in the form of an animal figure or a human head, while the part below bears a painted inscription running between two delicate palmettes placed at the handles. In this type the inscription often constitutes the only decorative element, with extremely sober, accurate characters. The third type of cup, known as Droop

or Antidoros cup, has more developed decoration, though it is still miniaturistic in form.

Some painters seem to have devoted themselves entirely to decorating these miniaturist cups: the painter of the cups by the potter Hermogenes, the painters who worked with the potters Tleson or Xenocles, or the painter Sakonides, who painted delicate and accurate small female heads. Others, however, also worked on large vases, for example, the painter of the *kylixes* made by Taleides, or another who worked with the potter Phrynos; other prominent vase painters like Exekias, the Nikosthenes Painter, and the Amasis Painter, only occasionally painted *kylixes*.

But beside this miniaturist taste, which was most successfully realized in cups and in some zonal friezes on large vases, Attic vase painters, masters of their technical and expressive means, also felt the need to manifest the vision of grandeur and sense of monumentality which had already flowered in the proto-Attic style and on the type of amphora with a single large metope. The so-called Acropolis 606 Painter (who takes his name from a *deinos* in Athens bearing that number), along with a small frieze of animal groups, spreads out a large epic scene of chariot clashes, in which the complexity of the motifs, the use of white and crimson, the decoration of the chitons worn by charioteers and warriors, and the robust, articulated, elegant horses create a scene that has the impetus and breadth of a great painting. The motif of horses and riders in monumental isolation also appears in the metopes of this painter's large amphorae, almost like a development from the Archaic vases with horse protomes. Another contemporary vase painter, Nearchos, appears to be a miniaturist in his spirited battle of pygmies against cranes, on a little *aryballos* in New York. However, in his *kantharoi* he attains a definite monumentality, supported by rich, rigorous, incised details, which culminates in his figure of Achilles saddling his horse.

Among the multiplicity of aspects that characterize this period is a particularly solid, statuesque plasticity that is reflected in the vast production of the vase painter Lydos between 550 and 530 B.C. (fig. 79). His female figures wrapped in their mantles retain the Archaic "penguin" stance; but his male nudes have the solid structure of contemporary Attic sculpture and they are conceived in clear spatial isolation, with a narrative vivacity and touches of elegance and grace. Theseus, the Attic hero, occupies the first place among the themes treated by these Athenian vase painters, whereas animal friezes tend to disappear.

Lydos also signed one of the Panathenaic

amphorae; these appeared after the foundation of the games in 566 B.C. and constitute a characteristic vase type in themselves. Their particular purpose as prizes and their symbolic decoration demanded not only that the shape never vary, but also the continued use of the black-figure technique as well as certain motifs — Athena Promachos on one side and, on the other, metopes of athletic scenes set between fighting cocks and inscriptions. As a result of this standardization, these vases present an interesting illustration, spanning several centuries, of the stylistic transformation of the Archaic language. The development can be traced from the first Panathenaic amphorae, in which Athena was not yet clad in Ionian costume, like that of Lydos or the heavy Burgon amphora, right up to the affected, archaizing mannerism of fourth-century examples.

The activity of the prolific vase painter who embellished the vases made by Amasis extends through the period of the Pisistratid tyranny from 560 to 526 B.C. In addition to eight signed vases we can point to ninety or so that seem to indicate his hand. Thus we can follow the artistic development of this personality through a great variety of vases and motifs. His first amphorae have unbroken profiles and the metopes hold five or six figures standing in a symmetrical, converging group, with scenes of arming, or of conversations, or Dionysiac subjects, or with tense, nude adolescents that recall kouroi. In his later amphorae with sharply defined necks, a form created under the influence of the models of the contemporary Exekias, the figures are limited to concentrated, elegant groups of two or three conversing in the middle of a light background (fig. 80). They are no longer framed in the space of a metope, but are set among refined, spiraloid ornament; and they wear more decorative garments, marked with three-dimensional folds. Dionysus, the fat, shaggy satyrs, and the pretty maenads with their varicolored costumes and flesh tones rendered by making use of the light ground color, triumph in lively groupings, showing thematic preferences that link the Amasis Painter with Lydos. A light note is struck by the romping dog that the artist introduces into many of his scenes. With his flowing decorative sense it was the Amasis Painter who best interpreted the Ionian taste that was influencing the Attic world, and declared itself in sculpture in the graceful, polychromed korai. Imitators of the Amasis Painter easily fell into mannerisms; a typical representative of this group is, indeed, known as the Affected Painter.

The other great vase painter of the time, Exekias, had a totally different temperament. With concentration and austere dignity, this master of a workshop modeled and painted his own vases, creating a new form of *kylix* with a low foot. He is also responsible for the creation of a wide cup with an unbroken outline, no rim, and exterior decoration of large apotropaic eyes; this remained the model for a series known as the "eye cups," not only in black-figured, but also in red-figured pottery. This painter's originality is revealed in his skillful use of the zone between the handles for scenes of epic combats, and in transforming the interior medallion of the *kylix* into a wide pictorial scene, in which the ship of Dionysus sails calmly in the dolphin-spotted sea against a coral-colored ground.

Exekias may also have created the calyx-krater on which, along with the journey of Heracles to Olympus, we find an epic combat over the body of Patroclus. Large vases were more suitable than *kylixes* for expressing the grandiose nature of Exekias' style, his epic themes, and his Homeric spirit. The series of amphorae certainly constitutes his most significant work (figs. 81, 82), along with clay plaques for tomb decoration, such as had previously been painted by Sophilos and Lydos. The long, ringing notes of the *epos* of the Acropolis 606 Painter are succeeded by a more austere and concentrated tone in the work of Exekias, who resumes epic and myth in the essential figures of the protagonists, increasing dramatic intensity and composed dignity. On his amphora in London, the Amazonomachy is resolved into the pathetic group of Achilles and Penthesilea, placed on the free, light ground and framed in the fine, elegant volutes that appealed so much to the Amasis Painter. Ajax and Achilles are also isolated and absorbed in a game of dice on the Vatican amphora; on the Boulogne amphora Exekias communicates epic, human drama by the solitude of Ajax, who resolutely fixes his sword into the ground for his suicide in the shade of the palm tree, the sole, mute witness to the scene.

Pathos, intense and human but noble and sustained, swells through the funerary scenes on painted clay tablets. A matchless balance of human and divine heightens the picture of the Dioscuri on the Vatican amphora; here also is the robust, well-articulated type of horse that Exekias represented lovingly in a series of examples ending with the original pose of the grazing horse on the Philadelphia amphora. With Exekias, black-figure technique reaches its zenith; the sure, plastic line is sustained by an elaborate interplay of minute incising in hair, clothing, and weapons, rivaling the finest chiseling of any bronze-worker. Many painters followed the style of Exekias, but none attained his stature.

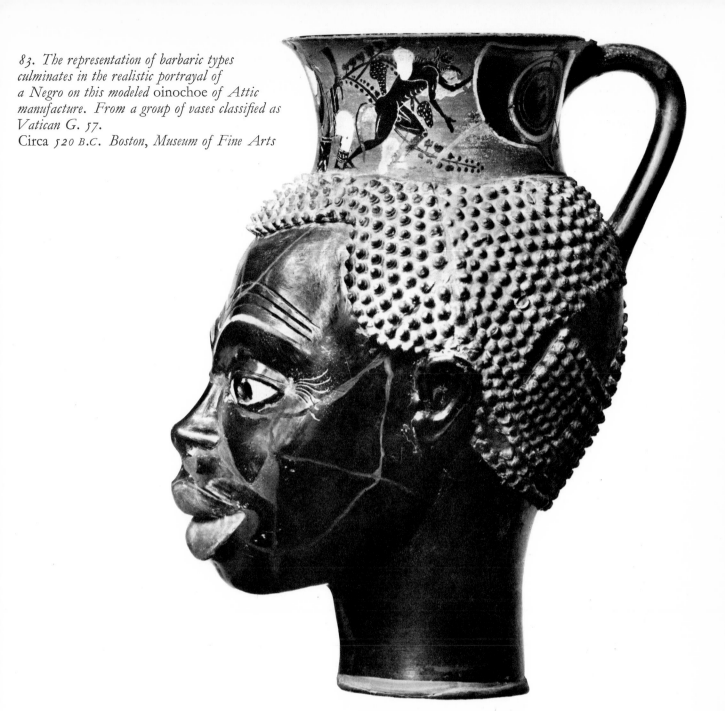

9. Creation of the Red-Figure Technique and the Late Black-Figure Style

In Athens about 530 B.C. a new pictorial technique was discovered which used red figures with a solid black background. The red figures were created by utilizing the color of the natural clay ground and surrounding the figures with the solid black background. The figure bore a thin overpainting in light red, and details within the red figures were expressed by painting in fine black lines, diluted glazes, and retouchings in white and crimson. The solid black figure had allowed only the addition of incised detail — a fundamentally calligraphic effect very close to drawing; but the figure formed by utilizing the light tone of the ground could be treated with a varied range of pictorial and plastic devices. These devices consisted of variations in the thickness of lines and in the thickness of the paint, which was used in heavy blobs for curly hair, and also in transparent touches of diluted pigment, achieving a new range of coloring that went far beyond the limits of the sharp, severe, two-color system. In sculpture an analogous difference can be distinguished in the frieze of the Siphnian Treasury: the sharp cut of the contour lines that characterizes the sculptor of the rape of the Leucippides and the judgment of Paris, on the one hand; and on the other the soft plastic sense that models coloristically the rich details in the works of the master of the gigantomachy and the gods watching the Homeric duel. The red figures on vases stand out against the black background like those that were carved on reliefs and on

95

84. An amphora of the type created by Nikosthenes, modeled by Pamphaios. The painting is by Oltos, who here experiments in the red-figure technique in scenes of satyrs and maenads, and on the neck figures of hetaerae. Circa *520 B.C. Paris, Louvre*

funerary steles, where the figures were seen against a background painted in a darker tone, usually red or blue. The inversion of the tonal relationships, with the light figures against a black background, can be compared with the practice in Etruscan goldsmiths' work, which contrasted figures executed in dust-fine granulation on a smooth ground, as well as luminous hammered figures against an opaque background covered with fine granulation. The latter technique appears in a boss from Vignanello, now in the Villa Giulia.

The fundamental change to red figures probably took place in the workshop of the potter Andokides toward the end of the reign of Pisistratus, and was the creation of an anonymous painter who has been called the Andokides Painter. At first, probably to accustom his clients to the novelty, he had to use the two techniques, one on each face of the same vase, a juxtaposition that clearly illustrates the difference between the old black-figure technique and the expressive possibilities of the new approach using red figures. The contrast becomes even more significant in the works of painters who remained faithful to the black-figure technique, continuing in isolation right up to the Persian Wars. Exekias had already experimented with all the most elevated representational resources of black-figure technique. However, none of the many painters who followed in the last quarter of the sixth century and the first decades of the fifth reached the same level, so that the survival of black silhouettes seems more a crystallization and decline. The only possible developments for the black-figure style were inevitably toward mannerism.

Thus, Lysippides, who painted "eye cups" and the black-figure parts of Andokides' "bilingual" vases, remains far from the coherency and vigor of line of Exekias, and even his minutely incised decoration is not an adequate compensation. The anonymous artist who painted black figures on the vases from the shop of Nikosthenes fell into boring monotony and returned to a miniaturistic style to decorate the bands that divided the new type of amphora created by his prolific potter. The Nikosthenic amphora is, in fact, a significant attempt at varying the structure of the traditional vase (fig. 84). It was inspired by metalwork forms, as can be seen from the broad, thin, band-like handles attached to the horizontal rim as if they were soldered on; even the horizontal, molded seams recall the joints between the various parts of metal bodies. This virtuoso technique, representing above all a structural mannerism, remained limited to this particular workshop, and ordinary amphorae followed

85. In this kylix *modeled by Hischylos, Epiktetos has painted on the inside an elegant horseman in the black-figure technique, decorating the exterior with satyrs in the red-figure style.* Circa *520 B.C. London, British Museum*

their own organic development in the two types, one with a distinct neck, and the other with a continuous uninterrupted profile. The structural division into various zones in Nikosthenic amphorae did not, in fact, allow for adequate development of the figured scenes, so that when the painter wanted to enlarge his figures he had to compromise and allow the figures to be cut into by the horizontal seam, a solution that cannot have appealed to many vase painters.

The experiments carried out by Athenian potters in this last quarter of the sixth century also included modeled vases. The variety of forms used by Archaic Corinthian potters for modeled vases was replaced in Athens by a concentration on the *kantharos* or *skyphos* types. These bore women's heads, carefully modeled by Charinos, and Negro heads, marked by a naturalistic characterization which presupposes the existence of models, perhaps among the slaves owned by the rich families of Athens (fig. 83). In these Negro-head vases the black pigment finds its most natural and meaningful application, its deep, glowing tone creating an effective contrast with the protruding lips left in the pink ground color and with the white of the eyes, while small clay globules provide a relief rendering of the tightly curled hair. The contrast becomes even more striking in the double-face vases that counterbalance a Negro head with a white female head.

In this period of transition, we see how a vase painter like Psiax experimented with various techniques. He painted some vases only with black figures; some entirely in red; other vases with both techniques, one on one side and one on the other; vases with black figures on a white or coral-color background; and even with red figures actually painted on the ground instead of utilizing the ground tone surrounded by black. Perhaps he succeeded best in expressing himself with black figures, reaching outstanding fineness of line, sure-handed, delicate strokes, and a miniaturistic tendency that created elegant figures of horses in a freshly conceived scene of a chariot attack. Thus, he succeeded better in developing traditional qualities of the black-figure technique with lightness and grace, than in innovating new techniques.

A feeling of greater liberty and a more relaxed style, though less accurate in execution, is exhibited by a prolific vase painter to whom about one hundred and thirty-five vases are attributed. Active in the last quarter of the sixth century, and adopting the black-figure technique exclusively, he was very close to Psiax and is known as the Antimenes Painter from a *kalos* inscription to a certain young Antim-

enes appearing on a vase with athletes taking showers under the portico of a fountain. In the abundant production and vast repertory of this painter it is interesting to note, among other things, the tendency to rejuvenate the figurative language. He accomplishes this by placing men in newly reduced proportions in definite settings, which are descriptive and human and conceived with a landscapist's approach. He represents the whole architecture of the fountain in the scenes of bathing adolescents or in scenes of gesticulating women arriving to fill their *hydriai*; the date palm and animals are depicted in the Apollo and Artemis scene; and he creates a fresh picture of an olive harvest on an amphora in Berlin.

In this final production using the black-figure technique, the most widely adopted shapes were the two types of amphorae and the *hydria*. These were usually decorated with a large scene on the body, with minor friezes above and below this scene and on the shoulders. Eye-patterned *kylixes*, small Nikosthenic amphorae, and series of *lekythoi* also continue into the fifth century. On the large panels of the bigger vases — especially a numerous group of *hydriai* classed under the name of Leagros, an ephebus popular among the generation of the end of the sixth century — scenes from the *epos* and myth become more frequent. The Trojan War, Achilles, the cycles of Theseus and Heracles, all appear. But the dominant subjects are quadriga groups, harnessing scenes, and women at the fountain. Retouching in white and crimson becomes rarer, and crowded scenes with bulky figures, often charged with a vigorous force, heighten the effect of the dark tonality of this production, which developed parellel to and in sharp contrast with the first red-figure work.

In a few of the painters of the Leagros group one can see attempts at translating into black-figure equivalents the achievements and effects of red-figure painting. Such is the case of the Madrid Painter, with his elaborate incising of hair, wreaths, and drapery, and other painters who insist on analytical anatomical details of torsos in tension. But generally speaking, all late black-figure work ends by falling into the conventional and the decorative, as with the Nikoxenos Painter and Eucharides Painter. The characteristic background, filled with vine shoots spreading in various directions, is found not only in Dionysiac scenes but also spreads over the characteristic *lekythoi* until the first decades of the fifth century. This motif illustrates the external, decorative interest in the late black-figure language.

The most valid and original achievements were to take place in the new language of

86. Horseman and archer from the retinue of Theanus going to meet Menelaus and Odysseus, who have come to Troy to request the return of Helen. Detail from a Corinthian krater. Circa 560 B.C. Naples, Astarita Collection

red-figure work, and if the Andokides Painter, though perhaps drawing much from his master Exekias, is responsible for this new technique, he certainly must have had a pictorial and coloristic temperament. Indeed, his draperies take on new values, not only in the soft volumes suggested by the arrangement of folds, but also in their lively coloring, that is accompanied by a generous use of crimson retouching, juxtapositions of dark and light zones, and decorations of crosses, stars, dots, and borders. His Artemis, delicately holding two voluted vine tendrils, exemplifies the Andokides Painter's refined, modulated grace.

The *kylix* underwent a development of its own at this time; the problem of its decoration was lovingly studied and elaborated on by various vase painters, but most of all by Oltos and Epiktetòs. Oltos painted over a hundred vases (fig. 84), mainly *kylixes* by the potters Kachrylion, Tleson, Pamphaios, Chelis, and Euxitheos. These vases reach a grandness of form and motif that culminates in the monumental Tarquinia *kylix*, more than 20 inches in diameter, over whose surface an animated, solemn assembly of deities unfolds, along with a scene showing Dionysus departing in his chariot among maenads and satyrs. In Oltos' output, he progresses from the insertion of one figure between the eye motifs under the handles, to figure groups, and ends by suppressing the eyes, freeing the space for a single frieze of figures like the one on the Tarquinia *kylix*. His figures have a solid, fullbodied structure, and are filled with vitality, while accents of elegance are shown in draperies, in palmettes, and bud ornament.

99

The contemporary Epiktetos painted about thirty *kylixes* and plates from the workshops of Hischylos, Nikosthenes, Andokides, Pamphaios, Python, and Pistoxenos, and treated not only the world of myth, but also themes of athletes, satyrs, and revelers, with endless variations. The compositional problem posed by the decoration of the interior of the cup, which was the exclusive preoccupation of the Hermaios Painter, who used a single figure, was a problem that also attracted Epiktetos (fig. 85). The latter showed continually renewed imagination in composing one or two figures in a studied, successful spatial equilibrium, so that the circular format, far from cramping and subordinating rhythm and arrangement, seems to be the most harmonious and functional framework for the scenes. Figures of satyrs, athletes, banqueters, hetaerae, and archers are arranged in reclining, standing, kneeling, bending, and dancing poses, back to back or facing each other, and are always organically related to the surrounding space, filled with a flowing, compositional harmony. This varied range of poses and figures is resolved in terms of the most extreme simplicity, based on a very clear, tense line, reducing details to their essentials. This passionate study of rhythm and space is realized in the prevalent profile treatment of figures, but it also led to experiments by Epiktetos in which figures were placed frontally, or seen from the back, or in a three-quarter view inviting foreshortening. Sometimes a leg is shown in perspective and even the foot begins to point forward in a foreshortened view, and the torso begins to turn obliquely into a three-quarter position. In these foreshortened representations anatomical detail serves to support and suggest the change of planes and the third dimension. Collarbones differ in length and position; chests and the vertical creases along the abdomen convey tension and receding planes. Though the eye on profile heads is still drawn as if seen frontally, the pupil now appears toward the inner corner of the eye. But the painters of large vases during the late sixth and early fifth centuries rationally developed foreshortening in the construction of the principal figures. This process was to culminate later in its full affirmation by the generation of artists from the period of the Persian Wars.

The mastery of foreshortening, never before achieved, now placed Greek art on a plane of absolute superiority, enabling it to create a universally valid figurative language. The various experiments of Attic vase painters from the end of the sixth century and the beginning of the fifth presumably reflect the efforts being made in contemporary painting.

Although we have no firsthand knowledge, this seems a legitimate assumption insofar as Pliny, echoing a Greek source, speaks of the Corinthian painter Kimon of Cleonae: Kimon is supposed to have perfected the discoveries of Eumares to the point of representing the *katagraphai*, which Pliny translates as *obliquae imagines* (probably to be interpreted as foreshortenings, rather than true perspective in terms of the principal views of the human body). Kimon depicted various positions of the head, raised, lowered, and thrown back, and is said to have differentiated the articulation of the limbs to show anatomical details such as veins. He was also the first to paint the folds and creases of garments. This anatomical research and treatment of drapery find parallels in the works of contemporary vase painters.

Euthymides, in contrast with Oltos and Epiktetos, was a painter of large vases — about twenty amphorae and *hydriai* — in which we see the development of a highly personal monumental style. He created panels of three or four rigorously drawn figures, with well-articulated nudes and generously cadenced drapery, all in a clear plastic isolation. Even the turbulent scenes of revelers or the rape of Corone by Theseus are composed with calm solemnity, like that of the static scene showing Hector being armed, with its exquisitely elegant gestures and feminine heads. Frontally viewed legs, figures with their backs turned, and three-quarter view torsos, whose numerous anatomical details are rendered in diluted glazes, confer spatial and plastic life on these well-constructed figures.

Euphronios also expresses himself well in large monumental vases, such as calyx-kraters and volute-kraters. He entered into a good-natured rivalry with Euthymides, the latter writing on a Munich amphora, "as Euphronios never could [paint]." Although Euphronios painted vases modeled by the potters Kachrylion and Euxitheos, he later became master of his own workshop, employing the Panaitios and Pistoxenos Painters, and Onesimos. He is the richest, most complex personality of his time. His fluid drawing, with its sure, articulated outlines, accompanies modeling in diluted glazes, and his drapery forms have a lively fullness. Athletic figures, the protagonists of many scenes, assume a structure that is elastic, vigorous, and at the same time graceful. They can be seen on the krater in Berlin in the most varied poses caught with lively naturalism. The Athenian ephebus is most elegantly expressed in the handsome figure of Leagros, who is shown on horseback almost in a light dancing rhythm, with his broad *petasos* and embroidered mantle, on the internal

87. *To decorate the internal medallion of this* kylix, *the Laconian painter known as the Hunt Painter has cut out a round portion from a narrative scene of the transporting of the body of a Spartan warrior.* Circa *550–540 B.C. Berlin, State Museums*

medallion of a *kylix* in Munich — a wonderful, sophisticated prelude to the Classical cavalcade of the Parthenon. A breath of poetry infuses the serene scenes of musical concerts, a vivacious playfulness animates scenes of revelers. A vigorous force invests the mythical battles of Heracles: against Geryon, the three-bodied monster, in the Munich krater; against the Amazons in the Arezzo krater; and against the Nemean lion in the Louvre plate. Monumental groupings of dramatic intensity are sustained by minute details, with refined pictorial effects; for instance, in the contrast between the thick, dark curls of Heracles and the fair, unkempt hair of the angry, beaten Antaeus. In the work of these Athenian vase painters of the end of the sixth century and the beginning of the fifth, are found the reflections of a new conception that continues to mature and will be affirmed by

the artists of the generation of the Persian Wars, marking the decisive and fundamental passage from the tenets of Archaic times to what is known as the Severe style.

10. Corinthian Vase Painting

A remarkable and coherent development led from the mid-sixth-century black-figure technique to the rich, expressive language of red-figure work in the last quarter of the sixth century, paralleling the accomplishment in sculpture. No other pottery industry had achieved the high quality of Attic production after the decline of this art in Corinth. The greatness and originality of Corinthian work had reached its zenith in the seventh century. Indeed, of little significance is the Orientalizing animal repertory which persisted in Corinth;

101

in the first quarter of the sixth century during the middle Corinthian period, it took on the massive and monumental forms of the so-called Heavy style, as well as the thin and mannered forms of the Delicate style. It is more rewarding and interesting to study the contemporary development of a narrative language in the scenes of hunting, battles, banquets, and the labors of Heracles on the larger vases with their black figures, and female heads and *gorgoneia* drawn in outline, and the use of white touches. These narrative scenes were to predominate until about 540 B.C. in late Corinthian style. Whereas in the first half of the sixth century Attic vase painters had

taken their inspiration from the Corinthians, now the situation was reversed, and the Corinthians tried to enliven their pale clay with a reddish-orange overglaze, and copied the palmette and lotus-flower ornaments. The austere Attic black-figure technique contrasts strikingly with the opulent polychromy, generously using white, yellow, and violet, that characterizes Corinthian pottery. These bright colors perhaps reflected the effects of contemporary full-scale painting.

The Astarita krater (colorplate, fig. 86), showing the embassy of Menelaus and Odysseus requesting the return of Helen, is the work of a Corinthian contemporary of the Athenian

88. *On this elaborate plate from Rhodes the epic narrative of the duel of Menelaus and Hector over the body of Euphorbus is transposed to an ornamental plane, placed among a profusion of decorative filling ornament. Circa 600 B.C. London, British Museum*

Kleitias, and illustrates the Corinthian pictorial qualities. These same qualities are also present in the precious painted wooden plaques dedicated to the nymphs of the grotto of Pitza, dating from 540 and 530 B.C. The figures of these plaques stand out against a white ground, accurately drawn with red outlines for the white-skinned women donors, and black outlines for their drapery, while the boys' skin is pinkish. There is vivid polychromy in the blue chitons and red mantles — which in one of the plaques are also decorated with Orientalizing animals and embroidered borders — and in the green of wreaths and boughs and the occasional touch of violet.

This typically Corinthian spirit — narrative and ornamental, pictorial and illustrative — is attested by Pausanias' description of the celebrated *Cypselus Chest* dedicated by the tyrant Cypselus in the Heraion at Olympia in the middle of the sixth century. Polychrome effects were obtained by using cedar wood, and figures gilded or in ivory with details in gold and black. A vast series of mythological themes were developed in five friezes accompanied, as in painted vases, by inscriptions. They included the marriage of Peleus and Thetis, which had also been treated by Sophilos and Kleitias; the departure of Amphiaraus, which is also to be found on a Corinthian krater and therefore perhaps reflects a common prototype; Perseus and the gorgons; Theseus and Ariadne; Ajax and Cassandra; Menelaus and Helen. Other themes treated were the myths of the Argonauts, Heracles, Marpessa, and Atalanta, the local myth of Pelops and Oenomaus, battles of Homeric heroes, and also strongly characterized personifications such as the ugly Adikia (Injustice) being strangled by Dike (Justice), Hypnos (Sleep), Phobos (Fear), and Ker, the demon with pointed teeth, who carries off the dead.

Reliefs of pierced ivory with gilding and decorative incised drapery, found mainly at Delphi and showing mythical themes like the departure of Amphiaraus, along with the motifs reflected in pottery, allow us to re-create the effect of this monumental Corinthian painting, developed in the most mature period of the narrative style.

Corinthian pottery in the second half of the sixth century no longer aimed at competing with or exceeding Athenian work, and limited itself to an output in the White style, consisting of a light ground with geometrical and floral elements.

11. Other Centers of Ceramic Production in the Sixth Century

Laconian pottery during the sixth century is marked by a striking narrative and pictorial interest, without the rigor of Corinthian work, but distinguished by a free, lively syntax. Under Attic influence the *kylix* develops a tall, slim form on a high foot, and becomes by far the most popular type of vase, with an original decoration very different from that used in Athens. In contrast to the logical structural composition of external decoration and central internal medallion of the Attic vase painters, Laconian painters conceived the

89. This spirited little figure is not in an athletic race but in flight. His abnormal structure characterizes him as a barbarian in the lively Ionic taste of the Fikellura style. From Camirus. Circa 540 B.C. London, British Museum

103

90. With great freedom of imagination, an
Ionic vase painter has made the interior
of this kylix into a little landscape painting.
Mid-sixth century B.C. Paris, Louvre

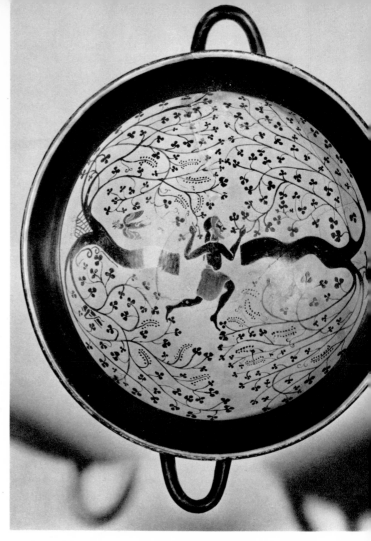

interior of the *kylix* as a continuous expanse
on which to place a narrative scene. Sometimes
artists tried to adapt the material to the circular
field by using a radial composition, but in
other cases the painters were not at all guided
by the shape of the vase and simply cut out
a circular piece from a composition created for
a rectangular frieze, as in a *kylix* in Berlin
by the so-called Hunt Painter, with the moving
scene of a dead warrior carried on the shoulders
of his comrades (fig. 87). A cargo ship, where
silphium is being weighed and loaded, is
daringly cut off in the same way on a fine
kylix dating from around 560 B.C. which can
be considered the masterpiece of its type. The
protagonist depicted in this scene is King
Arcesilas of Cyrene, shown in the middle of
an animated scene drawn from life and enlivened by darting birds, a monkey on the
flagstaff, and a panther under the king's stool.

Very often on the interior of *kylixes* an
exergue or half-moon section, such as that seen
at the base of figure 88, creates a supporting
plane for the frieze. At times two such half-
moon sections are placed opposite each other,
or the bottom one is divided by a band, thus
creating the space for a minor frieze. Frieze
compositions, one figured and the others floral,
dominate in the Laconian decoration of *hydriai*
imitating metalwork with the two sculptured
palmettes, masks, and bosses. Along with the
kylix the *hydria* was the most fashionable type
of vase in this area. The *hydria* from Ialysus
by the Hunt Painter, with a frieze of combatants and revelers, is the finest product
among these. The free narrative and compositional approach, the interest shown in less
common themes, the generous use of crimson
retouching that stands out against the creamy
ground color, and the black figures with rather
hard, unorganic incising, give Laconian ceramics an attractive, original quality that ac-
counts for their widespread export during the
first half of the sixth century. These vases
were exported to Samos and Rhodes, to Asia
Minor, Naucratis, Cyrene, and Carthage, to
Magna Graecia, Sicily, and Etruria, and as far
as Marseilles — without endangering, as Corinthian work had done, Attic supremacy.

91. Birds and fish are painted with an abstract
and decorative taste on this Cypriot oinochoe.
Seventh century B.C. Nicosia, Museum

On the Greek mainland in the sixth century only the pottery of Boeotia presented any noticeable local characteristics, with a delayed manifestation of the Orientalizing current, in a series of typical cups and plates on tall feet. These pieces achieved a sure-handed craftsmanship in the light grounds and decoration of birds drawn in panels, along with bands of daisies, palmettes, and geometrical elements. Corinthian, and later, Attic influences are seen in black-figure vases with revelers, animals, and a few figured scenes, but such efforts showed little strength in Boeotia.

The separation between the pictorial Western style of narratives and myths, centering around Corinthian and Attic work, and the largely ornamental Orientalizing styles of the islands and Ionia was more marked in the sixth than it had been in the seventh century, when both styles shared a common Orientalizing tendency. In spite of Corinthian influences in the Cyclades, the Orientalizing movement persisted there throughout the sixth century, with its spectacular ornament of volutes, large rosettes, swastikas hooked into running Greek key patterns, and figures having heads sketched in on the light ground, sparse incising, and decorated costumes. Nor was there any change in the form of the large amphora, whose wide neck and conical foot, ample surfaces, and heavy, unarticulated structure were well fitted to hold this exuberant decoration.

The predominant interest in ornament, and the taste for decoration rather than narrative throughout all the Eastern Greek world also explains the persistence of the Wild Goat style during the whole of the first half of the sixth century, — now with simplified ornament and untidily drawn animals. This style continued alongside a black-figure style influenced by Corinthian work, with hasty drawing and crimson retouching. Beside the animals that met the needs of this decorative trend, the human figure also began to appear, especially on plates, which provided surfaces large enough to carry whole scenes. However, human images were rare, and the general preference was still for black lines or concentric circles with radiating tongues, and animal, or filling motifs. The famous plate from Rhodes, dating from around 600 B.C., with the duel of Menelaus and Hector over the body of Euphorbus and thickly packed with filling ornament, is thus all the more exceptional (fig. 88). This work is thought to be an imitation of an Argive bronze relief. The angular, rigid formulation of the human figures shows the distance that lay between this decorative approach and the truly narrative style of Attica and Corinth.

Chios, which has recently been assigned a corpus of pottery formerly attributed to Naucratis, was also marked by a persistence of the Wild Goat style. During the first half of the sixth century there was also a survival of the technique of sketched forms on the light ground in the typical chalice-shaped vase of Chios, with a conical base, high flared lip, and horizontal handles. The ornamental taste here reaches a particular note of elegance and clarity, isolating an animal figure, usually a sphinx or a lion, which stands out against the pale ground on each of the two faces of the chalice. A narrative style also developed, with battle and *komos* scenes and the myth of Heracles, but this is distinguished by its pictorial sense and vivid polychromy rather than by accurate drawing. Corinthian influence established a black-figure style in Chios with sphinxes, lions, sirens, bulls, and revelers, but the chalice style represents the genuine, substantially ornamental, local trends.

The Wild Goat style is related in technique and conception to the production called Fikellura ware, after a center in Rhodes. This was widespread in Samos, Delos, Miletus, Naucratis, along the Black Sea coast, in Syria, and even in Italy, perhaps originating from Rhodes and Samos. The most characteristic vase form of Fikellura ware is the amphora, with a distinct neck and generous, semiovoidal body, offering large expanses of pale ground for decoration (fig. 89). This consisted of tendrils or meanders on the neck, radiating lines, tendrils or buds and, at first, animals on the shoulders, and generally a typical series of half-moon shapes surrounding the base. The main frieze consisted of broad, elegant volutes with palmettes, recalling the Cycladic taste, and isolated black silhouetted figures of animals, men, buffoons, pygmies, Negroes, satyrs, or fantastic creatures. The figures were placed on the light background and became progressively disengaged from the surrounding ornament, which was finally limited to the zones under the handles. These lively figures, always caught in sprightly movement, are not yet composed in scenes and have no illustrative function, so that they are often simply strange, semihuman forms, and appear to be no more than pretexts for vivid decorative images, in the elegant and free Ionian spirit.

Ionian vase painters did not resist the attraction of Attic black-figure *kylixes*, and when they attempted to imitate the form and technique of the Siana cups and lip-cups, they created works of great finesse, showing extreme elegance in the exterior ornament of myrtle, ivy, and buds, and with animals and birds on the interior of the *kylix*. However, the Ionians remained foreign to the Attic mythological and narrative repertory, and contrived, with great compositional freedom, to fill the interior surface with a carefree, purely ornamental composition. An example of this is a *kylix* in the Louvre (fig. 90), which shows a man walking about in the shade of two trees, which do not appear in perspective, but are flattened into a single abstract plane, creating a vivid arabesque effect.

The Ionian decorative approach affirms itself in a more native mode in the type of *kylix* from Rhodes, known as the Vroulia *kylix*. It is decorated exclusively with palmettes, lotus flowers, buds, and rosettes on the outside — often on the inside as well — between bands of triangular and plaited motifs, all incised on the black ground color and heightened with touches of crimson, in an imitation of the Corinthian black-polychrome style.

In this ornamental vision, which embraces all the Graeco-Oriental and island areas, we

92. This huge bronze krater (detail below) found in a Gallic tomb at Vix is a masterpiece of bronze relief sculpture, probably produced in Magna Graecia. End of the sixth century B.C. Vix, Museum

also find the persistence of the Orientalizing style in Crete, as well as in Cyprus where expressions were governed by Eastern and Phoenician influences. In Cyprus the geometrical repertory of rectilinear motifs and concentric circles, which had been transformed into a pictorial style using red, black, and white, survived on the typical barrel-shaped vases. Felines and original images of water birds or vultures are eloquently sketched in a few lines on the white ground of characteristic ovoidal *oinochoai* (fig. 91). By comparison, the occasional imitations of Attic vases, altogether too distant from this Eastern world

of ornament, appear distinctly insignificant.

Beside the free, refined, episodic interpretations to be found on Ionian cups, the narrative black-figure style was established by the middle of the sixth century in some workshops in Asia Minor, the best known of which was in Clazomenae. Clazomenaean amphorae and *hydriai* used black-figure technique to show processions of women, satyrs, revelers, chariots and horsemen, mythological scenes, friezes of animals, lotus flowers, and palmettes, and spots of white with a dot of black. This pottery distinguishes itself by a lively tone and vivid coloring with a generous use of white pigment

93. In this fine example of Chalcidian pottery, a controlled decorative sense has guided the painter in the composition of two heraldic cocks flanking entwined serpents. Second half of the sixth century B.C. Würzburg, University Museum

and crimson retouching, rather than by technical accuracy or draftsmanly precision.

While in this pottery of Asia Minor the Attic influence was remodeled with original touches, the Attic narrative style in black-figure, and later, red-figure technique, was imitated without being understood. It was translated into purely decorative formulas in friezes and battle scenes, chariot races and Amazonomachies decorating the typical clay sarcophagi that may have been produced in Clazomenae from about 530 B.C. until the first quarter of the fifth century. Incising, which constitutes the vital element in Attic black-figure silhouettes, was replaced by white lines; the figures are like stiff shadows; and there are slovenly imitations of red-figure technique. These figured scenes are interpreted on the same decorative plane as figures of animals, plaited ornament, or palmettes, all derived from the repertory of the Wild Goat style, with a mixing of typical Eastern motifs.

The high artistic level of the Dorian and Ionian styles inevitably had a profound influence on the cultures that came into contact with the Greek world. The Ionian influence was felt from the coast of Asia Minor to the colonies of the Black Sea, and did not fail to affect Achaemenid art, in architecture, sculpture, and glyptography, spreading along the coasts of Syria, Egypt, and Cyrenaica.

12. Sicily and Magna Graecia in the Sixth Century

Italy, already open to Greek colonization in the seventh century and to the active trade of the Greek mainland, the islands, and the coasts of Asia Minor, shows in the picturesque variety of her artistic cultures a lively reflection of how these outside influences were received. It is significant that the Dorian and Attic taste took root primarily in Sicily and Magna Graecia, and the Ionian in the Etruscan area. Sicily and Magna Graecia, profoundly influenced by Greece, at times arrived at a pure artistic language alongside inflections in the local dialect. The perfect adherence to Greek forms can be exemplified first and foremost by the products of the school of bronze-workers that arose in Tarentum, Locri, and Reggio, where there are records of the artist Klearchos, who is supposed to have belonged to the Daedalic school. Pausanias mentions an image of Zeus Hypatos in the Temple of Athena Chakioikos in Sparta, which Klearchos was supposed to have fashioned out of sheets of bronze nailed over a wooden core, in the *sphyrelaton* technique. Small figures, mirrors, and

94. *A pure late Archaic Greek style is assimilated in this polychromed terracotta figure of a seated Zeus from Paestum.* Circa 520 B.C. *Paestum, Museum*

bronze vases all bear witness to the flourishing activity of toreutic work in Magna Graecia from the sixth century on. It is indeed probable that the large bronze kraters with plastically decorated handles and fine modeling and incising — the most significant example of which is the colossal krater found in the tomb of a Gallic prince at Vix, near Châtillon-sur-Seine (fig. 92) — are to be attributed to a southern Italian center.

The Vix krater measures 5'4'' in height and its diameter is 4'2''; it weighs just under 440 pounds. The material found in this rich chariot tomb includes a Droop-type *kylix*, an Attic black-glaze *kylix*, an Etruscan bronze *oinochoe*, a silver phiale, and a center-bossed bronze basin, as well as torques, amber bracelets, and a magnificent gold diadem. These pieces date the burial toward the end of the sixth century. It has been a matter of debate as to whether

95. *One of five similar metopes showing couples of fleeing nereids, which form a unified theme on the temple at Sele. The refined and mannered Ionic style is here interpreted with a robust Italic accent.* *510–500 B.C. Paestum, Museum*

the krater was transported whole or in pieces, whether it was brought through Marseilles and up the Rhône and Saône, or over the Alps, and also whether it was made in Corinth, Laconia, or Magna Graecia. The letters incised

96. *The Etrusco-Ionic Paris Painter creates in this little scene one of the freshest and most pleasantly realized expressions of his colorful, sprightly style. Circa 540 B.C. New York, Metropolitan Museum*

on it seem related to the Locri alphabet, and it is most probable that the krater came from some Greek colony in southern Italy. This provenance seems all the more probable since Campania produced the krater in Munich which is over 25″ high, the Castellani krater in London, and a group of similar handles with gorgons in the Louvre and at Nîmes. Commercial traffic across the Ionian and Adriatic Seas and along the Egnatian Road could explain the discovery of two analogous kraters in the necropolis of Trebenischte in Yugoslavia, one, with a frieze of racing horsemen, over 25″ high, and the other over 26″ high. The vigorous style of the frieze of infantrymen and chariots that decorates the

Vix krater, and the accentuated profile of the small female figure, entirely wrapped in her peplos and mantle, that serves as a handle for the cover, find analogies in a small clay altar from Locri in the Reggio Museum (no. 6488), datable in the second half of the sixth century. These characteristics can perhaps be considered belated accents, with a light Italic inflection, of the artistic language of Corinth of the second quarter of the sixth century.

The so-called Chalcidian pottery (fig. 93) should probably be situated, not in Greece, but in some Chalcidian colony in Italy, most plausibly in the area of Catania, Messina, and Reggio Calabria. Had the workshop been in Etruria, as some have maintained, the less pure artistic ambient would probably have left some trace. This pottery develops through the entire second half of the sixth century in the works of various anonymous painters, and bears inscriptions in Chalcidian. It is executed in black-figure technique with perfect Greek stylistic expression. The absence of finds of this pottery in Euboea seems to rule out the attribution to Chalcis itself. Corinthian influences in the use of a white pigment and above all in the re-elaborated type of krater, represents the field in which the Italic taste is best expressed. In Paestum the polychromed clay cult statue of a seated Zeus (fig. 94) follows Attic types of about 530 B.C. It was perhaps originally placed beside a figure of Hera. Clay was probably also used for the pediments of the great temples, which may have provided the setting for a female torso with a vivacious decorated, sleeved costume, with a wavy *apoptygma*. Particular vigor is achieved by the late-sixth-century fragment of

97. On this Caeretan hydria *the herd of bulls stolen from Apollo by Hermes stands at the entrance to the grotto, which is hidden by branches on which a rabbit scampers away. The whole scene forms a vivacious little landscape picture.* Circa 540–530 B.C. *Paris, Louvre*

as well as Attic influences in the use of incising, the occurrence of so-called "eye cups," and the mythological language, could better be explained in the colonial setting of southern Italy. This colonial provenance would also justify the free, coherent affirmation of original touches in the interpretation of mythological scenes dominated by Heracles, in the prevalent ornament of rosebuds, interwoven palmettes, lotus flowers, and heraldic cocks among serpents twined into elegant volutes; and also in the preference for the motif of the frontally viewed quadriga, and for warriors and horsemen, which find parallels on the Vix krater.

In Sicily and Magna Graecia terracotta the group of Europa on the bull, a theme favored by the sculptor Pythagoras, who was active at Reggio. At Sele, after the flowering of Archaic sculpture in the metopes of the Treasury of about 560 B.C., the principal temple, dating from the end of the sixth century, shows the Doric order with Ionic influences. Ionic models also inspired the sculptures of the metopes of the temple. The predominant theme consists of graceful, pairs of nereids (fig. 95) presented in rhythmic flight, with tightly pleated drapery, like an elegant, dynamic ballet in which Italic accents ring out in the solid structure and in the rhythmic vivacity of the striding legs.

13. Archaic Etruscan Art and Ionian Influences

In Etruria the prevailing ornamental taste led naturally to a persistence of the entire Orientalizing repertory — often inducing scholars to date in the seventh century works which, after more detailed study, turn out to be from the sixth century. Grazing deer, griffins, sphinxes, panthers (two of which were often fused into a single head), birds, bulls, and lions continued to decorate the clay revetment panels of temples, *bucchero* ware, painted pottery, bronzes, ivories, bone carvings, goldsmith's work, and gems. These forms found a characteristic application in a series of carved panels of stone from Tarquinia, the use of which has not yet been determined. The panels are divided by triangular grooves into areas of horizontal figured friezes, or square figured areas framed with a plaited motif, or squares of projecting angular segments. This work recalls the syntax of embossed-gold covered *larnakes* (sepulchral chests) from the Attic Geometric period, and the arm-pieces of Corinthian bronze shields — work which was certainly unknown in Etruria. The flat relief of these panels from Tarquinia is hard, linear, and has analogies with intaglio technique. It may be that ivories and even textiles transmitted this type of decoration to Etruria, which is also to be found on sepulchral *cippi* (stone pillars) from Vulci.

Alongside the persistence of the Orientalizing repertory, the reactions of the Etruscan milieu to the various artistic currents of the sixth century are interesting. When the importation of Corinthian vases gave way to the massive importation of Attic black-figure work, in Etruria the most significant creations based on this influence are to be found in the pottery conventionally known as "Pontic," for at one time it was thought to have come from Greek colonies on the Black Sea, though in fact it was produced in Etruria, perhaps in Vulci, from the middle of the sixth century on. The animal friezes and the type of ovoid amphora show that out of the varied Attic production, the Tyrrhenian type of amphora had been chosen as inspiration precisely because of its prevailing ornamental repertory. The principal figured frieze around the shoulders and the dominant light background also betray open adherence to the Ionian taste. This assimilation of the spirit and language of Ionia is certainly to be connected with the activity of immigrant Ionian artists, but strong local inflections, misunderstandings in reworking myths and iconography, heavy coloring, and freedom of interpretation are all manifestations of Etruscan taste. The greatest of these vase painters, the Paris Painter, so called after his amphora in Munich bearing a lively scene of the judgment of Paris, is unimaginable except in Etruria, for only there was it possible for the artist to develop and justify the uninhibited, pungent humor of the scene. The same is true of the amphora in New York by the Paris Painter (fig. 96), where in a scene of dreamy, relaxed abandon, charming ladies wearing the tall veiled *tutulus* (conical hairdo), having hung up their pointed shoes, exchange secrets as they recline on beds set among boughs of myrtle. The scene on the reverse of this amphora presents the strange union of three characters, a dandified young man, a proud centaur, and a gesticulating old man with a caduceus. They are seen through the branches of a fantastic tree hung with rich fruit, and seem to be hastening to join the enticing group on the other side of the vase.

The work of Ionian artists in Etruria is attested by Greek inscriptions on the characteristic series of about thirty *hydriai*, perhaps produced at Caere (Cerveteri) in 540–530 B.C. and known as Caeretan *hydriai*. In the context of Ionian pottery, the closest parallels with these *hydriai* are to be found in the amphorae and *hydriai* of the Fikellura style by virtue of their expansive, semiovoidal form, flat shoulders, and decorative and expressive spirit. But different are the composition, the repertory, and the narrative taste, which is even more vital than that of Clazomenae. In this case again, only adaptation to the Etruscan environment could have given this Ionian master, creator of the Caeretan *hydria*, the distinctive style with which he expresses the Greek myths (fig. 97). Only in Etruria could the traditional scene of Heracles massacring the pale Egyptian followers of Busiris reach such explosive, expressive force, or become loaded with the tone of parody as in the Vienna *hydria*. Only there could a howling, gesticulating image of Ge rise up, as in the Louvre *hydria*, where Apollo and Artemis stride quickly forward, shooting arrows at Tityus. Nowhere else could the body of the dog in the Calydonian boar hunt on the other Louvre *hydria* have been shown sliced in two halves with the intestines bursting out under the deadly impact of the boar. In this vase, too, the landscape takes on free and fanciful notes, the heads and legs of the figures are expanded in curvilinear contours, and the ornament develops into large, ostentatious trellises of ivy.

Although the influence of the enormous number of imported Attic black-figure vases may, in the work of this Ionian master of the Caeretan *hydriai* and his pupils, have caused a

98. *Here in the hands of the Etruscan painter of the Tomb of the Bulls, the ambush of Troilus by Achilles becomes a polychromed fairy tale. Circa 530-520 B.C. Tarquinia*

weakening of the initial, vivid polychromy with its generous retouching in white and violet, Etruscan vase painters could not have imitated the Attic style, for they lacked the fundamental sense of its organic qualities. The rigorous, elevated Attic narrative language remained foreign to the spirit of the Etruscans, and the imitations to be found throughout the Etruscan black-figure production from the last decades of the sixth century — even in the work of the finest vase painters, such as the Micali Painter — are significant works only insofar as they depart from the Attic style. The native character manifests itself in hybrid structural forms of vases, in the processions of animals and fantastic creatures that predominate in the Tolfa group, in the misunderstanding of — as well as general disinterest in — myths, in the unorganic nature of the angular, disproportionate figures, and in motifs linked to local society and, ultimately, to the more barbaric, provincial forms of less cultivated artisans.

In these attempted imitations of Attic work, the essentially Etruscan qualities are less strong than in the creation of new vase forms, and in the black *bucchero* ware. One of the most important centers of *bucchero* production was Chiusi, where we find elaborate, baroque forms, imitations of metal vases, and rich, plastic

113

relief decoration with the favorite animals and monsters from the Orientalizing repertory, as well as mythological scenes, like Perseus and Medusa.

However, Etruscan art reached its most elevated tone in the works of the masters who assimilated Ionic teachings in the last decades of the sixth century, in wall paintings of the chamber tombs, beaten bronzes, and clay-modeling.

Tarquinia — where, according to tradition, the artist Demaratos immigrated with other Corinthians after the rise of Cypselus in Corinth — reveals a flourishing local school of painting, which has left us precious documents. Up to this time we lack documentation of Greek immigrant painters. Indeed, in light of the originality shown by Etruscan expression from its earliest appearance, the question of Greek artists loses significance. In the Tomb of the Bulls (colorplate, fig. 98), which dates from around 530 B.C., the mythological theme and iconographical tradition of the ambush of Troilus by Achilles, common in Archaic Greek art, becomes a pretext for covering the walls with a florid, ingenuous, exotic landscape of small trees, abstract shrubs, and a story-book palm, with an Etruscanized fountain in a vivid checkerboard pattern of white, red, and light blue. In this setting, which is framed by a border of buds in the "Chalcidian" taste, move the rounded Ionicizing figures.

Landscape becomes the absolute protagonist in the large, airy, vivacious, and carefree scenes of the Tomb of Hunting and Fishing (colorplate, fig. 99). Here dolphins flit upon the waves, above which birds flutter and hover in free flight, while the gesticulating fishermen and hunters with slingshots become tiny elements in a vibrant conception of nature. Only in Minoan-Mycenaean art can we find as open a conception of the life of the sea and sky, of the animals and flowers, represented with a lively naturalism although expressed in a fable-like atmosphere. In scenes of games, banquets, and dances, which constitute the themes of other tombs, small trees and flowering stalks are inserted to set the action in the open air among birds, wreaths, swags, and festoons.

The most elevated expression is reached by the painter of the Tomb of the Augurs of 520–510 B.C., in compositional coherency and expressive vigor, and in the colorful characterization of the figures, from the hieratic *tanasar* of the funeral lament, and the massive wrestlers, to the comic mask of the *phersu*. The lines which define the figures stretch assuredly in powerful, exuberantly plastic curves, very different from the more controlled, elusive Ionic line. The vigorous structure also marks the dynamic figures of dancers and acquires true monumentality in the banqueters of the Tomb of the Lionesses, of a decade later.

This dynamic, full-bodied, colorful pictorial language has no equivalent in Greek circles and can only be compared with the sculpture, similar in tone and expressive force, created by the Hellenized Italic sculptors of the metopes of the Treasury of Sele (figs. 55, 57). The attractive figure of a muscular dancing girl, apparently derived from a work by the painter of the Tomb of the Augurs and re-echoed in isolation in a different stylistic context in the later Tomb of the Jugglers, is far removed from Greek standards, with her smooth, robust limbs and the abstractly rounded curve of her stride (colorplate, fig. 105). She can be compared with the fleeing nereids of the temple of Sele from the end of the sixth century (fig. 95), though still showing the differences that separated the Hellenizing work of Magna Graecia from the genuinely Etruscan expression.

The solid, weighty Etruscan structure appears stiffened in the static, flat, and purely linear figures painted on clay funerary slabs from Caere, in the Boccanegra Collection in London, dating from around 550 B.C. and in the Campana Collection in the Louvre, from 530 B.C. But it takes on expressive modulation and turgid articulation in the embossed figures of laminated metal tripods and the bronze decorations of parade chariots, produced by the metal-workers of Caere and exported even to Marsciano and Castel San Mariano in Umbria. The skill and taste of Etruscan bronze-workers in this Ionicizing phase are also found in the elegant tripods with small cast figurines made in Vulci, and in the numerous series of small bronzes that adorned candelabra, incense burners, and handles of kraters and jugs, or were used as ex-votos or various kinds of ornament. These bronze adornments consisted of youths, warriors, offering bearers, dancing girls, satyrs, monsters, and animals. The Ionic models persist in these figures until the first decades of the fifth century, constantly being revitalized into new forms by their rhythm, pose, and modeling, and with characteristic Etruscan inflections, as in the gesticulating dancing girls with long, very curved fingers, whom we also find in paintings at Tarquinia and in the reliefs of sepulchral *cippi* from Chiusi.

The series of characteristic low reliefs in *pietra fetida* on sepulchral *cippi*, urns, and sarcophagi from Chiusi (fig. 100) begins under Ionic influence in the second half of the sixth century and lasts into the fifth. These reliefs exhibit, in their vast repertory of banquets,

99. Detail of the wall painting in the Tomb of Hunting and Fishing. More than the little fisherman, the real protagonists of this scene are the dolphins and birds rendered in abstract colors but full of life. 510–500 B.C. Tarquinia

contests, and hunting and funerary scenes, the elements that characterize the Etruscan syntax and expression: excited animation, decorative elegance, and narrative vivacity.

Ionian models were to linger on in the fifth century in the group of steles in *pietra serena* from Fiesole, showing banquets, dances, and animals. In Chiusi the plastic vigor formerly expressed in canopic heads also distinguishes the typical male and female statues in *pietra fetida*, hollowed out to serve as cinerary urns with removable heads covering the inner cavity intended to hold the ashes. These figures are seated on thrones, often flanked by sphinxes, and are sheathed in draperies conceived volumetrically in broad planes that recall the statues of the Branchidae in Miletus, but with more incisive, unsophisticated modeling. In heads and drapery we see traces of influence, first

from the Severe style, then from the Classical style of Greek art, in an Etruscanized and often eclectic version, which in certain of the more compelling works reaches a hieratic quality and a magical attraction (colorplate, fig. 142). Verve, plastic vigor, and effective decoration are sometimes to be seen in lions or other funerary sculptures carved in stone from Chiusi, Vulci, and other Etruscan centers, though they remain far from the original Greek spirit. Thus, the rectangular low-relief steles with figures of warriors, particularly from the areas of Volterra and Fiesole, seem heavy and rustic by comparison with the Greek types that inspired them. Examples of this are the stele of Aule Tite at Volterra, with its long, still Daedalic hair, or the stele of Larth Ninie from Fiesole, with its inflated, mannered Ionicism.

115

The most genuine Etruscan contributions of freshness, immediacy, and vitality are better seen in modeled clay in which Etruscan artists created their most successful works, rather than in stone for which the very different quality of rigid control is necessary. Among these works is the clay sarcophagus from Caere, now in the Villa Giulia, dating from the last decade of the sixth century (fig. 101). The deceased couple is shown reclining on a *kline* (banquet couch) in a pose borrowed from Greek art. The Greek hetaera is here replaced in Etruria by the wife, whose husband affectionately holds her arm. The pose can also be found in tomb paintings, including the Ionicizing works from the Tomb of the Old Man in Tarquinia. Ionic teachings are discernible in the elevated tone and the rounded structure of the forms, while the Etruscan

of prominent muscular ridges, the rib-like ornament of the drapery, the twisted, rope-like curls, and the sharp furrows of hair and pleats. Yet the final results are no less vital, even if much less sophisticated than the Greek.

Even though the Ionicizing taste lingers on in Etruria until the early fifth century, the influence of the Attic style already began to make itself felt toward the end of the sixth century, above all through the large-scale importation of red-figure pottery. The reflections in Etruscan art of an education aimed at a more controlled compositional and structural discipline, and a search for elegance and purity of line, are to be found in the paintings of the Tomb of the Baron from the end of the sixth century. In fact, the Attic influence is so strong here that the paintings have been referred to — erroneously — as the work of a Greek.

100. The Ionic cadence assumes mannered inflections in this dynamic ballet on a funerary urn from Chiusi, of pietra fetida with bronze lion protomes. Circa 510 B.C. Florence, Archaeological Museum

taste marks more decisively the eyes and lips, models the drapery and bands of the husband's hair with simple immediacy, in soft, smooth layers of clay, and also renders the long tresses of the wife as plastic braids rolled between the modeler's fingers.

Thus, by comparison with Greek models, such as the frieze from the Siphnian Treasury, the clay statues from the Temple of Apollo at Veii appear more full-bodied in their strong and exuberant structure, and more colorful in the vivid modeling of the unorganic network

In Italic territory, as one moves away from the areas of Greek influence, one finds manifestations of a native trend in art, lacking in rhythmic or compositional coherency, even if at times not without an expressive note. The most imposing specimen which, although it belongs to more recent times, still corresponds to Archaic conceptions, is the curious warrior from Capestrano (fig. 102), a work analogous to other fragmentary sculptures from this area of Picenum. The figure was carved in local stone on a monumental scale,

116

but its body structure appears no more than a mechanical enlargement of a schematic violin-shaped idol, with tubular arms and only the shin bones indicated as sharp ridges. There is an abyss between this static, unorganic conception, whose main expressive outlets lay in the minutely detailed, workman-like description of the armor ornaments and strange, immense, crested helmet, and the Greek kouros which here cannot be thought of as having exercised the slightest influence. This figure was painfully hacked out of the stone by means of primitive techniques, which could not dispense with the two side supports corresponding to the sides of the original block out of which the sculptor had carved the figure. Moreover, its Archaic appearance should not be allowed to mislead us about its date: the work is certainly far later than any comparable stylization from Hellenized areas.

14. Phoenician-Carthaginian and Greek Influences in the Celtic-Iberian Area

During the sixth century Greek artistic influence began to spread along the westernmost coasts of the Mediterranean, in Gaul and Spain. The

101. On this Etruscan sarcophagus of Ionicizing style, the deceased couple are represented at the eternal banquet. From Caere. Circa 510 B.C. Rome, Villa Giulia

ancient Mycenaean trade routes had already reached the southern part of Spain. A powerful commercial attraction was represented in the fabulous, gold-rich Tartessus region, on the southwest coast of Spain, which according to tradition was reached in the seventh century by the fleet of the Samian Colaeus.

The Phoenician trade routes and, most important of all, the strong expansion of Carthage, were responsible for a vast and intense Phoenician and Punic colonization, which had moved up the Iberian Peninsula, profoundly and basically affecting the Iberian culture and carrying with it the new Orientalizing style. This found its most significant expression in the lacy gold work using granulation and filigree, in the large belts, earrings, and diadems from Aliseda, which can be placed in the sixth century, with their decorative palmettes, rosettes, rosebuds, and spirals translated into ostentatious, provincial forms. As in all peripheral environments, the persistence of ornamental elements often leads to uncertainties in chronology, but we can see that this Punic-Iberian Orientalizing tradition remained active for a long time.

After the conquests of Cyrus and the fall of Phocaea in 540 B.C., the Phocaean wave first affirmed itself in the West with the foundation of Massilia (Marseilles), which promoted fierce rivalry between the Etruscans and Carthaginians. The Phocaeans then expanded into the colonies of Rosas, Ampurias, Hemeroscopeion, and Mainake along the Iberian coast. Pottery was imported from Corinth and also from Athens — black-figure first, and later, red-figure ware — and we find small bronzes, like the running Silenus in the Louvre, in a pure Greek Archaic style. But to find truly native reactions to these artistic importations, we must come down to the fifth and fourth centuries. Even the Iberian painted pottery, although it shows some Mycenaean traits, and some widespread motifs of pendulous semicircles and concentric circles analogous to those of the Greek proto-Geometric, together with other motifs of the Orientalizing type, it is certainly of a much more recent date and must be considered a belated provincial expression.

102. Italic funerary statue of a warrior,
6' 10'' high, from the necropolis of Capestrano.
Carved in stone with the armor painted in red.
On the lateral sustaining pieces is an
inscription in the language of southern Picenum.
Sixth century B.C. Chieti, Archaeological Museum

118

IV | The Transition from the Archaic to the Severe Style

The years between the end of the sixth century and 480 B.C. indeed mark a decisive period in history, with the end of the tyranny of the Pisistratids, the installation of the oligarchy, the reforms of Cleisthenes, and finally, the drama of the Persian Wars; these years also represent an important transition from the Archaic artistic vision, which corresponded to the court of the Pisistratids, to the new style established toward the end of the sixth century. Sculpture, more arresting and essential than the other arts, gives us the most striking evidence of this aspect of the new ideal, conventionally known as "severe," but the slow gestation and progressive elaboration of the various representational and expressive means that prepared the new language are most fully documented in the Athenian output of red-figure pottery, which reached its greatest heights in this period.

Forms became more refined: the low, heavy "eye cup" was discarded in favor of other types with smooth, unbroken lines that fused the slim foot into the widely flared dish in one flowing, sinuous outline; the interior medallion became surrounded by a border of meanders and small crosses. The amphora most in vogue was of small dimensions, with a distinct neck, and often with twisted handles in a type called Nolan amphora. The *pelike* (two-handled storage jar), with its continuous outline, receding shoulders, and wide rim, was created at this time. *Hydriai* became progressively rounder, and their expansive forms were related to those of the *stamnos* (another two-handled jar), while the chalice shape dominated the kraters.

The graphic style of vase painters invited a persistence of Archaic mannerisms, especially in drapery, anatomical representation, and composition. However, one can discern new traits that attest to the change in taste. Drapery tended to develop wider, looser folds, more closely following the movement and structure of the body with increased naturalism; mantles acquired an effect of weightier consistency. Heads lost their Archaic, pointed look as their structure became more rounded, their profiles straight, their jaws solid and firm. In male figures the hair was no longer dressed in rich, flowing locks and curls, but was arranged in a tight little cap-like coiffure separated by a line formed of the black background, and not by an incised line. In profile faces, the pupil was by now moved toward the inner corner of the eye, which tended slowly to open and later became triangular in form. At the end of the sixth century anatomy became increasingly analytical and rich in detail in order to sustain the growing dynamic life of the figures, which were placed in an infinite range of rhythms, with complete mastery of foreshortening.

The interest in anatomical study that characterizes this period, and is attested in the sources in reference to the painting of Kimon of Cleonae, finds precise parallels in contemporary three-dimensional work, not only in sculpture, which can be illustrated by the pedimental statues of Aegina, but also in reliefs, a typical example of which is the attractive late-sixth-century Athenian plinth, re-utilized in the wall of Themistocles (fig. 103). Here, observation of anatomical structure is pushed to the exaggerated representation of the nude in abstract muscular tension and contraction, as clearly scrutinized as if the figure were flayed. On this plinth the athletes playing ball can thus assume most varied poses, sustained by foreshortening and anatomical modeling.

On this same plinth the lively ball game and

after the ephebus who was acclaimed as *kalos* and who appeared on his vases and those of other painters of the time. His athletes are bursting with energy, and intense animation moves all his figures, whether in the drunkenness of the *komos* and the dance, or in scenes of amorous conversation. This dynamic force is present in the adventures of Theseus on the *kylix* in the Louvre and the satyr who is the protagonist in the inner medallion of his *kylixes*. The new sense of humanity also assumes a tender grace on the remarkable Louvre cup in the lyrical vignette of Theseus in the depths of the sea before Amphitrite.

In the work of Onesimos, another painter of cups (fig. 106), athletes predominate, along with horsemen, hunters, nude hetaerae, and revelers, with his only mythological scene that of Troilus. The *kylix* was the form also preferred by the Brygos Painter, a prolific vase painter to whom seventeen works have been assigned. All these are filled with passion and *brio*, giving a particular tone to his rich

103. The lively movement of the ball players on this plinth from the wall of Themistocles is underlined by the analytical treatment of the bodies and by the first attempts at foreshortening. End of the sixth century B.C. Athens, National Museum

the animated vignette of a dog and cat being goaded on by their elegant, idle masters show a new spirit of observation of the everyday world, which also provided a more humanized corpus of themes to the vase painters. Myth continued to satisfy the narrative taste, but there was an increasing preference for scenes from real life; the various aspects of life in the school and the palaestra; men's and women's baths; women's quarters and the world of the hetaerae; the *komos* (scenes of drinking and dancing) and the effects of drinking; the world of the satyrs, more lively and humorous than before, and the intense passion of the maenads.

All this was interpreted with acute interest by artists such as the Panaitios Painter, so-called

104. Detail of a discus thrower on a vase by the Kleophrades Painter with scenes of the palaestra. It illustrates the affirmation of foreshortening and the detailed rendering of anatomical details in Attic vase painting at the end of the sixth century. Tarquinia, National Museum

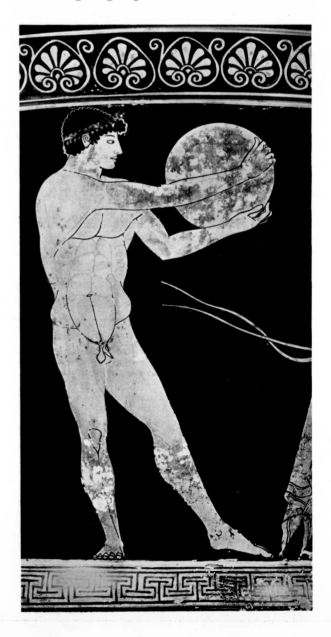

105. This dynamic figure of a dancer from the Tomb of the Jugglers, although full of expressive force, is far removed from the controlled and precise rendering of bodily movement found in contemporary Greek works. End of the sixth century B.C. Tarquinia

106. *This scene of the bath, set in an intimate and detached atmosphere, presents a most vivid and crystalline picture of a nude girl. Painted on the interior of a* kylix *attributed to the painter Onesimos. Circa 480 B.C. Brussels, Musée de Cinquantenaire*

repertory, which ranges from the *Iliupersis* depicted on the *kylix* in the Bibliothèque Nationale in Paris to the wild snarings of satyrs on the London *kylix*, and numerous *komos* and palaestra scenes. Douris, too, was a painter devoted to *kylixes*. He painted over two hundred vases, mainly from the workshop of Python, with grace and refinement, clear sure line, and a facile and inexhaustible inspiration. He presents us with figures of warriors

and Homeric heroes putting on their armor or fighting, as in the fine Vienna *kylixes*, Amazons on the Brussels *kantharos*, and satyrs on the London *psykter*. He also treated mythological themes, such as the myth of Jason on the Vatican *kylix*, the pathetic group of Eos carrying the lifeless body of Memnon —- foreshadowing the Christian motif of the Pietà — on the Louvre *kylix*, and many figures of robust athletes, ephebi, revelers, and naked girls bathing. The fame and excellence of

107. *Detail of a maenad in ecstasy from an amphora of the Kleophrades Painter. Rich pictorial effects are achieved by the use of diluted glazes. Found at Vulci. Circa 500 B.C. Munich, Antikensammlungen*

Douris explain why his style was imitated and his signature forged by the Triptolemos Painter.

It was, on the other hand, in large vases that the Kleophrades Painter preferred to express his exuberant, passionate humanity. In his output of over one hundred vases, he painted only twelve *kylixes*, depicting the mythical themes of Heracles, Theseus, and Homeric heroes, or the everyday subject of athletes. The traditional story of the destruction of Troy in the fascinating Vivenzio *hydria* in Naples becomes an urgent, arresting succession of episodes relived with a deep sense of humanity, as if infused with a breath of tragic pathos that even seems to bend down the palm tree between the altar of Priam and the disconsolate weeping woman who raises her arms and lowers her head in terror. On an amphora in Munich a satyr forgets his wild nature under the spell of the music of the double flutes, and drapes himself in the spotted skin of a fawn, while two maenads surrender themselves to the exalted intoxication of the revelings, opening their lips and throwing back their heads (colorplate, fig. 107). The style shows a grace in the drapery with its rhythmic groups of folds, and the application of diluted glazes creates pictorial tones in the fawn skin, in the short hair of the blonde maenad, who is contrasted with a brown-haired one, and in the violet-colored wreath her around head.

The Berlin Painter also chose large vases, rather than cups, when he placed his carefully drawn, crystalline, plastic figures in the abstract isolation of the black background of the broad surfaces. His style shows a great sense of balance and controlled concentration, culminating in his masterpiece, the amphora in Berlin with the group of Hermes, the lyre-playing satyr, and the fawn (fig. 108). On the other hand, Makron, a painter who specialized in *kylixes* and closely collaborated with the potter Hieron, had a completely different temperament. In the many-faceted panorama of Attic vase painting in this period, Makron is a significant personality by virtue of his extreme fluidity of line, his decorative exuberance, and his graphic virtuosity which is expressed above all in the drapery of female figures, achieving its most characteristic formulations in the two scenes whose respective protagonists are Helen, in the Boston *skyphos*, and the orgiastic maenads with puffed-out chitons, in the Berlin *kylix*. Makron seems to have found the maenads a congenial theme which he treated with more impetus and animation than did the Kleophrades Painter.

From the varied range of interpretations of the different vase painters in this period of enormous production, there emerges the funda-

108. A sophisticated satyr with a lyre and an elegant Hermes form a refined group on this amphora by the Berlin Painter. Found at Vulci. Circa 490 B.C. Berlin, State Museums

mental unity of the Attic graphic language, which, with an organic and autonomous development, was able to reach a very elevated expressive tone by means of the line, that translated every plastic, pictorial, or spatial effect. Even the large-scale painting, now lost, must also have been based essentially on drawing, probably using only a few fundamental colors, without shading. Thus there must have been a certain common vision shared by full-scale painting and the two-colored works of the vase painters, even though the two arts proceeded independently of each other, apart from the occasional thematic or compositional inspiration. However, the decorative problems of pottery were to become more complicated when the expressive means of full-scale painting were enriched during the fifth century.

V | The Severe Style and Its Artistic Conception

The Persian Wars and the defeat of the barbarians from the East at the battles of Marathon and Salamis represent a major historical event in the history of Western civilization, by definitively ensuring the survival of the Classical culture. The great concentration of energy rallied for these wars caused a new ferment in spiritual, religious, and artistic activity. This period saw the maturing of a new aesthetic vision that has been defined as "severe," for it coincided with the disappearance of the stylization which has falsely been interpreted as the "Archaic smile." But just as Archaic figures had been neither joyful nor laughing, these new works were not severe and sad, but were beginning to acquire an organic existence in space. The complete abandonment of the last residue of the Archaic conception of a figure constructed in parallel planes led to the achievement of full volumes, in which the mouth and eyes found their natural curves in depth, their just relationship with the structure of the rest of the head and with the modeling of the planes of the face.

The heroic conception of life held by the generation of the Persian Wars appeared translated into the clear, vigorous volumes of the Severe style. In contrast to the notable flattening of the planes and the cranial dome in Archaic works, this new style showed a spheroidal structure: in place of the pointed chin, a rounded, heavy jaw; the slim Archaic nose was transformed into a thick bony ridge; and the once acute angle of the face became more obtuse, replacing the accentuated Archaic profile with one that linked the smooth-stretched forehead to the ridge of the nose in a single straight line. A lively sense of volume rendered the eyelids thick and fleshy and swelled the full lips on the small mouth. An inner energy filled out the forms and gave tension to the smooth, luminous surfaces. Anatomical structure abandoned the extremely minute analysis that had distinguished the last phases of the Archaic style, and was coordinated into essential, organically articulated masses, with a modeling that was now volumetric instead of linear, and which outlined with simple clarity the muscles on the robust framework of the skeletal structure.

The art of the Severe period was dominated by the athletic ideal, which called for particularly broad, rounded, solid shoulders and powerful incurved backs. The upper torso was expanded by transforming the acute Archaic arched line over the stomach into a low, expanding arched curve beneath which the hollow abdomen was defined in broad corporeal sections. The line of the hip bone was prominently rendered, and the groin line took the form of a well-defined semicircle. Men's hair was gathered into a tight braid that ran around the head, merging into a cap of short curls which often spread over the braid in front; or it formed a single mass of short, flattened, flame-like or corkscrew curls. Women's hair was gathered into two parts with a thick knot at the nape of the neck, forming a heavy, clinging mass, calligraphically chiseled, often bound by a bandeau, or hidden by a snood.

The kore dedicated by Euthydikos on the Acropolis about 480 B.C. represents the first affirmation of the "severe" conception of rounded structures. The figure's coiffure and costume, however, still show Ionic modes, which were soon to disappear in the *peplophoros*, that is, in the type of female figure wearing a peplos, so characteristic of the Severe style. Indeed, in this period the Ionic cadences of the thin chiton and the light, pleated himation

gave way to the Dorian-Attic peplos, made of heavy material. The peplos, folded so that a short flap of it (*apoptygma*) hung over the chest and back, fitted closely at the belt around the waist, and fell in a few broad and heavy folds from the sturdy back down to the feet, assuming the rhythmic strength of the fluting of a Doric column. A few functional lines were created in this smooth drapery by the projection of the breasts and of the one flexed knee of these *peplophoroi*, which were either cast in shining bronze, sculpted in marble, or modeled in terracotta. Even in the interpretation of this theme on painted vases from the first half of the fifth century, the peplos kept its architectonic simplicity, though, in an attempt to stress movement, vase painters modified its plunging verticality with slanting borders and folds and inappropriately adapted the traditional Ionian gesture of lifting up one corner of the hem.

In the Severe ideal of the Attic masters of about 480 B.C., the male type is expressed in masterpieces like the *Blond Ephebus*, so called from traces of paint on his hair (fig. 109) — full-volumed and compact, yet tender and modeled with chiaroscuro effects — or the figure of the nude youth from the Acropolis, attributed to the sculptor Kritios and known as the *Kritios Boy* (fig. 110). The Archaic frontality in this youth is broken by the slight turn of the head, and the stiff Archaic pose with one leg put forward is here relaxed in the new position with the flexed right leg, which offers a subtle play of balance in the slight lowering of the corresponding hip. In its horizontal pectoral muscles and broad shoulders, however, the torso still shows a certain rigidity that remains characteristic of many creations of the Severe style.

Some statues, and series of small bronzes of athletes, discus throwers, and gods, and figurines used as handles for circular mirrors, as well as clay statuettes, show us the various

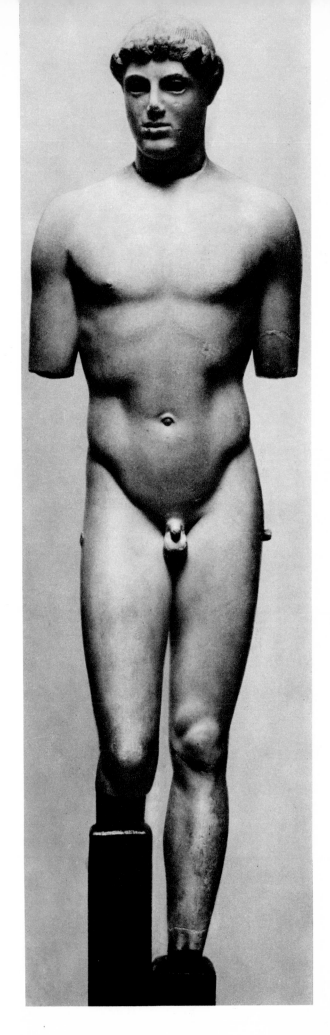

. *This head from the Acropolis, known as the* nd Ephebus, *has the robust structure typical* he Severe style *and is animated by a delicate* tic colorism of the surface. ca *480 B.C. Athens, Acropolis Museum*

110. The careful rhythmic articulation of this crystalline image of a youth from the Acropolis, attributed to Kritios and known as the Kritios Boy, *opens the new artistic horizon of the Severe style. Circa 480 B.C. Athens, Acropolis Museum*

stages of the slow, fascinating development of this weighty, poised rhythm, which is felt progressively through the whole posture of the figure in an organic articulation which curves the crease along the center of the torso, lowers one shoulder, and tilts the head slightly. The enthusiasm with which the masters of the Severe style tackled and developed this rhythmic problem was to culminate in the middle of the fifth century with the *Doryphorus*, or Spear Bearer, of Polykleitos. This work was to remain the most perfect solution and provide an unparalleled model for all future generations of artists, who were to learn from it.

The Severe ideal took tangible form more easily in bronze than in marble. Statistics gathered from plinths show that during the sixth century the numbers of statues in marble and in bronze were more or less equal, but those in marble became rarer after 480 B.C. Polychromed marble suited well the Archaic taste, whereas shining bronze was closer to Severe conceptions. Marble statues, for their part, were to loose the vivid polychromy for a more subdued effect produced by a delicate overpainting. Indeed, bronze sculpture flourished in the first half of the fifth century, and it goes without saying that a sculptor working in marble was also able to create works in bronze.

1. Sculptors and Bronze-Workers of the First Half of the Fifth Century

According to several sources, Kritios, the master who has been credited with the figure of the youth from the Acropolis (fig. 110), headed a school, teaching several generations of sculptors from various cities. His activity in Athens is documented by six signatures on bases, one of which carried the statue of Epicharinus, who according to Pausanias "practiced the race in armor." An example of the same type of victorious athlete in the contest of arms is the fine contemporary bronze in Tübingen (fig. 111). The name of Kritios is associated with that of his companion Nesiotes in the masterpiece of the Tyrannicides, Harmodius and Aristogiton, that took the place of the group by Antenor which was carried off by Xerxes. It may have been that the two sculptors were trained in the workshop of Antenor himself. We do not

know how work on this group was divided between the two artists: it is possible that Nesiotes cast in bronze the statues that we can reconstruct from several marble copies in Naples, New York, and in the Museo dei Conservatori in Rome, and from reproductions in various media, from painted vases to coins (fig. 113). The historical importance of this monument, and its particular function, that of replacing a group that the people of Athens had come to know and cherish, perhaps led the two artists to re-create the types of the Antenor group in their new Severe language. Indeed, it is possible that this work was distinguished from its Archaic predecessor only by the modeling, by the more contained and articulate stride of the figures, and by the treatment of hair, which is cut short in small, flame-like locks in the figure of Aristogiton, while Harmodius' head is covered in tight curls. The two images were conceived in a dynamic,

111. This fine small bronze figure represents a helmeted athlete at the moment he is about to enter into the contest of arms. Formerly his left arm held the shield and his right the weapon; the crest of his helmet is also missing. Circa *480 B.C. Tübingen, University Museum*

advancing rhythm, standing side by side on the square base, each figure perfectly contained in a plastic isolation, their poses expanded in the profile views. They did not yet constitute a genuine group constructed on an indivisible, coherent nexus, but were united only by their theme and their base.

Beside the weighty pose of static figures, artists of the first half of the fifth century also studied with equal enthusiasm figures in movement, for statues of runners and discus throwers. The open, dynamic rhythm of the Tyrannicides group was amplified in small bronzes representing Zeus hurling a thunderbolt, or Poseidon brandishing a trident, and culminated in the powerful bronze statue from Cape Artemision, dated about 460 B.C., one of the finest original works of the mature phase of the Severe style (fig. 114). The bearded head, with the hair still dressed with a thin braid, is slightly turned, its gaze fixed on the

112. Detail of the young Heracles from the metope with the Amazon from Temple E at Selinus. A comparison with the head of Harmodius evidences the influence of Greek models of the Severe style in Sicily.
470–460 B.C. Palermo, National Museum

point indicated by the outstretched left arm; the right arm is drawn back to hold a thunderbolt or trident. Because of its size and conception it is certainly the image of a god, and not, as has been suggested, simply a javelin thrower. Its attribution to the circle of the sculptor Kalamis is more convincing than the attribution to Myron, if we are to assign to Kalamis the type of Apollo known as the Omphalos Apollo, found in Roman marble copies including those in Athens and in the Choiseul-Gouffier collection. We can identify

113. Figure of Harmodius from the group of the Tyrannicides, conceived in accordance with the conceptions of the Severe style. Roman copy after the lost bronze which once stood in the Agora of Athens. Original created circa *477 B.C. Reconstruction, Rome, Museum of Casts*

129

the Omphalos type with the Apollo Alexikakos which the Athenians placed in the temple of the Agora after a plague, as a token of gratitude for advice from the Delphic oracle. The hair of this Apollo, with its fringe of curls falling over the brow, and the modeling of his nude body can indeed be compared with those of the bronze from Cape Artemision. This Apollo has the solemnity of a statue of a god as well as a solid, athletic vigor, and presents a more mature, relaxed pose than does Kritios' youth from the Acropolis (fig. 110).

Kalamis also created in Athens a celebrated bronze statue of Aphrodite, known as Sosandra, dedicated on the Acropolis about 465 B.C. by Callias, the son-in-law of Cimon. This figure so attracted the perceptive critic Lucian that he wrote of it three times in his *Dialogues*, admiring its serene, hidden smile and the dignity and elegance of its drapery, in comparison with the disheveled nakedness of the dancer Thaïs. The most likely of the various identifications proposed equates this work with a widely known type of draped female figure which was frequently copied in Roman times for portrait statues of Roman ladies, particularly in the Antonine period, as a paradigm of divine modesty and chaste beauty. Copies of the original from Baia (fig. 115) and Hama, and isolated heads, the finest specimen of which is in Pavia, all show us the solemn, contained grace of the original creation. The figure is clothed in a generous, heavy mantle that swathes the entire body in broad folds interrupted by the slight projections of the right knee and the hidden arm, the fold over the outstretched arm, and the crisp fold that forms a perfect oval of shadow around the emerging luminous face with its rigorously symmetrical waves of hair. This face is indeed unsmiling, but the pure and light freshness of the cheeks and the perfect drawing of the full lips are a focal point for us as our gaze runs over the broad surfaces of the cloak; and the expression of this face is intellectually interpreted by Lucian as a reflection of an inner, personal, divine smile.

Though Kalamis is supposed to have been a native of Boeotia — he worked in Tanagra, where he executed a Hermes *kriophoros* and a Dionysus, and the Boeotian Pindar employed him to make an image of Ammon in Thebes — he appears to have moved in completely Attic circles. Not only did he have contacts with Callias and Pindar, but also with Hieron, the Tyrant of Syracuse. Hieron, victorious in the Olympic games in 468 B.C., commissioned Onatas from Aegina to make a bronze quadriga and Kalamis to execute the two horses ridden by boys that flanked it.

The horse, along with the theme of the human figure, had been the center of interest for Greek artists from the Geometric period on, and pulsating and vibrant examples were created for the Acropolis at the end of the sixth century. Kalamis seems to have found this theme particularly sympathetic. According to Pliny, Propertius, and Ovid, he was unmatched in modeling horses in his numerous quadriga and biga groups of victors in the Panhellenic games. This theme was also in keeping with the heroic and agonistic ideals of the times, and it was cast in bronze in the same spirit that fills the verses of Pindar. From the numerous chariot monuments cast in bronze there remains only the figure of the charioteer and fragments of horses from the votive chariot celebrating the victory of Hieron at Delphi, dedicated by Polyzalus of Gela. The base of the work has survived and the signature of the sculptor Sothadas of Thespiae, found on another fragment, has been insecurely related to this base, but the style is not Attic and seems rather to stem from the Peloponnesus. The famous figure of the charioteer from this monument (colorplate, fig. 118) indeed sums up all the most salient characteristics of the Severe style in the solid, compact head, the tense surfaces of the face, the minute, calligraphic engraving in the close-clinging locks that stand out on the temples and cheeks, the architectonic simplicity of his chiton, and the vivid anatomy of the tensed arm and foot muscles. In the relief shown in figure 119 is represented the type of bronze chariot monument of which the Delphi charioteer once formed part.

Besides Kritios and Nesiotes, sources name the Athenian Hegias, who, together with Onatas of Aegina and Ageladas of Argos, is said to have been the master of Phidias. Hegias was known as one of the greatest bronze sculptors of the time. His personality remains unknown, however, and we can only deduce that his language must have represented the concise, pungent vigor of the first phase of the Severe style, since the practiced eye of Lucian, classing him with Kritios and Nesiotes, defines his work as "tight, muscular, hard, and chiseled with minute care." In the eyes of a critic like Quintilian, already far removed from the Classical spirit, the incisive, Severe character was to seem close to Etruscan art (*signia*

114. Poseidon or Zeus from Cape Artemision. In this bronze the athletic ideal of the Severe style is transferred to the divine plane. Circa 460 B.C. Athens, National Museum

131

115. At right: *Roman copy of the Aphrodite Sosandra of Kalamis. This copy is distinguished by the pure freshness of the features and a light coloristic effect in the folds of the mantle. Original created* circa 465 B.C. *Baia*

116. Lower left: *Roman copy of a type of Demeter, known from complete copies in the Museo dei Conservatori, Rome, and at Corinth. Original created by a great unknown Attic sculptor of the Severe style,* circa 470–460 B.C. *Rome, Antiquario del Palatino*

117. Lower right: *Roman copy of a type of Persephone, known from various copies, one of which is a headless statue in Corinth. It was probably paired with the Demeter of the type shown in figure 116, and created by the same unknown Attic sculptor,* circa 470–460 B.C. *Rome, Museo delle Terme*

118. Opposite: *Charioteer from the monument dedicated by Polyzalus of Gela at Delphi. The band around the head, symbol of victory, is inlaid with silver. This chiseled bronze is further enlivened by lips, lashes, and eyebrows of copper, and eyes of enamel.* Circa 475 B.C. *Delphi, Museum*

132

119. Relief from the agora of Cyrene which depicts the type of bronze chariot and rider erected in honor of agonistic victories. Cyrene, Museum

duriora et Tuscanicis proxima), but this judgment considered only the external appearances of clear, salient, anatomical features, without penetrating the differences in interpretation and style between the intellectualized Greek conception and the expressionistic Etruscan vision.

Sources indicate another characteristic interpreter of the Severe heroic ideal in Glaukias of Aegina. He worked in Olympia where he modeled a chariot for the victory of Gelon of Syracuse in 488 B.C., and three victorious pugilists. The figure of the pugilist Glaucus seemed to be fighting a shadow. Aegina had a celebrated school of bronze sculptors, and Pliny records the particular bronze alloy from

Aegina. Apart from the Archaic sculptor Kallon, the principal representative from Aegina of the Severe style was Onatas, from whom the Achaeans ordered the great votive offering with nine statues of heroes and Nestor for Olympia where there were five other works by Onatas. The Tar-

120. Apollo of Piombino, so named because found in the sea near Piombino. This bronze, bearing a dedicatory inscription to Athena, is difficult to place chronologically and stylistically, since it combines Archaic rigidity of pose with a particularly graceful profile and a soft, expansive modeling. Paris, Louvre

121. A good Roman copy in marble of the famous Discobolus *by Myron. The original bronze was created* circa *460* B.C. *Rome, Museo delle Terme*

antines commissioned Onatas, along with Ka-lynthos, to execute another monumental ex-voto at Delphi. Onatas was inspired by a primitive wooden *xoanon* for the statue of Demeter Me-laina, or "Black Demeter," in a grotto at Phi-galia. Since the originals of the bronzes by this Aegina master are lost, we can form an idea of the style of this school only from the sculptures of the Temple of Aphaia (figs. 51, 52, 59) and from an occasional isolated bronze head.

The austere Dorian spirit, in the Archaic period, shunned the more graceful expressions, and concentrated mostly on the nude male fig-ure, articulated with vigorous plasticity in clearly developed volumes. Now that the nude image of the athlete, symbol of the ethics of sport and the perfect *paideia* that created harmony between body and spirit, had become the center of artistic interest, it was possible to harmo-niously develop the Doric artistic premises which accorded perfectly with the conceptual world, the themes, and the artistic vision of the Severe style. Argos, Sicyon, Corinth, Sparta, and Elis were to count many bronze sculptors among their citizens. The great Argive school is represented by Eutelidas and Chrysothemis, who were responsible for statues of victorious athletes at Olympia, and by the famous Age-ladas, who seems to have had an exceptionally long working life from the end of the sixth

122. Copy in marble of Marsyas, after the lost bronze group of Marsyas and Athena created by Myron circa 450 B.C. Rome, Museo Barracco

century to 450 B.C., unless perhaps there were two successive artists of the same name. Ageladas, too, made bronze statues of the victorious athletes: at Olympia, Anochus and Timasitheus, and the quadriga of Cleosthenes; and at Delphi, bronze horses and Messapian women for the Tarantines. The motif of the nude Zeus violently hurling a thunderbolt, whose development can be followed in small bronzes and coins from the end of the Archaic period through the Severe style up to the great original work from Cape Artemision, met with outstanding treatment in the hands of Ageladas in his statue of Zeus Ithomatas, made for the Messenians exiled to Naupattus about 460 B.C.

A pair of charioteers beside horses were modeled in Olympia for the Arcadian, Phormis, by the Argive sculptors Glaukos and Dionysios, who also executed two offerings for Micythus with numerous bronze statues, among them the personification of the Homeric *Agon*, along with Homer, Hesiod, Orpheus, and divinities.

In Sicyon we have, along with Kanachos, the great master of the end of the Archaic period, his brother Aristokles. He founded a school which included Synon and his son Ptolichos of Aegina, and Sostratos and his son Pantias, all of whom created statues of victors at Olympia. The school of Kritios, too, gave rise to a long line of sculptors, among them Ptolichos of Corcyra, the teacher of Amphion of Knossos, whom the Cyreneans commissioned to execute the chariot of Battus at Delphi with personifications of Cyrene and Libya. Amphion taught Pison of Calauria, who in his turn had Damokritos of Sicyon as a pupil.

In the historical sources the personality of the sculptor Pythagoras stands out as one of the major artists of the Severe period along with Kritios and Nesiotes, Hegias, Kallon, and Onatas. Pythagoras seems to have interpreted in bronze the most typical ideals of his time. He was indeed the creator of a long series of statues of victorious athletes at Olympia: Leontiscus the Siceliot, Astylus of Croton, Euthymus of Locri, Dromeus of Stynphalion, Mnaseas of Cyrene, and Protolaus of Mantinea. He also executed a chariot with a Nike for Cratisthenes, the father of Mnaseas, and in Delphi he modeled the statue of a victor of the pancratium. The modeling of these nudes had to conform with the athletic conception, placing emphasis on the muscles, the network of veins, and very carefully chiseled hair, thus approaching the language of Kritios, Nesiotes, and Hegias, according to the tradition recorded by Pliny. But apart from this type of muscular, athletic nude, Pythagoras also seems to have been attracted by problems of expression, which he probably resolved through accentuating various tensions and rhythms of the body, since art at this time was far from imitating facial expression. In fact, the few experiments in expression and characterization remain on quite another level, that of particular demoniac and caricatural figures, found above all in the field of Athenian vase painting. The pain manifested in Pythagoras' statue of the wounded limping Philoctetes, or the fury of Eteocles and Polynikes, must have been expressed by forceful rhythmic arrangements and vivid modeling, which also gave elastic drive to his figures of Apollo Archer and Perseus. Diogenes Laertius does indeed tell us that Pythagoras searched

123. The pediments of the Temple of Zeus at Olympia have as the central axis and focal point of their compositions the imposing figure of a divinity. Here in the west pediment, with an imperious gesture, Apollo intervenes in the savage centauromachy. Circa 460 B.C. Olympia, Museum

124. A Lapith woman from the west pediment Olympia, shown as a centaur's hand seizes her by the hair. Her dense, heavy peplos falls in complicated folds which follow the movement of her body as she sinks on one knee.
Circa 460 B.C. Olympia, Museum

125. Young boy in a natural pose from the east pediment of Olympia. The compact rhythm of the composition is held together by the drapery which falls over his left arm and spreads in a fan shape on the ground beneath him. Circa *460* B.C. *Olympia, Museum*

126. Detail of the so-called Cladeus from the extreme right of the east pediment of Olympia. The smooth cap-like hair, at one time brought out by color, serves to accentuate the strong, vigorous modeling of the tense face. Circa *460* B.C. *Olympia, Museum*

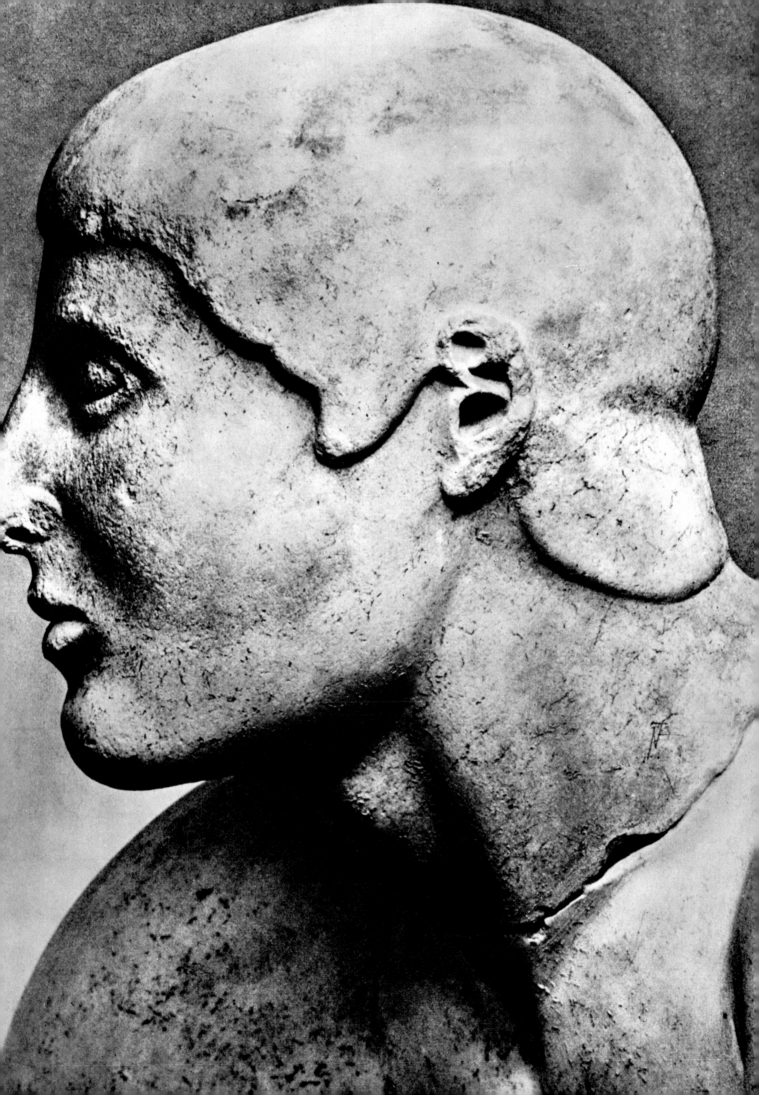

for symmetry and rhythm above all else; that is, he studied the articulation of the figure in space. Perhaps originally from Samos, Pythagoras emigrated to Reggio, where he was a pupil of Klearchos. Until Roman times one of his masterpieces remained in Reggio: the bronze group of Europa and the bull, the pride of the city, which was praised by Varro and Cicero.

Myron of Eleutherae, a pupil of Ageladas, was also very closely bound to this heroic, athletic world of the great bronze sculptors of the Severe style, and created bronze statues of victors at Olympia — Lycinus, Timanthes, Philippus, and Chionis — and pentathlon and pancratium victors at Delphi. But Myron did more than simply conceive his virile athletic figures in an articulated, poised stasis: he perceived them first and foremost in instantaneous, dynamic movement. With his work, the representational problem of the athlete acquired more complex and varied rhythm and movement, so that Pliny was prompted to call Myron *numerosior*, that is richer in rhythms, by comparison with Polykleitos. Myron multiplied the aspects of the image in space (*multiplicasse veritatem videtur*) in a rational pursuit of rhythmic composition (*in symmetria diligentior*). He was completely absorbed by the study of the body, showing no interest in the problems of expressing feeling (*corporum tenus curiosus animi sensus non expressisse*). And in the chiseling of the hair his style is still linked archaically to the Severe tradition. These descriptions recorded by Pliny apply perfectly to Myron's works, for example, the bronze statue of the runner Ladas — a victor in 476 B.C., celebrated in epigrams — who appears to be on the point of bolting off his plinth, and the famous *Discobolus* or Discus Thrower, known to us from Roman copies (fig. 121).

Painted vases offered a varied range of positions for discus throwers, but sculpture was more limited in its treatment of this theme. As we can see from small bronze figures, like the fine specimen in Peloponnesian style which is in New York, the discus thrower had to be a standing figure whose only variation of pose was to grasp the discus in either one or both hands. Myron, however, made his discus thrower bend forward, curving him daringly and compressing him between two parallel planes facing the spectator, in the tense, contained rhythm of the last phase of the throw, with the generous semicircle of the arms balanced by the powerful torso. Quintilian appreciated the novelty and difficulty (*novitas ac difficultas*) of this creation with its turning, complex rhythm (*tam distortum et elaboratum*), classifying Myron's images as being rhythmi-

cally freer (*molliora*) than those of Kalamis. Everything is concentrated in the lively, quivering modeling of the nude body, to which is subordinated the rigorously restrained treatment of the close-cropped cap of hair, chiseled in minute curls on the rounded structure of the head following the model of the Severe style. Myron's statues of gods included Heracles, Apollo, Dionysus, and Hecate, but we have only copies of his Athena grouped with the satyr Marsyas, the latter standing in the attitude of greed, insecure but dynamic, torn between the longing to pick up the flute dropped by the goddess and her divine prohibition. This group, formerly on the Acropolis, was held together by counterpoised, diverging rhythms. The shy, virginal simplicity of Athena, in whose figure the Severe treatment was softened by the looser drapery and the wavy hair flowing out from under the helmet, was contrasted with the wild nature of Marsyas, expressed in the muscular, tense nude with expressive, frowning face and hair that stands on end, as accurately chiseled as the beard (fig. 122).

Myron's vivid modeling must have conferred great animation on his famous bronze cow, widely celebrated by epigrammatists, who admired its *veritas*.

We know nothing of Myron's son, Lykios, remembered for statues of the pancratium victor Autholicus, the Argonauts, a boy blowing on a fire, a boy carrying a basin of water, and a group of Achilles and Memnon.

In the field of marble statuary the most notable and elevated creations we possess are represented by the outstanding complex of pediment sculptures and metopes from the Temple of Zeus at Olympia, in the famous Panhellenic sanctuary (figs. 123–128). In the second century A.D. Pausanias was not able to recognize the stylistic impossibility of attributing the east pediment to Paionios and the west pediment to Alkamenes, both artists of the generation following the unknown master who actually carved these marbles. While the erroneous declaration of Pausanias has led many critics astray, it has become increasingly clear that the absolute unity of conception and execution of the whole complex is the work of a

127. Lapith woman fighting the brutal grip of a centaur, from the west pediment of Olympia. The novel effects of her drapery are not patterns created by the garment alone, but are conceived and rendered in rapport with the vigorous movement of her body.
Circa *460 B.C.* Olympia, Museum

single, great genius; he seems to have sprung up suddenly in the Peloponnesus gifted in all the coloristic refinements of the chisel, and gave strength to the Severe ideal in works of a powerful monumentality. Local terracottas, like a full-volumed warrior torso or the akroterial group of Zeus and Ganymede, as well as small bronzes like the discus thrower in New York or the spinner in Berlin, can help us to understand the climate in which this artist may have grown up, but until now he remains a lone figure in his inimitable and highly personal style: vigorous in solid, organic nudes, and also capable of conveying the tender slimness of a boy or the soft fleshiness

wrinkles only in the pain of the Lapith savagely bitten by the centaur, in the old soothsayer's prediction of a tragic conclusion, or the worried sadness of Heracles faced with the trials he must undergo. When the representation of hair has a particular significance in terms of the subject, the master knew how to render with fine chiseling the lines of the thick mass of hair of the Lapith woman in the centaur's brutal grasp, or the ordered crown of curls that adds dignity to the solemn figure of Apollo, or again the thick cap of curls that emphasizes the robustness of the vigorous Lapith, or even the wavy locks that frame the incipient baldness of the soothsayer. But this

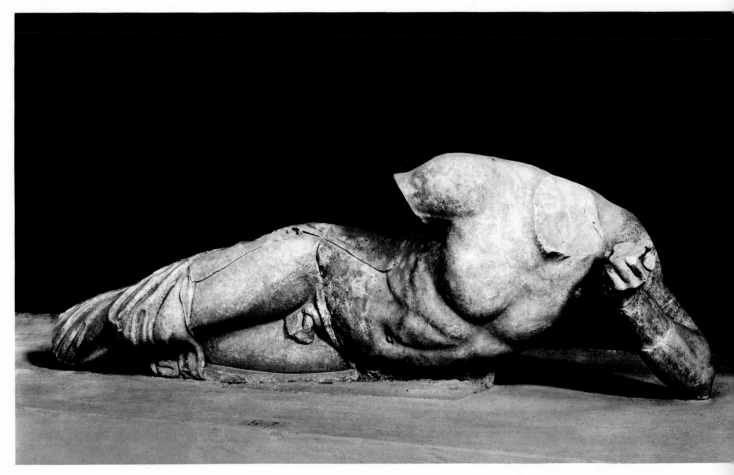

128. The so-called Alpheus from the east pediment of Olympia. A comparison of this figure with the angular figures from the Aegina pediments shows the evolution in rhythmic articulation that has taken place in the forty years which separates these works. Circa 460 B.C. Olympia, Museum

of an old man. His drapery was thick and full, and reached extreme simplicity in the peplos worn by his standing figures. When the figure was in movement, the sculptor experimented with new effects of rumpled folds, and scattered the hems with ingenious, rigorous ripples. The faces and brows of the Master of Olympia have a certain freshness, clear and crystalline, marked with a few

sculptor can also suppress detail to create the most absolute unity of mass in a supreme synthesis of volume and modeling as in the compact heads of Cladeus or Heracles, or the heads of Lapith women smoothly covered by the *kekryphalos*.

Pictorial models of the centauromachy, which could possibly have suggested to the sculptor the audacious compositional schemes and foreshortened, abbreviated poses, are invariably recast by him in new and essentially plastic terms. The agitated, complex composition, well adapted to the savage, convulsive struggle of the west pediment, intentionally contrasts with the poised stasis and isolated forms of the east pediment, more in keeping with the moment of solemn calm and tragic expectation preceding the chariot race between Pelops and Oenomaus. The harmony and richness of compositional solutions that the artist could produce are shown in the twelve metopes with the single theme of the twelve labors of Heracles. Compositional originality here joins forces with the new spirituality of the thematic conception, which introduces into the centauromachy the central and untraditional figure of Apollo who punishes the *hybris* and the thoughtless release of animal passion. This leads the drama of the cruel primitive legend of local heroes back to Zeus, the supreme judge, so that the symbolic subject of the

129. Detail of the largest known kylix. *Decorated by the Penthesilea Painter, on the outside with Homeric duels and on the inside with the exploits of Theseus, seen here in the central medallion with Pirithoüs. From Spina.* Circa *460–450* B.C. *Ferrara, Archaeological Museum*

Olympic *Agon* is raised to a divine plane. Similarly, a new sense of humanity dictated the choice of the most pathetic moment of each of the various labors of Heracles in the metopes. These are no longer conceived only as narrations of the culminating point of the struggles, but rather as the state of mind of the hero in relation to the completed effort, and to the confident support of a participating Athena.

The Master of Olympia gives strong characterizations in the faces of centaurs or the old soothsayer, as did Myron in his Marsyas and, later, Phidias in the centaurs of the Parthenon metopes. But these expressive experiments which turned away from beauty and concentrated on the ugly and demoniacal — finding widespread responses in the red-figured pottery of the period — still remain on the plane of general definitions of types and are not particular portrayals of individuals.

In the period of the Severe style, there was still no facial portraiture, an art which was to develop only in the fourth century B.C. The portraits of the *strategoi* were bearded heads with typecast features, characterized only by the Corinthian helmet. However, the herm of Themistocles, found at Ostia, seems to run counter to this trend: along with the structure of the head and the hair and beard chiseled in short locks, all in the purest Severe manner, this work presents round, deep-set eyes and a wrinkled brow, evidencing a search for expressiveness that seems dictated by a lively interest in characterization. But despite the fact that many scholars consider this portrait of Themistocles a copy of a genuine work of the Severe style, it seems more probable that it is a later, learned reconstruction of the neo-Attic school, inspired by fifth-century models but given the features of the man of thought and action which had been evolved in later portraiture.

2. Athenian Vase Painters of the First Half of the Fifth Century

In figurative art, as in literature, myth became humanized and dramatized; the Archaic narration was replaced by feelings of pathos and ethos. The Greek theater saw the rise of Aeschylus, and painting found in Polygnotos its *ethographos*, that is, its painter of mood and feeling.

To follow the path that leads in full-scale painting to Polygnotos and his colleague Mikon — from the Persian Wars to the mid-fifth century — we have only a few hints in literary sources and in Attic red-figure pottery.

Though still using the four fundamental colors, painters were now in full control of foreshortening, which they were also beginning to convey by shading. Vase painters showed truly painterly touches in using more complicated compositions which came from large-scale painting, in richer effects using diluted glazes, and in the use of a white ground on *kylixes*, *pyxides*, *alabastra*, and *lekythoi*. This more pictorial, narrative taste led to a preference for larger vases, the most popular being the Nolan amphora and the neck-amphora, the krater, *hydria*, *pelike*, and *stamnos*. It is significant that in precisely this period the *kylix* reached its greatest dimensions with the specimen from Spina, sumptuously decorated by the Penthesilea Painter with the myth of Theseus, and measuring more than 22 inches in diameter (fig. 129).

Trends among Attic vase painters became more numerous and varied. There were some painters who preferred simple compositions and isolated figures, such as the Nike, running women, women in their apartments, figures of Eros, or ephebi placed on the elongated bodies of *lekythoi* or *oinochoai*. This trend is seen in the work of the Bowdoin Painter, the painter of the Yale *lekythos*, or the Karlsruhe Painter who produced white-ground *lekythoi* and footless cups, or the Icarus Painter with his lively little figures. Other vase painters, however, had a more academic taste, which reached particular clarity and solemnity in the works of the Villa Giulia Painter. This tendency is expressed in static, elongated warriors putting on their armor, in ephebi and heroes on the *kylixes* of the Euaion Painter, and in more supple, modulated female figures by the Chicago Painter. This last painter has left us the balanced, elegant mythological panel on the Lecce *pelike*, which depicts Andrastus delivering the necklace of Harmonia to Eryphile. Andrastus is clad in a fine, embroidered chiton and Eryphile in a flowing peplos, with the characteristic note of a slim, mannered flamingo set between the two figures. Later, other vase painters, developing the stylistic features of the Myson circle, tended toward mannerism. Taking part in this trend was the Pan Painter who placed elaborate figures on amphorae and *lekythoi*, or composed lively mythological scenes with movemented figures in exuberant draperies on kraters, *hydriai*, and *pelikai*. The prolific Leningrad Painter belongs to this same mannered school, with his favorite *komos* and banqueting scenes on column-kraters, and so too the Agrigento Painter, who produced about forty of these kraters, mostly treating the *komos* theme. The *skyphos* shape, on the other hand, was exploited for figures of two or three

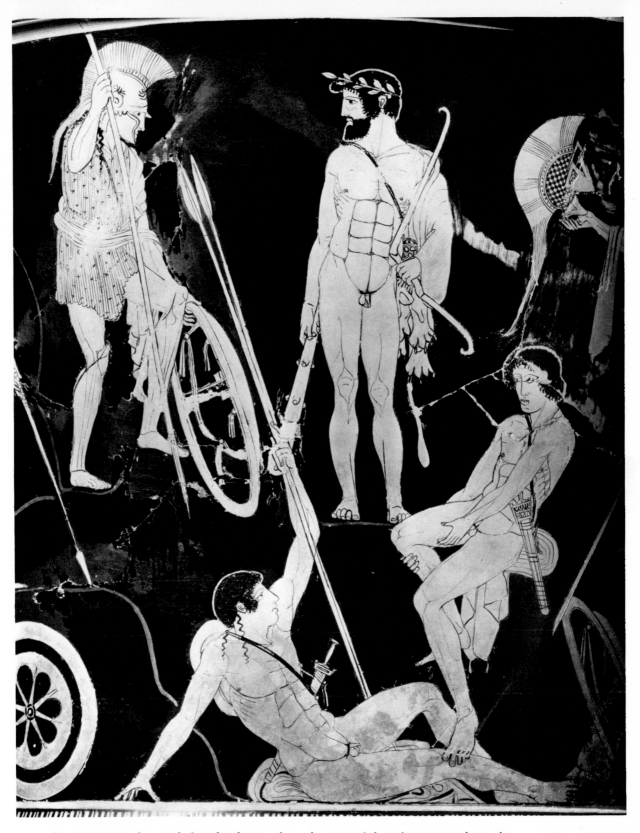

130. An expectant and anguished pathos hovers about these immobile and statuesque heroes by the Niobid Painter on this monumental calyx-krater found at Orvieto. Circa 460 B.C. Paris, Louvre

gods and for scenes of pursuit by the Lewis Painter and the Zephyr Painter. The *kylix* still continued to interest vase painters, and constituted the prevalent form for some of them. Among the artists treating the *kylix* was the Penthesilea Painter, but he also painted *skyphoi* and *pyxides* along with the controversial Pistoxenos Painter from whom he is none too clearly distinguished and who had a preference for white grounds.

Besides mythological motifs there were pursuits, lovers' meetings, and scenes of athletics and horsemanship. The new pictorial trends affirm themselves against white backgrounds, with shading obtained by the judicious use of diluted glazes, thus endowing bodies with vivid plasticity, and a coloristic effect. These qualities are well shown in the Penthesilea Painter's masterpiece, the *kylix* in Munich with the pathetic and romantic group, perhaps inspired by a large painting of Achilles at the very moment he stabs the beautiful queen of the Amazons and at the same time falls in love with her.

Another characteristic tendency can be seen in some vase painters whose conception is broad and solemn, and whose style is grand and noble, with isolated figures placed on large vases, particularly kraters. A typical representative of this style is the Boreas Painter, who takes his name from the scene on the volute-krater in Bologna with the rape of Oreithyia by Boreas, the god of the North Wind. The theme is significantly widespread in this period, and can be seen again in the work of the so-called Oreithyia Painter. It glorified the wind god, who was credited with the destruction of the Persian fleet, and whose cult was on the banks of the Ilyssus. About thirty kraters, as well as other vases, were produced by the prolific Altamura Painter, and the strong, sculptural quality of his figures, with their rich anatomical detail, conveys a desire to rival the effects of full-scale painting.

Spurred on by the conquests of full-scale painting in shading and expression, vase painters were trying to overcome the limits of draftsmanly perfection and two-color work, on which their traditional calligraphic language was based. The taste for presenting figures, shields, and other objects in illusionistic foreshortening, as well as the new compositional attempts at overcoming the abstract background and the single figure plane by scattering figures on several different levels indicated by rocks and stylized trees, bear witness to an approach inspired by contemporary painting. The Niobid Painter, so called because of his calyx-krater in the Louvre, is the most authoritative representative of this new pictorial language. Depicted on his krater is the slaying of Niobe's children by Apollo and Artemis, as well as a scene of heroes and gods, perhaps from the cycle of the Argonauts (fig. 130). His figures have the plastic and monumental grandiosity of the statues of the Master of the Olympia pediments. His composition has varying levels, landscape elements, and foreshortening. The figures of this vase painter, who was active around 460 B.C., attest to a new conception of space which must have stemmed from experiments carried out in pure painting.

3. The Painting of Polygnotos

Literary sources attribute these advances in painting to Polygnotos, but we cannot know if, as older painted vases seem to suggest, the way had in fact been prepared by preceding painters. We know nothing of the art of Polygnotos' father, the painter Aglaophon of Thasos. Of Kalliphon of Samos, we have only the mention of his attempt at characterization in the personification of Eris, the ugly goddess of Discord whom he depicted in a sea battle, according to Pausanias similar to the Eris that appeared between Ajax and Hector on the *Cypselus Chest*. The painting was in the Artemision at Ephesus, where Kalliphon had also represented Patroclus assisted by women as he fastened on his cuirass, a favorite theme among painters in the early phase of the Severe style.

Polygnotos, however, seems to have been the creator of a new compositional and spatial conception; this can be reconstructed on the basis of the detailed descriptions Pausanias gives of his large compositions in the Cnidian *Lesche* at Delphi, where the artist had been officially invited to paint the Underworld and the sack of Troy. We also have descriptions of large works in the Stoa Poikile, or painted portico, of Cimon's Athens where Polygnotos was given citizenship, as well as of mythological paintings in the Anakeion or sanctuary of the Dioscuri, in the gallery of the Propylaea, and outside Athens in Plataea and Thespiae. Pausanias clearly indicates the varied poses of the figures, placed on different levels among landscape elements, and gazing, now upward, now down. Pliny mentions the transparent garments of the women, their hair caught up in polychromed snoods, with partly open mouths, and less rigid, more varied types of faces. It is possible, moreover, that the representation of the characters' feelings, which won Polygnotos the epithet of *ethographos*, was expressed, as in the works of the Master of the Olympia pediments, in the general conception of the theme and the gestures of the figures, rather than in facial expressions.

The other great painter beside Polygnotos was his collaborator, Mikon, who created a series of works in Athens depicting the traditional centauromachy and Amazonomachy themes, and the myths of Theseus in the Hephaesteion, another Amazonomachy and the battle of Marathon in the Stoa Poikile, and the return of the Argonauts in the Anakeion.

In the fervid pictorial climate of the Athens of Cimon, it is no wonder that Attic vase painters, working to renew their own language, should have drawn inspiration from the rich figurative world of the Polygnotan school. It

148

131. The conquest of foreshortening achieved in full-scale painting of the Severe period gave new compositional life to the Amazonomachy. The representation of the theme seen here is inspired by the painting of Mikon. The decoration of this krater is attributed to the Painter of the Woolly Satyrs, who also gives a pictorial rendering of the centauromachy on the neck of the vase. Circa 460 B.C. New York, Metropolitan Museum

therefore seems legitimate to look for ideas and motifs from Polygnotos' and Mikon's painting in the enormous corpus of vases. A whole group of red-figure vases which develop the theme of the Amazonomachy show compositions of Amazons on horseback, or on their knees, or retreating (fig. 131). The fact that these motifs constantly recur in similar forms, bears witness to their derivation from a common archetype, diversely transmitted and reformulated. This archetype could indeed have been the painting of Mikon. Similarly, ne centauromachy theme, which showed the influence of pictorial models already in the monumental plastic interpretation on the west pediment at Olympia, is amply developed in a series of kraters exhibiting many traits attributable to the influence of full-scale painting. Some examples are the solemn and imposing centauromachy painted on a vase in Florence by a contemporary of the Master of Olympia; the centauromachy on a Louvre vase by a painter who has used daring foreshortening; and the centauromachy on a vase in Naples. All these works were influenced by the great pictorial compositions from the school of Polygnotos and Mikon.

The paintings of this school continued to offer vase painters sophisticated thematic and compositional elements, even after the mid-fifth century. However, there was a danger inherent in this attempt at rivaling the experi-

ments of pure painting: the danger of destroying the marvelous stylistic balance of the vase-painting language itself, and of distorting its true character as a graphic, two-color idiom, which had reached its highest level of quality at the end of the sixth century and the first decades of the fifth. Indeed, we shall see that after the different experiments of the second half of the fifth century, Athenian painted pottery fell into a rapid decline.

Though Polygnotos and Mikon were trained in the Severe style and represent its most extreme phase, they also marked the beginning of Classicism, which affirmed itself toward the middle of the century in the great figures of Phidias and Polykleitos. Although he took Athenian citizenship and always worked in Athens, Polygnotos came from Ionia, and perhaps traits like the transparent drapery and the ornamental grace of the polychromed snoods,

132. Central panel of the Ludovisi Throne.
The function of this work is uncertain.
Its theme and style evoke the mysterious and artistic environment of Magna Graecia under Ionic influences.
Circa *460* B.C. *Rome, Museo delle Terme*

133. The female nude, so often represented on Greek vases of the Severe period, either as a hetaera or a bather, finds here a rare plastic interpretation in this flute player of the Ludovisi Throne.
Circa *460* B.C. *Rome, Museo delle Terme*

150

134. Clay votive plaque from Locri with servant girls bearing objects for the marriage feast and rites in honor of Persephone-Kore, a legend which inspired many scenes of the vivacious repertory of the clay-modelers of Locri. Circa 460 B.C. Reggio Calabria, National Museum

mentioned in the sources, could be considered touches of Ionian taste. But in this painter Ionian vivacity still seems to have merged harmoniously with the monumental and ethic sense of Attic art.

4. Ionian Art of the Islands and Asia Minor

It is interesting to observe how the art of the pure Ionian areas of the islands and Asia Minor reacted to this fundamental tendency toward vigorous, solemn simplicity that characterizes

the Severe phase of the first half of the fifth century. Reliefs from the Prytaneion on Thasos, datable between 490 and 480 B.C., show Apollo with a lyre, the nymphs, and Hermes, who with a vivacious gesture leads in the Graces. Whereas the heads of the figures show a more solid, rounded structure, they are still linked to Archaic conceptions in their delicate grace, the pointed beard of Hermes, and the women's long hair. Even the Doric peplos, introduced into the varied range of costumes, assumes a slightly Ionicized transparency. Some funerary steles and a few reliefs from Naxos, Paros, and Samos illustrate the development of this har-

135. The sense of the colossal that inspired Sicilian architecture emanates from this fallen Atlas figure from the Olympieion at Agrigento. First half of the fifth century, B.C.

moniously rhythmic Ionian compositional language, with its soft modeling and elegantly cadenced drapery. The thick, heavy materials of the Severe Doric style were the very opposite of the light, transparent stuffs preferred in Ionia, and the new Severe taste was expressed only in the abandonment of the Archaic ornamental folds of drapery, and in the multiplication of more rigorously drawn fine engraving that conveys the lightness of the material and models the underlying forms of the bodies, which in their turn become fuller.

This Ionian interpretation of the Severe style is typified by the graceful stele from Paros dated about 460 B.C., now in New York, which shows a girl with elegantly chiseled hair holding two doves. Approaching nearer to the middle of the century, the headless Nike from Paros, wearing the peplos, and the *peplophoroi* from Xanthos have garments that are weightier, though they show Ionian influences in their flowing movement and soft modeling. In the last phase of the Severe style even the smooth cap-like hairstyle appears, as in a relief of a banqueting scene from Thasos, which nonetheless remains Ionian in its linear elegance.

Though Ionian influences can be traced in Thessaly and northern Greece, the work of this area is characterized by less harmony of proportions, and a heavier, summary modeling.

136. In this metope from Temple E at Selinus, the theme of Actaeon attacked by the dogs incited by Artemis is taken up by the Sicilian sculptor with vivacity and passion. Circa 470–460 B.C. Palermo, National Museum

5. Greek Artistic Currents in Sicily and Magna Graecia

In Italy, the Ionian current found a vital, refined expression in Magna Graecia, for instance in the famous marble triptych from the so-called Ludovisi Throne (figs. 132, 133). This carving, dated around 460 B.C., represents, in the central panel, the *anodos*, that is the annual resurrection of Persephone, and the other panels depict a hetaera with a flute — a theme dear to Attic vase painters — and a mantle-clad woman sacrificing. Delicate transparent drapery, calligraphically chiseled, striated hair, and tender, softly curving naked bodies are brought to a pitch of fresh, light grace in this Italic work.

Ionic modes and touches of the Severe style translated into a lively and uninhibited, cursive idiom formed the basis of the language of the clay-modelers of Locri, who produced an attractive series of votive plaques. These works were distinguished by a wealth of detail and a colorful interpretation. They illustrated offerings to the gods of Hades, the rape of Persephone, and marriages of gods, with some charming touches like the girl gathering pomegranates, or women unpacking marriage robes from decorated chests (fig. 134). Even the flourishing school of clay-modelers at

154

137. Female head of Parian marble from a metope of Temple E at Selinus. The inspiration of Greek models of the Severe style is evident. Circa 470–460 B.C. Palermo, National Museum

Medma in their clay statuettes and typical large half-figures of women showed influence of the Severe style. Indeed, under the influence of Greek models faces acquired a new solidity, and were framed in thick plastically treated hair, arranged either in a halo of curls, or in heavy, striated bands, and drapery took on a smooth consistency. The output of small bronzes, mirror handles, and bronze appliqués for vases, though adhering to the models of the Severe style, still showed an Italic accent in a greater vivacity and freedom of rhythm and graphic notation, whether in the decora-

tion of drapery, the animal skin worn by a satyr, or the gesture of a dancing girl.

After the Persian Wars, the ties between Greece and her colonies in Sicily and Magna Graecia became increasingly close, partly because of the danger of Phoenician expansion. Syracuse, Gela, Megara, Selinus, Sybaris, and Metapontum built treasuries at Olympia; the Deinomenids took part in the Panhellenic games at Olympia and Delphi; votive offerings and statues of Sicilian tyrants multiplied in Greek sanctuaries; and Pindar and Aeschylus both lived in Sicily for a time.

Solemn and splendid witnesses to this profound Hellenization are the temples which continued to be built during the fifth century in the major centers of Syracuse, Selinus, Agrigento, Himera, Segesta, Poseidonia, and Metapontum. The Ionic order was rarely used, but appears in two temples in Locri dating from the first years of the fifth century: one had an adyton (inner sanctuary) and a two-naved cella surrounded by a colonnade, whereas the other had a pronaos and opisthodomos (recessed porch in the rear) but no adyton. On the other hand, the Doric order flourished, and what it lost in refinement by its transplantation to Italy and the translation from marble into local limestone, it gained in monumentality by virtue of the imposing dimensions of the temples: the Temple G or Apollonion at Selinus was about 360 feet long by 164 feet wide, and the Olympieion at Agrigento measured about 361 by 173 feet. The latter was an altogether unusual creation, because of the gigantic atlantes (fig. 135) about 25 feet high, used instead of half-columns to support the heavy entablature of the heptastyle pseudo-peripteral temple, which probably had two entrances, and three naves separated by pillars. In many other temples, too, the Greek architectural canons were freely remodeled and adapted in a multitude of new formulations and solutions to suit the local taste, which also called for polychromed clay decoration. The plan was still peripteral, but often tended to give greater width to the ambulatory; this restricted the cella, which lost its corresponding symmetry of pronaos and opisthodomos, and acquired an inner sanctuary. The pronaos was generally more developed, gaining in depth and in the number of lateral columns, and often the line of columns around the outside of the building was doubled. The role assigned to the pronaos and the temple front seems to reflect an Italic attitude, a reaction against the balanced, all-around conception of the original Greek temple, stressing the front as a showpiece, and ideally making it face on to a square or down a street.

In the rigorous architectonic logic of the

Doric temple the interpretation and variation of motifs had to be limited so as to avoid altering their very essence. For this reason the unorthodox interpretations of this order found in Sicily and Magna Graecia have particular significance. These include peculiar ground plans; the insertion of a molding with palmettes in the capitals of the "Basilica" of Paestum; the adding of elements from the Ionic order, such as the ovolo moldings in the columns of the vestibule of the Temple of Athena at Paestum; in the same Temple of Athena, contrary to the canons of the Doric order, the triglyphs are displaced in relation to the axes of the columns; and in all the temples the decoration of the entablature was in polychromed terracotta.

Some sculptured metopes from the temples at Selinus likewise show that they were closely dependent on Greek models and at the same time far removed from them. Temple E at Selinus is one of the largest temples of this region, measuring roughly 220 by 82 feet. It is also one of the most regularly and harmoniously planned temples, with a cella and a pronaos organically aligned with the peristyle, just as the frieze divisions are related to the axes of the columns. The metopes from this temple are Greek in their mythological themes, their composition, and their general type. The young Heracles recalls Harmodius from the group of the Tyrannicides (figs. 112, 113); Artemis, determinedly setting the dogs on Actaeon (fig. 136), is as much a participant in the action as is Athena in the labors of Heracles on the Olympia metopes, although here the goddess is an enemy and not a friend; the solemn tone of the Master of Olympia is present in the metope with the marriage of Hera and Zeus (figs. 140, 141), the head of the latter recalling types such as the bronze from Cape Artemision (fig. 114). On the other hand, local taste shows through in various elements, for example, in the juxtaposition of tufa, from which the metopes themselves were carved, with Parian marble, used for the nude portions of the female bodies. This was a technical compromise imposed by the rarity of marble, and the effect must have been attenuated by the color that covered those areas executed in tufa. Other evidence of the local element appears in the retarded adherence to the Archaic, linear decorative conception of drapery, composed in mannered, swallow-tail folds; in the expressive force that emanates from the aggressive pose of Heracles seizing the Amazon's Phrygian bonnet and crushing down upon her foot (fig. 139); in the vivid structure of the hungry dogs turned upon Actaeon (fig. 136). Indigenous interpretation is also seen in the

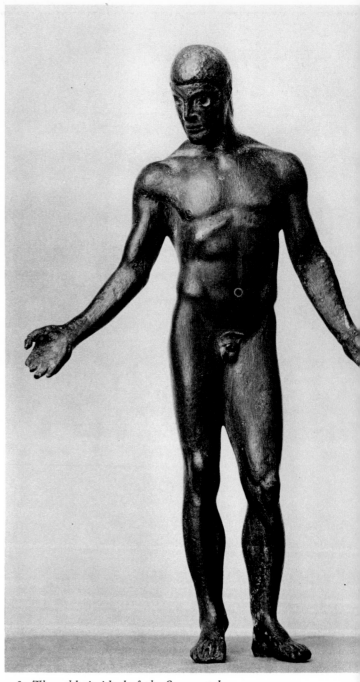

138. The athletic ideal of the Severe style is re-echoed in this fine Sicilian bronze statuette from Adrano. Circa 465 B.C. Syracuse, National Museum

139. Dynamic and oblique rhythms compose the struggle between the young Heracles and an Amazon wearing a cuirass on this metope from Temple E at Selinus. Circa 470–460 B.C. Palermo, National Muse

156

particularly vigorous plasticity given to marble and terracotta female heads based on Greek models of the Severe style (fig. 137).

The varied output of clay-modelers allows us to follow their acceptance of Greek influences, and a few isolated works, more striking than the others, show clearly the tone that Classicism took on in a Sicilian environment. There is a certain weightiness in the head, with its compact, chiseled hair, and slack, irregular line of the eyes; and a stylized treatment of the nude characterizes the marble ephebus from Agrigento by comparison with Greek models of the first twenty years of the fifth century. Perhaps the small bronze from Adrano in the Syracuse Museum (fig. 138) was inspired by a statue of some Sicilian victor in the Panhellenic games. The smooth cap of his hair brings us back to the bronze discus thrower in New York and to the style of the Master of Olympia; the vigorous masses of the muscles and the pre-Polykleitan rhythm, with both feet placed on the base, recall the athletic ideal of the great bronze sculptors of the Severe style around 470 B.C. On the other hand, the graceful ephebus from Selinus, about three feet tall and only slightly later in date, seems more Sicilian in its uncertain, unbalanced rhythm and less sure anatomical articulation; the treatment of the head transforms the original Severe-style model into a thin little face dominated by big, enameled eyes and topped by hair which has lost its rigorous Severe compactness and instead becomes an unorganic crown of separate locks.

140. This head of Zeus from the metope of Temple E at Selinus, representing the marriage of Zeus and Hera, follows closely the Greek models of the Severe style. Circa 470–460 B.C. Palermo, National Museum

141. The face of Hera from the metope of the marriage of Zeus and Hera is of marble, as are all the nude parts of the female figures in the metopes of Temple E at Selinus. Circa 470–460 B.C. Palermo, National Museum

142. Greek models of the Severe style inspired the head of this Etruscan cinerary statue in stone from Chianciano representing the deceased with her child. Fifth to fourth century B.C. Florence, Archaeological Museum

6. The Influence of the Severe Style on Etruscan Art

In Etruria Greek art continued to exert a profound influence during the fifth century, above all as a result of the importation of Attic red-figure pottery, preserved in large numbers in Etruscan tombs. Indeed, Greek art continued to nourish Etruscan art with a vital lifeblood that ennobled and raised its character. Etruria, however, unlike Sicily and Magna Graecia, was not colonized but remained entirely Italic, and thus there continued an unequivocal separation between Greek models and Etruscan interpretations.

The Severe style had a major impact in Etruria, and we can see clearly the transition from works created under the influence of Ionian models to those inspired by this new formal current in the first decades of the fifth century. Since, however, in this area these artistic elements did not develop from an organic, inner progression, but were only re-echoed or borrowed, the stylistic evolution does not rigorously adhere to the lines it had taken in Greece. Assimilation was more intense and advanced in some places than in others, for example in the coastal centers which were in frequent contact with Greek fashions, while it took place only later in inland centers. Imitation of Severe models already outdated in Greece could persist over long periods, and became linked to particular expressions in local crafts as at Chiusi or Veii.

There also existed contemporaneously with works influenced by this new current, others that still followed the iconographic development of Orientalizing and Archaic Ionian models. And elements of the Severe style could be eclectically combined with other more Classical ones. These Greek stylistic elements were for the Etruscans nothing more than expressive means found in the models that were successively put before them and then re-elaborated in the taste of the individual worker. As a result, the Greek myths almost always remain iconographic pretexts for ornamental treatment, and were often completely misunderstood, as can be seen, for example, in the scenes that the Etruscans were beginning to engrave on the characteristic bronze mirrors. The Etruscanized names of the characters often did not correspond to those of the original myth. In the same way, the typical motifs of athletic contests in the Greek palaestra — well known to the Etruscans through Greek vase painting — were taken up in Etruria with curious alterations and misunderstandings by painters of tombs and vases.

The elongated Ionian profiles, the tall, curving cranial dome, and the squat, heavy forms of Etruscan works of the end of the sixth century gave way in the first decades of the fifth century to more rounded heads with short hair, less slanting eyes, slimmer proportions in the body, and lighter, more richly pleated drapery. The influence of Severe style vase painters, from the Kleophrades Painter to the Brygos Painter, is attested to in the elegant paintings of banquets, dances, athletic contests, and chariot races in the Tarquinian tombs. But a comparison of Greek vase paintings with the painted frieze of athletic games in the Tomb of the Bigas at Tarquinia, from about 460 B.C., serves above all to point out how far syntax and style departed from the original, misunderstood models. Themes born in the Greek world of the gymnasium and the *paideia* were transformed by the Etruscans into popular spectacles with a crowd seated in a grandstand. While this tomb at Tarquinia aimed at Hellenic elegance, a more genuine, uncultivated spirit of greater immediacy appears in the motifs of athletic games in the Tomb of the Monkey at Chiusi, also from about 460 B.C., with its rough pugilists, a grotesque dwarf playing the flute, a lady sitting under a sunshade, a dancer with a candlestick on her head, and the monkey. This same spirit appeared again in late black-figure scenes on vases by the Micali Painter.

The influence of the Severe style of Greece penetrated as far as the Iberian and Gallic areas by means of painted vases and small bronzes. Among the most significant of these is a small bronze of a helmeted nude warrior from Majorca, whose large head shows a slightly provincial accent, and rather than a Graeco-Iberian work it should perhaps be thought of as a product of Magna Graecia. The traces of the Severe style that can be detected in some faces and various elements of Iberian sculptural work in reality represent late survivals of the Severe style mixed with Phoenician and native elements. An interesting provincialization of the Greek sphinx of the fifth century is the limestone sculpture from Agost. During this period the small terracotta figures of Phoenician inspiration did not rise above the level of a modest craft.

VI — The Classical Style and the Achievement of an Ideal Organic Naturalism

In Greece the transition from the Severe to the Classical style begins toward the middle of the fifth century. Like all great changes, this was brought about by innovators of genius who opened fresh horizons, interpreting the ideals of the time and inventing a new expressive language. Painting may have been the field in which these new artistic modes were first tried and realized, and the emergence of the personalities of Polygnotos and Mikon definitely marks a decisive step toward the Classical style.

The ancient chroniclers and historians echoed by Pliny roughly summed up the development of Greek art in chronological tables categorically divided into clear-cut stages, based on a division of time in terms of Olympiads. They also liked to present particular artists as the "discoverers" of certain expressive devices, as the initiators of new periods, who blazed the trails to be followed by others. But putting aside such mechanical chronological classification, it remains a truth that new impulses stem from great creative personalities and that only individual genius can dictate new directions and change the course of history.

So it was that in the field of town planning, Aristotle attributed the invention of the "dividing of the city" to Hippodamos of Miletus, notwithstanding the fact that examples of plans arranged on rectangular axes exist from earlier periods. Hippodamos was certainly a theoretical apologist of this system and gave a new stimulus to the study of town planning, the principles of orientation, and social criteria. He wrote treatises that he put into concrete form in the city of Piraeus and in the foundation of Thurii in 445–444 B.C., but his partici-

pation in Rhodes in 408–407 B.C. seems less probable. The influence of Hippodamos' system is to be found in the plans of various cities in Greece and Asia Minor, among them Miletus and Olynthus, as well as in Sicily and Magna Graecia, from Agrigento to Paestum, and from Naples to Pompeii.

The rational, mathematical, philosophical turn of Greek thought made town planning into a science: Hippodamos formulated its theory, Plato discussed it, Aristophanes mocked it, and Aristotle showed himself very interested in this problem. Despite progressive commercial developments, the agora, the center of the fifth-century city, still kept its predominantly political function. The Athenian Agora was embellished with monuments, and its west side was regularized. Although in the early years of the fifth century the Athenian *Ecclesia* (assembly of the people) moved to the Pnyx, plenary assemblies still met in the enclosure of the Agora; the many *ostraka* (potsherds used in voting) found in excavations bear witness to this political activity.

The fifth-century house developed living accommodations in wings around a courtyard that occupied half the site. On one side of the courtyard was the single portico, or *pastas*; beyond this was the dining room, or *andron*, which often had a vestibule decorated with simple paintings and polychrome pebble mosaics — sometimes, as at Olynthus, representing figured, mythological scenes. But apart from a few richer and architecturally sophisticated houses, the greater part of domestic building remained modest.

In statuary the transition from the Severe to the Classical style was largely the work of the

143. Reconstruction of the Doryphorus *created by Polykleitos, which permits an appreciation of the refined, complex play of rhythms of the lost original bronze. Munich, Glyptothek*

two great masters, Polykleitos and Phidias. While the former arrived at a fully Classical solution to the problems of the Severe style, the latter developed new conceptions with a more fervid imagination.

1. The Polykleitan Canon for the Representation of Man

In Polykleitos of Argos the spirit of the Peloponnesus combines with Athenian influences to reach a high point of perfection.

Phidias, on the other hand, became the most outstanding interpreter of the splendid climate of Pericles' Athens and the brilliant Attic artistic tradition. The most valid and significant aspect of the work of Polykleitos remains his rational study and fundamental resolution of the problem of the nude athletic figure, for which the artists of the Severe style had shown a predilection. The Argive master's interest in this type, which found its poet in Pindar and was treated frequently by bronze sculptors of the first half of the fifth century, is attested to by a series of statues of Olympic champions: Thersilochus of Corcyra, Aristion of Epidaurus, Cyniscus of Mantinea, Pythocles of Elis, Xenocles of Mainalos, and Antipatrus of Miletus. But Polykleitos' most perfect solution, according to ancient critics themselves, remained his *Doryphorus* (fig. 143, and colorplate, fig. 144). Other artists called this work "the canon," and took from it measurements and lines as though from a given law, recognizing, as Pliny says, that the merit was due to Polykleitos alone, for having given his theories concrete form in a work of art. We can re-create this figure from marble copies, including the Lancelotti marble, and the bronze herm from Herculaneum by the neo-Attic sculptor Apollonios. The accentuated tensions of the nude of the Severe style gave way here to a more naturalistic but vigorously organic form. Rhythm became freed of every residue of stiffness, the figure standing at ease with the axis of the body forming an S curve, the weight supported by one leg, while the other was bent and drawn back; the body leaned slightly to one side, giving a curve to the crease along the center of the torso and lowering the shoulder corresponding to the flexed leg; the head turned toward the side of the supporting leg; the left arm, which held the spear, was bent, whereas the right hung down along the tense thigh. Ancient critics understood the importance of the new rhythmic balance of this pose (*proprium eius est uno crure ut insisterent signa excogitasse*), which remained a characteristically Polykleitan formula and was soon widely imitated.

The new chiasmic relationship between tension and flexion, between arsis and thesis, which modulated the construction of the image seems ultimately to have been defined, according to Varro, as *quadratio*, that is, a harmonious tetradic regrouping of limbs, anal-

144. Basalt copy of the Doryphorus *of Polykleitos which richly renders the anatomical modeling of the original bronze. Florence, Uffizi*

ogous to the syntactical grouping of sentences in a literary text. From the earliest Archaic times Greek art had looked to the human figure for the archetype of universal beauty and harmony; the period of the Persian Wars had seen the first break appear in the rigid frontality of the Archaic kouros, and the *Doryphorus* stands at the end of this process, articulated in space with full, unhampered, rhythmic life. While the Sophist Protagoras, in his treatise on truth (*Aletheia*), proclaimed that "man is the measure of all things," Polykleitos studied the proportions of the human body, saw the dactyl as the unit of measurement, and put down the results in his treatise, which he called the *Canon*, and gave the most accomplished illustration of his theories in the *Doryphorus*, which can be thought of as the most significant symbol of the Classical spirit.

The unmistakable rhythm of Polykleitos' figures make secure the attribution to this artist of a certain type of Amazon that shows the master's typical chiasmic scansion of the limbs. The finest copy is in Berlin. According to the tradition handed down by Pliny, Polykleitos had executed this figure in a contest proclaimed by Ephesus in which Phidias, Kresilas, Phradmon, and Kydon also took part. The other competitors each judged Polykleitos second to himself, and this unanimity won the contest for Polykleitos. Among the various known types of Amazons, the Berlin type can be thought of as a female version of Polykleitos' canon, constructed with a rigorous counterpoint that composes even the tunic in rhythmic curves. Because of the particular requirement of showing the Amazon wounded, the artist made the concession of resting the left arm on a small pilaster — which, however, did not alter the balanced pose of the figure within itself — and placing the right hand on her slightly backward-tilted head. But pathos as such did not interest Polykleitos; he saw this subject above all as an essay in the rhythmic articulation of a female body, with a solid structure that remained very close to that of his ideal of the male athlete.

The pose in which the left arm rested on the hip gave an air of greater relaxation to a type of Heracles that was certainly the work of Polykleitos. It is known only through copies, including a torso in the Museo delle Terme, Rome, and a fine statuette in the Museo Barracco, Rome. If, as seems probable, we are to recognize Polykleitos' statue of the ephebus Cyniscus, an Olympic champion in 460 B.C., in a type known as the Westmacott Athlete, we see from the more delicate structure of the youthful body and his gesture of placing the wreath on his head that the master had contrived to discover softer inflections. The maturation of his style seems to culminate around 430 B.C. with his creation of the *Diadoumenus* (fig. 145), a youth binding his hair. Like the *Doryphorus*, this statue too is known through over thirty copies, bearing witness to its fame. The rhythm becomes more generous in the broad gesture with which the figure ties the victor's ribbon around his tilted head, creating a semicircle that crowns the curved torso in serene equilibrium. Compared with the earlier *Doryphorus*, the nude figure is more animated, the hair more plastically conceived. In the *Doryphorus* the short locks spread over the spherical skull, chiseled in a manner that is still linked to the Severe style; in the *Diadoumenus* the tightness of the narrow band is stressed by the hair, which swells with a new softness and curls out over the temples. This difference in tone was noted by the ancient critics, too, who called the *Doryphorus* a *viriliter puer* and the *Diadoumenus* a *molliter iuvenis*, a distinction that is to be referred, not so much to the respective ages of the two subjects, as to the stylistic qualities of these two creations.

This new softness and the chiaroscuro effects of modeling in the last works of Polykleitos are perhaps related to the master's maturation in an Attic environment, in contact with the achievements of Phidias. Polykleitos nonetheless remained a highly personal artist, profoundly different from Phidias. In the world of the Olympian divinities, subjects so dear to Phidias, Polykleitos ventured only rarely. Though he found the subject of Heracles congenial, where gods were concerned he limited himself to a figure of Hermes at Lysimachia, Zeus Meilichios at Argos, Aphrodite at Amyklae, and probably an Apollonian triad in Arcadia, but attribution of this last work is uncertain. Finally, perhaps about 420 B.C., at the end of his working life and certainly influenced by Phidias' colossal chryselephantine works, he created the gold and ivory statue of Hera, crowned with a diadem on which were represented the Graces and Horai, for the sanctuary of his native Argos. But the ancients themselves, as Quintilian attests, understood that Polykleitos' interest was in the human, not the divine, and that, while he ennobled the human image with supernatural, ideal beauty, he was incapable of expressing divine majesty (*nam ut humanae formae decorem addiderat supra verum, ita non explevisse deorum auctoritatem videtur*), so that his effigies lacked the grandeur and the Olympian nobility (*deesse pondus putant*) that Phidias was to breathe into his figures with such genius.

145. Roman copy of the Diadoumenus *of Polykleitos with a fine head. Fragments of the body reconstructed after the copy from Delos. Original created* circa *430 B.C. New York, Metropolitan Museum*

2. The Art of Phidias, the Supreme Expression of the Athens of Pericles

The Athenian Phidias, son of Charmides, was educated from an early age in the Attic school of the Severe style. His master was the Athenian Hegias and not, as a late tradition would have it, Ageladas of Argos, for the work of Phidias represents the maximum development of the purest Attic tradition and not, as in the case Polykleitos, Peloponnesian.

Phidias' early training in the Severe style still shows in his youthful works known to us through copies, for example the type of Apollo known as the Cassel Apollo (fig. 146), which probably echoes the Apollo Parnopios, dedicated as an ex-voto after the deliverance of Athens from a plague of locusts (*parnopes*). The plastic treatment of the hair, chiseled in short, curly locks around the forehead, the strong jaw, and fleshy lips are Severe elements assimilated from his masters, but the new movement in which the god presents himself to the faithful shows how the originality of the artist was beginning to take form. The bronze statue of the poet Anacreon, known through marble copies, including the one in

165

146. *Roman copy of the Cassel type of Apollo created by Phidias* circa *460–455* B.C. *This copy preserves the powerful structure of the lost original which still showed the young master's training in the Severe style. Rome, Capitoline Museums*

Copenhagen, was created for the Acropolis and is attributed to Phidias because of its precise similarities with the shield of his Athena Parthenos and the Parthenon metopes. The rhythm, the *chlaina* over the shoulders, the curly hair and beard recall Severe works from about 460 B.C. But innovation is manifest in the original interpretation that depicts this lyric poet as though transported by unheard music: Phidias has expressed as a state of mind the theme which Attic vase painters had formerly tried to convey by illustrating the sumptuous Ionian costumes of the poet slowly walking along with his lyre.

The *Anadoumenus* or boy binding a fillet on his head, which was at Olympia, probably dates from about 450 B.C. It is persuasively traced in the Farnese copy, now in the British Museum. This subject of the young victorious athlete tying on the fillet is treated by Phidias

147. *The head of the Athena Lemnia, created Phidias* circa *450* B.C., *is here seen in a Roman copy which renders with vitality the chiseling of the hair and the luminous planes of the face of the original lost bronze. Bologna, Civic Archaeological Museum*

in a calm, restrained, tender work, the head a softened version of the Severe style. It is probable that twenty years later Polykleitos, with his more accentuated amplification of rhythm and structure, developed this Phidian model in his own *Diadoumenus*.

Unfortunately, we know nothing of a bronze group of the eponymous heroes of the Attic tribes and of Miltiades between Athena and Apollo, which was erected at Delphi in this first period of the master's activity.

Phidias' attachment to his native Athens can be seen from the devotion with which he so often gave form to the protecting goddess of his city: in the statue for Pellene from his youthful period; in the gilt wood statue for the temple in Plataea that was erected with the booty from Marathon and decorated with paintings by Polygnotos and Onasias; in Athens as Athena Promachos, a colossal bronze, over 20 feet high, facing the Propylaea on the Acropolis plateau; as Athena Lemnia, again on the Acropolis; and finally, as Athena Parthenos in the chryselephantine colossus in the Parthenon. We have what may be a record of expenditure on material for casting the Athena Promachos, and also traces of the base of the statue. Coins with views of the Acropolis show the statue dominating the site like an armed sentry with the gold point of her lance

148. Metope I from the south side of the Parthenon. The vigorous head and torso of the centaur seem to indicate the direct intervention of the hand of Phidias. Circa 447–440 B.C. In situ.

sparkling in the sunlight, and as it was placed about 450 feet above sea level, it must have been visible to sailors a long way off, as soon as they rounded Cape Sounion. The Nike that stood on Athena's outstretched right hand was a symbol of victory; the rich shield — we cannot tell whether it was carried or placed on the ground — was chased with a relief of an Amazonomachy by the celebrated metal-worker Mys, after a cartoon by Parrhasios. The Athena Lemnia, on the other hand, was calm, virginal, and peaceful. This work was dedicated by the Athenian colonists who went to Lemnos about 450 B.C. Copies, including

the fine Palagi head in Bologna (fig. 147), enable us to understand Lucian's admiration for the pure outline of the face, no longer hidden by her helmet which she held instead in her right hand, and for the softness of her cheeks and the harmoniously modulated line of her nose. The aegis worn over the right shoulder and bound by her belt became an inoffensive ornament and, despite the severity of the over-all composition, even the peplos had a new looseness. By comparison with Phidias' figure of the *Anadoumenus*, a more plastic sense now shaped Athena's hair, held tight by a fillet and chiseled with a rigorous

149. Metope XXVI from the south side of the Parthenon. The Phidian modeling is here translated by a sculptor trained in the Severe tradition of robust nudes and sharp definition of outline. Circa 447–440 B.C. London, British Museum

150. Figure of the young Dionysus from the left-hand side of the east pediment of the Parthenon, posed with the limbs widely extended in a composition of calm solemnity. Circa 445–440 B.C. London, British Museum

symmetry, perhaps a little severe, but suiting the shy, simple, virginal beauty of the young goddess.

While all these works of the master's first period, up to about 450 B.C., still show the Severe elements to be expected from a pupil of Hegias, the new, original inventions from his own personality begin to develop with eruptive, vital strength under the intense stimulus provided by two demanding tasks: the creation of the mighty chryselephantine statue of Zeus at Olympia, and the immense mass of work Pericles commissioned for the monumental renovation of the Acropolis, inaugurated in 447 B.C. with the construction of the Parthenon.

Whereas the dating of the Zeus is debatable, the Parthenon project constitutes a sure, firm

151. At right, above: Phidias' treatment of drapery culminated in these three figures from the right-hand side of the east pediment of the Parthenon. Referred to as the Fates, these figures more probably represent Hestia, Dione, and Aphrodite. Circa 445–440 B.C. London, British Museum

152. At right, below: Cecrops seated on his serpent-tail beside his daughter Pandrosos, from the left-hand side of the west pediment of the Parthenon. Circa 445–440 B.C. In situ.

point in the artist's career. His style shows that he had meanwhile undergone a profound maturation, evident in the Parthenon marbles and other works from this second phase of his career.

170

154. Section of the west frieze of the Parthenon executed by a sculptor who also worked on sections of the south frieze. Circa 445–440 B.C. London, British Museum

Section of the south frieze of the ...enon with the cavalcade of the ephebi. ...ne seen here wears a cuirass.

445–435 B.C. London, British Museum

In his *Life of Pericles* Plutarch gives us a lively picture of the bustle of building activity on the Acropolis, concentrated above all on the construction of the main temple, the Parthenon, a symbol of the splendor of Athens under Pericles. The entire building was of

Pentelic marble, even the roof tiles. The whole great mass of the octastyle, peripteral temple, though no longer marked by the turgid force of Archaic Doric, which by then had become stiff, was technically perfect. It shows great refinement in its proportions, and in the optical adjustments provided by the curvature of the stylobate and the slight inclination of the columns. Though he departed from the rigid Doric canons, the architect Iktinos showed himself brilliantly able to reconcile the varied demands that faced him: cult traditions, references to the old Hekatompedon, pre-existing structures, and the problem posed in harmoniously and organically placing the colossus of the Athena Parthenos. He certainly worked in close collaboration with Phidias, who was the over-all director of operations (*episkopos*). The conception of the rich, figured decoration of the temple can only

155. Section of the south frieze of the Parthenon with a bull led to sacrifice. Circa *440–435 B.C. London, British Museum*

have come from Phidias, and he must also be given the credit for the organization of the whole workshop (*ergasterion*), handling the workmen, making maquettes, and controlling the realization of the project, with personal intervention in the most demanding parts of the gigantic undertaking.

The Parthenon was the first temple to have all its metopes carved, which here numbered ninety-two. And in order to narrate the solemn Panathenaic procession bearing the ceremonial peplos to Athena, symbolizing the devotion of all the citizens of Athens, Phidias introduced the Attic-Ionic element of the figured frieze into the Doric order, "Doricizing" it with the regulae and stretching it almost 500 feet around all the outer walls of the cella. The great pediments included over forty statues carved in the round. Obviously, Phidias could not have created all this sculpture with his

156. Section of the north frieze of the Parthenon with a cavalcade, executed by a sculptor of particular plastic vigor, who gives a characteristic curve to the mouths of the ephebi. Circa 440–435 B.C. London, British Museum

own hands, but every element sprang from his inexhaustible creative imagination. Stylistic analysis of the surviving marbles enables us to reconstruct the working procedure and methods.

The metopes (figs. 148, 149) which were executed first, so that they could be fitted into the side grooves of the triglyphs, were carved from Phidias' cartoons by artists of various stylistic formations, ranging from the Severe tradition to others better fitted to interpret Phidias' style. For the frieze (figs. 153–156) Phidias executed full-size, three-dimensional models for the east and west sides, the seated gods and the scene of the presentation of the peplos on the east and the preparations for the Panathenaic cavalcade on the west. The blocks were then carved in the workshop by various masters directing squads of *technitai*. For the frieze on the long north and south sides, Phidias limited himself to making cartoons which the various sculptors translated directly into stone on the blocks already set in place. Thus the east and west sides show greater unity and adhere more closely to the style of Phidias, while differences between the various hands are more frequent and noticeable on the long north and south sides. Detailed, three-dimensional models, perhaps reduced in scale, were made for the pediment statues (figs. 150–152), whose execution was directly supervised by the master himself, so that these groups achieve exceptional stylistic unity.

The entire decoration is a hymn to Athena. She is accompanied by Nike in the gigantomachy metopes on the east; she appears again among the divinities present at the sack of Troy in the north metopes; she is precisely referred to in the myth of Erichthonius narrated in the central south metopes; while the Amazonomachy of Theseus on the west metopes is set among the rocks of her Acropolis. The Panathenaic frieze could be considered a grandiose votive offering to Athena. Her miraculous birth from the head of Zeus is narrated in the east pediment, and her symbolic contest with Poseidon, ensuring her dominion over Attica, is represented in the west pediment.

A whole figural world of men, heroes, and gods springs from the intense genius of Phidias. He renewed the traditional motifs, breathed new spirit into the myths, made original versions of Attic legends, created logical rhythmic sequences in the metopes, and devised an infinite range of compositions in the friezes, from the varied, colorful harmonies of the preparation scenes to the stirring crescendo of the cavalcade itself. This procession included men leading bulls, the ambassadors of the games, flute players, water carriers, tray bearers, olive-branch carriers, the cadenced rhythms of the maidens and the eponymous tribal heroes, and finally, the solemn phalanx of deities. In the pediments Phidias gives us the most perfect and complex solutions of old compositional problems.

The physiques and the modeling of nude figures range from the delicate ephebi to the powerfully dynamic Poseidon of the west pediment. A new, sensitive treatment of flesh yields soft, eloquent expressions like the river god Cephissus. Drapery takes on new life in the mantle and peplos, composed in heavy clinging folds or fluttering in the most impetuous movements, arriving at a new conception of cloth in the fine, transparent garments with densely ruffled pleats that cover, yet reveal the forms of fully developed feminine bodies. This new type of drapery already appears in the metopes, for instance in the figures of Lapith women on the south side, and is developed in the east frieze in the figures of Aphrodite and Artemis, culminating in the refined lyricism of the "wet," clinging garments of Aphrodite and Dione (fig. 151) on the east pediment or in the Iris on the west. Hair assumes fluid, impressionistic forms, as in some ephebi on the frieze, or swells out in complex, sumptuous styles like those of the female deities. The horse, which had featured in abstract Geometric stylization, in the vibrant, muscular style of the Archaic period, and the tense compactness of the Severe style, found in the style of Phidias in the Parthenon its most elevated, absolutely unparalleled formulation. These equine images overflow with vigor and quivering energy, animated by an almost heroic spirit, from the subtle pictorial vibrations of the "stampede" of horses on the south frieze, to the dynamic bounding movement of the plastically conceived horses on the west frieze, and the enormous power of those carved in the round on the pediments.

These more intense and revolutionary accents in nudes, drapery, and modeling can only have come from the conception and hand of Phidias; they are indeed quite inimitable and are found in the work of no other artist of his circle. It is therefore legitimate to consider the "warmest" passages of the Parthenon marbles as reflecting the style, the supervision, and perhaps the very hand of the master. Certainly, in all the diversity of the centauromachy metopes, none of the helpers or pupils could have achieved the strength and effect of the carving that turned a block of marble into the head and torso of a centaur in the first south metope; it could have emerged from the stone only as the result of direct intervention by Phidias (fig. 148).

This rich world covering the exterior of the Parthenon was complemented by the image of Athena Parthenos, about 40 feet tall, which the faithful could contemplate in the spacious cella, framed by the inner marble colonnade. Small marble copies enable us to reconstruct this colossus. The eye was led up the deep folds of the peplos to the richly decorated breastplate and to the full oval of the face, surmounted by the great helmet with the triple crest and the visor decorated with animal protomes. A necklace, earrings, and sandals with centauromachy scenes completed the statue's decoration. The shield, too, which was at the goddess' side, was a precious work of art, for Phidias had imagined a gigantomachy on the inside and an Amazonomachy on the outside. These old themes acquired new content and new form. In the gigantomachy, the vault of the heavens, framed by Helius and Selene, separated the gods from the pyramidal mass of the giants and fitted into the curved upper half of the inner side of the shield. In the Amazonomachy, the battle was brilliantly set on the rocky slopes of the Acropolis, with ascending and descending waves of attackers and defenders around the central gorgon mask, with originally conceived groups of Amazons (fig. 157) throwing themselves into empty space, fighting their way upward and falling down head over heels. At the center Theseus and Daedalus, side by side, formed a group on diverging axes, around which the attackers broke apart. Contemporaries insinuated that in the Daedalus, characterized as a bald old man with the tunic of a craftsman, and in the Theseus, half hidden by his raised arm, the artist had represented himself and Pericles. The reliefs that decorated the front of the pedestal of the Athena Parthenos celebrated the goddess in the act of welcoming and adorning Pandora, the creature made by Hephaestus to distribute gifts to mortals, while the couples of Olympian spectators (known in neo-Attic reliefs), which re-echo the Parthenon types, are framed by Helius and Selene.

157. Neo-Attic copy of the pathetic group of the Amazon seized by the hair, that decorated the shield of the Athena Parthenos of Phidias, dedicated in 438 B.C. Piraeus, Museum

158. Roman copy of the bronze Amazon created by Phidias circa *435* B.C. *This head was found at the Villa of Hadrian, where a second copy of the same statue decorated the Canopus. Rome, Museo delle Terme*

Certainly from the period of the Parthenon is the Amazon, made by Phidias for Ephesus in competition with other artists. It is known from the Mattei copy, which is also the finest; from the headless statue found in the Canopus of Hadrian's Villa; and from the head from the same villa (fig. 158). The Parthenon style inspired the modeling of the Amazon's light, ruffled tunic, similar to those worn by the Amazons on the shield of Athena Parthenos, but there is an original touch in the left hem, which is tucked up and fixed to the belt so as to bare the forward left thigh and reveal the wound which can be seen in the Canopus copy. The injured leg is flexed and carries no weight, and the weight is further relieved by grasping the supporting lance with the hand, in a dynamic rhythm that sharply distinguishes this Phidian type from the other Amazons. The raised right arm frames the beautiful head, which seems a more mature re-evaluation of the head of Athena Lemnia, with fuller and more compactly rendered hair. The bronze herm from Herculaneum, identified with the Ephesus Amazon, is cold and devitalized, and gives us no opportunity of appreciating the modeling of the mouth and the harmonious line of the neck, so much admired by Lucian.

The most mature Parthenon phase can be

178

seen in the headless statue of Aphrodite Urania with the turtle under her foot (formerly in the Grimani collection and now in Berlin). The thin drapery of this figure finds precise parallels with that of the Parthenon pedimental figures. Since Phidias had treated this theme in two statues, one at Elis and the other at Melite, it is not implausible to consider this figure in Berlin a lively reflection of his original creations. Finally, the Parthenon phase also yielded the type of ephebus who rests a hand on his delicate, curly head, bound with a *taenia* or headband. This work is known in five copies, including the fine head in New York. We may perhaps recognize in this type the image of Pantarkes, the ephebus loved by Phidias, whom the master portrayed as a victor in the Olympic games.

But out of all this prolific production the artist's masterpiece remained, in the unanimous opinion of the ancients, the chryselephantine colossus of Zeus, considered one of the seven wonders of the world. Homer's god is supposed to have inspired Phidias for the statue which, according to Quintilian, equaled the god himself in majesty, and the beauty of the work added something new to traditional religion. Pliny tells us that Aemilius Paulus, too, was deeply moved when he saw Phidias' Zeus.

It is still undecided whether Phidias created his Zeus before the work on the Parthenon, begun in 447 B.C., or after the dedication of the Athena Parthenos in 438 and the subsequent legal proceedings around 432. We know that in Athens a hostile atmosphere had arisen against Pericles, who was accused of having used the League's treasury to gild and embellish Athens like a vain woman, and also against his friends Damon, Anaxagoras, and Aspasia, in the precarious political climate that degenerated into the Peloponnesian War, and Phidias too had to face accusations. First of all, Menon accused him of having appropriated gold and ivory intended for the Athena Parthenos — a charge which Phidias easily disproved by weighing the pieces in question, which he had made detachable. Then he was accused of impiety (*asebeia*) for having portrayed himself and Pericles as Daedalus and Theseus on the shield of the Athena Parthenos. According to one version, the artist was imprisoned and died in jail, but another says that he fled to Elis, where he was welcomed and honored. The second version is preferred by some critics, who date the Zeus in the period of the artist's last stay in Elis after his trial, and also see mature stylistic accents in parts such as the frieze of Niobe's children which decorated the crosspieces under the arms of the throne, and

which is known to us through various neo-Attic marble copies. Recent excavations of the workshop of Phidias on the Altis at Olympia have brought to light precious material illustrating workshop organization: small hammers for beating gold, lead lines, molds for the vitreous paste ornament of the god's cloak, clay molds for the various parts of the golden drapery, as well as a jug used by the master on which he had written his name. Even the style of drapery used in the clay molds is considered later than the Parthenon period. This late dating of the Zeus is further confirmed by painted pottery of about 420 B.C. found in the deposit. However, it can be observed that this ceramic fragment might well date from the time when all the material from the workshop was thrown out to leave the place clear for some new use, and indeed some years could have passed after the completion of the image before these things were discarded.

In the practice of chronographers, the date of maturity of an artist coincides with his masterpiece, and Phidias' maturity of 448 B.C. as seen in the Parthenon work should therefore correspond to the date of his Zeus. Also, it is less probable that the Temple of Zeus at Olympia, constructed by Lybon around 465 B.C., should have had to wait until after 432 to receive its main statue, and the erroneous calculation of the proportions of the colossus in terms of the cella seems to correspond better to the period preceding the perfected work of the Parthenon. Furthermore, if, as seems probable, the face of the statue corresponds to the Zeus shown on some coins of Elis from the fifty century, and not to the god appearing on coins from the classicizing period of Hadrian, then it still showed some traits of the Severe style, which would seem to confirm a date at the end of the first period of the master's activity. That is, at the time he had already manifested the new, soft, and pictorial language in his drapery, which we feel in the copies of the frieze of the Niobids from the throne of the Zeus, and in the molds of the golden mantle of the god, as well as in some metopes on the Parthenon. Indeed, these works would only have been separated by a very short time if the Parthenon was begun in 447 B.C. and the Zeus inaugurated in 448.

We do not have the elements to reconstruct the great statue, nor the throne with its decoration of statues, reliefs, and paintings by Panainos, which was minutely described by Pausanias. The group of the sphinx with the Theban youth that decorated the end of the arms is known through a basalt copy from Ephesus, showing originality in the humanization of the Sphinx, and the Phidian type of ephebus. Apart from this we know only the neo-Attic copies of the Niobid reliefs and echoes on painted vases of motifs from the birth of Aphrodite that decorated the base of the throne, typically set between Helius and Selene.

It seems more likely that we see the last phase of Phidias, not in the Zeus, but in the pediments of the Parthenon. The grandiose undertaking of the decoration of the temple and the creation of the Athena Parthenos perhaps mark the end of the career of this supreme artist, who disappeared in the tragic atmosphere of envy and jealousy, calumnies and political battles that took shape around his protector. Perhaps it was in the hope of glossing over the shameful end in prison of one of Athen's most celebrated sons that the Athenian historian divulged the legend of the flight to Elis. True or false, it would have been all the more plausible if the artist's masterpiece had already been there in the first place. Indeed at Olympia he had received great honors for this work which were transmitted to his descendants.

3. The Followers of Phidias

The creation of the new Parthenon style could not fail to have a profound effect on all the art of the times. It provided an infinite series of models, as well as the education of a large body of helpers and collaborators required by the sheer size of the undertaking; it offered also close contact between the master and his most favored disciples. And indeed we see the type of youth on horseback from the Parthenon imitated in votive reliefs and on marble funerary *lekythoi*. The group of vases inspired by Polygnotos was followed by a series of Attic red-figure vases inspired by the Parthenon style, and more modest vase painters simply copied directly motifs such as the groups from the Panathenaic frieze, a theme very dear to the Athenians.

The Phidian spirit and the Classical ideal gave substance to many votive reliefs of the second half of the fifth century, the most impressive example of which is the relief from Eleusis with Demeter, Persephone, and Triptolemus. A particular class is constituted by reliefs in which mythological themes are portrayed with three principal characters composed in calm, solemn attitudes: the tenacious affection of the two friends Theseus and Pirithoüs, shown with Heracles; the tender, indissoluble conjugal love of Orpheus and Eurydice, with Hermes; and the tragic filial piety of the daughters of Pelias beside the deceiving enchantress Medea. It has been suggested that these may have been ex-votos from actors victorious in dramatic contests, or that they decorated the altar of Pity in the Athenian Agora. The fundamental expression of the sadness of death and the hope of resurrection, seen in all these reliefs, could suggest works created for the decoration of some famous heroön in Athens. However this may be, it is certain that they were executed by the greatest sculptors from the circle of Phidias and widely copied as decorative panels for Roman patrons.

Drapery forms derived from the Parthenon sculptures, as well as a certain contained grace, and a new Classical conception lent dignity to funerary steles, which abandoned their narrow, elongated Archaic form and became broader, set in an architectonic framework of pilaster strips and a small gable, so that the low-relief group representing the deceased appeared as if placed inside a small shrine. The stele from Salamis with the Parthenon-inspired boy with a bird (fig. 159), though still unframed, can serve to represent the transition to the architectural type, a very pure example of which is the well-known stele of Hegeso in the National Museum in Athens, which combines the grandeur of its noble models with a tender elegance.

Disciples blessed with individual personalities, like Agorakritos and Alkamenes, naturally reached higher levels of originality than others, though they too remained faithful to the tradition of Phidias. We know nothing, however, of the disciple, Kolotes, who collaborated with the master on the statue of Zeus, and created an ivory table decorated with reliefs that was intended to carry the Olympic wreaths. Phidias is also supposed to have signed work by his pupils, so that in various sources some statues are alternately attributed to the master or his pupils. It is said that Agorakritos and Alkamenes competed with each other for a statue of Aphrodite, and when Alkamenes won, Agorakritos turned his own statue into an effigy of Nemesis for the temple at Rhamnus in Attica. The fragments of reliefs that decorated the base of this work by Agorakritos, depicting Helen led to Nemesis by Leda, show inspiration from Phidian conceptions, but are more voluminous in structure and modeling. The great gods of Olympus—Athena, Zeus, and Demeter—were also known to be themes adopted by Agorakritos, and among the most acceptable attributions to this sculptor is that of the imposing, softly modeled Zeus, known as the Dresden Zeus, which exists in several copies. It is a valuable example of an important work closely dependent on the Parthenon style.

159. The deceased ephebus is represented on this stele in the act of protecting a bird from the insidious cat. Only the sad face of the servant boy expresses the idea of death. Circa 440 B.C. Athens, National Museum

Sources and copies show that Alkamenes adhered just as closely to the majestic Classical conception of gods. His most celebrated work was the Aphrodite of the Gardens in the shrine on the banks of the Illissus. Pausanias' rather imprecise description and a series of contradictory hypotheses make its identification uncertain. The type is believed to be recognized in a herm from Leptis having a solemn and solid beauty of expression in its full, firm modeling; or in a type of figure seated on a throne, which is known through many copies and was used for iconic statues of Roman ladies, and even for the statue of the mother of Constantine. This latter type — calm, imposing, relaxed, with flowing rhythms and sumptuous coiffure, and soft, rich, Parthenon-style drapery — is a splendid creation descending directly from figures like the Aphrodite on the Parthenon frieze and pediment, and therefore substantially Phidian. There has also been a hypothesis identifying Alkamenes' Aphrodite of the Gardens with the Aphrodite *eximiae pulchritudinis*, which Pliny records as existing in the Portico of Octavia in Rome.

The work most certainly by Alkamenes is the Hermes Propylaios, known in several copies, which takes its name from its site near the Propylaea of the Acropolis. Here the artist seems to have aimed intentionally at Severe and Archaic styles to harmonize his work with the abstraction of the architectonic, solemnly hieratic type of the *perikalles agalma*, the beautiful image. The fine-chiseled knot of hair on the shoulders recalls those of the famous maidens of the porch of the Erechtheion, which renewed the Archaic, rigidly abstract theme of the Ionic caryatids with a humane sense of naturalism and a loose, articulated rhythm. These Classical korai cannot be imagined without the previous experience of Phidias' maidens on the Panathenaic frieze, which also inspired the drapery on the statue of Procne found on the Acropolis. Pausanias saw this sculpture and claimed it had been dedicated by a certain Alkamenes. If this is the artist of that name, and he carved the work as well as dedicated it, he reveals himself to be a follower of Phidias, but with a fuller, more solid structure in this work of secondary importance. The artist here used a closely knit group, with the boy Itys innocently hugging the legs of his mother, Procne, who is planning to immolate him because of a vendetta. Procne's anxious gesture with her raised forearm translates the intimate drama of the myth that tragedians were currently bringing to the theater.

Athens chose Alkamenes to create the cult statues of Athena and Hephaestus for the Hephaesteion, the Doric temple dominating the hill of Kolonos Agoraios. Begun before the Parthenon, this temple was completed about 425 B.C. The eighteen metopes with the adventures of Theseus and Heracles are in pre-Parthenon style. However, the frieze that adorns the deep pronaos on the side toward the Agora and the shorter frieze on the opisthodomos show clear influences of Phidias, with motifs imitated from the Parthenon. Alkamenes

decorated the front of the dark Eleusis stone base of the statuary group of Athena and Hephaestus with a relief showing the birth of Erichthonius, the son of the unrequited love of Hephaestus for Athena, which resembles the divine births in the work of Phidias. In the statuary group itself he created an Athena with her breastplate slung diagonally over the right shoulder, not without analogies with the Athena Lemnia of Phidias. The simple peplos and contained forms of Alkamenes' Athena constitute a harmonious rhythmic and formal counterpoint to the figure of Hephaestus with his succinct, slanting craftsman's tunic and his fine, bearded head in its conical cap.

Following in his master's footsteps, Alkamenes also created the chryselephantine statue of Dionysus for the sanctuary beside the theater of Athens. Alkamenes was probably the sculptor summoned to Olympia to carve the missing corner statues of the west pediment of the Temple of Zeus. Here, in the figures of Lapith women reclining on couches at the ill-omened banquet, he tried to imitate some motifs of the Severe style in order to harmonize with the work of the master of Olympia, but he reveals a mature Classical style, with studied expressiveness in the heads of the old nurses and the pure profiles of the younger Lapith women. Among the various anonymous statues of the time — products of the imposing and crystalline Classical spirit that Winckelmann called "noble simplicity and quiet grandeur" — the statue of Kore in the Villa Albani could also be ascribed to Alkamenes because of her close links with the Lapith women of Olympia. The type of Hera known through the Pergamon and Capitoline copies was also created in the same environment. Alkamenes also executed the statue of the god in the Temple of Ares in the Agora. This work has been identified with the type of the Borghese Ares in the Louvre, whose oblique rhythms might recall Alkamenes' Athena and Hephaestus, and even the Procne. The Louvre Ares, however, shows a new feeling, almost suffused with romanticism, in the curls falling over the temples, the richly engraved helmet, and the dreamy composure of the figure. These are all features which suited the lover of Aphrodite rather than the god of war, and they strike a note very different from the solemn majesty of Alkamenes.

Among the artists in this period of the full flowering of the Classical style was Kresilas of Cydonia in Crete. He may first have studied with Dorotheos in Argos, working with him at Hermione and at Delphi, but he absorbed and assimilated the Phidian atmosphere in Athens, where he lived and worked from 450 until 420 B.C. In fact, in addition to some

160. Roman copy of the bronze Amazon created by Kresilas circa 435 B.C. Rome, Capitoline Museums

offerings on the Acropolis sculpted by him, he executed the portrait of Pericles himself, attesting to the front-ranking position attained by this artist. This portrait, a type known in five copies, depicts the *strategos* in a pure Olympian conception, at once intimate and spiritual, bearing out the judgment of the ancients, echoed by Pliny, that the sculptor had further ennobled noble men by his art (*nobiles viros nobiliores fecit*). Kresilas was a participant in the famous competition for the Amazon of Ephesus, for which he produced the Amazon of the Capitoline type, which can certainly be attributed to him (fig. 160). This version of the Amazon theme fully reflects the artist's intimate, lyric temperament, which restrained inner feeling in the studied, serene balance that constitutes the very essence of Classicism, expressing pathos with only a slight external vibration, a particular modulation of rhythms. Veiled in pain and restrained grief, the fine head of the Amazon, framed in soft waves, is inclined toward the wound under her right breast, laid bare by her left hand. The rhythm of the body pivots around the vertical axis — the lance on which the Amazon is leaning — effectively displaced to one side.

Experiments with rhythmic expression of inner pathos must have preceded Kresilas' creation of the falling wounded man, the *Vulneratus deficiens*, in which, as Pliny says, one felt the degree of life the figure still had left in him. Among the various statues which critics assign to Kresilas, the attribution of the Velletri type of Athena holding the Nike in her outstretched left hand, known through several copies, seems particularly convincing because of the close resemblance to the Capitoline Amazon in the purity of the face and the soft, wavy hair flowing out from under the helmet.

From the most convincing reading of Pliny it would seem that at the contest for the Amazon of Ephesus, five sculptors, not four, took part. And it is probable that in the type of Amazon known from the inferior Pamphili copy we can identify the Amazon of Phradmon, who reworked the type created by his great compatriot Polykleitos. Phradmon may also have emulated this master in his statues of victorious athletes, such as Amertas, who was an Olympic champion, perhaps in 420 B.C.

Another type of Amazon, known from a reproduction on an architectural pilaster at Ephesus, seems rather to be a re-elaboration of Kresilas' Amazon with a different interpretation of the drapery, and should therefore be attributed to the sculptor Kydon.

4. Post-Phidian Mannerism

When a new artistic language is created through the efforts of a single great personality, the period of imitation and reformulation by his circle and followers is always succeeded by a trend that can be termed mannerist as a result of its accentuation and insistence on the most characteristic expressive elements of the master's style, sometimes reaching extreme forms. This phenomenon is first noticeable, after Phidias, in the more tormented types of nude, the tightly wrinkled diaphanous draperies, and in the accentuated pictorial effects of the centauromachy and Amazonomachy friezes that decorated the interior of the cella in the Temple of Apollo at Bassae, in the heart of Arcadia. The architect Iktinos, whose personality as an innovator appeared in the Parthenon, achieved even more original forms in this temple. The Doric peristyle, though somewhat stiffened, is here combined with the Ionic order of the cella with its semi-columns, and also in this temple the Corinthian order is used for the first time. The basket-shaped core of the Corinthian capital is surrounded with a double row of acanthus leaves out of which spring spiral tendrils, and at the four corners vertical volutes seem to support the abacus. The two-sided conception of the Ionic capital, which had necessitated the unorganic solution of the angle capital, was succeeded by the perfectly harmonious conception of the Corinthian capital, which can be viewed from any angle. But in the rigorous logic of the traditional Greek

161. Neo-Attic copy of an orgiastic maenad from the cycle created by Kallimachos circa 420–410 B.C. Part of a circular base from the Esquiline. Rome, Capitoline Museums

orders this new element was to find acceptance difficult. It began to affirm itself in some buildings in the fourth century B.C., then in Hel-

162. Nike unlacing her sandal, from the balustrade of the little Temple of Athena Nike on the Acropolis.
Circa *420 B.C. Athens, Acropolis Museum*

lenistic work, but was to appeal most of all to Roman architects because of its greater decorative value.

While Iktinos seems to have been the first architect to use the Corinthian capital, tradition claims its inventor to have been the sculptor Kallimachos, a typical representative of the post-Phidian mannerist current, in which this creation must, significantly enough, be placed. Sources describe Kallimachos as having a refined temperament, a critic never satisfied with himself (*semper calumniator sui*), whose principal gifts were elegance (*elegantia*), subtlety (*subtilitas*), and excessive, exaggerated diligence (*diligentia*) — so much so that he was called "the reducer of art into minute details" (*katatexitechnos*), an epithet which Pausanias meant in the sense of technical ability in working the marble drill.

These qualities emerge most strikingly in Kallimachos' cycle of orgiastic maenads, known from neo-Attic reliefs (fig. 161) which made wide use of this decorative theme. The Dionysiac impetus that shook the maenads on painted vases of the Severe style is here transformed into a rhythmic ballet among flowery cadences and virtuoso flourishes in the arabesqued, mannered linearism of the most diaphanous drapery. The same taste for over-refinement gives form to another cycle of dancers, also known from neo-Attic reliefs. These have swinging transparent skirts, and can be identified with the *Saltantes Lacaenae* or Spartan Dancers by Kallimachos. The type of Aphrodite known as the Fréjus Venus seems also to have come from the author of the maenads and dancers. This figure is conceived above all in terms of the elaborate grace of sheer draperies, which cling to the mature body as if soaked, and show the exaggerated development of the innovating achievements of Phidias.

We know these creations only through the smooth, cold modeling of copies from the Roman period, but the marble slabs from the balustrade that surrounds the Pyrgos at the entrance to the Acropolis, where, about 430–420 B.C., Callicrates built a little amphi-prostyle temple dedicated to Athena Nike, provide us with precious originals of this post-Phidian taste (fig. 162). In the atmosphere of the victories of Alcibiades in the last decade of the fifth century B.C., were created this swarm of Nikai, symbolic accompaniments of Athena and tokens of victory; they hold land and sea trophies, lead bulls to sacrifice, or move toward Athena, their thin draperies quivering in the wind in an elegant and elaborate pictorialism. Among the various sculptors who worked on this balustrade, the hand of Kallimachos is to be recognized in the finest parts. Indeed it was the style and taste of Kallimachos that created the balustrade as well as the frieze decorating the little Ionic Temple of Athena Nike. In the frieze we see the heroicized theme of Athenian victories over Eastern and other Greek enemies in the symbolic presence of the gods, who assume florid elegance and delicate inflections.

Phidian- and Parthenon-inspired modes appear in a softer, more conventional tone in the Erectheion, where figures illustrating Athenian myths sculpted in Pentelic marble are applied to the dark frieze of Eleusis stone. This frieze was begun about 408 B.C. and executed by modest Attic sculptors from various demes who were paid sixty drachmae per figure. The temple, which formed part of Pericles' plan for a monumental reconstruction of the Acropolis, may have been begun about 427, interrupted by the disasters that befell the Athenians in Sicily and then resumed in 409. The architect Philokles brilliantly resolved the difficult problem of creating an organic building that united the immutable requirements of worship: the salt-water spring of Poseidon, the *xoanon* of Athena Polias, the sacred olive tree of Athena, and the tomb of Cecrops. The Erechtheion, with its two pronaoi, the porch of the maidens, and the sanctuary of Pandrosos, constitutes a remarkable feat of logic and elegance, and of technical and functional refinement, obtained by abandoning the less flexible Doric order and using imagination and originality in exploiting elements from the richer Attic version of the Ionic order with its figured friezes.

In the virtuoso current to which Kallimachos belongs, the expressive possibilities offered by the fine draperies of Phidias are carried to their extreme form by the sculptor Paionios of Mende, in the creation of the Nike dedicated in Olympia by the people of Messene, probably in 425 B.C., of which we possess the original (fig. 163) and copies of the head. The Archaic Nike of Archermos was posed in the conventional "running on bent knees position," and Phidias had then made a Nike that looked as if it were descending with outspread wings on the hand of Athena or Zeus; but Paionios made her appear suspended in air, with one foot resting upon an eagle on top of a slim, tapered, triangular pilaster, in front of the Temple of Zeus. The wind that one imagines supporting the soft female body in flight gives the sculptor a pretext for turning the drapery into bravura passages. In places he virtually neutralizes it into diaphanous transparency, making it cling to the torso and right leg; elsewhere he turns it into a whirl of dense folds, as at the back, or stretches it out into the great veil formerly held in the raised left hand, in an audacious composition that ignores the technical limitations of marble while working it with a tender coloristic sense. Copies of the head of this statue show a firm, full structure. It is probable that Paionios had experimented with the Nike theme in the east akroterion of the Temple of Zeus, thus leading Pausanias to erroneously attribute to him the corresponding pediment.

A strong sea breeze seems to buoy up the generous swirl of light drapery that wraps the procession of nereids on the funerary monument at Xanthos in Lycia, built between 430 and 420 B.C. This style of drapery falls within

163. Flying Nike by Paionios, erected on a triangular pilaster about 30 feet high, which stood to the southeast of the Temple of Zeus at Olympia. Dedicated circa *425 B.C. Olympia, Museum*

the conceptions of Kallimachos and Paionios, and the suggestive force of this Classical language is evidenced by its spread as far as this region of Asia Minor, which had its own local traditions and was a dependency of the Persian Empire. The statues of nereids, freely placed between the columns of the peristyle that topped the quadrangular base of this monument at Xanthos, must have appeared intensely animated, like the procession of Nikai on the balustrade of the Acropolis. We may wonder whether they are the result of a profound assimilation of Athenian influences by local artists or the work of artists who had emigrated from Greece. The conception of the funerary monument itself, however, is typical of Asia Minor, derived from the Lycian type of tomb set on a high base, and in the friezes decorating the base and the cella the Oriental taste is clearly displayed. Here the local traditions of illustration and iconography are seen in the battle scenes and city sieges with architectural backgrounds characteristic of Lycian art.

Compared with the sparse, abstract indication of settings in Classical compositions, this type of detailed landscape relief appears as a singular phenomenon springing from the fusion of Greek formal experiments and Eastern tradition. In the art of the Babylonians, Assyrians,

164. Detail of a Lycian sarcophagus of Parian marble from the royal necropolis of Sidon with a scene of a boar hunt. End of the fifth century B.C. Istanbul, Archaeological Museum

165. Impression from a gem signed by the engraver Dexamenos of Chios. A masterpiece of extreme fineness that presents a physiognomic portrait of refined naturalism. From Cara in Attica. Circa 430–420 B.C. Boston, Museum of Fine Arts

187

and Achaemenids, the walls of the palaces were covered with reliefs exalting the dynast, and similarly in Lycian tombs there is a taste for friezes and panels celebrating the exploits of the prince. A tomb at Pinara shows the mountainous landscape, the battlements, gates, and towers, and the buildings inside the city, with their characteristic architecture, which resulted from the translation into stone of their original wooden structure; also depicted are the sarcophagus tombs of nobles. In the frieze from the Xanthos monument, the scenes achieve lively animation and compositional complexity, showing the rear gate of the besieged city, the walls with defenders and women, and the surrender before the satrap who is seated on a throne and shaded by a parasol. The closed, regular ranks of soldiers tiered with monotonous symmetry bring us back to the Oriental spirit. But the love for description inherent in the art of Asia Minor and Ionia here comes into contact with Classical teachings, producing noteworthy effects of perspective in the rich landscape background, placing towers and buildings diagonally, showing oblique stretches of wall, superimposing the buildings of the city on several levels, and faithfully reproducing the traditional Lycian funerary monuments crowned with sphinxes and lions.

The Lycian taste for narrative shows further in the quadrangular burial enclosure of the Heroön of Gjölbaschi, where the sculpted porous limestone friezes form a rich figural decoration with a juxtaposition of Greek mythological themes and war-like scenes exalting the deeds of the Lycian prince. In the traditional subjects — the Amazonomachy and centauromachy, the exploits of Theseus, Bellerophon, and Meleager, the rape of the Leucippides, the Seven against Thebes, and the slaying of the suitors by Odysseus — we see a convergence of the iconography of Polygnotos and Mikon. Classical compositions in a cursive, pictorial, mannered style are seen in the Lycian scenes of the siege and capture of the fortified city, presented in two registers, in accordance with Oriental syntax. There is also an attempt at conveying the local landscape, with the city perched on its rocky heights, the temple, the local costumes of the chiefs with the prince among them, enthroned beside the princess under a sunshade, and the marshaled regiments with tiers of soldiers and shields. All this is portrayed in a Classical figurative interpretation rejuvenated by pictorial and perspective conceptions that spring from the particular narrative tendencies of this region. Landscape treatment of this kind remains linked to the Lycian environment, and in the consequent organic development of the great mainstream

166. This long-haired homunculus with a large head and untrimmed goatee, seated before the gesticulating fox, creates an amusing caricature of Aesop. Kylix *attributed to the Bologna Painter 417. Vatican, Museo Gregoriano*

of Greek art we must wait until the Hellenistic period for a similar maturation of landscape elements.

A testimony indicative of the suggestive strength of the universally valid Classical art is provided by its spread into a region even more provincial and further from the Greek culture than Lycia: Sidon, the Phoenician city where the rich necropolis of the princes shows vivid reflections of pure Greek art in a sumptuous series of marble sarcophagi ranging from late Archaic to the Hellenistic period. A Phoenician artistic tradition already existed, and was particularly effective in the field of decoration, but when the people of Sidon wanted to raise funerary monuments worthy of the local princes, they called on artists with a Classical training, perhaps from Asia Minor. Thus, toward the end of the fifth century we find a sarcophagus of the typical Lycian architectural form, with the tall, ogival roof, decorated on the sides with reliefs in which youths seemingly from the Parthenon friezes are the protagonists of boar hunts (fig. 164) and Attic-inspired centauromachies spread out in thick, pictorial compositions in a softened, more graceful, Ionicized style. Through students, imitators, and artists of a younger generation, the language of Phidias continued to mature until it became transformed in its various environments, spreading into outlying regions, often transposed into Ionicized modes.

A sculptural work from the end of the fifth century, representing a refined, Ionicized interpretation of the ideals already expressed by Kallimachos or Paionios, is the unusual caryatid column, more than 30 feet high, at Delphi. The shaft of this column is covered with fleshy superimposed leaves, and the upper part is surrounded by the projecting figures of young dancing girls with transparent, flowing tunics, their heads bearing the tall, decorative, radial *polos*. We do not know how much these figures may contain motifs drawn from the Horai and Graces created by Phidias to top the throne of Zeus, but in any case this column remains an original conception, Ionian in its grace, perhaps the tall and animated support of a tripod, the symbol of the Delphic god.

5. Painters and Vase Painters of the Second Half of the Fifth Century

The intense artistic problems that were fermenting in this period, from the decline of the Severe style to the rise of the Classical style and to the phase of its mannerist evolution, were reflected with no less complexity in the field of full-scale painting, but there remain only the few notices in the literary sources, in addition to reflections of pure painting that are found on the pottery of the period.

Classical ideals were to inspire the work of Aristophon, the brother of Polygnotos, and also the work of Panainos, the brother and close collaborator of Phidias. Panainos painted the

167. Detail of the rape of the Leucippides on a hydria *by the Meidias Painter, in whose graphic style the post-Phidian language is developed in a mannerist tone.* Circa *420 B.C. London, British Museum*

throne of Phidias' Zeus with myths and symbolic personifications, and exalted the battle of Marathon in the large painting in the Stoa Poikile, in which, according to Pliny, he painted portraits of the leaders, though it is difficult to think that the characterization of these *strategoi* could have been truly physiognomic portraits. In the fifth century, the rare portrait image on the Boston gem (fig. 165) is an exceptional creation and due to the particular sensibility of the engraver.

In contrast to these painters of *ethos* there was Pauson, whom Aristophanes calls "very bad, the table guest of poverty," and who, according to Aristotle, depicted men as worse than they really were, unlike Polygnotos, who ennobled them. Aristotle therefore warned the young against looking too long at the works of Pauson, because of the ethical conception that lies at the foundation of art in Greek critical and philosophical thinking. In Pauson we see arising a new current, more liberal and free from preconceptions, running counter to the aristocratic and Classical current. This new approach could not be applied to the solemn themes of mythology, but found its outlet in subjects from everyday life on Attic red-figure pottery, sometimes offering strongly characterized images of barbarian slaves, of revelers, servants, and dwarfs, of grotesque personages derived from the comic theater, and straightforward caricatures full of humor and open-minded realism.

This aspect of Greek art is generally forgotten. But it should be remembered that the richness and complexity of accents and expressive procedures were not limited to the Homeric, noble, and Olympian, although these aspects of Greek culture dominated the great art linked to religion, or to votive or ceremonial ends. Indeed, there remains a whole field devoted to the other aspects, which we can call Hesiodic, Dionysiac, and popular.

At the moment when Polykleitos was giving the world his canonic, perfected formulation of the athletic image of man, we see the appearance on painted vases of the most degenerate figures of revelers. Far removed from the palaestra, more a frequenter of banquets, this personage is shown in the caricatural structure of a body shriveled with vice, tottering along on his puny limbs, with an abnormally large head. The exaltation of the athlete immortalized in the action of throwing the discus contrasts with the homunculus ironically portrayed with crude realism, straining away in the throes of constipation; the champion binding on his victor's ribbon is countered by the reveler bandaging his aching head. Thus while Kresilas portrayed Pericles as an Olym-

pian, comedians saw the type of *strategos* as an onion-head (*schinokephalos*) and Pauson turned his fresh eyes to representing men as they really appeared to him. Phidias portrayed even horses on a divine plane in the lyrical formulations of the Panathenaic frieze, but Pauson's horse wallowed in the dust. Beside Euripides was Aristophanes, and in figurative art, while artists were arriving at the summit of Classicism, with all its *pondus* and *ethos*, realism, passion, and caricature burst forth in full vitality in works of a more popular tone.

Even myth sometimes underwent a parodying interpretation, from the caricatural Aesop talking to the fox on the Vatican *kylix* (fig. 166), to the Cabiran black-figure vases of the late fifth century with Circe and Odysseus, Heracles, Cadmus, and the *mystai* transformed into stunted pigmy figures in a markedly grotesque spirit.

In the field of pure painting, however, Pauson's approach seems to have remained rather exceptional in the Classical atmosphere of his time, and was viewed with disfavor. Indeed, the greatest painters remained on an elevated ethical plane, idealized and typical in conception. Dionysios of Colophon tried hard to follow the ideals of Polygnotos.

Mastery of foreshortening posed problems of perspective, which was accordingly studied as an optical and mathematical problem. Agatharchos of Samos, a self-taught painter, experimented with perspective when painting the theatrical scenery for the tragedies of Aeschylus, and wrote a commentary on his work, which was to serve Anaxagoras and Democritus for their theories. Agatharchos as stage designer, *skenographos*, must have had a fine decorative sense, and indeed Alcibiades engaged the painter, who was certainly in his full maturity by then, to decorate his house. Alcibiades also had the younger painter Aglaophon, the son of Aristophon and grandson of the great Polygnotos, portray him in the allegorical vein of the times, with femininely beautiful features in the embrace of the personification of Nemea, and a second time crowned with the personification of the Olympian and Pythian games, a conceit which aroused general indignation. This conception of mannered *charis* that surrounded the circle of Alcibiades was also to be seen in contemporary pottery of the last decade of the fifth century, from the circle of the Meidias and Eretria Painters. These were popular works, but have iconographic concordances

168. White-ground funerary lekythos *decorated by a painter close in style to the Reed Painter.* Circa *430 B.C. Athens, National Museum*

169. *The orgiastic dance, perhaps in honor of Apollo Karneios, finds original and mannered rhythms in the graphic virtuosity of the drapery on this krater from Ceglie by the Karneia Painter. Circa 415 B.C. Taranto, National Museum*

170. *Silver coin of Syracuse with the head of the nymph Aretusa, by the engraver Kimon. Her face is modeled with a soft fleshiness and dolphins flit through her flame-like hair. Circa 410 B.C.*

171. Detail of the Mars from Todi, Etruscan bronze inspired by models of the Severe style. Dedicated, according to the Umbrian inscription, by Ahal Trutitis. The helmet is restored. Fourth century B.C. Vatican, Museo Gregoriano

shadow. He represented the various effects of shadow so that the eye of the spectator was held by the play of light in the painting. One can imagine the opportunities that a theme such as Ajax struck by lightning, painted at Pergamon, must have presented for treatment in terms of this light-oriented approach.

These relationships of light and shadow, these studies of chiaroscuro, are also at the basis of the painting of the great Zeuxis (*luminum umbrarumque invenisse rationem*, as Quintilian says). The rival of Zeuxis, Parrhasios, on the other hand, aimed at fineness and subtlety of outlines (*examinasse subtilius lineas traditur*), a functional line that rendered the plastic aspects of the body.

Zeuxis, as we know from Plato, was still a young boy when he arrived in Athens from his native Heraclea in Lucania, shortly before 424 B.C. His style had a solid, vigorous, Western and Attic construction (*grandior in capitibus articulisque*). Parrhasios of Ephesus, who came to Athens where he worked with Zeuxis in the period of the Peloponnesian War, retained an Ionian taste for flowing, elegant lines and refined grace. He was the soft, sophisticated esthete (*habrodiaitos*) who went about dressed in purple with a head-wreath and staff of gold. He cultivated symmetry, subtle expressive notations (*argutias*) in his faces, elegant coiffures, and beautiful mouths. Himerius contrasts the technical experience (*techne*) of Zeuxis with the psychological subtlety (*sophismata*) of Parrhasios. Zeuxis painted Zeus, Heracles as a boy, Penelope, Menelaus, Boreas, Pan, Marsyas, and Eros; he took pains to find five girls as models from whom to compose the beauty of Helen; and he created the complex picture of the family of centaurs. Parrhasios painted an Eros that seemed to have been fed all its life on roses, and chose themes with a pathetic and psychological content, like the pretended madness of Odysseus, the pain of the wounded Philoctetes, or the torment of Prometheus, and he did not hesitate to have a real slave tortured so as to study his expression. He also represented the many-sided, changing face of the Athenian populace succinctly suggested in a personification, as well as the panting and sweat of two heavily armed foot-soldiers. The broad conceptions and elaborate compositions (*megalographiai*) of Polygnotos are replaced in these paintings by a concentrated interest on one figure with its own particular expressive problem, or on a closed, simple composition of three figures, as was also common in contemporary reliefs.

With the loss of all the painting of these masters, painted pottery becomes a precious source of information about the trends of the

with Aglaophon's painting, particularly the group of Adonis languidly reclining in the lap of Aphrodite, on the *hydria* in Florence by the Meidias Painter.

Hand in hand with experiments in perspective went a study of chiaroscuro; much attention was devoted to the shading that gave depth and relief to the images. These problems seem to have been attacked in the last thirty years of the fifth century by Apollodoros, who is indeed called *skiagraphos*, the painter of

172. The Severe style and the art of Polykleitos are interpreted and transformed by the free plastic language of an Etruscan clay-modeler in this fresh head of a boy from Veii. Second half of the fifth century B.C. Rome, Villa Giulia

Inspired by the compositions and motifs of Polygnotos and the solemn world of Phidias in the Parthenon, mythological themes took on a more detached, calm tone. Scenes of musicians and women's quarters became more frequent, and intimate. An elegiac note of melancholy wrapped the funerary themes on white-ground *lekythoi*: groups now consisted of the dead person with his or her slave, just as on contemporary steles; the farewell of the warrior; the visit and offerings at the tomb; and Thanatos and Hypnos, Death and Sleep, carrying away the deceased, sometimes led by Hermes or ferried by Charon.

The serenity and dignity of this Classical atmosphere infused the many works of the Achilles Painter, who produced some of the finest white-ground *lekythoi*. The prolific Reed Painter, so called from the clumps of reeds he drew to indicate the banks of the River of the Dead, was a specialist in white-ground *lekythoi*. In some larger *lekythoi*, which seem to constitute a separate stylistic group, his line takes on an extreme fluidity and an exaggerated looseness, suggesting volumes and foreshortening, so that it has been compared with the line of Parrhasios. A heavy melancholy emanates from his male faces, whose hair is sketched in with coloristic dabs (colorplate, fig. 168).

Just as the thin transparency and fine pleating of drapery introduced by Phidias were elaborated by post-Phidian sculptors, so too were they translated graphically by the delicate brush of the Eretria Painter, an elegant miniaturist who treated myth and scenes of women's quarters with a refinement close to the atmosphere of Kallimachos and Parrhasios. At the same time these stylistic traits assumed an already mannerist inflection in the work of the Meidias Painter (fig. 167), who used finely intertwined drapery like spiders' webs, adorned with scrolls and flourishes and gilding, in depicting the myths of Aphrodite which unfold in a sensual, relaxed, idyllic atmosphere. The mythological themes of the great centauromachy and Amazonomachy scenes, following the development characteristic of the last decades of the fifth century, became mannered, as on the *kylixes* that Aristophanes painted in the workshop of Erginos, translating effects of full-scale painting into linear virtuosity.

It was above all in Athens in the second

times, even if its particular technique necessitated a different language. The rigor of draftsmanship of the pure outline, which had constituted the greatness of former masters of this art, was no longer enough. Vase painters now attempted to render the plastic relief and statuary grandeur of sculpture, and to approach more closely the coloristic, tonal, and spatial effects of pure painting. It was not only in red and black techniques that thick hatching, diluted colors, broken outlines, and elaborate gilding were used in an attempt at achieving pictorial effects: but now the technique using a white background became progressively common, with figures drawn, no longer exclusively in black, but also in pink, red, yellow, and blue. This technique was exploited above all for funerary *lekythoi* which, not being intended for everyday use, could keep the delicate overlays of varied colors.

173. Bronze Chimaera found at Arezzo in 1554. One right foot bears an Etruscan inscription. The restoration on the back of the animal (not shown) with a serpent biting the goat's horn is false. Fifth century B.C. Florence, Archaeological Museum

half of the fifth century that the most brilliant creative forces were concentrated and that Classical style reached its maturity. The diffusion of this style was vast and its penetration deep. In Italy one of the most significant manifestations of Classical Athenian influences was the creation of workshops producing vases painted with red figures, in a style and technique similar to those of Attic vase painters. It may have been that Athenian vase painters migrated to Magna Graecia after the mid-fifth century, yet the first production presupposes an Athenian training revived by local workers, who toward 425 B.C. produced two groups of vases, known as proto-Lucanian and proto-Apulian. The principal painters of the Lucanian production were the Pisticci, Amymone, and Karneia Painters (fig. 169), and of the Apulian group, the Dancing Girl Painter and the Sisyphus Painter.

Taranto was one of the most important centers of production. Large vases, monumental also in style, with complex scenes were favored. The Greek myths were developed, albeit sometimes in free variants, and a rich decorative repertory of palmettes and tendrils evolved. After the first, pure imitations of Attic work, we see Italic traits becoming increasingly evident in the lack of rigorous balance and harmony in the structure and proportions of bodies, in mannered inflections, and in a taste for the grandiose and the turgid.

In Campania, on the other hand, the imitation of Attic pottery gave rise to manifestations in a more popular tone on the vases of the Owl Pilaster group, so called because of their characteristic, distinguishing motif, particularly on the Nolan type of amphora. These were decorated with misunderstood Greek myths, depicted with clumsy, heavy figures.

The isolated Messapian society of southeast Italy continued with its geometric decorative treatment and its own peculiar forms, among them the characteristic *trozzella*, which became increasingly ornate and florid.

6. The Influence of the Classical Style on Etruscan Art

In Etruria the effects of red-figure pottery had been translated into a technique with figures overpainted in red on a black ground, in vases of the Praxias group, from the first half of the fifth century B.C. After this, vases with reserved red figures, that is, formed by the red ground surrounded by solid black, also appeared, but they were the modest products of a local craft, which showed Etruscan rather than Greek traits. On the other hand, Greek models found a different interpretation in larger, more important works, in which artists tried to adapt their approach to the Classical style. The political and commercial decline of Etruria resulted in less intense, more sporadic contacts with Greece, whereas the flow of Greek vases into the ports of the upper Adriatic continued, and at Spina and Numana, and inland at Bologna we find a rich series of Attic pottery from the Polygnotan to the later mannered style. In Etruria there was an anachronistic persistence of preceding styles, particularly the Severe style, which often makes dating difficult, but in some works there are clear echoes of the modes of the great Classical masters. The Umbrian-Etruscan Mars from Todi (fig. 171) can be taken as an example of the survival of the Severe style, which inspired the dignity on the youthful, full face of this Italic god; however, the torso, stiffly encased in the typically Etruscan cuirass, shows poor coordination in the limbs, which move in a vivacious unorganic rhythm that makes one aware of the difficulty Etruscan-Italic bronze workers found in adhering to the Greek ideals. Thus the Phidian type of Zeus developed into the Etruscanized terracotta version with fleshy eyelids, from Falerii. The influence of Polykleitos is particularly noticeable in some terracottas from Veii representing nude youths in poised rhythmic poses, and male and female heads with the characteristic rounded structure and full, oval face (fig. 172). But under the spontaneous, uncultivated hand of the Etruscan clay-modeler, rhythmic rigor slows down, anatomy is treated cursorily, and curly locks of hair are replaced by rustic blobs of clay indiscriminately stuck onto the solid skull. In the funerary sculptures from Chiusi, Severe modes are replaced by Classical in female heads, in sphinxes used to adorn chairs, and in attempts at softer, looser drapery folds. The Classical style gives a noble interpretation to scenes on the more carefully engraved mirrors, and to some small bronzes. Thus Greek models continued to represent a vital force in raising the tone of Etruscan art. Silens and centaurs, losing their Archaic stylization, reflect the new expressive forms. Without the Greek experiment, the creation of even so Etruscan a work as the magnificent bronze Chimaera (colorplate, fig. 173) from Arezzo would have been unthinkable. This piece interprets with a rough and flickering vitality the structure of its Greek model and translates the mane and fur in a flamboyant stylization, transforming the traditional Hellenic motif into a vigorous expression of Etruscan relief modeling.

VII | The Art of the Fourth Century and the Humanization of the Classical Ideal

Of the two great currents — the Polykleitan and the Phidian — that dominated the artistic scene from the mid-fifth century on, we are more familiar with the development of the school of Phidias up to its ultimate mannerist evolution. Sources yield only a few indications about the many pupils of Polykleitos, though their number alone bears witness to the vitality of this master's teaching.

We know from the sources that the followers of the Polykleitan tradition, who remained active into the fourth century, created athletic subjects and monuments to victors in war or games. These included quadriga and biga groups by Aristeides; athletes and warriors by Patrokles; a series of statues of Olympic and Delphic champions and the group of two boys cleaning themselves with strigils by Daidalos of Sicyon; the discus thrower and other statues of victorious athletes by Naukydes of Argos and his pupil Alypos of Sicyon, who was still working in the fourth century; and finally, the four athletic statues at Olympia by the younger Kleon of Sicyon.

The great offering dedicated by the Spartans at Delphi to celebrate the victory of Aegospotami in 405 B.C. had thirty-seven statues in two rows: the first included Lysander crowned by Poseidon, surrounded by Zeus, Apollo, Artemis, and the Dioscuri; the second row comprised the sea captains. This was a collective work by various bronze sculptors from the dominant Polykleitan school, which must have provided an interesting range of examples of the trends most prevalent in this circle of artists. But as these statues no longer exist, we cannot know in which direction the tradition of Polykleitos was developing. A work known in six copies, representing a discus thrower — one is in the Vatican and the head of another in the Museo dei Conservatori — has been referred, without justification, to Naukydes, but could perhaps legitimately be assigned to this post-Polykleitan circle. The meditative pose, the head bent in order to judge his distance, and the studied, curly hair, indicate a transformation of taste, from the external show of canonic elements in Polykleitos' rational articulation, to a freer, more varied rhythm, a more intimate concentration, a more refined, decorative approach. The canon of Polykleitos offered few opportunities for escape and transformation, but it had probably become relaxed, softened, and humanized among the master's followers, whereas the varied expressive elements of the language of Phidias had developed a more facile range of treatments, including even the most extravagant virtuoso work.

As in the case of the post-Phidian trend toward mannerism, the modification of the Polykleitan canon marks the end of a development. It coincided with a profound crisis that affected every part of political, spiritual, and religious life in the late fifth and early fourth centuries, with the spread of the philosophy of the Sophists, the criticism of the Olympian faith, and the twilight of the Homeric gods. Philosophers, too, switched their attention from physical problems to those of man, concentrating on morals and metaphysics; eloquence, reflecting the individual personality, became a form of art.

The renewal of the Classical conception took place along more humane, naturalistic lines. The *auctoritas* and *pondus* with which the Classical spirit had surrounded gods, heroes, and men were replaced by sentiment and expression. The most severe Olympic divinities lost their abstract solemnity and no longer appeared in a remote epiphany. At the same time there was a preference for those gods thought of as most closely participating in the feelings and passions of man: Aphrodite, Eros, Dionysus, Apollo, Asclepius, and Hygieia; Pan and the nymphs, Graces, and Muses. Artists were now attracted, not by the exalting, impressive undertakings of the pure hero Theseus, but by the romantic adventures of the pathetic Meleager. Men became even more eager to deify their own ideals and conceptions in allegories and personifications. The fury and vehemence of the savage centaurs of Mikon and Phidias had already died down in Zeuxis' idyllic painting; from now on satyrs were delicate, dreamy creatures of the woods. One no longer attempted the colossal chryselephantine effigies, and besides cult statues, ex-votos became more frequent. Artists began to think of decorating the altar as well as the temple, and there was an increasingly wide field of activity in votive reliefs, funerary steles, and portraits. The most important architectural and decorative enterprise of the fourth century was not a temple, but the Mausoleum of Halicarnassus, built to house the remains of a Carian prince. Though the political importance of Athens had declined, the city remained the most lively artistic center, attracting the greatest number of artists. Artists now, however, traveled more easily and worked in different cities, so that artistic centers multiplied. These tendencies were to become stronger during the second half of the fourth century, when the personality and conquests of Alexander the Great brought about a different political, economic, and cultural climate, and opened the new horizon of Hellenistic civilization.

1. Architecture and Town Planning

The creation of the various architectural orders had provided a harmonious, rational system that was convenient to apply and difficult to change without destroying it, although there had indeed been a noticeable progressive stiffening and slimming down of the Doric order during the fifth century. In a few cases, such as the Temple of Apollo reconstructed at Delphi after the earthquake of 373 B.C., the Doric order was retained as well as the original ground plan of the Alcmaeonids. Doric was also used in the hexastyle prostyle Temple of Artemis and the hexastyle Temple of Asclepius, both in Epidaurus, and in the hexastyle prostyle Temple of Athena at the Marmaria in Delphi.

But the taste of the new times did not fail to make itself felt in architecture. The combination of several orders, brilliantly pioneered by Iktinos, was harmoniously applied by the architect Theodoros of Phocaea toward the end

of the fifth century in the *tholos* of the Marmaria in Delphi. There were twenty Doric columns around the outside, and inside the cella, ten Corinthian columns on whose capitals the acanthus leaves and volutes were not yet organically fused. A more refined, mature expression of the two orders and the circular plan is to be found in the *tholos* of Epidaurus, created shortly after the middle of the fourth century by the architect Polykleitos the Younger, with the collaboration of twenty-two *technitai* from Argos, Athens, and other cities. Twenty-six outer Doric columns corresponded to fourteen inner Corinthian columns, and the new decorative conception can be seen in the more elaborate structure of the Corinthian capital, in the elegance and plasticity of the strongly shaded scrolls and palmettes that decorated the gutter with its lion mask, in the fine carving of the door frames, and in the colorism of the different materials: black Argos marble, white marble, and polychromed stucco. In the metopes, which were here curved, figural sculpture was replaced with elaborate, projecting rosettes. The Corinthian order was then applied to the outer peristyle of the *tholos* at Olympia, the Philippeion, which was dedicated to the Macedonian dynasty and contained the statues of the family of Philip and Alexander, made by Leochares.

A small, elegant *tholos* rises slimly from a tall, square limestone base to constitute the body of the choragic monument of Lysicrates in Athens from the year 334 B.C. The structure was destined to support a bronze tripod placed on the bunch of acanthus crowning the roof. The base of limestone, the steps in bluish Hymettus marble, and the *tholos* itself in white Pentelic marble, give us another example of coloristic researches. A desire to give the monument a lively movement, to heighten the tripod, and to enrich the decorative effect, dictated the choice of the Corinthian order in the columns placed against the circular wall of the cella, and led to the insertion of an Ionic figured frieze exalting Dionysus, the tutelary genius of the Greek theater.

Choragic monuments represent a new field for architecture in the fourth century. Along the Street of the Tripods in Athens, the monument with the six-columned Doric façade, by Nikias, was built in 319 B.C. Another by Thrasyllus, which was placed in front of a grotto, presented a sober façade *in antis* with freely interpreted Doric elements.

The intense participation of the Greek people in theatrical spectacles and the importance of the theater in Greek life are reflected in the architectural development of the theater building. In the fourth century, theater architecture developed an admirable harmony in the relationships between the generous rhythms of the seating area, the perfect circle of the orchestra, and the background provided by the *skene*, along with a perfect sense of functionalism and a rigorous application of the principles of acoustics. Two notable examples are the rebuilding of the Theater of Dionysus in Athens commissioned by Licurgus, and the theater at Epidaurus by Polykleitos the Younger.

A splendid monumentality characterized the most typical architectural expressions of Asia Minor, which showed a predilection for the Ionic order. The two most significant examples — considered two of the seven wonders of the ancient world — were the reconstruction of the colossal Artemision in Ephesus, after the fire started by Erostratus during the night of Alexander's birth in 353 B.C., and the Mausoleum of Halicarnassus, built by Artemisia for her husband, Prince Mausolus of Caria. The Artemision (about 360 by 170 feet) was rebuilt according to the original Archaic ground plan, with an eight-columned front and a nine-columned opisthodomos. The double row of columns decorating the front were carved on the lower part of their shafts as the Archaic ones had been. Twenty other columns, in front of and between the projecting walls of the cella, also bear carved relief on the lower part of their shafts. All this sumptuous plastic decoration at the level of the spectator took the place of the figured frieze of the entablature which, following the custom of Asia Minor, was lacking.

In like manner a series of friezes decorated the huge rectangular base (95 by 117 feet), and perhaps also the outer wall of the cella of the Mausoleum of Halicarnassus, while only a dentiled cornice adorned the Ionic entablature. Statues and lions decorated the intercolumniations, and a marble quadriga crowned the tall, stepped pyramid which, daringly placed on the light Ionic peristyle, seemed to hang in space. The architects Satyros and Pytheos found a way to organically combine the traditional elements of high-based Lycian funerary architecture with the canons of the Ionic order and the local taste for splendor, creating an original architectural work of powerful monumentality, which for a long time served as a model and an inspiration.

Besides the temples and public and private monuments, the city complexes themselves were becoming articulated in more regular and organic forms, developing the rectangular system of Hippodamos and the scenographic arrangement in terraces, depending on the demands of the site. The heart of the city, the agora, tended to lose more and more of its political function and to assume a commercial role. It became more regular in form, surrounded with porticoes of shops, though these were still not organized into a unified whole. Orators lamented the crowds of idlers and merchants that invaded the agora as political customs declined. The agorai of Megalopolis, Corinth, and Thasos illustrate this transformation. Ionian cities were more precocious in developing an organic and regular plan of the porticoed agora in terms of the urbanistic whole, as in Miletus and Priene during the fourth century.

2. Artistic Aspects of the Fourth Century

In figurative art, during the seventy years from the death of Socrates (399 B.C.) to that of Alexander the Great (323 B.C.), there was a particular development of the Attic qualities of grace, of chiaroscuro, of rhythmical ease, and soft naturalism, which culminated in the sculpture of Praxiteles and the painting of Nikias and Apelles. The problem of expressions, the pathos, the interpretation of feelings, was pursued by the sculptor Skopas and the painter Aristeides. The effects of fine drapery in the post-Phidian tradition were the subject of experiments, especially in the work of Timotheos. And the rational principles of Polykleitos concerning the structure and proportions of the human figure were developed by later sculptors, and found in Lysippos an expression of genius. Beside these main currents there flourished the varied personal tendencies of many individual artists: intense experimentation with composition, perspective, and, in painting, with lighting. In the fifth century the austere dynamic conceptions of the Severe style had been achieved most satisfactorily in bronze, but the softer, more colorful vision of the fourth century preferred marble, heightened by a thin overpainting known as *ganosis*. Abstract Archaic polychromy was replaced by naturalistic coloring that gave the marble warmth and emphasized the modeling.

One of the results of this pictorial development in art was, however, a decline in painted pottery, whose decorative principles depended on the vivid Archaic vision based on flat, fundamental colors, and the ideographic importance of drawing and line.

3. The Style of Praxiteles

The most original representatives of the great continuing tradition of Attic art were the sculptors Kephisodotos and Praxiteles. The art of the former can well serve to exemplify the transition from the ideals of the fifth century to the new atmosphere of the fourth century. Along with two fifth-century sculptors, Strongylion and Olympiosthenes, Kephisodotos executed a group representing the Muses on Mount Helicon. This theme introduces us into the Apolline atmosphere that appealed to the new times. The masterpiece of Kephisodotos, which we know through copies, was not an Olympian deity, but Eirene (fig. 174), the personification of Peace, which, after so many reverses of fortune and internal struggles, was once more beginning to smile on the Athenians after the congress of 374 B.C. This was not the fiery, colorful figure invoked by Aristophanes in the seething climate of the Peloponnesian Wars, but a solemn and benign mother bearing a cornucopia, the symbol of abundant harvests no longer destroyed by war. Eirene holds her infant son Plutus, the hope of increasing wealth, toward whom she affectionately bends her head. Her face is suffused with a new sweetness, and framed in rich waves and tightly rolled curls. The frontal pose is here dissolved into an intimate link that binds mother and son, almost as if in conversation. The heavy drapery is scanned by soft, rich folds which, in reaction to post-Phidian mannerism, restore consistency and dignity to the material. Awesomeness of interpretation is here softened by a new humanity.

With the disappearance of the greater part of the original work by Greek artists our knowledge of these creations necessarily depends on copies. These were generally executed for Roman clients by neo-Attic workshops in the Imperial period, thus the range of works reproduced reflects the taste of the purchasers and the Roman market. The extraordinarily high number of copies of statues by Praxiteles bears witness to the favor his art later found in Rome, where the artist was highly esteemed and loved, and consequently, he is the artist we know best. The elegant, graceful, sweet, sensual, smiling tone of his creations pleased the Romans, and the themes of his works were considered most suitable for decorating baths, villas, and gardens.

Praxiteles is the most typical representative of the Attic spirit of the fourth century — as Phidias was of the fifth — but though he was educated and worked in Athens, his fame summoned him to many other centers: Megara, Plataea, Thespiae, Elis, Olympia, Cnidus, and as far afield as Caria, and Parium in Mysia. All his work is directed toward an ideal of grace expressed by a new, personal vision in his choice of subjects, by the rhythm of his poses, and by his treatment of flesh and

174. Roman copy of the lost bronze original of Eirene and Plutus, created in Athens by Kephisodotos, circa 370 B.C. The restoration with the vase in her left hand is false; she originally held a cornucopia.
Munich, Antikensammlungen

drapery. Among the gods, he had a predilection for Aphrodite, Ares, the Eleusinian triad, the young Apollo, Artemis, and Hermes, while his satyrs are transformed into romantic youths. The humanized divinities of Praxiteles were no longer presented to the faithful in stiff, majestic attitudes; gods, satyrs, and men alike seem pervaded by a soft surrender, translated into new, poised rhythms which led to the typical and original Praxitelean pose, in which the body leans sinuously to one side, so that

175. Detail of a Roman copy of the Apollo Sauroctonus, *after the lost bronze created by Praxiteles, circa 360 B.C. From the Borghese Collection. Paris, Louvre*

it moves outside its own axis and needs a lateral support. After the more measured, sparing inflections that preceded it, this supple, oblique rhythm represents the final development of the psychologically and sentimentally oriented current in Athenian art, as opposed to the rigorous canons of Polykleitos. The nudes of Praxiteles become soft and fleshy with a delicately shaded modeling; eyes take on elongated lines and the lower eyelid becomes thinner, giving the gaze a dreamy, moist effect (fig. 175); garments, treated with a naturalistic feeling for the cloth, are draped in rich folds and studied arrangements, or hang in smooth, nonchalant simplicity. We can follow the development of Praxiteles' temperament from his youth to his maturity through the succession of his works. According to Pliny he reached his acme in 364–363 B.C., a date which perhaps corresponds to the creation of his masterpiece, the Cnidian Aphrodite.

The satyr pouring wine is a youthful work, known in over twenty copies, showing a delicate ephebus on whose curly head only the small pointed ears remain to show his animal nature. The pose is an elegant excuse for a calm, sinuous rhythm articulated with a slightly academic, refined elegance. A warmer, more sensual tone appears in the theme of the resting satyr, the *Anapauomenus*, whose fame is attested

176. *Small ivory copy from the second century A.D. of the original lost bronze of the Apollo Lycius attributed to Praxiteles. Found in the Agora in more than two hundred fragments.*
Athens, Agora Museum

177. *Roman copy of the lost original of the Aphrodite of Cnidus, created by Praxiteles. The head of this copy does not belong to the body. The right hand, left arm, feet, parts of the legs, and the vase are restorations.*
Vatican, Gabinetto delle Maschere

by the existence of over seventy copies. The rhythm of the figure is languid; posed leaning against a tree trunk, his face is framed with a thick cap of tiny curls and is tilted, as if enthralled by some rustic melody. A contrast is created between the luminous flesh of the smooth body and the rough animal skin over the chest. The tall, naturalistic tree trunk becomes an integral part of the theme in the *Apollo Sauroctonus* or Lizard Slayer. With soft, sinuous grace the young boy leans against the tree where there is a lizard that he is about

to transfix with his dart. The Apollo of Olympia of the Severe style appeared in solemn majesty as a sure, authoritative guarantee of salvation for the faithful; Praxiteles' smiling ephebus is beyond any rapport with

178. *Roman copy from Gabii of a lost original statue of Artemis, attributed to Praxiteles, in which some scholars have recognized the Artemis Brauronia from the Acropolis.*
Paris, Louvre

human spectators, he is completely engrossed in his own thoughts, and has the light elegance of an epigram while still remaining in a symbolic and divine sphere (fig. 175).

When Praxiteles revived the theme of Apollo on the slabs decorating an altar at Mantinea, probably produced in the master's workshop, he endowed his subject with a new dignity suited to the importance of the action. Here the god is shown as a solemn cithara player, seated and draped, about to punish the thoughtless, arrogant pride of Marsyas in the musical contest before the calm group of the Muses.

On the other hand, another version of the god, persuasively attributed to the artist's mature period, conforms more to his conception of languid abandon, and is represented by the type of *Apollo Lycius*, which Lucian admired in the gymnasium of Athens and described, though without naming the artist. In fact, this conception of the god, apparently resting after a long task, leaning on a pilaster with his bow in his left hand and his right arm raised and bent behind his head, with rich, wavy hair and a soft, full-volumed body, is plausibly attributable to Praxiteles. The many copies, including a small ivory in the Agora Museum (fig. 176), bear witness to the renown of the figure, which was to be reproduced many times during the Hellenistic period.

The same supple rhythm, thick, curly hair, and nude, youthful body was to find another appropriate theme in the figures of Eros by Praxiteles, exalted by rhetoricians and epigrammatists. Praxiteles' own preference went above all to the Eros he executed for Thespiae, and which he remodeled in even more supple forms in the bronze Eros from Parium.

The master's temperament found its most original, accomplished expression in the theme of Aphrodite in the statue acquired by the Cnidians (fig. 177). Aphrodite in the conceptions of Phidias, Alkamenes, and the other masters of the first Classical period was a goddess in a regal pose with a full, mature body wrapped in sumptuous, transparent drapery, and imbued with an Olympian atmosphere. She took on a more intimate note only in her maternal gesture toward Eros. Praxiteles' Aphrodite, on the other hand, is a woman shown completely nude, but absorbed in calm, modest concentration as she lays down her robes before the ritual bath. She is no longer an effigy destined for the enclosed space of the cella, but rather a figure to place in a pavilion open on all sides so that everyone could admire the body, as it seems the goddess herself would have wished — for, as Pliny said, its beauty was marvelous in every part. Phryne is traditionally supposed to have posed for this

179. Circular neo-Attic altar with twelve gods of Praxitelean type. Visible here are Hermes, Hestia, Apollo, Artemis, and Athena. Found in the sanctuary of Attis at Ostia. Augustan period. Ostia, Museum

work, whose fame is attested by the fifty or so copies. Lucian admired the figure's moist gaze, the perfect arc of her eyebrows, the purity of her brow, the smooth, full line of her hips, and the beauty of her legs, all the splendor and grace of her luminous body. After the female nudes of hetaerae, after the compact figure of the fifth-century Niobid from the Horti Sallustiani, Praxiteles achieved a richly shaded softness in his treatment of flesh.

A more simple, virginal grace, however, runs through his young Artemis in a smooth peplos, known as the Dresden Artemis, with a note of sweetness in the head. On the other hand, the so-called Artemis of Gabii (fig. 178) is a more mature work with richer drapery effects. The gesture of fastening her mantle has caused some authorities to recognize this work as the Artemis Brauronia of the Acropolis, since garments were dedicated to her. Praxiteles infused the divinities of Eleusis, Demeter and Persephone, with a calm, serene, composed elegance, and took particular pleasure in

180. Sarcophagus of the Mourning Women from the royal necropolis at Sidon. The sarcophagus has the form of an Ionic heroön, which is typical of Asia Minor, while the figures have a clearly Attic character. Circa 350 B.C. Istanbul, Archaeological Museum

wrapping them in garments with a richness of pleats and drapes. These female types of Demeter and Persephone by Praxiteles were to be much in demand among Roman ladies for use in portrait-statues. They were also reproduced, along with the full-bodied, curly-headed Triptolemus, in votive reliefs.

Praxiteles' particular taste for loose, well-draped garments, accompanied by the varied range of flowing, balanced rhythms, is also well exemplified by the Muses on the slabs from the altar of Mantinea, and by the series of twelve gods, clearly derived from works by Praxiteles, copied on a circular neo-Attic altar at Ostia (fig. 179). On this neo-Attic work we rediscover all the master's most typical modes in the conception and rhythms, in the curly-headed figures of Hermes, Hephaestus, and Ares, and in the full, soft, feminine figures, culminating in the veiled, seated Hestia, and in the characteristic cadences of the female garments. The influence of such Praxitelean draperies is evident on the monumental Sarcophagus of the Mourning Women from Sidon (fig. 180), attributed by scholars to various

circles of the fourth century. A triangular base for a choragic tripod found in Athens, though a modest work, also recalls this Praxitelean conception of drapery in the Nikai represented there, inspired by figures on the Parthenon frieze, and in the Dionysus with his sumptuously dressed hair who also appears on this base. This figure of Dionysus has been cited to justify the attribution to Praxiteles of another statuary type of the god, the Dionysus Sardanapalus, which gives a Classical interpretation of the Phrygio-Thracian Sabatius.

The slabs from Mantinea and the triangular base from the Street of the Tripods, though produced in the workshop of the master, are only secondary works and therefore we have no original that could show us the inimitable touch of Praxiteles' hand, so admired by the ancients. While it was once believed that the statue of Hermes with the infant Dionysus, found in the cella of the Heraion of Olympia where Pausanias recorded it as standing, was definitely an original work, this certainty has now been undermined. Observation of technical and stylistic considerations, like the

181. Head of a helmeted hero by Skopas, from the west pediment of the Temple of Athena Alea at Tegea. Doliana marble. Circa *350–340* B.C. *Athens, National Museum*

presence of the support, the unfinished back, and the contours of the base, have led to the postulation that it is a Hellenistic work by another Praxiteles of the second century B.C., who is known to us from some signatures. In view of the custom of passing on the art from father to son in the families of Greek sculptors, the work could still be admitted into the circle of Praxiteles, which was particularly large and active; and thus it could be considered a Hellenistic revival, by a descendant, of modes typical of his great ancestor. The shading achieves a tone of virtuosity in the languid head of Hermes, and the polishing offers an intense contrast with the rough, coloristic

modeling of the disheveled, curly hair, and the drapery, which the god gathers together over his arm as a pillow for the child Dionysus. This drapery, in its hollows and its loose sudden fall, constitutes a highly studied bravura passage.

4. The Style of Skopas

The consistent, unmistakable language of Praxiteles contrasts strongly with the varied range of expressive accents, including the most solemn Olympian tone and the most turbulent, agitated pathos, of the complex, many-sided

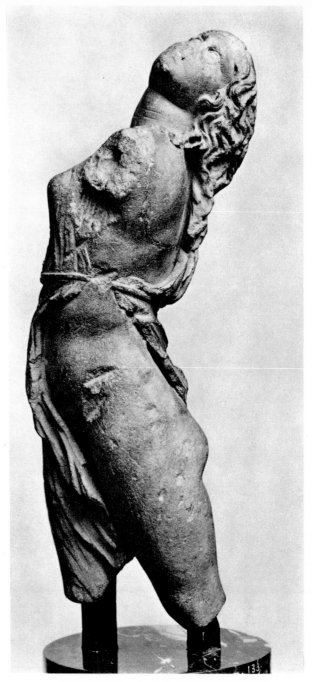

182. *Roman copy of Pothos, after the lost original created by Skopas. Found together with another copy as decoration in a Roman house. Rome, Capitoline Museums*

183. *Orgiastic maenad in a Roman copy after the lost original by Skopas. Although mutilated, this statuette is the best remaining document of the style of this sculptor. From Marino. Dresden, Albertinum*

personality of Skopas. Coming from a family of artists on the island of Paros, in which the name of the father, Aristandros, alternates with that of Skopas, his native Ionia may have given him his lively temperament and interest in expressive problems, though he was definitely trained in the Attic school and worked in Athens. He also worked farther afield, in Rhamnus, Megara, Thebes, the Peloponnesus, Argos, Elis, Sicyon, Gortys, and Samothrace, and in Asia Minor in the Troad, Ephesus, Pergamon, Cnidus, Halicarnassus, and Bithynia.

From his prolific output we still have the originals of some mutilated heads of pedimental statues he created for the Temple of Athena Alea at Tegea, that had burned in 395–394 and was rebuilt and redecorated by Skopas, perhaps 350–340 B.C. These fragments suffice to show us the expressive strength that animated his marbles with a new, personal conception of structure and modeling. The decoration of the temple was no longer inspired by the great myths of the Olympian gods, but derived from legends closely linked with the site itself. The Arcadian heroine Atalanta, taking part in

207

184. Section of the frieze representing an Amazonomachy from the Mausoleum of Halicarnassus, which has been attributed to Skopas on the basis of a comparison between the Amazon seen here in the center and the maenad illustrated in figure 183. Circa 350 B.C. London, British Museum

the Calydonian boar hunt, had won the animal's skin, kept in the Temple of Athena Alea, the priestess of which was Auge, the mother by Heracles of the hero Telephus. Skopas narrated the mythical hunt on the east pediment: Atalanta, Meleager, and Theseus on one side, and the wounded Ancaeus supported by Apochus on the other, who along with other heroes bear down on the centrally placed boar, whose vigorous snout has survived. The west pediment celebrated Telephus fighting Achilles in the plain of Caicus.

The curly head of a hero, another head with a helmet (fig. 181), and a head of Heracles, the last two certainly from the west pediment, show a single conception in their stereometric, square-cut, solid structure: in their eyes, set deeply in the shadowy cavities of their orbits; in the modeling of the tightly knitted brows; the short, half-open mouths; the head raised and sharply turned to one side; and in the rough hair with its small, disheveled curls. The artist had used these elements to create a new expressive language of dynamic force and intense pathos, well adapted to convey the excitement of the wild animal hunt and the heroic struggle. These themes offered a

varied scale of positions of assault and defense that could provide a harmonious solution to the problems of pedimental composition. We do not know whether a head with a torso clothed in a light tunic suggesting a graceful feminine figure comes from an akroterion or from the pediments, for unlike the other sculptures, which are in Doliana marble, these are in Parian marble.

There is no trace of the numerous divine effigies executed by the master — Asclepius and Hygieia, Hecate, Heracles, Athena, Aphrodite, Ares, Latona, Artemis, Dionysus, and Hestia — except for his lyre-playing Apollo, which was placed in the cella of the Temple of Apollo on the Palatine in Rome by Octavian in 28 B.C., where it was admired by Propertius. This figure is known through torsos, coins, and the representation on a marble base at Sorrento. By comparison with Praxiteles' Mantinea Apollo, Skopas' god, with the long tunic and wide

185. Detail of the statue of Mausolus from the Mausoleum of Halicarnassus. This figure attributed to Bryaxis.
Circa 352 B.C. London, British Museum

mantle that provides a backdrop for the figure, appears to have a new grandeur, a more opulent interpretation of the Classical ideal, as if in a musical *largo maestoso*, with the elaborate cadence of the rich knot of pleats above his belt. But just as Praxiteles had also envisaged an Apollo in the dreamy *Sauroctonus*, so Skopas portrayed the god with a mouse under his feet for the Temple of Apollo Smintheus at Chryse.

The attribution to Skopas of a type of Meleager which, to judge from the some twenty surviving copies, must have been very well known, seems quite plausible because of the romantic, pathetic tone of the work, expressed in the calm, balanced rhythm which is, however, moved by an inner agitation. We might think of this as a milder, melancholy version of the heroic heads from the pediments at Tegea. The delicate chiaroscuro in the Villa Medici copy may bring us closer to the original, or simply to the hand that sculpted this replica.

An interest in experiments in expression found subtle gradations in the conception of the statues which Skopas made for Megara, portraying Eros, Himeros, and Pothos who, according to the Platonic definition, personified the three states of amorous feeling. The first, Eros, was active love; Himeros represented the irresistible desire for the object before one's eyes; while Pothos corresponded to an anxious, tormented yearning for the absent or inaccessible loved one. In Attic pottery from the second half of the fifth century they appeared in Aphrodite's entourage as winged erotes. We can have no idea of the form the master gave to Eros and Himeros, but it seems that the type of Pothos that we know from gems and the twenty-seven marble copies which prove its fame, sprang from the inventive fantasy of Skopas (fig. 182). This Amorous Longing stands in a lordly pose, dropping his limbs in languor, as Archilochus wrote, and takes concrete form in the soft abandon of the supple body leaning on a Dionysiac thyrsus. There are clear inspirations from the contemporary works of Praxiteles in the unstably crossed legs, the pathetic backward tilt of the head, the passionate, deeply sunk eyes, and the half-open lips. The mantle which falls from his shoulder down to the symbolic goose fills the gap between the body and the thyrsus, and effectively contrasts with the soft flesh.

The pathos of Skopas acquired more fiery tones, moving from the world of Aphrodite to that of Dionysus in the statue of an orgiastic maenad (fig. 183), admired by rhetoricians such as Callistratus, and by epigrammatists. The Dresden statuette gives us a summary copy, but still shows the turbulent rhythm, the head thrown back, shaking out the tumul-tuous wave of unbound hair, and the motif of the light tunic open on one side to reveal the tense, muscular body. The refined cadence of Kallimachos' maenads (fig. 161) here takes on overpowering impetus, giving Dionysiac *enthusiasmos* its most lyrical interpretation.

Comparison of this maenad with the analogous motif of an Amazon who exposes the whole left side of her body in the violence of delivering a blow, seems to provide the one tenuous element that could lead to crediting Skopas with some parts of the Amazonomachy decorating the Mausoleum at Halicarnassus (fig. 184). It is recorded that he worked on the east side of the Mausoleum, while Leochares was responsible for the west side, Bryaxis the north, and Timotheos the south. In reality we do not know if this decoration comprised friezes, statues, or both, nor how the frieze panels showing Amazonomachy, centauromachy, and a chariot race were placed and distributed. Thus, despite attempts at recognizing the styles of the four sculptors in these marbles, the problem remains open.

Nor do we know the exact placing of the two colossal statues which have been supposed to represent Artemisia and Mausolus (fig. 185). In these Classical gravity of interpretation unfolded in a majestic treatment of drapery, pleated and divided by an endless variety of folds, rolls, and hems, in what can be thought of as a Hellenistic conception already at this time. The precise crown of curls on the statue alleged to represent Artemisia has an archaizing note, and the entire figure is indeed rather academic; but in the head of Mausolus one can already see an intense expressiveness of facial features, and the generally exotic nature of the head, with its long Eastern hair-style almost anticipates images of Christ.

5. The Sculptors of the Mausoleum of Halicarnassus

The three other sculptors working on the Mausoleum — Timotheos, Bryaxis, and Leochares — were all Athenians, though Bryaxis had adopted his nationality, for he was originally from Caria. The oldest must have been Timotheos, who was working on the decoration of the Temple of Asclepius at Epidaurus around 375 B.C., as we know from epigraphic records. Building work at Epidaurus lasted four years, eight months, and a few days, but in the third year the temple was already roofed, the cella walls were finished, and the thirty-four columns had been grooved. We know that Timotheos was paid 900 drachmae for executing the *typoi*. (There has been much dis-

186. One of the lateral akroteria from the west front of the Temple of Asclepius at Epidaurus. This figure of a mounted aura is attributed to Timotheos. Circa 375 B.C. *Athens, National Museum*

cussion over the interpretation of this technical word, which according to some means sketches, or clay or wax models for the pedimental sculptures, while others take it to mean reliefs decorating the sanctuary.) The sculptures on the east pediment of the temple were executed by Hektoridas for 3010 drachmae, and those on the west pediment by another sculptor. The pedimental fragments that remain indeed show stylistic differences, but it is also possible to assume that they were part of a unitary conception and that the models supplied were by Timotheos, only being translated into marble by Hektoridas and his colleague. From the east pediment representing the sack of Troy there have survived various fragments: the suffering head of Priam, who was perhaps being slain by Neoptolemus in the center of the composi-

187. An Attic original of the post-Phidian style. Perhaps an akroterion of a temple. Found in the Agora at Athens to the north of the altar of Zeus Agoraios. Tentatively thought to come from the Hephaesteion. Athens, Agora Museum

188. Central akroterion from the west front of the Temple of Asclepius at Epidaurus, representing Epione with the goose. Attributed to Timotheos. Circa 375 B.C. Athens, National Museum

tion; the torso of Palladium, to whom Cassandra was clinging; the torso of the figure of Ajax, which occupied the right-hand side of the pedimental space; the draped body of a Trojan woman carrying a wounded man who was placed near Priam on the left-hand side; Andromache clasping Astyanax to her body, heavily draped and kneeling in perspective; and a kneeling archer shooting an arrow toward the center. The varying positions dictated by the dramatic episode of the tragic night offered all the elements for a harmonious solution of

the syntactical problem of decorating a pediment, as did the Amazonomachy on the west side. From the west pediment a fine torso of Penthesilea on horseback can be reconstructed as having dominated the center of the composition, bending over a fallen warrior and framed by two other Amazons converging on horseback, of which have survived the head of the horse on the left, and the turning torso of the Amazon on the right, in the process of being dragged down by a Greek. Other kneeling and wounded figures could have organically filled the far corners of this pediment, using arrangements borrowed from painting to create a composition tighter than that of the sack of Troy on the east pediment.

The architect of the Temple of Asclepius at Epidaurus, Theodotos, was also a sculptor, and received 2240 drachmae for executing the akroteria on the east side, while Timotheos was paid the same amount for those on the west. The size of the payment indicates the importance that these summit ornaments had taken on as the decoration of the temple became more and more elaborate. From the pieces that have survived we see that Theodotos used for his central akroterion a figure of Iris descending in flight, like the Nike of Paionios at Olympia, but with an original, more studied composition of drapery which wraps like a veil about the wings and stretches between them, and rises up to form a billowing drape on the thigh, with fine, neat folds. As lateral akroteria, Theodotos carved two youthful figures on horseback, of which one torso and one head have been preserved. There is a harmonious correspondence with the akroteria on the west by Timotheos. These included two mounted aurae (winds) at either side, and the central akroterion represented a dynamic figure of Epione, the wife of Asclepius and dispenser of health-giving potions, with the goose (fig. 188). In this figure, too, a wind seems to envelop her from below, making the light chiton cling to the body, then billow above the waist and twist the cloth over her chest. In the aura (fig. 186), drapery caught by the wind, furrowed and flattened, becomes the most significant expressive element, composed of tangled knots, razor-edged ridges, clinging transparencies, and fluttering hems, in an almost baroque animation, which was to undergo further development in the Hellenistic period.

Thus in the first quarter of the fourth century the post-Phidian tradition in drapery gained new, vividly contrasting effects in the work of Timotheos, who also seems to have made allowance for the fact that his statues would be seen at a distance from below. This conception also marks a fine headless statue of a woman that was found in the Athenian Agora (fig. 187) and has justly been placed in the post-Phidian current. Precisely because of the treatment of drapery, with rich effects of pleats, rolls, and wind-blown, veil-like portions, as well as the comparison of the head with those of the aura from the Temple of Asclepius, one is very tempted to follow the attribution to Timotheos of a creation showing Leda embracing her swan (fig. 189). This figure, known in copies and remodeled during the Hellenistic period, in its passionate, languid tone

189. Roman copy of a lost original of Leda and the swan, known through some twenty replicas and attributed to Timotheos. The neck and head of the swan are restored. Rome, Capitoline Museums

recalls the Pothos by Skopas, and illustrates the trends followed by artists in the fourth century.

Timotheos' Artemis, which later stood beside Skopas' Apollo and the Latona of Kephisodotos the Younger in the Temple of Apollo on the Palatine (all three reproduced on the base at Sorrento), is another typical expression of the artistic climate. The type of the so-called Dresden Artemis of Praxiteles, and the type of Artemis on the circular altar at Ostia (fig. 179) which is derived from Praxiteles', is enriched in Timotheos' version by more tightly wrinkled drapery and the plastic interplay of crossed

190. Detail of the Apollo Belvedere. *Hadrianic copy of a lost bronze original, which has been attributed to Leochares. Found at the end of the fifteenth century, perhaps at Anzio, and placed in the Vatican Belvedere by Pope Julius II. Vatican Museums*

191. Statuette of Serapis. Roman copy which re-echoes the famous work by Bryaxis. Ostia, Museum

straps over the chest. The rhythm, too, becomes more complex, with the bent legs and the lateral support with a torch again recalling Skopas' Pothos. The pose becomes sinuously relaxed with the projecting right hip on which the hand rests, in a cadence often used by Praxiteles. Thus even the dynamic virgin huntress, whom Archaic, Severe, and Classical art preferred to view as an active participant in the struggle against the giants, and the attentive companion of Apollo in the fight with Heracles and the cruel slaughter of Niobe's children, abandoned her bow in the romantic world of the fourth century and took up a torch; this provided a convenient support for her body in the languid repose that was now preferred to the tension of action.

A confirmation of the community of ideals among fourth-century masters is shown by the uncertain attribution to Timotheos or Leochares, in the same ancient sources, of the colossal acrolith representing Ares which was placed on the summit of the acropolis at Halicarnassus, where both artists had been active on the Mausoleum. Timotheos had made an effigy of Asclepius for Troezen, which the people con-

sidered to be a portrait of Hippolytus, who had died in their city. This was perhaps because the youthful type of beardless Asclepius, conceived by Skopas in Gortyn in Arcadia, had been adopted by Timotheos for the Troezen figure, in accordance with the more humane ideals of the fourth century. It might be interesting to note that the important image of Asclepius for the great temple at Epidaurus, the center of his cult, had in any case been entrusted to an artist of the Classical and Phidian traditions, Thrasymedes, an expert in the chryselephantine technique, who wanted his figure to be solemn and bearded, with the *pondus* and *auctoritas* of Phidias' colossi. Thrasymedes, from Paros, represented the god enthroned, holding a scepter in one hand and caressing the head of his sacred serpent with the other. The throne of the god was decorated with the myths of the Argive heroes, such as Bellerophon slaying the Chimaera, or Perseus beheading the Medusa. Thrasymedes must have been intensely committed to the Phidian ideal, for one tradition attributed the effigy to Phidias himself, notwithstanding the fact that the work was made half a century later. Yet, while echoes of this type of Asclepius are to be seen in reliefs in Epidaurus, he is here seen in a more relaxed pose, with crossed legs and drapery which is more elaborate and varied. From inscriptions we know that Thrasymedes had also decorated the doors of the temple which were incrusted with gold and ivory, as well as the ceiling of the cella.

The Classical tradition of statues of the great Olympian gods continued in Leochares, an Athenian. He created several effigies of Zeus: as Zeus Polieus on the Acropolis, placed beside Demos in Piraeus, and with a thunderbolt in the statue that was later taken to Rome for the Capitoline. He also represented Apollo several times: as *Alexikakos* in Athens; with a fillet, also in Athens; and in a statue at Syracuse. But even in the work of Leochares the new spirit takes concrete form in the theme of the rape of Ganymede, shown as a tender little boy delicately held by the eagle and carried upward as the bird flies off toward Olympus. The modest copy in the Vatican and echoes in other monuments can give us only an idea of the virtuosity of the compositional rhythm of this work, the pathos of the child's upturned, curly head, the sense of color in the contrast between the light, childish nude standing out against the wings and plumage of the eagle, with effects dear to Hellenistic epigrammatists.

Leochares, who had a predilection for the theme of Apollo, has been assigned a characteristic image of the god, known through copies, the best known, most complete of which is the *Apollo Belvedere* in the Vatican (fig. 190), and although lacking in elements that could make the attribution secure, the figure is indeed indicative of an approach that harmonizes with the taste shown in his Ganymede. The *Apollo Belvedere* is an archer and not, as Skopas and Praxiteles had liked to portray him, a cithara player. The awesomeness of the infallible judge is here transmuted into the studied force of a handsome actor with luxuriant, curly hair, who displays his grace before the spectators in accordance with the romantic spirit of the fourth century, which also proved very agreeable to the Neoclassical taste of Winckelmann. A similar dynamism, emphatic and elaborate in tone, is to be seen in the type known as the Versailles Artemis, which has been compared with this Apollo.

Nothing is preserved of the portraits of Leochares, who executed the image of the trader Lyciscus, a family group on the Acropolis, the bronze statue of Isocrates at Eleusis, and statues of the family of Alexander the Great in the Philippeion at Olympia. The

chryselephantine technique used in this last group suggests a Classical tone. As we have no originals by Leochares, the attributions to him of the slabs from the Mausoleum of Halicarnassus must remain uncertain.

Nor can these reliefs from Halicarnassus provide us with any knowledge of the style of the other sculptor who worked at the Mausoleum, Bryaxis from Caria. The three horsemen carved on a base in Athens bearing this artist's name are of little value to us. From the sources, Bryaxis seems to have worked within the Classical conception of Olympian divinities, which he carved in five images at Rhodes, later representing Zeus and Apollo at Patara, Dionysus at Cnidus, Asclepius and Hygieia at Megara, a much-admired Apollo with lyre at Antioch, and a Serapis, his masterpiece, executed for the Serapeion at Alexandria under Ptolemy I, de-

192. Headless statue of Apollo Patroüs attributed to Euphranor. Found on the west side of the Agora. Circa 350 B.C. Athens, Agora Museum

scribed by Clement of Alexandria and later destroyed by the Christians. This work, on the threshold of Hellenistic conceptions, enables one to guess at the transformation of the Classical ideal into a theme that springs from a significant religious syncretism between Zeus-Hades and Osiris-Apis. It was executed in a technique which strove to express the chthonic nature of the god with new coloristic effects in the bluish tone of the nude, and a luministic preciosity in the gems and metals that composed the figure. The face of the Lord of the Land of the Dead was entirely shadowed by locks of hair falling over his brow, crowned by the *modium* (corn measure), a symbol of fertility. The images of Serapis we possess may indeed represent diverse re-modelings (fig. 191), but it is still probable that in their fundamental common characteristics — the rich, voluminous hair and beard, the gravity and solemnity of tone — they can be traced back to the celebrated work of Bryaxis. All these stylistic elements are to be found again in the grandiose, anonymous creation which has been approximated with the work of Bryaxis, the Otricoli Zeus. In this figure the inner calm, verging on gloom, that is seen in the Serapis is transformed into explosive energy that ruffles the hair and wrinkles the planes of the brow.

6. Versatility of Euphranor

Beside the more original, famous figures such as Praxiteles and Skopas, the spirit of the period found another typical representative in the versatile, hard-working Euphranor (*docilis et laboriosus*). Versatile indeed, for he was not only a sculptor in stone, bronze, and clay, but also a painter, and a theoretician on problems of symmetry and color. Though he carved images of gods, it was most of all in figures of heroes, closer to the conceptions of the fourth century, that he revealed new accents, conferring on them particular *dignitas*. In the theme of personifications, he sculpted Virtus and Hellas, and painted Demos and Democracy beside Theseus. Psychological interest was evidenced in his statue of Paris — in which he contrived to express at the same time the judge of goddesses, the lover of Helen, and the slayer of Achilles — and again in his painting of the feigned madness of Odysseus, a theme that Parrhasios had already treated. His sensitive treatment of flesh occasioned the remark that his painted Theseus must have been fed on real meat. The Apolline ideal gained one of its most impressive interpretations in Euphranor's work, as can be seen in

193. Roman copy of the Apoxyomenus. *The original lost bronze was created by Lysippos,* circa *320 B.C. Vatican Museums*

the headless statue of a cithara player found in the Temple of Apollo Patroüs in the Agora (fig. 192). The solemn, flowing drapery recalls the Palatine Apollo by Skopas, but monumentally amplified. Euphranor also attempted portraiture in his images of Philip and Alexander in quadrigas. Complicated compositions of battle scenes, which centered mainly around the battles in which Alexander was a protagonist, were common at that time, such as Euphranor's painting in the Kerameikos of the battle of Mantinea, which took place in 362 B.C.

As Parrhasios had done before him, Euphranor studied symmetry. He seems also to have

194. Roman copy of the original lost bronze of Eros nocking the arrow in his bow, attributed to the first period of activity of Lysippos. Found along with another copy forming part of the decoration of a nymphaeum at Ostia. Ostia, Museum

195. Reduced copy from the first century B.C. of the lost original bronze Hercules of the Farnese type. The creation of the type is attributed to the mature period of Lysippos. Found in the sanctuary of Hercules Curinus at Sulmona. Chieti, Archaeological Museum

experimented with a new canon of the human figure, with slimmer, more graceful proportions, but according to the ancients, this paring down of limbs made the heads and joints appear too large.

7. The New Canon of Lysippos

It was Lysippos of Sicyon who gave harmonious and organic expression to a new canon of the human figure, a canon which adhered to the new conceptions and taste of the fourth century. Pliny tells us that the sculptor showed the utmost diligence in studying the problem of symmetry, replacing the structure of the ancients with a new system of proportions. Taking Polykleitos' *quadratio* and the chiasmic rhythms of the Polykleitan athlete, he transformed them by making the head smaller and the body slimmer, so that the figure appeared taller. The disharmonies of Euphranor's canon

217

196. *Roman copy of the portrait of Socrates which Lysippos is supposed to have created* circa *350 B.C. This portrait type has been reconstructed as the head of a seated figure in the collection at Copenhagen. Rome, Museo delle Terme*

197. *Detail of the so-called Sarcophagus of Alexander with scenes of battles and hunts. Found in the royal necropolis at Sidon; probably intended as the sarcophagus of Abdalonymus. The influence of the Lysippan creations exalting Alexander are seen in such details as the one illustrated here. End of the fourth century B.C. Istanbul, Archaeological Museum*

were thus corrected in Lysippos' new version, which is best illustrated in the sculptor's *Apoxyomenus*, the athlete scraping himself with a strigil, known through the fine Vatican copy (fig. 193), the original of which had been placed in front of the baths of Agrippa, and was much admired by Tiberius. The figure acquires a new impetus. The flexed leg is no longer drawn back, as in the works of Polykleitos, but is now placed to one side. Poised stasis is abandoned in this pose; instead, the sinuousness of the torso endows the statue with an elastic, ascending rhythm; the inner dynamism is scanned by the outstretched arm, conveying a new, three-dimensional space.

The tension and movement that enfold the entire body could no longer be crowned by the smooth Polykleitan cap of flattened curls; instead the head is covered with thick, disor-

derly locks of hair which re-echo the vibrations that give life to this new athletic ideal. Ancient critics, recorded by Pliny, indeed recognized that Lysippos had made a great contribution to the art of statuary by giving the hair a special expressive function and by devoting profound study to even the most minute details (*argutiae operum custoditae in minimis quoque rebus*). His canon, as Lysippos himself said, aimed at reproducing men as they appeared to the eye, whereas Classical artists had represented them as they were. The mathematical, rational canon of Polykleitos thus became transformed according to optical principles subjected to expressive ends, a step which marks the passage from the Classical to the Hellenistic style. Symmetry was replaced by eurhythmy, reality gave way to appearance, rationality to fantasy, and tactile values optical ones.

218

A tenser, less mature version of this Lysippan conception of the athletic figure is to be found in the statue of the Thessalian prince Agias, champion in numerous games; this was erected in Delphi, along with many other statues of members of his family. The statue of Agias is a reproduction of the work created by Lysippos for the town of Pharsalus, a fact documented by an inscription. To the master of the *Apoxyomenus* it also seems reasonable to attribute the dynamic, tense image of another type of athlete, known in copies, who bends down to lace his sandal, presenting complex rhythmic articulation and a vibrant nude body.

In Thespiae, Praxiteles' Eros was brought face to face with Lysippos' version of this same theme, to be recognized in the statuary type of Eros nocking the arrow in his bow, the fame of which is proved by the existence of about forty copies (fig. 194). This juxtaposition must have brought into evidence the profound difference between these two artistic temperaments: Praxiteles' languid, sinuous boy was shown in dreamy repose; Lysippos'

figure is tense and elastic, with intersecting rhythms, and soft, vibrantly disordered locks of hair.

Rhythmic daring, thematic imaginativeness, and particular elaboration of the hair, which was shaven at the nape and tumbled over the face to express the blindness and the elusive, mercurial nature of Opportunity, are basic features of the sculptor's allegory of this subject, his figure of *Kairos*, which was widely praised in rhetorical and epigrammatic literature of ancient times. Lysippos portrayed his subject as a boy with winged heels perched on a wheel, and in his hand he carried a razor on which he apparently balanced a pair of scales. The type known from an academic relief in Turin, a fragment in Trau, another in Athens, and a late medieval echo on an ambo in Torcello, could be equated with Lysippos' Eros.

The athletic canon of Lysippos was to take on a variety of forms in the five statues of Olympic champions recorded to have been at Olympia itself. It is natural that in the field of mythical heroes the sculptor should have

198. Roman copy of a portrait of Plato, known in eighteen replicas, believed to have been created by Silanion and dedicated in the Academy of Athens, perhaps after Plato's death in 347 B.C. Geneva, Boehringer Collection

199. Original bronze portrait of a pugilist, considered to be the head of the statue of the Olympic victor Satyrus of Elis, modeled by Silanion, circa 330 B.C. Athens, National Museum

been particularly attracted by Heracles, that image of vital energy. Indeed, he produced numerous works exalting Heracles in his labors: at Alyzia in Acarnania; in bronze at Sicyon; and on a colossal scale in the seated statue at Taranto, which was moved to Rome and later to Constantinople. Lysippos also treated Heracles in miniature forms, as in the Heracles Epitrapezios, a silver ornament made as a table decoration originally executed for Alexander, which later belonged to Hannibal and then to Sulla and Novius Vindex. Martial and Statius sang the praises of this work, which is known in several copies. The Heracles Epitrapezios, with its expansive rhythm and joyous tone, holds a *skyphos* in his hand, as an invitation to be congenial company. This figure contrasts with the colossal figure, known as the Farnese Heracles after the copy by Glykon in the Farnese collection in Naples, shown standing in an immobile, balanced position, plunged in a tired, melancholy meditation, in accordance with the new romantic conceptions (fig. 195). With their lively narrative sense, Archaic artists had seen Heracles as the hero in the throes of action, and the Master of Olympia, who lived and breathed the atmosphere of drama, had envisaged the hero imbued with the pathos of his adventures and the manifestations of divine will. On the other hand, Lysippos, living in the climate of the very first years of the Hellenistic age, was attracted by the state of mind of the hero meditating on his fate. This psychological, romantic note strikes one as all the more lyrical and pathetic in Lysippos' Heracles. The subtle and controlled expression of feeling is effectively contrasted with the exuberant exaltation of physical energy seen in the expressionistic, almost exaggerated, modeling of the baroque nude, and the tormented treatment of the hair and beard; these features are essential and cannot be attributed to the copyist.

We know nothing of Lysippos' numerous interpretations of Zeus, including a colossal statue at Taranto; nor have we any trace of his representations of Apollo and Dionysus; nor his Helius from the quadriga at Rhodes. Certainly the ardent, heroic personality of Alexander the Great must have proved congenial to Lysippos' temperament, for the artist represented him several times in isolated statues, like the famous Alexander holding a lance, or in groups, such as that of the battle of the Granicus (later moved to Rome), and the lion hunt commissioned by Craterus at Delphi, of which we can form an idea from indirect echoes in a polychromed narrative version on the so-called Sarcophagus of Alexander (fig. 197). Created by an Athenian sculptor, this work was found in the princely burial place at Sidon. It

was perhaps the sarcophagus of Abdalonymus, whom Alexander had installed on the throne of Sidon. From the many portraits of Alexander there may be echoes of Lysippos in the Azara herm in the Louvre, and in the Acropolis and Geneva heads. The artist contrived in this work to express the character of his sitter in the torsion of the head, the hair rising from the brow, the upturned gaze, and the inspired, vibrant tone: he thus gave life to a type of heroic portrait that was to be remodeled in the time of the Diadochi and developed far and wide in the Hellenistic and Roman worlds.

Beside the heroic conception of the divine Alexander, Lysippos had also given a psychological interpretation of the satyr-like face of Socrates. This portrait by Lysippos has been identified with the type in which the philosopher is shown seated, but leaning forward in a tense rhythm expressing inner disquiet, the face ennobled by nervous, pensive concentration (fig. 196), constituting a prototype for the many statues of philosophers created during the Hellenistic period. From the portrait idealized according to the Classical concepts of the typically beautiful, we thus pass during the fourth century to the physiognomical and psychological portrait, and heroic portraiture.

8. Other Sculptors of the Fourth Century

Occasionally artists, like Demetrios of Alopeke, who was active from the end of the fifth to about the middle of the fourth centuries, had shown leanings toward realism, as had some vase painters and the painter Pauson. Demetrios portrayed the physical decadence of the old priestess Lysimache and the paunchy, bald Corinthian *strategos* Pellichus with, as Quintilian says, an excess of *veritas*. But Socrates urged the investigation of the soul and the individual, and artists began to portray not only physical, but also moral features, seeing the face as the expression of the spirit.

Thus Silanion, a skillful bronze worker, in his portrait of the bronze sculptor Apollodoros, managed to represent the maniacal character of this eternally dissatisfied artist, who often broke up his finished works, and was considered a madman. Silanion himself said that he had succeeded in rendering in this bronze,

200. Detail of an original bronze statue of an ephebus, with eyes of stone. Found in the sea off Anticythera. This work shows elements of various styles of the fourth century B.C., but substantially of the Attic school. Athens, National Museum

201. *Detail of the enthroned Demeter from Cnidus, attributed by some scholars to Leochares. Circa 340–300 B.C. London, British Museum*

202. *Base and sculpted lower drum of a column from the Artemision at Ephesus, which was rebuilt after the fire of 356 B.C., with work continuing for several decades. London, British Museum*

not the man himself, but the very image of wrath. Silanion's interest in portraiture is also expressed in the iconic statues of Corinna and Sappho — the latter admired by Cicero as an elegant and elaborate work — and in the portrait of Plato, known to us through copies (fig. 198). This portrait of Plato was commissioned by Mithridates and dedicated to the Muses in the Academy of Athens. We do not know if this was before or after the death of the philosopher in 347 B.C. The acme of Silanion is fixed by Pliny in 325–321 B.C.; this would make it possible to assume that the bust was dedicated shortly after Plato's death. The noble conception of the bearded face is enlivened by an intimate, thoughtful concentration, with a wrinkled brow and vividly modeled cheeks. Silanion even used a mixture of bronze and silver to render the pallor on the face of his dying Jocasta.

Considering the strong tendency to characterization and expression in the portraiture of Silanion, one is strongly attracted to the hypothesis that the splendid bronze head of a pugilist from Olympia (fig. 199), portrayed with vigor-

ous realism in the battered nose and the magnificently carved bristling hair, is in reality a fragment of the statue of Satyrus of Elis modeled by Silanion. He is known to have executed other statues of victorious athletes at Olympia and had indeed interpreted the heroic ideal in his statues of Theseus and Achilles.

The taste for naturalism and realism even led Lysistratos, the brother of Lysippos, to use plaster casts of faces, taking molds in wax and retouching them to obtain a perfect likeness.

Alongside these great figures, literary sources also record a swarm of minor artists, who are now nothing more than names to us, but still bear witness to the general intensity of artistic activity and the variety of schools in this period. The personal innovating language of the great must have had a considerable influence on the minor figures, and left a strong imprint on the entire artistic output of the times. Even in the most noteworthy anonymous works we can trace reworkings of the more significant modes of leading artists. The fine original bronze of an ephebus (fig. 200), fished out of the sea off Anticythera and coming from a

203. *Attic funerary stele representing a
deceased youth, absorbed and detached from the
world, while his old father looks at him with
intense pain, the little slave boy is broken-
hearted, and the dog sniffs about. Second half
of the fourth century* B.C. *Athens, National Museum*

204. *Roman copy of the portrait of Euripides,
known in twenty-five replicas, after an original
of particularly fine modeling. Farnese herm,
with inscription. The nose is restored.*
Circa *320* B.C. *Naples, National Museum*

sunken ship loaded with works of art for the
Italic market, has Praxitelean touches in the
curly hair, while the loose, ascending rhythms
of the pose approach the style of Lysippos
and the torso shows a Peloponnesian robustness. This figure, who once held something
in his raised right hand, has been variously
interpreted as Hermes, or as Paris holding the
golden apple, or perhaps Perseus holding the
head of Medusa. Praxiteles is echoed in the
rhythm and theme of another bronze, this one
found off the coast of Marathon. It perhaps
represented Hermes playing with a turtle held
in the palm of his outstretched hand: not a god
to be invoked, but a work made to be admired
as an epigram, like the *Apollo Sauroctonus*.

The taste for intense play of chiaroscuro develops vivid tonal contrasts in the fine enthroned Demeter from Cnidus, now in London
(fig. 201). The head, sculpted in gleaming
Parian marble with refined shading reminiscent
of Praxiteles, stands out strikingly against the
body, which is of a local marble rendered

opaque by the many folds of the drapery.
The new romantic conception of the goddess
is affirmed in the mild, gentle face which, un-
aware of the onlooker, is absorbed in a
faraway vision, with the liquid gaze of the
round, deeply set eyes in the manner of Skopas.
The pathetic and softly modeled head of Asclepius from Melos, now in London, is also intensely coloristic in conception, and the lan-
guorous gaze combines with the rich mane of
curls in an exuberance that is already Hellenistic. This rich, soft, modeling is also seen in
the well-known portrait of Euripides (fig. 204).

Well-arranged drapery, falling in elegant
hems and folds, soft, adolescent nudes, loose,
poised rhythms, and heads pathetically raised
or bent in intimate meditation, are elements
that also characterize the figures sculpted in
high relief on the lower part of the shaft
of the columns along the grandiose front
of the Artemision at Ephesus (fig. 202). The
appearance in Pliny of the name of Skopas,
cited as the creator of one column, is perhaps

223

205. Lateral figures from the painting of the sacrifice of Iphigenia, from the House of the Tragic Poet at Pompeii. At left, Agamemnon covers his face in order not to see the sacrifice of his daughter. At right, Calchas is seen in a pose which betrays his inner agitation. These figures reflect motifs from the famous painting by Timanthes of the fourth century B.C. Naples, National Museum

the result of an error arising from a confusion between the words "Scopa" and "scapo," the latter meaning the lower part of a column, but the figures do recall Skopas. Sculpture found new fields in the sumptuous architecture of the Asiatic centers, while on the Greek mainland the art remained more sober.

In Attica there were no funerary monuments to compare with the Mausoleum at Halicarnassus: tombs were decorated only with steles. The steles, however, increased in number and richness, developing the form of a shrine with a small gable and pilasters and increasing the

depth of the relief so that figures were carved almost in the round. The tone of these works was that of dreamy melancholy and quiet pathos (fig. 203). The single figure became more rare, and groups of two in conversation were often enlarged with more figures. The stylistic in-

206. Pompeian wall painting of Perseus liberating Andromeda after he has slain the monster. Re-elaboration of the original painting by Nikias created in the second half of the fourth century B.C. Naples, National Museum

fluences of the great masters, elaborated in the main Attic workshops, were variously reflected in these steles, some of which reach a nobility and intensity of expression, until a decree of Demetrius of Phaleron between 317 and 307 B.C., limiting their use, led to a decline in production. Even at the beginning of the fourth century the stele of the horseman Dexileos, who died in battle at Corinth in 394 B.C., still shows references to the Parthenon frieze and the Classical compositions of the second half of the fifth century. That of the warrior Aristonautes, plastically emerging with dynamic impetus from the dark hollow of the shrine, datable in the second half of the fourth century, is more influenced by the battle groups of Lysippos. The draperies and women's heads on these steles frequently re-echo the softness of Praxiteles. The youthful bodies of athletes and huntsmen range from Praxitelean modes to those inspired by Lysippos. Sometimes the hollow, shadowy eyes in the style of Skopas strikes a more intense note of inner pain in the head of an old man or woman. These accents are always purely expressive rather than attempts at portraiture: notwithstanding the new interest in the individual and the physiognomic image, the dead person was always heroicized on these funerary steles.

The models provided by the divine effigies created by the greatest masters were imitated in votive reliefs and in the figurative panels at the top of slabs bearing decrees. The vitality of the styles created by the great masters is also attested to by their widespread re-elaboration in an infinity of craft works: small bronzes, the embossed covers of circular bronze mirrors, terracotta statuettes, engraved gems and goldsmiths' work. This varied, lively craft activity forms a rich thread running through the history of artistic developments, and provides a precious source of motifs which throw light on the complexity of the Classical world. In studying the Archaic period, since we lack information about particular artistic personalities, recourse to every manifestation of figural art is a prerequisite if we are to circumscribe and understand the various artistic currents that period. In later epochs, however, with the rise of individual great masters who created particular expressive forms, and the aid offered us by literary sources, the movements that determined the development of Classicism, can more easily attract the interest of the student to the fundamental forces directing this historical process. For our purpose, a study of the minor arts is less essential in these later periods.

9. The Great Painters and Schools of Painting of the Fourth Century

In the field of painting, while painted pottery was reaching the end of its remarkable development and falling into a decline, the first quarter of the fourth century witnessed a remarkable flourishing of full-scale painting, which can be reconstructed from literary sources and from the occasional, indirect, distant echo in Pompeian painting. Huge, complex, narrative paintings (*megalographiai*) on walls of the fifth century were succeeded by works painted on panels of wood — easel painting. The decorative and commemorative frescoes decreed by the *polis* gave way to votive pictures and works commissioned by private patrons. These were now the independent creations of painters shut up in their studios, which became intellectual meeting places, visited by monarchs and other important people. Alexander frequented the studio of Apelles, and, when he began to make blundering statements about art, the painter invited him to hold his peace, pointing out that even the boys mixing the colors were laughing at him. The same Alexander gave his favorite, Pancaspe, to Apelles, who was in love with her, so that he could paint her nude portrait. At a banquet in Alexandria Apelles could reply with his art to Ptolemy. During the siege of Rhodes in 304–305 B.C., Demetrius Poliorcetes stationed sentries around the studio of Protogenes to protect the painter, and often left military operations to watch the artist paint. King Cassander commissioned Philoxenos of Eretria to paint the battle of Alexander against Darius.

Study led to perfecting the techniques of encaustic and tempera; new varnishes and overpaintings were tried out; treatises were written on color and on the problems of composition and perspective.

The subjects of paintings, as in sculpture, show a humanized conception of the gods, a preference for genre themes, allegories, and personifications, portraits, and complex battle scenes, virtuoso perspective work, spatial illusionism, problems of lighting and color, the representation of moods and feelings, and the psychological interpretation of character.

Praxiteles' famous Cnidian Aphrodite cor-

207. Detail of the mosaic of the battle of Alexander the Great against Darius, from House of the Faun at Pompeii. The composit is derived from a painting attributed to Philo of Eretria, painted for King Cassander in the fourth century B.C. Naples, National Museum

responds to the equally celebrated Aphrodite Anadyomene rising naked from the sea, wringing out her wet hair, painted by Apelles, who had used Pancaspe as his model. The satyr of Praxiteles, the *Anapauomenus*, is a theme revived by Protogenes, whose satyr held the pipes as a symbol of serene tranquillity. Painters, like sculptors, conceived satyrs as idyllic, bucolic creatures; the Theban Aristeides painted a crowned satyr holding a *skyphos*, ready to drink; Philoxenos represented three in lascivious poses; Nikomachos depicted satyrs seducing maenads; and perhaps the so-called *Aposkopeuon* Satyr, clad in a wild animal's skin, painted by Antiphilos, an Egyptian, is to be understood as spying upon a maenad, shielding his eyes with his hand (*aposkopeuein*). Timanthes, in Gulliver fashion, showed satyrs using their staffs to measure the gigantic thumb of a sleeping Cyclops, to give an idea of the size of the protagonist of his little painting.

The athletic ideal that culminated in the work of Lysippos met with as much interest in painting, and Eupompos painted a champion with his palm; Euphranor's pupil Antidotos, who is said to have studied rhythm with more diligence than variety, painted a wrestler, a warrior with a shield, and a flautist; while Protogenes painted an athlete and Apelles a nude hero. Pliny says that with this last work Apelles had defied Nature to do better; his observation brings us back to the search for naturalism in sculpture of the period, the soft, fleshy nudes.

Among the divinities preferred by painters at this time were Aphrodite, Apollo, Artemis, Dionysus, Asclepius, and Hygieia; among the heroes, Heracles. The new conception of this hero, which was to be seen in the works of Lysippos, was also reflected in the famous painting by Apelles, which showed the hero alone and viewed from the back. He was therefore not seen in action, but remote from the spectator, perhaps in a static and isolated concentration. This rear-view position must also have provided a pretext for an illusionistic treatment of the face, turned in bold foreshortening toward the spectator.

The soft ephebi of Praxiteles may have found equivalents in the Hyacinth painted by Nikias, which was admired by Augustus and Tiberius, or in Protogenes' Ialysos, or in the boys painted by Pausias on small encaustic panels. When someone insinuated that the theme and dimensions of Pausias' pictures were dictated by the slow process of the encaustic technique, the artist replied by painting the *Hemeresios*, a picture of a boy painted in one day, proving that his own taste created the work, not the technique.

The most pathetic and romantic episodes of myth were the ones that most interested painters and sculptors. They did not choose the tragic, violent part of the action, but the moment that expressed the protagonists' feelings, the concept of the theme. In his famous picture of the sacrifice of Iphigenia, Timanthes did not aim at illustrating the cruel moment of the slaying of the virgin, but rather at illustrating the psychological gradation of feelings, from the sadness of Calchas, the melancholy of Odysseus, the lamentation of Menelaus, to Agamemnon covering his head in grief. For this work the painter won the admiration and praise of rhetoricians from the Hellenistic period to the time of Quintilian and Valerius Maximus. Timanthes' creation is reflected in the lateral figures of Agamemnon and Calchas in the sacrifice of Iphigenia, from the House of the Tragic Poet at Pompeii (fig. 205).

From echoes in a series of paintings in Pompeii and Rome we see that Nikias' painting of the liberation of Andromeda from the sea monster did not represent the culminating moment in which Perseus slew the monster, but the following episode, in which the hero helps the maiden to climb down from the rock to which she had been chained (colorplate, fig. 206). The drama has been transformed into an idyll: the hero is now an accomplished knight, the heroine a romantic, dreamy maiden. The brown tone of the hero's skin contrasts with the whiteness of the heroine's, and his red cloak with the delicate yellow and violet of the mantle worn by Andromeda. Similar interpretation was given to the painting of Io guarded by Argos, which became a mute, romantic communion between the seated girl, who is animated by a pathetic uneasiness so that she draws back her body and raises her head, and the handsome, athletic guard who seems passionately intense in his complex, Lysippan pose. The onlookers so often included in earlier narrations disappeared; all was concentrated upon the protagonists. Relationship with the spectator gave way to the exchange of feelings between the characters.

Pliny, echoing a Greek source, says that the Theban, Aristeides, painted the soul and the feelings (*animum et sensus*), which the Greeks called *ethe*, the passions of men (*perturbationes*), and he revealed in this a temperament that could be equated with that of Skopas. In Aristeides' picture of a child trying to find the breast of its wounded, dying mother in a siege scene, the woman's figure showed her sadness, and her fear that her child might suck blood instead of milk. Another painting had a supplicating figure that seemed to be speaking, most probably with the lips parted just as

208. *Polychrome pebble mosaic with the scene of a stag hunt, signed by Gnosis. Decoration of a house in Pella. First half of the third century B.C.* In situ.

Skopas, too, expressed pathos. Aristeides painted other pathetic works: one showed a girl dying for love of her brother, another, showing a sick man, was very much praised.

The search for expression and taste for the pathetic led to the choice of these elegiac, passionate, and funereal themes. But these were offset by joyful, idyllic, and calm subjects, like Pausias' Glycera weaving wreaths of flowers, known as the *Stephanoplokos*. This contrast was a characteristic of the time, stemming from the breakdown of the rigorous Classical balance. The fifth-century ideal was an absolute control over passions, an exaltation of man toward the Olympian sphere, an ethical, noble conception of life and art. But

the fourth-century ideal enjoyed showing human passions, the manifestations of every aspect of the spirit: art became the companion of life.

The personality of Alexander the Great and the tumultuous military undertakings of the time offered interest and incentive for battle scenes, in accordance with the heroic ideal which is another aspect of the spiritual climate of the period. Through the fine mosaic copy from the House of the Faun at Pompeii (colorplate, fig. 207) we can appreciate the celebrated picture, attributed to Philoxenos of Eretria, representing the battle of Alexander against Darius. We can see here the syntactical complexity, the skillful use of foreshortening, the effects of light and of relief obtained with a

229

few fundamental colors, as well as the accurate study of costumes and weapons, and, although the scene is composed on a neutral ground, the creation of spatial illusionism. This work was comparable to the battle groups by Lysippos. Aristeides of Thebes painted a battle against the Persians, with a hundred figures, for each one of which he had insisted on a contract payment of ten minas from Mnason, the tyrant of Elatea; and an equestrian battle is listed among the works of Euphranor.

The heroic ideal was offset by an interest in everyday life, and while some artists painted battles, others drew their inspiration from more humble themes. Among the latter, the most characteristic representative is Peiraikos, who gained considerable fame with his pictures of barber shops and shoemaker shops, donkeys, arrangements of food, and so on. Indeed, he was called *rhyparographos*, or the painter of humble things, though his paintings sold for higher prices than the works of the greatest masters. In the same way, Antiphilos painted the interior of a woolen mill with women at work. This was the beginning of a taste for genre pictures and still lives, which was developed during the Hellenistic period and is reflected in Roman mosaics and paintings.

With Antiphilos it seems that caricature, which previously had been only an occasional manifestation of vase painters, became a genre in itself in a type of humorous pictures known, according to Pliny, as *grylloi*. This name and its origin are still the object of discussion, and various authors have suggested either the caricature of one Gryllos, or the grotesque dance motif of Egyptian origin, known as *gryllismos*. Be that as it may, the comic, parodying, caricatural vein became fashionable in the fourth century, and a pupil of the great Apelles, Ktesilochos, made himself famous with an irreverent, burlesque work representing Zeus moaning in labor with his head bandaged and surrounded by godly midwives, as he gives birth to Dionysus. Such parodies of myth, which had already appeared on Cabiran vases in the late fifth century, became highly developed in the Hellenistic period.

In this many-sided spiritual climate, while on the one hand there was an interest in the most simple and realistic aspects of life, on the other there developed sophisticated conceptions of abstract personifications and elaborate allegories. Apelles' personifications of Thunder (*Bronte*), Lightning (*Astrape*), and the Thunderbolt (*Keraunobolia*) were perhaps based on a rich play of lighting effects. Lucian tells us that a studied gradation of colors in the faces distinguished the personifications in the allegory of Calumny, emulated by Botticelli.

Another genre that became as widespread in painting as in sculpture was the portrait. Personalities of the time were portrayed by the greatest artists: Alexander was often painted by Apelles, Protogenes, and Antiphilos; Epaminondas was painted by Aristolaos, the son of Pausias; Menander, the satrap of Caria, and King Antigonus were portrayed by Apelles; King Antigonus was also painted by Protogenes; Leontion, a female disciple of Epicurus, was painted by Aristeides and by Theoros, who also portrayed King Demetrius. To kings and princes we must add various portrait types: philosophers; men of letters; actors such as Gorgosthenes, whom Apelles painted; priests, for instance Megabyzus, portrayed by Nikias and Apelles; the Thesmothetai of Protogenes; courtesans like Pancaspe; and even self-portraits, as in the case of Apelles.

The themes of many paintings would indicate a Caravaggesque preoccupation with vivid contrasts of light and shadow, from Antiphilos' boy blowing on a fire, to Aetion's old woman carrying a lamp. Nikias, as Pliny tells us, took great care in the play of chiaroscuro (*lumen et umbras custodiit*) and aimed above all at giving his paintings a semblance of relief. In the picture of Alexander with the thunderbolt, Apelles had painted the fingers so that they seemed executed in relief, and the lightning seemed to be sparking out of the painting. Foreshortening was developed to the point of virtuosity by Apelles in his painting of Heracles seen from behind, and in his portrait of King Antigonus, whom Apelles had placed in an oblique pose, in order not to show that the king had only one eye, "so that what his body lacked should rather seem to be missing from the picture." Pausias' famous painting of an ox showed the animal from the front, yet one could still appreciate its size because the illusionistic effect of the foreshortening was accompanied by a bold inversion of light and dark in relation to the volumes — the projecting parts were not painted light to contrast with the dark shadowed hollows, but, instead, the animal was shown all black and a vivid effect of relief was obtained by breaking up the planes (*in confracto solida omnia*).

Along with the perfecting of techniques there was the minute care taken by Protogenes, who painted his Ialysos with four layers of color; the fluidity of touch, the *facilitas* of Antiphilos; and the unrivaled speed of execution in the work of Nikomachos, who finished his monument to the poet Telestes in a few days, with remarkable skill. This rapid procedure indicates a new pictorial trend, opposed to Classical tradition. The heir to this tradition in the fourth century was most outstandingly the school of Sicyon, founded by Eupompos and carried on by his pupil Pamphilos, who was learned in all the sciences, in mathematics and geometry, and who introduced the study of *graphike*, that is, of painting on wood, into the schools as one of the liberal arts. This tradition culminated later in Apelles, who, although coming from Ephesus and thus of Ionian origin, assimilated the teachings of the Sicyon school and kept himself in training with drawing exercises every day. According to the famous anecdote, worthy of Vasari, Apelles and Protogenes held a contest to see which of the two could hatch the greater number of strokes on one very fine line. In the House of Augustus on the Palatine in Rome, there was a finished painting that "contained nothing but lines that were barely visible on the surface, like a vast empty frame, placed among so many outstanding works, and for that very reason, admired and celebrated more than all the others" — an early form of abstractionism.

This tradition still held draftsmanship to be the basis of painting. A learned and scientific attitude was adopted in the study of the application of colors. And Apelles invented transparent varnishes that protected the painting like a sheet of glass and toned down colors that were too bright, creating a crystalline clarity.

On the other hand, sources tell us that greater liberty and variety characterized the Attic-Theban school of painting with Nikomachos, Philoxenos, Aristeides, and Nikias, the last of whom seems to have been the interpreter in painting of the ideals realized in sculpture by Praxiteles, to whose statues, in fact, he applied the color. Even greater vivacity distinguished the work of Ionia and Asia Minor. Between the Attic-Theban school and the school of Ionia and Asia Minor there were active contacts.

The *facilitas* of Antiphilos, the *celeritas* of Nikomachos were not simply quicker, more economical ways of painting, but the expression of having moved beyond the Classical draftsmanship and coloring, by different chromatic values that aimed at new effects of lighting, space, and illusion. Philoxenos, imitating and surpassing the speed of his master, Nikomachos, thus arrived at a summary type of painting, defined as *compendiaria*.

Notwithstanding the various interpretations of this term, it seems it should be understood as meaning a sort of painting in splashes of color, founded less on *perigraphe*, that is, on outline and drawing, and more on the free, unconstrained combination of colors. Petronius attributes this invention to Egyptian audacity, and the Alexandrian painter in this period, Antiphilos, fits well with these interests and

experiments in lighting and abridged statement.

Precious echoes of the themes, compositions, and effects of pure painting of the fourth century and early Hellenistic period are to be found in the mosaics of small, multicolored pebbles, which had first appeared in the fifth century and now enjoyed particular popularity, showing remarkable technical and artistic advances. Specimens found in Olympia, Olynthus, Sicyon, Corinth, and most of all in Pella, the birthplace of Alexander the Great, display a rich repertory of geometrical ornament, palmettes, bunches of grapes, tendrils, and flowers in the borders of the large central panels which contained animals, hunting scenes, duels, Amazonomachies, and characters from myth and legend such as Theseus and Helen.

In these mosaics fine strips of lead were used to define some outlines and details, and a studied, precise choice of the various shades of the few fundamental colors found among the pebbles, along with a complex over-all texture, enabled mosaicists to achieve striking pictorial results. The rather linear style of the earlier mosaics gave way to fully shaded, vividly plastic works, which rivaled contemporary painting. The dark blue-gray tone in the background of the figured scenes bears witness to their inspiration from painting.

The scene of the stag hunt, with the animal attacked by a dog and falling under the blows struck by two athletic huntsmen, found at Pella, is signed by the mosaicist Gnosis. This mosaic is the equal of any painting in the richness of its effects (fig. 208). The minute, naturally smoothed and rounded stones of these mosaics create a warm, shaded, impressionistic tone, like a sort of pointillist painting. In the third century B.C., however, the introduction of small marble cubes (*tesserae*), artificially cut to shape, led to the creation of the new type of tessellated mosaic, which permitted a sharper and more complex pictorial effect, a more extensive chromatic range, and a more minute gradation of tones. This technique culminated in the virtuosity of the *emblema vermiculatum*, that is, the picture composed of very tiny cubes of marble which followed the chromatic structure of the image, and vied with easel painting to become true painting in marble.

10. The Decline of Attic Vase Painting

Faced with the richness of expressive means used in painting, the decorative resources used in Athenian painted pottery must have seemed increasingly unsatisfactory and outdated. The crisis in this art, already hinted

209. *Detail of a monumental Apulian volute-krater by the Lycurgus Painter. A warrior scene of vivacious Italic taste is seen within the architectural setting of an Ionic heroön.* Circa *350 B.C. Vatican Museums*

at in the second half of the fifth century, became profound and led to its final decline in about the period of the death of Alexander the Great. Already in the late fifth century, the aphrodisiac and mannered world of the Meidias Painter, and the somewhat more Classical repertory but with delicate youths and flowing outlines of the Deinos Painter, had ushered in a little of the artistic atmosphere of the fourth century. While the style of the Meidias Painter, as happens to every form of mannerism, was becoming exhausted, it was easier for the modes represented by the Deinos Painter to survive into the first part of the fourth century, and one of the most characteristic representatives of this development is the

Jena Painter. Vase painters took their inspiration from the same mythological world expressed in the major arts. The dominant themes were those of Aphrodite, Apollo, Dionysus, the Eleusinian divinities, Heracles, the garden of the Hesperides, Thetis surprised by Peleus, banquets, and scenes of women's apartments and the palaestra. As in contemporary sculpture and painting, the figures take on supple, sinuous rhythms like those of Praxiteles, or slender elastic forms like those of Lysippos; profile heads are replaced by foreshortened or perspective views; fluid, curvilinear poses of the figures seem to follow the progressively more curving lines of the vases. Vase painters attempted to imitate the drapery

210. *Fragment of a Paestan calyx-krater by the painter Assteas. The scene is a parody showing a fierce and frightened Ajax clinging to the image of Pallas Athena and hotly pursued by an ugly and shrewish Cassandra, while the female sacristan of the sanctuary looks on in horror.* Circa 350 B.C. Rome, Villa Giulia

211. *Paestan calyx-krater by Assteas with a phlyax scene representing the young Gymnilus and Cosilus who try to pull the old miser Charinus off his safe, while the servant Carion looks on. The scene is shown on a stage.* Circa 350 B.C. Berlin, State Museums

212. *Fragment of a krater with a phlyax scene showing a sprightly old man before a door. In the style of Assteas. Mid-fourth century* B.C. Gela, Museum

effects of the great masters with fine, broken lines, ornamental elements, elaborate gathers, and the appearance of lightness and transparency. Among the dominant vase forms were the *pelike*, with a longer neck and a rim that is expanded to correspond to the widest diameter of the body, the *lekanis*, the aryballoid *lekythos*, the *hydria*, and the volute-krater and calyx-krater. The transformation of vase shapes tended toward a studied elegance and grace with accentuated curves.

Full-scale painting had definitely shown the possibilities of perspective, illusionistic and spatial experiment, and effects of lighting and relief to be obtained by the play of colors. Vase painters tried to approach this pictorial vision by arranging their figures on several planes, crowding their scenes, and inserting architectural motifs in the distance. But they could not achieve true spatial and perspective solutions without destroying the very nature of vase decoration. They tried to imitate illusionist relief effects, making wider use of diluted glazes, using white with yellow and brown touches for the main protagonists of the scenes, like Aphrodite and Eros, or Thalos, so that they stand out within the limited means of vase decoration. The resulting conventional compromise conveys the intrinsic impossibility of vying with pure painting.

The final stage in this process was the attempt at modeling figures in relief on vases, perhaps in imitation of either relief sculptures or vases of beaten and engraved precious metals. A vase reproducing the contest between Athena and Poseidon, inspired by the west pediment of the Parthenon, presents only the two figures of the protagonists in relief, but the vase painter Xenophantos modeled all the figures in relief on two aryballoid *lekythoi* from Kerch. Greek colonies in the Crimea represented an important outlet for Attic pottery in the fourth century, and even attracted emigrant Attic potters. And, indeed, a whole class of Attic pottery, among the most characteristic of the fourth century, is given the name of Kerch vases. Because of these new contacts, new themes appeared in the decorative repertory, for instance, griffins and Arimaspians. Xenophantos covered the entire surfaces of his *lekythoi* with hunting scenes of Persians, arranged on several planes among palm trees and executed in polychrome relief.

The progressive formal decline can be traced down to the summary, unorganic sketches that can be seen, for example, in the long-hallowed motif from Classical tradition of three nude or draped youths that were used during the fourth century with monotonous regularity to decorate the backs of many vases. Such figures are a clear demonstration of the exhaustion of this vase-painting style, despite pictorial and plastic experiment seen in the more important scenes executed by the vase painters.

In the last quarter of the fourth century, figural decoration, which had made its appearance in the Dipylon style in the eighth century B.C., disappeared after five centuries of brilliant development. Athenian vase painters gave up trying to make their pots into works of art, and limited themselves instead to tectonic and structural values, glazing the entire surface in shiny black, a traditional type of work which until then had played a secondary role by comparison with figured decoration. The forms were more noticeably influenced by those of metalwork, which the shiny, one-tone effect of the black glaze also imitated. A type of pottery of rather heavy shapes and using a black ground, and known as West Slope ware from a site facing the Acropolis in Athens — although examples have been found also in Corinth, Asia Minor, and southern Russia — developed from the end of the fourth to the first century B.C. The upper part of the vase had a decoration in white and yellow of floral motifs of ivy, laurel, vines, and buds, and geometric ornament of checkers and rectangles. But this production never went beyond the level of a modest craft.

11. The Flowering of Italiot Vase Painting

Within the context of the diffusion and developments of the Classical ideal through the ancient world, in the field of vase painting the results of the grafting of the Attic style onto the native Italic tradition in Magna Graecia, at the end of the fifth century B.C., offers special interest. After the first, strongly Atticized manifestations from the workshops of Apulia and Lucania, with the increasingly rare importation of Attic pottery into Italy, the Italiot spirit emerged and developed a very rich ceramic production in Apulia, Lucania, Campania, as well as in Sicily. The repetition of ornamental elements and shapes of vases has made it easy to distinguish a whole series of painters and stylistic groups.

This could be considered a variant on a provincial level of Attic vase painting, since the greater part of the themes, techniques, and models that inspired it were Greek. But the similarities are less significant than the differences, which constitute the original, authentic expression of Hellenized Italiot culture. Indigenous characteristics are shown, for example, in a whole series of large vases evidenc-

213. *Wall painting from a chamber tomb at Paestum with two gladiators in combat. Third century* B.C. *Paestum, Museum*

ing a retarded interest in the language of Polygnotos, in a vast repertory drawn from Classical mythology, and in themes manifestly influenced by the great tragedians of the fifth century. This monumental trend expresses itself in large volute-kraters and enormous amphorae, and develops through the work of the Sarpedon Painter, the Painter of the Birth of Dionysus, the Iliupersis Painter, and Lycurgus Painter, culminating in the most mature and important of these personalities, the Darius Painter. His monumental volute-krater at Naples, executed about 325 B.C., with the entire Persian court represented on three registers, along with personifications and divinities, and other kraters by this same painter showing the sacrifice of Trojan warriors, the myth of Medea, and the Land of the Dead, are expressions of the luxuriant, exuberant

flowering of the Greek seed on Italic soil, while Attic vase painting was reaching its end.

Alongside the series of vases with mythological scenes was a very large series of Apulian vases, generally smaller in size, which bear a repertory of generic figures of the Dionysiac world such as satyrs, maenads, women initiates into the cult of the god, youths, erotic figures, warriors, and scenes of offering and cult at the sepulcher, with the funerary heroön at the center of the composition (fig. 209).

Myths also abound in the Lucanian production; often depicted were Heracles and Busiris, episodes from the cycle of Heracles, the madness of Lycurgus, the daughters of Proetus, and Dionysiac scenes. Popular also were themes that derived from the theater and particularly those from the Orestes cycle, as in the work of the Coephoroe Painter, who repeated several times the meeting of Orestes and Electra at the tomb of Agamemnon; genre scenes; couples in conversation; offering and cult scenes; scenes of women's quarters.

The Apulian style shows many influences and derivations, as in the work of the Primato Painter, the most important and prolific vase painter, to whom about one hundred and fifty vases are attributed, including some on a monumental scale. He had a preference for flying erotes, palm boughs, and birds. Ninety vases have been assigned to the Naples 1959 Painter, who treated figures of women and youths. A hundred or so vases are given to the Roccanuova Painter, active until about 320 B.C., who did not treat myths, but preferred generic figures of youths and women.

Myth, even if often freely interpreted, was treated on Campanian vases, and especially in the oldest group centered around the Capua workshops with the Cassandra Painter, the Capua Painter, and the Ixion Painter. The centers of Avella and Cumae, on the other hand, used the usual repertory: couples in conversation; scenes of funerary rites; Dionysiac scenes; figures of warriors wearing the costumes and arms of the Oscans, with feathers at the sides of the helmet and cuirasses with circular plates and belts; as well as female figures and softly modeled youths.

The Apulian and Lucanian monumental style arrives at remarkably fine detail and elaborate drawing, but the great mass of Italiot production is characterized by a diminishingly organic treatment of forms and body structure. Facial profiles lose their Greek line to take on an unmistakable Italic look, pointed or chubby in form and with astonished or overemphatic expressions. Drapery becomes progressively far removed from Hellenic rigor, and assumes forced, mannered, eccentric forms and ostentatious ornament. The exuberant, decorative, provincial taste is translated into an abundance of fill-in motifs, objects, animals, floral elements, twigs, wreaths, and dotted lines, which spread over the ground between the figures. The most characteristic expression of this Italiot taste for ornament is perhaps the floral trellis formed of wavy stems with numerous tendrils, generally twisted into corkscrew spirals enlivened with buds, flowers, corollas, palmettes, and dentate leaves, in complex flourishes and arabesques that spread over the necks of vases, often framing a woman's head seen in three-quarter view or full face, or over the inside of a dish. Other elaborate compositions of palmettes and tendrils spread out under the handles. From the fluidity, the showy elegance, the care taken over detail in these floral flourishes, one realizes that they constituted

the most important element for these vase painters. Even the motif of the male or female head, which recurs often in Italic vase painting, and also in the work of Etruria and the upper Adriatic, is found in Greece only during the Archaic period. It is an indication of the provincial taste for abstracting the human figure from its mythological or narrative context and turning it into an ornamental motif, a cipher, a decorative symbol like a floral motif. In later Apulian and Campanian production, most of all in Etruria and the upper Adriatic, graphic disorganization, progresses toward abstraction.

In tune with the lively Mediterranean and Italiot climate are the attractive plates with a central depression and a reversed rim, all decorated with various sorts of fish drawn with vivid naturalism, very widespread in late Apulian and Campanian production. Though the inspiration for this type may have come from Attica, the conception is purely local.

The most colorful, original expression of the Italiot climate in vase production, however, is the series of about a hundred and fifty phlyax vases with motifs inspired by popular comedies, the *phlyaxes*. These vases were produced mostly in workshops of Apulia and Paestum, Campania, and Sicily (figs. 210–212). Forms included bell-shaped kraters and calyx-kraters, as well as *skyphoi* and *oinochoai*. In this field too, though precedents, albeit rare, do exist in Greece at the end of the fifth and the beginning of the fourth centuries, the richness of the products, the novelty of the themes, the fresh, spontaneous, inexhaustible vein of humor and farce that animate these vases bear witness to their originality, and evidence a spirit congenial to the native temperament. Mythological parodies, adventures of Heracles, misadventures of Zeus, all the themes of slaves and old men, courtesans and parasites, market places and banquets, thieves and beatings, that comprise the substance of comedy and farce, and the comic actors with padded costumes, wigs, and the masks typical of the popular Italic theater, are represented on the vases.

Humor as well as the comedy thus lead to a highly expressive language of caricature, representing a colorful interlude in the rigorous counterpoint of the Classical concert. The Greeks' rational study of rhythm is countered by the more carefree gesticulation, and their organic structure by the most extreme deformation. Wittily abnormal masks are created, with tousled hair, wagging beards, winking eyes, hooked or snub noses, acutely arched eyebrows, with the most fiery, free expressionism. The typically beautiful is opposed by the individualized and ugly. Assteas and Py-

214. Wall painting from a tomb at Ruvo with a chain dance of veiled women winding around the deceased, their costumes painted in an alternation of bright colors. Second half of the fourth century B.C. Naples, National Museum

thon, vase painters of Paestum, were the most sophisticated, witty exponents of this trend.

Attic vase painters of the fourth century had tried to make their principal figures and details stand out by using a white pigment; the Italiots, whose technique was less bound by tradition, let themselves go with the most vivid polychromy, using white and yellow, red and brown, and in the later Campanian pottery, pink, peacock, and a light greenish-blue. They used white with varied retouching for funerary shrines, architectural elements, and for women's skin, with details in yellow, but they also made lavish use of polychromy for all the figures, filling motifs, and floral trellises, in a somewhat heavy taste, but bright, eye-catching, gay, and typically Italic. Vase decoration was conceived in wholly chromatic, pictorial terms; draftsmanship as the supreme criterion was a thing

of the past. This trend culminated in Siceliot production, especially in the work of the Lipari Painter and his circle, with about a hundred vases datable between 320–300 B.C. These include *pyxides, lekanai,* nuptial *lebetes,* and *lekythoi,* with a whole repertory of scenes of women's quarters, with the bride's toilet, Nikai, isolated female heads, vine trellises, and other floral elements. This pictorial conception is very different from that of Attic vase painters, who had created the polychrome *lekythoi* in the second half of the fifth century, using a white background and maintaining rigorous draftsmanship highlighted by a discreet range of delicate colors. In Italiot and Siceliot vase painting there is a vivid palette ranging over white, yellow, and red, generously applied sky-blue, orange, and green, extending over the black background with a development of

is often more refined. This Italic production of the fourth century arrives at a felicitous expression sprung from the Classical root and often marked by a fluidity of technique.

12. Italiot Funerary Wall Painting

Lucania and Campania in the fourth century present also a rare and precious body of wall painting (colorplates, figs. 213, 214). This work formed the decoration of tombs constructed of rectangular blocks of cut stone, often with pointed roofs. The colors were applied in fresco technique on a thin layer of white plaster and were usually limited to black, red, and yellow, with figures in outline, the bare parts of the bodies left in the light ground color with some thin overpainting. The walls

the red-figure technique that transforms graphic values into a chromatic effect of splashes of color that Attic vase painters had never attained.

Even in the Italiot vases, however, one feels the exhaustion of this decorative style, and, while figured ornamentation lasted longer here than in Greece, toward the middle of the fourth century a new development appeared, which was to continue through the third century: the creation of vases entirely covered with a shiny black glaze in refined shapes imitating metalwork, known as Gnathia ware. The principal center of production was perhaps Taranto. Even in this work Italiot taste was less sober than Greek, and did not renounce decorating the vases with some overpainted ornament in cream or white with polychrome touches, representing flowering sprigs, vine leaves, small objects, and little figures of erotes, maenads, satyrs, animals, and masks. This decoration resembled gold appliqués or inlaid or embossed friezes on bronze vases. Gnathia ware finds a parallel in Greek pottery in the so-called West Slope ware, but Gnathia ware

of the tomb usually had a dado painted in red with wavy black lines separating it from the figured scene above. The figure scene was framed at the top with parallel lines in red, stylized olive branches, and *kymatia*. The triangles created in the short sides by the sloping roof were decorated with a large palmette. On the long sides we most often find biga races and contests between pugilists or gladiators, which are to be interpreted as games in honor of the dead man; on the short sides, scenes of relatives with the dead man, whom we see returning victorious from the wars, or else in his chariot on the journey to Hades, or lying in state, often lamented by weeping women, or in the case of a woman, enthroned, with her maids, in the process of dressing her hair or contemplating her reflection in a mirror. We can trace reminiscences of Greek compositions in the chariot races, duels, and in the groups which recall Attic funerary steles, but the flavor of these paintings remains authentically Italic. In fact, there is an Italic ring to these naïve race scenes scanned with Ionic columns, with the two horses prominently painted, the nearer in black, the farther in yellow; in the gestures of the weeping women in their red costumes; in the plump, common faces of the bejeweled deceased women; in their costumes with the turban and veil, as well as in the showy details, and the great yellow *kalathoi* decorated just like works of the local craftsmen; and above all, in the warriors and gladiators.

The warriors are described with care in their costumes and offer interesting documentation on the Oscan and Samnite armies. They return victoriously on horseback or on foot, carrying the decorated, bloodstained tunics of their defeated enemies hung on lances as standards, along with pieces of armor attached to their spears, like trophies from some lethal hunting party. They advance proud, pompous, and be-plumed, sometimes preceded by the standard-bearer with the gaudy banner, making live again the processions of the Campanians after their victories over the Samnites. A cruel Italic realism appears in the ferocious combats of gladiators, the bleeding wounds inflicted by javelins thrown from a distance, and the close fighting of the duel (colorplate, fig. 213). Pathetic notes underline the dying or fallen gladiators, or a horseman carrying his dead comrade over his shoulder, the lifeless head hanging down. In many murals pomegranates are seen hanging in the background of the paintings, giving the scenes a clearly funerary significance.

The Etruscan expansion in Campania during the sixth century and the analogies with Etruscan tomb painting have generally led scholars to consider the tombs of Paestum, Capua, and other centers of Magna Graecia as creations influenced and suggested by the Etruscan tradition in painting. But apart from the chariot races, the thematic material of Campanian paintings is quite unlike that found in Etruria, and the style is profoundly different. The inspiration instead emanates from the Greek world, and one of the oldest paintings of this region, with two figures playing checkers, and also the typical *prothesis* scenes, show themselves clearly derived from Greek

217. *Detail of the wall painting from the François Tomb at Vulci. The Etruscan artist has struck a spontaneous and realistic note in this small, fat man with a bird. Third century* B.C. *Rome, Torlonia Collection*

vases. Taste and style link these works closely to the painted pottery of Apulia, Lucania, and Campania, in which one also finds the typical warrior figures. These funerary paintings are thus a manifestation of Italiot artistic culture.

13. Italiot and Etruscan Reactions to Greek Artistic Trends of the Fourth Century

The influence of the great Greek masters of the fourth century endowed the figured terracottas of Sicily and Magna Graecia with a new tenderness of tone and softness of modeling. A particularly rich series is presented by the terracottas of Taranto. In female heads we most often find the characteristic traits of Praxiteles, for these had a great appeal and, indeed, had become international. An original re-elaboration of Greek styles is to be found in the sculptured friezes of soft stone from Taranto (fig. 216), used to decorate tombs. The ease with which this stone could be carved led to a freedom of expression and effects, with strong, sharp hollows, piercing,

218. Lid of a sarcophagus from Vulci with the deceased husband and wife embracing in the sleep of death, shown as on a bed with a cover. First half of the third century B.C. Boston, Museum of Fine Arts

219. Lid of a sarcophagus from Caere with the deceased laid out with a crown, wearing a necklace and bracelet decorated with bullae, and holding a libation bowl in his right hand. Late fifth to early fourth century B.C. Vatican, Museo Gregoriano

220. *Faliscan volute-krater attributed to the Aurora Painter, with a scene of the rape of Thetis by a stocky Peleus. In his haste Peleus overturns a cist with toilet articles and terrifies the maids.*
Fourth century B.C. *Rome, Villa Giulia*

and incision, and the rich modeling that pleased provincial taste. In the Italic vision we can also recognize echoes of post-Phidian mannerism in some female figures, as well as elements from Attic funerary steles. The modes of Skopas and Lysippos can be seen in the frequent combat scenes. Later, the accents of the Hellenistic baroque are traceable in third-century reliefs of an eclectic, highly colored, expressive language. There are purer accents in the field of metalwork, Tarantine and

Campanian bronzes, and in silver and gold work with vigorous lion masks decorating bracelets, earrings, and necklaces, with tiny women's heads in the pendants of earrings with filigree rosettes. Particularly fine execution is to be seen in the magnificent gold rings with engraved, elliptical settings, produced mostly in Taranto and in other centers of Magna Graecia. Dominant themes in these works are graceful female figures, sometimes of a type derived from the style of the Meidias Painter, shown seated playing with a small bird, or standing and leaning in sinuous, muse-like poses, dancing so that their short skirts swirl out, crouched for the bath, standing or kneeling as Nikai, or perhaps in the isolated portrait head. More rare are the mythological motifs of Perseus or Odysseus.

A refined Hellenic language is conserved in the coinage of Sicily and Magna Graecia, in the types and styles used, and in the fineness of the engraving, which after the splendid flowering of the fifth century (fig. 170) continue to represent the most pure and perfect expression of Classical culture on Italic soil.

In Etruscan territory too, influences from the Severe and Phidian styles which had persisted were replaced by those of the Greek masters of the fourth century. But the political and economic decline that began with the capture of Veii by the Romans in 396 B.C., and the progressive loss of dominion of the seas, slowed down the Etruscan contacts with Greece, so that Hellenic influences became more sporadic and less intense, giving a more varied and multiform character to Etruscan production. The difference between works created by more cultivated artists, with a closer adherence to Greek models, and works expressing the local, popular taste, became more pronounced. The progressive decrease of imported painted pottery from Attica interrupted one of the principal sources of experience with Greek works. At the same time, intermediary Hellenizing influences became stronger through a greater familiarity with works from Magna Graecia. This is proved, for example, by a group of Etruscan red-figure vases, termed "Campanianizing" because of their clear dependence on Campanian models. Yet, other Etruscan red-figure vases, as for example, *kylixes* and kraters from Vulci, demonstrate the strongly provincial elaboration of Attic themes and styles, with a reduction of highly traditional motifs into cursive, narrative forms. The major part of Etruscan vase production surrendered, however, with greater freedom to native taste and conceptions. This can be seen in the series of kraters made in Volterra, exported also to Perugia, and in the closely related series of

241

221. Detail of the Ficoroni cist with the ship the Argo *on which one* Argonaut *is sleeping, two others are seated, and a fourth descends the ladder, following an iconographic motif which goes back to the painting of Polygnotos. Second half of the fourth century* B.C. *Rome, Villa Giulia*

kylixes attributed to Chiusi or Volterra, in which Greek myths became Etruscanized and a local repertory made its appearance. Figures lost their organic structure and fluidity for more eye-catching solidity; women became loaded with overpainted jewelry and adopted Etruscan costumes; drapery was enriched with heavy, striped hems and ornament; palmettes, triangles, and large pointed leaves alike were all filled with hatching. This was a draftsmanly style, cursive and linear, enlivened with details added in white or yellow, and a fine hatching emphasized all the figures. The aim was a showy effect whose best representative was the Hesion Painter.

The grand pictorial tradition in Tarquinia seems to have weakened during the fourth century, at least so we must assume from the rare examples that have been found to date, and certainly Etruscan prosperity must have suffered a severe blow with the struggle begun by Rome for the progressive conquest of Etruria. The first and oldest chamber of the fourth-century Orco Tomb nonetheless preserves for us the fine fragment with a head of a lady of the Velcha family, seated on a bench. This was drawn by a hand still pure and certain, with reminiscences of the Severe style, to which Etruscan artists always turned when aiming at an effect of nobility. The head of this woman with the curl of her full lips is shown as if veiled by a shadow of sadness, thus contrasting with the joyous tone of Ionic-influenced paintings. She seems instead in harmony with the popular conception of the dark Land of the Dead, peopled by Lasae, Charun, Tuchulcha, and other infernal demons, who now figured in Etruscan funerary scenes. Even the banquet no longer takes place in the open air among flowery branches and festoons, but has been pushed into the shadowy recesses of the Underworld dominated by the gods of death. But in Orvieto the traditional motif of the banquet in the Land of the Dead finds a colorful amplification with the slaves busying themselves in the kitchen, and the pantry where game and quartered oxen are hung with a naturalism typically Etruscan.

Hellenic pictorial influences are attested at Tarquinia in the fine marble sarcophagus with an Amazonomachy accurately painted on its four sides, in a language of notable purity that has led many to think of a Tarantine artist, while others would have it attributed to an Etruscan. It is an attentive imitation of the pictorial models supplied by great painting, with accurate drawing and a rich chromatic scale. The high level of the model, however, makes one feel only more acutely the lack of spontaneity in this provincial imitation.

In the other important center, Vulci, the François Tomb (fig. 217) with the famous pictures of the sacrifice of Trojan prisoners shows us an interesting Etruscanization of noble Greek motifs, with the insertion of Etruscan figures like the winged spirit Vanth, and the horrible griffin Charun, while the general pathos and studied chiaroscuro in the figures point to

fourth-century stylistic models. Since the elements of this scene reappear in works of other Etruscan crafts, it has been thought that they were elaborated in a painting executed by a Hellenized Etruscan artist in some Etruscan city, which could originally have inspired the tomb decoration. The scenes from local history with the tragic struggle of the Etruscans, Vibenna and Mastarna, against the Tarquins of Rome are more mechanically subdivided into pairs, so that the traditional battle compositions, although losing in organic form, acquire more realistic accents and expressive effects.

The art of terracotta modeling, especially in antefixes and pedimental statues, shows a conventional, facile assimilation of the fundamental Hellenic styles. In more important works it arrives at an effective strength in modeling, as in the monmuental group of winged horses from the great temple of Tarquinia. Sculpture in stone acquires greater significance and originality, especially in the sarcophagi produced at Caere, Tarquinia, and Vulci. These works are typified by the hieratic figure of a bearded, cloaked magistrate on the lid of a sarcophagus in the Vatican, which still shows traits of the Severe style in the noble, incisive, linear head

222. Bust of a bearded man identified as a copy of the portrait of Pythagoras set up in the Roman Forum in 343 B.C. The original was probably created by an Etrusco-Italic artist. Ostia, Museum

243

(fig. 219); or by the reclining couple in an embrace of eternal sleep on the sarcophagus from Vulci, where the woman's head is an imitation of Greek types, while the husband's is more Etruscan and expressive, with his sadly curled lips and the naturalistic, unadorned cap of smooth, striated hair (fig. 218).

In Etruscan sarcophagi, when the defunct is lying on the lid he is always represented as if lying on a bed. In similar Punic sarcophagi from Carthage, the defunct is imagined as a standing statue with base, now laid on its back on the lid of the sarcophagus. Furthermore, the lid is not flat, but in the form of a pitched roof. Although Greek influence is felt in the figures, the conception of the whole is far from the organic Classical spirit.

In the area that runs from Falerii to Praeneste, that is, to the north and to the south of Rome, there was a wider and deeper acceptance of Hellenic influences, even though the greater part of these influences passed through Magna Graecia. This was perhaps because the Etruscan element in this more southerly environment was less deep-rooted and dominant. The Faliscan area produced painted pottery which, especially in the works of the earlier painters, such as the Aurora Painter (fig. 220), who depicted the myths of Eos and Cephalus, Peleus and Thetis, Leda and the swan, and Aphrodite and Adonis, attained outstanding elegance and fluidity. But even when forms took on a more provincial tone, as in kraters with the *Iliupersis* or in the characteristic Dionysiac cups with Faliscan inscriptions inviting one to drink, or in later vases with little female figures overpainted in white, the taste is still closer to the Italiot taste of Apulian and Campanian vases, than to the true Etruscan. This greater correspondence between the Faliscan environment and Hellenic conceptions is also evident in the fine terracottas of the third century from the Scasato Temple at Falerii, with stylistic elements from the Greek masters of the fourth century and the early Hellenistic period.

In the fourth century Praeneste, though Etruscan-influenced, showed closer adherence to Greek forms, as is demonstrated particularly well by the bronze cists which were used to hold women's toilet articles, a characteristic product of the highly developed local craft. The lid and cylinder that formed the body were decorated with fine engraving, as were Etruscan mirrors, while the handles and feet, often in the form of statuettes, were cast separately. The masterpiece among these works, the celebrated Ficoroni cist in the Villa Giulia (fig. 221), graphically translates the Greek pictorial composition of the landing of the Argonauts in the land of the Bebryces. With its

223. Limestone statue of an offering bearer, known as the Gran Dama. *Iberian art of monumental stature and coordinated compositional language. From the group of statues of Cerro de los Santos. Fourth century* B.C. *Madrid, Archaeological Museum*

224. Detail of the so-called Dama de Elche. *The exceptional quality of this work evidences its greater dependence on coherent Hellenic form and models of the Severe style. Fourth century* B.C. *Madrid, Prado Museum*

244

typical fourth-century Greek syntactical and stylistic elements, it is to be thought of in terms of a taste analogous to that of the most Attic-influenced Apulian vases. The signature tells us that it was made, not in Praeneste, but in Rome, by the artist Novius Plautius, for Dindia Macolnia as a gift for her daughter. The gold fibula, of an Etruscan type, found at Praeneste, dating from the seventh century B.C., has an archaic Latin inscription stating that it was made by a certain Manius for one Numerius. It could be that Novius Plautius was a Romanized Campanian artist; certainly the principal stream of Hellenic art in this part of Latium flowed from Magna Graecia.

14. Art in Rome During the First Republican Period

Although Rome lay in the Faliscan-Praenestine cultural area, and was the center for workshops like that of Novius Plautius, and perhaps also for potters, the city still could not provide an atmosphere suitable for the rise of indigenous works of art, and depended on Etruscan and Campanian artists for decorating temples, for furnishings, and votive statues.

Their strenuous struggles against the Etruscans, Volsci, Equi, Gauls, and Samnites left the Romans no leisure to cultivate the delights of the arts. "The ancient Romans," said Strabo, "cared nothing for beauty, for they were too taken up with greater, more necessary things." Even the works of art plundered from conquered centers of a higher cultural level were considered not as luxury objects, but as votive offerings to be dedicated to the gods. When in 396 B.C. Camillus captured and sacked Veii, the Romans, in the words of Livy, "began to carry off the sacred offerings and statues of the gods more as believers than as robbers," and when Camillus, deviating from this behavior, decorated the doors of his own house with bronze panels taken perhaps from Veii, he was accused of a crime by Spurius Carvilius. Thus it was that Titus Quintius dedicated on the Capitoline the statue of Jupiter he had carried off from Praeneste in 380 B.C.

The Roman house was still simple and poorly equipped. Customs were frugal, the images of the Lares still rough, and tombs were modest, bearing only inscriptions. The *Lapis Niger*, which was thought to be the tomb of Romulus, in the Forum, is a simple altar with ante placed on podia of expansive, curvilinear, archaic forms. The ante perhaps once supported two lions. Other architectural works, walls, bridges, terraces, podia, canals, and cisterns, were purely functional. Only in the temples of

the gods, which were multiplying in Rome, were any concessions made to art. These temples were still in the Etruscan-Italic style with stone podia and polychrome terracotta decoration. Another concession, indicative of the Roman mentality of the time, was made for statues honoring and celebrating historical personages or distinguished citizens. Tradition refers these statues to an earlier period, but they were erected from the fourth century on, in the Forum and in the most sacred and prominent places.

Rome, coming into contact with peoples of a higher degree of civilization, now felt the need to show her own titles of glory before the people she had conquered. Etruscan artists probably received the commissions for the statues of the kings, of Titus Tatius, Horatius Cocles, Mucius Scaevola, Clelia on horseback, Tanaquil, the vestal Gaia Taratia, Tarpeia, the Three Sibyls, Junius Brutus, and the ambassadors of Veii slain by the Fidenates. To these figures were later added statues erected by the descendants of the *gentes* to their illustrious founding fathers, in accordance with a usage that was to last through the entire Republican period, with the equestrian statues of Furius Camillus, Gaius Menius, and Marcius Tremulus, and the figures of Lucius Caecilius Metellus, Publius Junius, and Tiberius Coruncanius.

Commemorative portraiture was, indeed, to be the most truly Roman artistic expression. It was the first to be treated, and was to remain, along with the historical relief, the most elevated and significant aspect of Roman art. Though the rustic Rome of this first Republican period was not yet attracted by the fascination of Greek art and the names of great artists, the Romans nonetheless looked admiringly on the brilliant Greek thinkers and politicians. Proof of this is the erection, justified by consultation with the Delphic oracle, of statues of Pythagoras and Alcibiades, the wisest and the strongest of the Greeks, on either side of the Comitium in the Forum, in 343 B.C., during the Samnite War. If the small bust from Ostia, from the period of Caesar (fig. 222), is a possible echo of the portrait of Pythagoras, then these bronze, re-created portraits of philosopher and statesman were perhaps the work of Etruscan artists. In the bust from Ostia, the Severe touch used in hair and beard, the string-like eyebrows, the rough, linear taste recalling the bearded head of the Caere sarcophagus (fig. 219), all point to Etruscan work.

225. Fragment of a vase decorated in the Iberian style. From Elche. Third century B.C. Madrid, Archaeological Museum

The rough, vigorous language of the Republican period was perhaps expressed in the simple images stamped on the *aes grave*, the bronze libral standard and its fractions, which showed heads of deities and prows of ships, symbols of Rome's rising naval power, that would soon control the Mediterranean and thus have direct contact with Greek civilization.

15. The Influence of Classical Art in the Celtic-Iberian Area

In the more westerly provincial setting of the Iberian area, Hellenic artistic influence began to play a larger role and give new dignity to local sculpture, which was still executed in limestone or terracotta. Phoenician works, such as the Cathaginian sarcophagus from Punta de la Vaca, now in the Cadiz Museum, show inspiration from Greek types: the solemn, bearded head on the sarcophagus, though probably dating from the fourth century, recalls archaizing models like the Hermes Propylaios of Alkamenes. Clear influences from Magna Graecia are discernible in sculpture, especially in terracotta. Above all, some limestone sculptures, stimulated by Hellenic work, attained a vigorous, expressive language, though they are still far removed from the measured, organic rigor of Greek creations. The group of sculptures from the sanctuary of Cerro de los Santos is particularly interesting. Some pieces date from the Hellenistic and Roman periods, but others indicate a flourishing activity that can be set in the fourth century: datable perhaps in the fourth century is the *Gran Dama*, 4′ 6″ high, which is the most elaborate work of this group (fig. 223). The sculptor contrived to express a sense of hieratic solemnity in this rigid figure, shown offering a vase which she holds in both hands. The drapery is composed with a lively architectonic and decorative sense, framing the figure in the rhythmic cadences of the descending hems of the mantle in symmetrical zigzag folds that are echoed in the smaller pointed tucks seen below the hands. The drapery is further elaborated by incising, and the figure wears lavish jewels, necklaces, and pendants. The motif of a female offering-bearer is repeated in some statuettes, which find a certain modest expressive logic in the lines of their drapery folds schematized into geometrical formulas. The finest creation, which is surely to be ascribed to Hellenic inspiration, remains the well-known bust of the *Dama de Elche* (fig. 224), which has been variously dated, but probably belongs to the fourth century. This Iberian princess, whose body must also have been punctuated rhythmically with folds zigzagging down the mantle

in which she was swathed, shows a fascinating delicacy in the fine features of her face, Hellenic in its grace. This is emphasized by the contrast with the exotic splendor of her diadem and the enormous wheel-shaped ornaments she wears, in addition to the pendants and the triple necklace that form a striking frame about her head, like an idol overloaded with jewels. Jewels were also used profusely in Phoenician clay statuettes of women, and indeed constituted the principal interest of the clay-modelers, who molded them in great detail with strong chiaroscuro effects, along with the decoration of floral and plant forms in women's garments. Similarly these clay-modelers could draw particular effects from beards and thick, coloristically rendered hair of male figures, though bodies remained schematic and unorganic. Iberian bronzes, too, present warriors and donors in forms that are virtually always summary and modest, and only attain more colorful notes in the compact forms of figurines of women wrapped in their mantles, or in the occasional lively gesture of a warrior.

The fourth century perhaps marks the greatest flowering of Iberian painted pottery (color-plate, fig. 225), which also continues through the Hellenistic period. In the various regional styles of Andalusia, Verdolay, Archena, Lyria, Valencia, Catalonia, and Aragon, and even in southern France, we can trace a common taste, profoundly different from the Classical style, tending toward ornamental arabesques and an unorganic, childish vivacity in figured scenes. Geometric and floral motifs combine and merge with traditional Orientalizing elements in a thickly packed, luxuriant decoration in which spirals entwine with vine tendrils, floral trellises, and abstractly hatched plumage that recalls late Mycenaean ornamental work. Human figures and fantastically winged animals make their appearance. The thick network of linear decoration, dictated by a *horror vacui*, approaches the effects of textiles. The figured scenes frequent in the pottery of Lyria, Archena, and Valencia exhibit warriors, horsemen, huntsmen, and dances with men and women, among a thick fill of rosettes, buds, tendrils, and an intricate network of vegetal elements and volutes. Narrative interest is subordinated to ornamental considerations and does not lead to an organic figurative language. The merit of this Iberian decoration remains its lively arabesque effect, revealing its distance from the Classical root and its provincial nature.

All the decorative art of the Celtic area of the La Tène period remains on an abstract, ornamental level, replacing the earlier rectilinear geometrism with an originally developed, fantastic curvilinear repertory.

VIII | The Art of the Hellenistic Period

1. The New Ideals

The Hellenistic period, which can be considered as the period from the death of Alexander the Great (323 B.C.) to the battle of Actium (31 B.C.) and the creation of the Roman Empire by Augustus, saw profound historical changes in politics, society, religion, and literature, and these changes naturally had profound repercussions in the arts. The life of the *polis* melted into the wider context of the states that rose out of the subdivisions of the great empire of Alexander. Art was called upon less often to give concrete form to the religious, commemorative, and votive ideals of the community of citizens; its main function now was to exalt the Diadochi and the various kings and princes of the larger, autonomous states. The Parthenon had been a monument donated by all the citizens of Athens: the great monuments of Pergamon were the dynastic expression of the Attalid.

In the process of shaking off its social links with the *polis*, art changed from a cooperative effort into virtuoso work: it became an individual rather than a civil undertaking. Stripped of religious content, art now assumed value as decoration. The primitive and unified aesthetic content — the result of a synthesis of culture and myth, of the world of gods, heroes, and men — was replaced by various genres, just as culture after Aristotle was divided into specialized branches of activity. The spread of Greek thought over a much larger area, embracing non-Greek peoples, imposed a transformation of the Greek language into the Alexandrian *koine*, and art, too, in turn became internationalized. Indeed, in the last phase of the Hellenistic period art tended increasingly toward a basic common tone, albeit through a many-faceted proliferation of schools and movements, ending in an artistic *koine* that reached from Gandhara to Spain.

In the Classical period of the fifth and fourth centuries a few great personalities among painters, sculptors, and bronze workers had created new expressive forms and a particular figurative language, which had been assimilated and elaborated in the works of a highly developed artisan class, forming a unitary, organic artistic scene. The late fourth century had already shown symptoms of a break in this unity, which continued to split up during the Hellenistic period into a multiplicity of accents and tones. Beside the great masters swarms of minor and independent figures sprang up, and not only did art develop into certain schools, but, continually handed down from father to son in certain families, it gradually became a trade. With the first art collectors in the more progressive courts, and later among Roman clients, we see an industrialization of art work. The market for decorative works, copies, and remodeled versions of original pieces grew immensely. Mechanical methods of reproduction were more widespread, from tracing to the use of cartoons and plaster models, which led to a broad diffusion of Greek culture, and thus influenced the formation of a common taste.

Artists traveled more widely, so that works and ideas were more easily exchanged. Sculptors of different nationalities worked side by side on the same projects and the exceptional example set by the four who collaborated on the Mausoleum in Halicarnassus in the fourth century was followed by the numerous artists from Athens, Rhodes, Tralles, Pergamon, and other centers, who worked together on the great Pergamon projects.

Apart from these political, economic, and

social factors, Hellenistic art reflects the profound change in the spiritual climate of the times. Deities, already considerably humanized in the fourth century, were conceived in an even more terrestrial vein, even becoming the subject of genre works, or were conceived with a new solemnity aimed at grandiosity, or with a presence foreign to Classical modes; in either case the result was by now conventionalized. The most original Hellenistic versions of gods were to be those that represented a drunken Dionysus leaning on a young satyr, or Aphrodite as a woman crouching in her bath, ostentatiously baring her thigh, or taking off her slipper to give the impudent young Paniscus a lesson. The Dionysiac and Aphrodisiac aspects in this art were to prove the most original and lively, because they were closest to the human passions. Apollo, in the more significant works, became an increasingly languid cithara player, discarding the solemn peplos of the fourth century to show his soft, fleshy nude torso emerging from a mantle arranged with studied negligence about his flanks. In the Hellenistic period Artemis is first and foremost a huntress, but her tunic and mantle are draped with careful elegance, in rolls, hems, and folds. The Muses assume a prominent position, no longer shown as a uniform, discreet procession following Apollo Musagetes, but as distinct personifications of the various arts and sciences that constituted the specialized fields subdivided and pursued by Hellenistic culture. In their honor the place where men of learning lived and ate together was called the Museum, and the sanctuaries of the Muses multiplied. The Three Graces, whom Classical poets and artists had conceived in the chaste elegance of well-draped mantles, holding each other by the hands in a rhythmic dance, now bared their bodies and showed themselves to the onlooker, linked in an affected, languid embrace. The nymphs made up a light-footed ballet with Pan or were invited to dance by impetuous young satyrs. They appeared in graceful drapery, or stripped of all clothing as joyful bathers, the carefree protagonists of numberless bucolic scenes, joking with satyrs and sometimes allowing them closer embraces and more passionate kisses, but nonetheless resisting the satyrs' lascivious impetuosity. The nereids flitted upon the waves together with young tritons, now covered by their silky robes, now letting them slip down to reveal their blooming young bodies. Tyche, the goddess of fortune, became a dominant figure as a symbol of good luck and a protective personification of the city. Similarly, Nemesis found more worshipers in the Hellenistic period, as a magical force to be invoked before the various undertakings of life, and thus acquired the most varied attributes.

The world of heroes was no longer animated by the spirit of courage and battle, but by love. Even in the fourth century the ideal champion was no longer Theseus, but Meleager; Hellenistic protagonists were the heroes of sentimental and pathetic romance. The Archaic and Classical rape episode was replaced by scenes of tender idyll, refined courtship, and passionate seduction. Art in the sixth and fifth centuries had exalted the bloody, fatal efforts of Pelops to win Hippodamia, the irresistible determination of Theseus to carry off Antiope, the intelligent tenacity of Peleus in conquering the elusive Thetis, the divine force of Boreas flying away with Oreithyia, and the youthful, chivalrous passion of the Dioscuri carrying off the Leucippides. Hellenistic artists, on the other hand, were more moved by the amorous adventures of Apollo and Daphne, of Leander swimming the dangerous sea to visit Hero, the sighs of Polyphemus for the beautiful Galatea, the sleeping Ariadne discovered by an admiring Dionysus, the mute yearning of Selene for her handsome Endymion, the tender, bucolic loves of Daphnis and Chloë, or the childish embraces of Eros and Psyche. Archaic art had celebrated couples, and narrated marriage processions: Hellenistic art exalted lovers. In literature and figurative art love took on all sorts of tones and nuances, from the most audacious to the most ingenuous, the most explosive to the most tranquil, spanning the extremes of tenderness and sensuality, of idyll and pathos, of rusticity and refinement. The philosophical attitude of the fourth century had made the distinction between the three aspects of love: Eros, Himeros, and Pothos. Inspired by the literary fable, Hellenistic art created the ambiguous, bisexual figure of Hermaphroditus, summing up all the desires in nature; born of Aphrodite and Hermes, his double nature was the result of his indifference to the love of the nymph Salmacis, who persuaded the gods to mingle her body with her beloved's.

The dreamy atmosphere that was seeping into fourth-century works was transformed into sleep in Hellenism. Artists gave concrete form to the innocent sleep of Eros, the soft languor of Ariadne, the calm of Endymion, the heavy, troubled sleep of the worried satyr, and the sensual, voluptuous surrender of Hermaphroditus.

Grief and lamentation had been expressed in Archaic art with the violent gestures of beating the breast or brow, or tearing the hair. Classical art had chosen silent, calm meditation, drooping, shrouded heads, and crossed hands, creating closed, balanced rhythms. Skopas had pioneered a representation of pathos, slightly opening the mouth, wrinkling the forehead, and setting the eyes in deep shadow. Hellenistic art produced a whole varied gamut of pathetic expression, from the subdued, ingenuous grief of Eros to the exaggerated howling, twisted faces that culminated in the Laocoön.

While joy had been expressed through gestures from Archaic times on, the smile as a facial expression was a creation of the Hellenistic age, leaving us the dazed smile of the drunken old woman, the sparkling grins of satyrs, the fresh smiles of young boys, and the lighthearted expressions of nymphs.

Though in this new Hellenistic world every psychological and physical aspect of man was investigated, man ceased to be the exclusive center of speculative and artistic interest. Archaic culture and art had made man the measure of all things; Hellenistic, like Minoan-Mycenaean art before it, considered him as one subject in the immense setting of nature, whose manifold elements were being studied by scientists, whose varied forms were being described by men of letters. At the beginning of the Hellenistic period Theophrastus wrote about the characteristics of man, and at the same time, he also wrote treatises on plants and stones. Now the artist sensed new attractions in an animal or plant, a rock or a spring, a view of land or sea; and the backgrounds of paintings and carved or incised reliefs lost the abstract neutrality against which Archaic and Classical art had placed gods, heroes, and men, beyond the confines of time and space, in the ideal, mythical conception of the time. Occasionally Classical art had situated a scene with rare, isolated architectural and landscape elements, virtually reduced to stylized abstract symbols, and the Lycian landscape relief had been a purely local phenomenon. Now Hellenistic art was to create true landscape, organic and unified, composed of specific elements, though still conceived in intellectualistic terms. Not only were landscape backgrounds called on to localize narrative scenes, but the setting was also identified with the protagonists in small paintings and reliefs of an idyllic, bucolic nature; these have a literary parallel in Hellenistic poetry from Theocritus to Herodas, Bion, Moschus, and the epigrammatists.

Slaves and people of humble condition had never been taken into account in the conception and repertory of Classical art, except in particular scenes on painted vases, or to emphasize, on rare occasions, the profound difference between Greeks and barbarians, between the near-godly aristocracy of the *kalos k'agathos* and those who did not belong to the heroic world of Greek *paideia*. But in the Hellenistic age, an old shepherd, a fisherman, a Negro, a peasant, or a slave boy could provide subjects every bit as interesting as the *strategos*, the citizen, the philosopher, or the prince.

Man was no longer depicted solely in images of flourishing beauty, but shown in all his physical conditions, from blooming youth to the most repulsive decrepitude. Things ugly were no longer only the subject of occasional caricature, but the object of expressive, artistic interest. Just as medical science was studying and describing the maladies of man, dissecting bodies and examining their innermost structures, art began to reproduce sickness and physical deformities with the most pitiless realism. Along with the spread of anecdotal stories, biographies, and works of synthesis that classified and illustrated figures from the various domains of the past, we have the multiplication of portraiture: from the heroic tradition of Lysippos, to the learned tradition of reconstructed portraits of great personages of the past, to the psychological approach used to portray philosophers, poets, and men of letters, to the naturalistic, veristic, and virtuoso types, and finally the taste for the exotic and the barbarous.

While literature was turning to the epyllion, the mime, and the epigram, Hellenistic art was similarly developing the genres which had begun to attract artists in the fourth century. Just as the epigram was no longer dependent on an external occasion, but had acquired an independent, intrinsic lyrical value, the small genre scene became a form of art sufficient in itself. The range of treatments exploited by Hellenistic art became richer and broader, adding to traditional approaches the fanciful, the sophisticated, the virtuosic, the ingenious, and the allegorical. Much admiration was lavished on the colossal and on the microscopic.

The learned, cultivated, scientific spiritual climate led to an awakening of historical interest in the past and art, too, often took on an academic, classicizing, turn. While the trends most characteristic of the fourth-century masters were being developed, one also began a cultivated re-evocation and imitation of the various styles of preceding centuries, from the Archaic and Severe to the Phidian, inevitably in a conventional and artificial manner. The Archaic style, which was more difficult to understand and re-create in its abstract synthesis, became archaizing or was remodeled with greater originality in archaistic forms. The fourth century's naturalistic mastering of drapery and nude figures was further developed along expressionist and virtuoso lines.

2. Evolution of the Architectural Orders and the New Expression of Hellenistic Architecture

Hellenistic architecture still made use of the three traditional orders, but the Doric, where it survived, seems to have been drained of its original meaning and was stylized into elongated forms, tall, slender columns, rigid in the capitals, impoverished in the entablature, where the metopes no longer provided a field for sculptural experiment. The elongation of the Hellenistic Doric column conflicted with its original structure; to mask this elongation the grooving of the lowest third of the shaft was sometimes eliminated, forming a smooth sleeve that broke up the continuity of the shaft; the fluting was even at times abolished completely, thus transforming the canonic type still more radically. The Ionic order, on the other hand, was developed with originality between the third and second centuries B.C. by the architect Hermogenes, who studied the relationships between the intercolumnar spaces, the *ratio intercolumniorum* mentioned by Vitruvius, and established a module of two and a half diameters, known as eustyle. Hermogenes also introduced the figured frieze into the Ionic order in Asia Minor, carrying on the refined Archaic experiments of the Greek mainland, and leaving an example in the great Temple of Artemis Leukophriene at Magnesia.

With its greater decorative character, the Corinthian order was more widely used in the Hellenistic period, and in 174 B.C. found its most grandiose realization in the Temple of Zeus Olympios in Athens, the Olympieion reconstructed through the good offices of Antiochus Epiphanes, King of Syria. It is not insignificant that its architect, Cossutius, was of Italic origin; the Corinthian order was to prove the most attractive to Roman taste and underwent considerable developments in Roman architecture.

The Olympieion remains the most grandiose and splendid Corinthian temple, built entirely of Pentelic marble, 340 by 130 feet, with a forest of 104 columns, almost 53 feet high, arranged in three rows on the fronts and two along each side. Thus, because of a Syrian king, Greece in the Hellenistic period could vie with the grandiosity of the dipteral Ionic temples of Asia Minor, the Didymeion of Miletus, the Artemision at Ephesus, and the Heraion of Samos, discarding the traditional Classical dimensions. The very size of the undertaking meant that work on it took a very long time, and the temple was only finished under the Emperor Hadrian in the second century A.D.

The Hellenistic age, moving increasingly further from the purism of Classical architecture, was in search of new forms. Even if the date of the first appearance of the composite capital — a combination of the Corinthian acanthus with Ionic volutes, very widespread throughout Roman architecture — is uncertain, we have examples of Hellenistic capitals with new figured elements, with palmettes, and capitals of an Egyptianizing, exotic taste such as the palm-leaf capitals on the Stoa of Attalus in Athens or the papyrus capitals of the Pergamon porticoes.

Temple plans showed greater freedom and variety, and often tended to have more spacious peristyles. Pedimental decoration became less important, as did the decoration of the metopes, on which figural decoration was finally renounced for pure ornaments of floral elements and shields.

On Samothrace, in the famous sanctuary of the Cabiri, the *Megaloi Theoi* or Great Goddesses, the particular aim was to create a grandiose, impressive circular hall that could hold all the participants in the ceremonies held during the annual international festivals, which were attended by ambassadors from many countries. Between 289 and 281 B.C. Arsinoë, the wife of King Lysimachus, saw to the building of the marble rotunda, over 60 feet in diameter, known as the Arsinoeion. This structure represents a significant transformation of the usual religious *tholos*. Previously, the *tholos*, which held the cult statue of the god, had been conceived primarily as external architecture, and decorated with a peristyle; the Arsinoeion, on the other hand, was planned in terms of its internal space, and did away with the peristyle by transforming it into a decorative pilastered gallery superimposed on the tall marble wall. These new architectural forms were thus more free to incorporate elements from the traditional orders. In the Arsinoeion the pilasters of the external blind gallery carried a Doric entablature and were closed at the foot by parapets decorated with patera motifs and ox skulls, while the corresponding semi-columns inside the temple were Corinthian with an Ionic entablature. On the outer cornice, decorated with vine tendrils and lion-mask gargoyles, was placed the conical roof, whose tiles were graduated in size, with *anthemion* antefixes. Only Roman architecture, with the invention of the arch and the agglomerate cement dome, was to achieve, in the round halls of the baths and in the Pantheon, a new, organic structural solution to the architectural problem that was presented by the large, circular interior space.

With the decline of the ancient religious observances and the multiplication of the exigencies of life, the architect found many other fields of activity, and temples no longer absorbed all the finest energies of the *polis* as they had during the Archaic period.

The Hellenistic theater developed the architecture of the *skene*. In the pre-existing theaters, as, for example, in Athens, the *skene* was often rebuilt with a new *proskenion*. A greater dignity was given to the *skene* by architectonic perspectives of columns, as in the theaters of Asia Minor, at Priene, Pergamon, and Ephesus, and in the later examples at Thermessus and Aspendus.

Another important building which was probably developed during the Hellenistic period was the *bouleuterion*, which presented problems at once similar to and different from those of the theater. Both buildings had to provide seating accommodation; but the theater, which was sacred to Dionysus, had to cater to large audiences, while only the smaller number of the citizens' council, the *boule*, had to be contained in the *bouleuterion*, though in a few minor centers, like Thoricus or Rhamnus, the theater served for both purposes. But whereas the theater was open to the sky, the *bouleuterion* was roofed, and the building was therefore conceived differently, as an enclosed space, an interior architecture. The principal problem was constituted by the roof, and was usually resolved by supporting the wooden covering on four pillars, sometimes with a raised lantern in the center. This was a solution similar to that found in the Mycenaean *megaron*, and, indeed, the only solution possible in the rectilinear, architraved Greek architecture which, based on the trilith system, had not yet developed the arch and vault with which the Romans were daringly and brilliantly to cover large spaces.

The hall of the *bouleuterion* gradually acquired an internal organic unity, which became articulated in terms of the demands made by seating capacity, visibility, lighting, and decoration. This was accomplished within the limits of the simplicity and sobriety that characterized the Greek architectonic language, and was free from all the decorative superstructures that, by contrast, were to be the great indulgence of the Romans. The development of the *bouleuterion* from the Classical period to Hellenistic times shows the change from wooden to stone seats; and from tiered seating set at right angles to each other around three sides of the hall, as in the Hellenistic *bouleuterion* at Priene, to the type in which the tiers of seats are slightly curved, under the influence

of the theater *cavea*, as in the other Hellenistic *bouleuteria* in Thermessus and Cretopolis. The tiers of seats were even at times arranged in a full semicircle, as already in the late fifth-century *bouleuterion* at Athens up to the monumental example at Miletus dating from 175–174 B.C. Attempts were made to eliminate the obstacle to complete visibility constituted by the four central columns placed on the floor by moving them into the tiers of seats. One also tried to achieve a flat, horizontal ceiling and to divide the upper part of the inner front with windows, enlivening the spaces between with semi-columns corresponding to the pilasters on the outside, as at Miletus, or, as at Priene, placing an exedra between the doors, and thus creating a façade articulated on two storeys.

The *bouleuterion* is the most significant creation of an enclosed space in Greek architecture. The temple, though fulfilling the function of sheltering the cult statue within the cella, was conceived primarily as an architecture of exteriors. Porticoes, too, though creating spacious covered ambulatories, often with colonnades and shops, were organized in terms of the columned façade. The gymnasium, which occupied so important a place in Greek life and culture, starting with the famous Academy, Lyceum, and Cynosarges in Athens, was originally a complex of shaded gardens with fountains, altars, statues, tracks, and open spaces for the various games, with simple *apodyteria*. When the layout became more sophisticated and physical culture was accompanied by philosophical and literary activities, the gymnasium was extended with porticoes and colonnades, some covered rooms, courtyards, peristyles, and small baths, often, as at Delphi and Pergamon, arranged in terraces. In the Hellenistic period the gymnasium, as seen in the important examples in Olympia and Delos from the third century B.C., assumed a grandiose, organic development which was to reach its culminating point in Pergamon, but was still based fundamentally on these elements of open architecture. We shall see how the Roman baths, which took the place of the Greek gymnasium, were to develop from just the opposite architectural conception, that of the creation of large enclosed spaces, using new technical means.

With the fervor of the Hellenistic dynasts, libraries multiplied, from the famous Alexandria Museum to those in Pella and Antioch, and those founded by Mithridates and by the Attalids in Pergamon.

Only during the Roman period was the library to acquire its own particular architectural development.

The element that became increasingly widespread and grandiose in Hellenistic architecture was the portico; this found application in gymnasia, and it also surrounded, framed, and embellished town squares, particularly the agorai, linking the various façades, closing the sides in perspective effects like theater wings, and generally giving architectural unity to the whole area. The agorai that were built in the Hellenistic cities presented a regular, symmetrical plan, and pre-existing complexes were regularized. The Athenian Agora, between 159 and 138 B.C., received on its east side, the monumental Stoa of Attalus II, 350 feet long, with shops, and a complex of two stoai along its entire south side. While these latter had Doric columns, the Stoa of Attalus was built on two levels, with Doric columns on the lower level and Ionic above, corresponding respectively to an inner row of Ionic columns on the lower floor and to columns with palm-leaf capitals on the upper floor.

Porticoes developed the superimposition of levels and architectural orders, and buildings and façades began to be articulated on two or three storeys, with horizontal divisions. The balustrade of the upper floor was sometimes decorated with rich relief freizes with thick arabesque of weapons, as at Pergamon. Porticoes on several storeys were also used when they were backed up against terraces, for example on the west side of the agora at Alinda of the second century B.C. In this case the stoa was built on three storeys and the colonnade of the third was on the level of the square above. At Aegae, a three-storey portico was also used; here a slope on one side of the square was exploited and connected with a two-storey shop building, supported by a portico on the level of the square.

The agora, regularized into a quadrangular plan surrounded by porticoes, became progressively integrated as a harmonious, organic part of the orthogonal network of the Hellenistic city. It corresponded to the grid of the streets but tended to be cut off from the flow of traffic, becoming an enclosed area, a grandiose peristyle reached through monumental gateways, as in Cnidus, Cos, and Aphrodisia. Once more the agora discovered its essentially political and monumental role as a meeting place, a promenade where the various buildings, altars, and statues were now arranged in a more orderly alignment along the sides. The increased commercial functions were centralized in other peripheral agorai; on Delos there was the Agora of Theophrastus, and the Agora of the Hermaistai, the so-called Agora of the Italians of the second century B.C. — the collegial seat of the Italic colony — which is a

typical example of a unified, enclosed square with peristyle. We have a grandiose monumental example in Ephesus, where the agora is about 400 feet square, laid out at the end of the fourth century and progressively embellished with Ionic and Corinthian porticoes and two gateways.

This new architectural outlook is also reflected in the plan of the Hellenistic house, which in its most typical and widespread form

226. Roman copy of a portrait of Menander, after a lost original of vibrant and refined plasticity, created in the third century B.C. Boston, Museum of Fine Arts

always presents an inner peristyle with Doric or Ionic columns, around which the various rooms are arranged. These buildings have as many as three storeys, and are carefully decorated with mosaics and wall paintings. Priene, Delos, Rhodes, Cos, and Pergamon have preserved many specimens of this domestic architecture, and even the most sumptuous villas are only enlargements of the fundamental elements of the house.

The picture of Hellenistic architecture is as varied and many-sided as that of the other arts: a diversity of forms were offered in fu-

water, and sumptuously decorated with marble and bronze.

While the temple to the gods was losing its importance for sculptors and painters, the decorative field offered by other buildings was broadening to include private houses and vast, impressive palaces, tombs, collegial centers, libraries, gymnasia, gardens, porticoes, theaters, and squares. In the Archaic and Classical periods artistic activity had been concentrated on sanctuaries, but now it had the entire city as its object. The city became an organic architectural unit; its regular plan developed the norms laid down by Hippodamos, of a rectangular grid, or development in terraces, the most monumental example of the latter type being the Attalid city of Pergamon, conceived with a scenographic taste.

227. Roman marble copy of the statue of Demosthenes. The lost bronze original by Polyeuktos once stood in the Athenian Agora. The hands were originally clasped together; the restoration with a scroll is false.
Vatican, Braccio Nuovo

228. Detail of a Roman copy of one of the Niobids from a group known in many replicas. The original was created by an artist of the third century B.C. working in the Praxitelean-Skopadic current.
Rome, Capitoline Museums

nerary monuments, such as the heroön, and the Alexandrian hypogeum, the plan and decoration of which seem to reflect local domestic architecture; or in particular edifices, such as the octagonal marble Tower of the Winds in Athens, a water clock constructed in the first century B.C. by Andronicus Cyrrhestes; or the colossal lighthouse built on the little island of Pharos at Alexandria by Sostratus of Cnidus, which stood about 360 feet high, daringly placed at the end of the break-

3. Developments of the Praxitelean and Skopadic Currents

In the vast artistic panorama of the Hellenistic world the stylistic traditions of the great masters of the fourth century can be seen in the works of their most direct disciples, in the remodeling by a vast circle of minor artists, and in the work of the major centers of artistic activity, such as Athens, Alexandria,

255

Rhodes, Pergamon, and other cities of Asia Minor. The style of Praxiteles seems to have had the greatest influence on a long series of Hellenistic works, which developed the fundamental principles of the master and carried them to their extreme consequences.

The sons and pupils of Praxiteles, Kephisodotos the Younger and Timarchos, whose *acme* is placed by Pliny in the hundred and twenty-first Olympiad (296–293 B.C.), were both very active in Athens and various other cities, where they often worked together. Kephisodotos sculpted statues of gods, such as Aphrodite, Asclepius, Apollo, and an Artemis which was in Rome. His Latona, which was in the Temple of Apollo on the Palatine in Rome, is known through its representation on the Sorrento base. The ample drapery and forms of this figure seem to recall the Hestia of his grandfather, Kephisodotos the Elder. The softness of Praxiteles' nudes became a virtuoso element in the art of his son, who created a famous erotic group in Pergamon, a noble *symplegma*, in which "the fingers seemed to press real flesh, not marble." As we know from one of the mimes of Herodas, the two brothers carved statues that were dedicated by Eutias in the famous sanctuary of Asclepius on Cos, and if their hands can be recognized in some fragments of the Asclepieion, they show themselves to be their father's sons in the delicate surface treatment and the interplay of chiaroscuro effects. The importance gained by portrait sculpture is attested to by the series of portraits recorded in the sources as executed by these two sculptors. These include the wooden figures of Lycurgus and his sons, the portraits of poetesses such as Myro of Byzantium and Anyte of Tegea, and the statue of the comic writer Menander.

Beside conventional images of Menander in paintings, mosaics, and reliefs, one is struck by a series of forty-three copies of a head, in herms and busts of the Roman period. The poet's features are shown with a refined modeling enlivened by an inner energy expressed in the deep orbits of the eyes, the wrinkled brow, and the soft, vibrant locks of hair. In this portrait (fig. 226) the intensely coloristic treatment of the planes joins forces with a dynamic sense stemming from the Lysippan tradition: these stylistic traits could well fit the personalities of the sons of Praxiteles. In view of the fame of this work, it could be identified with the statue in the Athens theater, though some critics prefer to view it as a reworking by an artist of the late second century B.C.

In the field of late Hellenistic portrait sculpture one work stands out, its fame proved by forty-two copies: the statue of Demosthenes,

229. *Detail of the Aphrodite of Melos, known as the* Venus de Milo, *found in 1820. Parian marble. Mid-second century* B.C. *Paris, Louvre*

raised by the Athenians in the Agora about 280 B.C., which sources attribute to an otherwise unknown sculptor, Polyeuktos (fig. 227). The work's profound fascination resides in the extreme and rigorous simplicity of the pose and drapery, the lively naturalism of the face, and the intense, psychological expression.

Fifty years earlier another great artist had succeeded in expressing the nobility and fame of Sophocles, using an open, dynamic pose, and achieving elegant refinement in the draped mantle, whose rich cadences shrouded and exalted the solemn structure of the body, in a

230. Landolina Aphrodite, found in 1804 in a niche of a nymphaeum near Syracuse. Copy in Parian marble of a type known in various examples. Second century B.C. Syracuse, National Museum

tone animated by sustained, coherent, and flowing rhythm. Polyeuktos reached the same degree of effectiveness in portraying the tormented nature of Demosthenes, who is caught in a moment of painful concentration, meditating on the sad fate of Athens. His head is bowed and hands are clasped in a rigorously closed rhythm, while the mantle wraps round the slender body with expressive negligence,

231. At right: Esquiline Aphrodite, found in 1847 at the Villa Palombara on the Esquiline. First century B.C. Rome, Capitoline Museums

257

232. *Roman marble copy of the bronze Aphrodite created by Doidalsas in the second half of the third century* B.C. *Found at Hadrian's Villa. Rome, Museo delle Terme*

233. *Reduced Roman copy in marble of the Aphrodite by Doidalsas, somewhat slimmer in the body, but with a rich and elaborate treatment of the hair. Ostia, Museum*

not as a drape, but as a simple cover, and rich modeling animates the planes of the lean face and wrinkles the high brow of the thinker. The work is a lyrical formulation of the contrast between the unconquerable energy of the sitter's mind and his lack of physical strength, evoked again in the epigram on the base of the statue, lamenting that if Demosthenes' strength had been equal to his wisdom, the Macedonian Ares would never have taken over the Hellenes.

The post-Praxitelean current that spread from Athens in the first years of the Hellenistic period merged with Skopadic characteristics in a group of Niobids known in several copies (fig. 228), which must have been thought a harmonious decoration for landscaped gardens. It is indicative that the ancients themselves were uncertain whether to attribute the similar

group in the Temple of Apollo Sosianus in Rome to Praxiteles or to Skopas. This uncertainty suggests a characteristic mixture of stylistic modes, probably the work of an artist of the third century B.C. In this work the concentrated rhythmic syntax of the Phidian frieze unfolded its episodic figures in more complex, loose, theatrical groupings; draperies became more complicated, with fluttering veils and hems, and post-Praxitelean forms merged with the expressive elements of Skopadic faces in accordance with the tragic pathos of the theme.

The soft nude torso, which rises from its folds of drapery in a colorful contrast, in the celebrated Aphrodite of Melos, known as the *Venus de Milo* (fig. 229), certainly could not have been conceived without the fundamental experience of Praxiteles' Cnidian Aphrodite (fig. 177). The Hellenistic accent of the outstanding unknown artist who created this work is expressed in the flowing, sinuous, rising rhythm of the figure. The type reappears in groups of an epigrammatic tone, showing the goddess in the act of teaching Eros, poised on a pilaster by her side, how to shoot an arrow; if this particular conception goes back to the original creation, it shows the new idyllic content in the conception of Aphrodite.

The isolation and tranquil pose of Praxiteles' Cnidian Aphrodite continued to serve as a model for Hellenistic sculptors in various centers. Indeed, from the inspiration of this figure were produced the lighter, fleshier, dreamy type of the Medici Aphrodite; the more imposing naturalistic type, with elaborate coiffure, of the Capitoline Aphrodite, probably a work of the second century B.C. from Asia Minor; the baroque and sensual Landolina Aphrodite of Syracuse (fig. 230), with virtuoso work in the deeply carved drapery that forms a backdrop for the legs and contrasts with the smooth nude body, which many authors have identified as the famous Syracusan Callipygia; the completely naked type of the famous Aphrodite Anadyomene from the baths of Cyrene, created perhaps about 100 B.C., with a slightly academic tone; and finally, the Esquiline Aphrodite (fig. 231), in which the lively naturalism of the immature body, in a search for Archaic conciseness, is combined with the tone of the Severe style of the head, in the classicizing, archaizing current of the first century B.C.

In this rich series of Hellenistic Aphrodites a place apart is reserved for the figure cast in bronze by Doidalsas of Bithynia for King Nicomedes in the second half of the third century B.C. The goddess is shown naked, crouching down to have water poured on her back, with voluptuous pleasure expressed in the half-open lips of her graceful face (figs. 232, 233). In this highly talented interpretation, the genre motif is translated into a contained and complex rhythmical composition, built round the flowing, continuous line of the tense back and crossed limbs, which enables the artist to draw new effects from the soft, fleshy nude, with its opulent folds and smooth surfaces, crowned by the sumptuous, sophisticated play of the braided and disordered hair.

This type appealed greatly to the Romans for the decoration of baths and gardens. A mingling of the crouching type of Aphrodite with the Anadyomene type appeared in late Hellenistic Alexandria, in statuettes with a delicate modeling, which becomes evanescent in languid Alexandrian marble heads.

The virtuoso rhythm of a figure turning to the back, very popular in the Hellenistic period,

234. Roman marble copy after the original lost bronze of the Tyche of Antioch, created at the beginning of the third century B.C. by Eutychides, and known in some twenty replicas. Vatican, Galleria dei Candelabri

gave rise to the witty type of the young satyr looking at his tail, and also became a skillful pretext for placing Aphrodite in the same position, baring her back and side in a gesture that has been equated with a dance step, but is instead a typical pose of the affected sensuality of late Hellenism.

The chaste conception of Phidias' Aphrodite Urania was revived in the Hellenistic period in statuettes that bare the torso and elongate the leaning body in a sinuous rhythm. The nude body of the goddess was conceived as a pearl held between the two halves of a shell, alluding to the goddess' origins in the surf of the sea. This theme appears from the fourth century through the Hellenistic period in clay statuettes, and later, in painting, mosaics, and

259

gems. Finally, there is an extreme, completely earthly humanization in the type of Aphrodite found in bronzes and terracottas, in which the goddess is placed on one foot, in a daring, unstable pose, bending her nude body to tie the lace of her sandal.

4. Developments of the Lysippan Current

Transmitted through a succession of disciples of the master, the influence of the artistic ideals of Lysippos remained very strong throughout the entire Hellenistic period. Lysippos' son Boedas was famed for a worshiping figure that has been traced in the bronze boy in Berlin, clearly influenced by Lysippos. The other son, of Lysippos, Euthykrates, had a more austere approach than his father, and imitated his proportions mainly for their elegance, and like his father treated the theme of Alexander's hunting expeditions. The disciple Daippos revived the subject of the athlete with the strigil in his *Perixyomenus*, and executed statues of victorious athletes. Tisikrates, a pupil of Euthykrates,

235. Winged Nike of Samothrace poised on the prow of a ship, originally part of the nymphaeum at the sanctuary of the Great Gods. Work datable circa *200 B.C., attributed to the school of Rhodes.*
Rhodian marble. Paris, Louvre

236. Roman copy of the Muse Polyhymnia, after the lost original from a series probably created by the sculptor Philiskos in the third century B.C. The transparent mantle and heavy, sumptuous chiton reveal the style of Rhodes or Asia Minor. Rome, Capitoline Museums

237. *Tanagra figurine. Terracotta group of two seated, mantled women. Third century B.C. London, British Museum*

sition, scanned by the lines of her carefully arranged mantle, but the rhythm is tense and restless, as if stressing the figure's anxious gaze, fixed on distant aims, with her head held erect under its crown of turreted walls, while her foot rests on the shoulder of the fluid and youthful figure of the swimming Orontes. This highly successful creation, filled with inner energy and imaginative content, follows the line of development of the art of Lysippos. The temperament of Eutychides seems to have favored the theme of personifications of rivers: his statuary interpretation of the Eurota was considered artistically more fluid (*liquidiorem*) than the river itself. Eutychides' pupil, Kantharos of Sicyon, must also be set in the mainstream of the Lysippan tradition; he executed statues of victorious athletes at Olympia in the third century B.C.

was so close to the style of Lysippos that it was difficult to tell their works apart; he was the portraitist of King Demetrius Poliorcetes and of Peucestes, the savior of Alexander. Xenokrates, a pupil of Tisikrates or Euthykrates, excelled his masters in the volume of his output and was a theoretician and critic of art, one of Pliny's main sources. In contrast with the anecdotal, rhetorical, ecphrastic, and chronographic histories of Douris, Antigonos, and Apollodoros, the critical content of the writings of Xenokrates is notable; he based his judgments on concrete elements, on the problems of rhythm, proportion, optical correction, line, and color, all elements that had formed the basis of Lysippos' art and that were developed and studied in the work of this later follower.

One of the most important direct pupils of Lysippos to be mentioned is the Sicyonian Eutychides, a painter and a sculptor in bronze and stone, who flourished during the hundred and twenty-first Olympiad (296–293 B.C.), when he may have executed his masterpiece, the bronze Tyche of Antioch, the city founded on the Orontes in 300 B.C. (fig. 234). The personification of this raw, new city holds sheaves of wheat, and sits on a rock in a closed compo-

238. *Tanagra figurine. Terracotta statuette of a woman in a transparent mantle and heavy chiton, wearing a hat. In the style of the third century B.C. Boston, Museum of Fine Arts*

261

239. *Tanagra figurine. Terracotta statuette of a mantled dancer. Third to second century* B.C. *Munich, Antikensammlungen*

240. *Bronze statuette of a veiled dancer, here seen in a full view (above, at right) and in a detail of her head and shoulders. The figure is completely wrapped in a fringed mantle, with virtuoso rendering of its transparent material. Late third century* B.C. *Probably Alexandrian. New York, Walter C. Baker Collection*

A direct pupil of Lysippos, Chares of Lindos, went on to create one of the seven wonders of the world, the famous Colossus of Rhodes, a bronze placed at the harbor mouth of Rhodes, about 290 B.C., which was destroyed by an earthquake in 224 B.C. In this work the traditions of bronze sculpture, the athletic nude, and Lysippan proportion were transposed onto a colossal scale in the image of Helius, protector of Rhodes, who here discarded the

almost a palpitating symbol of the victories of the Rhodian fleet against Antiochus III.

In the third and second centuries B.C. the problem of female draperies seems to have found an original treatment, marked by a refined virtuoso taste, in the circle of a certain artistic language shared by Rhodes, Cos, Delos, and the various centers of Asia Minor, such as Miletus, Magnesia, and Priene. Not only did drapery acquire a complex flow of deep

241. Detail of the group of the Gaul who kills his wife and himself. Marble copy of the original Pergamene bronze, created circa 230 B.C. Rome, Museo delle Terme, Ludovisi Collection

242. Group of Menelaus holding the body of Patroclus. Roman marble copy of an original bronze of the third century B.C., known in various replicas. The position of the restored head of Menelaus is false; it was originally more raised and turned to the side. Florence, Loggia dei Lanzi

traditional charioteer's tunic in a new, Hellenistic conception.

Perhaps another artist from this fervid milieu on Rhodes, Pythokritos, can be credited with the creation, about 200 B.C., of the famous winged Nike of Samothrace (fig. 235). This figure stood in a nymphaeum, mirrored in a shallow pool of water, and impetuously jutted forward on its plinth formed by a ship's prow, surrounded by space and modeled by the wind which twists and turns the flying draperies —

folds, rich borders, sculptural whirls, tangles, and knots, but there was also a transformation in the consistency of the mantle which, instead of being heavier than the tunic, became of silken softness and, clinging to the body, created a whole new range of transparent, veil-like effects (figs. 236, 238, 240). The mantles, which perhaps reproduce the famous textiles woven on Cos, adhere to the body and underline its elongated structure, with the very high, slim waist, the extremely narrow shoulders contrast-

263

243. *Roman copy of a bearded head, after an original Hellenistic work of the second century* B.C. *Ostia, Museum*

244. *Head of the crouching Scythian from the group of the flaying of Marsyas. Copy after an original Pergamene work of the late third century* B.C. *Florence, Uffizi*

ing with the opulent hips and thighs that swell out in soft curves, and the characteristically pronounced projection of the hip corresponding to the supporting leg.

These same elements also form the figures of the Muses from the series that can be assigned to the Rhodian sculptor Philiskos, and which is recorded by Pliny to have stood in the Portico of Octavia in Rome. These figures of the Muses are known through statuary copies, an outstanding example of which is the composed grace of the meditative Polyhymnia (fig. 236). They are also reproduced on the relief by Archelaos of Priene, where they appear above the allegory of the Apotheosis of Homer, in accordance with the typically symbolic conceptions of the Hellenistic age. A similar virtuoso elegance in drapery and rhythm also modulates the celebrated clay statuettes known, after their main center of production, as Tanagra figurines, although they were also produced in other Hellenistic centers (figs. 237–239). These small, graceful figures are rather like languid fashion models. Analogous figures were often used in the representation of deceased women on late funerary steles in the Ionian islands and Asia Minor.

5. Pergamene Art

A concentration of political and economic energies in Pergamon gave rise to a particularly intense activity in the arts, fostered by the court of the Attalids. Indeed, Pergamene art,

which can be classified as dynastic and commemorative, constitutes one of the most important chapters in the history of the arts of the Hellenistic period. The general atmosphere of victory that followed the annihilation of the Gallic invaders took concrete form in a series of votive offerings, and the great Altar to Zeus and Athena Nikephoroi. The glorious deeds of the Attalids, transposed to a mythical plane, are dedicated to the gods. The Galatomachy, battle of the Greeks and the Gauls, is placed on the same level as the gigantomachy and Amazonomachy themes, together with the by this time symbolic struggle against the Persians. In Roman art the commemoration of the Imperial *res gestae* was instead to take concrete form in state-commissioned monuments illustrating military and political events with historical realism. By comparison with the variety of accents in the art of other centers, Pergamene art, precisely because of its courtly nature, achieved a substantial unity of style and expression, which is often defined in the convenient formula "Pergamene baroque," though the work in question was carried out by artists of varied origins.

For the offerings of Attalus I (241–197 B.C.) and Eumenes II (197–159 B.C.) representing Galatomachies, Pliny records the names of the sculptors Isigonos, Stratonikos, Phyromachos, and Antigonos, the last being the author of theoretical works on bronze statuary. In the copies of the first great offering of Attalus I erected in Pergamon, the Gaul who kills his wife and himself, now in the Museo delle Terme (fig. 241), and the Dying Gaul of the Capitoline Museum, the vivid ethnic portrayal of the figures — conveyed in the shaggy hair and mustaches and in the Celtic torques worn by these proud barbarians — loses its illustrative episodic character, so that the figures become universal artistic material, symbols of heroic epos and dramatic pathos. The influence of Lysippos flows through the supple, vigorous nude of the Dying Gaul, in an audacious rhythmic and spatial composition. The Gaul with the body of his slain wife in the Museo delle Terme is on the same conceptual and artistic level as the group in which Menelaus holds the inert body of Patroclus and anxiously gazes over the battlefield, known through the famous "Pasquino" torso in Rome and the copy in the Loggia dei Lanzi in Florence (fig. 242), and

In the offering dedicated by Attalus II (159–138 B.C.) on the Athenian Acropolis, figures were more numerous, but were only two cubits high. The Asian marble of the copies has led to the suggestion that the originals may actually have been in Pergamon, dedicated by Eumenes II and copied later for Athens. There is a wider rhythmic range in these statues, which illustrate four battle themes, and the modeling has a more extreme, incisive character, while the tone is more turgid and pathetic. Pathos takes on a melodramatic content in the group described in sources, representing a child caressing its dead mother, a highly praised work of the sculptor Epigonos, who is also said to have produced a figure of a trumpeter. These subjects relate to the themes of the offering and to the artistic climate of the city of Pergamon. Epigonos also executed a chariot

245. Detail of the gigantomachy from the east side of the main frieze of the Pergamene Altar, with Zeus hurling the thunderbolt at the serpent-footed Porphyrion, who is seen from the back. First half of the second century B.C. Berlin, Pergamon Museum

which has been linked with the name of Antigonos. On the other hand, a more academic, decorative approach is to be seen in syntactical analogies between the groups of Achilles holding the dying Penthesilea and Artemis holding Iphigenia with the doe, which can both be reconstructed from fragments of copies.

in honor of the Olympic victory of Attalus.

It is probable that the group of Marsyas hanging from the tree, on the point of being flayed by the Scythian, should also be attributed to the Pergamon circle; the crude dramatic content of this theme found a response in Hellenistic expressionism and offered interesting

265

246. Detail from the Telephus frieze of the Pergamon Altar showing the building of the coffin which was to enclose Auge, who is seen above, seated on a rock, wrapped in her mantle. First half of the second century B.C. Berlin, Pergamon Museum

opportunities for ethnic characterization in the crouching barbarian (fig. 244), and for virtuoso work in the taut, stretched limbs of the nude satyr.

The heights reached by Pergamene art, however, can be appreciated better from the original slabs of the frieze of the great altar than from this series of copies. Begun perhaps in 181 B.C., when the *Nikephoria* feasts were instituted, the Altar of Zeus and Athena at Pergamon was finished about 159 B.C. under Attalus II, with hastily done passages in the Ionic colonnade and the minor frieze of the inner portico. The main frieze, 7 feet 6 inches

high and almost 400 feet long, was executed in the workshops of various sculptors, some of whose signatures have been preserved, including, among other fragmentary signatures, those of Dionysiades, Melanippos, Orestes, and Theorretos. The artists were of different nationalities and worked under the direction of a single master who conceived and roughed out the models, arriving at an exceptional harmony and a substantial unity of style, except for slight differences of touch and technique.

The vast, complex narrative of the immanent struggle between the gods and the giants is distributed with skill and an organic, cosmic vision. Beginning with Oceanus and the terrestrial and marine gods in the west, the narrative continues with the gods of night and the stars on the north, then with those of light and the luminous heavens on the south, culminating with the Olympian gods on the principal east side, where Zeus and Athena were placed in the southern half, in relation to the visual focal point presented to the faithful as they entered the sacred enclosure. A rich imagination multiplies the monstrous animal forms of the giants, and the figures are woven into a titanic, tangled concatenation, in a scene invested with a chaotic, superhuman impetus (fig. 245). The nude here becomes a weighty scansion of powerfully structured masses; drapery seems invested with a violent wind liberated by the clash of cosmic forces, and wraps around all the participants, with rich modeling, coloristic pleating, deep-cut folds, knots, and tangles. The drill bites deeply into the marble to create strong cavities and deep shadows, and the relief has the vivid bodily presence of carving in the round. The work moves from the full, soft plumpness of women's faces to the distorted planes of the faces of the more mature giants. Skopadic elements in this Pergamene style are developed until they become pure spasm and fury in the shrieking mouths, the deep-set, rolling eyes, and the eyebrows contracted into sharp angles, while hair and beards frame the faces with squirming, disorderly locks. A refined chiseling in wing feathers, animal skins, serpent scales, and many other details gives added preciosity and enriches the fiery, agitated tone of the frieze.

247. *Wall painting from Herculaneum representing Heracles discovering the infant Telephus suckled by a doe. Copy of a Pergamene painting of the second century* B.C.
Naples, National Museum

248. *Roman copy of a type of Artemis known in four other replicas. After an original work from Asia Minor, perhaps Pergamon, of the second century* B.C.
Rome, Antiquarium del Palatino

From the strong plastic character of this gigantomachy decorating the outer plinth of the Altar, exposed to strong outdoor light, we pass to the pictorial treatment of the frieze beneath the inner portico, about 5 feet high, and stretching for about 250 feet, which narrates the myth of the hero Telephus (fig. 246). While the gigantomachy on the main frieze has a neutral, Classical background, the complex mythological story of Telephus has a landscape setting, with rocks, trees, and architectural elements that localize the action and link it together, permitting an organic distribution

249. Portrait of Mithridates VI Eupator, King of Pontus, represented as Heracles wearing the lion skin, similar to heads on coins of Odessus. Circa 80 B.C. Paris, Louvre

of the figures on more than one plane, with a sense of spatial illusionism not uninfluenced by painting, then flourishing in Pergamon. Indeed, an original painting in Pergamon seems to have served as model for a copy in Herculaneum (fig. 247) representing Heracles discovering the infant Telephus being suckled by the doe on Mount Parthenius, seen against a landscape background dominated by the solemn, seated figure of Arcadia. The group of Heracles and Telephus in this painting shows precise correspondences with the same group in the Telephus frieze of the Altar.

A typical Hellenistic pictorial genre, the still

life, finds an original interpretation in Pergamon in the virtuosic realism of the mosaic artist Sosos, who created the celebrated *asarotos oikos* or the "unswept room." Using tiny, varicolored pieces of marble, he represented in a floor mosaic the debris of a meal and all the other odds and ends that are usually left to be swept away, as if they were still lying on the floor. This veristic theme appealed greatly to the Romans, who had many copies made of this mosaic, including one signed by Herakleitos, which is now in the Lateran Museum. The taste for illusionistic effects and chromatic virtuosity that marked the Hellenistic pictorial culture was also affirmed in the mosaic picture by the same Sosos at Pergamon. He depicted a dove drinking, rendering the water darkened by the shadow of the bird's head, while other doves in full light perch on the rim of the basin, a motif that is certainly reflected in the celebrated Capitoline *emblema* mosaic from Hadrian's Villa and in other copies.

It has been suggested that the mosaic with the doves recalls the Homeric cup of Nestor, and that originally it was the *emblema* from the center of the *asarotos oikos*. It would thus constitute a single pavement inspired by funerary symbolism, that Sosos created for some place dedicated to the cult of the heroes in Pergamon.

As in Alexandria, the foundation of the Pergamon library was a further stimulus for pictorial art applied to the illustration of scientific books. Collecting began to take hold in the cultured circles of Pergamon, and the masterpieces of the fifth century, such as the Athena Parthenos, were copied and remodeled. The myth of Heracles liberating Prometheus became an imaginative allegory in a classicizing group from the first century B.C., in which the hero is a portrait and symbol of Mithridates VI Eupator, who reconquered Asia from the Romans and resided in Pergamon, honored by the Greeks as their liberator (fig. 249).

So strongly original and expressive a language as that of the Pergamon Altar could not fail to have a widespread influence on contemporary art. For example, the giants on the frieze seem to have inspired the conception of the emphatic, magniloquent, agitated Daedalus, apparently watching tragedy overtake his son, known through a copy found in Amman. There is still a close relationship between the Pergamon giants and the famous Laocoön group executed by the Rhodian sculptors Agesandros, Athenodoros, and Polydoros (fig. 250), showing the contacts and mutual influences between Rhodes and Pergamon in the seething activity of the Hellenistic world. The tragedy and spasmatic pain shown in Laocoön's face is composed of the same expressionist elements

250. *Plaster reconstruction of the Laocoön group,*
with the right arm of Laocoön restored to its
original position, bent behind his head.
Rome, Museum of Casts
Restoration: Vergara Caffarelli

251. *Head of Odysseus from the grotto of Sperlonga.*
In the virtuosity of the rendering of the dense
shadows and the vital plastic conception
brimming with pathos, this work is very close
to the Laocoön. Sperlonga, Museum

252. Detail of a bronze representing a boy jockey, found in the sea off Cape Artemision. Original Hellenistic work of the third century B.C. Athens, National Museum

to be found in an Enceladus and in the Earth goddess Ge, on the Pergamon Altar, with corresponding values of contrasting nudes and exaggerated rhythms. The syntactical complexity of the high relief of the gigantomachy is daringly transferred into the round with a sense of space in the "marvelous knot" of the Laocoön, which greatly impressed Pliny. The dating of this group in the first century B.C., proposed by many authorities, seems therefore to move it closer to that of the Pergamon Altar, and the question of the chronology and activity of Agesandros, Athenodoros, and Polydoros is opened once more with the discovery of sculptures and signatures in the grotto at Sperlonga, which had been converted into a sculpture museum in the time of Tiberius.

253. Copy in bronze of a portrait of an unknown Greek personage, conventionally called the Pseudo-Seneca, and known in thirty-six replicas. Original created circa *230 B.C. Naples, National Museum*

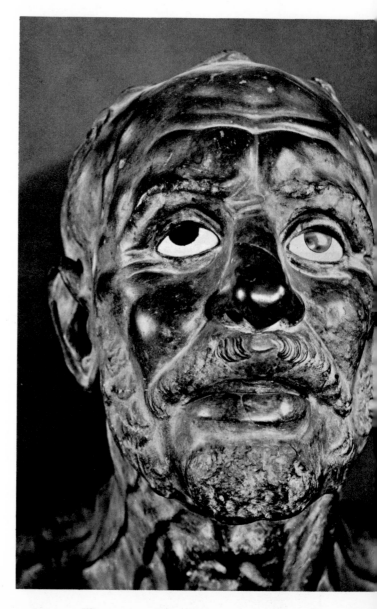

254. Detail of a copy in black marble of an old fisherman, after an original Hellenistic bronze of the second century B.C. Paris, Louvre

255. Roman marble copy of a portrait of Homer, known in twenty-five replicas. After an original Hellenistic work of the second century B.C. In its virtuoso veracity, this head is close to the Laocoön in style. Naples, National Museum

Many of these Sperlonga marbles, patiently recovered during excavations in the grotto, present the exuberant, baroque characteristics of the mature Hellenistic style, as in the agitated head of Odysseus (fig. 251), the grandiose group of Scylla with the companions of Odysseus, and the pilot on the prow of his ship, or the colossal fragments of a nude, perhaps a Polyphemus.

The decorative, dynamic theme of Scylla had been treated in painting by Nikomachos and the unknown Phalerion, and Hellenistic sculptors had transposed this motif into marble to make of it one of those complex, elaborate groups, meant to be set among gardens and fountains, that so delighted the theatrical taste of the times. These rich groups were sought after by Romans, and the Scylla group was placed in a reflecting pool, as in the grotto of Sperlonga and the Canopus of Hadrian's Villa.

In addition to the Laocoön and Scylla groups, there was the theme of the sufferings of Dirce at the hands of Amphion and Zethus, which had been treated in painting, and in the late Hellenistic period appeared in a sculpted marble version. This elaborate virtuoso group, pyramidal in composition and with a landscape setting, was created by the sculptors Apollonios and Tauriskos of Tralles. These sculptors were the sons of Artemidoros, but were adopted by the Rhodian Menekrates, active in Pergamon, a situation which confirms the known contacts between these two Hellenistic centers. The colossality and decorative qualities of this marble group corresponded well to Roman taste, as can be seen in the copy now in Naples known as the *Farnese Bull*, which was intended as an architectural decoration for the center of the huge hall of the Baths of Caracalla.

A further transposition of a fourth-century pictorial theme into sculpture would appear to be the sleeping Ariadne, known through the Vatican copy. The figure unfolds in a series

256. Small female head with the soft and delicate modeling typical of the Praxitelean-influenced art of Alexandria. From the Serapeion of Alexandria. End of the third century B.C. Alexandria, Archaeological Museum

of crossing lines of the legs and arms and the
drapery which is arranged in elegant, elaborate
folds and loops, the result of the sumptuous
vision of the style of Asia Minor, well suited
to a landscaped setting among the rocks and
plants of a garden.

6. Hellenistic Rococo and Verist Virtuosity

Beside this baroque trend, which reached its
most accomplished and elevated expression in
Pergamon, another tendency, sometimes termed
"rococo," began to take shape in the middle
Hellenistic period. One of the first significant
works representing this movement is the figure
of a boy clutching his pet goose, which Pliny
recorded as the work of the sculptor Boethos
of Chalcedon in Bithynia, and, if we are to
judge by the number of copies that have survived, was greatly admired by the Romans.
The original bronze group with its pyramidal
composition and twisting rhythm, contrasted
the light, soft nude body of the child with the
opaque colorism of the goose's downy plumage,
and the theme took on the playful quality of
an epigram. The boy clutching his pet goose
is a theme created by the Hellenistic spirit.
This same spirit gave birth to a new vision
of Heracles: whereas Archaic artists had portrayed the hero wrestling the lion, the Hellenistic age preferred rather to see Heracles as
a sturdy infant strangling the serpents.

This famous Boethos should perhaps be identified with the artist of the same name who
signed the imaginative bronze personification
of Agon (athletic contest) as a boy placing a
garland on his head, and leaning against an
archaistic herm, which was found in the cargo

of an ancient ship sunk off Mahdia in Tunisia.

Putti, ephebi, satyrs, nymphs, tritons, nereids, dancing girls, shepherds, and peasants were the protagonists in this rococo trend, which was also reflected in a large number of statuettes and groups in polychromed terracotta. The seated nymph ready to join in the dance with a leaping satyr, the satyr turning around to look at his tail, the dancing girl balanced daringly in her giddy, spinning rhythm, the lighthearted group of a running girl carrying another on her shoulders in the children's game of *ephedrismos*, the vibrant bronze of a young jockey with outstretched arms and legs (fig. 252) fished out of the sea off Cape Artemision — these are only a few of the more imaginative creations of this artistic trend.

A particular aspect of this trend is constituted by the idyllic and bucolic motifs: old shepherds, peasants, fishermen, and their animals were the protagonists, whether in isolated statues or in landscape reliefs set among rocks, rustic altars, and knotted, twisted trees. All these elements went to form a refined language of apparent rusticity and Arcadian simplicity, which, however, reveals itself to be extremely intellectualized, allusive, lyrical, and precious, in a soft, impressionistic style. Animals, conceived with a fresh sense of naturalism, appeared not only in these landscape reliefs, but also in isolated carvings and bronzes, which were later to be copied and remodeled in abundant quantities for Roman clients who were to place them in their houses, gardens, and fountains. The nude figures of old shepherds and fishermen became virtuoso pieces of anatomical study; artists excelled themselves in rendering the extremes of physical decay, flaccid flesh, hanging folds of skin, protruding veins, sharp, pointed bones, and the play of wrinkles, with an extreme verism that is essentially intellectual in conception (fig. 254). This trend is memorably illustrated by the bony, wrinkled, drunken old woman, sitting down and joyfully hugging her bottle, of the early second century B.C., attributed to one Myron.

This current of virtuoso verism also embraces some portraits. These include the so-called Pseudo-Seneca, a highly elaborate work in which an unknown sculptor portrayed an unknown sitter (fig. 253), and the blind Homer (fig. 255), which could be attributed to the Laocoön circle in Rhodes.

The need to remain close to physical reality led to restrained tones in other portraits of illustrious Hellenistic personalities, such as the so-called Chrysippus, or the Hippocrates, though the subjects were invariably conceived in terms of an intellectualized vision. A fresher realism sometimes animates the faces of contemporary figures, as in the surprisingly vivid presence of Euthydemos of Bactria; for other princes and dynasts, however, artists were to prefer remodeling the heroic conception of Lysippos.

7. Alexandrian Art

In Alexandria the extreme consequences of the Praxitelean tradition is seen in small female heads and statuettes of marble of a subtle modeling treated with a very delicate surface effect (fig. 256). Certain aspects of these works also indicate a convergence with Lysippan tradition. On the other hand, a work like the head of the Gaul from Gizeh shows affinities with the Pergamon offerings, but in a sketchy, shaded modeling typical of Alexandria. The portraits of the Ptolemies imitate those of Alexander the Great, and Libyan princesses, despite all their carefully curled hair, acquire a Hellenic tone.

The panorama of the Nile presented material for an Alexandrian type of artistic creation, showing all the seething, many-sided life of the great river, with the typical flat-bottomed, baldaquin-bedecked boats, pavilions on the banks and the smaller islands, palm groves, clumps of papyrus reeds, water lilies, Negro pygmies, and all the various fauna, including hippopotami, crocodiles, elephants, camels, birds, and cranes, as well as inexhaustible scenes of hunting, banquets, and everyday life, comical, lascivious, burlesque, but always lively and animated. The types of the Negro and the pygmy were the protagonists of complicated landscape scenes in painting, mosaic, reliefs, gems, and stucco work, and were re-developed in statuettes, small bronzes, and terracottas, creating a vast repertory that spread through the craft circles and was to have a long life in the Roman world.

Statuettes of Negro boys, whether as strolling vendors or street singers, or in the relaxed rhythms of lazy, somnolent calm, are lyrical, realistic, and psychological interpretations of aspects of life in Alexandria. Masterpieces in this category are the listless, melancholy little Negro boy musician in the Bibliothèque Nationale in Paris (fig. 257), the four pathetically grotesque statuettes of the *placentarii* in Pompeii, and the lascivious, caricatural small bronzes of dancing pygmies from Mahdia.

Though the painted and mosaic originals of this varicolored Nilotic world have disappeared, we find living echoes of them in works from the Roman period, like the great Barberini mosaic in Palestrina (colorplate, fig. 259) or the paintings of the columbarium of the Villa Pamphilii, apart from other more modest extracts and vulgarizations.

The fertile Nile was personified in statuary in the well-known, sumptuous group in the Vatican, where the classicizing copyist has toned down the original effect of the solemn, bearded god of imposing portliness, who reclines in a soft rhythmic pose most fitting to a great river, while sixteen baby boys, symbolizing the cubits that the river rises each year, clamber over his great body, climb onto the Egyptian sphinx against which the god is leaning, and even into his cornucopia.

The Hellenization of some gods from the Egyptian pantheon led artists to confer Greek forms on the appropriate cult effigies and, together with Serapis, Isis became a well-draped, Hellenized figure, and Harpocrates a plump adolescent. The assimilation of Isis into many local divinities in the Hellenistic world, such as Atargatis, Aphrodite, Hera, Selene, Tyche, and Nemesis, gave her cult universality and caused the number of her images to multiply greatly. These images of Isis reflected all the most typical artistic trends. In Alexandria she took on the form of a Praxitelean Demeter. In the third century B.C. was established the type of Isis with a fringed mantle knotted on her chest in the typical sacred knot of Isis. In this type the light, densely folded material of her garments form slanting, crossed lines, and a complicated effect of folds and edges, and her right hand is raised to hold the sistrum, while she carries the situla in the other hand. There are many versions of this type, the most refined and elaborate of which is the Catajo Isis in Vienna, which is thought to be a product of Rhodes of the second century B.C. The type of the Pharia Isis, placed on a ship's prow, was more turbulent and baroque, while in other types a dominant classicizing, academic tendency is evident. The figure of Isis acquired a large variety of aspects dictated by later religious syncretism.

The shaven head which distinguishes some male portraits in granite and basalt from the late Hellenistic period has led to their being considered priests of Isis, but they belong rather to a characteristic type of portrait in which the traditional Egyptian technique leads to a stereometric conception and compact style, while still conceived with the naturalistic vision proper to the Hellenistic *koine*.

Obviously the artistic culture of Alexandria was also bound to express itself through pictorial activity, and generated the summary, personal style of Antiphilos. In this freer, more open Hellenistic world, a woman painter also is recorded: Helena, the author of a painting of Alexander's battle of Issus, which approaches the tradition of Philoxenos and the Pompeian mosaic in the House of the Faun. We know nothing of Polemon and a certain Demetrios, who had a studio in Rome in the second century B.C., where Ptolemy VI Philometor stayed as a guest. Steles painted with spatial rendering, funerary paintings with vivacious panels

260. *Monumental marble candelabrum in imitation of bronze models. The shaft is surrounded by acanthus leaves and on the faces of the base are Classical types of Zeus, Hera, and Hermes. An example of the final development of the decorative neo-Attic style under Hadrian. From Hadrian's Villa. Vatican, Galleria delle Statue*

in a free, impressionistic style, walls painted with decorative partitions, and fine mosaics, including the allegorical bust of Alexandria by Sophilos, still survive to bear witness to Alexandrian activity in the field of painting. The refined taste of this society is also reflected in the splendid products of metalwork, goldsmiths' work, gem carving, cameos, and glass.

8. The Classicizing Movement in Athens and the Neo–Attic Sculptors

The fresh energies awakened by the activities of the maritime centers of Rhodes and Delos, and the new life of the dynastic courts of the Ptolemies in Alexandria, the Seleucids in Syria, the Attalids in Pergamon, and the royal families of Pontus and Bactria, had brought about a vast and complex flowering of artistic manifestations. Politically and economically in decline, old Athens still carried the weight of an ancient and glorious tradition, and was still live and productive in literature, philosophy, and the arts. With an erudite orientation toward the past, Athens as an artistic center nurtured a learned, academic, classicizing tendency. So it was that the Attic models of fourth-century masters still served for the great statue of Themis by Kairestratos, dedicated by one Megacles in Rhamnus in the first years of the third century B.C. In this figure of Themis the solemnity of fifth-century effigies, like the figure of Nemesis by Agorakritos in the same sanctuary at Rhamnus, is brought together with a soft, Praxitelean head wearing the high coiffure found on deceased women of fourth-century Attic funerary steles, while the broad rolls of pleats in the Hellenistic drapery are treated with a cold and compact linearism. The Classical composition of the seated, draped figure, together with the Hellenistic decorative sense shown in the wild-animal skin, characterize the statue of Dionysus used to decorate the choregic monument of Thrasyllus, a work by Thrasykles of 271 B.C. The inner energy and vigorous modeling of works like the Serapis of Bryaxis or the Otricoli Zeus become toned down to a calm and academic conception in the head of Zeus on an acrolith in the temple at Aegira sculpted by the Athenian Eukleides. This artist followed the Classical spirit and moved in the Olympian sphere of great deities, executing effigies of Demeter, Aphrodite, Dionysus, and Eileithyia for Bura in Achaea between the third and second centuries B.C.

In the second century B.C. similar ideals gave substance to the art of Damophon of Messene,

261. Detail of the marble Borghese krater. Roman copy of the first century A.D., after an original bronze of the first half of the second century B.C. From the same bronze original is also derived a marble neo-Attic vase from Madhia, showing this same group of a young satyr holding the drunken Silenus. Paris, Louvre

exclusively dedicated to sculpting statues and reliefs of the greatest of the Olympian gods. His style is known to us through fragments of heads and draperies from the colossal acrolith of a group of Demeter and Despoina, seated between Artemis and Anytus, carved for the Arcadian sanctuary of Lycosoura. Damophon restored Phidias' celebrated statue of Zeus, and emulation of the great master is to be seen in Damophon's broad treatment and striving for the grandiose, which, however, gave academic results. The emulation of Phidias is also visible in the technique of the acrolith, which provided an economical substitute for chryselephantine work, and he imitates the master in the fine chiseling on the mantle of Despoina, which bears a minute decorative repertory of Nikai carrying candelabra, nereids on sea monsters, grotesque dancers, floral motifs, and garlands. This decorative work, however, is not unrelated to Hellenistic relief modeling. Damophon aspired to Classical grandeur, attempted coloristic accents in the full-volumed heads of Demeter and Artemis which were conceived in terms of the Praxitelean tradition, and gave yet another treatment and expression to the head of Anytus. Thus the work as a whole is eclectic and not coherent in style because of this variety of incompletely assimilated tendencies. Perhaps the sight of Kolothes' celebrated ivory table in Olympia sparked the desire in Damophon to create a similar work in the sanctuary at Megalopolis — where he had already carved many images of gods — adorning his table with the typically Hellenistic motifs of Horai, Pan playing a syrinx, Apollo with a cithara, and nymphs caring for the infant Zeus and carrying overflowing water jars. One is tempted to attribute to Damophon, who was active in Arcadia, the stele found there at Cleitor, and to interpret the work as an image of Polybius of Megalopolis, whom we know was honored with statues in Olympia and Pallantion, and with steles at Megalopolis, Mantinea, Lycosoura, and Tegea.

Academically inclined chronographers and theoreticians like Apollodoros, the author of a history of art arranged in terms of Olympiads, generations, and the *acme* of individual artists, viewed the classicizing movement in the Attic school, which became particularly prominent in the second century B.C., as a renaissance of the great Classical ideals that had marked the finest flowering of Greek art. These ideals were considered to have degenerated and become obscured as a result of the new Hellenistic trends, and to have been definitively exhausted around 297 B.C., the period corresponding precisely to the ascendance of Pergamene art. Coming after this "death of art" — *"cessavit deinde ars"* in the words of Pliny — the classicizing trend which appeared in Athens in the second century B.C. was indeed thought of as a rebirth, personified by two families of artists in which the names of Eucheiros and Euboulydes alternate in one, and Polykles, Dionysios, Timokles, and Timarchides in the other.

One Euboulydes, active between the third

and second centuries B.C., had sculpted the seated figure of Chrysippus in the naturalistic, expressionist style normally used for portraying philosophers, poets, and men of letters. This field constituted one of the activities then most widely practiced by sculptors, who produced more and more statues and herms of such figures. But the true content of this so-called Classical renaissance of the chronographers is revealed to us by the cold, immobile, vacuous head of Athena sculpted by another Euboulydes, perhaps the grandson of the former. A statue of Apollo, of the well-known type with the cithara, known in several copies including the statue from Cyrene, could be identified with the Apollo by Timarchides, from the second century, which had been taken to the Temple of Apollo Sosianus in Rome. It is a typically Hellenistic creation in which the post-Praxitelean tradition is tempered with a virtuoso contrast between the polished surfaces of the soft, plump nude and the deep furrows of the curls and rich folds of the drapery, the whole conceived in a tone of languid restraint.

The large number of signatures of neo-Attic sculptors and the lack of major works bear witness to the fact that the greater part of artistic production had become a mere craft. Many of these sculptors were in reality copyists, reworkers of creations from the past, executing herms, wellheads, basins, bases, reliefs, and candelabra, all decorative works destined for export to Italy, as we can see from the cargoes

262. Metope with the chariot of Helius from the hexastyle Doric Temple of Athena at Troy. Variously dated in the third and first centuries B.C. Berlin, Pergamon Museum

263. Askos *from Canosa with painted decoration and modeled masks, horse protomes, and Nikai.* 31 inches high. Third century B.C. *London, British Museum*

decoration of small framed panels (fig. 157). Phidias' pathetic figures in the frieze of the Niobids from the throne of Zeus were adapted in various ways, and were even recomposed in an arbitrary medallion-shaped composition, in a false and eclectic landscape arrangement. The figures from the base of the Athena Parthenos, beside being utilized in friezes, were placed singly on the faces of a marble candelabrum of the type shown in figure 260. The central group from the east pediment of the Parthenon was translated into relief on a circular wellhead, and also divided into framed marble panels. The centauromachy from the sandals of the Athena Parthenos was used on a marble vase. Copies were made of the reliefs from the plinths of Agorakritos' Nemesis, of Alkamenes' statues of Athena and Hephaestus, of the mythological three-figure groups, of the famous relief of the Eleusinian triad, and of the Nikai from the balustrade surrounding the Temple of Athena Nike on the Acropolis. Particularly favored for their refined and decorative grace were Kallimachos' orgiastic maenads (fig. 161) and his Spartan Dancers with the *kalathiskos*. All this decorative repertory is divided, combined, and recomposed in various ways on panels, wellheads, plinths, vases, and friezes; the elegant *rhyton* in marble, signed by Pontios, in the Capitoline Museums, is one of the most characteristic examples.

Sometimes we must postulate a pictorial model for certain relief scenes, like the seduction of Helen with Aphrodite and Eros, which seems in the vein of the Meidias Painter. The grace and softness of fourth-century art and the rich Hellenistic repertory provide neo-Attic workers with many motifs such as figures from the Dionysiac and Apolline cycles, or the marine *thiasos*.

There is, on the other hand, a particular interest on the part of these neo-Attic sculptors in Archaic art, although the abstract content of this art was by then too far removed from the Hellenistic spirit, and even with the erudite and learned manner of the neo-Attic style it was impossible to revivify the full significance of Archaic art. Beginning already with Alkamenes' Hermes Propylaios we can trace a certain archaizing tendency. Originally, this deliberate archaizing was usually adopted for particular reasons, as in the herm, or in the

of sunken ships fished out of the port of Piraeus, and off Anticythera and Mahdia. Able sculptors, masters of every technique and versed in every style, they were well equipped to cater to all the tastes of their Roman collector-customers.

The choice of models and their application provides an interesting index of taste and preference. From the great art of the fifth century, the Severe style is represented only by copies of reliefs with the Three Graces clad in the peplos, attributed to the sculptor Sokrates. The figured world of Phidias was much admired and provided many decorative themes. The dynamic groups from the Amazonomachy on the shield of Athena Parthenos had already been copied by Timokles and Timarchides in the shield of their own Athena made for Elatea, and later these groups, divorced from their original context, served as models for the

264. *Etruscan painted terracotta bust, perha representing Apollo, inspired by the Lysippa style. From the Scasato temple at Falerii.* 22 inches high. Late third century B.C. *Rome, Villa Giulia*

Palladium which was invariably manneristically stylized on Panathenaic amphorae, or in other figures of gods on amphorae and *oinochoai* produced by the Panathenaic circle. However, these various archaizing accents were not composed into a consequent, organic style until the second century B.C., when neo-Attic artists, freed from problems of content, remodeled the Archaic modes of swallow-tailed drapery, long-ringleted coiffures, and the characteristic rhythms of the Archaic style into new, superficial, purely ornamental forms, based on an exaggerated, decorative line. Gods, Graces, nymphs, and Pan were transformed into figurines for a mannered ballet on tiptoe, given rhythm by the diverging hems of their robes and their long, curving figures. There is a still more generic and eclectic interpretation of the Archaic style that resuscitated the corkscrew curls and Ionic drapery. This is seen in statues marked by a refined, though empty academism, and was to find its last development on Roman soil.

This classicizing current, which radiated from Athens in the second century B.C., did not fail to influence the late work of other centers. Evidence of this seems to be provided by the frieze on the Ionic Temple of Hecate in Lagina, from the first years of the first century B.C., where even in complex scenes with superimposed planes, the figures are still represented frontally, placed in terms of a prevalently static conception. This trend can also be traced in the conventional nature of the gigantomachy scenes, groups of gods, and typical Amazon-like personifications of cities, including Rome, which were to undergo a wider development in Roman art. Even the last art of Rhodes is not without classicizing touches and a characteristic tendency toward refined mannerism can be seen in the very elaborate types of fauns, Priapus, and Dionysus and the Bacchantes.

9. The Artistic *Koine* of the Hellenistic World and Its Diffusion

The very wide diffusion of the common artistic language or *koine* of the Hellenistic period is documented by its various degrees of acceptance, and the reactions it produced in even the most outlying regions. Oriental grandiosity and Hellenic forms, a syncretism of Persian and Greek religion, are expressed in the solemn tumulus of the Hierothesion, raised by Antiochus I, king of Commagene, 6000 feet up on the Anti-Taurus, known as Nemrud Dagh. This monument dominated the entire kingdom of Commagene, as an exceptional example of *pietas*, with a desire to forge a link between all the civilized peoples of East and West. On the two terraces were colossal seated statues in the Oriental style of hieratic, stylized immobility, but with heads marked by an incisive modeling. They showed Zeus Oromazdes, a fusion of the Olympian god with the Persian Ahura Mazda; the personification of Commagene with a cornucopia, ears of wheat, and a *kalathos*, in accordance with Greek conceptions; and a significant juxtaposition of Apollo, Mithras, Helius, Hermes, Artagnes, Heracles, and Ares. A naturalistic head of Antiochus on the relief decorating the altar is accompanied by a typically Oriental expression in the relief with the lion, representing the horoscope of the King. In this unique, monumental complex East and West genuinely did meet, in a work suggestive of the fabulous.

Greek naturalism was responsible for the splendid series of portraits of the kings of Bactria on the coinage of this kingdom, which bear legends in Greek and reproduce statuary types of gods drawn from Lysippan tradition. In this region the Greek influence mingles with the Oriental tradition in fine silver medallions showing the lively figure of an elephant of war, in gold and silver cups, and in goldsmiths' work.

In far-off Gandhara, formerly conquered by Alexander, Hellenistic art contrived to permeate the Indian tradition, and under the influence of Greek anthropomorphization, the traditional, symbolic, nonrepresentational image of Buddha took human and Apolline forms.

In the West of the ancient world, the Celtic and Iberian areas were coming into increasingly frequent and close contact with the Hellenistic artistic current. The *neapolis* at Ampurias with its regular groundplan comes to

265. Top left: Detail of a small Etruscan alabaster urn from Volterra with a baroque version of the centauromachy in a very high relief. Second century B.C. Volterra, Museum

266. Top right: Detail of the lacerated head of Actaeon on a small Etruscan alabaster urn from Volterra. Hellenistic models are here interpreted with a rustic plastic vigor. Second century B.C. Volterra, Museum

267. Below: Detail of the head of Charun on a small Etruscan alabaster urn from Volterra. The fierce Etruscan demon with equine ears here grabs one of the horses of Enomaus. Second century B.C. Florence, Archaeological Museum

resemble Hellenistic cities with the Doric stoa and agora, and in the Temple of Asclepius of the same town a marble effigy 7 feet high repeats the pure, classicizing forms of the early Hellenistic period. A bronze statuette from Jaén, now in Madrid, showing a satyr playing the double flutes, exemplifies the assimilation of Hellenistic modes by local bronze-workers, revealed in the elongation of the limbs and the tunic that covers the body. But Hellenistic influences remain on a provincial level, and the more genuine, direct expressions of the native Celtic and Iberian cultures are of greater artistic significance. These include the plastic vigor and unorganic expressivity of the limestone high reliefs from Osuna, with flute players and warriors; the effective, abstract stylization of funerary sculpture; the primitive symbolism of severed heads and animals from the region of Provence of the pre-Roman period. The most original Celtic decorative expression, an inheritance from the La Tène period, is to be seen in the ornamental abstraction on weapons, mirrors, vases, and goldsmiths' work. The genuine artistic values of this culture indeed rest on an indigenous, native culture profoundly separated from and foreign to the Classical spirit. The most significant proof of this is to be found in Celtic coins. During the Hellenistic period they began to imitate Macedonian golden staters with heads of Apollo and bigas driven by Philippus, but the models were rapidly transformed into an abstract, ornamental nature, arriving at the most fantastic arabesques. All Celtic decoration, even when it shows Hellenic sources, is expressed in elements that have no typological parallels in the traditional Classical repertory: the palmette becomes a three-petaled lily and the more fantastic motifs simply cannot be described in terms of precise floral or naturalistic elements, but only approximately equated with flower buds, fish bladders, tears, or flames. These forms occur within a syntax dominated by the use, developed to the extreme, of the curved line, the volute, the spiral, and the wheel motif, in a sinuous interweaving, with endless combinations of interlacing and linear openwork. The already dazzling effects of this flamboyant style were further enriched by pierced work and the use of corals and, later, enameled inlay.

Although the Hellenistic art invaded the Celto-Iberian area, the local art still remained well outside the Classical tradition.

Italy, on the other hand, became a true province of Hellenism. Statuary, terracottas, and works of varied and rich crafts carried the imprint of the Hellenistic koine. Although these works, in the assimilation of Hellenic modes, do not modify the general picture of Hellenistic art, they do furnish documentation for the history of Italic taste, inasmuch as this taste departs from or reacts against the strong Greek influx. The degree of Hellenization can be gauged from the work of the clay-modelers of Centuripae, which, from the third century B.C., reflects all the typical stylistic and typological repertory of Hellenism, with light, languishing Aphrodites, flying figures of Eros, Psyches, dancing fauns, characters from the world of comedy and farce, caricatures, and grotesques. Thousands of terracottas from Sicily and Magna Graecia are only the vulgarization of Hellenic types, but this assimilation of the common denominator of Hellenistic art became transformed into a sonorous Italic accent in the graceful, draped female figurines and animal protomes which came to crown the showy and baroque askoi from Canosa, produced by Daunian-Messapian craftsmen (fig. 263).

The most characteristic and genuine aspects that color the picture of Italic art are represented precisely by the indigenous popular currents that escaped Greek formulas to a greater or lesser degree: whether in the linearism of sculptures in soft Tarantine stone; in the heavy, incisive plasticity of the summary but eloquent Campanian mother-figures, carved in tufa, who are seated and virtually fused into one piece with their thrones, while holding in their wide embrace numerous babies swaddled tight as cocoons; in the jutting beards, the protruding ridges of eyelids and eyebrows on the bewildered peasant heads of Campanian terracottas; or in the expressive unorganic rhythms in small bronzes of Heracles, Italic warriors, or donors shown in the act of offering. Further indigenous elements are to be found in the later Campanian paintings, with their victorious warriors and bloodstained gladiators, or again in the exuberant polychrome and relief decoration of the pottery of Centuripae, as well as in the local tempera paintings with Hellenizing Dionysiac scenes, or busts and heads in native style, which also appear on funerary shields.

10. The Flowering of Etruscan Art in the Hellenistic Period

Etruria, too, participated in this widespread stylistic koine of Hellenism, which left its mark on the greater part of artistic production,

268. Etruscan terracotta portrait in a strong and sober style, of fresh and spontaneous naturalism. From Caere.
First century B.C. Rome, Villa Giulia

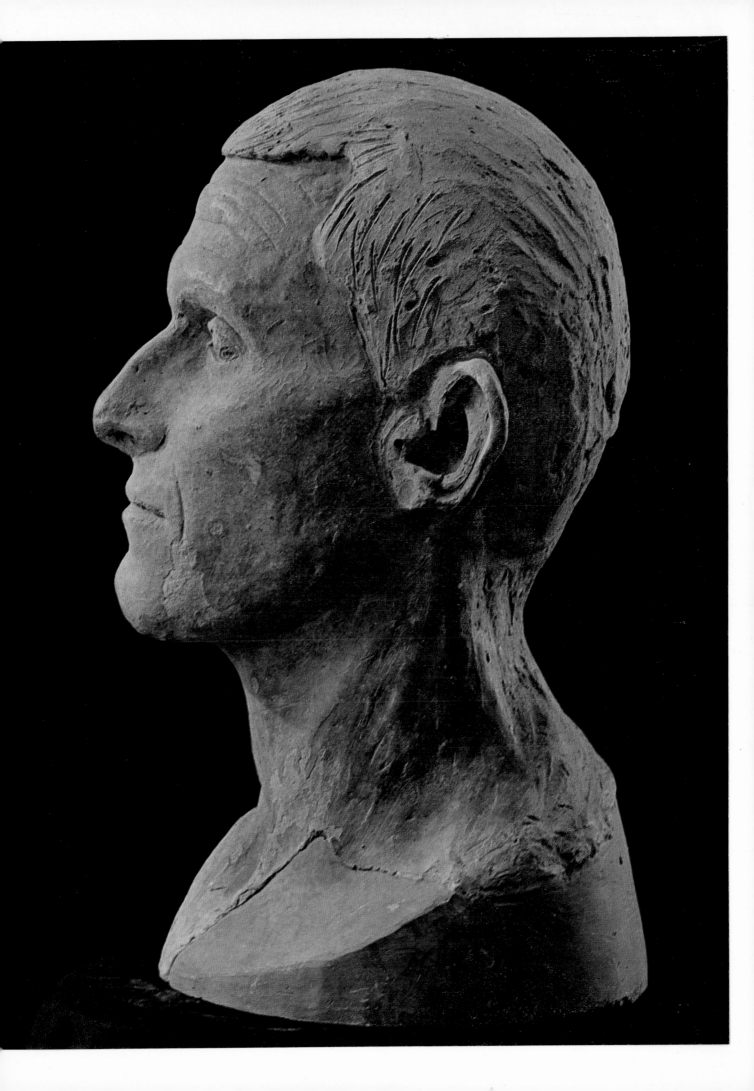

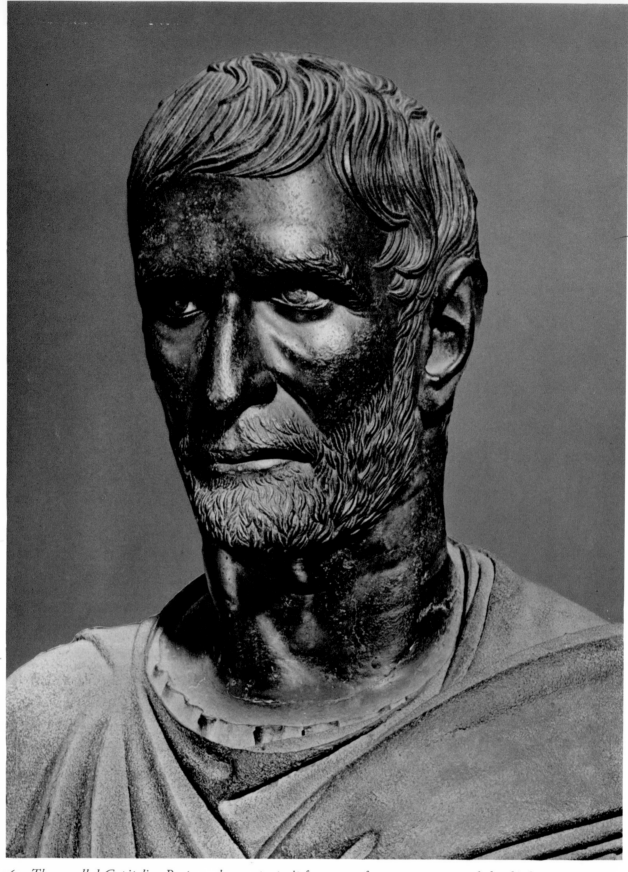

269. *The so-called Capitoline Brutus, a bronze portrait from some funerary monument of the third to the second century* B.C. *Created by an artist of the Etrusco-Italic tradition. Rome, Capitoline Museums*

more intensely in the works of greater importance such as the clay decorations of temples, bronzes, and tomb paintings. The Hellenistic language with its free naturalism was easier to speak than the abstract, transcendental, Archaic idiom, the rigorous, compact, Severe style, or the heroic, Olympian Classical expression; and Etruscan clay-modelers now attained effects of Hellenic purity under the belated stylistic influences of the fourth-century master and the principal Hellenistic trends. A woman's head in the Vatican achieves the coherency of an early Hellenistic Aphrodite; male and female heads from Arezzo have a Hellenic structure; and a melancholy head of a pedimental figure of a boy in a Phrygian cap is on the same level as the softest, most romantic expression of Hellenism; a bearded, crowned head in Orvieto from San Leonardo has an academic serenity and the balance of a classicizing Zeus of the late Hellenistic period.

The Faliscan region, increasingly open to Hellenic influences, produced at the end of the third century B.C. a fresh, vigorous image born from the teachings of Lysippos, in the well-known male bust, perhaps of Apollo, from the Scasato temple in Falerii, now in Villa Giulia, with its deep, gazing eyes, rich, curly hair, heroic rhythm, and pathetic tone (colorplate, fig. 264). A graceful figure with bowed head is in the post-Praxitelean tradition, and an antefix representing Diana, both from the same Scasato temple, is a lively image of pure Hellenistic grace.

While in Hellenistic Greece pedimental decoration in marble was reduced to ornamental elements, in Etruria it had a remarkable flowering in terracotta. Following Classical examples the Etruscans created figures in the round, like those from Falerii, but the Hellenistic experiments in pictorial landscape narrative led to a preference for unified high-relief compositions with scenes set on several planes animated by numerous figures, tightly packed and emerging from the background. This type of Etruscan pediment was also accepted in Etruscanized areas. In Telamon a temple commemorating perhaps the victory against the Gauls in 225 B.C. presents the mythical battle of Thebes, which is developed symmetrically to either side of the central figure of the winged Genius, with the diverging chariots of Amphiaraus and the fleeing Adrastus, framed by typical Lasae, which bear witness to the Etruscan elaboration of Hellenistic motifs of a baroque style. At Luni, a Roman colony founded in 176 B.C., pediments, which must be dated at the time of the founding, with the Niobids, the Muses, Apollo, and other gods, are even more infused with classicistic, soft, graceful elements. And in Civitella Alba, in the Marches, two clay pediments from the second century B.C. develop two typically Hellenistic themes: one of a Galatomachy, battle of Greeks and Gauls, referring to the sack of Delphi and recalling conceptions dear to Pergamene art; and the other showing the rediscovery of Ariadne and her marriage to Dionysus, another theme familiar to Hellenistic painters and sculptors.

In the field of painting, draftsmanship in the Classical tradition and a chiaroscuro modeling persist in the figures of the later, second chamber of the Orco Tomb in Tarquinia, with the Land of the Dead peopled with Greek as well as Etruscan mythological personages, with a curly-headed Theseus, Odysseus, Sisyphus, Memnon, the three-headed Geryon in an Etruscan cuirass, Hades with a fine profile wearing a wolf-skin on his head, a Persephone of Hellenistic grace but with snaky hair, and a livid, Etruscan Tuchulcha shaking a serpent.

As in the fourth century, banquet scenes continued to be set in this underworld. The banquet scene from the Tomb of the Shields at Tarquinia has the graphic, cursive style that is to be found in some Campanian pottery, rising to expressive accents in the face of the man shown in three-quarter view with an aquiline nose, the beard hatched in, and the eyes downcast. The style degenerates, however, in the more typecast women's faces, mere conventional imitations of the grace of their Hellenic models, compensating for the lack of expression with an entirely superficial play of ornament, details, and reproductions of the showy Etruscan jewelry of the times.

Greek painting constituted the principal source for the scenes on the small clay urns from Chiusi, on the carved tufa urns from Chiusi and Perugia, and on similar urns in alabaster from Volterra. The clay urns from Chiusi were molded by stamping and then retouched. This technique led to a plastic relief with a smooth background, in the Classical spirit, while in the more easily worked tufa and alabaster, the Etruscan chisel indulged in a taste for strong contrasts (figs. 265–267), with deep shadows which detach the figures from their background so that they stand out and seem to advance toward the onlooker. The mythological themes chosen, among them scenes of cruel battles from the Theban and Homeric cycles, sacrifices, and funerary rites, are all pervaded with a striking animation that camouflages the modest nature of the craft style and confers an Etruscan tone on the Greek models. Iphigenia is dragged horizontally to the altar; intestines burst from the wounds of Eteocles and Polynices; costumes have very detailed Etruscan elements, emphasized by vivid polychromy; and Lasae and demons mingle with Greek personages and welcome the deceased to the underworld.

The deep hollows, the high relief of the figures, their varied grouping, sometimes in circular arrangements, sometimes on several levels, stretching out or leaning forward, have led to the hypothesis of an Etruscan elaboration of spatial problems, considered as the premise for the development of the Roman historical relief. But not only had this illusionism and landscape relief been experimented with before in Hellenistic art, but also nowhere in this artisans' art of Etruria do we find organic composition or coherent development. It is rather a case of improvised, varied, and often contrasting expressions of an uninhibited mode of narrating with technical facility in the soft tufa or alabaster. The gesticulation and external excitement that animate these Etruscan figures must not be confused with the intellectualized study of expression by the Greek masters. Thus, what these Etruscan urns exhibit is the very free echoing of some Hellenistic compositional and expressive modes, even though the Etruscan imagination of itself does sometimes fortuitously appear in a case of foreshortening or in some pose which in audacity outstrips Hellenistic experiments.

The reclining figures of the dead placed on the lids of these small urns and on stone or clay sarcophagi — in which Greek models are not consulted, but the spontaneous, unsophisticated Etruscan tradition is followed — provide many conventional examples of a stylistic poverty counteracted by the abundance of wreaths and jewels that cover the dead person. Some, however, show a veristic search for expression that aims at giving the appearance of a portrait, although only in a few of the best and most important sarcophagi was there a real attempt to convey the features of the deceased. This is a fluid, summary style, which becomes almost impressionistic when rendered in terracotta. All attention is concentrated on the head, and the body is reduced to approximate, symbolic forms and flattened out on the lid, in a perfunctory, careless execution that leaves the thumb prints and tool marks unerased on the clay. The style becomes rougher and more incisive in stone sarcophagi. At times these have a hieratic tone,

as in the dead woman idealized in the aspect of a Greek maenad, but wearing Etruscan jewelry from her necklace with *bulla* to her Gallic torques, on the lid of a limestone sarcophagus from the Tomb of the Triclinium in Tarquinia, from the middle of the third century B.C.; or, as in the striking sarcophagus of Parthunus at Tarquinia, a tone of immediate verism pins down the type of the *obesus Etruscus* supporting his melancholy head with his hand, while the soft, heavy mass of his halfnaked body slumps and spreads over the bed.

Similar expressions of characterization are to be found in the numerous clay heads cast in molds and retouched by hand, used as ex-votos in the Etruscan and Italic areas. The type of these heads is varied by the addition of a few details executed with vivacity and immediacy of touch, in a linear style with a few particulars brought out in color.

Expressive freedom and a naturalistic taste were basic Etruscan qualities, which made portraiture their most congenial artistic expression (colorplate, fig. 268); when these qualities were combined with Greek formal principles, Etruscan art could produce some very felicitous results, most of all in the more important bronze statuary. The head of the so-called Capitoline Brutus (fig. 269) probably represents one of the honorary portraits of Roman personages created by an Etruscan artist of the third to second century B.C. Because of its rough, vigorous, incisive style, it appears different from a Hellenistic portrait, but equally valid, and perhaps more intense and aggressive in its impact. On the other hand, the soft, Italic bronze head from near Bovianum, from the second century B.C., is more Hellenistic and sophisticated, while other portraits, like the one of a boy in Florence and the head of a beardless young man from Fiesole in the Louvre, seem already to fit into the Roman artistic climate.

IX | The Contrast Between Greek Influence and the Ideal of the *Civis Romanus*

Rome was to wait longer than other centers before accepting and assimilating the Hellenistic influence, but in the end it was there that this influence had its most important development and produced the most valid works, giving life to the creation of Roman art. After forging a widespread common artistic language and leaving a Hellenic imprint on the entire ancient world, the elevated Greek tradition in its manifestations in the East ceased to be a renewing force, and did not give rise to any substantially new contributions, though it contributed to keeping alive the artistic experience and spiritual values of Classicism, which were to play a major role in the formation of Byzantine art.

Hellenism planted its most vital seed in the West, on Italic soil, nourished it, and brought about the vigorous germination of Roman art, after a slow maturing process that had developed during the third and second centuries and bore fruit in the first century B.C.

After the period when Rome had called on Etruscan and Italic artists for the few artistic requirements of the city's sober life, geared to the struggle for conquest, contacts with Greek art became increasingly close and direct. From the third century on, Greek art began to exercise its fascination on the Roman spirit, which recognized and admired the level and fame achieved by Greek culture. These contacts gradually became established through conquests in Italy and the East, the importation of works of art, the immigration of artists, and the penetration of Greek thought, progressively overcoming the tenacious resistance shown by the Roman mentality, which considered art as a corrupting influence, and an activity unworthy of the *civis Romanus*. With the development of a literature in Latin came inevitably a knowledge of the Greek literary masterpieces of the historians, rhetoricians, poets, and dramatists. Andronicus translated the *Odyssey* into Saturnian verse; Plautus took the Greek comedy as his model. Acceptance of Greek thought was easier and more spontaneous because the Romans readily admitted the strength and importance of history to document and evoke great deeds; of eloquence to give vigor and nobility to political struggles and judicial activities; of the epic to celebrate the legends and splendors of Rome; of poetry to comment on sentiments in a convivial tone, and to create the funerary epigram and religious litany; and of comedy to cheer people's souls. The literary arts were soon given status in Rome, and with the centralizing force that was later to lead to the creation of the Roman Empire, Rome accepted and Romanized its first poets, who were Italic: Andronicus perhaps from Taranto, Ennius from Rudiae, Naevius from Campania, Plautus from Sarsina, and Pacuvius from Brindisi.

While "the muse with winged step had been introduced among the proud, warlike people of Rome," many ethical preconceptions were still long to be invoked against figurative and decorative art. It was recorded as an exceptional, discreditable case when in 303 B.C. a Roman, Caius Fabius Pictor, decorated the Temple of Salus on the Quirinal with paintings, and Valerius Maximus was much later to ask why a man of so noble a family, already rich in glory, should ever have thought to seek fame through things so humble, through so unworthy an activity.

287

1. The Influx of Greek Works of Art into Republican Rome

During the third and second centuries B.C. there was on the one hand an increasing influx of Greek works of art and progressively widespread surrender to the delights of the arts, and on the other hand, the renewal of professions of faith, *virtus*, and *pietas* opposing any aesthetic pleasure.

In 212 B.C. statues and paintings looted by Marcus Marcellus after his capture of Syracuse were carried through Rome in triumphal pomp, and the city, according to Plutarch, "neither knew nor possessed, before then, any of these objects of luxury and refinement, nor did it take any pleasure in masterpieces of grace and elegance, but was filled with barbarous weapons and bloodstained hostages, and crowned with triumphal monuments and trophies, no happy or serene spectacle for timid and refined visitors." Many praised Marcellus, "who had enriched the city with a spectacle of pleasure, Hellenic grace, and the varied aspects of art." But the old guard had more esteem for Fabius Maximus, "who had carried nothing of that kind from Taranto, but had taken only money and wealth, leaving the statues where they stood and letting the Tarantine people keep their angry gods." Indeed, they criticized Marcellus first and foremost for having made Rome hated and envied, for he had seemed to be leading not only men, but also gods in captivity through the city, and for having filled the Romans with idleness and gossip and led people to talk urbanely about artists, when they were more used to fighting and killing and tilling the fields, free from any softness and frivolity, like Euripides' Heracles, "simple and straightforward, fit only for important things." Livy considered this moment as the beginning of admiration for Greek works of art, and it appears that Marcellus was most proud of what he had done.

The influx of works of art went hand in hand with the increasingly frequent succession of conquests. Statues came from Capua in 212 B.C.; objects of gold and silver, and statues, including Lysippos' Heracles, arrived from Taranto in 210 B.C. According to Annaeus Florus, prior to the triumphal procession of Marcellus Rome had seen processions of the herds of the Volscians, the flocks of the Sabines, the chariots of the Gauls, and the broken weapons of the Samnites. Now works of art became the greatest part of the triumphs over rich Eastern centers. A great mass of refined relief works in chased gold and silver

sparkled in the triumphal procession of Titus Quintius Flamininus after his victory over Philip V of Macedonia in 194 B.C. Gold and silver treasures, golden crowns, coins, swords, and one hundred and thirty-four statues figured in the triumph of Lucius Scipio Asiaticus in 188 B.C., and precious tables, richly decorated triclinium couches, and sumptuous garments in the triumph of Cnaeus Manlius in 186 B.C. "In Asia," Sallust commented, "the army of the Roman people assuaged itself first with love and wine, then in admiration of statues, painted pictures, and chased vases."

Works of art continued to accumulate, with the booty from Ambracia for the triumph of Marcus Fulvius Nobilior over Pyrrhus in 189 B.C., and two years later, with the triumph over the Aetolians, which brought in two hundred and eighty-five bronze statues and two hundred and thirty in marble; and in 168 B.C. with the triumph of Lucius Aemilius Paulus over Perseus. In this way Rome acquired Greek originals such as an Athena of Phidias, and the cycle of Hellenistic Muses from Ambracia, and later, with the triumph of Quintus Caecilius Metellus over the Macedonians in 146 B.C., the group of Alexander the Great in battle by Lysippos was taken to Rome. Statues and votive offerings were looted by Publius Scipio Africanus in the sack of Carthage, and in 146 B.C., when Lucius Mummius took Corinth, notwithstanding his proverbial ignorance in matters of art, the Roman general took care to strip the rich city of all its works of art and celebrated Corinthian bronzes.

The censor Marcus Porcius Cato is the most representative exponent of the conservative attitude. He defended the *Lex Oppia*, anti-luxury law, forbidding excess in jewelry, multicolored garments, and vehicles with more than one horse, and he generally inveighed against the growing admiration for Greek works of art: "The more the fortunes of our Republic grow happy and propitious from day to day — and we have already crossed Greece and Asia, lands rich in every kind of flattery and vicious pleasure, and we have laid our hands on their royal treasures — the more I am horrified, for fear that these riches may have conquered us instead of our having conquered them. Believe me, these statues from Syracuse are pernicious for our city. Already I hear far too much praise and admiration of works from Corinth and Athens, and scorn for the clay images of Roman gods. But I still prefer our own gods, and that they be gracious, and I hope that they will continue so if we make sure they remain in their rightful places."

But Cato's *virtus* was countered in Rome

itself by the *humanitas* of the circle of the Scipios, which was by then open to Greek culture. The divine effigies in Etruscan-style polychromed terracotta, which still dominated the city in temple pediments and cellas, may have satisfied *pietas*, but their rustic nature was all too evident when compared with Greek masterpieces.

2. Architecture and Commemorative Monuments in Rome

Rome in the third and second centuries B.C. must have presented a most singular contrast with, on the one hand, great wealth and many Greek works of art brought back after Roman victories, and on the other hand, the simple, austere picture presented by the city itself. Rome had been rebuilt in haste, without any over-all plan, after the Gallic fire of 390 B.C. The first preoccupations had been to surround the city with walls of tufa, to reconstruct the temples, and cover the *Cloaca Maxima*. The first aqueduct was created in 312 B.C., and the road to the South was fortified under the censor Appius Claudius. In 272 the city was to have its second aqueduct, the *Anio Vetus*, followed by that of the *Marcia* in 144 B.C., and the *Tepula* aqueduct in 129. It was not until the second century, however, that anyone thought of regularizing and embellishing the Roman Forum: the Basilica Porcia was built in 170 B.C., that of Fulvia Aemilia in 179, and the Basilica Sempronia in 170, the Rostra were erected, and the Curia was several times rebuilt. The first masonry bridges were also built in the second century B.C.: the Pons Aemilius in 142, and the Pons Milvius in 109.

All their works of public utility, and the temples on massive stone podia, with clay decorations in an architecture of stone, tufa, and terracotta must have made Rome very different from the splendid cities of Asia Minor, all of sparkling white marble, thick with columns, and planned with regularity or a scenographic sense. But this sober, austere Roman architecture carried in itself the vital technical principles of cement and brick-making, the keystone arch, and the concrete vault, with a constructional system different from that used in Greece and well suited for monumental development. A noteworthy expression of Roman architecture in the second century B.C. is the Porticus Aemilia, an enormous warehouse near the Tiber, built in 192 and remodeled in 174, measuring 1600 by 190 feet, with arcades on pilasters, and divided transversely into fifty bays covered with cement barrel-vaults, creating an enclosed, organically articulated, functionally monumental space.

In addition to its applications in harbors, bridges, and aqueducts, the arch became an architectonic element in its own right as a part of the support for honorary statues. In 196 B.C. Lucius Stertinius erected two arches carrying gilded statues in the Forum Boarium, and one with Spanish trophies in the Circus Maximus. Another arch was raised in 190 B.C. by Publius Scipio on the Capitol, with gilded statues, horses, and fountains. In 121 B.C. yet another was raised on the *Via Sacra*, this time due to Quintus Fabius Maximus.

This honorary function was also fulfilled by the most ancient type of monument, the column carrying an iconic statue. That of Gaius Menius was created in 338 B.C. Columns with rostra were erected on the Capitol to commemorate the naval victories of Gaius Duilius, in 260 B.C., and Marcus Aemilius Paulus, in 225 B.C.

In the field of architecture concessions were thus made to the requirements of commemorative and honorary procedures, but at the same time the Senate, at the instigation of Publius Cornelius Scipio Nasica, prohibited as an immoral extravagance the construction of permanent theaters, despite the passion for the theater shared by all Roman society. The theater begun by the censors Valerius Messalla and Cassius Longinus on the slopes of the Palatine was ordered to be destroyed, being "useless and harmful to the habits of the public." Even the Circus Maximus and the Circus Flaminius were only to have simple facilities, and gladiatorial contests took place in the area of the Forum. Public baths were still small and unadorned.

The importance of family life led to the transformation of the Roman house, which centered around the traditional dark *atrium*, by replacing the *hortus* and *viridarium* which were beyond the *atrium*, with a Hellenistic peristyle, more airy and pleasant. Walls began to be covered with plaster and painted to imitate marble panels and cornices. This particular type of wall decoration is conventionally known as the First style of Roman wall painting, which was derived from Hellenistic work and which is known principally from examples in Pompeii.

3. Roman Triumphal Painting

The Romans began to appreciate the political role of art, as well as its religious and commemorative functions. From the third century B.C. on, the political function of art is represented by the triumphal painting that was used to give the populace illustrations of victorious campaigns and of the countries in which they had taken place. Paintings representing the campaigns against the Carthaginians and against Hieron of Syracuse were exhibited by Valerius Messalla in 264 B.C. on the side of the Curia Hostilia. Pictures of victorious soldiers banqueting at Beneventum in the Second Punic War were commissioned in 214 B.C. for the walls of the Temple of Liberty, by Titus Sempronius Gracchus. In 201 B.C. Publius Scipio Africanus had an exhibition of triumphal paintings and in 188 B.C. Lucius Scipio showed pictures on the Capitol of his exploits in Asia. A geographical map of Sardinia and scenes from the war there were placed in the Temple of Mater Matuta by Titus Sempronius Gracchus in 174 B.C.

In 168 B.C. Lucius Aemilius Paulus asked the Athenians for a painter to commemorate his victorious campaign against the Macedonian king, Perseus, and a philosopher to instruct his sons. Metrodoros was sent to him, as being the best man on both counts. The Romans could no longer ignore Greek culture, and Metrodoros, a philosopher and painter, was a characteristic example of the erudite, academic leanings of second-century Attic art. We can form an idea of the artistic trend Metrodoros must have followed, from the frieze on the tall base of the monument to Aemilius Paulus in Delphi, which illustrates the war against Perseus in a style that shows minute care in the details of Macedonian weapons and pictorial foreshortenings, but remains smooth, polished, conventional, and cold.

In the *fabula praetexta*, "*Paulus*," the poet Pacuvius exalted the enterprises of the Roman general. Pacuvius, like Metrodoros, was also a painter, and was perhaps chosen by Aemilius Paulus himself to decorate the Temple of Hercules in the Forum Boarium, which the general probably had restored after the victory of Pydna. Art was increasingly appreciated by the more cultured Romans, though generally speaking it still was not considered a worthy occupation for a Roman citizen. Pacuvius, however, came from the more openminded, Hellenized society of Magna Graecia; and the case of the painter Lucius Mallius, recorded by Macrobius as being active in Rome in the third and second centuries B.C., was still completely exceptional, so much so that Pliny could truthfully say that until then he had found no trace of any Roman citizen of any rank having been a painter. The other painters recorded in Rome in the third and second centuries were all foreigners: Theodo-

tos, who according to Naevius, used a large brush (and therefore broad strokes) to paint altars with figures of Lares, was a Greek; Marcus Plautius came from Aisa Minor, and became a citizen of Ardea; Demetrios, from Alexandria, had the nickname of *topographos*, which makes one think of maps and landscape views, a type of work that could certainly have been exploited in triumphal painting.

Triumphal painting was probably the result of the convergence of various artistic forces, Greek, Italic, and even Roman. It was the expression of a Roman mentality, finding an immediate, passionate response among the people by virtue of its explanatory, illustrative, commemorative, and social character. In 146 B.C. Lucius Hostilius Mancinus, who had been the first to enter Carthage, had paintings exhibited illustrating the city and its destruction; he went himself to the exhibition in the Forum, and delivered a commentary to the crowd on the various details. He thus incurred the resentment of Scipio Aemilianus, perhaps because Mancinus had omitted reference to the help he had received from Scipio. Similarly, Lucius Scipio's triumphal paintings had caused pain to his brother because his son had been made prisoner by Antiochus in the battle illustrated.

The importance and fame of triumphal painting in Roman society are shown by the fact that Mancinus was rewarded with the consulate for his courteous appearances before the people to explain his paintings.

The complete disappearance of these triumphal paintings makes it impossible for us to study the various sources and elements that were combined in this narrative language that grew up in the climate of Republican Rome. Perhaps some inspiration from these paintings is reflected in the work of the modest painter of a tomb on the Esquiline. The tomb was probably that of some military leader. In a fragment of the wall painting (colorplate, fig. 270) we see a composition in tiered zones illustrating scenes of combat and a meeting and parley between two chiefs, Marcus Fannius, who may have been a Samnite, and Quintus Fabius (this latter figure has also been identified as Maximus Rullianus). In this tomb decoration, beside battle compositions derived from a more sophisticated tradition, we see companies of soldiers tightly arranged in

270. Roman wall painting from a tomb on the Esquiline in Rome, with battle scenes and the meeting of the chiefs, Marcus Fannius and Quintus Fabius. First century B.C. Rome, Capitoline Museums

several ranks, following a compositional principle that also appears in paintings from late Etruscan tombs, for instance, in the crowd of dead people in the Tomb of the Typhon, in Tarquinia. There is also greater freedom in proportional relationships, so that the protagonists are shown larger than the other figures, and are placed on the front plane, in accordance with syntactical principles that were to be amply developed in historical reliefs of the Roman Empire.

4. Honorary Portraiture

The general acceptance in the Roman world of honorary portraiture in the form of statues, or surmounting iconic columns or arches, is attested to by the measures taken in 179 B.C. to move some of the honorary statues that had been placed on the Capitol, and by the order of the censors in 158 B.C. which demanded the removal of all statues of magistrates erected in the Forum without a special plebiscite or decree of the Senate.

New forms of portrait statuary were maturing as a result of contact with Greek art. Roman military leaders, magistrates, and businessmen who saw the cities, ports, and sanctuaries of Greece became familiar with examples of Classical and Hellenistic portraiture, and acquired the ambition to have themselves depicted in bronze or marble along the same lines as these Greek models. Accordingly, the Romans began to abandon their togas of citizenship to have themselves portrayed in the nakedness of Greek heroes and athletes. The sculptors Dionysios and Timarchides endowed the Roman Gaius Ofellius Ferus with a Praxitelean body in a statue at Delos. For the gold coin struck to commemorate his victory over Philip V of Macedon, Titus Quintius Flamininus had his image portrayed by a Greek artist who designed a classicizing head of heroic interpretation, while the reverse of the coin bore a Nike copied from the type seen on the Macedonian staters of Alexander.

Pliny records the introduction of the type of portrait statues with the subject depicted in heroic nudity, known as "Achillean" portraits. These nude figures held spears, like the ephebi of the gymnasium. Pliny also notes that the Greeks usually left the body bare, whereas the Roman military custom was to add breast-plates. The bronze statue of the so-called Hellenistic Ruler, in the Museo delle Terme in Rome, is a typical example of an "Achillean" statue, which the Romans adopted not only in the East, but also in · Rome. The more conservative elements in Roman

271. Bronze statue of the Umbro-Etruscan Aulus Metellus, known as L'Arringatore *or* The Orator. *Cast in six pieces. From the region of Lake Trasimeno. First century B.C. Florence, Archaeological Museum*

society, however, maintained the toga-clad type, which at that time was also appearing in Etruscan sculpture, as can be seen from the famous bronze of Aulus Metellus known as *L'Arringatore*, or *The Orator*, shown with the gesture of the Roman *adlocutio* (fig. 271). This work dates from the period of Sulla.

292

Another field of Greek art which was quickly and easily accepted in Roman society was that of various metalworks: finely engraved gold and silver pieces, silver tableware, and bronzes known as "Corinthian" bronzes, passionately coveted by the Romans, who had first come to know them as part of the spoils of war. These precious objects satisfied utilitarian and practical demands, and also the taste for decoration and love of luxury that had become dominating factors in the spirit of the new masters of the world, enriched by all their victories and henceforth forgetful of Cato's precepts.

5. Numismatic Art

Coinage also had a role of growing importance in the life of the state, and here decorative means had to be harnessed to a practical end, so as to make the proper impression in the vast field that was opening to Roman trade. The Romans understood the utility of the means offered by art in the new domain of coinage, which came to assume political and commemorative functions as well. When, about 297 B.C., Roman-Campanian didrachma coins were first struck in the Capua mint, artists from Magna Graecia, trained in the Hellenic tradition, produced the first formulation of the Roman she-wolf with the twins, in an elegant plastic style; the reverse bore a Hellenistic head of Hercules. Greek elements also show in the Roman silver denarii, which appeared about 269 B.C., with religious subjects like the head of Rome, the Dioscuri, the cart of Diana, and the figure of Victory.

But during the second century B.C. coinage developed a more national, historical character, and gods were replaced by symbols alluding to Roman victories: the legionary eagle, the standard, wreaths, and Gallic helmets and swords. The Roman denarius became a means of commemorating the military, political, and religious glories of the *gens* who issued the coins, calling on the engraver's art to create symbols showing family coats of arms, like the elephant head and Macedonian shield for the families of the Caecilii Metelli and of the Quintii, the *apex* and *lituus* for the Postumii and Servilii families, the ship's prow for the Fabii family, and the anchor for the Julii, narrating the more significant episodes on the reverses. In the second half of the second century B.C., Sextus Pompeius Fostlus inserted a small vignette of the she-wolf with the twins under the fig tree, the *ficus ruminalis*, with the woodpecker in the tree and Faustulus dressed as a shepherd, the minter relating his own family name to that of Faustulus. The soft, refined style of the Campanian version of the she-wolf here becomes rough and incisive, reflecting the artistic climate of Rome.

These various contrasting artistic elements — the indigenous, native Roman culture, the Etrusco-Italic tradition, the influences of Magna Graecia and the various Hellenistic centers, and the influx of works of different artists and artistic currents — made of Rome a singular meeting ground where an exceptionally eclectic atmosphere was created, overflowing with energy and with great possibilities for action and reaction. This led to the slow maturation during the first century B.C. of an art that can truly be called Roman.

X | Artistic Trends Under Sulla and Caesar and the Formation of Roman Art

The periods of Sulla and Caesar in the middle of the first century B.C. saw the germination of the first seeds of an artistic language which, although reflecting the strong eclecticism of the artistic environment of Rome, showed certain new characteristics. Architecture, confronted with the necessity of rebuilding the temples of Latium and embellishing the new capital of the ancient world, embarked on a long, varied series of experiments, and produced an original, monumental means of expression.

1. The Development of Architecture

Greek architectural elements were translated by the Romans into stone, tufa, travertine, and later, marble, but were freely reinterpreted and mingled with Italic, indigenous features. "Some architects," said Vitruvius, "take their disposition of columns from the Tuscan order, and use it with the Corinthian and Ionic orders." There was a preference for figured and floral capitals, and traditional Italic friezes with vegetal motifs, while the metopes of Doric entablatures were decorated with various kinds of weapons.

The solemn, severe façade of the Tabularium, which rose behind the Forum on the slope of the Capitoline, with its broad arcades flanked with semi-columns, and the inner rooms covered by cloister vaults, represents the most authentically Roman aspect of architecture under Sulla.

The peripteral temple, which was the most accomplished, consistent expression of Greek temple architecture, was less favored than the prostyle temple, or a plan with wings, or the pseudo-peripteral temple. The Greek temple, of which all four sides were important, was replaced by the temple conceived frontally, placed against a background. Roman ritual needs, and the theatrical taste of the people, kept the temple raised on the high podium, of Etruscan and Italic tradition. The *capitolium* which was built in every Roman city as an expression of the religious unity of all Roman citizens, was constructed at the end of the forum, following an axial composition, with architectonic wings on either side, thus marking the profound difference between the Roman square and the Greek agora. The isolated temple planned to be viewed from all angles, the most perfect example of which is the Greek *tholos*, was adopted in Rome only in particular cases: as for instance the Temple of Vesta in the Forum, whose circular form is dictated by a ritual allusion to the primitive wooden hut; or else the circular form was suggested by its position in the landscape, as the round temple at Tivoli in an open position on top of a high rocky cliff; or the circular temple on the open side of the Tiber in the Forum Boarium. But even to this type of circular temple the Roman taste preferred the addition of a façade transforming it into a prostyle plan, as in Temple D in Largo Argentina, in Rome, a form which was to be reduced during the Empire to a closed brick rotunda with a pronaos in the monumental example of the Pantheon.

In the period of Sulla, constructional techniques replaced the heavy *opus quadratum*, of large blocks, with the *opus incertum* and *opus quasi reticulatum*, which used small units of tufa. Under Caesar, the finer, regular *opus reticulatum* was adopted, which allowed an easier and more flexible articulation for structures with apses, niches, and vaults, while still more daring experiments in vaulting were to be carried out with cement agglomerate.

Hellenistic scenographic planning, as at Pergamon, provided the inspiration for Sulla's rebuilding of the sanctuary of Fortuna at Praeneste. But Hellenistic models were here interpreted in a Roman vein, with free use of the various architectural orders, barrel-vaulted roofs over corridors and stairs, and a new conception of interior space, as in the severe halls with podia. The circular structures crowning this superb scenographic creation of ascending terraces is here completely functional, as was the grandiose gray marble statue, imitating bronze, which it contained and which perhaps served less as a cult effigy than as the culminating akroterion. This feminine figure, caught in a turbulent wind that modeled her light drapery, effectively interpreted Hellenistic creations.

During the period of Sulla the attempt to lighten the somber effect of stone and give it a more precious note of polychromy, by the use of imported colored marbles, was still viewed with disapproval and considered, as Cato might have said, a reprehensible luxury. The orator Lucius Lucullus was called "the Palatine Venus" for having dared to decorate his own *atrium* with columns of Hymettus marble, and in 178 B.C. Marcus Lepidus was reproached for having laid floors of Numidian marble in his house. But polychrome marble was ultimately to exert a strong attraction on the Romans, almost as much as silver and gold. Lucius Lucullus imported marble from Melos and gave it the name *Lucullaeum*; and in 58 B.C. Scaurus used it for his *atrium*, and decorated the *scaena* of his temporary theater with colored marbles, mosaics, vitreous paste insets, gilded wood, textiles, and paintings. Mamurra had his house faced with Charistian marble and the new white marble from the quarries of Luni; these were opened about 50 B.C., making marble easier to obtain and contributing to the transfiguration of Roman architecture under Augustus.

Already in the fourth century B.C., in the plans of new colonies, Rome had adopted an orthogonal plan, not unrelated to that of the military *castrum*; and from the period of Sulla, there are interesting examples of regularized plans with broad vistas, as at Ostia. But the capital itself had developed haphazardly. The plans for the city promoted by Caesar foresaw an urbanistic reorganization of the Campus Martius and the center; because of the dictator's death, the plan was not carried out, but Caesar had still succeeded in expropriating, at great cost, the area next to the old Forum, to create a monumental square which constitut-ed the first element of the grandiose complex of the Imperial Fora. This new Forum of Caesar was still presided over by a god, whose temple constituted the axial focus and backdrop of the square as a whole. Caesar honored the protectress of the *gens Julia*, Venus Genetrix, with an octastyle marble temple; its columns of *giallo antico* in the cella, a cult statue by the Greek sculptor Arkesilaos, and paintings representing Ajax and Medea by the Greek Timomachos, provided a classicizing note in the typical combination of a Hellenized atmosphere within the Roman setting of the forum, which included a row of utilitarian *tabernae* running along either side of the monumental area.

Under the influence of Hellenism and the phil-Hellene Pompey, the interdict against permanent theaters was finally overcome. The Theater of Pompey was not, like the theater of Athens, dedicated to Dionysus but to Venus Victrix, in whose honor a temple was raised above the *cavea*, conceived almost as a grandiose access stairway. With its quadriporticoes, exedrae where the Senate could meet (and where Julius Caesar was assassinated), and its collections of works of art, the Theater of Pompey was a sumptuous monument vying with the finest Hellenistic theaters. There was a major difference, however, for there was no longer the need to find a natural slope on which to build the sloping *cavea*: with the Roman cement technique of barrel-vaulting, it was possible to construct the entire complex artificially, with circular corridors and a curving façade divided into several tiers of arcades framed by semi-columns or pilasters, with a superimposition of architectonic orders. In this way the theater could fit functionally and organically into the urban plan, and present a grandiose façade that was an original Roman contribution to architecture and a striking note of monumentality for the face of the city. The orchestra, which had already become less important in the Hellenistic theater, was further reduced to a semicircle in the Roman theater, and attention was more and more concentrated on the *scaena*, which took on a complex architectural development. The Roman stage was progressively to lose all illustrative connection to the action, which in Imperial times was most frequently variety shows, mimes, or dancing. The high podium decorated with reliefs and the *frons scaenae* became a striking array of niches with statues of the Muses and

272. Detail of a fleeing woman from the monumental frieze of the Villa of the Mysteries at Pompeii. Period of Caesar. In situ.

Apollo, culminating in the imposing decorative masses of the theaters of Asia and Africa in the second and third centuries A.D.

The combination of two Roman *caveae* face to face produced the amphitheater for gladiatorial spectacles, formerly held in the Forum, and Scribonius Curio, in 53 B.C., is supposed to have constructed an ingenious specimen with two mobile wooden *caveae* which functioned as separate theaters when back to back, and formed a single amphitheater when facing each other. But while the presence of a temple to Venus had justified the permission of permanent constructions for theaters, Rome had to wait until the time of Vespasian for a permanent amphitheater. Amphitheaters, developing the theater's semicircular façade into a wide ellipse, did not provide an axial focal point, but rather produced an uninterrupted, circular architectural monument. This was naturally more difficult to fit organically into a rectilinear city plan; as it needed surrounding space, it was better suited for sites in the outskirts of cities, which were also more convenient with respect to the noise from spectacles, the transport of wild animals, and the arrival of great crowds of spectators.

The new *Horti Luculliani* and *Horti Sallustiani* which opened in Rome created vast, monumental parks and were so richly set with sculptures that Juvenal speaks of *horti marmorei*. In private villas also, the art of gardening, the *ars topiaria*, was cultivated, with trees and shrubs artfully trimmed into ornamental and figurative shapes, *nemora tonsilia*, with statues, fountains, pools, ponds, aquariums, water displays, grottoes, and exedrae. Intellectuals like Cicero liked to show their love for Greek culture by giving Greek names to the various parts of their houses: the gymnasium, the lyceum, the academy, the *xystus* (open colonnade), and the *biblioteca* (library) in which they placed portraits of Plato and Aristotle.

2. The Decorative Arts

Besides *negotium* (business), the Romans now began to appreciate enlightened *otium* (leisure), and luxury was more widespread. The flow of wealth and of works of art continued with the triumph of Sulla in 81 B.C.; with that of Lucius Licinius Lucullus, who brought back Kalamis' Apollo from Apollonia, and decorated his house with paintings and statues; and with Pompey's return from Asia with precious furnishings and engraved gems.

Engraved gems became a passion with the Romans, who were attracted by all things precious and decorative. Gem collections were formed, from that of Scaurus, a praetor in 56 B.C., to Pompey's collection, which was taken from Mithridates and dedicated on the Capitol; the collection of Caesar was dedicated in the Temple of Venus Genetrix, and that of Marcellus placed in the Temple of Apollo on the Palatine. Greek engravers came to Rome to work. The use of rings with signet stones became widespread. And pearls were increasingly sought after, so that the shops of the *margaritari* (dealers in pearls) opened up along the *Via Sacra*. Pompey had an image of himself set with pearls carried through the streets, and in 48 B.C. Caesar had to promulgate a law regulating their use, though he himself presented a pearl worth six million sestertii to the mother of Brutus. Golden rings, once the symbol of a determined rank, tended to become signs of wealth, and appeared more and more frequently on the fingers of the rich. Roman jewelry became increasingly eye-catching, and to the traditional Hellenistic motifs were added smooth hemispherical elements in bracelets, gems set in pendants and brooches, and pearls in earrings; the Etruscan gold *bulla* also continued to be used.

Silverware, works in gold, candelabra, precious appliqués for triclinium couches, and all the products of Greek chased metalwork became highly prized by the Romans, who went to any lengths to obtain them. Caius Verres monopolized this market in Sicily, where he was governor from 73 to 70 B.C., using the services of the metal-worker Tlepolemos and the painter Hieron, both from Cibyra, who smelled out everything like hunting dogs, following up every *objet d'art* they heard of and laying hands on them by fair means or foul. For eight consecutive months Verres shut up a host of goldsmiths and metal-workers in a workshop in Syracuse to remodel all the riches he had looted, making golden vases and basins in which he had them set decoration stripped from thuribles and plates. He had also assembled a gem collection with the rings confiscated from the citizens. His house in Rome and his villas were filled to overflowing with rugs, tapestries, bronze couches, candelabra, trophies of engraved cuirasses

273. Detail of the wall painting in the triclinium of the House of the Vettii at Pompeii. Example of the so-called Fourth Pompeian style of wall painting, with fantastic architectural elements and figural motifs. In the panel below is Apollo as the slayer of the serpent, and Diana with the sacrificial bull. Circa A.D. 65–70. In situ.

and helmets, gigantic ivory tusks, and even bamboo canes from the Athenaion in Syracuse.

The Temple of Felicitas, the Monument of Catulus, the Portico of Metellus, the Theater of Pompey, and the Forum of Caesar became museums of works of art, but the houses of wealthy Roman citizens, like the villa of Scaurus at Tivoli, also became increasingly rich in precious objects. "Originally it was of rustic simplicity," commented Ovid, "but now Rome is all gold and possesses all the wealth of the conquered world." These objects of Roman *luxuria* were a direct inheritance from Hellenistic taste, revived with more intensity and exuberance in Rome. In the historical context of the Classical world they attest to the spread and survival of the Hellenistic tradition, and are indications of the artistic trends of Roman society.

3. Painting and Mural Decoration

In the field of painting during the first century B.C., beside Hellenistic traditions there appeared new aspects which were local developments and manifestations of the emergent Roman art. It is true, there were Greek painters working in Rome, among them Iaia of Cizicos, who specialized in female portraits on ivory and wood panels, and for whom Roman ladies most willingly sat. There were also the Greeks Sopolis and Dionysios, specialists, for their part, in portraits of men, so that Dionysios was known as *anthropographos*. Serapion, who had exhibited an enormous painting in the *Tabernae Veteres*, and Arellius, author of mythological paintings with goddesses to whom he gave the features of his own mistresses, also worked in Rome. It is true that the works of Classical painters were keenly sought after and fetched very high prices, and it is equally true that Greek works were drawn upon for copying, and reworking into monumental paintings. The figures of gods, mythological cycles, scenes from the *Iliad*, and the adventures of Odysseus are cited by Vitruvius as decorative themes used in Roman houses. The fine pictorial cycle from the *Odyssey* from a house on the Esquiline with inscriptions in Greek is a precious relic of the atmospheric, fablelike, landscape painting made for a Roman house in the time of Caesar after a Hellenistic model, probably Alexandrian of the second century B.C.

The architectural and decorative development of the Roman house presented the new need for painted decoration covering many walls and large spaces, and neither the panels of Classical tradition, nor even a succession

274. *Detail of a wall in the so-called House of Livia on the Palatine, decorated in an architectural style with podium, columns, and festoons. Above the white panels behind the columns runs a yellow monochrome landscape frieze of Hellenistic inspiration. End of the first century B.C. In situ.*

of several pictures in a cycle, could meet this demand. Hellenistic artists had decorated walls with imitation marble structural elements; Rome evolved a decorative system that divided the available space into ornamental, architecturally relevant sections which could provide an organic setting for single paintings of the Classical type, or for the continuous rhythm of the figured frieze.

The more severe taste of the period of Sulla dictated a mural style with illusionistic architecture of podia, columns, and entablatures, a typical example of which is to be found in the House of the Griffins, as well as in the so-called House of Livia (fig. 274), both on the Palatine. But the desire for richer and more varied decoration led to the transformation of this architectural style, called the Second Pompeian style, into an increasingly abstract ornamental composition of architectural motifs, giving the walls a chromatic, rather than structural, quality, with fine, glossy encaustic backgrounds in black, red, or yellow. In this style, known as the Third style, many examples of which are to be found in Pompeii, columns became slender floral shafts, light, fantastic elements framing the delicate, floating figures seen against the monochrome backgrounds. While the expert grace to be found in .this Third style is a result of Hellenistic teachings, the syntax is Roman. Miniaturistic details reveal Egyptian inspiration. Egypt was dear to Pompey and Caesar, just as it was to be to Napoleon, and this gave rise to a wave of Egyptian taste, as in the Napoleonic *style empire*. The taste for fantastic decorative elements was even further developed in the Fourth Pompeian style (colorplate, fig. 273).

The idyllic, bucolic Hellenistic landscapes of religious character, along with views of ports and towns in a more realistic Roman treatment, were used for panels and friezes. A very fine example is the luminous and impressionistic monochrome frieze on a yellow ground from the House of Livia (fig. 274). Because of its largely miniaturistic nature, however, this type of painting could not be expanded to cover an entire wall. Roman painting created a new type of naturalistic landscape, articulated in ample, unitary views over the walls of the house, that suggested openings in the calm, enclosed, domestic setting onto airy backdrops of gardens richly planted with fruit trees, ornamental shrubs, and pergolas of greenery, with fountains and exedrae; these examples of the *ars topiaria* are in a taste presaging that of the eighteenth century. This realistic landscape, which forms part of the range of experiments in mural decoration mentioned by Vitruvius in his treatise, written between 31 and 27 B.C., was to be developed in the Augustan and Flavian periods (colorplate, fig. 285).

Lastly, painting was called on at an official level, to interpret Roman themes, not only in triumphal scenes, like those exalting the victories of Pompey over Mithridates, or the exploits of Caesar, but also to commemorate the history of Rome and the legends of its origins, Roman themes which counterbalanced Greek mythology. There are modest reflections of a pictorial cycle illustrating the legends from Aeneas to Romulus and Remus, in the frieze of a columbarium on the Esquiline, dating from the first century B.C. This frieze bears Latin inscriptions and has realistic scenes in Roman style, such as the building of the walls of Alba Longa and Lavinius, along with Hellenistic reminiscences in the female types and in the battle groups.

The development of decorative mural painting in private houses corresponds to the evolution of mosaic floor decoration, in which Hellenistic tradition predominates in the refined *emblemata*, often imported ready-made on slabs of terracotta, and in the figured compositions. But the Roman style is expressed in the simpler black and white geometric mosaics, and in the pavements with touches of color provided by fragments of polychrome marble used to highlight the crushed potsherd floors of the old Republican tradition.

4. Sculpture and the Classicizing Trend

In sculpture, as in painting, we see on one side the continuing flow of the great Hellenistic current, and on the other the slow emergence of a Roman artistic language. In Rome the greatest sculptors were still Greek, like Claudius Avianus Evander, who restored the head of Artemis by Timotheos on the Palatine, or Pasiteles, a native of Magna Graecia and a typical representative of the cultured, refined, classicizing milieu. He was an art historian and an expert in all techniques, working in all media, and for all his works he executed a preliminary clay model. Artists no longer attacked the marble directly, but first worked out the forms in wax; the immediate force of the Classical chisel thus gave way to the ductile grace of classicizing work, and the imaginative vigor was replaced by a soft and delicate imitation of nature. Pasiteles made life studies from real animals in cages. This artist was the head of a school and one of his pupils, Stephanos, in a statue of a nude adolescent, shows himself a practitioner of the most academic Classicism, taking early fifth-century works as his models, but rendering their severe compactness mawkish and empty, perhaps to make his works more acceptable to Roman taste.

On the other hand, Stephanos remodeled Hellenistic types in his statues of the nymphs, which decorated a spring of the *Aqua Appia*, and belonged at one time to Caius Asinius Pollio. In a funerary group in the Museo delle Terme, perhaps representing a mother and son, and conventionally known as Orestes and Electra, one of Stephanos' pupils, Menelaos, imitated fourth-century Attic types and produced the coldest form of Classicism, presaging academic work of the nineteenth century.

The art of the Greek Arkesilaos was also well suited to satisfy Roman tastes. He sculpted animals, like the rococo group of a lioness with Amors, which Varro owned and admired. He also modeled kraters, demanding one talent

275. *Funerary portrait of a mature man in a hard, direct realism which notes the facial paralysis of the subject's twisted lips. First half of the first century* B.C. *Ostia, Museum*

276. *Copy of the official portrait of Pompey, dedicated in the Curia of the Porticoes of the Theater of Pompey,* circa *53* B.C., *in a style of sophisticated, soft modeling. Copenhagen, Carlsberg Glyptothek*

in payment just for a plaster model, and sculpted effigies of gods, from Venus Genetrix in the temple of the Forum of Caesar to the figure of Felicitas for which Lucullus paid one million sestertii.

Greek tradition became implanted in Rome mainly as a result of the classicizing, ornamental trend fostered by the influx of neo-Attic work. The Romans looked on sculpture largely in terms of decoration and illustration related to architecture. They placed statues in niches, apses, and colonnades. They sought for symmetrical arrangements, even going so far as to couple pairs of reproductions of one and the same work, sometimes even reversing the pose of a statue so as to obtain an exact symmetrical balance, as in the copy of the figure of Pothos in Florence. They liked to arrange statues in cycles in an architectonic rhythm, as can be seen from the series of the Muses on the *frons scaenae* of theaters, groups like the labors of Hercules, and the personifications of the fourteen provinces that adorned the so-called *Ad Nationes* portico of Augustus; statues were also grouped in landscape compositions set in gardens and pools.

The choice and placing of sculptures recorded in the library of Asinius Pollio corresponds to these very conceptions of symmetry and architectural relationships. Cicero's de-

mands to Atticus were also based on the criteria of the suitability of sculptures to the environment to be decorated: reliefs to be set in *atrium* walls, wellheads and herms for gardens, and a herm of Athena, which was judged most suitable for the gymnasium and fitted in so well that the setting seemed dedicated to her. Indeed, Cicero protested, to those who sent him statues of bacchantes, that he admitted they were graceful, but he could not decide where to put them; if at least they had been Muses, he added, they could have gone in his library. He was also at a loss to dispose of a statue of Mars, which he felt unsuitable for a man who professed peace as he did.

As can be seen from the examples in Pompeii, the same illustrative criteria often governed the choice of Greek paintings to be copied and reworked on the walls of the various rooms of the houses: the models were above all from the fourth century and the Hellenistic period.

Greek Classicism not only supplied the inspiration for cult and decorative statuary, but also pervaded portraiture in the first century B.C., creating the soft, cultivated, refined, psychological images of a Cicero and a Pompey (fig. 276; this has been tentatively attributed to Pasiteles); the baroque and virtuosistic work conventionally called a head of Sulla; and portrait statues with Lysippan bodies shown in heroic nudity, as that of Cartilius Poplicola in Ostia, or the similar statue of a citizen in Cassino, and the proudly posed Roman citizen from Delos, with his bald head and protruding ears. The accentuation of the tendency toward realism made this juxtaposition of faithfully portrayed faces and idealized bodies an even more strident contrast.

5. The Affirmation of a Roman Artistic Language in Sculpture and Coinage

Beside this strong classicizing trend under Sulla and Caesar, we can also find expressions of a Roman style, particularly in portraiture and in funerary and historical reliefs. Statues of toga-clad figures, reliefs in tufa, in travertine, and later in marble, showing the faces of the deceased, were executed in a rough, dry, linear style which outlined drapery

Roman portraiture from the time of Sulla and Caesar veracity was rendered with immediacy, without the slightest trace of artifice (fig. 275, 277). The crude realism of certain bony, wiry, rough, tight-lipped faces has suggested inspiration from the wax masks that were molded on the face of the deceased and kept in cupboards in the *atrium*, like a gallery of the ancestors of the *gens*, to be brought out and paraded at family funerals. But death masks were not at the root of the verist style which, in fact, was an Etrusco-Italic and Latin tradition. In the same way, there is no need to search for the sources of bald, bony Roman portraits in the late Alexandrian portraits of the so-called priests of Isis, nor to assume a relationship between the modeling of Republican heads and the stereometric vision of Egyptian portraits in granite and basalt which are in keeping with the technique in hard stones.

The same stylistic traits of this Roman funerary and honorary portraiture are to be

277. Portrait of a wrinkled old man, showing virtuosity in the clear and harsh veristic rendering of the folds of the skin. Circa 45 B.C. Osimo, Palazzo Municipale

278. Copy of an official portrait of Agrippa in a Hellenistic style, created in Rome between 28 and 13 B.C. From Gabi. Paris, Louvre

in stiff, sharp folds, modeled the bone structure of the faces with a rustic vigor, and emphasized the network of wrinkles.

The verist elements in Hellenistic portraiture were rendered with cultured virtuosity in terms of intellectualistic conceptions; while in

found in the faces of personages commemorated on silver denarii, as in the austere, rough, incisive, unadorned heads of Domitius Ahenobarbus, Claudius Marcellus, Antius Restio, Quintus Arrius, and even some portrait types of Caesar; however, these same qualities

C·FVLVIVS·SALVIS·HARVSPEX·S·D·D

appeared in certain marble heads of Caesar that are classicizing in conception.

The freshest and most vital vein of native Roman art, which was to broaden into the great current of Imperial art, can be found in the series of legendary and historical scenes on the reverse faces of silver denarii of the first century B.C. Among the subjects treated are the sacrifice of Numa; the rape of the Sabines; the punishment of Tarpeia; the procession of Brutus with the lictors; and the consecration of a treaty with a Roman taking the oath on a piglet, a theme revived by the Italic insurgents between 91 and 89 B.C. Other themes are the dedication of the *spolia opima* to Jupiter Feretrius; voting in the *Saepta*; a peasant leading oxen to symbolize the distribution of land to veterans by Marius; the *dextrarum iunctio* (joining of hands) between Rome, shown as an Amazon, and Italy, bearing her cornucopia; duels on horseback and on foot; Jugurtha and Boccus kneeling before Sulla; Aemilius Paulus with the trophy to which Perseus and his sons are tied; and reproductions of civic monuments like the *Sacellum Cloacinae*, the viaducts of the Via Aemilia, the Temple of Vesta, or the Villa Publica in the Campus Martius.

The small dimensions of the coin meant that these scenes had to be limited to essential elements, but they were treated with lively realism and the unsophisticated, but effective and spontaneous language characteristic of native Roman art. Equally fundamental themes, compositions, and concepts will form the basis of the historical relief of the Imperial period. The narration of census-taking, and the *lustratio* or purification with the typical Roman sacrifice of the *suovetaurilia* to Mars in an important official monument, such as the so-called Altar of Domitius Ahenobarbus, in the Louvre (fig. 279), was perhaps entrusted to a Greek sculptor, who used Pentelic marble to treat the Roman theme against a neutral background, in a rather dry, restrained, classicizing style. However, a certain syntactical timidity and lack of vivacity in this relief would seem to indicate an artist not wholly at ease with a subject outside his repertory, whereas in another subject, with a long Hellenistic tradition, that of the marine *thiasos* represented on the slabs of this same altar that are preserved in Munich (fig. 280), he can deploy his talents more surely. The result is less soft and flowing than that obtained by the neo-Attic sculptor who treated the same marine subject on the finely executed marble vase from Santo Spirito, now in the Museo delle Terme, in Rome, which is from the end of the second century B.C. The slabs from the altar of Domitius Ahenobarbus have been variously dated in 115, 86–87, 54, and 42 B.C., on uncertain historical, antiquarian, and stylistic grounds. These slabs probably date from the first half of the first century B.C. The two different themes, mythological and historical, combined on one work, provide a concrete example of the Roman and Hellenistic aspects of the Roman artistic world at the end of the Republican period.

For less important reliefs and altars from the periods of Sulla and Caesar, Roman sculptors were already employed, using first travertine, then marble, still with rough, linear modeling similar to that found in funerary portraiture. An interesting votive relief of the haruspex Fulvius Salvis (fig. 281), from the Sullan sanctuary of Hercules in Ostia, uses this style in a colorful, uninhibited narration of three consecutive scenes that show an Archaic bronze statue of Hercules being netted and fished out of the sea, the consulting of an oracle, and, probably, the coronation of the victorious general who had made the consultation. This type of continuous narrative, which Greek vase painters, painters, and sculptors had used only for episodes from mythical cycles, was now transferred onto a realistic plane, a step of fundamental importance for the later development of the Roman historical relief.

In marble works we find a more classicizing tone. An archaizing, dry and linear neo-Attic style served for the Roman theme of a warrior making a sacrifice to Mars on a Caesarean plinth from Civita Castellana. On the other hand, a more lively pictorial sense characterized the base showing a sacrifice, also from the period of Caesar, in the Galleria

279. Slab from the frieze of the so-called altar of Domitius Ahenobarbus with the scene of the sacrifice of the suovetaurilia *to Mars. First half of the first century B.C. Paris, Louvre*

280. Slab from lateral frieze of the so-called altar of Domitius Ahenobarbus with the marine thiasos *of Poseidon and Amphitrite, tritons and nereids. First half of the first century B.C. Munich, Glyptothek*

281. Relief in travertine dedicated by the haruspex Fulvius Salvis in the sanctuary of Hercules at Ostia. From the period of Sulla. Ostia, Museum

Borghese. A tight, linear Roman imitation of the neo-Attic cycle of reliefs with dancing girls is to be found on the slabs from Via Praenestina in the Museo delle Terme. But at the opposite extreme there is the Tomb of the Baker Eurysaces, outside the Porta Maggiore in Rome. The structure of this tomb is inspired by the form of an oven, constituting a realistic Roman theme, and the relief scenes illustrate the baking of bread. This trend of a more craftsman-like style of work, which continued throughout the Empire, was always to show more uncultivated, authentic, popular, and expressive characteristics; it often contrasted strongly with the more important official art, and thus enriched the scale of expression in the over-all historical picture of the arts.

At the end of this period, in the field of

carried out under Tiberius. The Roman theme is treated with varied accents. Some have a Roman ring to them, and follow local traditions: the flight scene in the rape of the Sabines, which seems to stem from the scene on the denarius of Lucius Titurius Sabinus of 72 B.C.; the tragic immobility of Tarpeia, half buried under the heavy Sabine shields, again resuming the theme of the same coinage, but with a face that seems inspired by a Niobe, and she wears a Selene-like mantle; or the scene of the construction of the walls of a city (fig. 282), with workmen whose faces are naturalistically characterized, recalling the analogous scene on the painted frieze from the Esquiline. There is, however, a classicizing note in other features of this frieze, such as the richly modeled heroic nude figures of combatants; the knotted tree trunk derived from

282. Slab of the frieze decorating the Basilica Aemilia in the Roman Forum, with the scene of the construction of the walls of a city in the presence of a female divinity. Circa 35 B.C. Rome, Antiquarium of the Forum

official art we have the interesting remains of the marble frieze with the legends of Rome that decorated the interior of the Basilica Aemilia in the Forum. This frieze is perhaps datable in the period between the restoration of the Basilica in 55 B.C. and the rededication in 34 B.C., while other work, we do not know how extensive, was necessary after the fire in the Basilica in 14 B.C., and still more was

bucolic reliefs; and the use of rocks as a supporting plane rather than as a natural element of the setting; the classicizing head of Titus Tatius resembles the heads of Mars; and the female types and the gods or personifications have soft, idealized faces, and drapery in the Praxitelean tradition. Perhaps this artist was not a Roman sculptor versed in neo-Attic lore, but a Greek sculptor who adapted his own classicizing temperament to the Roman theme and here presented aspects of the local figurative tradition. Nevertheless, this frieze must be considered as an expression of Roman art, for it is a product of the new historical climate of the city. Roman art stems precisely from the confluence of these varied types of creative energy, and the accumulation of different movements and traditions; in this formative, eclectic period they are still distinguishable but they will be continually assimilated in an increasingly organic fusion.

This Roman art was continually nourished by Classical art that ennobled native qualities and conferred a universal value on the new artistic language. The Classical contribution, though filtered through classicist culture, remained live and active from the time of Augustus through that of Marcus Aurelius and was particularly intense in the period of Hadrian. It only began to weaken with Commodus, when local Roman energies came to assume the pre-eminent place in official art and expressive tendencies matured that were far removed from the organic naturalism that lay at the roots of Classicism. The abandonment of the Classical principle, the appearance in the philosophy of Plotinus (A.D. 205–270) of the concept of the soul as judge of beauty — consisting no longer in Classical symmetry but in expressive vividness — mark the first true profound crises in the total tradition of Classical art. Up till that time Classical art had had a substantial unity and consistence, identifiable with the great mainstream of figurative culture that first radiated from Greece and then from Rome, beside which all the collateral artistic manifestations or peripheral and provincial areas remained altogether secondary. This crisis led to the new, diversified, expressive world of the late Empire, which was divided into the various areas of the provinces where different artistic tendencies could take shape, from the Iranian and Scythian movements in the East and South of the Empire, to Celtic abstract, ornamental trends, in the North and West. However, the part of the inheritance of Roman art that was to be transmitted with universal validity was always to embody a live, active survival of Classical teachings.

6. The Roman Mentality in the Judgment of Art

The active acceptance of Classicism in Rome entailed an adaptation of this tradition to the Roman mentality, which was different in many ways from that of Greece. The most significant manifestations of Roman art were official in character, consisting of public works commissioned by the Senate, the People, or the magistrates. In its most striking aspects, Roman art was an art of the state, an arm of the political propaganda of the Empire. What counted most in figured monuments was the Imperial dedicatory inscription, not the artist's signature. Roman art was essentially anonymous. In contrast to the abundance of names of Greek artists we know the names of only a few Roman artists, and even these names are not of the greatest masters responsible for the most important undertakings, but of secondary artisans in the various fields of sculpture, painting, mosaic, chased metalwork or gemengraving, and, above all, of architects.

The great Greek masters enjoyed considerable fame among the cultivated Roman public, but artistic activity was still considered not really worthy of a Roman citizen. It was only for eccentric or snobbish entertainment that occasionally an emperor practiced an art as a dilettante. Nero decided to try his hand at sculpture and painting as well as music. According to Aurelius Victor, Hadrian was a painter, sculptor, and bronze-worker, comparable to Polykleitos and Euphranor; he was bold enough to make the plan of the Temple of Venus and Rome, and would not tolerate the architect Apollodoros' criticism of the excessive size of the effigies. Marcus Aurelius is supposed to have taken painting lessons from Diognetus; and Heliogabalus, who liked to present himself as a pastry-cook, perfumer, tavern-keeper, shopkeeper, and slave-trader, sent a large picture by him to Rome, representing himself in the act of making a sacrifice; Alexander Severus practiced painting as well as geometry and singing, and Valentinianus painted, and modeled in clay and wax.

Apart from the dilettante activities of various emperors, however, it was still exceptional for Roman citizens to practice art; a certain nobleman, Quintus Pedius, whom Caesar had named as his heir along with Augustus, was urged to take up painting on the advice of the orator Messalla and with the approval of Augustus himself, but only because he had been dumb from birth. Pliny, in fact, records as exceptional cases the left-handed Venetian knight Turpilius, fine paintings by whom existed in Verona, and the praetor and proconsul of the Narbonne district, Titidius Labeo, who amused himself by painting small pictures but earned himself the laughter and scorn of his contemporaries because of his activity. The few names of painters and sculptors recorded in the sources and inscriptions are those of plebeians and freedmen; but significantly enough, a certain number of full Roman citizens appear along with freedmen among the signatures of architects, proving the greater consideration accorded to architecture by the Romans, who saw it as the realization and blending of *utilitas* and *decor*, the useful and the beautiful, according to the Roman maxim, *"nisi utile est quod facimus, stulta est gloria"* (unless what we make be useful, the glory is foolishness).

In Diocletian's *Edict of Prices*, which fixed the wages of the various trades, a *marmorarius*, a marble-worker, and a *musearius*, to be interpreted perhaps as a mosaic-worker for the finer wall decorations, earned 60 denarii; a *tessellarius*, who laid floor mosaics, 50 denarii; and a mason also 50 denarii; a wall painter, *pictor parietarius*, was paid 75; and a painter of figured scenes, *pictor imaginarius*, 150 denarii; this scale bears witness to the modest level of this decorative activity.

We know none of the authors of the great artistic works of Rome, and we can reconstruct no single career. Only stylistic analysis enables us occasionally to assemble groups of works which could have come from the same workshop, as, for example, sarcophagi. When attempts have been made to define the creative personality corresponding to a determined artistic trait, conventional names have had to be adopted, as in the case of the "Master of the Exploits of Trajan," or the "Master of the Exploits of Marcus Aurelius."

During the Empire ethical preconceptions against art continued to make themselves heard, despite the fact that the political ends of art were well appreciated, and that there was by then a flourishing trade in antiques, with public auctions, exhibitions, and even forgeries. Indeed, amateurs and collectors were more numerous than ever before, and some of them were setting themselves up as authorities capable of recognizing real Corinthian bronzes at a glance. Yet, for Seneca, artists were still *ministri luxuriae*, dispensers of luxury; art lovers were children who wasted time in play; expenditures on paintings and Corinthian bronzes were mad and immoral: "All these statues," he exclaimed, "all these columns that support nothing, used as decoration because of our mania for spending!" In the *Historia Naturalis* by Pliny the Elder, the most personal passages of the books devoted to the arts consist of condemnations of luxury in comparison with antique *virtus*, and invective against the passion for works of art. In Pliny's opinion the old clay statues of the gods were more to be admired for their modeling, art, and solidity, more sacred than gold, and certainly more pure. However, he justifies and admires portraiture, which contrives to record the image of the *gens*, and shows the faces of famous men; he appreciates *imagines clipeatae* and honorific monuments, but most of all, architectonic monuments that combine usefulness with grandiosity, such as the Roman aqueducts, "than which nothing more remarkable has existed on land or sea in the world."

Those Romans who studied Greek philosophy took little interest in aesthetics, and in this field, too, the Roman attitude toward art reveals itself. When Horace touches on aesthetic problems in his *Ars Poetica*, he does not follow the Epicurean line of thought of Philodemus of Gadara, who was active in the circle of Lucius Piso and had managed to overcome the dualism of form and content, and the utilitarian ends of art, by pleading for the poetic and the fabulous, on the grounds that everything is real providing it is effectively represented. Horace, on the other hand, followed the Peripatetic and Stoic theories, close to those of Philodemus' opponent, Neoptolemus of Parium; art had to delight and be useful at the same time, and to reproduce the true and the truthful by eschewing the irrational and the fantastic for logic and simplicity, avoiding all excesses and adhering to the happy medium. Otherwise it would fall into mere vain play, false appearances, aberrant dreaming, and futile amusements which, however attractive, were more fitting for boys than for men.

This, then, is the cultural setting of Roman art, which with the advent of Augustus will be raised to the dignity of an art of a vast empire.

XI Augustan and Julio-Claudian Classicism

In the Augustan period (27 B.C.–A.D. 14) architects were called upon to give the new capital a more monumental face. From this time on, Luni marble was used in Rome instead of tufa or travertine, so that Augustus could boast of having found the Republican city all in clay and brick, and left it in marble. It was, indeed, in the field of monumental architectural enterprises that the Roman spirit expressed itself most originally. The Hellenistic town-planning based upon abstract rationality was replaced with a more varied adaptation in accordance with concepts of practicality and monumentality. In the Forum of Augustus the Temple of Mars Ultor was placed against the great wall that isolated this forum from adjoining areas, and the axial nature of the forum was emphasized by sumptuous lateral halls with porticoes. For the Mausoleum of Augustus the Etruscan burial mound form was used, but developed on a grandiose scale. The *Ara Pacis* or Altar of Peace created a new architectural type with its marble enclosure, perhaps in imitation of the temporary wooden structure erected for the actual founding ceremony. The great obelisk raised in the *Solarium* on the Campus Martius initiated the series of these Egyptian monuments that were daringly ferried from the Nile to the banks of the Tiber to create a characteristic exotic, picturesque note in the townscape of Rome. The old Roman Forum was enriched with the Temple of the Divine

283. Detail of the panel on the west side of the Ara Pacis Augustae, showing the pious Aeneas sacrificing. 9 B.C. Rome, Museum of the Ara Pacis

Julius, and on the Palatine Augustus erected the Temple of Apollo.

In the monumental remodeling of Rome, Augustus was helped by Maecenas, who rehabilitated the Esquiline with parks, and by Agrippa, who embellished the southern part of the Campus Martius with the Pantheon, the Baths of Agrippa with gardens, the quadriportico of Vipsanius Agrippa, and the Portico of the Argonauts which held a gallery of painting where he exhibited his *Descriptio Orbis*, a monumental map of the Empire.

Plans were made to provide more aqueducts for the city from the springs of the *Aqua Julia*, *Aqua Virgo*, and *Aqua Alsietina*, which were to feed new baths and fountains.

In the Forum of Augustus copies of the Erechtheion Caryatids and statues of figures from the history of Rome, with their inscriptions, represent the two facets of the art of the time: the classicizing and the native Roman.

1. Classicism and Native Roman Tradition in the Creation of the Augustan Style

Official art was inspired by typically Roman conceptions, but took on forms that sprang from Greek experience. The ideals of the

284. Impression from the Gemma Augustea, *with the coronation of Augustus, represented as Jupiter; below, the erection of a trophy. Double-layered onyx intaglio in a classicizing style. Beginning of the first century* B.C. *Vienna, Kunsthistorisches Museum*

285. Detail of wall painting from the Villa of Livia at Prima Porta, with a view onto a garden with a variety of plants and birds. Augustan Period. Rome, Museo delle Terme

Pax Romana, the fertility of the land, the *magna parens frugum, Saturnia Tellus, magna virum*, piety toward the gods, the triumph over barbarism, and exaltation of the emperor are common themes throughout literature and art.

The *Aeneid* and the *Georgics* are the best commentaries to the *Ara Pacis*, which was dedicated on January 30th in 9 B.C., to commemorate the peace of the Empire. On this monument Roman legends were exalted in the person of the pious Aeneas sacrificing to the Penates (fig. 283), and in the Lupercal, both on the west side, and in the personification of Rome itself, balanced by the panel of Tellus, or Earth, on the east side of the exterior of the enclosure. All the most refined achievements of the Hellenistic bucolic relief converge in these panels. In this extremely elegant Augustan decorative conception the vegetal ornament of Hellenistic inspiration undergoes a new, elaborate development that thickens it into heavy festoons on the inner face of the enclosing wall, while on the lower half of the exterior of the enclosing wall it spreads out into arabesques of acanthus forms with soft, illusionistic planes. This same taste and style can be seen in the vegetal ornament on the precious silverware from the Augustan treasures of Boscoreale and Hildesheim, or in the more modest imitations found on Aretine vases.

The frieze of the Imperial procession that runs round the upper half of the outside of the marble enclosure is executed in the expert Greek tradition, while the varied, free, and lively close-packing of the figures reveals the influence of the more naturalistic narrative mode of the Etrusco-Italic tradition. A more cursive, incisive style is seen in the small frieze with sacrificial scenes on the altar within the enclosure.

The exaltation of the emperor victorious over the barbarians, raised to a superhuman plane, became from this period on the dominant motif of Roman commemorative art. It was even used to make a complex composition out of a cameo, in the precious *Gemma Augustea*, the double-layered onyx work now in Vienna (fig. 284), which has been attributed to Dioscurides, Augustus' official engraver. The Hellenistic tradition of gem-carving here rose to a new monumentality, Roman in conception, to honor Augustus in allegorical, and at the same time historical, forms. The Emperor, as Jupiter, is seated beside the figure of Rome; as ruler of the inhabited universe, he is crowned by *Oikoumene*. Behind the throne are Tellus and Oceanus. The enthroned deities are perhaps watching the triumph of the young Tiberius over the Ger-

286. Statue of Augustus wearing the cuirass and cloak of a general, in the pose of the adlocutio. *Formerly heightened with color.*
Found 1863 in the Villa of Livia at Prima Porta. Circa 20-17 B.C. Vatican, Braccio Nuovo

manii. In the lower register soldiers are erecting a trophy in the presence of barbarian prisoners.

In this Imperial environment even a silver cup can become a refined commemorative and allegorical monument, for instance the cups from Boscoreale. On one of these cups Augustus, seated on his *sella curulis*, receives a statue of Victory in homage; and again, seated on his *sella castrensis*, he receives the submission of the barbarians. On another cup Tiberius celebrates and makes a sacrifice. While on two cups found at Hoby, which are now in Copenhagen, a Greek metal-worker Cheirisophos, in the purest Hellenistic style, represented the ransom of Hector's body, and Philoctetes at Lemnos.

An academic Classicism with elegant neo-Attic moldings is found in the marble altars dedicated to the Lares, such as that of the *Vicus Sandalarius*, now in the Uffizi in Florence; while in others the reliefs show a more incisive, fresh style with a sense of space, as in the altar representing a sacrifice, in the Museo Nuovo of the Museo dei Conservatori in Rome.

The refinement and ornamental elegance of this Hellenizing Augustan milieu marked the entire output of altars with garlands (fig. 288), of decorative reliefs, wellheads, candelabra, vases, bronzes, and silverware, all of which present the most delicate, subtly shaded modeling and daringly rich high relief in the naturalistic vegetal motifs of vine leaves, ivy, olive boughs, and acanthus leaves. The same taste appears in engraved gems, cameos, monochrome marble *pinakes*, or plaques, with Classical linear compositions from Herculaneum, and in stucco work, as in the very fine specimens from a house at the Farnesina now in the Museo delle Terme. Wall painting develops the finely drawn miniaturistic ornament of the so-called Third Pompeian style, or classicizing panels on white grounds, and we see the emergence of naturalistic backgrounds with views of gardens, though the finest example, from the Villa of Livia at Prima Porta (colorplate, fig. 285), now in the Museo delle Terme, has been quite unconvincingly dated in the Flavian period.

The creation, on certain fixed occasions of an emperor's reign, of an official portrait type, which is generally precisely recorded by the various issues of coins, was to have profound effects on portraiture as a whole. The official type spread and naturally became current in the provinces as well as in the capital, providing a stylistic model which inevitably tended to set the tone for the entire portrait production of the time. Thus also the emperor's manner of dressing his hair, or of shaving his beard or letting it grow, almost always became the prevailing mode of the period. Women's coiffures, too, underwent various changes, and every type that became the fashion of the period provides useful information for chronology.

The Roman naturalistic sense eschewed the abstract, architectonic form of the Greek herm for portraits and instead adopted the bust, which may have been linked to an Etrusco-Italic tradition. The form of the bust underwent a typological development and, starting with the limited form of the Republican and Augustan periods — cut off in a half-circle below the neck — grew to include the shoulders in the first century A.D., the upper arms and chest in the second century, and included the entire chest in the late Empire.

The portraits of Augustus that we possess number one hundred and forty or so. We see that the dominant influence is Classicism in its various interpretations, from the heroic tone of the Diadochi to the pathetic expressions of works from Asia Minor, to classicizing academism, and to the more realistic Italic approach. Italic naturalism and Greek Classicism combine happily in the official statue of Augustus from Prima Porta in the Vatican (fig. 286), where the Roman type of figure wearing a cuirass takes on a Polykleitan rhythm, transformed into the latin pose with outstretched right arm, the gesture of public address or, *adlocutio*. In the decoration of the ceremonial cuirass, Hellenistic modeling gives life to the historical scene of the restitution of the standards taken by the Parthians from Crassus in the battle of Carrae, and to the allegories of Heaven and Earth. In the statue of Augustus from Via Labicana, the Emperor, in his sixties, is shown as Pontifex, with veiled head. The melancholy face is more human than heroic, and softer, more coloristic, and vibrant in treatment. This work can be considered one of the most vivid and mature specimens of Augustan portraiture.

A common tone can be traced in the other Roman portraits of the time, and in those of women the coiffure presents a high, smooth, rolled-back curl at the center in imitation of Octavia; the coiffure then becomes wavy, with curls over the forehead, in the style of Livia. A warmer color sense at times enlivens certain portraits in terracotta, free of the academic approach that usually dominated work in marble.

2. The Affirmation of an Imperial Art in the Provinces

The *Pax Romana* provided favorable conditions for the artistic development of the provinces. At Athens it was decided to affirm the Empire by honoring the cult of Rome and Augustus in the sacred precinct of the Acropolis. But a certain discretion and taste for the Classical led to the construction of a small marble *tholos*, whose peristyle did not conflict with the neighboring solemn mass of the Parthenon; and an academic imitation of the Ionic order used in the Erechtheion was adopted in order to harmonize the building with its surroundings.

287. Relief from west side of the Mausoleum of the Julii at Saint-Rémy-en-Provence, with a battle scene around a nude fallen hero, re-echoing the Greek composition of the struggle over the body of Patroclus. Augustan period. In situ.

The Roman agora in Athens, which was completed by Augustus with the Doric propylon in honor of Athena Archegetis, repeats the Hellenistic plan with a peristyle, instead of adapting the Roman forum type of layout. The transformations made in the old Classical Agora, however, betray Roman conceptions. The intention was to complete the regularization begun in the late Hellenistic period, with the rectilinear rows of porticoes on the south and west sides, by heightening the lower, northeast side, dismantling the Temple of Ares and re-erecting it on the east-west axis, and creating a central axis with the bulk of the Odeion, built by Agrippa about 15 B.C. When it came to building in Greece a new city, Nicopolis, in Epirus, to commemorate the victory of Actium, the Romans used the planning and the techniques of Roman architecture.

In the Eastern provinces, with their ancient culture, Roman activity fitted into the classicizing artistic current; but in the Western provinces of the Three Gauls, which Caesar had opened to Roman civilization, a vital premise for European culture, the Roman spirit declared itself more directly in the planning of new colonies. Celtic villages were transformed into urban organisms that were to develop during the Empire, with aqueducts, fora, amphitheaters, theaters, baths, basilicas, monumental gateways, and triumphal arches. Arles, Autun, Vienne, and Nîmes, with their walls and gates, Orange, and Augusta Emerita in Lusitania, are all examples of Romanization under Augustus. A daring, original monumentality marks the aqueduct of Segovia, over 900 feet long. The submission of forty-four Alpine tribes was commemorated in the grandiose trophy of the Alps at La Turbie, over 150 feet high. On its square base was placed a *tholos* with niches for statues, The *tholos* carried the tall, conical roof crowned with a bronze statue of Augustus surrounded by prisoners.

The small city of Glanum, now Saint-Rémy-en-Provence, had begun to develop already in the second century B.C., and in the period of Sulla there rose a porticoed forum and, as in Italy, houses with peristyles and pavements of crushed terracotta sherds. In the first years of Augustus' reign an arch was erected at the entrance to the main street, perhaps dedicated by veterans of the sixth legion, and decorated with sculptured groups of prisoners. The modeling of these groups reveals Hellenistic influences, which are also discernible in the four great reliefs from the base of the nearby mausoleum belonging to the Romanized Julii family of Provence. The base of the mausoleum, decorated like a monumental sarcophagus with garlands held by putti (fig. 287), carried a tetrapylon crowned with an open *tholos* which held the statues of the deceased. This type of mausoleum has points in common with that of the Istacidi at Pompeii, and with one at Aquileia, the base of which has shallow false arcades and lions at the corners, and with another near Nettuno. There is great variety in tomb structures of this period and Hellenistic models were re-elaborated in accordance with Roman taste, as in the type with an open shrine surmounted by a pyramid at Sarsina, belonging to Antonius Marcus Obulaccus, analogous to the pinnacled tomb of the Curii in Aquileia, from the first half of the first century A.D.

In the reliefs on the base of the Mausoleum of the Julii (fig. 287), inspiration from Hellenistic pictorial compositions leads to a learned, complex syntax in the animated battle scenes;

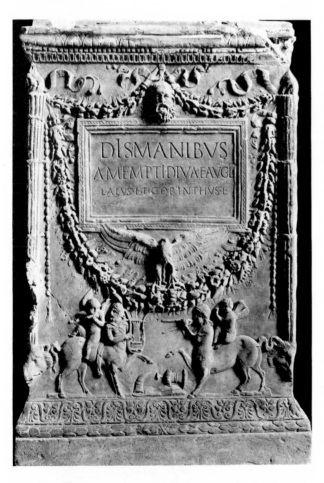

288. Funerary altar of Amemptus, the freedman of the Empress. At the angles, symbolic motifs of torches; also masks, garlands, centaurs, and amors, all of a refined, delicate, and precise modeling. First decade of the first century A.D. *Paris, Louvre*

these re-echo Classical motifs such as the struggle for the body of Patroclus, the Calydonian boar hunt, and the death of Adonis, mixed with toga-clad figures and other Roman elements. An incision like a black pen stroke forcefully outlines the figures. We are face to face here with a Hellenistic tradition surviving in a provincial Romanized setting; the great Classical inheritance still offers inexhaustible material for these decorative and symbolic scenes.

However, during the first century A.D., in works more closely linked to the demands of the soldiers and colonists, a Roman style begins to assert itself in the provinces. This can be seen in the widespread series of military grave steles: one type bore a frontally viewed centurion, standing, or in half-bust, shown with all his medals and decorations and the insignia of command, in a sober, but effective portrait style; another type depicted the horseman bending over his fallen enemy, in which reminiscences of Classical groups are reworked in a provincial style and modeling, showing similarities with the reliefs figuring the socalled Thracian Rider which are found over a wide area along the Danube.

During the first century A.D. Rome created many cities in the provinces of the North, based on the plan of the military *castrum*, or camp, and the heart of many modern Germanic and Gallic cities still retain this plan.

In Africa, Cyrene still maintained close contact with the Hellenistic currents through Alexandrian Egypt, but Rome asserted itself in all the cities of the coast as far as Mauretania, in city plans, aqueducts, arches, baths, and amphitheaters. In the Augustan period Juba II, educated in Rome and installed on the throne of Mauretania by Augustus, attempted to imitate Augustan ideals in customs, coinage, and intellectual life. As a writer and lover of things Classical, he surrounded himself with copies of originals by fifth-century Greek masters and by neo-Attic works, creating collections at Caesarea and Volubilis.

3. The Classicizing Trend in Julio-Claudian Art

The classicizing trend of the Augustan period persisted all through the reign of the Julio-Claudian emperors — Tiberius, Caligula, Claudius, and Nero. Portraits of Tiberius (A.D. 14–37) are modeled with Classical crispness, and an academic sense of plasticity makes Imperial figures stand out against the smooth background in a relief in Ravenna, as do the figures of Mars, Venus, and a young prince in a similar relief from Carthage. Classical types are used for the personifications of fourteen Asiatic cities rebuilt after the earthquake of A.D. 17, on a plinth at Pozzuoli, intended to support a colossal statue of Tiberius erected in A.D. 30. The allegory of fertile Earth exalted in the Tellus relief on the *Ara Pacis* reappears in a scene with a Julio-Claudian emperor as Triptolemus making an offering to Ceres, on a silver patera from Aquileia, now in Vienna, thus transforming this plate into a piece of Imperial propaganda.

Occasionally a note of greater realism and color is to be discerned in the later portraits of Caligula (A.D. 37–41), though in this classicizing climate they never quite represented the *foeditas* (hideousness) and *torvitas* (grimness) that sources attribute to this Emperor's appearance.

The ships found in Lake Nemi with their sumptuous decoration of gilded copper tiles, bronzes, and mosaics, inlay work, and paintings are a typical expression of Caligula's bizarre splendor, which seems to have vied with the Hellenistic opulence of the famous tent of Ptolemy II Philadelphus.

The search for characterization becomes more intense in portraits of Claudius (A.D. 41–54), which show a thoughtful concentration, psychological expression, and more mobile planes, lingering over the signs of advancing age, even when the Emperor is idealized as Jupiter in the statue now in the Vatican Rotunda. It is as if the aim were to go deeper than the polished academism of Augustus and Tiberius, just as the limpid serenity of the Augustan poets was succeeded by the psychological insight, the humanity, and the passion of Seneca, the strong moralism of Persius, and the pathos of Lucian.

The motifs of personifications of cities and provinces remained one of the most characteristic themes of Roman art. Claudius, who was interested in Etruscan civilization, erected in Caere (Cerveteri) a marble monument to the Lucumonic cities of Etruria, representing them

289. Right-hand terminal slab of a frieze with a sacrificial procession of the Vicomagistri; toga-clad figures crowned with laurel, and four young boys in tunics with their heads veiled and holding statuettes of Lares and of the Genius of the Emperor. Found in Rome near the Cancelleria. Period of Tiberius. Vatican, Gabinetto dell' Apoxyomenus

in personifications. A fragment of this monument has survived with the figures of Vetulonia, Tarquinia, and Vulci, in the Lateran Museum.

The historical relief continued the soft, classicizing style of the Augustan period, but the panels in the Villa Medici and the Capitoline Museums which have been connected with the *Ara Pietatis Augustae*, ordered by Tiberius in A.D. 22 and consecrated in A.D. 43, show a more complex, varied syntax, and mark the introduction of architectural backgrounds with faithfully reproduced temples that give the scenes precise topographical value, and thus replace the Hellenistic bucolic background with the realistic Roman setting.

Work on official monuments was done above all by Greek sculptors. In secondary works, however, we often find a less cultivated, more immediate, authentically Roman style. The procession of the Vicomagistri, on the frieze from the Palazzo della Cancelleria, now in the Vatican (fig. 289), has thickset proportions and rough modeling, and there is a freer, more airy space above the figures' heads, which are no longer stiffly aligned. Funerary reliefs are conceived in a more realistic key: a vivacious, spontaneous tone marks reliefs showing scenes of shops and arts and crafts, among which the two scenes showing cloth merchants, now in the Uffizi, are particularly accurate and naturalistic, while a relief from Avezzano, done in a popular style, shows a landscape view of a town set on a hill.

Roman engineers constructed the imposing mass of Claudius' new harbor, north of the mouth of the Tiber, and erected the four-storeyed lighthouse. They provided Rome with two aqueducts, the *Aqua Claudia* and the *Anio Novus*, with the powerful rhythm of their stone arches. The architects of Tiberius initiated the transformation of the Palatine into a sumptuous Imperial residence. Town-planning had to meet the need for new solutions to problems raised by the rebuilding of the many quarters of Rome, destroyed in the fire that broke out in the night of the 18th of July, A.D. 64, and lasted nine days. The new masterplan, the *forma aedificiorum urbis novae*, called for by Nero, ordered the widening and straightening of streets, laid down rules for the placing of balconies and windows on street façades, and forbade lightweight construction and the use of wooden laths. This last measure in particular stimulated the development of building in brick, a solid medium which made it possible to increase the height of buildings so that it was now easier to erect multi-storeyed houses and the great masses of the baths.

The ideals that had inspired Augustus' policies had been interpreted by poets and artists;

the fanatical personality of Nero (A.D. 54–68), in whom the attitudes of Hellenistic and Oriental monarchs met with the Roman concept of master of the Universe, who aspired to be musician, poet, painter, and sculptor, was to exhaust itself instead in a few extravagant, maniacal undertakings, the most startling example of which is still the construction of his Golden House, or *Domus Aurea*. Nero called

290. Black and white mosaic of the "cave canem"; others known also in the House of Paquinius Proculus and the House of the Tragic Poet at Pompeii, and in the Cena Trimalchionis *of Petronius. From Pompeii. First century A.D. Naples, National Museum*

on his architects to create a complex, sumptuous palace extending from the Palatine to the Caelian, with porticoes, gardens, pools, baths, and vast halls and audience chambers. In connection with this architectural work we still have records of the names of Severus and Celer, who built the palace, and the painter Fabullus, who decorated it. New forms were achieved in the general plan and the elevations, in octagonal rooms with fenestrated vaults, radial halls, and the celebrated *coenatio rotunda*, with its rotating dome imitating the vault of the heavens.

Fabullus himself seems a character well fitted for the pompous, extravagant life of Nero's court for, according to Pliny, who drew on a contemporary Greek source, he painted for only a few hours each day and in grand solemnity, always dressed in his toga even when he was perched on the scaffolding, and produced works in a style that contrived to be grave

291. Wall painting from Pompeii depicting the riot between the Pompeians and the Nucerians in the amphitheater of Pompeii in A.D. 59. Naples, National Museum

and severe, florid and fresh at the same time. The *Domus Aurea*, Pliny adds, was the prison of Fabullus' art, for no work of his existed elsewhere. The critical language of Pliny's report seems to indicate a type of painting in contrasting tones, unlike Augustan Classicism; and perhaps, among the paintings that remained in *Domus Aurea*, the gilded dome that was reproduced by Francesco d'Olanda in the sixteenth century may reflect the art of Fabullus. It shows a generous use of vivid colors, fiery red and azure blue, with gilded stucco work, and small panels painted with a light touch.

4. Decorative and Popular Trends in Painting and Sculpture

Mural painting, as can be seen in the houses of Pompeii, was indeed tending toward a greater degree of fantasy and exuberance in its archi-tectonic frames. It produced complex theatrical effects; the ornamentation became more baroque, and developed the use of large, centralized mythological scenes imitating works by Greek masters. The brushwork took on an increasingly impressionistic, summary touch with light strokes of color, especially in small figured or landscape panels, in a development of the generically Hellenistic style, whose Alexandrian ancestry is recorded by Petronius himself, the arbiter of elegance in Nero's court.

The moralistic tirades against luxury of the time in the writings of Seneca, and the satirical parody of the rich parvenu freedman in Petronius' *Cena Trimalchionis*, give us a colorful picture of the role played by art in Nero's society. The decoration of Trimalchio's house reflects contemporary taste, with classicizing paintings representing Hylas and the nymphs, the rape of Ganymede, Apollo and Narcissus, all the romantic myths dear to the Romans; copies

318

of paintings by Zeuxis and Apelles; the cycles of the *Iliad* and the *Odyssey*. There were also paintings in the Roman style, with more popular subjects, such as the realistic chained dog at the entrance (*cf.* fig. 290), gladiatorial contests, and a narrative cycle of the life of Trimalchio, the master of the house: he began in the slave market, was brought to Rome as a boy under the protection of Minerva, learned his first lessons, was appointed administrator by his master, and was then shown in apotheosis with Mercury lifting him up by the chin to sit in judgment, assisted by Fortune who showered him with gifts, and by the Fates weaving his life in gold threads.

Pompeii and Ostia present an abundant secondary production of shop signs, and scenes from everyday life in the forum. The gladiatorial battles in the house of Trimalchio can be compared with the realistic perspective view showing the Pompeian amphitheater during the riot that broke out between the Nucerians and Pompeians in A.D. 59 (fig. 291), and with Pliny's account of the paintings that covered all the walls of the public porticoes of Anzio, illustrating in life-size portrait figures the gladiatorial spectacle, a work donated by a freedman of Nero in that city. Pliny also records that the use of such paintings goes back to Gaius Terentius Lucanus, who dedicated, in the sanctuary of Diana, a painting of the gladiatorial games that he had given in the Forum in honor of his grandfather. Funerary paint-

ings in Campanian hypogea with gladiatorial duels take us back to the iconographic tradition and Italic taste of the fourth century B.C. Even the "*cave canem*" motif in the house of Trimalchio finds precise equivalents in the famous black and white Pompeian mosaics (fig. 290). The continuous narrative cycle of the life of Trimalchio described by Petronius reflects the narrative mode of historical reliefs and, later, of sarcophagi reliefs illustrating the childhood and life of the deceased.

Even the funerary monument that Trimalchio wanted for himself is a typical example of the conceptions of illustrative realism that dominated Roman tomb decoration, in which the inscription had to detail the entire *cursus honorum*, with statues of the husband and wife and reliefs narrating the life and occupation of the deceased. In Trimalchio's case we have ships in full sail, and he appears seated in a tribunal with *toga praetexta* and five golden rings, in the act of distributing money from a bag to the people, along with triclinium couches, the little dog, the broken pitcher, the weeping boy, and gladiatorial combats. The importance of gladiatorial contests is attested to by the precious nature of the ceremonial weapons, like the two Pompeian helmets on which the Greek motif of the *Iliupersis* is balanced by the more patriotic theme of the submission of the barbarians to Roman rule.

The passion for silverware, of which Trimalchio was a "*studiosus*," for Corinthian bronzes, and precious glass is satirized by Petronius, and it mirrors the widespread luxury and the love for decorative art.

5. Portraiture in the Time of Nero

In the field of portraiture Nero inspired some extravagant manifestations, like the colossal bronze statue 119 feet high cast by Zenodorus, showing the Emperor as the Sun; or the gigantic portrait painted on a canvas of 120 feet, which was exhibited in the *Horti Maiani* and destroyed by lightning.

In official portraits sculptors tried to give their images of Nero a heroic, pathetic tone, raising the face and lifting the gaze in an interpretation of the Hellenistic ideal of the emperor; but they gave a realistic reproduction of the characteristic tiers of hair over his forehead. Generally speaking, however, this Neronian expression did not spread through contemporary portraiture, and while the official images of the two Agrippinas (mother and

292. Portrait of a boy of the Neronian period. Rome, Museo Barracco

319

daughter) retained a classicizing flavor, portraits of other Romans of the time gradually lost their academic character. The expert modeling tended to develop a simpler, more lively tone, with expressive psychological naturalism, creating masterpieces like the Domitius Corbulo in the Capitoline Museums, and the Pompeian bronze portraits of Norbanus Sorex, who must have been an actor, and Caecilius Jucundus, a banker of Nero's time. In painting, the popular tone of immediate realism was caught in portraits like that of a couple from Pompeii.

In Romanized Germania, at Mainz, the *canabari* had a column erected, the work of Samus and Severus, dedicated to Jupiter, *pro salute imperatoris*; the column was perhaps raised to commemorate Nero's escape from the conspiracy led by Caius Piso, and it consisted of a double plinth which carried a shaft of five blocks carved with figures of gods from the Roman pantheon. The votive column of former times was thus transformed into a figured monument, and the religious concept converged with a commemorative function.

XII | Naturalism and Colorism in Flavian Art

The naturalistic current, which followed more closely the Roman tradition, rose to a higher official level with the portraits of the Emperors Vespasian (A.D. 69–79) and Titus (A.D. 79–81). Stripped of all heroic or idealized content, their features were recorded with an expressive, direct realism in a bourgeois conception which took pleasure in rendering the lively fullness

293. *Copy of an official portrait of Domitian, created* circa *A.D. 70.*
From Isola Sacra. Ostia, Museum

294. *Portrait of a Flavian lady with a diadem coiffure and the seminude body of an Aphrodite. Found outside Porta San Sebastiano in Rome. Rome, Capitoline Museums*

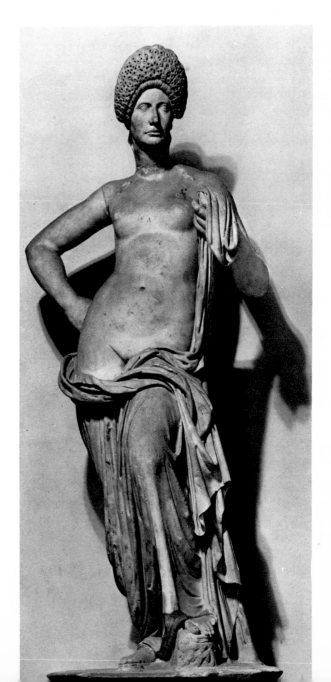

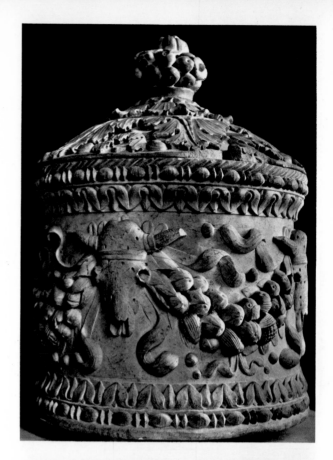

of clean-shaven faces on massive necks; this was done with soft coloristic effects, very different from the precise Augustan Classicism. But the ambitious, restless personality of the Emperor Domitian (A.D. 81–96), *dominus et deus*, made a different imprint on official portraiture; the realistic features of the projecting chin, the thin mouth, the curving nose, were interpreted in an idealized composition inspired by the Hellenistic type of monarch (fig. 293). Like Nero, Domitian longed to be represented in colossal forms, and had a massive bronze equestrian statue erected in the Forum, of which only the base, measuring 18 by 36 feet, remains. The statue was destroyed, as were many others, in the *damnatio memoriae* of the tyrant, but it lives on in the rhetorical lines of Statius. The allegorical concepts favored by Imperial propaganda were expressed in this statue by the statuette of Minerva that Domitian held in his right hand — Minerva, the protective goddess of the Flavian dynasty, was holding out her shield to strike terror into the enemy — and by the figure of the Rhine under the raised hoof of the Emperor's horse, symbolizing his victory over the Chatti. This exaggeration, however, remained particular to the portraits of Domitian, most all of which were destroyed by the wrathful people, but it survives in colorful terms in the writings of Pliny the Younger and Juvenal.

Flavian portraiture was distinguished by a refined chiaroscuro, a vibrant sensitivity in the modeling of the face (figs. 296, 297, and 314), and a play of coloristic effects achieved with the drill, which found particular expression in the tall diadems of curls that crowned women's faces with the baroque Flavian coiffure (fig. 294).

Naturalism and colorism give life to vegetal ornament (fig. 295), which acquired illusionistic touches and became more warm and intense by comparison with the rigorous elegance of similar motifs in Augustan and Julio-Claudian art, using festoons of fruit and flowers, interlacing vine tendrils, roses, lemons, and quinces, on altars, cinerary urns, ornamental panels, or pilasters. Products of the expert crafts of the times show a noticeable stylistic consistency in this decorative repertory, and also achieve a very lively, detailed realism, as in the little scenes that illustrate the builder's trade, funerals, cremations, and the apotheosis

296. Bust of an old Roman man, with an acanthus leaf at the base. Flavian period. Ostia, Museum

of the deceased in reliefs from the tomb of the Haterii of the period of Domitian.

Official works remain, on the other hand, more closely linked to the temperament of the various masters, and thus differences of tone are easier to come by, especially in a period in which no single artistic personality has emerged who shaped the style of all the art of his time with works of major importance. In this way, the historical reliefs of the Flavian period show contrasting aspects in the two most important monuments remaining to us, the Arch of Titus, erected *in summa sacra Via*, at the highest point of the Sacred Way, after A.D. 81, and the reliefs found under the Palazzo della Cancelleria in Rome, now in the Vatican.

The Arch of Titus elaborated the Augustan type of commemorative arch by inserting relief panels in the inner archway. These panels illustrate the triumphal procession following the conquest of Jerusalem (fig. 298). There is a new illusionistic sense in the superposition and gradation in the planes of the relief, and

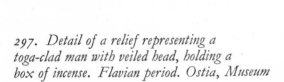

297. Detail of a relief representing a toga-clad man with veiled head, holding a box of incense. Flavian period. Ostia, Museum

298. Detail of a relief on the Arch of Titus in the Roman Forum, showing the seven-branched candelabrum from the Temple of Jerusalem carried in triumph. After A.D. 81

in the open space above the heads of the figures; these are no longer uniformly aligned along the upper edge of the relief in the Classical manner that was still followed in the frieze of the *Ara Pacis*, but are more freely arranged so as to leave an empty space above, cadenced by the slanting spears, standards, and looted trophies. The illusionism of the scene is sustained by the obliquely placed arch toward which the impressive cortege marches, localizing the scene and suggesting depth and movement. In these scenes referring to the precise historical event of Titus' triumph after his victory over Jerusalem in A.D. 71, costumes, standards, the seven-branched candelabrum, and the trumpets from the Temple of Jerusalem — which must have also characterized the triumphal landscape paintings recorded by Josephus Flavius — are all treated in the one relief with the most exact realism; in the other,

299. Detail of the portrait of Vespasian, from the Cancelleria relief shown in figure 300.

realism is combined with the personification of Victory crowning Titus, who is seen standing in the quadriga guided by the personification of Rome, in accordance with the typical concepts of Imperial propaganda. The vibrant modeling, which is left unpolished, and the thick shadows of the drapery indicate an approach in keeping with the dominant coloristic vision of Flavian art.

A different, classicizing style informs the two large reliefs found beneath the Palazzo della Cancelleria, prepared for an unknown monument in honor of Domitian; this monu-

ment was perhaps never built, for the slabs were found propped against the wall of an earlier tomb, that of Aulus Hirtius, in the Campus Martius. One of them, according to the most convincing hypothesis, presents an idealized *profectio*, or setting forth, of Domitian: Victory clears the way, followed by the striding figures of Mars and the protectress, Minerva; the personification of Rome urges the Emperor onward with one arm, and personifications of the Genius of the Senate and the Genius of the Roman People salute the Emperor. The other relief represents an idealized, symbolic meeting between Domitian and Vespasian, over whose head Victory is holding a rich, jeweled crown (fig. 300). The scene is an ostentatious proof of the legal transmission of power from the triumphant Vespasian to the young prince, Domitian; it does not take place in the presence of war-like gods, but is watched by the seated figure of Rome and by the Vestals, along with the Genius of the Senate and the Genius of the Roman People who symbolize the participation of the whole city. The figures are spread out against a neutral background, and there is a lack of spatial interest; but the work is dominated by a sharp, accurate, classicizing modeling with engraved details on armor, standards, and costumes.

Differences in execution might be attributed to various hands that executed the models of a single artist, rather than to the work of two or more independent masters. Two remarkable portraitists were responsible for the lively, coloristic head of Vespasian (fig. 299), and, on a portion of the relief not shown here, the remodeled head of Domitian, made into a portrait of Nerva (A.D. 96–98) when the memory of Domitian was condemned.

This classicizing official style is also to be found in similar figures of soldiers on two reliefs from Pozzuoli, now in Berlin and Philadelphia, belonging to a monument from the time of Domitian, and in the grandiose figure of a winged Minerva that decorated a pilaster on the remodeled main gate of Ostia.

Domitian had dedicated a temple to Minerva, the Flavian protectress; this formed the axis of the new Forum Transitorium in Rome, brought to completion under Nerva. The Forum Transitorium lay between the Forum of Augustus and the Forum of Peace dedicated by Vespasian. Vespasian's Temple of Peace, however, stood in the center of a colonnaded square, in accordance with the Greek tradition; the Forum Transitorium marks the return to the Roman plan. The restricted space suggested the use of projecting columns rhythmically placed along the walls to give an illusion of space behind them. This arrangement is also typical of the decorative use made of columns in Roman architecture. The frieze that runs around the broken entablature realistically narrates, not the myths of Minerva, but the works and trades protected by the goddess, rendered in an incisive, plastic style.

Flavian architecture, apart from these Imperial fora, produced the most grandiose and

stored to the people by the construction of a building that had a great appeal for the mass public, in accordance with the Imperial policy of *panem et circenses* (bread and circuses). Under Titus, new baths were built; another monument for the spectacles dear to the populace was built by Domitian, the Stadium in the Campus Martius, which still survives, transformed into the lovely Piazza Navona.

300. Detail of a relief found under the Cancelleria in Rome, showing Vespasian and Domitian between lictors, with the Genius of the Senate personified as a bearded man and the Genius of Rome with a cornucopia. Flavian period. Vatican, Cortile delle Corazze

harmonious form of the amphitheater, in the Colosseum. Elegant and severe, with its rhythmically tiered arcades distinguished by the ornamental elements of the various architectural orders, and decorated with statues, this was a structure at the same time functional and monumental. The Colosseum was constructed on the spot of the artifical lake of the *Domus Aurea*; the land that the tyrannical Nero had seized for his extravagant palace was thus re-

We know the name of the architect Rabirius who erected on the Palatine the sumptuous *Domus Flavia* with its solemn halls rich in marble. The plans of Flavian constructions took on a more active articulation, animated with niches, columns, rib-vaults, and aediculae. The vigorous Flavian sense of colorism was affirmed in architecture by rich entablatures and moldings, with strong chiaroscuro effects created by the use of the drill.

325

Greek Teaching and Roman Tradition
in the Imperial Art of the Trajanic Period

The importance and sheer magnitude of the *res gestae* of Trajan during his reign of nineteen years (A.D. 98–117) offered a wide field for figurative commemoration. The great projects desired by the Emperor provided a very strong impulse for the monumental arts, and stimulated and concentrated new creative energies; in Rome under Trajan the arts flourished, presenting a coherent and organic picture which can be compared with that of the period of Pericles in Greece. And just as Pericles found in Phidias the master best fitted to figurally interpret the ideals of his time, Trajan had his own, unknown artist, who created a particular narrative language to express in marble the complex tale of his Emperor's exploits.

1. The Master of the Exploits of Trajan

We know that Apollodoros of Damascus was Trajan's official architect, and followed him in his military expeditions, building the famous bridge over the Danube, and in Rome an odeum, a circus, and baths; and creating in Rome the great Forum of Trajan that completed the series of Imperial fora with the most complex and monumental of them all. The Forum of Trajan comprised an entrance arch; the square with the equestrian statue of Trajan; the Basilica Ulpia with a sumptuous forest of columns up and down five naves; beyond was a courtyard with a library to either side, and in the center stood the famous column of Trajan with an historiated, helical frieze; and closing the courtyard, the Temple of the Divine Trajan. In addition there were the hemicycles, to either side of the square, and the great brick mass of the market buildings which extended over the slopes of the Quirinal, ending in a vast vaulted hall with booths.

Architecture and sculpture were closely linked in this work, which constituted a splendid affirmation of the power of the Empire victorious under its *optimus princeps*. It has been thought that Apollodoros may have been responsible for the conception of the figured decoration as well as the architecture proper. The main sculptural work was the Column of Trajan, illustrating the various stages of the two wars against the Dacians in A.D. 101–102 and 105–106, the narration of the respective campaigns separated by a figure of Victory recording the successes on her shield. This monument was set in the general plan of the Forum according to a precise sense of function, and its conception must have been presided over by the architect. The inscription on the column actually states the relationship of the height (100 feet) of the column to the corresponding mass of excavation and embankment that was necessary to level the site for the future Forum; this certainly reveals an essentially architectonic mentality, and stresses the importance assigned in the Roman scale of values to urbanistic works, monumental creations deemed more worthy of remembrance than a work of art. Apollodoros, who had followed the campaigns, could also be credited with all the realistic details of bridges, forts, encampments, and cities, which give valuable local color to the narration; but we cannot tell whether he was himself enough of an artist to give life to this grandiose figured chronicle by drawing all the cartoons, or if, as Iktinos had done with Phidias, he called in a sculptor to make the model and to organize the workshop in which the final version in marble was produced. The lack of any documentation in this

301. Base of the Column of Trajan decorated with Roman and barbarian arms and armor, worked into an arabesque-like composition of precise and refined modeling. Dedicated in A.D. 113. Rome, Forum of Trajan

anonymous Roman art obliges us in our uncertainty to use the conventional title, the Master of the Exploits of Trajan; he remains the greatest artistic personality known till then in Rome.

He showed nothing less than genius in giving monumental scale to the ancient Republican tradition of the honorary column with an iconic statue. In this case the monument also had to serve as the Imperial tomb, with a chamber for the urn hollowed out in the base. And his solution showed high originality: to imagine a gigantic papyrus scroll illustrating the *res gestae* of the Emperor, dragged out of one of the neighboring libraries, as it were,

and wrapped around the axis of the column, covering its groovings (which were visible only at the very top) and thereby almost translating painting into marble relief. Indeed, he was all the more of a genius because the *volumen* with illustrations in the form of a continuous frieze did not, in fact, exist at that time; it was to appear much later, and then only under the influence of the historiated column. As his point of departure the artist must have taken the idea of a scroll with illustrations divided by columns of text, and translated it into a marble low-relief frieze; this made possible the long, complex narrative of the wars winding round the column. The Hellenistic

302. At left: *The Romans forming a testudo for an assault against a Dacian fortress during the first Dacian war.*
Detail from the Column of Trajan

303. Above, at left: *Roman soldiers setting up a ballista with bulwarks formed of tree trunks, outside of a small fort.*
Detail from the Column of Trajan

304. Above, at right: *Roman soldiers presenting severed Dacian heads to Trajan.*
Detail from the Column of Trajan

305. At right: *Submission of the Dacian chiefs to Trajan, who is seated on the raised platform or* suggestum *among standard-bearers, at the end of the first Dacian war.*
Detail from the Column of Trajan

306. At left: *Trajan addressing his troops.*
Detail from the Column of Trajan

307. Below, at left: *Heads of Dacians on
pikes, in front of a Roman fort during the
first Dacian war.*
Detail from the Column of Trajan

308. Below: *The suicide of Decebalus at the
arrival of the leaping Roman horseman,
at the end of the second Dacian war.*
Detail from the Column of Trajan

experiments in narrative mythological friezes, like the Telephus frieze at Pergamon, were transformed into a realistic Roman language (figs. 301–309). With this the tradition of triumphal painting may also have converged, for the background is enriched with indications of landscape, precise topographical allusions, and a lively sense of space; with varied, cartographic representations of rivers, bird's-eye views of camps, or perspectives of forests and cities. These animate the story and hold it together in an uninterrupted flow of episodes, from the crossing of the Danube on the bridge of boats to the dramatic suicide of Decebalus which concludes the narrative.

The recurring figure of Trajan — at the head of marching columns, supervising the construction of camps, offering sacrifices, addressing

his soldiers or guiding them in skirmishes, receiving the surrender of the barbarians, and watching executions — provides a unifying nexus in the gripping rhythm of the scenes of this epic, whose heroic protagonist is the entire Roman army. Notes of drama and tragedy, pathos and idyll, solemnity and vitality, rejoicing and ceremony, alternate in a varied scale of expression, achieving particular intensity in the scenes of the tortures inflicted on naked

Roman prisoners by Dacian women; in the presentation of severed barbarian heads to Trajan; the search for wounded in the Dacian field; the assault of an enemy fortress by forming a testudo of overlapping shields; the flight of the Sarmatians in their heavy scale-patterned armor; the Emperor's audience with barbarian ambassadors in their long, splendid, exotic costumes; and finally, in the impressive pause of the complex scene of the Dacian surrender at the end of the first campaign, based on the effective contrast between the vertical lines and solemn calm of the group consisting of the seated Trajan surrounded by officers and standard-bearers, and the oblique lines and confused mass of the kneeling Dacians, their shields on the ground and arms outstretched in an invocation of Imperial clemency.

This figurative historical language finds a literary equivalent in the historical prose of Tacitus, who combined Latin *gravitas* with rhetorical education, and shows dramatic vigor and descriptive richness, absolute judgments and psychological insights. He exalts the wisdom of Trajan, illustrates the ways and the life of the Britons and Germans, inserts striking speeches, and evokes with expressive realism such scenes as the sack of Cremona, the triumphal entry of the Vitelliani into Rome, the remains of the massacre of Teutoburg, and the assassination of Britannicus.

On the Column of Trajan the vigorous portrait interpretations of Trajan, Decebalus, and other higher officers is accompanied by an expressive characterization of Roman soldiers and barbarian ethnic types, with a faithful reproduction of costumes, weapons, and standards. In this historical narrative the only personification is the imposing, solemn Danube, who emerges from his bed and invites the Romans to pass.

Despite the various hands in the execution of this work, a substantial stylistic unity emerges throughout the entire frieze. This represents the creation of a figurative patrimony that was to inspire all the art of the period. The fundamental characteristics of the Trajanic style return, with stronger plasticity and in a more thickly packed composition, in the elaborate frieze representing a synthetic commemorative rendering of the decisive Dacian triumph of Trajan, bursting through the barbarian ranks on his horse before being crowned by Victory (fig. 310). This frieze once decorated the Forum of Trajan but was dismantled into several strips, two of which were later incorporated into the Arch of Constantine.

More vigorous relief, as befitted architectural decoration, marks the panels that decorated the piers and attic of the sumptuous arch erected

at Beneventum to commemorate the opening of the Via Trajana in A.D. 114, completed three years later under Hadrian. These reliefs illustrate the works achieved by Trajan in Italy and the Empire. Here, according to the tenets of Imperial propaganda, the historical events are commemorated in an allegorical tone, and therefore personifications of the Genius of the Senate, the Genius of the Roman People, Honor, and the Provinces, as well as the gods make their appearance. Vivid realism, as in the animated scene of the *institutio alimentaria*, the establishment of gifts of food to the children of the poor, with fathers carrying children on their shoulders, is mixed with solemn figures wearing turreted crowns who personify the various cities (fig. 311). Trajan's provident institution had also been celebrated in a bronze

309. Portrait of a Dacian chief who witnesses the gathering of the wounded during the first Dacian war. Detail from the Column of Trajan

group in the Roman Forum showing the Emperor enthroned before a figure of Italy carrying two infant boys.

The rich thematic material presented by Trajan's long reign thus transformed even the

312. At left: Relief from the Monument at Adam-Klissi, showing a family of barbarians on a cart. Trajanic period. Reproduced from a cast in the Museo della Civiltà Romana, Rome, after the original in the National Museum, Bucharest

313. Below: Imago clipeata *with a portrait of a man wearing the hairstyle of the end of the Flavian period. Ostia, Museum*

310. Opposite, upper: *Relief depicting Trajan charging into a group of Dacians. This relief, originally in the Forum of Trajan, was reused on the Arch of Constantine.*
Circa A.D. *110. Rome, Arch of Constantine*

311. Opposite, lower: *Relief on the Arch at Beneventum showing the* institutio alimentaria, *or the establishment of gifts of food to the children of the poor by Trajan. A.D. 114–117*

arch into a figured monument by multiplying its historical panels. The abundantly illustrated arch that was placed at the entrance to the Forum of Trajan, which can be seen in a stylized reproduction on a coin, must also have had this form.

Art under Trajan achieved a felicitous balance and an intimate fusion of Latin traditions and Greek artistic culture, of Classicism and naturalism, producing a wholly Roman style. In the field of portraiture, too, we have harmonious, expressive manifestations in the plain, sober, humane portraits of Trajan and the Empress Plotina, whose hair was dressed in smooth bands, restrained and simplified in comparison with Flavian styles, and also in portraits of private citizens, and funerary works. The *imago clipeata*, which according to a Roman tradition inserted the portrait head into a frame formed by a shield (fig. 313), reached vigorous, highly effective forms in specimens from Ostia dating from Trajan's reign.

The technique of brick construction, now fully developed, allowed for a monumental expansion in architecture: in private houses; in utilitarian buildings like the *horrea* for storing grain and other foodstuffs; and in public baths, as can be seen from the Baths of Trajan on the Collis Oppius in Rome. The plan of the baths was transformed by placing a court lined with porticoes, exedrae, and apses round three sides of the organic, symmetrical, central body that contained the various bathing halls; these took on round, elliptical, or apsidal forms, with cross-vaulted roofs, niches, and columns. Trajan's engineers created a daring artificial hexagonal harbor at Ostia, linking it to the port built by Claudius and with a new branch of the Tiber, providing a safe port adequate for the intense traffic which was then converging on the Imperial capital from every corner of the Mediterranean.

2. Aspects of Trajanic Art in the Provinces

In all the provinces the architecture of Trajan's period left noteworthy evidence in the form of new cities and new buildings. Some letters that Pliny the Younger, in his capacity as *legatus pro praetore* in Bithynia, wrote to Trajan between A.D. 111 and 112, provide interesting information about Imperial activity in this field. Pliny asked the Emperor to send a hydraulic engineer or an architect to Nicomedia to build an arched aqueduct, partly from reused stone blocks, partly in brick; he planned another aqueduct at Sinope; he criticized the projects of the few local experts for a gymnasium in Nicaea, judging it too complicated and large, inefficient and clumsy; he spoke of the baths in Claudiopolis; and proposed to add a colonnade and porticoes consecrated to Trajan in the bath to be built at Prusa. In his *Panegyricus* to Trajan, Pliny contrasted the mad spending of Nero and Domitian on their palaces with Trajan's intense architectural activity devoted to the public good. He described the rich towns of Laurentum, Etruria, and Como, surrounded by parks, with marble pavilions and paintings showing views onto gardens where birds perched on the branches; he recorded the gardens of Regulus in Rome, with their immense porticoes, and the statues along the Tiber.

In the East the Hellenistic monumental tradition was developed in the grandiose complex of the Trajaneum, which was installed on the topmost terrace at Pergamon, with the peripteral temple placed in the square surrounded with porticoes, silhouetted against the dramatic view of the surrounding landscape. In Africa, the Roman *castrum* survived in the regular division of the monumental cities of Timgad

and Lambaesis. Spain, Trajan's native country, linked ever closer to the Empire to which she had already given Lucan, Martial, Seneca, and Quintilian, was enriched with new monuments in Trajan's reign, ranging from single-vaulted arches, as at Barà, to triple-vaulted arches, as in Caceres. The architect Gaius Lucius Lacer built the six-arched bridge which still stands over the Tagus at Alcantara and proclaimed in the inscription that it would "last as long as the world."

The various monuments of Trajan's time scattered throughout the Empire represented fundamental characteristics of Trajanic architecture, with greater Hellenism persisting in the Eastern provinces and more typically Roman forms in the West; but the elaborate monument that was raised at Adam-Klissi in Dobrudja to celebrate, like the Column of Trajan, the Dacian victories, was completely original. The gifted architect erected the tall, crenelated cylinder over 300 feet in diameter, topped by a conical scallop-tiled roof that supported a colossal trophy, creating a harmonious fusion of the concept and tradition of the Etrusco-Roman burial mound, exemplified in the Mausoleum of Augustus and the minor tombs of Caecilia Metella or Munatius Plancus, and the function of a triumphal monument. This composite monument, tumulus and trophy, took on the appearance of a closed, crenelated fortress, as the symbol of the scene of the battle itself. To the originality of the architectural conception was, however, juxtaposed the poverty of the decorative sculptures executed by two groups of local artists in Sarmatian limestone (fig. 312). From the schematic battle scenes on fifty-four panels, and the figures of the prisoners tied to trees between the twenty-six merlons of the parapet, an ingenuous, uncultured, provincial, linear language emerges in the stiff drapery, unorganic structure, and summary modeling; it only comes to life in gestures, in ethnic characterizations, and in the reproduction of costumes.

The Column of Trajan and the Monument of Adam-Klissi are the most obvious demonstration of the extreme poles reached by art in one and the same period: on one side, a profound assimilation of Classical culture, while the other remained completely ignorant of it. This is a situation that gives us the true measure of the value of Classical heritage.

314. Portrait of a woman with a rich coiffure of the Flavian period. Rome, Torlonia Museum

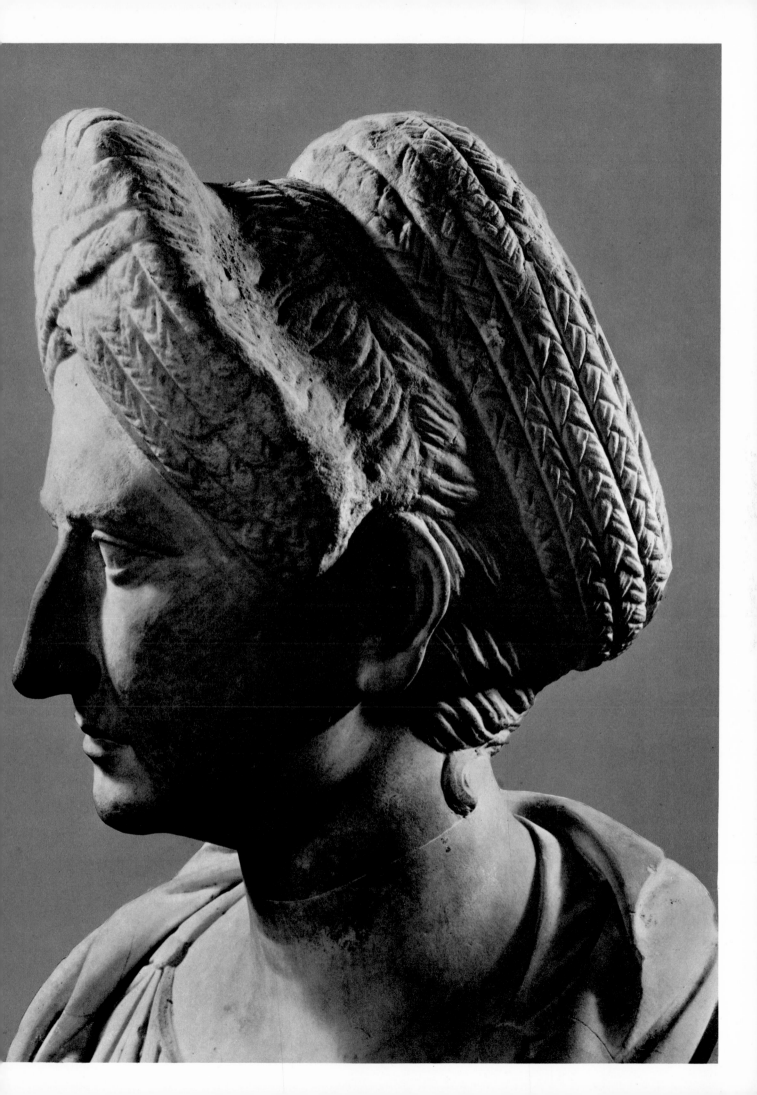

XIV | The Classicizing Character of Hadrianic Art

Classical culture fused harmoniously with Latin tradition in Trajanic art; in the following reign of Hadrian (A.D. 117–138), art assumed a more intensely classicizing character, in accordance with the ideals cherished by the new, phil-Hellene Emperor. Trajan's personality had marked the art of his time with his exploits and the fervor of his undertakings; Hadrian, instead, influenced art by his intellectual and political attitudes. Hadrian had a great familiarity with painters, he was known as "*Graeculus*," and was also called, in the words of Philostratus, "the spur of the Sophists." And indeed, he was enthusiastic about the neo-Sophist movement, which aimed at reviving Classical Attic prose, thus giving rise to an archaizing style.

The most numerous and characteristic portraits of Trajan are statues of the Emperor wearing the cuirass in the Roman tradition. On the other hand, the rich series of portrait statues of Hadrian include only a few in cuirass, like those from Olympia and Hierapydna. Instead, Hadrian, who reintroduced the fashion of the beard in imitation of the Greek philosophers, was most often portrayed as Mars, either in heroic nakedness, or deified. Hadrian's numerous journeys through the provinces, especially to the eastern parts of his Empire, led to the erection of many honorary statues in which the official type took on stylistic shades of the various localities: idealized and crowned with pine branches in the portrait at Cyrene; expressive in Pergamon; heroic in Vaison; colossal in Egypt; with rich chiaroscuro in Athens; and archaizing in style at Ostia (fig. 315). Even the regular features of the Empress Sabina seem fixed in Classical, idealized composure, and in the fine statue in Ostia she assumes the body of a fourth-century Ceres, following the fashion, by then popular among Roman ladies, of having herself portrayed as a Hellenic goddess. At another time, portrayed together with Hadrian, she assumes the type of Venus Genetrix while her husband is shown as Mars.

Classical ideals play an even greater part in the series of portraits of the deified Antinous, the handsome Bithynian adolescent who was the Emperor's favorite (fig. 317). Hadrian wanted to foster a cult of Antinous after the youth's early, mysterious death, and sculptors portrayed his soft, feminine, fleshy forms, assimilating them into the types of Dionysus, Osiris, Vertumnus, Adonis, Sylvanus, and Ganymede, reworking Polykleitan, Hellenistic, and archaizing modes. The sculptor Antonianos of Aphrodisia represented Antinous as Silvanus in a relief with the Classical tone of an Attic stele. All the portraiture of the time was steeped in this Classicism, sometimes academic and cold, sometimes more romantic and coloristic (fig. 318).

A proof of the Hellenic aspirations of artistic culture is the vast multiplication of copies of statues by Greek masters, produced by neo-Attic sculptors and the school of Aphrodisia. The rich marble quarries of Aphrodisia had favored the rise of an intensely active community of copyists, portraitists, and decorators from the Augustan period on, who found easy outlet for their work in Rome, especially during the Flavian period, and continuing under Trajan and Hadrian. Their work was executed with an expert, even virtuoso, technique, and an eclectic, ornamental style. Aristeas and Papias, who executed the very elaborate group of centaurs for Hadrian's Villa, are typical representatives of this school.

Reliefs of mythological themes for wall decoration were of a cold, restrained academism (figs. 320, 321). Marble candelabra were transformed into splendid, monumental shafts of acanthus leaves with bases adorned with classicizing figures of gods (fig. 260). The many Egyptian-inspired sculptures found at Hadrian's

337

Villa complete the picture of these artistic tendencies, reviving in external, entirely conventional and decorative forms, the most typical elements of Egyptian statuary, drained of all content. The diffusion of the cult of Isis was to contribute to the multiplication of these Imperial remodelings of the Egyptian style.

One source of transmission of Greek iconography and the classicizing taste was the thematic material used in the decoration of sarcophagi; these sarcophagi, after the occasional late Trajanic examples, appeared more frequently and finally, with the adoption of interment under Hadrian and the Antonines, became a characteristic product. We still have not enough information to establish whether the production of these sarcophagi began in Athens or in Rome, but in either case their diffusion was rapid. Attic sarcophagi in Pentelic marble from the time of Hadrian were imported into Italy. The most characteristic forms are those with Dionysiac scenes acted out by putti, or those on which softly modeled putti hold festoons of fruit and flowers.

In addition to imitations of Attic sarcophagi, Rome developed a type in Luni marble, the faces and sides of the casket decorated with an iconographic repertory derived mainly from fourth century B.C. and Hellenistic pictorial cycles, reworked in high relief in a close, continuous composition. The tragic destiny of death was symbolized by the massacres of the Niobids, by Orestes, Medea, the unconsolable sorrow of Alcestis, and of Laodamia, or by the enigmatic fate of Oedipus and the Sphinx. Besides such battle scenes as the agitated gigantomachy drawn from Pergamene tradition, the turbulent rape of the Leucippides, and the adventures of Peleus and Thetis, there are symbolic allusions to the journey to Elysium and the joys of afterlife such as bacchic themes with satyrs and maenads, and Dionysus and Ariadne, or marine themes of tritons and nereids. Amors and figures of Victory support festoons, and above the swags are inserted symbolic mythological scenes, or comic and tragic masks constituting an allegory of life as a theater stage.

The reign of Hadrian did not offer bellicose exploits for commemoration. Trajan had led campaigns; Hadrian traveled through all the provinces of his vast Empire between 121 and 134 A.D. The circular relief medallions from a monument of the Hadrianic period, later incorporated into the Arch of Constantine (figs. 316, 317), show Hadrian, depicted in a soft, balanced, classicizing style, making sacrifices and offerings to Apollo, Artemis, Hercules, and Sylvanus, and hunting boars, bears, and lions. Hadrian did not hold with being represented at the head of his troops, preferring scenes of allegorical lion hunts, like a new Alexander the Great, or scenes of sacrifice to the god of music and song, to the goddess of the hunt, to the gods of invincible strength or the fertility of the fields. His most significant work, a defensive move against the barbarians rather than an aggressive measure, was the great wall across Britannia, known as Hadrian's Wall.

Hadrianic coins constitute the most representative monuments of the policies and propaganda of Hadrian. They bear numerous personifications of the concepts of liberality, justice, peace, happiness, concord, and mercy, of providential gifts of unity and solidarity in the Empire, and the brotherhood of all Roman citizens. In the series of coins issued between A.D. 134 and 138, Hadrian is shown ceremonially arriving in a province that is personified by a female figure who welcomes him and makes sacrifices, or he is seen as the Restorer being thanked by the kneeling figure of a province.

Shortly after A.D. 130, when Hadrian completed the construction of the Olympieion at Athens, which had dragged on for centuries, he had a series of bronze statues of the Provinces placed around the gigantic colonnade, as if to symbolize the presence of the entire Empire and place the Panhellenic cult on a universal plane. Numerous statues of Hadrian, including the colossal figure erected by the Athenians, were raised in cities all over Greece. The grandiose effigy of Zeus commissioned by Hadrian for the cella of the Olympieion was inspired by Phidias' example, and was perhaps reproduced on Hadrianic coins.

1. Architectural Activity Under Hadrian

Hadrian made special plans for Athens, creating the whole new monumental area which was reached through the gateway that combined the traditional Roman arch with the airy rectilinear Greek attic. In addition to the baths, the Temple of Zeus, and a palaestra, the complex included the sumptuous library with interior porticoes of a hundred Corinthian columns, halls, and the west façade decorated with fourteen more Corinthian columns, placed on dadoes against the wall above which ran the entablature with angular breaks over the columns, in the same manner as in the Forum Transitorium of Nerva in Rome. The theater of Dionysus in Athens was remodeled along Roman lines with a wide stage decorated with reliefs in honor of Dionysus, composed of classicizing figures on a neutral ground.

Hadrian was seconded in his works of reconstruction in Athens and the rest of Greece by Herodes Atticus, a philosopher and rhetorician, who built the Odeum on the slopes of the Acropolis, and the marble stadium. Athens honored him with seventeen statues, while others were dedicated to him in Olympia, Corinth, and Alexandria in the Troad. His bearded portrait, with the soft treatment of his thin cheeks and thick hair, is one of the most characteristic specimens of portraiture of the time of Hadrian and the Antonines.

While Hadrianic architecture in Greece took on a prevailingly Classical tone despite certain Roman features, in Rome and in the Western provinces spatial structures and brick techniques underwent major transformations. The intense building activity led to the multiplication of factories producing bricks marked with the seal of Hadrian. In the villa that Hadrian built at the foot of Tivoli, the names of its many structures evoked the monuments admired by the Emperor in the course of his travels: the Serapaeum, the Canopus, the Academy, the Lyceum, the Stoa Poikile, and the Vale of Tempe. Its brick architecture, however, expressed a Roman conception, here affirmed with fervid imagination, with the complexity of the plans, the predilection for curved and moving lines, for round and polyfoil halls, for apses, exedrae, and colonnades, and for barrel-vaults, cross-vaults, baldaquin vaults, and undulating domes. Stucco work, marbles, paintings, mosaics, and decorative statues made of this villa an Imperial residence. The Classical mentality found a significant opportunity to express itself in the series of statues decorating the edge of the pool of the Canopus, where copies of Amazons and fifth-century male figures alternated with caryatids copied from the Erechtheion (fig. 319), Hellenistic Silenus figures, personifications of the Nile and the Tiber, and the Hellenistic group of Scylla rising from the water.

It was during Hadrian's reign that Roman

example of Augustus, readopting the mound type of tomb, which he placed along the axis of the new bridge over the Tiber. The Mausoleum of Hadrian exists today in the form of the Castel Sant'Angelo.

Apart from these grandiose, monumental works, Hadrian's period also saw developments in domestic architecture. In Roman society the middle class was becoming increasingly important and thus a new type of house appeared. The patrician *domus* transformed the plan of *atrium* and peristyle into a house with halls and courtyards surrounded with pilastered porticoes of brick; the middle-class dwelling was

318. Portrait bust, showing a soft and coloristic plasticism. Circa A.D. *135–140. Ostia, Museum*

319. Detail of a Hadrianic copy of the type of caryatid on the porch of the Erechtheion, used as decoration of the Canopus of Hadrian's Villa at Tivoli. Antiquarium of Hadrian's Villa

spatial architecture created its technical and artistic masterpiece, the gigantic, coffered concrete dome of the reconstructed Pantheon.

In following through the program of monumental reconstruction of the Campus Martius, Hadrian extended the temple and porticoes of Marciana and Matidia between the Pantheon and the Flaminia. And since the Forum of Trajan had completed the monumental complex in the heart of the city, he chose to leave a testimonial to the splendor of his Empire on the summit of the Velia, drawing up himself the plans for the gigantic decastyle Temple of Venus and Rome, almost an echo of the Athenian Olympieion. For his own mausoleum Hadrian decided to follow the

an apartment in a large, multi-storeyed block, the construction of which was made possible by advances in brick and cement techniques. The development in height changed the face of the city, as can be well seen in Ostia. This new type of apartment-house block radically transformed the preceding type of plan of domestic building, whose various parts, gravitating inward, had been clearly differentiated; now the individual apartments were all of equal size, and were made up of five or more similar rooms, usually with a larger one, intended as a living room, at the corner. Rooms no longer gave onto the *atrium*, which had disappeared, but onto a corridor instead; the rooms did not receive light from the interior of the building, but from windows which were now aligned on the outer façade, often scanned by rows of balconies supported on brackets. Access was by stairs, and when the block was really large, the façades were multiplied by inner courtyards, brightened with gardens and fountains; at times these became full-blown city blocks of apartment buildings with garden courts, all virtually the same, combined in a single organic complex governed by principles similar to those of the most modern systems of town-planning.

aspect, with pilastered porticoes of brick which are recalled by the Medieval and Renaissance center of Bologna.

2. Pictorial and Mosaic Decoration

The decorative requirements of these middle-class dwellings determined the development of a style of wall painting that renounced the complex compositions of the Flavian period. This decoration was limited to panels divided by bands of color generally in tones of red and yellow; or to a white ground with light,

320. Detail of a relief depicting Amphion and Zethus. Zethus, an enthusiast of the hunt, is seated with a dog at his feet beside a shrine of Artemis, while his brother Amphion, a musician, presents the lyre to him.
Circa A.D. 130–140. Rome, Palazzo Spada

321. Detail of a relief depicting Paris and Oenone seated by the port with a ship, beneath which is the personification of a river shown here.
Circa A.D. 130–140. Rome, Palazzo Spada

Along the streets there were often pilastered porticoes that supported the upper floors. These created roomy covered walks onto which opened shops. With its rear workshop and its mezzanine room reached by an internal stair, the shop became the simple dwelling of the artisan and the small tradesman, who also at times set up house in the attics under the eaves of the buildings. In the East, the Hellenistic tradition was retained in marble colonnades along the street, and architraved structures; in Rome, streets took on a different

schematic divisions in the architectonic tradition, with garlands and ribbons and an occasional scene rapidly sketched in an impressionistic style, showing animals, idyllic landscapes, seascapes, and still lives. On the other hand, painting of a more elevated sort maintained a classicizing Hellenistic style, but the mythological scene tended to disappear, giving way to delicate, refined landscapes. Ceiling decoration became richer, often with ornamental and figured stucco work, typical examples of which are to be found in the Antonine tombs of the Valerii and the Pancratii on the Via Latina (fig. 322). A similar

322. *Stucco vault of the tomb of the Valerii, with nereids and sea monsters in the tondi and amors and rosettes in the squares. Antonine period. Rome, Via Latina*

style is seen in the painting of some of the older parts of the catacombs, as in the catacomb of Domitilla (fig. 368).

In the East, during the time of Hadrian and the Antonines, the art of mosaic developed the great Hellenistic tradition of polychrome mythological scenes rivaling painting, with refined *emblemata* and ornamental compositions, richly exemplified in the houses of Antioch. In the West, large, accurate geometrical divisions predominated in the Germanic area, with panels and polychrome figured medallions; in the Gallic and Iberian regions, there was a broader development of figured compositions. In Rome, fine *emblemata* and small polychrome pictorial landscape panels were supplemented by an interesting development of the black and white technique, not only in a rich range of geometrical patterns in the humbler pavements of rented houses and secondary quarters, but also in the immense mosaic carpet patterns used for larger spaces. In the geometrical repertory the meander pattern found symbolic application in the allusion to the Cretan labyrinth, in the center of which was often represented a Minotaur; this particular type of geometric composition permitted a broad spread of the pattern, while the stylized motif

of a turreted, crenelated wall, taken from Hellenistic tradition, served as a border.

The creation of the new, vast, interior architecture, culminating in the great halls of the baths, demanded a new decorative conception of the mosaic art, with a more functional relationship to the room decorated; this was supplied by simplified, stylized pictorial motifs executed in a linear, black and white treatment. The closed, and well-defined syntax of the polychrome pictorial panel unfolded into open compositions of floral arabesques, with tiny leaf and flower elements, stylized into fine trellises, in which birds, masks, and other small figurative elements were inserted. In the mosaics of the great baths, on the other hand, much use was made of marine figures of tritons and nereids, and a rich repertory of fish derived from Hellenistic tradition but realized with a new, original, linear stylization. There was also a considerable development of vast geometrical divisions in lozenges, polygons, and rectangles, which often recalled the forms used in the coffers of the ceilings. At other times motifs of tiny stylized leaves or geometrical elements based on tapestry composition were used. All these elements could be multiplied freely to cover the vast surface to be decorated.

XV Classicism and Colorism in the Art of the Antonines

The traits that characterized the art and architecture of the period of Hadrian were to develop with harmony and coherency during the long reigns of Antoninus Pius (A.D. 138–161) and Marcus Aurelius (A.D. 161–180).

In the Temple of the Divine Hadrian, erected in the Hadrianic area of the Campus Martius and dedicated in A.D. 145, were reliefs with twenty figures of the Provinces characterized by an ethnic realism, interpreting the political ideals of Hadrian, to which ·Antoninus Pius also adhered. In 139 A.D. Antoninus had a series of coins struck that showed thirteen personifications of Lands and Provinces, perhaps using the same artist who had worked on the analogous series issued by Hadrian.

Historical relief was no longer used in great continuous friezes, but only in isolated panels, following the stylistic tradition of the Trajanic arches; the modeling was more concise, accurate, and academic in the reliefs of the period of Antoninus Pius, softer and more coloristic in the period of Marcus Aurelius. From an arch, perhaps leading to the Hadrianic area of the Campus Martius, are four panels, two of which were reused in the late Arco di Por-

Detail of the horses of the Imperial quadriga from a relief panel showing the Emperor Marcus Aurelius riding in triumph, ed in a very rich and soft plasticism. Circa A.D. 176–177. Rome, Capitoline Museums

324. *Relief panel showing the submission of the barbarians to Marcus Aurelius, with Pompeianus riding next to the Emperor.* Circa A.D. 176–177. Rome, Capitoline Museums

the Emperor's statue at the summit of its grandiose granite shaft, the decoration was limited to the base. Repeated on two sides of the base is a circular parade of horsemen. This parade is set against a classicistic neutral background, but seen in a conventionalized perspective achieved by the device of placing the procession on rocky ledges.

The theme of apotheosis in which the figure is transported through the air has a precedent in the so-called *Grand Camée de France*, in the Bibliothèque Nationale in Paris, which was believed to be Tiberian but is now dated A.D. 136, as its protagonist has been interpreted as a figure of Hadrian, camouflaged by later remodeling.

The exploits of Marcus Aurelius were to be glorified after his death in his great spiral column, but they were also commemorated, perhaps soon after his triumph over the Germans and the Sarmatians in A.D. 176, in three panels now in the Capitoline Museums; these represent the Emperor in a triumphal quadriga (fig. 323), sacrificing, and receiving the submission of barbarians (figs. 324, 325). In the scene of the submission of the barbarians the mounted figure of Marcus Aurelius repeats the type and style of his bronze statue now in the center of the Piazza del Campidoglio.

Portraiture in the Antonine period was throughout imbued with a soft, naturalistic plasticism, which in some ways resembles nineteenth-century work, especially in the calm, serene faces of Antoninus Pius and Faustina

togallo, representing the *adventus*, the *adlocutio*, the surrender of the barbarians to Hadrian, and the apotheosis of the Empress Sabina. The scene of the apotheosis is located in the Campus Martius, personified by a young reclining figure who perhaps formerly held an obelisk that is now abraded; the Empress rises from the funeral pyre and soars toward the heavens, supported by a torch-bearing, winged female genius, in the presence of Hadrian.

This same motif is found in the apotheosis of Antoninus and his wife Faustina on one side of the base of the honorary column, erected in the Campus Martius near the *Ustrina Antoninorum*, which is reproduced on coins. On the base of this column, now in the Vatican, the Imperial couple is being raised to the heavens by a winged male genius flanked by eagles, and below are seated the personification of the Campus Martius with an obelisk, counterbalanced by the solemn seated personification of Rome. The reign of Antoninus Pius was marked by no warlike enterprises, and on this honorary column, which carried

325. *Detail of the head of the soldier, in the left foreground of the relief shown in figure 324.*

326. *Portrait of Faustina the Elder modeled with a very delicate surface effect in a classicizing taste.* Circa A.D. 138–140. *Ostia, Museum*

327. *Funerary relief of a husband and wife in the pose of* dextrarum iunctio, *with putti holding garlands as a symbol of apotheosis.* Circa A.D. 150–160. *Ostia, Museum*

328. *Relief showing an animated scene of a shop with fruit, chickens, and rabbits, and two monkeys on the counter to attract customers. Example of popular art in the Antonine period. Ostia, Museum*

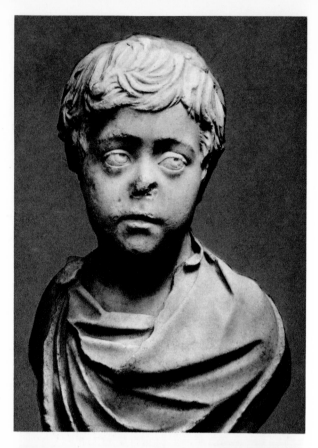

329. *Portrait bust of a boy showing an extremely soft and delicate modeling.* Circa A.D. *160. Ostia, Museum*

330. *Portrait bust of Volcacius, with a strong coloristic contrast between smooth, luminous surfaces and the dark mass of drilled curls.* Circa A.D. *180. Ostia, Museum*

the Elder (fig. 326) who launched the fashion of the coiffure with a braid of hair twisted around on the top of the head, and of Faustina the Younger, with her heavy, undulating bands of hair and fleshy face. More striking tonal contrasts appear in the heads of Marcus Aurelius and Lucius Verus (A.D. 161–169), with deep drillings, particularly in the thick curly hair of Lucius Verus, who shows a romantic, sensual, melancholy face. The spread of the philosopher type of the Hellenistic baroque tradition influenced official portraiture, particularly under Marcus Aurelius. Asiatic artistic influences contributed to modifying the more restrained Attic-influenced Classicism, and accentuated the coloristic effects of late Antonine art. Sarcophagus reliefs also showed greater contrasts of light and shadow.

1. Aspects of Art Under the Antonines in the Eastern and Western Provinces

The sumptuous, fluid, picturesque taste of Asia Minor found characteristic expressions in the decorative work of sculptors of the school of Aphrodisia. Among the artists of this school in the second century we have the signatures in Greek of Flavius Zenon, Flavius Chryseros, Flavius Andronikos, and Lucius Atinas Syneros. Friezes of festoons held up by putti and female figures, pilasters decorated with floral scrolls, and sculptured brackets adorned the architectural monuments of Aphrodisia. The motif of the garland and the festoon became characteristic of a type of Asiatic sarcophagus, found from Perge to Alexandria.

The translation of Roman conceptions into this style of Asia Minor is seen in the historical reliefs that decorate a dismantled monument celebrating the victories of Lucius Verus over the Parthians. The reliefs of this monument, erected at Ephesus, are now in Vienna (figs. 331, 332). In this transference to the East of a Roman type of monument there appears — apart from the urbane iconography of the Imperial family in the scene of the adoption of Lucius Verus, the sacrifice, and the Provinces and personifications — the Hellenistic tradition; this shows through in the scenes of the Emperor's apotheosis on a chariot, flanked by gods who accompany him, and above all in the battle scenes with daring pictorial foreshortening and lively contrasted modeling, and with intensely expressive effects, particularly in the faces of the barbarians.

In the provinces of North Africa and of the East, the Hellenistic heritage remained more live and productive; this is attested, for instance, by the splendid mosaics of Antioch and Apamea, and of various African centers. But in both the East and in North Africa there also existed other aspects due to the presence of native, indigenous expression on the edge of these areas of Classical culture. A characteristic phenomenon is the funerary sculpture of Palmyra, closely linked to the architectonic decoration of chamber tombs, with busts in high relief on the slabs that closed the individual tombs, and with the major groups of the figures of the deceased reclining on the couch of the funeral banquet. Here is an independent renaissance of the Etruscan type of sarcophagus, and perhaps there are Roman influences in the form of the busts. The artists of Palmyra, foreign to the organic Classical approach, express themselves with a stereometric conception in the heads, and no dynamic articulation in the bodies; they used an ornamental linearism to render drapery, whose simple calligraphic formula was enlivened with a decorative display of women's jewelry. There was, moreover, a studied over-all architectonic rhythm in these works, which

331. Detail of a Roman soldier whose face is classicistic, similar to that of Antinous; from a relief of the monument erected at Ephesus to commemorate the victories of Lucius Verus over the Parthians. Circa A.D. 166–170. Vienna, Belvedere

also lies at the basis of the paintings, in other tombs: these paintings usually show a Victory standing on the globe holding medallions or figures of the deceased, in a rigid frontality and hieratic, Oriental conception.

Semitic and Iranian elements, merging with Hellenistic tradition and Roman influences, gave a particular coloring to the art of another important caravan center on the edge of the Classical world, Dura Europos, which flourished during the Empire. The numerous paintings decorating temples, houses, the synagogue, and the Mithraeum provide precious documentation from the first century A.D. to the late Empire. A prevalent Syrian-Oriental vision runs through the solemn figures of Konon and his family set against architectural backgrounds, priests in their tall, conical head-dresses, and sacrificing figures framed between twisted columns, in the paintings from the Temple of Zeus Theos at Dura Europos which

332. Detail of a head of a barbarian in a baroque style which is a distant echo of the Hellenistic style of Pergamon; from a relief of the same monument commemorating the victories of Lucius Verus. Circa A.D. 166–170. Vienna, Belvedere

347

dates from the second half of the first century A.D. These figures are marked by hieratic frontal poses, with exotic notes in their Iranian costumes, and with a taste for draftsmanship and polychromy. But in paintings at Dura Europos from the time of Severus, showing the sacrifice of the tribune Terentius, the influence of Roman historical relief makes itself felt in the parade of soldiers headed by their standard-bearer, although the scene is cast in a a more abstract, Oriental conception; this becomes more evident in other sacrificial scenes, in which figures of different scales of size are conventionally juxtaposed. At the end of the third century A.D. Sasanian influence dominates in the two-color paintings of battle scenes, with groups of horsemen in the motif of the Iranian gallop, and in Mithraic paintings.

In Egypt, Roman influences are noticeable

with vistas on nymphaea, monumental arched gateways, and with tetrapylons at crossroads; this tradition also continued in porticoes, temples, houses, and tombs. Consoles to support statues were incorporated in the columns that lined the streets of Pompeiopolis, Anazarbus, Apamea, and Palmyra. In Syria the rectilinear entablature was broken by curving it into an arc over the central pediment. This type of pediment appeared in the Temple of Hadrian at Ephesus and became very widespread, above all from the time of Septimius Severus on. The most original, imaginatively planned, and decorated works, the most grandiose and splendid, were to be found in the architectural complex of the sanctuary at Baalbek, where deep niches gave movement to the Antonine peristyle and the cella of the mid-second-century Temple of Bacchus. This temple was

333. Relief from a Rhenish funerary monument showing an animated scene of the collection of taxes. From Neumagen. Second half of the second century A.D. Trier, Landesmuseum

in the naturalism, in the coiffures, and in the faces painted on panels, first with encaustic, then in tempera, for mummy masks found mainly in Fayum. In these Fayum portraits one follows the trends in Roman portraiture right up to the late Empire, from a vivid, colorful verism to a stylized abstraction.

The most genuine and original aspects of Roman architecture contrived to impose themselves in the East and West alike, in aqueducts, amphitheaters, baths, triumphal arches, and the development of the *frons scaenae* of theaters.

In the East, however, the Hellenistic architectural tradition was to continue to develop its town-planning with long, colonnaded streets,

enriched with decorative sculptures and had an unusual, hexagonal vestibule, which was to gain a turreted pronaos under Septimius Severus. Niches are also a feature of the bizarre little circular Temple of Venus with its pronaos, set on a podium with a peristyle; both the podium and entablature curve concavely between the columns of the peristyle.

A singular proof of the free evolution and intermingling of Hellenistic and Oriental traditions is furnished by the fantastic, scenographic, and architectonic tomb façades carved in the living rock at Petra, with colonnades, superimposition of storeys, broken pediments, *tholoi*, and curvilinear and rectilinear elements.

334. *Stone mask decorating the central shield of a pediment on the Temple of Sulis-Minerva; it resembles the type of head of Oceanus, but has a knot of serpents. End of the second century* A.D. *Bath, Museum*

In the provinces of the West the poverty of the indigenous culture permitted a more immediate acceptance of the principles and forms of Roman architecture; the only changes were the adaptation of the style to local materials and rare expressions of native tradition. The new Roman technique of brick construction was even adapted to the special form of Gallic circular temples with an external gallery.

During this apogee of the Empire in figurative art there were, in addition to mosaics in villas, town houses, and baths, many examples of plastic art in Germany, Gaul, and Britain. The prevalent influence in funerary steles, portraits, altars, and decorative sculptures was Roman. Steles with legionaries and horsemen from the first century A.D. were replaced in the Gallic region, and particularly along the Rhine, by family groups set in small shrines with decorated borders. The funerary altar gave way to the monument with pilasters, a rich example of which is provided in the tomb of the Secundinii, a family of cloth merchants in Trier, from A.D. 250. The Roman conception of the *imago clipeata* shows through in medallion steles or shield steles with the bust of the deceased; these spread from Noricum to Dacia and Macedonia, where this form persisted until the fourth century. These medallion steles presented certain regional variants: in

Noricum they were protected by a pitched roof and plastically modeled; in Dacia they were roofless and executed in a flatter, more decorative style. Medallions multiplied, occasionally being arranged in several rows on rectangular steles, particularly in the valleys of the Struma and the Vardar. Sometimes local customs gave these funerary steles an exotic aspect; in Pannonian work from the Vindobona region, the sculptured heads were crowned with large, furry, bicorn hats.

A certain unity of artistic culture embraces sculptural work in the Danubian and Illyrian areas, which also included northern Italy: steles, portraits, and funerary architecture show some common stylistic and typological traits.

In some of the least sophisticated work local expressive tendencies predominated, as in reliefs and sculptures representing local gods and barbarian themes. The provincial character of these works always shows in a weakening of the organic and syntactical qualities that constituted the basis of Classicism.

The most felicitous reception of the organic naturalism of Classical tradition by way of its Roman forms is to be seen in a group of Rhenish sculptures from the second century A.D.; these include the well-known boat loaded with wine, and reliefs showing tax collection (fig. 333), school scenes, ladies at their toilette, and bread-vendors. The departure from the formal ideal in costumes and ethnic types adds to the attractiveness of these works, with their illustrative spontaneity, since the basic stylistic principles remain intact.

An instructive example of how Classical iconographic motifs and teachings were interpreted in the least cultured barbarian areas is provided by the pediment of a temple in Roman Britain dedicated to Sulis-Minerva, at Bath. The Classical plan with composite capitals had been adopted, and the intention was to create a pedimental relief decoration with symbolic reference to the temple cult. Minerva is suggested by the shield held by a figure of Victory who rests on a globe, and by the owl below, which crowned a helmet, the helmet perhaps being originally balanced by another helmet of barbarian form. The *gorgoneion* on the shield, however, has been transformed into an eclectic male mask (fig. 334) with mustache and beard, inspired by heads of Oceanus, with the tongue-like hair

and the serpents of a Medusa head; perhaps it was intended to personify the god of the medicinal waters that made the site of Bath an important thermal center. The same conception also inspires two tritons, derived from Hellenistic marine processions, whose twisting, serpentine tails harmoniously fill the corners of the pediment. The type of pedimental decoration using a central shield is Hellenistic-Roman in origin, and this unknown artist succeeded in obtaining a harmonious composition based on bilateral symmetry, translating his models into a linear low relief. Thus in this remote setting, we see a singular convergence of classicizing culture and the Celtic substratum. The influence of naturalism also confers a certain dignity on the head of the young god Antenociticus (fig. 335), found in a small, apsed temple on Hadrian's Wall, at Condercum, the modern Benwell, in which the Celtic roughness of the modeling in the heavy, tumbling locks of hair, and the thick, clearly outlined eyelids, strikes a note analogous to late Etruscan heads, since the common basis of provincial characteristics is always their lack of adherence to the Classical spirit.

335. Stone head of the young god Antenociticus from a temple at Condercum, the modern Benwell. Newcastle upon Tyne, King's College, Museum of Antiquities

XVI

Expressionism in Late Second-Century Art
and the Beginning of Late Antique Conceptions

The historical panels in the Capitoline Museums that relate the triumphs of Marcus Aurelius (figs. 323-325) mark the climax in the development of naturalistic, organic Classicism. In the group of monuments that was perhaps planned by Marcus Aurelius but completed only after his death in A.D. 180 by his son Commodus (A.D. 180–192), is revealed instead a style of a completely different tendency; the Column of Marcus Aurelius, and a series of eight reliefs later reused in the Arch of Constantine, are what remain of these works.

1. The Master of the Exploits of Marcus Aurelius

The Column of Marcus Aurelius (figs. 336–339, 341-343), completed before A.D. 193, intentionally repeats the form of the Column of Trajan; the narrative of Marcus Aurelius' two campaigns against the Germans and Sarmatians (A.D. 172–173 and 174–175) begins, like the Column of Trajan, with a scene on the Danube, perhaps alluding to the events of A.D. 172; and the figural narration of the two campaigns is likewise separated by a figure of Victory. The eight panels reused in the Arch of Constantine (figs. 340, 344, 346), which seem to have come originally from an arch, develop the themes and compositions of the traditional historical relief. Yet, notwithstanding close relationships with past monuments, there are clear differences, all the more evident as their thematic and iconographic resemblances to previous monuments are so striking.

The number of windings of the helic frieze is reduced from the 23 on Trajan's Column to 21 on that of Marcus Aurelius, while the height of the frieze increases from 41 to 49 inches; this allows for greater clarity and legibility of the scenes, the number of which are also correspondingly reduced. The pictorial

low relief of Trajan's Column becomes an incisive high relief in that of Marcus Aurelius; the soft modeling in the former monument

336. The Column of Marcus Aurelius, shown as it appeared at the time of the Renaissance; here, in this fantastic view of Rome by Enea Vico, we see not only the Column but the original base, which was destroyed in the late sixteenth century in the course of Domenico Fontana's renovations.

337. *Three registers of the helic frieze of the Column of Marcus Aurelius, showing scenes from the first campaign against the Germans and Sarmatians. Circa* A.D. *180–190. Rome, Piazza Colonna*

becomes hard and rough; the drill bites into the marble, gouging out beards, hair, and armor, incising the stiff folds of the draperies, the undercutting around the figures, and the sinuous curves of the waves on the rivers.

Composition is more schematized and the variety of motifs gives way to repetition, as in the rhythm of marching scenes; landscape details appear less frequently, and views are more conventional. The characteristic formation of the testudo, represented at an angle on Trajan's Column, is represented frontally on the Column of Marcus Aurelius, and the bare torso of Victory is turned toward the onlooker with the same frontality that prevails also in representations of the Emperor. Trajan appeared at the head of his armies and among his soldiers; Marcus Aurelius is presented on a more detached plane that emphasizes the majesty of the Emperor; he appears in full face, flanked by his faithful, valiant general Pompeianus and another officer, who are shown in three-quarter poses, as side wings to offset the central presence of the Emperor. The soldiers in the scene of the *adlocutio* are no longer grouped to one side, as they were on the Column of Trajan, when the Emperor turned toward them in profile; now they form a semicircle and stand around below the pre-eminent, centrally placed, frontal figure of Marcus Aurelius in the new static conception which presages representations of Christ among the Apostles.

There is no longer any trace of the feeling of humanity and of pity for the barbarians that infuses Trajan's frieze, and the narrative of war becomes cruel and merciless. The bodies of the barbarians are twisted in angular, distorted rhythms. The fluidity of Trajan's relief contrasts with the brusquely broken lines and volumes of this later work. The naturalistic structure is dispersed into the most excessive, forced expressionism, which culminates in the vigorous, hallucinatory heads of captured Sarmatians. The narrative becomes more vivid and dramatic, and assumes miraculous overtones in the bizarre personification of the dripping Jupiter Pluvius in the scene of the rain that overwhelmed the Quadians (fig. 343), and the ruination of the enemy's equipment, struck by lightning, in the scene referring to events of A.D. 172.

This style, which subordinates organic composition to expressionism, unites the Column of Marcus Aurelius with the eight panels reused in the Arch of Constantine, even if the difference of dimensions and purpose imposed on these panels a more restrained modeling.

338. Roman soldiers composed in the clear, symmetrical rhythm of the march; second campaign against the Germans and Sarmatians. Detail from the Column of Marcus Aurelius

339. Barbarian woman trying to escape with her child during the annihilation of a village; first campaign against the Germans and Sarmatians. Detail from the Column of Marcus Aurelius

353

340. At right: *Detail of Roman soldiers listening to an address by Marcus Aurelius, from a relief reused on the Arch of Constantine. Circa A.D. 180–190. Rome, Arch of Constantine*

341. Below, at left: *Barbarian women clutching their children as the Roman soldiers take them prisoners; from the second campaign against the Germans and Sarmatians. Detail from the Column of Marcus Aurelius*

342. Below, at right: *Head of a barbarian horseman, rendered with a rapid and vibrant modeling; he turns to look at his pursuers, during the second campaign against the Germans and Sarmatians. Detail from the Column of Marcus Aurelius*

By comparison with the earlier panels of Marcus Aurelius in the Capitoline Museums, the scene of sacrifice is more tightly packed and agitated in the later works; the *Liberalitas* scene is conceived frontally; while the portrait of Pompeianus has the vigor of the small, rapid images on the Column of Marcus Aurelius.

Certain large sarcophagi of Roman officers, with thickly packed scenes of battles against barbarians, seem to have been produced by the same workshop as the reliefs of Marcus Aurelius from the Arch of Constantine, and speak the same expressive language. The style of the Column also succeeds in transforming Greek iconographical motifs by giving them the syntactical and formal stamp of Roman

354

art: for example, the myth of Meleager on the sarcophagus of Perugia is definitely the work of a sculptor from the Column workshop. This art of the early years of Commodus' reign does not adopt a polemical attitude toward the past; in fact its aim is to adhere as closely as possible to the example of its predecessors. The different results when treating the similar themes is, therefore, not due to an intentional reaction against the Classicism of the Antonines, but rather to the nature of the expressive means employed. The theory that considers this stylistic trend as a reflection of the personality of Marcus Aurelius, and associates the frieze with passages from his *Meditations* is anachronistic; for Marcus Aurelius, conservative and aristocratic, a deeply humane man inspired by Stoic principles, would if anything have followed the Classicism of his times, whereas this style matured after his death, in the first years of the reign of Commodus. Nor can

exercised a normative influence in urban circles.

The workshops which realized the official monuments from the times of Trajan and Marcus Aurelius had been organized under the guidance of and the experience of artists trained in Greek culture. Gradually a certain Roman artistic personality had built up and now, with the decline in the number of Greek immigrant artists, more purely Roman masters were entrusted with the group of monuments ordered by Commodus in honor of the Divine Marcus. We thus see the affirmation in full liberty of the tendency toward unorganic expressivity, which was an innate Latin trait, as previously it had been in Italic and Etruscan art. Until this time, it had been tempered and ennobled in the official sphere by the more elevated classicizing naturalism.

In these official monuments Commodus appeared only in the scene of the submission of the barbarian chiefs on the base of the Column

343. *Personification of the rain god Jupiter Pluvius who miraculously and beneficently showers the Romans and furiously sweeps the Quadians and their horses into a whirling stream, during the first campaign against the Germans and Sarmatians. Detail from the Column of Marcus Aurelius*

this change be attributed to an influence of provincial "military" art, for the considerably rougher, less cultivated artistic environments of the provinces at this time could never have

of Marcus Aurelius, which was destroyed by Domenico Fontana's restoration (fig. 336). His portraits, however, follow the highly contrasted and intensely coloristic style of

355

344. *Detail of a barbarian boy who clings to his father, in the scene of submission to Marcus Aurelius; from a relief reused on the Arch of Constantine.*
Circa A.D. 180–190. Rome, Arch of Constantine

345. *Bust of Commodus as Hercules, wearing the lion skin and carrying a club, with the golden apples of the Hesperides in his left hand. From the Villa Palombara on the Esquiline.*
Rome, Capitoline Museums

346. *Detail of a relief reused on the Arch of Constantine, representing the investiture of a bearded king by Marcus Aurelius. The rich use of the drill in the hair and beards produces strong chiaroscuro effects.*
Circa A.D. 180–190. Rome, Arch of Constantine

historical relief, and although his portrait busts are of necessity more accurately modeled, they reveal their relationship with the relief style in the effective over-all contrast between the luminous polished surfaces of the skin and the curly hair, densely worked with the drill. The similarities of style can be seen here in the juxtaposition of a bust of Commodus with a detail from one of the reliefs of Marcus Aurelius from the Arch of Constantine (figs. 345, 346). This bust of Commodus as Hercules, is a famous example of the baroque style of portraiture of the end of the second century.

The decline of the Hadrianic-Antonine style and its replacement by the coloristic and exuberant style of Commodus and Septimius Severus can easily be traced in the series of sarcophagi decorated with motifs from the traditional Hellenistic cycle of Dionysus, that were found in the tombs of the Calpurni Pisoni family near Porta Pia in Rome. In these works, the greater part of which are now in the Walters Gallery, Baltimore, we can see a progressively deepened undercutting of the figures and a concentration on polish and coloristic effects. This lively plastic sense also characterizes the Asiatic type of sarcophagus, which was decorated with statuary figures in shadowy shrines, framed by twisted columns and gables, triangular or arched, with moldings deeply pierced and carved out. A splendid specimen of this type, datable around A.D. 169, is the sarcophagus at Melfi with the portrait of the dead woman on the lid, and of gods in the niches.

XVII

Severan Artistic Splendor
and the Art of the Late Empire

The new artistic principles that had been affirmed at the end of the second century mark the beginning of Late Antique conceptions which were to develop during the third century, and which represent a departure from the Classical ideal that had remained profoundly effective up to this time.

Septimius Severus (A.D. 193–211) initiated a series of emperors of provincial origins; and the army, constituted largely of provincial elements, came to play an increasingly important part in deciding the fate of the Empire. Centurions' sons became members of the Senate, the Second Parthian Legion was installed by Septimius Severus on Mount Albano, and the cults of Mithras, Sabatius, and Jupiter Dolichenus, which were practiced among the military, became more widespread. Septimius Severus, however, tried to associate himself with the old dynasty of the Antonines and keep their ideals alive. In his first portraits he followed the fashion and tone of Marcus Aurelius, and also had himself portrayed, in a bronze statue from Cyprus, in heroic nudity with a Lysippan athletic body. In his more mature portraits, however, when he wished to assume, following the traditional idealization of Imperial majesty, an appearance inspired by divine types, he did not choose Apollo or Jupiter or Hercules; he was an African who was married to the Syrian Julia Domna and closer by far to the Eastern spirit, and he chose to be assimilated to Serapis, from whose representations he adopted the hair style, with locks falling over the brow.

Leptis Magna, where Septimius Severus was born, and many other African centers, were now bustling with an intense activity in monuments, promoted by Imperial propaganda;

347. Portrait of Septimius Severus, detail from a panel showing the Emperor and his two sons before statues of divinities, from the Arch of Septimius Severus at Leptis Magna. Circa A.D. 203

while the lively spiritual ferment, which was to make Africa the stronghold of Christianity,

357

348. Upper: *Panel with the sacrifice of a bull in the presence of Septimius Severus and Julia Domna, from the Arch of Septimius Severus at Leptis Magna. Circa* A.D. *203. Tripoli, Museo del Castello*

349. Lower: *Detail of a panel on the Arch of Septimius Severus in the Roman Forum, with the scene of the* adlocutio *above, and below, the representation of a siege with battering rams. Circa* A.D. *203*

the tenth anniversary of the Emperor's reign and to commemorate his victories in Arabia. At this same time a four-faced arch honoring Septimius Severus was built at the intersection of the *cardo* and *decumanus* in Leptis Magna. The reliefs of the Roman arch (figs. 349, 351) show the decadence of the urban style into rough, unorganic forms, their hard, strong modeling emphasized by the drill. The reliefs of the Arch of Leptis Magna (figs. 347, 348, 350) contain survivals of the classicizing vision in the shaded modeling of the faces, the sharp clarity of the nudes, and the linear play of

350. Detail of a group of toga-clad men in a panel showing the Emperor and his two sons before statues of divinities, from the Arch of Septimius Severus at Leptis Magna. Circa A.D. 203

351. Detail of a group of Roman officers standing behind the Emperor in the scene of the adlocutio, *on the Arch of Septimius Severus in the Roman Forum. Circa A.D. 203*

generated the personality of Tertullian of Carthage, the city which, in A.D. 200, was also to see the birth of Cyprian.

The Arch of Septimius Severus of A.D. 203, in the Roman Forum, was erected to mark

drapery folds that shows a design of shadows in a fine, calligraphic taste, produced by the adept use of the drill.

Both monuments represent an architectural enrichment of this type of honorary triumphal

359

352. *Portrait statue of Julia Domna, whose body is copied from a Greek statue type of Demeter of the fourth century B.C., while the head is a realistic portrait of the Empress wearing a wig. Circa A.D. 218. Ostia, Museum*

arch. In the Roman Arch of Septimius Severus, pierced by three archways, the artist used a composition that resembles a continuous frieze cut into four parts and placed one above the other in order to create large, unified narrative scenes, under the influence of the elaborate figured chronicle of the helic column. The figures are placed on rocky ledges (fig. 349), and an attempt is made to group them harmoniously and link them together with fragmented overlapping planes, transitional passages, and centrally placed cityscapes, and with a rough, pitted background that is an abstract, coloristic solution of the pictorial landscape background. We know that Septimius Severus had had triumphal paintings exhibited to the public, but these panels from the Arch of Septimius Severus are inspired by relief and not painting.

In the Arch of Leptis Magna, which follows the Oriental form of the tetrapylon, the classicizing tradition preserves the smooth, neutral background in the battle and cult scenes on the inner archways, and in the four long panels on the attic containing scenes exalting the *Concordia Augustorum*, one façade showing the *adventus* of Septimius Severus, one the sacrifice in honor of Julia Domna, one the investiture of Geta, and the fourth the triumph of Caracalla. Frontality predominates in all these ceremonial scenes, and in the *adventus*, after the two ranks of horsemen shown in profile, the Imperial quadriga is placed in a forced frontal perspective. The confused, agitated Roman narrative contrasts with the clear, hieratic African work in which Septimius Severus, seated like the Jupiter in the Capitoline triad, but dressed as Serapis, appears between Minerva and Julia Domna, who is in the guise of Juno.

Severan taste was sumptuous and theatrical: architecture became intensely coloristic, with grandiose buildings animated by niches, apses, and vistas of columns; sculpture showed a profusion of floral and figured decoration, all drilled with strong hollows that make the modeling of the figures stand out against

353. *Portrait of Caracalla; a copy — which has been said to be a Renaissance copy — of an official type known in nine replicas, and datable circa A.D. 211–215. From the Farnese Collection. Naples, National Museum*

their shadowy background; and painting was characterized by vivid colors and broad black strokes outlining the figures, in the same way that relief figures were surrounded by deep, drilled furrows.

The daring multi-storeyed mass of the imposing, columned façade of the *Septizodium* at the eastern corner of the Palatine, offered a sumptuous sight for those coming up the broad, colonnaded street that was the continuation of the Via Appia. In Leptis Magna,

the gigantic architectural complex of the Severan Forum was decorated with rich ornament from the skilled hands of sculptors from the school of Aphrodisia, culminating in the magnificent floral and figured pilasters of the Basilica. In Rome, the Arch of the Money Changers, a singular honorary monument with an architraved doorway carrying Imperial statues, dedicated by the *argentarii* or money changers in A.D. 204 in the Forum Boarium in honor of Septimius Severus and Julia

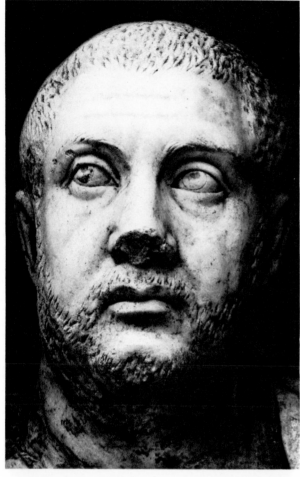

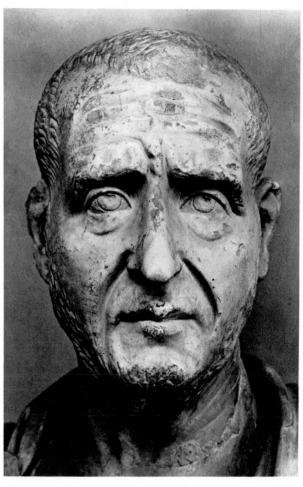

354. Above, at left: *Portrait on the lid of the sarcophagus said to be that of Balbinus.* Circa A.D. *238.* *Rome, Museum of the Catacombs of Pretextatus*

355. Above, at right: *Portrait of Decius, rendered with a dry and incisive realism.* Circa A.D. *250. Rome, Capitoline Museums*

356. At left: *Portrait of Alexander Severus, modeled with rich chiaroscuro effects yet still maintaining firmness in the forms.* Circa A.D. *230–235. Rome, Torlonia Museum*

Domna, was covered with figured reliefs, pilasters with floral decoration, and deeply carved moldings, with vivid plastic effects.

Thermal architecture reached its most monumental form under Caracalla (A.D. 211-

361

217) in the famous Baths of Caracalla in Rome, with gigantic masses of brickwork, immense cross-vaults, and luxurious decoration in marble and mosaic.

In keeping with the ostentatious taste of this period were the new feminine coiffures worn by Julia Domna (fig. 352) and other third-century empresses; Julia Domna wore heavy, thick rows of curls around her head which were cleverly contrived wigs, often gilded. Caracalla banished the long beard and dreamed of becoming another Alexander the Great, posing with his head turned in a heroic manner; but in official portraits the inner Classical dynamism was transformed into a violent passion, so that it became the grim, frowning mask of the tyrant (fig. 353).

In A.D. 212 Caracalla, with the Antonine constitution, bestowed Roman citizenship on all free subjects of the great Empire, and the new political position thus assumed by the provinces went hand in hand with the multiplication of provincial artistic movements and their mutual interaction.

Official portraits of emperors constitute the

357. Detail of a barbarian couple beside a trophy, at the corner of a sarcophagus with a battle between Romans and barbarians. From Portonaccio. Circa A.D. 190. Rome, Museo delle Terme

358. Portrait of a boy with a compact cap of hair, worked with light, coloristic incisions. Circa A.D. 250. Rome, Museo delle Terme

most significant aspects of third-century art, and allow us to follow its stylistic development. The lively plasticity of the images of Caracalla was progressively attenuated in forms that were always more compact, closed, and tense in the portraits of Heliogabalus (A.D. 218–222) and then of Alexander Severus (A.D.

222–235), with less relief given to the hair and short beard (fig. 356). This style ended by losing all plastic naturalism in the images of succeeding soldier emperors. The sharply outlined solid caps of hair were marked only by short cuts and scratches of the chisel, which also etched in the beard on the planes of the face. The faces of Imperial portraits developed a nervous, gloomy contraction, with knitted brows, deep wrinkles, and pupils hollowed out with the drill, from the massive Maximinus Thrax (A.D. 235-238), to Pupienus (A.D. 238), to the full, fleshy Balbinus (A.D. 238) (fig. 354) and the more compact heads of Gordian III (A.D. 238–244), to the even more frowning, rough figures of Philippus the Arab (A.D. 244–249), Decius (A.D. 251) (fig. 355), and Trebonianus Gallus (A.D. 251–253). These crudely realistic faces modeled in an anti-Classical manner, when placed on bodies of Jupiter, Mars, Hercules, Sylvanus, and athletes — while female heads with complicated coif-

curred in the earlier classicizing iconic statues.

Apart from portraiture, the numerous series of sarcophagi reflect the artistic currents of the times. Besides those decorated with reliefs of Classical-influenced mythological works imported from Attica or made in Rome, outstanding among which were the scenes of the Amazonomachy, sea·battles, the Achilles myth, and the Dionysiac and marine cycles, we find increasing numbers of typically Roman creations. Sarcophagi tended to gain in height and, instead of the frieze decoration used under the Antonines, to develop broader, more complex compositions. Historical relief and painting influenced the new style of sarcophagus reliefs. Echoes of third-century painting can be discerned in a group of miniatures with thickly packed, agitated masses of troops, in

359. Battle scene from the Ambrosian Iliad, *inspired by traditional Hellenistic compositions through the intermediary of Roman re-elaborations of the third century A.D. End of the fifth or beginning of the sixth century A.D. Milan, Ambrosian Library*

360. Sarcophagus with a battle between Romans and barbarians; the commander on horseback has been identified as Ostilianus, the second son of Decius, who died in A.D. 251. Rome, Museo delle Terme, Ludovisi Collection

fures rose above the bodies of Venus, Ceres, Omphale, Hygieia, and figures of Muses — rendered only more strident the stylistic break with the Classical ideals, which had not oc-

the codex of the *Ambrosian Iliad* (fig. 359). Similarly, on sarcophagi, battle scenes framed by trophies and the pathetic figures of prisoners (fig. 357) became an intricate, tight

361–362. Details from a sarcophagus decorated with a lion hunt.
Circa A.D. 250. Rome, Palazzo Giustiniani

mass of figures with pronounced deformations and audacious foreshortenings (fig. 360).

There was a preference for the type of sarcophagus with a central medallion holding the portrait of the deceased or of the deceased married couple. These portrait medallions were held by centaurs, tritons, Victories, or putti as an expression of apotheosis, and the rest of the decorated surface was covered with the strigel motif or festoons. Further representations on sarcophagi included realistic circus races with circus monuments, alluding to the contest of life. Military *virtus* was now transformed into the courage of wild animal hunts. The classicizing motif of Alexander at the hunt, revived by Hadrian, became colored with Roman accents: the lion was joined by boars and deer in a more complex, closely woven scene conceived in new, allegorical terms. The poet Oppian dedicated his *Cinegetica* to Caracalla, who delighted in boar hunts, and the hunting theme flourished on a numerous series of sarcophagi with agitated figures and a dense play of the drill (figs. 361, 362). The motif of the lion attacking his prey was taken to decorate the sides of elliptical sarcophagi, or reduced to a single protome, with a progressively vigorous, ornamental stylization of the mask and mane in deeply chiseled grooves, in examples dating from A.D. 240 to 270 (fig. 371).

1. The Grandiose Artistic Conceptions of Alexander Severus

The reign of Alexander Severus (A.D. 222–235) saw the introduction on sarcophagi of a decorative syntax with large, plastic figures which developed until the time of Gallienus (A.D. 253–260), representing hunting scenes, the myths of Penthesilea, Endymion, Mars, and Rhea Sylvia; or with images of the deceased persons, as in the sarcophagus said to be that of Balbinus in the Museum of the Catacombs of Pretextatus (fig. 354). Allegorical historical scenes were also used, as in the monumental sarcophagus from Acilia in the Museo delle Terme in Rome (figs. 364, 365), on which is depicted the presentation of Gordian III (A.D. 238–244); the young Emperor is seen in a

363. Monumental figured capital from the Baths of Alexander Severus, constructed A.D. 227. Vatican, Cortile della Pigna

364

of this period. Also from the period of Alexander Severus must be the polychrome mosaic with thick-set, massive, grandiose, realistic figures of athletes and gymnasts, from the baths, now in the Lateran Museum. These scenes represent one of the new themes which, along with gladiatorial scenes, were introduced into the history of the mosaic art and were also developed in reliefs. Alexander Severus, a Syrian but educated in Greek culture, was very fond of the palaestra (*palaestes primus fuit*) and a typical expression of his athletic and monumental ideals is the original creation of the type of colossal capital from the Baths of Alexander Severus, which he constructed in the Campus Martius in A.D. 227. One of these capitals, now in the Cortile della Pigna of the Vatican (fig. 363) is decorated with a muscular, baroquely expansive statuary

364–365. Details of the sarcophagus from Acilia, showing the Genius of the Senate, with a thick full head of hair and beard, pointing with outstretched hand to the young Gordian III. Circa A.D. 238. Rome, Museo delle Terme

portrait of lively realism that contrasts with the classicizing polished heads, with hair and beards worked with the drill, of the spiritualized, allegorical figure of the Genius of the Senate, and philosopher types, in the tradition of Asia Minor.

The grandiose conception of these sarcophagi corresponds to an attitude peculiar to Alexander Severus who, according to the *Historia Augusta*, had numerous colossal statues erected in Rome, summoning artists from many centers to execute them. Since we know that he completed and decorated the Baths of Caracalla, it is probable that sculptural groups such as the Farnese Bull and the colossal Heracles by Glykon from the Baths are

figure of a victorious pugilist, flanked by referees and tibia players.

In painting, too, as in mosaic, large isolated figures made their appearance during this period, for example, the ceremonial figures of tunic-clad slaves painted in a house on the Via dei Cerchi in the period between Alexander Severus and the Gordians. The slaves are shown preparing to serve a meal under the guidance of their banquet master; they emerge in plastic isolation against an architectural background which still retains a certain element of perspective. Other examples are the solemn figures, perhaps of Apostles, in the hypogeum of the Aurelii family, inspired by the type of the Greek philosopher (fig. 367).

366. Wall painting of Mary with the Infant Christ, in the Catacombs of Priscilla, Rome. Third century A.D.

367. Wall painting of a figure, possibly an Apostle, in the hypogeum of the Aurelii, Rome. Circa A.D. 235

2. Iconographic and Stylistic Aspects of Christian and Mithraic Art

With the progressive affirmation of the new faith, the images of Christ multiplied. Christ was shown as Master in painting, and later, on sarcophagi, in a type inspired by the motif of the bearded philospher, while He appeared as the idealized, youthful, Apollonian type in New Testament cycles, beginning with the resurrection of Lazarus and the meeting with the Samaritan woman. The Greek tradition of Orpheus inspired the iconography of the Christ-Orpheus, who had changed stones and

368. Painting on the vault of a cubicle in the Catacombs of Domitilla, Rome, consisting of linear partitions, small birds and trees, fine tendrils and garlands; in the central tondo is the figure of the Good Shepherd. Third century A.D.

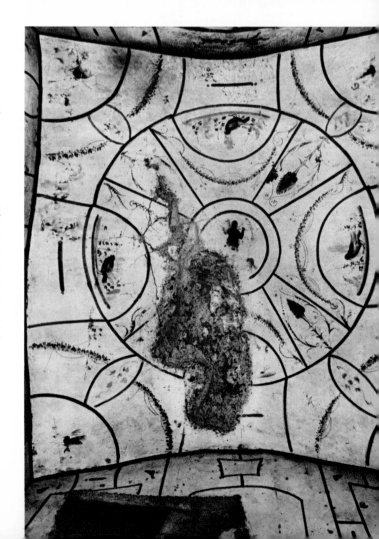

366

animals into men, and presenting Him, in the most ancient paintings, surrounded by sheep. The Classical type of the *kriophoros* is revived in painting and sculpture with Christ as the youthful Good Shepherd carrying the lamb on his shoulders. The figure of Mary also appeared in third-century catacomb painting in the mother and child group, with the Child Jesus in her lap (fig. 366); and in the scene of the adoration of the Magi, who advance toward the enthroned Virgin with hands outstretched, in a composition derived from the theme of conquered barbarians paying homage to an emperor; and finally in Nativity scenes, which began to appear on Christian sarcophagi shortly before the middle of the fourth century.

Christianity created a vast iconographical repertory in the popular narrative tradition. Using a style of thick strokes and strong shading, artists illustrated in catacomb painting — and after the mid-third century also on sarcophagi — scenes from the Old and New Testaments, beginning with Daniel in the lion's den and Jonah and the whale. Widespread use was also made of the type of sarcophagus decorated with the seasons or with putti. Among the most significant manifestations of the popular tendency are the animated scenes in the hypogeum of the Aurelii, with realistic backgrounds of cities and countryside treated in a conventionalized perspective.

Decorative wall painting documented by the catacombs (fig. 368), by the houses of Ostia, and by a few examples in Rome, show a progressive linear stylization of architectural and perspective ornament, turned into fine, schematic forms, and simple framings.

By comparison with the new expressions dictated by Christianity there is little artistic interest in the work connected with the other mystical religion, the cult of Mithras, which was until the fourth century Christianity's most persistent, serious rival. During the third century the cult of Mithras, in addition to paintings in vivid colors and symbolical mosaics, produced numerous reliefs and sculptures of Mithras and the bull, as well as small scenes narrating this Oriental god's birth from the rock, the miracles of water bursting from the cliff-face, the capture and immolation of the bull, the meeting with the sun, the mystical banquet, and Cautes and Cautopates as *dadophoroi* spirits. The style of these works remained on a provincial, craft level, not only in those produced in the various provincial areas of the Empire, but also in Mithraic works from Rome, rather similar to the reliefs of the Thracian Rider god from the Balkan and Nordic regions.

369. Portrait of a bearded man of the period of Gallienus. Circa A.D. 250. Rome, Torlonia Museum

3. Spiritualized Classicism Under Gallienus

After the rough, vigorous expressive trend which Roman art had developed in the period from Maximinus Thrax (A.D. 235–238) to Trebonianus Gallus (A.D. 251–253), the Classical leaning which reappeared with a polished plasticity after the mid-third century can only be referred to the new ideals cherished by the Emperor Gallienus (A.D. 253–268). He was sufficiently attached to things Greek to have himself named magistrate of Athens, and mystical enough to have himself initiated into the Eleusinian mysteries. This quasi-divine monarch sprinkled his hair with gold dust and wore a crown of sun rays. A cultivated and philosophically inclined man, he was the friend of Plotinus. The short-haired, youthful type of his official portraits are related to earlier conceptions; but the image of Gallienus which appears after A.D. 260 reveals Classical aspirations in its full volume, in the movement of the hair, in the clear surfaces of nude flesh, the coloristic chiseling of the short beard, and in the pathos of the raised head turned to one side, while the upturned, inspired gaze conveys the new spiritual conception of the *religiosissimus Augustus.*

Some portraits of the intellectual Empress Salonina, wife of Gallienus, are imprinted with idealism by comparison with other, more realistic works. The philosophical ideals of the time are reflected in sarcophagi, where the deceased was wont to appear as a philosopher among the Muses and personifications, and his wife often took the part of the ninth Muse. To be dated in the Gallienic period are the elaborate Torlonia sarcophagus (fig. 370) and

370. Detail of a sarcophagus decorated with philosophers and Muses, with masks in the background. Circa A.D. 250–260. *Rome, Torlonia Museum*

371. Elliptical sarcophagus with lions attacking their prey at the ends, and pastoral scenes in a style of relief that gives the effect of openwork. Circa A.D. 270. *Rome, Museo delle Terme*

the so-called sarcophagus of Plotinus in the Lateran Museum, as well as the sarcophagus in the Museo delle Terme at Rome, characterized by its personifications of Annona (or Agricultural Produce), of the Port of Rome, of Abundance, and of Africa, belonging to some high official in the Roman foods office, shown in the *dextrarum iunctio* with his wife.

In Greece, Asia Minor, and Rome itself, portraiture developed the type of the neo-Platonic *homo spiritualis*, with an elongated face, polished, shaded planes, and an inspired gaze. Three portraits of a type of philosopher found in a meeting hall in Ostia have been though to be images of Plotinus.

The link between this spiritualized classicizing trend and the particular Gallienic climate is demonstrated by the short duration of its vitality in the following decades; it can still be traced in the soft, pompous plasticity of the portraits of Postumus (A.D. 260–268) and the classicizing tone of the head of Tetricus (A.D. 270–273). But the portraits of Claudius Gothicus (A.D. 268–270) show a return to the vigorous pre-Gallienic expressionism, with stronger, firmer tones.

Plastic concentration became schematized by a rude incisive touch, which reached expressive force in the images of Aurelianus (A.D. 270–275) on the coinage.

4. Stereometric Vision in the Plastic Arts Under the Tetrarchs

The last developments of this trend were reached by the stereometric vision that dominated the plastic arts under the Tetrarchs. Heads took on compact, geometric solidity; the solid caps of hair were sharply delimited, beards were pitted and incised in a hard and abstract calligraphic manner, and drapery folds were sculpted with stiff symmetry. All portraiture on the coins and in sculpture under the tetrarchy of Diocletian (A.D. 284–305), Maximian (A.D. 286–305), Constantius Chlorus (A.D. 292–306), and Galerius (A.D. 293–311), was marked by this conception. This compact, schematized style was realized in marble and bronze, and also proved well adapted to the hardness of the porphyry, provided by the Imperial quarries in Egypt. Porphyry, the color of which recalled Imperial purple, became increasingly popular for expressing the majesty of the emperor in portraits, such as that called either Maximian or Galerius in the Cairo Museum, and it was used for statues, sarcophagi, and in architecture.

Two monumental porphyry sarcophagi, now in the Vatican and conventionally known as the sarcophagi of Saint Helena and Saint Constantia, were decorated by Egyptian sculptors of the Alexandrian circle who translated, using high relief against a smooth Classical background, the motifs of Roman historical relief into the compact, tectonic vision that was typical of the times and was also close to the Egyptian stylistic tradition. From mosaics and reliefs they took the motifs of putti gathering grapes, along with garlands seen on sarcophagi from Asia Minor and Alexandria, expressing these elements in a clear-cut, volumetric, decorative style.

A characteristic expression of this art of the Tetrarchs is seen in the two porphyry groups, one in Venice and the other in the Vatican, each representing both the two Augusti and the two Caesars immortalized in the symmetrical embrace that symbolized the *Concordia Augustorum* in the difficult political climate of a government divided into four parts (fig. 372). The special techniques required to work porphyry, as well as certain barbarianized features and the Eastern background of the sculptors, make it difficult to place these works in a chronological framework.

In this same fashion the two Augusti and the two Caesars were all present and honored as a symbol of the unity of the Empire in the celebration of the exploits of Galerius on the four-faced arch erected at Salonica. Galerius had a palace in Salonica and wanted to erect a monument there to record his Armenian campaign in which, after suffering defeat at Carrae, he had managed in A.D. 298 to conquer Narsetes. He chose the tetrapylon form, traditional in the Oriental cities of Asia Minor and Africa, which he set into the city's monumental center at the crossroads of the important artery of the Via Egnatia and the street that led to the great round brick Imperial mausoleum, which was later to be transformed into the church of Saint George. The piers of such arches usually bore architectural decoration with vertical elements such as trophies, or with medallions, or with niches as in the Arch of Janus Quadrifrons erected a little later in the Velabrum in Rome; but in this Arch of Galerius at Salonica the piers were covered with historical reliefs (figs. 373, 374), no longer limited to framed panels, but forming deep friezes one above the other, running round all four faces of each pier, so that they could be admired by any passer-by who went through the monument. It is as if the frieze of the illustrated helic column had been cut up and recomposed in tiers on these piers. We must not dismiss the possibility that this tetrapylon, which seems to translate the Tetrarchic concept into a decorative architectural form, may have been intended precisely as a counterpart of the Column of Trajan, with its exaltation of the Trajanic victories over the Dacians; for Galerius, who was born near Serdica, was himself a Dacian who had risen to Imperial majesty, and was accused of nationalism. Indeed, this Arch of Galerius also commemorated a Roman army in which it appears that Dacians, recruited by Galerius after the first defeat, formed the most loyal and courageous contingent.

Galerius' short expedition into Armenia did not provide the artist with many subjects; on the other hand, the subdivision into registers and faces justified the lack of a continuous narrative and the alternation of genre and symbolic scenes from Imperial propaganda. These scenes were certainly all conceived by a single master and then executed by various workers. The historical relief shows the syntactical and stylistic revolution wrought by the new ideals of the late Empire: the concept of the *majestas Augusti* is expressed in the dimensions of the figure of the Emperor, which is much larger than the soldiers or citizens; he is placed in full face in the *adlocutio*; enthroned on a raised *cathedra* on the chariot in the *adventus* (fig. 373); indeed, even landscape motifs, views of cities, and encampments are proportionally reduced, not for reasons of perspective, but to accentuate the greatness of the emperor.

373. Above: *Detail of the Arch of Galerius at Salonica showing two friezes. Above, the* adventus *of the Emperor; below, a scene of battle between Romans and barbarians.* Circa A.D. *305–310*

374. At right: *Detail of the head of a Persian on the Arch of Galerius at Salonica.*

The traditional iconographic motif of the emperor on horseback charging into a group of barbarians is transformed into a composition with the Romans standing above and the enemy fallen beneath them (fig. 373), in a hierarchic conception characteristic of the late Empire. Ceremonial scenes were spread out in a frontal

At left: *Detail of the porphyry figures* o *Augusti in symmetrical embrace. Period* Tetrarchy. *Venice, Piazzetta di San Marco*

composition, which isolates the Tetrarchs in abstract majesty in the scene of *Pietas Augustorum*, with the kneeling personifications of Armenia and Mesopotamia on either side, flanked in their turn by Oceanus and Tellus. There is similar frontality in the scene of a sacrifice to Hercules and Jupiter, with gods and personifications against a discreet background of arcaded porticoes. The lower register of the piers carries the recurrent motif of Victories isolated in niches, similar to the figures in niches on Oriental sarcophagi of the Sidamara type and other pagan and Christian sarcophagi of the time. Touches of realism in armor, standards, Persian costumes, elephants, the dromedary with captive women, panthers, and other wild animals sent as a tribute by the Persians to the Emperor characterize some scenes, but the tone of the reliefs is no longer that of an animated, continuous historical narrative; the chronicle of war is transformed into a symbolical allegory of the solemn, ecumenical conception of the Empire. The unorganic modeling, though vigorous and contrasted, aims at an over-all effect. A Tetrarchic painting preserved in the *sacellum* of a Roman camp at Luxor shows the two Augusti and the two Caesars dominating the scene, isolated in a central niche toward which files of dignitaries and soldiers with horses converge from either side. This pictorial composition is less tense and rigid than that of the reliefs, but it is arranged in the same hierarchic fashion.

Although in the East the concept of Tetrarchic rule was commemorated in the Arch of Galerius at Salonica; in Rome commemoration followed the Republican tradition of the honorary column carrying an iconic statue. On the occasion of the tenth anniversary of the reign of Diocletian, four such columns were erected behind the Rostra in the Roman Forum, with statues of Diocletian and Galerius on one side and Maximian and Constantius on the other; a column carrying the image of Jupiter, the protector of the dynasty, was placed in the center, as can be seen in the schematic reproduction of the Forum in the frieze of the Arch of Constantine. The surviving plinth of the column of Constantius has a rough plastic modeling on the secondary side showing the *suovetaurilia*; this contrasts with the graphic style of the other sides in which outlines and drapery are defined with the drill — not to save labor, but to satisfy the taste for sharp shadows that draw rather than model the structure. From now on structure loses the organic unity of the Classical tradition, becoming always more decomposed in the Late Antique conception.

5. Magnificence and Monumentality in Tetrarchic Architecture

Late Imperial architecture, however, retained a solid, organic monumentality. At the end of the third century, its most significant expressions were: the enormous ring of over six miles of turreted brick walls, with massive gates, which enclosed Rome, a work of Aurelian (A.D. 270–275); the solemn, single hall of the Curia of the Senate, rebuilt by Diocletian, with the development in height characteristic of the late Empire, and with a polychromed floor in *opus sectile* which bears witness to a renewed taste for color; the colossal baths dedicated by Diocletian in Rome in A.D. 305–306, which represent the culminating point in the development of Roman thermal installations, with the spacious, dignified, cross-vaulted halls that survive to this day in the structure of the church of Santa Maria degli Angeli; and the imposing palace that Diocletian, a Dalmatian, built beside the sea at Spalato, where he retired and died in 316.

Nero had flaunted the gilded splendor of an Oriental potentate's palace in his *Domus Aurea*; in his Villa at Tivoli, Hadrian attempted to revive Classical ideals; Septimius Severus gave concrete form to the theatrical baroque of his time in the *Septizodium*. Diocletian — the practical man who reorganized the army, divided the Empire's provinces into dioceses, and introduced the Tetrarchic organization of the Empire — conceived of his palace at Spalato as a military camp, a quadrangular *castrum* within a ring of compact, turreted walls like a massive fort with three gates; only on the side facing the sea was the structure lightened and opened by a loggia 500 feet long. Within the palace walls two colonnaded streets intersected one another at right angles to divide the complex into four geometrically symmetrical parts; these were occupied by a large peristyle, the block of apartments, the temple, and the octagonal mausoleum.

The more isolated villas of the late Imperial governors and *potentiores* in the provinces of Africa, Syria, and Gaul became turreted fortresses with towers flanking façades which bore loggias. There was a different plan for country houses: in a villa at Desenzano on the banks of Lake Garda, for example, an octagonal room of Roman type on one side of the central peristyle corresponded to a triconch room of Eastern type on the other. In the safe and pleasant countryside of Sicily the sumptuous villa at Piazza Armerina has been variously attributed to Maximian, as a retreat after his abdication in A.D. 305, or to patricians who

375. Detail of the mosaic of the Great Hunt in the villa of Piazza Armerina. Fourth century A.D.

held vast terrains in this region such as the Nicomachi family or the *gens Sabucia*, or else to Claudius Mamertinus, the governor of Africa and Illyria; but the plan of this villa was developed during the fourth century.

While in the second and third centuries the *domus* or individual house had acquired a porticoed brick inner court, and constructional principles were developed which created the *insula* or apartment block, in the late Empire there was a return to the traditional Republican plan that grouped the wings of the building around a peristyle or garden. The new Late Antique approach in domestic architecture is seen in loggias, in open colonnaded rooms, and in the taste for curved apses, polychrome floor decoration in marble and mosaic, and inlaid marble work on walls, known as *incrustatio*. Columns no longer carry architraves, but support brick arches. Series of these arches are arranged in perspective vistas that open onto nymphaea that in turn are decorated with niches, as in the House of Amor and Psyche in Ostia — a prelude to Romanesque modes. Capitals assume smooth, stylized leaves and abandon the canonical forms of the Corinthian and Composite orders; the architectural orders inherited from Classical tradition were superseded in the late Empire, transformed by the ornamental effect of splendor and color that was substituted for the old architectonic principles.

6. Mosaic Decoration

In its varied scenographic articulation, rich in interior vistas, the villa of Piazza Armerina presents the courtly plan of an apsed hall opening off the rear side of a large central peristyle, typical of formal palaces. The Roman forms of the thermal installations are cunningly camouflaged off one corner of the main peristyle, and the refined curving walls of the lateral peristyle that terminates in the triconch hall have an Oriental form; the monumental entrance has a nympheum, and leads to the semicircular portico of the forceps-shaped atrium. The Hellenistic tradition predominates in the fourth-century mosaic decoration that covered all the vast floor of the villa, which was perhaps the work of African masters. The corridors and long, broad wings demanded decorative motifs that could be harmoniously multiplied over the surfaces to be filled: thus, use was made of minute floral and geometrical elements that could be woven into a tapestry-like composition, or medallions bearing animal masks or busts set into a continuous floral ornament or interlacing motif. Figured mythological, bucolic, or realistic scenes had to be limited to the central *emblema*, or to a large panel surrounded by geometrical motifs, but could not be spread over too large an area. In the villa of Piazza Armerina, a rich repertory of the traditional Hellenistic mythological themes was used to decorate smaller rooms, exedrae, and apses with scenes of Arion, Orpheus, Eros and Pan, Daphne, Cyparissus, Hesion, Endymion, Lycurgus and Ambrosia, Polyphemus and Ulysses, and the labors of Hercules. Sometimes pictorial motifs such as the baroque-like fallen giants, treated with violent, plastic expressionism, were extracted from the context of their original composition and scattered over the abstract field of a large apse. When figured polychrome decoration had to be developed over larger surfaces, the artist called on circus races which could be extended in length, or *venationes* — hunting scenes, or animal combats in the circus — whose motifs could be multiplied and adapted to varying syntactical arrangements, or gladiatorial contests. The gladiatorial theme, traditionally and authentically Roman, acquired a more brutal, abrupt style, a fine example of which is found in the Tetrarchic mosaic in the Villa Borghese.

The enormous complex of the Great Hunt mosaic, with the hunt and capture of wild African animals for the circus, assumes a very particularly narrative and realistic tone in the villa of Piazza Armerina (colorplate, fig. 375), giving a lively, direct, clear illustration of the various phases of the story, with luxuriant color, rich costume details, and landscaped backgrounds; this contrasts with the Hellenistic tone of the Little Hunt mosaic in the same villa.

Roman accents animate the mosaics with scenes of daily life: *mutationes vestis* (the changing of clothes), *unctiones* (anointings), and persons being massaged in the baths of Piazza Armerina, or the mosaic with bikini-clad girl athletes, of the fourth century.

For the round or polygonal rooms that characterize the architecture of the late Empire, there was a preference for mosaics with radial partitions of the field, into which cycles of figures of seasons or months might be inserted. Figured calendars were also created, with the Months set in frames, and Aion was often joined with the Seasons. In geometrical frames, often imitating the divisions of coffered ceilings, and in medallions outlined by ribbon or braid motifs, were placed in appropriate symmetry, the Four Winds, the Four Factions of the Circus, the Seven Sages, the Seven Planets, and the Nine Muses. The allegorical trend of the late Empire multiplied personifications in symbolic scenes, busts, and medallions representing new concepts such as *Megalopsychia* (Magnanimity), *Soteria* (Salvation), *Opora* (Fertility), *Apolausis* (Joy), *Ananeosis* (Renewal), and *Amerimnia* (Security). Besides geometrical settings imitating architectural cofferings, or intertwining garlands and curving ribbons, syntactical unity was also achieved by arabesque-like pergolas of vines, often enlivened with amors and harvesting putti, that sometimes spread over the floor surface, as at Piazza Armerina; these were also placed more realistically in mosaic ceiling vaults, as at Santa Constanza in Rome. The floors of Christian basilicas were to seek a unified composition through geometrical divisions which could contain scenes with allegorical animal motifs, busts, sacred scenes, personifications, and portraits, such as the magnificent pavements in the basilicas of Aquileia.

It is probable that Oriental textile patterns may have suggested the tapestry-like composition of small flowered and geometrical motifs, petals, and rosettes, that became widespread during the fourth century. A new form of mosaic in late Syrian and Palestinian art is provided by topographical representations accompanied by explanatory inscriptions; these are conventional cartographic views similar to illustrated itineraries, typical examples of which are the mosaics in Antioch, Jerusalem, and Madaba.

VIII | Eastern and Western Aspects of Art in the Reign of Constantine

With the new, strong impulses that made themselves felt in art in Rome and Constantinople, the reign of Constantine (A.D. 306–337) marks a new stage in the history of Roman art.

Official portraiture reflected the new Apolline ideal of the Emperor; wishing to be associated with Augustus as the founder of the new Empire, he shaved off his beard and took on an idealized, youthful appearance. Whenever there was a desire to give official art added dignity, there was inevitably a return to the organic nature of the Classical tradition. Thus, after the abstract expressionism, the stereometric structure and the conventional notation that had marked portraiture under the Tetrarchs, Constantinian portraiture showed a new classicizing conception in its broad, smooth surfaces, the return to plastically modeled hair, and its calm, serene facial expressions. When the official type of the image of Helena, the mother of Constantine, became widespread, at Rome her portrait head was set on the body of a seated Aphrodite from the school of Phidias; but in Constantinople she appeared in an iconic statue set on a column.

The panorama of art in the late Empire is varied and complex because of the diverse nature of the society and the culture. The subdivision, already favored by the Tetrarchic system, of vital centers and their zones of influence led to the multiplication of capitals in Nicomedia, Trier, and Milan, the growing development of the cities of Africa, Syria, Gaul, and Britain, and the two main poles of the Empire: ancient Rome, and the New Rome which Constantine inaugurated in A.D. 330, transforming the Byzantium of the Greeks into the splendid Constantinople.

The Eastern and Western capitals of the Empire, Constantinople and Rome, were each the center of a different basic artistic current, and these two currents, the Eastern and the Western, diverged more and more with the passage of time, despite reciprocal influences and frequent interaction. Western art, follow-

ing the ancient Italic tradition, was always to remain less organic, harder, and more incisive and impressionistic; whereas art in the East, more in tune with the still living Hellenistic

376. Detail of the portrait statue of Maxentius from the College of the Augustales at Ostia. Beginning of the fourth century A.D. Ostia, Museum

tradition, was to be characterized by an organic, soft, classicizing, spiritualized tone.

The intense architectural activity in the two capitals also developed two different hallmarks. In Rome the constructional principles of brick-

377. Portrait of Constantine, a reworking on one of the Hadrianic medallions inserted in the Arch of Constantine in Rome. A.D. 315

building, and the sense of space, still produced grand and monumental works such as the Baths of Helena, or those of Constantine on the Quirinal; the Sessorian Palace with its great apsed hall and walls pierced by arcades; and the Castrensen amphitheater. Most important of all was the Basilica of Maxentius, perhaps intended for ceremonial use, which rose near the *summa sacra via* in the Roman Forum. This building no longer relied on colonnaded naves, but consisted of a single vast interior space covered with gigantic cross-vaults, built according to the system perfected in thermal architecture, and with a spacious apse that served to frame the colossal acrolith of Constantine. Maxentius, the pagan Emperor defeated by Constantine in A.D. 312, who termed himself *restitutor urbis suae* and aspired to be the defender of paganism, also rebuilt the gigantic temple of Venus and Rome, originally built by Hadrian and burned down in A.D. 283 under the Emperor Carinus. In Maxentius' rebuilding, rich marbles were used to decorate the great apsed cellae surrounded by peristyles. He also built the massive Circus along the Via Appia, 1500 feet long and 220 feet wide, with its turreted end-structure; and he erected the neighboring circular mausoleum, with pronaos and quadriportico, for his son Romulus, who died in A.D. 309. Max-

entius also commemorated his son in the circular heroön, the Temple of the Divine Romulus, on the Sacred Way in the Roman Forum.

For mausolea and nymphaea fourth-century Roman architecture created elaborate organisms with a centralized plan, enlivened with deep niches, pierced at the top by arcades and windows; there were original solutions in the transition from polygonal interiors or exteriors to daring circular cupolas, achieving a perfected, harmoniously articulated enclosure of unified internal spaces. The heavy mound-tomb of Etruscan tradition was transformed in these mausolea into a round cella, or inner space, following the example of Hadrian's Pantheon. This form of building had a significant flowering in the late Empire. In the West there are many examples; from the Mausoleum of Diocletian in Spalato to the tomb and to the heroön of the Divine Romulus (transformed by Constantine into an entrance structure for the *Templum Sacrae Urbis*), the mausoleum known as the Tor' de' Schiavi on the Via Prenestina, and the Mausoleum of Saint Helena, from about A.D. 330, to the great hall or nymphaeum of the Horti Liciniani, known as the Temple of Minerva Medica; Eastern examples include the Mausoleum of Galerius at Salonica, and a later manifestation was to appear in the Mausoleum of Theodoric in Ravenna, of the seventh century, in which inspiration drawn from barbarian tents and monolithic cupolas merges with the Roman structural form.

These Roman buildings embodied the forms that were to mature into the architecture of Christian baptisteries and centrally planned churches, while Christian basilicas were to revert to naves with colonnades, architraves, and pitched roofs, in the tradition of the Classical temple and the civil basilica.

This Roman architectural style is the basis for the various monumental constructions that rose in the main cities of the West, from Milan to Trier. At Trier the baths repeated the traditional plan, and the Palatine Basilica was conceived as an interior space similar to the Roman Curia, while the Porta Nigra embellished its turreted structure with tiers of arcades framed in semi-columns.

In Constantinople, Roman constructional principles governed the design of thermal establishments, and the brick construction of the tiers

378. Portrait of a Roman woman wearing a ri[...] coiffure. Fourth century A.D. Rome, Torlonia Museum

of encircling corridors in the *Sphendone* of the Hippodrome; but when it came to creating a new Forum of Constantine they did not adopt the rectangular Roman plan, but rather the circular arrangement used in the cities of Asia Minor, such as Gerasa, and Apamea. The new forum was ringed by colonnades, with entrance arches giving on to the *Mese* which was the principal colonnaded street, similar to the great porticoed thoroughfares of Asia Minor and Syria. Thus the forum really constitutes an enlargement of the *Mese* at this point. There was therefore no need for a temple to set the axis and create a backdrop, as it had in the Roman forum plan; instead, the focal point of the square was represented by a porphyry column surmounted by a bronze statue of Constantine in the paganized guise of Helius, but carrying a globe surmounted by a cross, the symbol of the new faith.

and Western barbarians, introduced by a trophy-bearing figure of Victory, were offering tribute. The Roman theme of submission to the Empire was here expressed in a soft, refined relief, in the allegorical, ceremonial forms that suited the Eastern mentality.

In Rome the Arch of Constantine, dedicated in 315, provides the most elaborate and sumptuous conclusions of the development of this type of Roman architectural and decorative monument. As if to symbolize the continuity and renewal of the Empire impersonated by Constantine, the plastic decoration of this arch incorporated, in harmonious syntactical and architectural unity, historical reliefs from the times of Trajan, Hadrian, and Marcus Aurelius, while the friezes are from the time of Constantine and represent scenes of the Emperor going forth from Milan, the siege of Verona, the victory at the Milvian Bridge, the triumphal entry into Rome, and scenes

379. *Frieze on the Arch of Constantine in Rome, showing the scene of the* liberalitas; *the Emperor is seated on the raised* cathedra, *distributing gifts in a symmetrical and hieratic composition. A.D. 315*

A Mannerist Renaissance drawing records for us the relief decoration on the base of this column: a bust of Constantine, surrounded by sun rays and set in a wreathed medallion, was placed above the enthroned Tyche of the city, to whom the young sons of two Eastern

of oration and of the distribution of gifts in the Forum (fig. 379). Altogether the figural decoration, old and new, of this arch constitutes a precise and intentionally coordinated anthology, showing the most salient stages in the development of Roman historical relief.

XIX Popular and Classicizing Currents in the Art of the Fourth Century

The friezes on the Arch of Constantine reveal a profound separation from the classicizing Eastern conception. In the syntax of these reliefs the laws of perspective and spatial illusionism are abandoned, and conventional laws of visibility and hierarchic order, abstractly expressed through dimensional relationships, are substituted. The divergence from the Classical ideal also shows in the volumetric modeling; rough, massive, unorganic structure; large, compact heads showing an uncouth realism; drapery folds indicated by sharp, deep furrows made with the drill. This style stemmed from the current of popular art, of which this represented an official formulation. Sculptors in Roman workshops, who had been acquiring increasing importance and autonomy during the third century, now graduated from the secondary production of shop reliefs, funerary steles, portraits, and sarcophagi, to official commissions which had formerly been given to artists more directly reared in the Classical artistic culture. While the bustle of work for the embellishment of the new capital in the East was attracting artists from Classical circles all over the Empire to Constantinople, in Rome the process of using artists of the native Roman tradition, that had started in the first years of the reign of Commodus, found a natural outlet in the friezes of Constantine. The Classical culture that still sustained the sculptors of the Column of Marcus Aurelius had been weakening progressively during the third century under the impact of the new spiritual ferments — mystery cults, and Christian and mystical movements — and under provincial and popular pressures. The classicizing aspirations of emperors such as Alexander Severus or Gallienus, and of the pagan aristocratic circles, remained sporadic and artificial in Western art and in the end had less significance than the new expressions stemming from the native movement which, though less cultured, could interpret with greater originality and faithfulness the expressive demands made by a restless people.

The conversion of Constantine, and his edict of 313 that recognized the Christian religion, offered a fresh impulse to art, inspired by the new faith. Christ appeared as a bearded *basileus*, and with the Imperial attributes, he gave the law to Peter who received it in draped hands in accordance with Imperial ceremony, the applauding figure of Saint Paul at his side; this composition perhaps appeared in the apse of the first basilica of Saint Peter. In miracle scenes, however, which were often arranged in two registers on sarcophagi, Christ continued to be represented in the youthful, beardless type (fig. 381), and the Nativity scene also made its appearance.

In the first decades of the fourth century pagan and Christian sarcophagi with more closely packed scenes, and a central conch shell framing the busts of the deceased, fall in the same artistic current as that seen in the friezes of the Arch of Constantine. This style is also to be found on carved consoles and architectural decorations.

Many catacomb paintings also belong to this popular tradition, such as the lively realistic scenes from the hypogeum of Trebius Justus in which builders, laborers, and overseers are seen against realistic architectural backgrounds and country landscapes. And a similar style marks the paintings from the

House of the Nymphaeum at Ostia as well as the North African mosaics of rural and rustic scenes (fig. 380).

Courtly painting, on the other hand, such as the ceiling panels in the palace of Trier with figures of personifications and putti, has a more classicizing tone. In painting, too, we see the spread of ceremonial motifs with large figures. The solemn, frontally placed goddess

The subject of ceremonial banquet bearers, already developed in third-century painting, was interpreted in this fourth-century taste; new versions were developed, with large figures placed in abstract settings. The paintings, known through drawings, from a house near the Lateran Baptistery, and those in the ample and colorful example in the wall paintings of a tomb at Silistra, ancient Durostorum, in

380. *Detail of a mosaic from Caesarea (Cherchell) showing a scene of plowing and sowing in a vivacious narrative style, rendered with a vigorous expressionism. Third century A.D. Cherchell, Museum*

in the Barberini panel in the Museo delle Terme, formerly thought to represent the city of Rome but instead representing a solemn enthroned Venus with Victory in her hand and Amor and Psyche behind her shoulders, was perhaps inspired by the effigy restored by Maxentius in the Temple of Venus and Rome. Rome is enthroned in another painting, from a nymphaeum near the Capitol, framed by figures of interceding Provinces bearing tribute in their hands that are veiled like those of the Magi in Christian art.

the far-off Lower Mesia in Bulgaria, give proof of the contact between Eastern and Western artistic trends. The wall paintings of this tomb, in framed panels with a white ground, show male and female servants, clad in tunics like medieval pages, who bear the various necessities for the symbolic banquet and converge upon their master and his wife, shown in the central panel. The style combines realistic details with an allegorical abstraction. In the lunette of the tomb, peacocks flank a krater, recalling catacomb motifs, and the

381. Detail from the sarcophagus of Junius Bassus, showing Christ's entry into Jerusalem. A.D. 359. Vatican Grottoes

painting on the barrel-vault is divided into coffers decorated with birds, flowers, and hunting scenes, in the same way that birds and flowers decorate painted tombs in Philippopolis in Thrace.

The taste for these paintings with large isolated figures is also to be found in Africa in the full-bodied, heavily shaded candle bearers, wearing rich tunics decorated with circles and bands; these figures form the decoration of a painted tomb from the first half of the fourth century at Gargaresh in Tripolitania, along with a portrait medallion, a circus scene, and other motifs, including two peacocks on either side of a tablet bearing inscriptions.

In the East as in the West, the greater part of the larger polychrome mosaics still depended on the Hellenistic tradition. There was, however, a progressive decomposition and stylization of pictorial chiaroscuro, and a progressive increase in the size of the *tesserae*, or pieces of marble used to form the mosaic; gradually mosaics approached the taste for figured inlay and *opus sectile*.

Marble facings and marble *incrustatio* on walls, which had been so widely used in the third and fourth centuries, were now commonly imitated or feigned with painting. Painted panels of simulated polychrome marble are to be found in houses, catacombs, and chamber tombs even in the most distant regions, at Kerch, Salona, and Serdica. And similar decoration in both painting and marble passed into use in Christian basilicas.

Christianity in the third century had been a clandestine religion, persecuted and poor, followed mainly by the humblest people; consequently it had developed an art which spoke to these social groups in a popular narrative language. As it acquired freedom and rights, however, making converts in the governing, cultured, and aristocratic classes, it was possible to build cemeteries and basilica churches; the religion progressively transformed its artistic tone, moving closer to courtly, official work. Christian art was no longer limited to modest decorations for dark catacombs, but now expressed itself in paintings and mosaics decorating the apses and walls of churches, and in relief sculpture on sarcophagi for illustrious patricians. The new sense of dignity slowly modified the popular inflection, introducing classicizing accents and a more accurate plasticism; bodies and drapery were rendered more organically, and iconographical motifs of Imperial Majesty were adapted to express Divine Majesty. The Christian sarcophagus of the *praefectus Urbi* Junius Bassus, from the middle of the fourth century, exemplifies this renewal of Classicism (fig. 381); it is also to be seen in portraits, and was to culminate in the period of Theodosius.

The name of a certain Junius Bassus who was consul in 331 is linked with the basilica which was discovered and destroyed on the Esquiline; richly decorated with marble wall facings of *opus sectile*, which had geometrical and figured panels attesting to the taste of the fourth century for sumptuous polychromy (colorplate, fig. 382). The mythological theme of Hylas and the nymphs, the Roman theme of the consul placed frontally in a biga and set between the factions of the circus, and the traditionally Oriental motif of a tiger sinking its teeth into its prey, are all certainly represented in an allegorical key and conceived in the geometricized vision of marble inlay based on a vivid juxtaposition of colors. Another example of *opus sectile* attesting to the vitality of Late Antique art is provided by a hall in Ostia dating from the end of the fourth century, with floral friezes of acanthus leaves enlivened with flowers, birds, butterflies, and spirals from the Classical tradition of painting, and similar panels with lions and tigers; into this decoration is inserted a hieratic, bearded bust of Christ.

During the fourth century, before Rome was sacked by the barbarians, the magnificence of the city reached its peak, and the *Regionary Catalogues* list, in the period of Constantine, 11 fora, 11 baths, 10 basilicas, 28 libraries, 36 triumphal arches, 19 aqueducts, 22 large equestrian statues, 80 gilded effigies, 74 chryselephantine statues, 3785 iconic statues, and an infinity of other sculptures. Ammianus Marcellinus records the admiring stupefaction of Constantius II when confronted with the marvels of the *Urbs* during his visit in 367. New arches were still erected in the second half of the fourth century: one dedicated to Gratianus Valentinianus and Theodosius, in 382, near the Ponte Elio; to Valentinianus and Valens, near the Ponte Sisto; and to Arcadius, Honorius, and Theodosius, in 405. And the embellishment of the city continued by giving new monumentality to the gateways of the Aurelian wall between 402 and 405. Finally the sack of the city by Alaric in 410 was to strike the first grave blow to the artistic riches of Rome.

382. *Panel of a marble wall-facing of* opus sectile, *representing a tiger sinking his teeth into a young bull. From the Basilica of Junius Bassus on the Esquiline. First half of the fourth century* A.D. *Rome, Capitoline Museums*

XX

The New Development

of the Historical Relief in the East

Constantinople, which Constantine had enriched with works of art looted from all the main centers of the East, continued to expand into a vast urban organism that pivoted on the axis of the colonnaded *Mese* within the great ring of Constantine's walls; and to embellish itself with monuments in emulation of the old capital of the Western Empire. This Imperial program included the new Forum Tauri, which Theodosius (A.D. 378–393) placed on the extension of the *Mese*. The Forum Tauri was consciously inspired by Trajan's Forum in Rome: as a Spaniard, Theodosius hoped to be compared with his great compatriot Trajan, whom sources tell us he resembled in physique and dress.

1. The Helic Column of Theodosius

Indeed, the monument Theodosius chose to commemorate his own wars and triumphs against the Scythians and other barbarians was, precisely, a helic column placed in the center of his new forum. The surviving fragments of reliefs from this column — which was destroyed by Bayazid II at the beginning of the sixteenth century to make way for the baths — were incorporated in the walls of the baths; they show processions of soldiers, battles, boats on rivers, and soldiers kneeling in the act of prayer or for clemency, their shields marked with the *Chrismon*, the monogram of Christ (*chi* and *rho*). These fragments can perhaps be referred to the part of the helic frieze recording the campaigns against the Grutungians and Ostrogoths which were led by Theodosius and his general Promotus along the lower Danube, and ended with the triumph in Constantinople in 386. But it is

also probable that part of the same frieze is recorded in a late sixteenth-century Mannerist drawing in the Louvre; this drawing may be derived from a drawing made before the destruction of the column, for it shows a triumphal procession that seems to pass from the *Hebdomon* across the *Kampos*, toward the walls and eastern quarters of Constantinople.

It would have been difficult for these generic war scenes to provide enough inspiration and subject matter to fill the long frieze, and the commemoration of the Emperor's glory was now conceived above all in terms of the triumph, rather than the narrative of war. The campaigns themselves were increasingly entrusted to generals; and the majesty of the Emperor, who was progressively detached from his army, was shown only in the triumphal episode, which became transformed into a series of ceremonies occurring between the *Hebdomon*, the Golden Gate, and the Hippodrome: acts of homage, the presentation of the golden crown, the submission of barbarian chiefs, the show of booty, and the people's ovation.

The columns of Trajan and of Marcus Aurelius recounted the *virtus* of the emperor at the head of his troops; the Column of Theodosius, besides its scenes of war, exalts and eternalizes the ceremony of triumph.

The Hippodrome was the most active center of Constantinople; within it took place the most popular spectacles, the factional sporting contests and political events, and all the most lavish of the Imperial ceremonies. On the *spina*, which Constantine had embellished with the historic treasure of the bronze serpent-shaped support of the tripod of Platea, taken from Delphi, Theodosius erected the Egyptian obelisk on a marble base; on this were reliefs representing the actual erection of the monument itself, and the Emperor in the Imperial loggia or *kathisma*, between his sons Honorius and Arcadius, court dignitaries in chlamys and togas, and the Imperial bodyguards (fig. 383). From his loggia he watched races, dancing, and ceremonies in the arena and received the homage of Eastern and Western barbarians.

On this obelisk base the invariable frontality of the poses, the hierarchic order and paratactical syntax, the isolation of the Imperial group, the absence of spatial depth, and the crystal clarity of the composition are the results of the new concepts. The soft, fluid modeling seen here is achieved without use of the drill, and has a refined, classicizing effect on the full, rounded, youthful heads and fine, calligraphic drapery folds; these qualities are also found in the fragments from the Column of Theodosius, and they reappear in the statue of Valentinian II (A.D. 375-392) from Aphrodisia. This style is very different from the sharp, incisive, drilled, volumetric trend of Western art of the period of Constantine.

2. The Helic Column of Arcadius

Just as Rome had two helic columns, Constantinople could also boast of a second column which, during the reign of Arcadius (A.D. 395-408), was erected in accordance with the program of his dynasty; it stood in the center of the great new forum built on the newest section of the *Mese*, repeating the plan of the Forum Tauri. This column, dedicated in 402, received its statue of Arcadius only in 421 during the reign of his son, Theodosius II. The shaft of the colum was demolished by Ahmet I in 1717 and only the worn base remains, but a series of sixteenth and eighteenth-century drawings by Lorichs, Cassas, and an anonymous artist in the Freshfield Collection enable us to trace the development of the figured frieze.

This historiated column, which is said to have been identical with that of Theodosius — together they constituted the two marvels of the city — has significance only in terms of monumental architecture and town-planning; the historical and chronographical aspects have become weak and conventionalized. The frieze is no longer a realistic commemoration of military glory, but an abstract exaltation of Imperial majesty. The turbulent reign of the timid Arcadius, a victim of the courtly intrigues of Rufinus, Eutropius, and Eudoxia, knew nothing but barbarian invasions and compromises with the enemy, and it even

383. Detail of the base of the obelisk of Theodosius, showing the Emperor in the kathisma *or Imperial loggia, with his sons Arcadius and Honorius and court dignitaries, watching the spectacle in the Hippodrome of Constantinople. Circa A.D. 390. Istanbul*

suffered the occupation of Constantinople by the Gothic troops of Gaina. In fact, the popular uprising against the barbarians in 401, and the pursuit and naval victory on the Bosphorus under the command, not of Arcadius, but of the general Fravita, was the only historical event that the artist could find to record in the commemoration of the Emperor's reign.

Because of the limitation of the theme, the number of windings of the frieze was reduced to 13, in comparison with the 23 of Trajan's Column, but the height of the frieze was doubled; similarly, the 119 scenes of the Column of Trajan were replaced by a more unified presentation of a few motifs of battles and marches alternating with ceremonial scenes. The flight of the Goths from Constantinople with the city and its most important monuments represented in the background; the march with shepherds and herdsmen; and the naval battle in the straits of the Bosphorus — all have lively animation and are interwoven with pictorial and landscape elements in the Hellenistic tradition. The Emperor appears in ceremonial scenes surrounded by chlamys-clad dignitaries and Imperial bodyguards to watch the flight of the Goths; or together with Eudoxia he witnesses the reassembling of the army; or in the final apotheosis; or in the representation of the Imperial group in the *kathisma*, where even Honorius, Emperor in the West (A.D. 395–432), is present in order to affirm the unity of the Empire; these scenes are symmetrical, frontal, paratactical compositions, and the general tone is abstract and hieratic in accordance with Late Antique conceptions. The syntactical unity on which the continuous Roman narrative style had been based was by now disintegrated. Modeling, however, remained soft and fluid in this Eastern courtly art.

On the three sculptured sides of the base of the column both the Emperors, Arcadius and Honorius, are shown side by side; and with a rigid sense of hierarchy the relief is divided into four registers. On the lowest level are supplicating barbarians and trophies; on the second level are the homage and tribute of Eastern and Western barbarians and the Provinces; the Emperor in Glory is seen in the third tier; and the cosmically framed exaltation of the symbol of the cross appears at the top.

3. The Imprint of Christianity in Late Imperial Art

The closing of the temples dedicated to pagan gods, the destruction of their effigies, and the end of the Olympic games were decreed by Theodosius; this marked the final decline of pagan religion and Classical *paideia*. The art of the court from then on was impregnated with the new Christian concepts: on the Column of Arcadius an angel chased Gaina from the gates of Constantinople, and the Emperor, crowned by Victory, trampled the demoniacal serpent to show that his victory was not merely over barbary, but over evil itself. The *Chrismon*, the new emblem on the shields of the army, was exalted on the base of the column

and adorned the angles of its double capital. The victory of the army is brought about by Divine Providence, and *Virtus* gives way to *Divinus Favor*, military skill to miracles. The emperor, as the representative of God, is invincible; the title of *triumphator gentium barbarorum* is no longer connected with warlike deeds but with the general nature of his mission; the emperor is *semper victor*, *semper triumphator*. The narration of historical reality, which had been at the foundation of Roman art, now gives way to an exaltation of the transcendental nature and universality of the Empire, laying the foundations for Byzantine art which was to celebrate the celestial empire, Christ "victorious and triumphant."

The typological resemblance between the columns in Rome and those in Constantinople serves to underline the profound transformation in form and content that had taken place during two centuries in the two different environments of East and West. The other honorary columns, with statues in silver, bronze, and marble, which were still raised in quantities in Constantinople, and in the Roman Forum until the Column of Phocas, no longer bore carved illustration; the *Chrismon* on the wreathed medallions held by Victories was the only motif, repeated on each side of the base of the Column of Marcian (A.D. 450–457) in Constantinople.

4. Classical Trends in Late Imperial Art of the Court

While Rome was sacked by Alaric in 410, in 413 Constantinople was still expanding, with the colossal turreted walls, 50 feet high, erected around the city by Theodosius II (A.D. 408–450), who also rebuilt Santa Sophia with a basilican plan and a pillared pronaos. The city continued its monumental development as the opulent capital of the Eastern Empire. The great Imperial palace begun by Constantine became an immense courtly residence, with gardens, peristyles, ceremonial apartments, baths, churches, barracks, terraces, and its own mint. A whole courtly art developed in sculpture, painting, floor and wall mosaic, illuminated manuscripts, silver work, and ivory work. These products maintained the classicizing imprint that was suitable to the aristocratic class for whom they were made, and in harmony with the ideals and spirituality of the culture of the time — in which Homer became a literary cult. In the output of engraved and beaten silver we can see, from the fourth to the sixth and seventh centuries, the persistence of the Hellenistic tradition with pagan gods, landscapes, and marine scenes; this tradition takes on a florid decorative effect in engraving, and mannerist inflections in the modeling and structure of images, and it becomes progressively drained of naturalistic and pictorial content. In other silver pieces, and above all in the *missoria*, silver plates with Imperial figures, we find the frontal, hierarchic compositions in the courtly, ceremonial tradition; the same stamp also characterizes the figures of consuls, in their richly embroidered costumes, on the wings of ivory diptychs and on engraved glass. Silver treasures were easily transported and, as they comprised the patrimony of governors, magistrates, and wealthy families, they spread into all the provinces of the Empire, thus contributing to the diffusion of the courtly style.

In Rome, too, where there was no longer any opportunity for the creation of historical reliefs in which the popular expressive style of the Arch of Constantine might otherwise have developed, artistic production tended to be ennobled with a classicizing tone in which Oriental influences were also operative. And this was so both in the art that served triumphant Christianity and in that which expressed the survival of paganism among the aristocracy. Claudian, the classicist poet of the intellectual circle of the Symmachi family, was the representative of this particular culture; he wrote the mythological poems *Gigantomachia* and the *Rape of Proserpine*, and produced Imperial panegyrics and short satirical epic poems. Likewise, classicizing figures and representations of Asclepius, Hygieia, and the Muses appeared in the ivory diptychs of the Symmachi and Nicomachi families (fig. 384). Portrait sculpture, too, conserved the clarity of organic, classicizing modeling, especially in Imperial and aristocratic images.

However, in spite of this common classicizing tendency — romantically invoked by the intellectualistic pagan restoration of the Emperor Julian the Apostate (A.D. 361–363), and culminating in the period of Theodosius (A.D. 378–393) — differences between East and West can be seen in this courtly art. The ivory diptychs from Rome, Milan, and Ravenna have a more plastic, vigorous style; those from Constantinople tend always more toward a flattened relief — *rilievo schiacciato* — modeled in surface patterns, draftsmanly, calligraphic, and

384. Wing of an ivory diptych of the Symmachi family, showing a woman sacrificing; in a pure classicizing style. Circa A.D. 400. London, Victoria and Albert Museum

precious. A taste for forms ever more graphic, even miniaturistic in details, produced the
refined Oriental coinage. In the East, toga-clad
statues present elaborate, symmetrical, linear
stylization in their folds; faces become inspired
and spiritualized, taking up again the philosopher type and culminating in the exacerbated,
expressionist accents of the elongated, large-
eyed faces of fifth-century figures from Aphrodisia and Ephesus. In Rome, the structure of
the figures was more robust and the drapery
modeled more incisively, as can be seen in the
two statues of magistrates in the act of casting
the *mappa circenses*, the cloth thrown down as
signal for the commencement of the games, in
the Museo dei Conservatori in Rome, from the
end of the fourth century; and again in the
statue of a toga-clad figure from Ostia (fig. 385),
perhaps Vincentius Ragonius Celsus, which,
however, is in the more popular artistic style,
with drapery in hard, angular, drilled furrows
and a rough realistic face.

Western polychrome mosaics were more
schematized and chromatically decomposed
than Oriental work, which was more closely
linked to the Classical tradition. And in Constantinople the mosaics of the Imperial Palace,
which have now been dated in the sixth century, still used Hellenistic motifs against the
abstract, scale-patterned background.

While this art of the court had preserved a
Classical imprint in East and West, albeit with
two different accents, in the Western provinces,
apart from the limited demands of courts and
governors — who could easily have arranged
for the visit of the occasional artist from outside, or for direct importation of their products
— art was destined to satisfy the needs of the
modest local population. It increasingly lost
touch with the Classical tradition, and showed
progressively an unorganic conception of structure, a linear approach to drapery, and general
decorative tendencies.

With the breaking up of the Roman Empire
and the affirmation of new ethnical substrata,
Classicism as a force became weakened and
died out, leaving the field free for the spread
of other cultural currents and the rise of a
new artistic language which marked the transition to medieval culture. The basically ornamental abstraction of Celtic art burst forth
once more in the Christian art of Ireland,
flourishing from the fifth to the seventh cen-

*385. Portrait statue of a toga-clad man, in a
rough, realistic style. From the baths of the
forum of Ostia. Perhaps Vincentius Ragonius
Celsus. End of the fourth century A.D.
Ostia, Museum*

turies, with the characteristic interwoven arabesques of their miniatures. The wide circle of barbarian kingdoms that stretched from central Asia, around the northern boundaries of Italy to Germany, Scandinavia, and Gaul, and down to the Africa of the Vandals, found their most natural modes of expression in gold work; this adorned fibiae, brooches, belts, and horse saddles and trappings; it embellished weapons; and bejeweled the chiefs of these nomadic peoples. The style of these ornaments drew upon an abstract heritage that combined elements from many sources: Iranian, Scythian, Syrian, Sarmatian, and Celtic motifs, animal and geometric elements, and interlacing ornament. These goldsmiths used varied techniques: splendid filigree work, deep engraving, vivid inlays, flashing set gems, granular decoration, and cloisonné work filled with vitreous paste or enamel. Motifs included openwork arabesques, spiral tendrils, and stylized quadrupeds, and later, complex, interlacing ribbon forms of Syrian and Coptic derivation, all foreign in conception and completely opposed to Classical taste. The *barbaricari*, private and state-employed goldsmiths mentioned in the *Codex Theodosianus* and the *Notitia Dignitatum*, were the artists most representative of this new barbaric world.

But in the more lively, pulsating heart of the Mediterranean world, based on the foundation of Classical culture and the centuries-old Hellenistic tradition, on Roman historical relief, and on the Eastern courtly art, there was a new spiritual climate that was to see the birth of Byzantine art.

Glossary

ABACUS The uppermost element of a capital, quadrangular in shape, on which rests the architrave (*q.v.*).

ACME The Greek word used by ancient chronographers to designate the period of years considered to include the height of an artist's career.

ACROLITH A statue in which stone (or marble) is used together with other materials; usually the head and nude parts of the body are of stone, the rest of wood.

ACROPOLIS The hill in ancient Greek cities on which were situated the principal temples. *The* Acropolis refers to that of Athens.

ADLOCUTIO In Roman imperial iconography, the representation of the emperor in the act of making a public address.

ADVENTUS In Roman imperial iconography, the representation of the triumphal arrival of the emperor.

ADYTON The inner sanctuary of a temple, generally a separate room to the rear of the cella (*q.v.*).

AEDICULA (*pl.* AEDICULAE) A niche or a window in the form of a miniature temple front, framed by a pair of small columns or pilasters supporting a pediment (*q.v.*).

AES GRAVE The bronze weight standard of early Republican Rome, cast in circular form and having a distinct type on each side; valued by weight.

AGON The Greek word for contest, used here specifically in reference to the great public athletic contests of ancient Greece.

AGORA (*pl.* AGORAI) A public square or market place in ancient Greek cities; analogous to the forum (*q.v.*) of Roman cities. *The* Agora refers to that of Athens.

AKROTERION (*pl.* AKROTERIA) An architectural decoration, figurative or ornamental, crowning the top or placed at the corners of the triangle of a pediment (*q.v.*).

ALABASTRON (*pl.* ALABASTRA) A small, handleless perfume or ointment container of slim ovoid body, with a narrow opening surrounded by a wide rim.

ALTIS The enclosed sacred area at Olympia which contained the temples of Hera and Zeus.

AMAZONOMACHY A battle of Greeks and Amazons.

AMPHI-PROSTYLE A type of temple with a columned portico (*q.v.*) in front and rear only.

AMPHORA (*pl.* AMPHORAE) A tall vase for oil or wine, with an opening always considerably narrower than the body, and two vertically attached handles. From the foot the body swells out up to the shoulders, and from this point either tapers to the rim in a continuous profile, or in an abrupt curve which forms a distinct neck. See also NIKOSTHENIC AMPHORA and NOLAN AMPHORA.

AMPULLA The name given to a widely varying vase form which very generally consists of a more or less globular body, a narrow, elongated neck, and a vertically attached handle.

ANAX The word designating a Mycenaean prince.

ANDRON The dining room of the ancient Greek house.

ANTAE (*pl.*) The projecting pilasters forming the forward termination of the lateral walls of a cella (*q.v.*) or other structure. When the lateral walls of the cella in a temple are thus terminated, the temple is described as *in antis*.

ANTEFIX The architectural ornament which appears repeatedly along the lower edge of a roof and masks the end of each semicircular covering tile of the roof.

ANTEPAGMENTUM (*pl.* ANTEPAGMENTA) One of the decorative terracotta slabs attached, usually in a continuous row, to the entablature of an Etruscan temple.

ANTHEMION A type of very conventionalized floral motif used in ancient architectural decoration.

ANTIDOROS CUP See DROOP CUP.

APEX Latin word used here in its specific meaning as the name of a type of hat worn by certain Roman priests (the *flamines*): a close-fitting cap, ornamented on top with a short spike of olive wood and a woolen thread.

APODYTERION (*pl.* APODYTERIA) The dressing room of a gymnasium or bathing establishment.

APOPTYGMA The fold of the peplos (*q.v.*) which falls as a flap from shoulders to waist.

APOSKOPEUEIN The Greek verb meaning to peer out, shielding the eyes from above with the hand.

391

APSE A semicircular termination of a room, a building, or a recess in a wall.

ARA PACIS The Altar of Peace, Rome; constructed by Augustus, 13-9 B.C.

ARA PIETATIS AUGUSTAE The Altar of Imperial Piety, Rome, built first century, B.C.

ARCHITRAVE The wooden beam or stone lintel which extends from column to column; in the Classical system of architecture the lowest member of the entablature (q.v.).

ARS TOPIARIA The art of gardening.

ARYBALLOS (pl. ARYBALLOI) A small ointment container, with or without handles, having a round or ovoid body, and a small neck with a wide, thick rim.

ASKOS (pl. ASKOI) A small vase in the form of a wineskin. The body is wider than it is high, with a handle attached from one side to the top, and a small opening at the other side; often taking the shape of an animal.

ATLANTES (pl.) Sculpted male figures employed in architecture in place of columns or pilasters; also called telamones. Cf. CARYATID.

ATLAS FIGURE The singular form of atlantes (q.v.).

ATRIUM In an ancient Roman house, the entrance hall or court, roofed around the four sides but having a rectangular opening to the sky in the center.

AUCTORITAS Latin word literally meaning excellence, used frequently in ancient critical writings to signify the quality of excellence in a work of art in the sense of the supreme dignity of its conception. Cf. PONDUS.

AUGUR Etruscan or Roman priest concerned with the interpretation of the will of the gods through the observation of the flight of birds, or celestial signs. Cf. HARUSPEX.

AULE Greek word meaning courtyard.

BAND-CUP A type of Little Master cup (q.v.). The concave lip passes into the body in a smooth curve. The decoration consists of a lip band painted all black, and a frieze in the handle zone, with a figure or small group between palmettes. All the lower part of the cup is black except for a reserved (q.v.) stripe on the lower basin. The interior is usually painted black.

BASILEUS Greek word for king.

BASILICA (pl. BASILICAE) In ancient Roman architecture, the exchange hall and court of justice. A rectangular building with the principal entrance in one of the long sides, and usually having aisles around the interior. At one or both ends, or at the center of one of the long sides was a raised area or recess used as a tribune.

BIGA An ancient two-horsed chariot.

BOULE The citizens' council in ancient Greek towns.

BOULEUTERION The meeting place of the boule (q.v.).

BUCCHERO WARE A type of Archaic Etruscan pottery of fine black clay, with only incised and relief decoration.

BULLA (pl. BULLAE) A boss-shaped pendant used in Etruscan and Roman necklaces and other jewelry, usually of laminated gold.

CALDARIUM A chamber with hot water baths in a Roman bath establishment. See FRIGIDARIUM and TEPIDARIUM.

CALYX-KRATER A krater (q.v.) with a body that rises in a convex curve toward the rim, and has handles attached at the base of the body.

CAMPUS MARTIUS The ancient name for the flat area of the city of Rome bordered by the Capitoline, Quirinal, and Pincian hills, and the Tiber.

CANABARI (pl.) The inhabitants of the towns that sprung up around the permanent Roman military encampments; so named after the type of huts (canabae) in which they lived.

CANOPUS Name of the famous garden suburb of ancient Alexandria, and hence the name given to the Egyptian-inspired sculpture gardens and pool of Hadrian's villa at Tivoli.

CAPITOLIUM The principal temple of ancient Rome, on the Capitoline hill, dedicated to the Roman triad of Jupiter, Juno, and Minerva. The name was extended to such a temple set up in every Roman town.

CARDO The cardo and decumanus were the principal, central cross streets of a Roman town. The decumanus usually ran east-west; the cardo, north-south.

CARYATID The sculpted figure of a maiden used in place of a column to support an entablature (q.v.).

CASTRUM A Roman military camp.

CATHEDRA A chair with back and arms, used by important personages in ancient Rome; in the Christian era, the cathedra became the seat of the bishop.

CAVEA The seating area of a theater.

CELERITAS The Latin word for rapidity.

CELLA The enclosed room or actual sanctuary within a temple where the cult statue was placed.

CENTAUROMACHY Battle of Greeks and centaurs.

CHARIS The Greek word for grace or charm.

CHARUN One of the frightful, tormenting demons of the Etruscan world of the dead; he has equine ears and usually carries a hammer.

CHATTI (pl.) The members of a particular ancient Germanic tribe.

CHIASMIC An adjective derived from the Greek word chiasma, meaning a cross formed by a vertical and a horizontal. It is here used to describe the rhythms in the equilibrium of ancient Greek statuary that have a diagonal crisscross relationship in reference to the horizontal and vertical axis. See QUADRATIO.

CHITON The long or short tunic worn by Greek men and women.

CHLAINA A long double mantle attached on one shoulder, worn in ancient Greece.

CHLAMYS A short mantle fastened on the right shoulder, worn in ancient Greece.

CHORAGIC MONUMENT In ancient Greece, a monument erected in honor of the leader of a dramatic chorus.

CHOROS The chorus of the ancient Greek drama which commented upon and participated in the action of the play.

CHRISMON The monogram of Christ formed by the Greek letters chi and rho: ☧

CHRYSELEPHANTINE Made of, or decorated with, gold and ivory.

CIPPUS (pl. CIPPI) A type of Etruscan funerary monument consisting of a cylindrical or rectangular stone shaft, usually bearing figurative relief decoration. Used also by the Romans.

CIRCUS An ancient Roman course for horse races

and chariot races. The long parallel sides and one semicircular end were fitted with seats; the other end was rectangular and contained the stables for the competing horses. The course was divided in two down the center by the *spina* (*q.v.*).

CIST A tall, circular, metal receptacle with lid, used for toilet articles.

CIVIS ROMANUS A Roman citizen.

CLOACA MAXIMA Canalized stream draining the northeast section of ancient Rome into the Tiber by way of the Forum. Its regulation is ascribed to the fifth century B.C.

CLOISONNÉ A technique for decorating metal by pouring multicolored enamel or paste into areas which have been outlined on the metal ground by metal strips.

CLOISTER VAULT A vault composed of four convex sections, or coves, meeting in the vertical-diagonal planes; the axial sections of the vault are arched, and the horizontal courses of stone diminish in width from base to crown.

COENATIO ROTUNDA Literally: round dining-room. The name described specifically the famous round dining-room with revolving dome in the *Domus Aurea* (*q.v.*).

COLUMBARIUM A type of vaulted tomb structure lined with niches in which were placed the cinerary urns of the dead.

COLUMEN The central, main wooden roof beam of an Etruscan temple.

COMAST CUP A type of *kylix* (*q.v.*) common in Corinthian pottery of the very early sixth century B.C. and appearing in Attic black-figure pottery around 580 B.C. It has a flaring foot, a short stem, and a short, distinctly offset lip. The lip is decorated with rosettes bearing incising; the frieze on the body generally bears figures of dancers, actors in padded costumes, or revelers, *i.e.* scenes of the *komos* (*q.v.*); the interior is painted black.

CONCORDIA AUGUSTORUM Harmony among the emperors, a concept of Roman imperial propaganda.

CORBEL A block of stone, often decorated, which projects from a wall and supports some structural beam within.

CORNICE The uppermost horizontal member of the entablature (*q.v.*); also the two sloping moldings of the triangle formed by the pediment (*q.v.*), in this latter case more exactly called the raking cornice.

CRENELATION The openings which appear regularly and repeatedly along the top of a battlement or wall

CUIRASS A piece of armor covering the body from neck to hips, and consisting of a breastplate and back piece.

CURIA The Senate House of ancient Rome.

CURSUS HONORUM The series of public deeds and offices of a Roman magistrate.

DADOPHOROI In the Mithraic religion, the two youths, Cautes and Cautopates, dressed in Phrygian costume, who appear to either side of Mithras, the former bearing an upright torch and the latter bearing a torch held upside down in symbolic reference to the sun in the East and West.

DAMNATIO MEMORIAE In Roman law, a penalty for crimes against the state, which implied the canceling of the memory of the condemned after death by destroying his images and erasing his name from inscriptions.

DECASTYLE A temple having ten columns along the front.

DECUMANUS See CARDO.

DENTILED CORNICE A cornice with small rectangular blocks running along its lower edge, which translate into stone the ends of the roof joists of primitive wooden temples.

DEXTRARUM IUNCTIO Literally: the joining of right hands. In ancient Rome the representation of couples in this pose was a symbol of the marital union.

DIADOCHI A name referring collectively to the generals of Alexander the Great among whom his empire was ultimately partitioned, establishing the principal political boundaries of the Hellenistic world: Antigonus I, Antipater, Cassander, Lysimachus, Ptolemy I, Seleucus I.

DEINOS (*pl.* DEINOI) A large wide-mouthed bowl, which served as a wine vessel; having a rounded, footless bottom, it was supported by a stand or tripod.

DEINOMENIDS Name referring collectively to the tyrants of Syracuse in the fifth century B.C., sons of Deinomenes: Gelon, Geron, Polyzalus, Thrasybulus, and Geron's son Deinomenes.

DOMINUS ET DEUS Latin phrase meaning lord and god, titles attributed to the emperor in ancient Rome.

DOMUS The Latin word for house.

DOMUS AUREA Literally: golden house. Name given to Nero's enormous villa in Rome because the façade of the vestibule was gilded.

DROMOS A long, narrow passage like that leading into ancient chamber tombs.

DROOP CUP (pronounced Drope) A type of Little Master cup (*q.v.*). Its decoration is more elaborate than the lip-cup or band-cup. At the handle level there is usually an upper frieze with a chain of buds and below this a frieze of animals or other ornament. All the lower parts of the basin are decorated, usually with rays at the base of the basin. The interior is decorated with a medallion. Named after its first classifier.

ECHINUS The convex circular molding which supports the abacus (*q.v.*) in a Doric capital.

EMBLEMA VERMICULATUM A mosaic panel executed in an extremely refined technique using very tiny pieces of marble, which is then set into the center of a larger and less finely executed floor mosaic.

ENNEAPYLON The "nine gates" of the Mycenaean Acropolis of Athens.

ENNEASTYLE A temple plan having nine columns along the front.

ENTABLATURE In the Classical architectural system, the whole complex of horizontal elements above the columns, comprising architrave, frieze, and cornice.

ENTHUSIASMOS Greek word meaning fanatical, almost inspired, delirium or passion.

EPHEBUS (*pl.* EPHEBI) Greek word referring to a youth who had reached the age of eighteen, at which time he became inscribed on the citizen rolls of Athens.

EPOS Greek word for the heroic epic of ancient Greece.

ETHOS Greek word denoting the noble, sublime, and composed expressions of the human soul. *Cf.* PATHOS.

EUSTYLE A temple plan in which the space between the columns is two and a quarter times the lower diameter of the columns.

EXEDRA (*pl.* EXEDRAE) A rectangular or semicircular recess in the interior or exterior wall of a building.

EYE CUP A type of Attic black-figure *kylix* (*q.v.*) created in the third quarter of the sixth century B.C., having a short stem and a wide shallow basin of continuous and unbroken profile, and decorated on the outside with large eyes at the level of the handles. Found also later in the red-figure technique.

FABULA PRAETEXTA A serious drama on a Roman historical subject.

FACILITAS The Latin word for facility, ease.

FICUS RUMINALIS The fig tree on the Tiber where Romulus and Remus drifted ashore, and under which they were suckled by the she-wolf.

FILIGREE A technique of jewelry decoration using fine wires.

FORUM (*pl.* FORA) The principal public square of a Roman town. *The* Forum refers to the Roman Forum.

FRIEZE In the Classical system of architecture, the portion of the entablature between the architrave and the cornice (*q.v.*). The word is also used generally to describe any band with figurative or ornamental decoration.

FRIGIDARIUM A chamber with the cold water bath in a Roman bath establishment. See CALDARIUM and TEPIDARIUM.

FRONS SCAENAE The façade of the stage building of an ancient Roman theater.

GALATOMACHY A battle between Greeks and Gauls.

GENS (*pl.* GENTES) The patrician families of ancient Rome.

GIALLO ANTICO A type of yellow marble used in ancient Roman building; coming principally from Numidia it was known as *marmor numidicum*.

GIGANTOMACHY A battle between the gods and the giants.

GORDION CUP A type of Attic black-figure *kylix* (*q.v.*) of the mid-sixth century B.C., which in its form and decoration seems to provide a transition to the Little Master cups (*q.v.*). In profile it is more squat than the Little Master types. Its exterior decoration consists of a black lip and a single frieze around the body; the interior bears a figured medallion with an elaborate frame. Named after the Phrygian city where one such cup was found.

GORGONEION The representation of the Gorgon, Medusa, usually in the form of a mask.

GRANULATION A technique of jewelry decoration which employs tiny balls of gold.

GUTTAE (*pl.*) Small tapering peg-like elements which appear in the Doric entablature (*q.v.*) on the underside of the mutules (*q.v.*), and also under the regulae (*q.v.*).

HARUSPEX Etruscan or Roman priest concerned with the ascertaining of the divine will by the examination of the entrails, particularly the liver, of sacrificial animals. *Cf.* AUGUR.

HEBDOMON A seaside suburb seven miles to the west of ancient Constantinople.

HELIC COLUMN A column decorated with a continuous narrative relief in the form of a frieze which spirals upward around the shaft of the column.

HEPTASTYLE A temple having seven columns along the front.

HERM A square pillar surmounted by a sculpted head.

HEROÖN A funerary monument built to honor a hero.

HETERA (*pl.* HETERAE) A courtesan of ancient Greece.

HEXASTYLE A temple having six columns along the front.

HIMATION A heavy mantle worn by men and women in ancient Greece.

HIPPODROME The Greek word to describe the equivalent of the Roman circus (*q.v.*). *The* Hippodrome refers to that of Constantinople which was very large and served also as the main center of public and political activities and imperial ceremonies.

HORREUM (*pl.* HORREA) A warehouse for storing grain.

HORTUS (*pl.* HORTI) Latin word for garden.

HUMANITAS Latin word meaning human nature, in the sense of the intellectual nature of man. Used here in contrast to *virtus* (*q.v.*).

HYBRIS Greek word denoting violent, animal passion.

HYDRIA (*pl.* HYDRIAI) Primarily a water carrying jar, with one vertical handle on the back for pouring, and horizontal handles for lifting on either side of the shoulders. The body of the jar is wide through the shoulders and tapers at foot and neck.

HYPOGEUM (*pl.* HYPOGEA) An underground chamber, usually for funerary purposes.

ILIUPERSIS The sack of Troy.

IMAGO CLIPEATA (*pl.* IMAGINES CLIPEATAE) A type of Roman portrait in which the bust appears within a frame formed by a circular shield.

IN ANTIS See ANTAE.

INCRUSTATIO The inlaid marble work on walls or floors of Roman buildings. See also OPUS SECTILE.

INSULA The Latin word denoting the apartment block in Roman domestic architecture.

INTERCOLUMNIATION The distance between the columns of a colonnade which is determined by a given proportion to the lower diameter of the column.

ISOCEPHALY The conception of the design in ancient relief sculpture in which all heads are arranged on one horizontal line.

KALATHISKOS A small *kalathos* (*q.v.*).

KALATHOS A circular wicker basket with straight upright sides and a flaring rim; also the name of a vase having this shape.

KALOS INSCRIPTION Type of inscription found on Attic vases which acclaimed as "beautiful" (*kalos*) some particular *ephebus* (*q.v.*).

KALOS K'AGATHOS Greek phrase expressing the beauty and nobility of the soul.

KAMPOS In ancient Constantinople, a large plain near the *Hebdomon* (*q.v.*) for the reunion and training of military troops.

KANTHAROS A stemmed drinking cup having a body with deep, straight, upright sides, and two high vertical handles which rise up from the rim and curve downward to the base of the body.

KATHISMA Greek word for seat; in particular, the imperial loggia of the Hippodrome (*q.v.*) of Constantinople, which was connected to the imperial palace by a covered passage.

KEKRYPHALOS A hair-net or scarf that wrapped and tied about the head of a woman in ancient Greece, smoothly covering the hair.

KERCH VASES A class of Attic red-figure pottery of the fourth century B.C., so named after the excavation site of Kerch, in the Crimea, where many examples were found.

KLAFT A long, heavy Egyptian hair-do with regular rows of horizontal waves.

KLINE Greek word for a banqueting couch.

KOINE Greek word literally meaning a common language. Its original meaning is extended to cover a cultural expression or artistic style common to a variety of peoples.

KOMOS A banquet, with revelling and merry-making.

KORE (*pl.* KORAI) Greek word meaning maiden, which has been adopted to denote Archaic Greek statues of standing maidens. *Cf.* KOUROS.

KOTHON A *pyxis* (*q.v.*) supported by three feet. Also called *tripod-pyxis*.

KOTYLE A small drinking cup, similar in shape to a small *skyphos* (*q.v.*).

KOUROS (*pl.* KOUROI) Greek word meaning a youth, which has been adopted to denote Archaic Greek statues of standing youths. *Cf.* KORE.

KRATER A deep, wide-mouthed bowl with a foot, used for mixing wine. The body is sometimes shaped like an inverted bell, with horizontally attached handles just below the lip of the rim. For other variants, see VOLUTE-KRATER and CALYX-KRATER.

KRIOPHOROS Greek word meaning ram-bearer.

KYLIX (*pl.* KYLIXES) A footed, and usually stemmed, drinking cup with a wide basin to which are attached two horizontal handles. Profiles vary greatly according to period and style, from a relatively deep to a very shallow basin, and from a very marked lip to an unbroken profile without any distinct lip.

KYMATIA (*pl.*) A decorative molding so named for its contour resembling that of a wave.

LARES The Roman household deities.

LARNAKES (*pl.*; *sing.* LARNAX) Small rectangular sepulchral chests of ancient Greece.

LASAE (*pl.*) In the Etruscan world of the dead, minor winged female divinities, often with individual names.

LEBES (*pl.* LEBETES) A large bowl which in its simple form is the same as a *deinos* (*q.v.*). The nuptial lebes is a specific type of large *deinos*, having two high handles which rise above the mouth of the vase, and an attached stand.

LEGATUS PRO PRAETORE An ancient Roman title given to magistrates charged by the senate or emperor to undertake some special work: in the senatorial provinces they were assistants to the governor; in the imperial provinces the *legatus Augusti pro praetore* was the governor.

LEKANIS (*pl.* LEKANIDES) A basin-shaped bowl with a lid and two horizontal handles.

LEKYTHOS (*pl.* LEKYTHOI) A one-handled vase of narrow, ovoid body, angular shoulder, narrow neck, and thick-rimmed lip. The smaller form was the standard oil jug; the large form, often decorated in the white ground technique, was a funerary vase.

LESCHE In ancient Greece, an informal meeting place, which often resembled the form of a stoa (*q.v.*).

LEX OPPIA A Roman anti-luxury law carried in 215 B.C. by the tribune Gaius Oppius and repealed in 195 B.C.

LIBERALITAS In Roman imperial iconography, the representation of the emperor in an act of imperial largess.

LIP-CUP A type of Little Master cup (*q.v.*). The concave lip is sharply offset from the body. Both the lip frieze and handle frieze are reserved (*q.v.*), and divided from one another by a thin black line; the lip band bears a single figure, a small group, or no decoration at all; the handle frieze usually bears palmettes and an inscription. The lower part of the cup is black except for a narrow reserved stripe on the lower basin. The interior is usually painted all black.

LITTLE MASTER CUP A class of Attic black-figure *kylix* (*q.v.*) of the second half of the sixth century B.C. bearing miniature decoration, and constituting a further, more refined development of the Siana cup (*q.v.*). The class has three principal forms: band-cup, lip-cup, and Droop cup (*q.v.*); all have a stem and an offset lip.

LITUUS The curved crook or wand borne by an augur (*q.v.*).

LUPERCAL The cave or grotto at the foot of the southwest corner of the Palatine hill in which the she-wolf suckled Romulus and Remus. It gave its name to the priests, *Luperci*, and to the festival of the *Lupercalia*. Used here to describe the representation of Romulus and Remus suckled by the she-wolf.

LUSTRATIO The performance of the *lustrum*, or purification ceremony, which the censors conducted every five years in ancient Rome.

MAJESTAS AUGUSTI The majesty, dignity, and greatness of the emperor, a concept of Roman imperial propaganda.

MEANDER A continuous decorative motif like a rectangular spiral; known also as fret or key pattern.

MEGALOGRAPHIA (*pl.* MEGALOGRAPHIAI) The Greek word for large, multifigured paintings of complex composition.

MEGARON The principal hall in a Mycenaean palace or house.

MELISSA In Greek mythology, a nymph whose name means "bee"; together with her sister Amalthea she cared for the infant Zeus by feeding him honey.

MESE In ancient Constantinople, the great central artery that crossed the whole city.

METOPE In the frieze (*q.v.*) of the Doric order, the sunken panel, usually decorated in relief, that appears between two triglyphs (*q.v.*).

MOSCHOPHOROS Greek word meaning calf-bearer.

MOUND-TOMB A tomb structure having one or more underground chambers, covered above ground by a dome-like mass of earth, often with a masonry wall encircling the base of the mound.

MUTULES The projecting slabs placed on the underside of a Doric cornice (*q.v.*) above each metope and triglyph (*q.v.*).

MYSTAI (*pl.*) Greek word for the initiates in a religious cult.

NEAPOLIS Greek word meaning new city.

NIKEPHORIA A feast in honor of Nike, celebrating a victory.

NIKOSTHENIC AMPHORA An amphora (*q.v.*) with a conical neck which flares out to form the shoulders of the vase, and at this point is attached to the body by a seam. It is also characterized by thin band-like handles that curve out directly from the rim and bend down to join the shoulders. This shape was developed in the Attic workshop of Nikosthenes in the late sixth century B.C., but is found also in Etruscan *bucchero* ware (*q.v.*).

NOLAN AMPHORA A particular form of relatively small amphora (*q.v.*), having a distinct neck, simple foot, and often twisted handles. It was a common form in the late sixth and early fifth centuries B.C. Named after the excavation site of Nola, in southern Italy.

NYMPHAEUM (*pl.* NYMPHAEA) Literally a sanctuary of the nymphs, but used generally in ancient architecture to denote a decorative ambient with plants, flowers, and running water or a fountain.

OBESUS ETRUSCUS Literally: fat Etruscan. A phrase found in a verse of Catullus (XXXIX, 11).

OCTASTYLE A temple having eight columns along the front.

ODEUM A small roofed theater, used principally for musical performances.

OIKOUMENE A female personification of the civilized, inhabited world.

OINOCHOE (*pl.* OINOCHOAI) A one-handled wine jug with a round or ovoid body, a distinct and relatively narrow neck, and often a trefoil mouth.

OLLA (*pl.* OLLAE) A bulbous bowl with foot and tall stem; a typically Italic vase shape.

OLPE (*pl.* OLPAI) A tall one-handled pitcher or jug, with a body that swells out near the base and tapers toward the opening.

OPISTHODOMOS The recessed porch at the rear of a temple.

OPTIMUS PRINCEPS Literally: great and good leader. A title granted to Trajan in recognition of the glorious exploits and achievements of his reign.

OPUS INCERTUM In Roman architecture, a wall of lime and rubble, faced with irregularly shaped stones.

OPUS QUADRATUM In Roman architecture, a wall made of rectangular blocks of stones, with or without mortar joints and frequently secured with dowels or clamps.

OPUS QUASI RETICULATUM In Roman architecture, a wall faced with almost regular-cut small square stones, held together with mortar.

OPUS RETICULATUM In Roman architecture, a wall of fine-cut square stones, generally of tufa, set diagonally and joined with mortar.

OPUS SECTILE A technique employing the inlay of various colored marbles to create a figurative or ornamental decoration on floors or walls.

ORCHESTRA The place of action of the chorus in the ancient Greek theater, generally circular in plan. In the Roman theater this area is very much diminished and semicircular.

ORESTEIA The legends of the hero Orestes.

OSTRAKA (*pl.*; *sing.* OSTRAKON) Potsherds; used in ancient Greece for voting.

PAIDEIA Education in ancient Greece, in the sense of its whole complex of moral and cultural values.

PALAESTRA An open area for athletic training, used especially for boxing and wrestling. It can be a building in itself or part of the larger complex of the gymnasium.

PALLADIUM The rigid and Archaic representation of Athena as Athena Promachos, protectress of heroes, which became standard for cult statues and representations on Panathenaic amphorae (*q.v.*).

PANATHENAIC AMPHORA An amphora (*q.v.*) with a relatively narrow neck, and broad body which tapers sharply toward the foot. From the mid-sixth to the second century B.C. the type conserved the same form, and the traditional black-figure decoration consisting usually of the Archaic representation of Athena Promachos on one side and a representation of the contest on the other. Used as a prize in the contests of the Panathenaea, the Athenian feast held every four years in honor of Athena.

PANCRATIUM In the Greek athletic contest, a game combining wrestling and boxing.

PASTAS In the ancient Greek house, a long narrow room onto which other rooms opened; it opened onto a courtyard through a row of several pillars.

PATERA The Latin word for a libation bowl, broad and shallow in form, without handles, and usually having a boss in the center. Also the name for a circular decorative motif representing a libation bowl. *Cf.* PHIALE.

PATHOS Greek word denoting the passionate, emotive expressions of the soul. *Cf.* ETHOS.

PAX ROMANA The Roman Peace, a concept of Roman imperial iconography.

PEDIMENT The triangular termination of the space created by a gabled roof; often, in Greek buildings, bearing sculptural decoration.

PELARGIKON The Mycenaean wall of the Acropolis of Athens.

PELIKE A wide-mouthed, two-handled jar; the profile of the body is continuous, swelling out near the base and tapering through the shoulders.

PEPLOPHOROS (*pl.* PEPLOPHOROI) A female figure wearing a peplos.

PEPLOS A heavy garment worn by Greek women, fastened on both shoulders.

PERIPTERAL A temple plan having a covered colonnade on all four sides.

PERISTYLE A colonnade which completely surrounds either a building as in a peripteral temple (*q.v.*), or an open space, usually a courtyard within a building.

PETASOS A hat with a very broad brim worn by men in ancient Greece.

PHERSU Etruscan word found in an inscription in the Tomb of the Augurs, indicating a masked actor.

PHIALE The Greek word for a libation bowl, broad and shallow in form, and without handles. Often there is a boss in the center, in which case it is described as *mesomphalos*. *Cf.* PATERA.

PHLYAX VASES South Italian red-figure vases of the fourth century B.C. decorated with scenes from a type of popular comedy called *phlyax*.

PIETAS Latin word for piety, in the sense of respect for the gods, country, and family.

PIETAS AUGUSTORUM The piety of the emperors, a concept of Roman imperial propaganda.

PIETRA FETIDA Name of a soft, bituminous sandstone found in the area of Chiusi.

PIETRA SERENA Name of a variety of hard sandstone found in Tuscany having a bluish gray color.

PINAX (*pl.* PINAKES) A plaque, used for decoration or as a votive offering.

PITHOS A large earthenware storage jar, without handles or foot.

PLACENTARII (*pl.*) Realistic grotesque and obscene statuettes of bread vendors, known through examples found at Pompeii.

PODIUM (*pl.* PODIA) A continuous pedestal or platform at the base of a structure or against a wall.

POLIS Greek word for city.

POLOS A high, cylindrical, "pill-box" headdress worn by Greek women.

POLYCHRYSOS Literally: rich with gold. Word used in the Homeric description of Mycenae.

PONDUS Latin word literally meaning equilibrium and the balancing of weight, frequently used in ancient critical writings to describe the quality of gravity or importance of a work of art.

PONTIFEX A Roman high priest, a pontiff.

POROS A type of soft limestone from Piraeus used for the pediment figures of the Archaic temples of the Acropolis in Athens, and for many buildings.

PORTICO A covered colonnade or arcade surrounding all or part of a building, or placed along a street, or around an open square or courtyard.

POTENTIORES The rich upper class of ancient Roman society.

POTNIA THERON The mistress of the beasts; used of Greek representations of a goddess (usually Artemis) holding an animal in each hand.

PRAEFECTUS URBI The Roman military officer, selected from among the senators of consular rank, who commanded the urban cohorts; he also had the criminal jurisdiction over those disturbing public order.

PROFECTIO In Roman imperial iconography, the representation of the setting forth of the emperor for a military campaign.

PRONAOS The entrance porch of a temple.

PROPYLON In the architecture of ancient Greece, a gate or gate building, generally with columns.

PRO SALUTE IMPERATORIS Latin phrase meaning in honor of the emperor.

PROSKENION A one-storey façade placed between the orchestra and the *skene* (*qq.v.*) of an ancient Greek theater.

PROSTYLE A type of temple with a columned portico (*q.v.*) at the front only.

PROTHESIS The lying-in-state of the dead.

PROTOME The representation of the head and forepart of an animal, or in the case of a human figure the head and upper part of the body, used for decoration. Thus a fuller, more three-dimensional representation than the simpler mask.

PSEUDO-PERIPTERAL A temple having a colonnade on all sides, the columns of which on some sides, usually the lateral ones, are not free-standing but engaged in the wall of the *cella* (*q.v.*).

PSYKTER A vase of mushroom shape, used as a wine cooler.

PYRGOS Greek word for a bastion or tower. *The Pyrgos* refers to the bastion of the Acropolis in Athens on which is situated the Temple of Athena Nike.

PYXIS (*pl.* PYXIDES) Small box, usually round, with a lid which has a central knob; used for toilet articles.

QUADRATIO The name given in ancient rhetorical exposition to a figure with a double antithesis, the terms of which are crisscrossed. The word was thus applied by ancient critics of art to the chiasmic (*q.v.*) rhythms of statues.

QUADRIGA The ancient four-horsed chariot.

QUADRIPORTICO A four-sided portico (*q.v.*) which completely surrounds a rectangular open space.

REGULAE (*pl.*) The narrow strips of stone placed beneath the triglyphs (*q.v.*) in a Doric architrave (*q.v.*).

RELIGIOSISSIMUS AUGUSTUS The very pious emperor, a concept of Roman imperial iconography.

RESERVED In vase painting, the term used to describe a decoration utilizing the ground color of the clay of the vase, the design being formed by outlining, or by blacking out all around the contours of the design.

RES GESTAE The Latin term for great public exploits.

RESTITUTOR URBIS SUAE Literally: savior of his city. *Restitutor* was a Roman title conferred upon emperors who had saved a city or part of the Empire from disaster.

RHYTHMOS A term used in ancient critical writings meaning the just position and sequence of two quantums or movements or other elements which are different and discordant one to the other, but reconciled by their periodic recurrence.

RHYTON A horn-shaped drinking vessel, often in the form of an animal head.

ROSTRA (*pl.*) Literally: beaks of ships. Name given to the orator's platform in the Roman Forum because it was decorated with the beaks of ships captured in the battle of Antium in 338 B.C.

SACELLUM A small religious sanctuary.

SACELLUM CLOACINAE Small circular shrine dedicated to Venus Cloacina, situated on the south side of the Roman Forum near the portico of the Basilica Aemilia, over the spot where the drain flowed under the basilica into the Cloaca Maxima (*q.v.*).

SAEPTA The *Saepta Julia* was the voting precinct of ancient Rome situated in the Campus Martius (*q.v.*).

SCAENA The stage and the stage building of a Roman theater. *Cf.* SKENE.

SELLA CASTRENSIS In ancient Rome, a folding stool used by the emperor in the military encampment (*castrum*) during the campaigns.

SELLA CURULIS In ancient Rome, a folding stool used by magistrates, and the attribute of the higher magistrates, including the emperor; the seat of justice.

SEPTIZODIUM The monumental façade facing the Via Appia, which Septimius Severus added to the imperial palace on the Palatine. The monument was referred to also as *Septizonium*, but research seems now to have proved that the official title was *Septizodium*, perhaps referring to the seven planets.

SIANA CUP A type of Attic black figure *kylix*

(*q.v.*) of the second quarter of the sixth century B.C. It has a relatively tall stem and an offset lip. It may have a band of ivy or animal figures or other decoration around the lip, and a separate figure frieze around the body. At times, however, one wide frieze covers both body and lip. The lower part of the basin can have decoration, but usually it is all black interrupted only by a narrow reserved (*q.v.*) band; stem and foot are also painted black. The interior bears a large figured medallion with an elaborate frame. Named after a site in Rhodes where two such cups were found.

SIMA The gutter of a building.

SISTRUM A metal rattle, used in religious rites, especially those of Egyptian divinities.

SITULA (*pl.* SITULAE) A deep, circular, bucket-shaped vessel, usually of bronze.

SKENE The stage building of a Greek theater.

SKYPHOS (*pl.* SKYPHOI) A deep, footless drinking cup with two horizontally attached handles at the rim.

SOLARIUM A monumental sundial that formed a whole public square in the Campus Martius (*q.v.*); the pointer, erected in 10 B.C., was an Egyptian obelisk of the Pharaoh Psammetichus II.

SPHENDONE Name given to the southwest, semicircular end of the *Hippodrome* (*q.v.*) of Constantinople.

SPHYRELATON TECHNIQUE The method used in making certain Archaic Greek images, whereby plates of hammered metal are nailed to a wooden core.

SPINA The axial rib down the center of the circus or hippodrome (*qq.v.*), marked at the end by the turning points (*metae*), thus dividing the race course in two.

SPOLIA OPIMA The Latin term meaning spoils of war.

STAMNOS A jar, similar in shape to an amphora (*q.v.*), but with two handles attached horizontally and the neck reduced to a strong rim.

STELE An upright slab bearing inscriptions or relief decoration, frequently used as a funerary monument in ancient Greece.

STOA (*pl.* STOAI) In ancient Greek architecture, a portico (*q.v.*) with a rear wall and one or more rows of columns in the front, set along a street or about a public square.

STRATEGOS (*pl.* STRATEGOI) In ancient Greece, a general term for the commander of an army or a fleet.

STYLOBATE The top step of a temple which forms the platform on which the columns are placed.

SUOVETAURILIA A Roman religious sacrifice of a pig, sheep, and bull.

SYMPLEGMA The representation of an interlocked pair of figures, usually erotic.

TABERNAE (*pl.*) The stalls or shops of a Roman market.

TABERNAE VETERES Literally: the old shops. Name given to the market stalls on the south side of the Roman Forum, built already in early Republican times and later displaced by the building of the Basilica Julia.

TAENIA Greek word for a band or fillet; may refer to a headband, or to the projecting band of stone at the top of a Doric architrave (*q.v.*).

TANASAR Etruscan word found in an inscription in the Tomb of the Augurs; it would seem to indicate some sort of priest, but its precise significance is not known.

TECHNITAI Greek word for technicians, here used to distinguish the workshop members from the artist actually creating the designs of a project.

TEPIDARIUM A chamber with warm water baths in a Roman bath establishment. See CALDARIUM and FRIGIDARIUM.

TESSELLATED Made up of tesserae (*q.v.*), as a mosaic.

TESSERAE (*pl.*) The small cubes, usually of marble, used to make a mosaic.

TETRAPYLON An archway with four portals, as at the intersection of two roads.

THESAUROS The treasury building of a Greek religious sanctuary in which the precious objects of the cult were housed.

THESMOTHETAI The six junior archons, or chief magistrates, of ancient Athens, whose functions were mainly judicial.

THIASOS The Greek word for a sacred procession.

THOLOS The Greek word for a circular building.

THURIBLE A censer used in religious ceremonies.

THYRSUS A staff surmounted by a dried bunch of vine leaves or a dried pinecone, used in the Dionysiac rite.

TOGA The official garment of a Roman citizen; a heavy semicircular white cloth draped over the body and covering the left arm while leaving the right arm free.

TOGA PRAETEXTA The official garment of a Roman magistrate, distinguished from the ordinary toga (*q.v.*) by a purple border.

TOREUTICS The art of metal working in relief, or by embossing, or chasing.

TRIGLYPH In the frieze (*q.v.*) of the Doric order, the slightly projecting rectangular slab, usually carved with vertical grooves, which is placed between the metopes (*q.v.*).

TROZELLA Literally: little wheel. Characteristic type of amphora (*q.v.*) with geometric decoration found in Apulia. Its tall handles are decorated with a wheel-like ornament, whence the name.

TUCHULCHA One of the frightful, tormenting demons of the Etruscan world of the dead; he has wings and serpents for hair, and a vulture's beak.

TURMS The Etruscan equivalent of the Greek Hermes.

TUTULUS High conical headdress worn by certain priests. Also the name of a high female hair-do held by a band, worn particularly by Etruscan women, and often veiled.

URBS Latin word meaning city, especially the city of Rome.

USTRINA ANTONINORUM A square platform surrounded by a double enclosure, remains of which were found near the site of the column of Antoninus Pius in the Campus Martius (*q.v.*). The structure perhaps contained the funeral pyres of Antoninus Pius and his wife Faustina.

VANTH In the Etruscan world of the dead, a minor female divinity, usually represented with wings, and serpents for hair.

VELIA Ancient Roman name for the hill which rises east of the Roman Forum on which are situated the Arch of Titus and the Temple of Venus and Roma.

VIRIDARIUM The Latin word for a garden composed exclusively of trees and shrubs.

VIRTUS Latin word meaning manliness, in the sense of the best of the physical and moral nature of man. Used here in contrast with *humanitas* (*q.v.*), to describe the rigid and military ideals of the old Roman Republic.

VOLUMEN A book in the form of a scroll.

VOLUTE An ornamental motif in the form of a spiral curve.

VOLUTE-KRATER A krater (*q.v.*) with tall vertical handles which, from the shoulders of the vase, rise up above the rim and terminate in decorative volutes (*q.v.*).

WEST SLOPE WARE A type of Greek pottery having a black ground color and floral and geometric decoration in white and yellow, made from the late fourth to the first century B.C. Named after an excavation site facing the Acropolis in Athens.

XOANON (*pl.* XOANA) A primitive, rigid, wooden image of a deity.

BIBLIOGRAPHY

ENCYCLOPEDIAS AND DICTIONARIES

Cabrol, F., and Leclercq, E., *Dictionnaire d'archéologie chrétienne et de liturgie*, Paris, 1924–.

Daremberg, C., and Saglio, E., *Dictionnaire des antiquités grecques et romaines*, 9 vols., Paris, 1887–1916.

Enciclopedia dell'arte antica, classica e orientale, 7 vols. Rome, 1958–1967.

Encyclopedia of World Art, New York, 1960–.

Roscher, Wilhelm H., *Ausführliches Lexicon der griechischen und römischen Mythologie*, 9 vols., Berlin-Leipzig, 1884–1937.

Thieme, U., and Becker, F., *Allgemeines Lexicon der bildenden Künstler von der Antike bis zur Gegenwart*, 37 vols., Leipzig, 1907–1950.

HANDBOOKS AND GENERAL WORKS ON GREEK ART

Akurgal, Ekrem, *Die Kunst Anatoliens von Homer bis Alexander*, Berlin, 1961.

Arias, Paolo E., *La Grecia nell'impero di Roma*, Rome, 1940.

Beazley, John D., and Ashmole, Bernard, *Greek Sculpture and Painting to the End of the Hellenistic Period*, New York, 1966.

Bianchi-Bandinelli, Ranuccio, *Archeologia e cultura*, Milan, 1961.

———, *Storicità dell'arte classica*, Florence, 1943; 2d ed., Florence, 1950.

Boardman, John, *Greek Art*, London, 1964.

———, Dörig, J., Fuchs, W., and Hirmer, Max, *Die griechische Kunst*, Munich, 1966.

Brunn, Heinrich, *Geschichte der griechischen Künstler*, 2d ed., Stuttgart, 1889.

Bulle, Heinrich, *Der schöne Mensch im Altertum*, Munich, 1922.

Carpenter, Rhys, *The Esthetic Basis of Greek Art of the Fifth and Fourth Centuries B.C.*, rev. ed., Bloomington, Ind., 1959.

———, *Greek Art, A Study of the Formal Evolution of Style*, Philadelphia, 1962.

Curtius, Ludwig, *Die klassische Kunst Griechenlands*, Potsdam, 1938.

Della Seta, Alessandro, *I monumenti dell'antichità classica*, I: *Grecia*, 2d ed., Milan, 1931.

———, *Il nudo nell'arte*, Milan-Rome, 1930.

Deonna, Waldemar, *Du miracle grec au miracle chrétien*, Basel, 1946.

———, *L'expression des sentiments dans l'art grec*, Paris, 1914.

Ducati, Pericle, *L'arte classica*, Turin, 1927.

Garcia y Bellido, Antonio, *Hispania Graeca*, Barcelona, 1948.

Giglioli, Giulio Q., *Arte greca*, Milan, 1955.

Grube, G. M. A., *The Greek and Roman Critics*, London, 1965.

Hafner, German, *Geschichte der griechischen Kunst*, Zurich, 1961.

Hamann, Richard, *Geschichte der Kunst von der Vorgeschichte bis zur Spätantike*, Munich, 1952.

Hamann, Richard, *Griechische Kunst*, Berlin, 1949.

Herzog, August, *Studien zur Geschichte der griechischen Kunst*, Leipzig, 1888.

Klein, Wilhelm, *Geschichte der griechischen Kunst*, I–III, Leipzig, 1904–1907.

Langlotz, Ernst, *Ancient Greek Sculpture of South Italy and Sicily*, New York, 1967.

———, *Die Darstellung des Menschen in der griechischen Kunst*, Bonn, 1941.

Matz, Friedrich, *Geschichte der griechischen Kunst*, Frankfort, 1950.

Michaelis, Adolf, and Wolters, Paul, in H. Springer, *Handbuch der Kunstgeschichte*, I: *Das Altertum*, 12th ed., Leipzig, 1926.

Neumann, Gerhard, *Gesten und Gebärden in der griechischen Kunst*, Berlin, 1965.

Perrot, Georges, and Chipiez, Charles, *Histoire de l'art dans l'antiquité*, VI–IX, Paris, 1894–1914.

Pollitt, J. J., *The Art of Greece (1400–31 B.C.): Sources and Documents*, Englewood Cliffs, N.J., 1965.

Rayet, Olivier, *Monuments de l'art antique*, II, Paris, 1884.

Richter, Gisela, M. A., *A Handbook of Greek Art*, 2d ed. rev., London, 1960.

Ridder, André de, and Deonna, Waldemar, *L'art en Grèce*, Paris, 1924.

Rodenwaldt, Gerhart, *Die Kunst der Antike: Hellas und Rom*, Berlin, 1927.

Rumpf, Andreas, and Mingazzini, Paolo, *Manuale di storia dell'arte classica*, Florence, 1945.

Salis, Arnold von, *Die Kunst der Griechen*, 2d ed., Leipzig, 1922.

Schefold, Karl, *Griechische Kunst als religiöses Phänomen*, Hamburg, 1959.

———, *Meisterwerke griechischer Kunst*, Basel, 1960.

Schuchhardt, Walter H., *Die Kunst der Griechen*, Berlin, 1940.

———, *Griechische Kunst*, Frankfurt, 1964.

Schweitzer, Bernhard, *Zur Kunst der Antike*, I–II, Tübingen, 1963.

Scranton, Robert, *Aesthetic Aspects of Ancient Art*, Chicago, 1964.

Seltman, Charles T., *Approach to Greek Art*, London, 1948.

Tarbell, Frank B., *History of Greek Art*, New York, 1896.

Walters, Henry B., *The Art of the Greeks*, New York-London, 1906.

Willers, Heinrich, *Studien zur griechischen Kunst*, Leipzig, 1914.

Winckelmann, Johann J., *Gedanken über die Nachahmung der griechischen Werke in der Malerei und Bildhauerkunst*, Dresden, 1755. English trans. by H. Fuseli, *Reflections on the Painting and Sculpture of the Greeks*, London, 1765.

———, *Geschichte der Kunst des Altertums*, Dresden, 1764; new eds., Berlin, 1913, and Vienna, 1934.

Winter, Franz, *Kunstgeschichte in Bildern*, I: *Das Altertum*, Leipzig, 1912–.

Woodcock, George, *The Greeks in India*, London, 1966.

Zervos, Christian, *L'art en Grèce*, Paris, 1946.

GREEK ART: SOURCES

Becatti, Giovanni, *Arte e gusto negli scrittori latini*, Florence, 1951.

Blake, K. J., and Sellers, E., *The Elder Pliny's Chapters on the History of Art*, London, 1896.

Choisy, Auguste, *Vitruvius*, 4 vols., Paris, 1909.

Ferri, Silvio, *Plinio il Vecchio: Storia delle arti antiche*, Rome, 1946.

———, *Vitruvio*, Rome, 1960.

Frazer, James G., *Pausanias's Description of Greece*, 6 vols., London, 1913.

Hitzig-Blümner, *Pausanias*, I, Berlin, 1896; II–III, Leipzig, 1901–1907.

Jücker, Hans, *Vom Verhältnis der Römer zur bildenden Kunst der Griechen*, Bamberg, 1950.

Kalkmann, August, *Die Quellen der Kunstgeschichte des Plinius*, Berlin, 1898.

Loewy, Emmanuel, *Inschriften griechischer Bildhauer*, Leipzig, 1885.

Marcadé, Jean, *Recueil des signatures des sculpteurs grecs*, I–II, Paris, 1953–1957.

Overbeck, Johannes, *Die antiken Schriftquellen zur Geschichte der bildende Künste bei den Griechen*, Leipzig, 1868.

Pliny the Elder, *Natural History*, English trans. by H. Rackham (Loeb Classical Library), 10 vols., Cambridge, Mass., 1938–1962.

Pollitt, J. J., *The Art of Greece (1400–31 B.C.): Sources and Documents*, Englewood Cliffs, N.J., 1965.

Schweitzer, Bernhard, *Platon und die bildende Kunst der Griechen*, Tübingen, 1953.

———, "Xenokrates von Athen: Beiträge zur Geschichte der antiken Kunstforschung und Kunstanschauung," in *Schriften der Königsberg Gelehrten Gesellschaft*, 9, I, 1932. Reprinted in Bernhard Schweitzer, *Zur Kunst der Antike*, Tübingen, I, 1963.

Vitruvius, Pollio, *On Architecture*, English trans. by F. Granger (Loeb Classical Library), 2 vols., London, 1931–34.

GREEK ARCHITECTURE

Åkerström, Åke, *Die architektonische Terrakotten Kleinasiens*, Lund, 1966.

Anderson, William James, Spiers, R. Phené, and Dinsmoor, William B., *The Architecture of Ancient Greece: An Account of Its Historic Development*, rev. ed., New York, 1927.

Andrae, Walter, *Die ionische Säule: Bauform oder Symbol*, Berlin, 1933.

Anti, Carlo, *Teatri greci arcaici, da Minosse a Pericle*, Padua, 1947.

Arias, Paolo E., *Il teatro greco fuori di Atene*, Florence, 1934.

Basile, Giovanni Battista F., *Curvature delle linee dell'architettura antica*, 2d ed., Palermo, 1896.

Bell, Edward, *Hellenic Architecture: Its Genesis and Growth*, London, 1920.

Benoît, François, *L'architecture: Antiquité*, Paris, 1911.

Berve, H., Gruben, G., and Hirmer, M., *Greek Temples, Theaters, and Shrines*, New York, 1962.

Bethe, Erich, *Prolegomena zur Geschichte des Theaters im Altertum*, Leipzig, 1896.

Bieber, Margarete, *Die Denkmäler zum Theatherwesen im Altertum*, Berlin-Leipzig, 1920.

———, *The History of the Greek and Roman Theater*, rev. ed., Princeton, 1961.

Borrmann, Richard, *Geschichte der Baukunst*, I: *Altertum*, Leipzig, 1904.

Bötticher, Karl G. W., *Die Tektonik der Hellnen*, 2d ed., I–II, Berlin, 1869–1881.

Brooks, Alfred M., *Architecture: Our Debt to Greece and Rome*, Boston, 1924.

Bundgaard, Jens A., *Mnesicles*, Copenhagen, 1957.

Cali, François, *L'ordre grec*, Paris, 1958.

Chipiez, Charles, *Histoire critique des origines et de la formation des ordres grecs*, Paris, 1876.

———, *Le système modulaire et les proportions dans l'architecture grecque*, Paris, 1891.

Choisy, Auguste, *Histoire de l'architecture*, I, Paris, 1899.

Crema, Luigi, *Manuale di storia dell'architettura antica*, Milan, 1962.

Cultrera, Giuseppe, "Architettura Ippodamea: Contributo alla storia dell'edilizia nell'antichità," in *Memorie dell'Accademia dei Lincei*, XVII, 1923–1924.

Delbrück, Richard, *Hellenistische Bauten in Latium*, I-II, Strasbourg, 1907–1912.

Delorme, Jean, *Gymnasion: Étude sur les monuments consacrés à l'education en Grèce, des origines à l'empire romain (Bibliothèque des Écoles Françaises d'Athènes et de Rome*, vol. 195), Paris, 1960.

Demangel, Robert, *La frise ionique*, Paris, 1933.

Dinsmoor, William Bell, *The Architecture of Ancient Greece*, 3d ed., London, 1950.

Donaldson, Thomas L., *A Collection of the Most Approved Examples of Doorways from Ancient Buildings in Greece and Italy*, London, 1833.

Dörpfeld, Wilhelm, and Reisch, Emil, *Das griechische Theater*, Athens, 1896.

Doxiadis, Konstantinos A., *Raumordnung im griechischen Städtebau*, Heidelberg, 1937.

Drerup, Heinrich, *Griechische Architektur zur Zeit Homers*, Berlin, 1964.

Durm, Josef, *Constructive und polychrome: Details der griechischen Baukunst*, Berlin, 1880.

———, *Handbuch der Architektur: Die Baukunst der Griechen*, 3d ed., Leipzig, 1910.

Ebert, F., *Études épigraphiques sur l'architecture grecque*, Paris, 1883–1884.

Fensterbusch, Curt, *Das griechische Theater in klassischer Zeit*, Leipzig, 1927.

Feuger, L., *Die dorische Polychromie*, Berlin, 1886.

Fiechter, Ernst R., *Antike griechische Theaterbauten*, Stuttgart, 1930–.

———, *Die baugeschichtliche Entwicklung des antiken Theaters*, Munich, 1914.

Frickenhaus, August, *Die altgriechische Bühne*, Strasbourg, 1917.

Fyfe, Theodore, *Hellenistic Architecture: An Introductory Study*, Cambridge, 1936.

Gardner, Percy, and Blomfield, Reginald, *Greek Art and Architecture*, London, 1922.

Gerkan, Armin von, *Griechische Städteanlagen*, Berlin-Leipzig, 1924.

———, and Müller Wiener, W., *Das Theater von Epidauros*, Stuttgart, 1961.

Goodyear, William H., *Greek Refinements: Studies in Temperamental Architecture*, New Haven, 1912.

Grinnell, Isabel H., *Greek Temples*, New York, 1943.

Gropengiesser, Hildegund, *Die pflanzlichen Akrotere klassischer Tempel*, Mainz, 1961.

Gruben, Gottfried, *Die Tempel der Griechen*, Munich, 1966.

Haigh, Arthur E., and Pickard-Cambridge, Arthur W., *The Attic Theatre*, 3d ed., Oxford, 1907.

Hambidge, Jay, *The Parthenon and other Greek Temples: Their Dynamic Symmetry*, New Haven, 1924.

Hauck, Guido, *Die subjectiv Perspektive und die horizontalen Curvaturen des dorischen Stils*, Stuttgart, 1879.

Haverfield, Francis. J., *Ancient Town-Planning*, Oxford, 1913.

Hodge, A. Trevor, *The Woodwork of Greek Roofs*, New York, 1960.

Kähler, Heinz, *Der griechische Tempel*, Berlin, 1964.

Kohte, Julius, *Die Baukunst des klassischen Altertums*, Brunswick, 1915.

Koldewey, Robert, and Puchstein, Otto, *Die griechischen Tempel in Unteritalien und Sicilien*, Berlin, 1899.

Krauss, Friedrich, *Paestum: Die griechischen Tempel*, Berlin, 1941.

———, and Herbig, Reinhard, *Der korinthisch-dorische Tempel am Forum von Paestum*, Berlin, 1939.

Krell, Paul F., *Geschichte des dorischen Stils*, Stuttgart, 1870.

Krencker, Daniel, and Zschietzschmann, Willy, *Römische Tempel in Syrien*, Berlin-Leipzig, 1938.

Krischen, Fritz, *Die griechische Stadt: Wiederherstellung*, Berlin, 1938.

Laloux, Victor, *L'architecture grecque*, Paris, 1888.

Lappo Danilewski, O., *Untersuchungen über den Innenraum der archaischen griechischen Tempel*, Wurzburg, 1942.

Lattermann, H., *Griechische Bauinschriften*, Strasbourg, 1908.

Lawrence, Arnold W., *Greek Architecture*, Baltimore, 1957.

Lechat, Henri, *Le temple grec*, Paris, 1902.

Leroux, Gabriel, *Les origines de l'edifice hypostyle (Bibliothèque des Écoles Françaises d'Athènes et de Rome, vol. 108)*, Paris, 1913.

Libertini, Guido, *Il teatro greco e la sua evoluzione*, Catania, 1933.

Lichtenberg, Reinhold von, *Die ionische Säule als klassisches Bauglied rein hellenischen Geistes entwachsen*, Leipzig, 1907.

Luschan, Felix von, *Entstehung und Herkunft der ionischen Säule (Der Alte Orient, XIII)*, Leipzig, 1912.

McDonald, William A., *The Political Meeting Places of the Greeks*, Baltimore, 1943.

Marquand, Allan, *Greek Architecture*, New York–London, 1909.

Martienssen, R. D., *The Idea of Space in Greek Architecture*, Johannesburg, 1956.

Martin, Roland, *Manuel d'architecture grecque, I: Materiaux et techniques*, Paris, 1965.

———, *Recherches sur l'agora grecque (Bibliothèque des Écoles Françaises d'Athènes et de Rome, vol. 174)*, Paris, 1951.

Mauch, Johann M. von, *Die architektonischen Ordnungen der Griechen und Römer*, 7th ed., Berlin, 1875.

Mercklin, Eugen von, *Antike Figuralkapitelle*, Berlin, 1962.

Müfid Mansel, Arif, *Stockwerkbau der Griechen und Römer*, Berlin-Leipzig, 1932.

Müller, A., *Das attische Bühnenwesen*, Gütersloh, 1916.

Mussche, H. F., *Greek Architecture*, Leiden, 1964.

Neppi Modona, Aldo, *Gli edifici teatrali greci e romani*, Florence, 1961.

Orlandos, Anastasios, *Les materiaux de construction des anciens grecs*, I, Paris, 1966.

Pennethorne, John, *The Geometry and Optics of Ancient Architecture*, London-Edinburgh, 1878.

Penrose, Francis C., *An Investigation of the Principles of Athenian Architecture*, 2d ed., London, 1888.

Perrot, Georges, and Chipiez, Charles, *Histoire de l'art dans l'antiquité*, VII–VIII, Paris, 1898–1903.

Pickard-Cambridge, Arthur W., *The Theatre of Dionysus in Athens*, Oxford, 1946.

Praschniker, Camillo, *Zur Geschichte des Akroters*, Brno, 1929.

Puchstein, Otto, *Die griechische Bühne: Eine architektonische Untersuchung*, Berlin, 1901.

———, *Das ionische Kapitell*, Berlin, 1887.

———, *Die ionische Säule als klassisches Bauglied orientalischer Herkunft*, Leipzig, 1907.

Raphael, Max, *Der dorische Tempel*, Augsburg, 1930.

Rave, Paul O., *Griechische Tempel*, Marburg, 1924.

Rider, Bertha C., *The Ancient Greek House*, Chicago, 1964.

———, *The Greek House: Its History and Development from the Neolithic Period to the Hellenistic Age*, Cambridge, 1916.

Riehl, Hans, *Griechische Baukunst*, Munich, 1932.

Riemann, Paul, *Zum griechischen Peripteraltempel*, Dürm, 1935.

Robert, Fernand, *Thymele: Recherches sur la signification et la destination des monuments circulaires dans l'architecture religieuse de la Grèce*, Paris, 1939.

Robertson, Donald S., *A Handbook of Greek and Roman Architecture*, 2d ed., Cambridge, 1954.

Rodenwaldt, Gerhart, and Hege, Walter, *Griechische Tempel*, Berlin, 1941.

Roux, Georges, *L'architecture de l'Argolide aux IVe et IIIe siècles avant J.-C. (Bibliothèque des Écoles Françaises d'Athènes et de Rome, vol. 199)*, Paris, 1961.

Schede, Martin, *Antikes Traufleisten-Ornament*, Strasbourg, 1909.

Schlikker, Friedrich W., *Hellenistische Vorstellungen von der Schönheit nach Vitruv*, Berlin, 1940.

Schultze, Rudolf, *Basilika*, Berlin-Leipzig, 1928.

Scranton, Robert L., *Greek Architecture*, New York, 1962.

———, *Greek Walls*, Cambridge, Mass., 1941.

Shoe, Lucy T., *Profiles of Greek Mouldings*, Cambridge, Mass., 1936.

———, *Profiles of Western Greek Mouldings*, Rome, 1952.

Solon, Léon V., *Polychromy, Architectural and Structural*, New York, 1924.

Spiers, R. Phené, *The Orders of Architecture, Greek, Roman and Italian*, 3d ed., London, 1897.

Tatham, Charles H., *Etchings of Grecian and Roman Architectural Ornament*, London, 1893.

Theuer, Max, *Der griechisch-dorische Peripteraltempel*, Berlin, 1918.

Tiberi, Claudio, *Mnesikles, l'architetto dei Propilei*, Rome, 1964.

Valéry, Paul, *Eupalinos, or the Architect*, London, 1932.

Vetter, Max, *Der Sockel: Seine Form und Entwicklung in der griechischen und hellenistisch-römischen Architektur und Dekoration*, Strasbourg, 1910.

Volkert, Karl, *Das Akroter, I: Archaische Zeit*, Frankfurt a. m., 1932.

Warren, Herbert L., *The Foundations of Classical Architecture*, New York, 1919.

Weickert, Carl, *Das lesbische Kymation*, Leipzig, 1913.

———, *Typen der archaischen Architektur in Griechenland und Kleinasien*, Augsburg, 1929.

Wiegand, Edmund, *Vorgeschichte des korinthischen Kapitells*, Würzburg, 1920.

Wolfer Sulzer, Lucie, *Das geometrische Prinzip der griechisch-dorischen Tempel*, Winterthur, 1939.

Wycherly, Richard E., *How the Greeks Built Cities*, London-New York, 1949.

Wymer, J. E., *Marktplatzanlagen der Griechen und Römer*, Munich, 1916.

GREEK SCULPTURE: GENERAL WORKS

Alscher, Ludger, *Griechische Plastik*, 4 vols., Berlin, 1954–1957.

Arndt, Paul, and Lippold, Georg, *Photographische Einzelaufnahmen antiker Skulpturen*, Munich, 1893–.

Beazley, John D., and Ashmole, Bernard, *Greek Sculpture and Painting to the End of the Hellenistic Period*, New York, 1966.

Biesantz, Hagen, *Die thessalischen Grabreliefs*, Mainz, 1965.

Blümel, Carl, *Griechische Bildhauer an der Arbeit*, (4th ed.), Berlin, 1953. English trans., *Greek Sculptors at Work*, London, 1955.

Brunn, H., and Bruckmann, F., *Denkmäler griechischer und römischer Skulptur*, Munich, 1888–.

Budde, Ludwig, and Nicholls, R., *Catalogue of Greek and Roman Sculpture: Fitzwilliam Museum*, Cambridge, 1964.

Buschor, Ernst, *Die Plastik der Griechen*, Berlin, 1936.

Carpenter, Rhys, *Greek Sculpture*, Chicago, 1960.

Collignon, Maxime, *Histoire de la sculpture grecque*, I–II, Paris, 1892–1897.

———, *Les statues funéraires dans l'art grec*, Paris, 1911.

Conze, Alexander, *Die attischen Grabreliefs*, 4 vols., Berlin, 1890–1922.

Cook, Robert M., *Niobe and Her Children: A Subject of Greek Art*, New York, 1964.

Friis Johansen, Knud, *The Attic Grave-Reliefs of the Classical Period*, Copenhagen, 1951.

Furtwängler, Adolf, *Meisterwerke der griechischen Plastik*, Berlin, 1893. English trans. by Eugenie Sellers, *Masterpieces of Greek Sculpture*, London, 1895.

Gardner, Ernest A., *Handbook of Greek Sculpture*, London-New York, 1920.

Gerke, Friedrich, *Griechische Plastik in archaischer und klassischer Zeit*, Zurich-Berlin, 1938.

Greifenhagen, Adolf, *Antike Kunstwerke*, Berlin, 1966.

Hausmann, Ulrich, *Griechische Weihreliefs*, Berlin, 1960.

Kähler, Heinz, *Das griechische Metopenbild*, Munich, 1949.

Karageorghis, Vassos, *Sculptures from Salamis*, I, Nicosia, 1964.

———, and Vermeule, Cornelius C., *Sculptures from Salamis*, II, Nicosia, 1966.

Kekulé von Stradonitz, Reinhard, *Die griechische Skulptur*, Berlin, 1922.

Kraay, Colin M., and Hirmer, Max, *Greek Coins*, New York, 1966.

Lacroix, Léon, *Les reproductions de statues sur les monnaies grecques*, Liège, 1949.

Lapalus, Étienne, *Le fronton sculpté en Grèce des origines à la fin du IVe siècle*, Paris, 1947.

Lawrence, Arnold W., *Classical Sculpture*, London, 1929.

Lehmann, Phyllis (Williams), *Statues on Coins*, New York, 1946.

Lippold, Georg, *Kopien und Umbildungen griechischer Statuen*, Munich, 1923.

Loewy, Emmanuel, *Die griechische Plastik*, Leipzig, 1911.

Lullies, Reinhard, and Hirmer, Max, *Greek Sculpture*, New York, 1960.

Moebius, Hans, *Die Ornamente der griechischen Grabstelen klassischer und nachklassischer Zeit*, Berlin, 1929.

Murray, Alexander S., *A History of Greek Sculpture*, London, 1890.

Muthmann, Fritz, *Statuenstützen und dekoratives Beiwerk an griechischen und römischen Bildwerken*, Heidelberg, 1951.

Neugebauer, Karl A., *Antike Bronzestatuetten*, Berlin, 1921.

Picard, Charles, *Manuel d'archéologie grecque; La sculpture*, I–III, Paris, 1935–1948.

———, *La sculpture antique*, I–II, Paris, 1923–1926.

Reinach, Salomon, *Recueil de têtes antiques*, Paris, 1903.

———, *Répertoire de reliefs grecs et romains*, 3 vols., Paris, 1909–1912.

———, *Répertoire de la statuaire*, 5 vols., Paris, 1916–1924.

Reutersward, Patrik, *Studien zur Polychromie der Plastik: Griechenland und Rom*, Stockholm, 1960.

Richter, Gisela M. A., *Three Critical Periods in Greek Sculpture*, New York, 1951.

———, *The Sculpture and Sculptors of the Greeks*, New Haven, 1930; 2d ed. rev., 1950.

Rodenwaldt, Gerhart, *Das Relief bei den Griechen*, Berlin, 1923.

Schoder, Raymond V., *Masterpieces of Greek Art*, New York, 1965.

Schuchhardt, Walter H., *Die Epochen der griechischen Plastik*, Baden-Baden, 1959.

———, *Griechische Plastik*, Berlin, 1938.

Studniczka, Franz, *Die griechische Kunst an Kriegergräbern*, Leipzig-Berlin, 1915.

Wace, Alan J. B., *An Approach to Greek Sculpture*, Cambridge, Eng., 1935.

Waldmann, Emil, *Griechische Originale*, Leipzig, 1914.

PORTRAITS

Arndt, Paul, and Bruckmann, Friedrich, *Griechische und römische Porträts*, Munich, 1891–.

Babelon, Jean, *Le portrait dans l'antiquité d'après les monnaies*, Paris, 1942.

Bernoulli, Johann J., *Die erhaltenen Darstellungen Alexanders des Grossen*, Munich, 1905.

———, *Griechische Ikonographie*, Munich, 1901.

Bieber, Margarete, "The Portraits of Alexander the Great," in *Proceedings of the American Philosophical Society*, XCIII, 1949.

Boehringer, Robert, *Das Antlitz des Genius, Homer*, Breslau, 1937.

———, *Homer, Bildnisse und Nachweise*, Breslau, 1923.

———, *Platon, Bildnisse und Nachweise*, Breslau, 1935.

Buschor, Ernst, *Das hellenistische Bildnis*, Munich, 1949.

Crome, J. F., "Das Bildnis Vergils," in *Atti e Memorie della R. Accademia di Mantova*, 1935.

Delbrück, Richard, *Antike Porträts*, Bonn, 1912.

Hafner, German, *Späthellenistische Bildnisplastik: Versuch einer landschaftlichen Gliederung*, Berlin, 1954.

Heintze, Helga von, *Das Bildnis der Sappho*, Mainz-Berlin, 1966.

Hekler, Anton, *Die Bildniskunst der Griechen und Römer*, Stuttgart, 1912.

———, *Bildnisse berühmter Griechen*, Berlin, 1942; 3d ed. rev. by H. von Heintze, Berlin, 1962.

Hinks, Roger P., *Greek and Roman Portrait-Sculpture*, London, 1935.

Imhoof-Blumer, Friedrich, *Porträtköpfe auf antiken Münzen hellenistischer und hellenisierter Völker*, Leipzig, 1885.

Kekulé von Stradonitz, Reinhard, "Strategenköpfe," in *Altertümer der K. Preussischen Akademie der Wissenschaft*, 1910.

Koepp, Friedrich, "Über das Bildnis Alexanders des Grossen," in 52 *Berliner Winckelmannsprogramm*, Berlin, 1892.

Lange, Kurt, *Herrscherköpfe des Altertums*, Berlin, 1938.

Laurenzi, Luciano, *Ritratti greci*, Florence, 1941.

Lippold, Georg, *Griechische Porträtstatuen*, Munich, 1912.

Lorenz, Thuri, *Galerien von griechischen Philosophen- und Dichterbildnisse bei den Römern*, Mainz, 1965.

Michalowski, Kazmierz, *Les portraits hellénistiques et romains (École française d'Athène. Exploration archéologique de Délos, fasc. 13)*, Paris, 1932.

Newell, Edward T., *Royal Greek Portrait Coins*, New York, 1937.

Pfuhl, Ernst, *Die Anfänge der griechischen Bildniskunst*, Munich, 1927.

Poulsen, Frederik, *Greek and Roman Portraits in English Country Houses*, Oxford, 1923.

Richter, Gisela M. A., *Greek Portraits: A Study of their Development (Collection Latomus, XX)*, Brussels, 1955.

———, *The Portraits of the Greeks*, 3 vols., London, 1965.

404

Rosenbaum, Elisabeth, *A Catalogue of Cyrenaican Portrait Sculpture*, London, 1960.

Schefold, Karl, *Die Bildnisse der antiken Dichter, Redner und Denker*, Basel, 1943.

_____, *Griechische Dichterbildnisse*, Zurich, 1965.

Schweitzer, Bernhard, "Griechische Porträtkunst: Problem und Forschungsstand," in *Acta Congressus Madvigiani*, 1957. Reprinted in B. Schweitzer, *Zur Kunst der Antike*, Tübingen, II, 1963.

_____, "Studien zur Entstehung des Porträts bei den Griechen," in *Abhandlungen der Sächsischen Akademie*, XCI, 1940. Reprinted in B. Schweitzer, *Zur Kunst der Antike*, Tübingen, II, 1963.

Studniczka, Franz, *Das Bildnis des Aristoteles*, Leipzig, 1908.

Suhr, Elmer G., *Sculptured Portraits of Greek Statesmen with a Special Study of Alexander the Great* (The Johns Hopkins University Studies in Archaeology, XIII) Baltimore-London-Oxford, 1931.

Traversari, Gustavo, *Statue iconiche femminili cirenaiche*, Rome, 1960.

Visconti, Ennio Q., *Iconographie grecque*, Paris, 1808.

Waldhauer, Oskar, *Über einige Porträts Alexanders des Grossen*, Munich, 1903.

Wulff, Oskar, *Alexander mit der Lanze*, Berlin, 1898.

SCULPTURE OF THE ARCHAIC PERIOD

Akurgal, Ekrem, *Griechische Reliefs des VI Jahrhunderts aus Lydien*, Berlin, 1942.

Blümel, Carl, *Die archaische-griechischen Skulpturen der Staatlichen Museen zu Berlin*, Berlin, 1963.

_____, *Griechische Skulpturen des sechsten und fünften Jahrhunderts v. Chr., Staatliche Museen zu Berlin*, Berlin-Leipzig, 1940.

_____, *Katalog der griechischen Skulpturen des fünften und vierten Jahrhunderts v. Chr.*, Berlin, 1928.

Borda, Maurizio, "Kyprios Character: Aspetti della scultura arcaica cipriota," in *Rendiconti della Pontificia Accademia*, XXII, 1948.

Budde, Ludwig, *Die attischen Kouroi*, Würzburg, 1939.

Buschor, Ernst, *Altsamische Standbilder: Bilderhefte antiker Kunst*, I–V, Berlin, 1934–1960.

_____, *Frühgriechische Jünglinge*, Munich, 1950.

Caputo, Giacomo, "Tre xoana e il culto di una sorgente sulfurea in territorio Geleo-Agrigentino," in *Monumenti Antichi dei Lincei*, XXXVII, 1938.

Casson, Stanley, *The Technique of Early Greek Sculpture*, Oxford, 1933.

Charbonneaux, Jean, *La sculpture archaïque*, Paris, 1938.

Conze, Alexander, *Zur Geschichte der Anfänge griechischer Kunst*, Vienna, 1870.

Demargne, Pierre, *La Crète dédalique*, Paris, 1947.

_____, *Naissance de l'art grec*, Paris, 1964.

Deonna, Waldemar, *Les Apollons archaïques*, Geneva, 1909.

_____, *Dédale ou la statue de la Grèce archaïque*, I–II, Geneva, 1930–1931.

Dickins, Guy, *Catalogue of the Acropolis Museum*, I, Cambridge, Eng., 1912.

Dörig, J., and Gigon, O., *Der Kampf der Götter und Titanen*, (Bibliotheca Helvetica Romana), Olten-Lausanne, 1961.

Dunbabin, Thomas J., *The Greeks and their Eastern Neighbours*, London, 1957.

Gotsmich, Alois, *Studien zur ältesten griechischen Kunst*, Prague, 1930.

Grace, Frederick R., *Archaic Sculpture in Boeotia*, Cambridge, Mass., 1939.

Hampe, Roland, *Frühe griechische Sagenbilder in Böotien*, Athens, 1936.

Heberdey, Rudolf, *Altattische Porosskulptur*, Vienna, 1919.

Homann-Wedeking, Ernst, *Die Anfänge der griechischen Grossplastik*, Berlin, 1950.

_____, *Das archaische Griechenland*, Baden-Baden, 1966.

Invernizzi, Antonio, *I frontoni del tempio di Aphaia ad Egina*, Turin, 1965.

Janni, Pietro, *La cultura di Sparta arcaica*, Rome, 1965.

Jenkins, Romilly J., *Dedalica: A Study of Dorian Plastic Art in the Seventh Century B.C.*, Cambridge, Eng., 1936.

Kähler, Heinz, *Das griechische Metopenbild*, Munich, 1949.

Karo, Georg, *Greek Personality in Archaic Sculpture*, Cambridge, Mass., 1948.

Karousos, Christos, *Aristodikos: Zur Geschichte der spätarchaisch-attischen Plastik und der Grabstatuen*, Stuttgart, 1961.

Krahmer, Gerhard, "Figur und Raum in der ägyptischen und griechish-archaischen Kunst," in *28 Hallisches Winckelmanns programm*, 1931.

La Coste-Messelière, Pierre de, *Au Musée de Delphes, recherches sur quelques monuments archaïques et leur décor sculpté*, Paris, 1936.

Langlotz, Ernst, *Die archaischen Marmorskulpturen der Akropolis*, Frankfort, 1930.

_____, *Frühgriechische Bildhauerschulen*, Nuremberg, 1927.

_____, and Schuchhardt, Walter H., *Archaische Plastik auf der Akropolis*, Frankfort, 1943.

Lechat, Henri, *Au Musée de L'Acropole*, Lyons, 1903.

Loewy, Emmanuel, *Die Naturwiedergabe in der älteren griechischen Kunst*, Rome, 1900. English trans. by John Fothergill, *The Rendering of Nature in Early Greek Art*, London, 1907.

Luca, Gioia De, "Kouroi in Italienische Museen," in *Antike Plastik*, III, 2, 1964.

Milchöfer, Arthur, *Die Anfänge der Kunst in Griechenland*, Leipzig, 1883.

Minto, Antonio, "Figure virili arcaiche (kouroi) del Museo Archeologico di Firenze," in *La Critica d'Arte*, VIII, new series III, 1943.

Müller, Valentin, *Frühe Plastik in Griechenland und Vorderasien: Ihre Typenbildung von der neolithischen bis in die griechisch-archaische Zeit*, Augsburg, 1929.

Niemeyer, Haus Georg, "Attische Bronzestatuetten der spätarchaischen und frühklassischen Zeit," in *Antike Plastik*, III, 1, 1964.

Payne, Humfrey, and Young, Gerard, *Archaic Marble Sculptures from the Acropolis*, London, 1936.

Poulsen, Frederik, *Der Orient und die frühgriechische Kunst*, Leipzig-Berlin, 1912.

Raubitschek, Antony E., *Dedications from the Athenian Acropolis*, Cambridge, Mass., 1949.

Richter, Gisela M. A., *Archaic Attic Gravestones*, Cambridge, Mass., 1944.

_____, *Archaic Greek Art*, New York, 1949.

_____, *Kouroi: A Study of the Development of the Greek Kouros from the Late Seventh to the Early Fifth Century B.C.*, New York, 1942; 2d ed., London, 1960.

Rodenwaldt, Gerhart, *Altdorische Bildwerke in Korfu*, Berlin, 1938.

_____, Schleiff, H., and Rhomaios, K., *Korkyra*, I–II, Berlin, 1939–1940.

Rumpf, Andreas, "Endoios, ein Versuch," in *La Critica d'Arte*, III, 1938.

Schefold, Karl, *Griechische Plastik*, I: *Die grossen Bildhauer des archaischen Athen*, Basel, 1949.

_____, *Myth and Legend in Early Greek Art*, New York, 1967.

Schrader, H., Langlotz, E., and Schuchhardt, W. H., *Die archaische Plastik auf der Akropolis*, Frankfort, 1939.

Schuchhardt, Walter H., *Archaische Giebelkompositionen*, Freiburg, 1940.

——————, *Archaische Plastik der Griechen*, Stuttgart, 1957.

Zancani-Montuoro, P. and Zanotti-Bianco, U., *Heraion alla foce del Sele*, I–II, Rome, 1951–1954.

SCULPTURE OF THE SEVERE STYLE

Alscher, Ludwig, *Götter vor Gericht*, Berlin, 1963.

Arias, Paolo E., *Mirone*, Florence, 1940.

Baroni, Fiorenza, *Osservazioni sul Trono di Boston*, Rome, 1961.

Becatti, Giovanni, *Il maestro di Olimpia*, Florence, 1943.

Beyen, Hendrik G., and Vollgraff, Carl W., *Argos et Sicyone: Études relatives à la sculpture grecque de style sévère*, The Hague, 1947.

Brunnsäker, Sture, *The Tyrant-Slayers of Kritios and Nesiotes*, Lund, 1955.

Buschor, Ernst, and Hamann, Richard, *Die Skulpturen des Zeustempels zu Olympia*, Marburg, 1924.

Della Seta, Alessandro, "La genesi dello scorcio nell'arte greca," in *Memorie dell'Accademia dei Lincei*, XII, 1906.

Dörig, Jose, "Kalamis-studien," in *Jahrbuch des Deutschen Archäologischen Instituts*, 1965.

Hafner, German, "Ein Apollon-kopf in Frankfurt und die Niobiden-gruppe des V Jahrhunderts," in *Deutsche Beiträge zur Altertumswissenschaft*, XVII, Baden-Baden, 1962.

Hege, Walter, and Rodenwaldt, Gerhart, *Olympia*, London, 1936.

Langlotz, Ernst, *Frühgriechische Bildhauerschulen*, Nuremberg, 1927.

——————, *Das Ludovisische Relief*, Mainz, 1951.

——————, *Zur Zeitbestimmung der streng-rotfigurigen Vasenmalerei und der gleichzeitigen Plastik*, Leipzig, 1920.

Orlandini, Piero, *Calamide*, Bologna, 1950.

Paribeni, Enrico, *Museo Nazionale Romano: Le sculture greche del V secolo*, Rome, 1954.

Pfuhl, Ernst, "Spätjonische Plastik," in *Jahrbuch des Deutschen Archäologischen Instituts*, L, 1935.

Polacco, Luigi, *L'Atleta Cirene-Perinto*, Rome, 1955.

Poulsen, Vagn H., "Myron: Ein stilkritischer Versuch," in *Acta Archaeologica*, XI, 1940.

——————, "Der strenge Stil," in *Acta Archaeologica*, VII, 1937.

Rodenwaldt, Gerhart, *Olympia*, Berlin, 1936; 2d. ed., 1941.

Stucchi, Sandro, "Nota introduttiva sulle correzioni ottiche nell'arte greca fino a Mirone," in *Annuario della Scuola Archeologica Italiana di Atene*, XXX–XXXII, new series XIV–XVI, 1952-1954, (1955).

SCULPTURE OF THE CLASSICAL PERIOD: SECOND HALF OF THE FIFTH CENTURY

Arias, Paolo E., *Policleto*, Milan, 1964.

Becatti, Giovanni, "Postille partenoniche," in *Archaeologia Classica*, 1965.

——————, *Problemi Fidiaci*, Milan-Florence, 1951.

Berger, Ernst, *Parthenon Ostgiebel*, Bonn, 1959.

Bianchi Bandinelli, Ranuccio, *Policleto*, Florence, 1938.

Binnebössel, Rosemarie, *Studien zu den attischen Urkundenreliefs*, dissertation, Leipzig, 1932.

Blümel, Carl, "Der Fries des Tempels der Athena Nike, in der attischen Kunst des 5 Jahrhunderts v. Chr.," in *Jahrbuch des Deutschen Archäologischen Instituts*, LXV–LXVI, 1950–1951.

Blümel, Carl, *Die klassischen griechischen Skulpturen der Staatliche Museen zu Berlin*, Berlin, 1966.

——————, *Römische Kopien griechischer Skulpturen des fünften Jahrhunderts v. Chr.*, Berlin, 1931.

Brommer, Frank, *Die Skulpturen der Parthenon Giebel*, Mainz, 1963.

——————, *Die Metopen des Parthenon*, Mainz, 1967.

Buschor, Ernst, *Pferde des Phidias*, Munich, 1948.

Caputo, Giacomo, *Lo scultore del grande bassorilievo con la danza delle Menadi in Tolemaide*, Rome, 1948.

Carpenter, Rhys, *The Esthetic Basis of Greek Art of the Fifth and Fourth Centuries B. C.*, rev. ed., Bloomington, Ind., 1959.

——————, *The Sculpture of the Nike Temple Parapet*, Cambridge, Mass., 1929.

Charbonneaux, Jean, *La sculpture grecque classique*, Paris, 1943.

Devambez, Pierre, *L'art au siècle de Périclès*, Lausanne, 1955.

Diepolder, Hans, *Die attischen Grabreliefs des 5 und 4 Jahrhunderts v. Chr.*, Berlin, 1931.

Dohrn, Tobias, *Attische Plastik vom Tode des Phidias bis zum Werke der grossen Meister des IV Jahrhunderts v. Chr.*, Krefeld, 1957.

Eichler, Fritz, *Die Reliefs des Heroon von Gjölbaschi-Trysa*, Vienna, 1950.

Himmelmann-Wildschnitz, Nikolaus, *Studien zum Ilissosrelief*, Munich, 1956.

Hofkes-Brukker, Chartine, "Die Nike des Paionios und der Bassaefries," in *Bulletin van de Antieke Beschaving*, 1961.

Kenner, Hedwig, *Der Fries des Tempels von Bassae-Phigalia*, Vienna, 1946.

Kjellberg, Lennart, *Studien zu den attischen Reliefs des V Jahrhunderts v. Chr.*, Uppsala, 1926.

Kleemann, Ilae, *Der Satrapen-Sarkophag aus Sidon* (*Istanbuler Forschungen*, XX), Berlin, 1958.

Koch, Herbert, *Studien zum Theseustempel in Athen*, Berlin, 1955.

Langlotz, Ernst, "Alkamenesprobleme," in *108 Berliner Winckelmannsprogramm*, Berlin, 1952.

——————, *Aphrodite in den Gärten*, Heidelberg, 1954.

——————, *Phidias und der Parthenon*, Stuttgart, 1965.

——————, *Phidiasprobleme*, Frankfort, 1947.

Laurenzi, Luciano, *Umanità di Fidia* (*Studia Archaeologica*, III), Rome, 1961.

Liegle, Josef, *Der Zeus des Phidias*, Berlin, 1952.

Mallwitz, Alfred, and Schiering, Wolfgang, *Die Werkstatt des Pheidias in Olympia*, Berlin, 1964.

Noack, Friedrich, "Amazonstudien," in *Jahrbuch des Deutschen Archäologischen Instituts*, XXX, 1915.

Orlandini, Piero, "Kresilas," in *Memorie dell'Accademia dei Lincei*, VIII, vol. IV, fasc. 5, 1952.

Poulsen, Vagn H., *Phidias und sein Kreis*, (*Ny Carlsberg Glyptothek, Publications*, no. 3), Copenhagen, 1942.

Praschniker, Camillo, *Parthenonstudien*, Augsburg, 1928.

Rizzo, Giulio E., *Thiasos*, Rome, 1934.

Rodenwaldt, Gerhart, *Köpfe von den Südmetopen des Parthenon*, Berlin, 1948.

Schmidt, Eva Maria, "Der Kasseler Apollon und seine Repliken," in *Antike Plastik*, V, 1966.

Schrader, Hans, *Phidias*, Frankfort, 1924.

Schweitzer, Bernhard, "Prolegomena zur Kunst der Parthenonmeister," in *Jahrbuch des Deutschen Archäologischen Instituts*, LIII, 1938; LIV, 1939; "Pheidias der Parthenonmeister", *ibid.*, LV, 1940.

Thompson, Homer A., "The Altar of Pity in the Athenian Agora," in *Hesperia*, XXI, 1952.

——————, "The Pedimental Sculpture of the Hephaisteion," in *Hesperia*, XVIII, 1949.

SCULPTURE OF THE CLASSICAL PERIOD : FOURTH CENTURY

Adriani, Achille, "Alla ricerca di Briasside," in *Memorie dell'Accademia dei Lincei*, VIII, vol. I, fasc. 10, 1948.

Amelung, Walter, *Die Basis des Praxiteles aus Mantinea: Archaeologische Studien*, Munich, 1895.

————, "Saggio sull'arte del IV sec. a. C.," in *Ausonia*, III, 1908.

Arias, Paolo E., *Skopas*, Rome, 1952.

Becatti, Giovanni, "Un dodekatheon ostiense e l'arte di Prassitele," in *Annuario della Scuola Archeologica Italiana di Atene*, 1939–1940, (1942).

Blinkenberg, Christian, *Knidia: Beiträge zur Kenntnis der Praxitelischen Aphrodite*, Copenhagen, 1933.

Blümel, Carl, *Hermes eines Praxiteles*, Baden-Baden, 1944.

————, *Römische Kopien griechischer Skulpturen des vierten Jahrhunderts v. Chr.*, Berlin, 1938.

Collignon, Maxime, *Scopas et Praxitèles*, Paris, 1907.

Crome, J. F., *Die Skulpturen des Asklepiostempels von Epidauros*, Berlin, 1951.

Kabus-Jahm, Renate, *Studien zu Frauenfiguren den vierten Jahrhunderts vor Christus*, Dissertation Freiburg 1962, Darmstadt, 1963.

Klein, Wilhelm, *Praxiteles*, Leipzig, 1898.

————, *Praxitelische Studien*, Leipzig, 1899.

Marella, Maria Luigia, *Ricerche e studi sulla scultura greca del IV secolo*, Rome, 1939.

Pfuhl, Ernst, "Bemerkungen zum Kunst des vierten Jahrhunderts," in *Jahrbuch des Deutschen Archäologischen Instituts*, XLIII, 1928.

Rizzo, Giulio E., *Prassitele*, Milan, 1932.

Schlörb, Barbara, "Timotheos," in *Jahrbuch des Deutschen Archäologischen Instituts*, Ergänzungsheft XXII, 1965.

Süsserott, Hans K., *Griechische Plastik des vierten Jahrhundert v. Chr.*, Frankfort, 1938.

Webster, Thomas B. L., *Art and Literature in Fourth-Century Athens*, London, 1956.

SCULPTURE OF THE HELLENISTIC PERIOD

Adriani, Achille, *Documenti e ricerche di arte alessandrina*, I: *Sculture monumentali del Museo Greco-romano di Alessandria*, Rome, 1946.

————, *Repertorio d'arte dell'Egitto greco-romano*, I–II, Palermo, 1961.

———— *Testimonianze e momenti di scultura alessandrina*, Rome, 1948.

Andrén, Arvid, "Il torso del Belvedere," in *Opuscula Archaeologica*, VII, 1953.

Becatti, Giovanni, "Attikà: saggio sulla scultura attica dell'ellenismo," in *Rivista dell'Istituto di Archeologia e Storia dell'Arte*, VII, 1940.

Bieber, Margarete, *The Sculpture of the Hellenistic Age*, New York, 1955; enlarged ed., 1961.

Bienkowski, Piotr R., *Les Celtes dans les arts mineurs gréco-romains*, Cracow, 1928.

————, *Die Darstellung der Gallier in der hellenistischen Kunst*, Vienna, 1908.

Borda, Maurizio, *La scuola di Pasiteles*, Bari, 1953.

Borrelli, Licia, "Una scuola di manieristi dell'ellenismo rodio-asiatico," in *Rendiconti dell'Accademia dei Lincei*, VIII, vol. IV, 1949.

Bruns, Gerda, *Der grosse Altar von Pergamon*, Berlin, 1949.

Bulle, Heinrich, "Archaisierende griechische Rundplastik," in *Abhandlungen, Bayerische Akademie*, XXX, 1918.

Cultrera, Giuseppe, *Saggi sull'arte ellenistica e romana*, I: *La corrente asiana*, Rome, 1907.

Deubner, Otfried, *Hellenistische Apollogestalten*, Athens, 1934.

Dickins, Guy, "Damophon of Messene," in *Annual of the British School of Athens*, XII, 1905–1906.

————, *Hellenistic Sculpture*, Oxford, 1920.

Dimitriou, Penelope, *The Polychromy of Greek Sculpture to the Beginning of the Hellenistic Period*, New York, 1951.

Dohrn, Tobias, *Die Tyche von Antiochia*, Berlin, 1960.

Folman, Michel, *Introduction à l'étude de la sculpture archaïsante*, Montpellier, 1935.

Forti, Lidia, *Le danzatrici di Ercolano*, Naples, 1959.

Fuchs, Werner, "Die Vorbilder der neuattischen Reliefs," in *Jahrbuch des Deutschen Archäologischen Instituts*, Ergänzungsheft XX, 1959.

Goethert, Friedrich W., and Schleif, Hans, *Der Athenatempel von Ilion*, Berlin, 1962.

Hauser, Friedrich, *Die neuattischen Reliefs*, Stuttgart, 1889.

Herkenrath, Emil, *Der Fries des Artemisions von Magnesia*, Berlin, 1902.

Holden, Beatrice Mills, *The Metopes of the Temple of Athena at Ilion*, Northhampton, Mass., 1964.

Horn, Rudolf, "Hellenistische Köpfe," in *Römische Mitteilungen des Deutschen Archäologischen Instituts*, LII, 1937.

————, "Stehende weibliche Gewandstatuen in der hellenistischen Plastik," in *Römische Mitteilungen des Deutschen Archäologischen Instituts, Ergänzungsheft*, II, 1931.

Johnson, Franklin P., *Lysippos*, Durham, N.C., 1927.

Kähler, Heinz, *Der Fries vom Reiterdenkmal des Aemilius Paulus in Delphi*, Berlin, 1965.

————, *Der grosse Fries von Pergamon*, Berlin, 1948.

————, *Pergamon*, Berlin, 1949.

Karousos, Christos, "Archaistikà," in *Archaiologikon Deltion*, X, 1926.

Klein, Wilhelm, *Vom antiken Rokokò*, Vienna, 1921.

Krahmer, Gerhard, "Die einsichtige Gruppe und die späthellenistische Kunst," in *Nachrichten der Gesellschaft der Wissenschaften zu Göttingen, Philol. hist. Klasse*, 1927.

————, "Stilphasen der hellenistischen Plastik," in *Römische Mitteilungen des Deutschen Archäologischen Instituts*, XXXVIII–XXXIX, 1923–1924.

Laurenzi, Luciano, "Problemi della scultura ellenistica: La scultura rodia," in *Rivista dell'Istituto di Archeologia e Storia dell'Arte*, VII, 1940.

Lawrence, Arnold W., *Later Greek Sculpture and its Influence on East and West*, London, 1927.

Lehmann, Phyllis (Williams), *The Pedimental Sculpture of the Hieron in Samothrace*, New York, 1962.

Luschey, Heinz, *Funde zu dem grossen Fries von Pergamon*, Berlin, 1962.

Mansuelli, Guido A., "I Cleomeni ateniesi, un'officina neo-attica nell'ambiente romano del I secolo a. C.," in *Rendiconti dell'Accademia delle Scienze di Bologna*, VI, vol. VI, 1955.

Maviglia, Ada, *L'attività artistica di Lisippo*, Rome, 1914.

Möbius, Hans, *Alexandria und Rom*, Munich, 1964.

Müller, Wolfgang, *Der Pergamonaltar*, Leipzig, 1964.

Napp, Adolf E., *Der Altar von Pergamon*, Munich, 1936.

Noshy, Ibrahim, *The Arts in Ptolemaic Egypt: A Study of Greek and Egyptian Influences in Ptolemaic Architecture and Sculpture*, London, 1937.

Pinkwart, Doris, *Das Relief des Archelaos von Priene und die Musen des Philiskos*, Kallmünz, 1965.

————, " Das Relief des Archelaos von Priene " in *Antike Plastik*, IV, 1965.

Richter, Gisela M. A., *Three Critical Periods in Greek Sculpture*, New York, 1951.

Rohde, Elisabeth, *Pergamon: Burgberg und Altar*, Berlin, 1961.

Rumpf, Andreas, "Boethoi," in *Österreichische Jahreshefte*, XXXIX, 1952.

Salis, Arnold von, *Der Altar von Pergamon*, Berlin, 1912.

————, "Löwenkampfbilder des Lysipp," in *112 Berliner Winckelmannsprogramm*, Berlin, 1956.

Schede, Martin, "Zu Philiskos, Archelaos und den Musen," in *Römische Mitteilungen des Deutschen Archäologischen Instituts*, XXXV, 1920.

Schmidt, Eduard, *Archaistische Kunst in Griechenland und Rom*, Munich, 1922.

————, *Der grosse Altar zu Pergamon*, Leipzig, 1961. English trans., *The Great Altar of Pergamon*, Leipzig 1962.

Schober, Arnold, *Der Fries des Hekataions von Lagyna* (*Istanbuler Forschungen*, II), Baden bei Wien, 1933.

————, *Die Kunst von Pergamon*, Vienna, 1951.

Schrammen, Jakob, *Altertümer von Pergamon*, III, 1: *Der Grosse Altar*, Berlin, 1906.

Schreiber, Theodor, *Der Gallierkopf des Museums in Gizeh bei Kairo*, Leipzig, 1896.

————, *Die hellenistischen Reliefbilder*, Leipzig, 1894.

————, *Die Wiener Brunnenreliefs aus Palazzo Grimani: Eine Studie über das hellenistische Reliefbild mit Untersuchungen über die bildende Kunst in Alexandrien*, Leipzig, 1888.

Schuchhardt, Walter H., *Die Meister der grossen Friese von Pergamon*, Berlin, 1925.

Schwarzenberg, E., *Die Grazien*, Bonn, 1966.

Schweitzer, Bernard, "Die Menelaos-Patroklos Gruppe: Ein verlorenes Meisterwerk hellenistischer Kunst," in *Die Antike*, XIV, 1938. Reprinted in Bernhard Schweitzer, *Zur Kunst der Antike*, Tübingen, 1963.

————, "Das Original der sogenannten Pasquinogruppe," in *Abhandlungen der Sächsischen Akademie der Wissenschaften, Philol. hist. Klasse*, XLIII, no. 4, 1936.

Sichtermann, Hellmut, "Der Knabe von Tralles," in *Antike Plastik*, IV, 1965.

Sjöqvist, Erik, "The Early Style of Lysippus," in *Opuscula Atheniensia*, I, 1953.

Squarciapino, Maria, *La scuola di Afrodisia*, Rome, 1943.

Stähler, K. P., *Das Unklassische im Telephosfries*, Münster, 1966.

Stark, Karl B., *Niobe und die Niobiden*, Leipzig, 1863.

Studniczka, Franz, "Artemis und Iphigenie," in *Abhandlungen der Sächsischen Akademie der Wissenschaften, Philol. hist. Klasse*, XXXVII, no. 5, 1926.

Visscher, Fernand de, *Herakles Epitrapezios*, Paris, 1962.

Watzinger, Carl, "Das Relief des Archelaos von Priene," in *63 Berliner Winckelmannsprogramm*, Berlin, 1903.

Webster, Thomas B. L., *Hellenistic Poetry and Art*, London, 1964.

Winnefeld, Hermann, *Altertümer von Pergamon*, III, 2: *Die Friese des grossen Altars*, Berlin, 1910.

Winter, Franz, *Der Alexandersarkophag von Sidon*, Strasbourg, 1912.

————, *Altertümer von Pergamon*, VII: *Die Skulpturen*, Berlin, 1908.

GREEK TERRACOTTAS

Besques-Mollard, Simone, *Catalogue raisonné des figurines et reliefs en terre cuite grecs, étrusques et romains, Musée National du Louvre*, Paris, 1954.

Breitenstein, Niels J., *Catalogue of the Terracottas, Cypriote, Greek, Etrusco-Italian and Roman: Danish National Museum*, Copenhagen, 1941.

Burr, Dorothy, *Terracottas from Myrina in the Museum of Fine Arts, Boston*, Vienna, 1934. See also, Thompson, Dorothy Burr.

Campana, A., *Museo Campana: Antiche opere in plastica*, Roma, 1851.

Charbonneaux, Jean, *Les terres cuites grecques*, Paris, 1936.

Chéhab, Maurice H., *Les terres cuites de Kharayet*, Paris, 1951–1952.

Froehner, Wilhelm, *Terres cuites d'Asie de la Collection Julien Gréan*, Paris, 1886.

Graindor, Paul, *Terres cuites de l'Égypte gréco-romain*, Antwerp, 1939.

Higgins, R. A., *Catalogue of the Terracottas in the Department of Greek and Roman Antiquities, British Museum*, London, 1954.

Hutton, Caroline A., *Greek Terracotta Statuettes*, London, 1899.

Jacobsthal, Paul, *Die Melischen Reliefs*, Berlin, 1931.

Kaufmann, Carl M., *Graeco-ägyptische Koroplastik*, Leipzig-Cairo, 1915.

Kekulé von Stradonitz, Reinhard, *Die antiken Terrakotten von Sizilien*, Berlin-Stuttgart, 1884.

Kleiner, Gerhard, "Tanagrafiguren," in *Jahrbuch des Deutschen Archäologischen Instituts*, Ergänzungsheft XV, 1942.

Knoblauch, Peter, *Studien zur archaisch-griechischen Tonbildnerei in Kreta, Athen und Böotien*, Bleicherode am Harz, 1937.

Koester, August, *Die griechischen Terrakotten*, Berlin, 1926.

Laumonier, Alfred, *Les figurines de terre cuite*, (*École Française d'Athène, Exploration Archéologique de Délos*, fasc. 23), Paris, 1956.

Laumonier, H., *Catalogue des terres cuites du Musée Archéologique de Madrid*, Bordeaux, 1921.

Lengyel, Ilse Schneider, *Griechische Terrakotten*, Munich, 1936.

Lenormant, François, *Collection Camille Lecuyer, terres cuites antiques trouvées en Grèce et en Asie Mineure*, Paris, 1882.

Levi, Alda, *Le terracotte figurate del Museo Nazionale di Napoli*, Florence, 1921.

Mendel, Gustave, *Catalogue des figurines grecques de terre cuite, Musées impériaux ottomans*, Constantinople, 1908.

Neutsch, Bernhard, "Studien zur vortanagräisch-attischen Koroplastik," in *Jahrbuch des Deutschen Archäologischen Instituts*, Ergänzungsheft XVII, 1952.

Panofka, Theodor, *Terrakotten des Königliche Museum*, Berlin, 1842.

Paul, Eberhard, *Antike Welt in Ton: griechisch und römische Terrakotten des Archäologisches Instituts in Leipzig*, Leipzig, 1959.

Perdrizet, Paul, *Les terres cuites d'Égypte de la Collection Fouquet*, Nancy-Paris, 1921.

Pottier, Edmond, *Diphilos et les modeleurs de terre cuites grecques*, Paris, 1909.

————, *Les statuettes de terre cuite dans l'antiquité*, Paris, 1890.

————, and Reinach, Salomon, *La nécropole de Myrina*, Paris, 1887.

Poulsen, Vagn H., *Catalogue des terres cuites grecques et romains, Ny Carlsberg Glyptothek*, Copenhagen, 1949.

Quarles van Ufford, L., *Les terres cuites siciliennes: Une étude sur l'art sicilien entre 550 et 450*, Assen, 1941.

Robinson, David M., *Excavations at Olynthus*, IV: *The Terracottas of Olynthus found in 1928*, Oxford, 1931.

————, *Excavations at Olynthus*, VII: *The Terracottas of Olynthus found in 1931*, Baltimore, 1933.

————, *Excavations at Olynthus*, XIV: *Terracottas, Lamps and Coins found in 1934 and 1938*, Baltimore, 1952.

Sieveking, Johannes, *Die Terrakotten der Sammlung Loeb*, Munich, 1916.

Stoop, J. M. W., *Floral Figurines from South Italy*, Assen, 1960.

Thompson, Dorothy Burr, "The Origin of Tanagras," in *American Journal of Archaeology*, LXX, 1966.

————, *Troy: The Terracotta Figurines of the Hellenistic Period*, Princeton, 1963.

Van Ingen, Wilhelmina, *Figurines from Seleucia on Tigris*, London, 1939.

Walters, Henry B., *Catalogue of the Terracottas in the British Museum*, London, 1903.

Weber, Wilhelm, *Die Ägyptisch-griechischen Terrakotten: Königliches Museum zu Berlin*, Berlin, 1914.

Winter, Franz, "Die Typen der figürlichen Terrakotten," in *Die Antiken Terrakotten*, Berlin-Stuttgart, 1903.

GREEK AND ITALIC POTTERY

Åkerström, Åke, *Der geometrische Stil in Italien*, Lund, 1943.

Albizzati, Carlo, *Vasi antichi dipinti del Vaticano*, Rome, 1925.

Alfieri, N., Arias, P. E., and Hirmer, M., *Spina*, Milan-Florence, 1958.

Amyx, Darrell A., *Corinthian Vases (University of California Publications in Classical Archeology*, I), Berkeley, Calif., 1943.

Arias, Paolo E., "Storia della ceramica di età arcaica, classica ed ellenistica e della pittura di età arcaica e classica," in *Enciclopedia Classica*, ser. III, vol. XI, Turin, 1963.

————, and Hirmer, Max, *A History of 1000 Years of Greek Vase Painting*, New York, 1963.

Baur, Paul V. C., *Catalogue of the R. Darlington Stoddard Collection of Greek and Italian Vases, Yale University*, New Haven, 1922.

Beazley, John D., *Attic Black-Figure; a Sketch*, London, 1928.

————, *Attic Black-Figure Vase-Painters*, Oxford, 1956.

————, *Attic Red-figured Vases in American Museums*, Cambridge, Mass., 1918.

————, *Attic Red-Figure Vase-Painters*, New York, 1942; 2d ed., 1963.

————, *Attic White Lekythoi*, London, 1938.

————, *Der Berliner Maler*, Berlin, 1930. English trans., *The Berlin Painter*, Berlin, 1964.

————, *Campana Fragments in Florence*, Oxford, 1933.

————, *The Development of Attic Black-Figure*, Berkeley, 1951.

————, *Etruscan Vase-Painting*, Oxford, 1947.

————, *Greek Vases in Poland*, Oxford, 1928.

————, *Der Kleophrades-Maler*, Berlin, 1933.

————, *Der Pan-Maler*, Berlin, 1931.

————, *Potter and Painter in Ancient Athens*, Oxford, 1946.

Beazley, Sir John D., and Magi, Filippo, *La raccolta Benedetti Guglielmi nel Museo Gregoriano Etrusco*, Vatican City, 1939.

Becatti, Giovanni, *Meidias, un manierista antico*, Florence, 1947.

Benndorf, Otto, *Griechische und sizilische Vasenbilder*, Berlin, 1883.

Benson, Jack L., *Die Geschichte der korinthischen Vasen*, Basel, 1953.

Bernardini, Mario, *I vasi attici del Museo Provinciale di Lecce*, Bari, 1965.

Bernhard, Maria L., *Les vases grecs au Musée E. Majewski à Varsovie*, Warsaw, 1936.

Bloesch, Hansjörg, *Formen attischer Schalen*, Bern, 1940.

Borda, Maurizio, *Ceramiche Apule*, Bergamo, 1965.

Brann, E. T. H., *Late Geometric and Protoattic Pottery: Mid 8th to late 7th century B.C. (American School of Classical Studies at Athens; The Athenian Agora*, VIII), Princeton, 1962.

Brommer, Frank, *Satyrspielen*, Berlin, 1959.

————, *Vasenlisten zur griechischen Heldensagen*, Marburg, 1960.

Bothmer, Dietrich von, *Amazons in Greek Art*, Oxford, 1957.

Brauchitsch, Georg von, *Die panathenäischen Preisamphoren*, Leipzig, 1910.

Bruhn, Ada, *Oltos and Early Red-Figure Vase Painting*, Copenhagen, 1943.

Buschor, Ernst, *Attische Lekythoi in der Parthenonzeit*, Munich, 1925.

————, *Grab eines attischen Mädchens*, Munich, 1939.

————, *Griechische Vasen*, Munich, 1940.

————, *Griechische Vasenmalerei*, Munich, 1921. English trans. by G. C. Richards, *Greek Vase-Painting*, London, 1921.

Cambitoglou, A., and Trendall, A. D., *Apulian Red-Figured Vasepainters of the Plain Style (Monographs on Archaeology and Fine Arts*, X) New York, 1961.

Caskey, L. D., *Geometry of Greek Vases*, Boston, 1922.

————, and Beazley, John D., *Attic Vase Paintings in the Museum of Fine Arts, Boston*, I–II, Boston, 1931–1954.

Catteruccia, Luigi M., *Pitture vascolari italiote di soggetto teatrale comico*, Rome, 1951.

Collignon, Maxime, and Couve, Louis, *Catalogue des vases peints du Musée National d'Athènes*, Paris, 1902–1904.

Conze, Alexander, *Melische Thongefässe*, Leipzig, 1862.

Cook, Robert M., *Greek Painted Pottery*, London, 1960.

Corbett, P. E., "Preliminary Sketch in Greek Vase Painting," in *Journal of Hellenic Studies*, 1965.

Corpus Vasorum Antiquorum, since 1922 to the present there have appeared some one hundred fascicules. For a concordance of the first seventy-four see: J. W. Crous, *Konkordanz zum Corpus Vasorum Antiquorum*, Rome, 1942.

Courbin, Paul, *La céramique géometrique de l'Argolide*, Paris, 1966.

Courby, Fernand, *Les vases grecs à reliefs*, Paris, 1922.

Crous, Jan W., *Konkordanz zum Corpus Vasorum Antiquorum*, Rome, 1942.

Davison, Jean M., *Attic Geometric Workshops (Yale Classical Studies*, XVI), New Haven, 1961.

Del Chiaro, Mario A., *The Genucilia Group*, Berkeley, Calif., 1957.

Desborough, Vincent R. d'A., *Protogeometric Pottery*, New York, 1952.

Diepolder, Hans, *Der Penthesilea-Maler*, Leipzig, 1936.

————, "Der Pistoxenos-Maler," in *110 Berliner Winckelmannsprogramm*, Berlin, 1954.

Dohrn, Tobias, *Die schwarz-figurigen Etruskischen Vasen*, Cologne, 1937.

Ducati, Pericle, *Pontische Vasen*, Berlin, 1932.

————, *Storia della ceramica greca*, Florence, 1923.

Dugas, Charles, *La céramique grecque*, Paris, 1924.

Dumont, Albert, and Chaplain, Jules, *Les céramiques de la Grèce propre*, Paris, 1888.

Fairbanks, Arthur, *Athenian Lekythoi*, New York, 1907–1914.

Forsdyke, Sir Edgar J., *Catalogue of the Greek and Etruscan Vases in the British Museum*, I, 1: *Prehistoric Aegean Pottery*, London, 1925.

Forti, Lidia, *La ceramica di Gnatia*, Naples, 1965.

Frickenhaus, August, "Lenäenvasen," in *72 Berliner Winckelmannsprogramm*, Berlin, 1912.

Furtwängler, Adolf, *Beschreibung der Vasensammlung in Antiquarium, K. Museums zu Berlin*, Berlin, 1885.

————, and Reichhold, Karl, *Griechische Vasenmalerei*, Munich, 1904–1932.

Gerhard, Eduard, *Auserlesene Vasenbilder*, Berlin, 1840–1858.

409

Gerhard, Eduard, *Etruskische und Kampanische Vasenbilder*, Berlin, 1843.

————, "Rapporto Volcente," in *Annali dell'Istituto di Corrispondenza Archeologica*, III, 1831.

————, *Trinkschalen und Gefässe des Königlichen Museums zu Berlin*, Berlin, 1848–1850.

Graef, Botho, and Langlotz, Ernst, *Die antiken Vasen von der Akropolis zu Athen*, Berlin, 1925–1933.

Greifenhagen, Adolf, *Eine attische Schwarzfigurige Vasengattung*, Königsberg, 1929.

————, *Griechische Eroten*, Berlin, 1957.

Guerrini, Lucia, *Vasi di Hadra* (*Università di Roma, Seminario di archeologia e storia dell'arte greca e romana, Studi Miscellanei*, no. 8), Rome, 1964.

Hackl, Rudolf, and Sieveking, Johannes, *Die Königl. Vasensammlung zu München*, I, Munich, 1912.

Hahland, Walter, *Vasen um Meidias*, Berlin, 1930.

Hambidge, Jay, *Dynamic Symmetry: The Greek Vase*, New Haven, 1920.

————, *The Elements of Dynamic Symmetry*, New York, 1926.

Hampe, Roland, *Ein frühattischer Grabfund*, Mainz, 1960.

————, *Frühe griechische Sagenbilder*, Athens, 1936.

————, and Winter, A., *Bei Töpfer und Töpferinnen in Kreta, Messenien und Zypern*, Mainz, 1962.

————, and ————, *Bei Töpfern und Zieglern in Süditalien, Sizilien und Griechenland*, Mainz, 1965.

Hancarville, D., *Collection of Etruscan, Greek and Roman Antiquities from the Cabinet of the Honorable Wm. Hamilton*, Naples, 1766–1767.

Hartwig, Paul, *Die griechische Meisterschalen des strengen rotfigurigen Stils*, Stuttgart, 1893.

Haspels, Caroline H. E., *Attic Black-figured Lekythoi*, Paris, 1936.

Hemelrijk, J. M., *De Caeretaanse Hydriae*, Rotterdam, 1956.

Heydemann, Heinrich, *Griechische Vasenbilder*, Berlin, 1870.

Hoffmann, Herbert, *Attic Red-figured Rhyta*, Mainz, 1962.

————, *Tarentine Rhyta*, Mainz, 1966.

Homann-Wedeking, Ernst, *Archaische Vasenornamentik*, Athens, 1938.

Hoorn, Gerard van, *Choes and Anthesteria*, Leiden, 1951.

Hoppin, Joseph C., *Euthymides and his Fellows*, Cambridge, Mass., 1917.

————, *Handbook of Attic Red-figured Vases*, Cambridge, Mass., 1919.

————, *A Handbook of Greek Black-figured Vases*, Paris, 1924.

Inghirami, Francesco, *Pitture di vasi etruschi*, Fiesole, 1825–1833; 2d ed., 1852–1856.

Jacobsthal, Paul, *Ornamente griechischer Vasen*, Berlin, 1927.

Jahn, Otto, *Beschreibung der Vasensammlung*, Munich, 1854.

Jatta, Giovanni, *I vasi italo-greci del Signor Caputi di Ruvo*, Naples, 1877.

Johansen, Knud F., *Les vases sicyoniens*, Paris, 1923.

Kardará, Chrysoula, *Ροδιακὴ Ἀγγιοραφία*, Athens, 1963.

Klein, Wilhelm, *Euphronios*, Vienna, 1886.

————, *Die griechischen Vasen mit Lieblingsinschriften*, Vienna, 1890; 2d ed., 1898.

————, *Die griechischen Vasen mit Meistersignaturen*, 2d ed., Vienna, 1887.

Kretschmer, Paul, *Die griechischen Vaseninschriften*, Gütersloh, 1894.

Kübler, Karl, *Altattische Malerei*, Tübingen, 1950.

Lacroix, Léon, *La faune marine dans la décoration des plats à poissons*, Verviers, 1937.

Lambrino, Marcelle F., *Les vases archaïques d'Histrie*, Bucharest, 1938.

Lane, Arthur, *Greek Pottery*, London, 1948.

Langlotz, Ernst, *Griechische Vasen in Würzburg*, Munich, 1932.

————, *Griechische Vasenbilder der strengrotfigürlichen Vasenmalerei*, Heidelberg, 1922.

————, *Zur Zeitbestimmung der strengrotfigurigen Vasenmalerei und der gleichzeitigen Plastik*, Leipzig, 1920.

Lenormant, Charles, and De Witte, J. J., *Élite des monuments céramographiques*, Paris, 1844–1861.

Leroux, Gabriel, *Lagynos*, Paris, 1913.

————, *Vases grecs du Musée archéologique de Madrid*, Bordeaux, 1912.

Lücken, Gottfried von, *Greek Vase Paintings*, The Hague, 1921.

Lullies, Reinhard, *Griechische Vasen der reifarchaischen Zeit*, Munich, 1953.

Luschey, Heinz, *Die Phiale*, Bleicherode, 1939.

Millingen, James, *Ancient Unedited Monuments*, I: *Painted Greek Vases*, London, 1822.

————, *Peintures antiques et inédites de vases grecs*, Rome, 1813.

Mingazzini, Paolo, *Vasi della Collezione Castellani*, Rome, 1930.

Minto, Antonio, *Il vaso François* (*Accademia Toscana di scienze e lettere*, "*La Colombaria*," *Studi VI*), Florence, 1960.

Nicole, Georges, *Catalogue des vases peints du Musée National d'Athènes*, Paris, 1911.

————, *Meidias et le style fleuri*, Geneva, 1908.

Pace, Biagio, *Ceramiche ellenistiche di Centuripe*, Palermo, 1923.

Pagenstecher, Rudolf, "Die Calenische Reliefkeramik," in *Jahrbuch des Deutschen Archäologischen Instituts*, Ergänzungsheft VIII, 1909.

Panofka, Theodor, *Die Vasenbilder Pamphaios*, Berlin, 1848.

————, *Von den Namen der Vasenbildner in Beziehung zu ihren bildlichen Darstellungen*, Berlin, 1849.

Papaspiridi, Semni Karouzou, *Ἀγγεῖα τοῦ Ἀναγυροῦντος*, Athens, 1963.

————, *The Amasis Painter*, Oxford, 1956.

————, *Ten White Lekythoi in the National Museum*, Athens, 1959.

Passeri, Giovanni B., *Picturae Etruscorum in vasculis*, I–III, Rome, 1767–1775.

Patroni, Giovanni, *Catalogo dei vasi del Museo Campano*, Capua, 1902.

————, "La ceramica antica nell'Italia meridionale," in *Atti dell'Accademia di Napoli*, XIX, Naples, 1897.

————, *I vasi dipinti del Museo Vivenzio disegnati da Costanzo Angelini nel 1798*, Rome-Naples, 1900.

Payne, Humfrey G., *Necrocorinthia*, Oxford, 1931.

Pellegrini, Giuseppe, *Catalogo dei vasi dipinti delle collezione Palagi e Universitaria*, Bologna, 1900.

————, *Catalogo dei vasi greci dipinti delle necropoli felsinee*, Bologna, 1912.

Perrot, Georges, and Chipiez, Charles, *Histoire de l'art dans l'antiquité*, IX–X, Paris 1911–1914.

Peters, Karl, *Studien zu den panathenäischen Preisamphoren*, Berlin, 1942.

Pfuhl, Ernst, *Malerei und Zeichnung der Griechen*, Munich, 1923. English trans. by John D. Beazley, *Masterpieces of Greek Drawing and Painting*, New York, 1955.

Philippart, Hubert, *Collections de céramiques grecques en Italie*, I–II, Brussels, 1932–1933.

————, *Les coupes attiques à fond blanc*, Brussels, 1936.

Pottier, Edmond, *Catalogue des vases antiques de terre cuite*, I–III, Paris, 1866–1906.

————, *Vases antiques du Louvre*, Paris, 1897–1922.

Poulsen, Frederik, *Die Dipylongräber und die Dipylonvasen*, Leipzig, 1905.

410

Rayet, Olivier, and Collignon, Maxime, *Histoire de la céramique grecque*, Paris, 1888.

Reinach, Salomon, *Répertoire des vases peints grecs et étrusques*, Paris, 1899–1900; 2d ed., 1922–1924.

Richter, Gisela M. A., *Attic Red-figured Vases: A Survey*, rev. ed., New Haven, 1958.

————, *The Craft of Athenian Pottery*, New Haven, 1923.

————, and Hall, Lindsley F., *Red-figured Athenian Vases in the Metropolitan Museum of Art*, New Haven, 1936.

————, and Milne, Marjorie J., *Shapes and Names of Athenian Vases*, New York, 1935.

Ridder, André de, *Catalogue des vases peints de la Bibliothèque Nationale*, Paris, 1902.

Riezler, Walter, *Weissgrundige attische Lekythen*, Munich, 1914.

Robinson, D. M., Harcum, C. G., and Iliffe, J. K., *A Catalogue of the Greek Vases in the Royal Ontario Museum of Archaeology in Toronto*, Toronto, 1930.

Robinson, Edward, *Museum of Fine Arts, Boston: Catalogue of Greek, Etruscan and Roman Vases*, Boston, 1893.

————, *Handbuch der Archäologie*, IV, 1: *Malerei und Zeichnung*, Munich, 1953.

Rumpf, Andreas, *Chalkidische Vasen*, Berlin-Leipzig, 1927.

————, *Sakonides*, Leipzig, 1937.

Schaal, Hans, *Griechische Vasen*, Bielefeld, 1928.

————, *Griechische Vasen aus Frankfurter Sammlungen*, Frankfort, 1923.

Schäfer, Jörg, *Studien zu den griechischen Reliefpithoi des 8-6 Jahrhunderts v. Chr. aus Kreta, Rhodos, Tenos und Boeotien*, Kallmünz, 1957.

Schefold, Karl, *Kertscher Vasen*, Berlin, 1930.

————, *Untersuchungen zu den Kertscher Vasen*, Berlin, 1934.

Schiering, Wolfgang, *Werkstätten orientalisierender Keramik auf Rhodos*, Berlin, 1957.

Sechan, Louis, *Études sur la tragédie grecque dans ses rapports avec la céramique*, Paris, 1926.

Seltman, Charles T., *Attic Vase-Painting*, Cambridge, Mass., 1933.

Sichterman, Hellmut, *Die griechische Vase: Gestalt, Sinn und Kunstwerk*, Berlin, 1963.

————, *Griechische Vasen in Unteritalien, aus der Sammlung Jatta-Ruvo*, Tübingen, 1966.

Smith, Cecil H., *Catalogue of the Greek and Etruscan Vases in the British Museum*, III: *Vases of the Finest Period*, London, 1896.

Smith, Henry R. W., *Der Lewis-Maler*, Leipzig, 1939.

————, *New Aspects of the Menon Painter*, Berkeley, Calif., 1929.

————, *The Origin of Chalcidian Ware (University of California Publications in Classical Archaeology, I)*, Berkeley, Calif., 1932.

Technau, Werner, *Exekias*, Munich, 1936.

Thiersch, Hermann, *Tyrrhenische Amphoren*, Leipzig, 1899.

Tillyard, E. M. W., *The Hope Vases*, Cambridge, 1923.

Tischbein, W., *Collection of Engravings from Ancient Vases... now in the Possession of Sir Wm. Hamilton*, Naples, 1791–1795.

Trendall, Arthur D., *Frühitaliotischen Vasen*, Leipzig, 1938.

————, *Paestan Pottery*, London, 1936.

————, *Phlyax Vases*, London, 1959.

————, *South Italian Vase Painting*, London, 1966.

————, *Vasi antichi dipinti del Vaticano: Vasi italioti ed etruschi a figure rosse*, I–II, Vatican City, 1953–1955.

Tuchelt, Klaus, *Tiergefässe in Kopf und Protomengestalt (Istanbuler Forschungen, XXII)*, Berlin, 1962.

Union Académique Internationale, *Classification des céramiques antiques*, Paris, 1927.

Ure, Percy N. *Black-Glaze Pottery from Rhitsona in Boeotia*, London–New York, 1913.

Villard, François, *La céramique grecque de Marseille (Bibliothèque des Écoles françaises d'Athènes et de Rome, vol. 195)*, Paris, 1960.

————, *Les vases grecs*, Paris, 1956.

Walters, Henry B., *Catalogue of the Greek and Etruscan Vases in the British Museum*, I, 2: *Cypriote, Italian and Etruscan Pottery*, London, 1912.

————, *Catalogue of the Greek and Etruscan Vases in the British Museum*, II: *Black-figured Vases*, London, 1893.

————, *Catalogue of the Greek and Etruscan Vases in the British Museum*, IV: *Vases of the Latest Period*, London, 1896.

————, *History of Ancient Pottery*, London, 1905.

Webster, Thomas B.L., *Der Niobiden-Maler*, Leipzig, 1935.

GREEK AND ROMAN PAINTING

Aletti, Ezio, *La tecnica della pittura greca e romana e l'encausto*, Rome, 1951.

Arias, Paolo E., "Storia della ceramica di età arcaica, classica ed ellenistica e della pittura di età arcaica e classica," in *Enciclopedia Classica*, sec. III, vol. XI, Turin, 1963.

Aurigemma, Salvatore, *L'Italia in Africa, Tripolitania*, I, 2: *Le pitture di età romana*, Rome, 1962.

Balil, Alberto, *Pintura helenistica y romana (Bibliotheca Archaeologica, III)*, Madrid, 1961.

Beazley, John D., and Ashmole, Bernard, *Greek Sculpture and Painting to the End of the Hellenistic Period*, New York, 1966.

Bendinelli, Goffredo, *Le pitture del Colombario di Villa Pamphili (Monumenti della pittura antica, Roma, V)*, Rome, 1941.

Beyen, Hendrik G., *Die pompejanische Wanddekoration vom zweiten bis zum vierten Stil*, I-II, The Hague, 1938–1960.

————, *Über Stilleben aus Pompeji und Herculanum*, The Hague, 1938.

Bianchi-Bandinelli, Ranuccio, "Continuità ellenistica nella pittura di età medio e tardo-romana," in *Rivista dell'Istituto Nazionale di Archeologia e Storia dell'Arte*, 1953.

————, *Hellenistic-Byzantine Miniatures of the Iliad*, Olten, 1955.

————, "Tradizione ellenistica e gusto romano nella pittura pompeiana," in *La Critica d'Arte*, VI, 1941.

Blanckenhagen, P. H. von, Alexander, C., and Papadopulos, G., "The Paintings from Boscotrecase," in *Römische Mitteilungen des Deutschen Archäologischen Instituts*, Ergänzungsheft, VI, 1962.

Borda, Maurizio, *La pittura romana*, Milan, 1958.

Boyce, George K., "Corpus of the Lararia of Pompei," in *Memoirs of the American Academy in Rome*, XIV, 1938.

Brown, Blanche R., *Ptolemaic Paintings and Mosaics and the Alexandrian Style*, Cambridge, Mass., 1957.

Bulas, Kazimierz, *Les illustrations antiques de l'Iliad*, Lvov, 1929.

Bulle, Heinrich, "Eine Skenographie," in *94 Berliner Winckelmannsprogramm*, Berlin-Leipzig, 1934.

Burbel, P., *Griechisch-Aegyptische Mumienbildnisse der Sammlung Graf*, Vienna, 1922.

Croisille, J. M., *Les natures mortes campaniennes*, Brussels, 1965.

Curtius, Ludwig, *Die Wandmalerei Pompejis*, Leipzig, 1929.

Dawson, Christopher, M., *Romano-Campanian Mythological Landscape Painting (Yale Classical Studies, IX)*, 1944.

Diepolder, Hans, "Untersuchungen zur Komposition der römisch-campanischen Wandgemälde," in *Römische Mitteilungen des Deutschen Archäologischen Instituts*, XLI, 1926.

Dorigo, Wladimiro, *Pittura tardo-romana*, Milan, 1966.

Drack, Walter, *Die römische Wandmalerei der Schweitz*, Basel, 1950.

Du Mesnil du Buisson, Robert, *Les peintures de la synagogûe de Dura-Europos*, Rome, 1939.

Eckstein, Felix, *Untersuchungen über die Stilleben aus Pompeji und Herculaneum*, Berlin, 1957.

Eibner, Alexander, *Entwicklung und Werkstoffe der Wandmalerei*, Munich, 1926.

Elia, Olga, *Le pitture del Tempio d'Iside* (*Monumenti della pittura antica, Pompei, III-IV*), Rome, 1941.

————, *Le pitture della Casa del Citarista* (*Monumenti della pittura antica, Pompei, I*), Rome, 1937.

————, *Pitture di Stabia*, Naples, 1957.

————, *Pitture murali e mosaici del Museo Nazionale di Napoli*, Rome, 1932.

Felletti-Maj, Bianca M., *Le pitture delle Case delle Volte dipinte e delle Pareti Gialle* (*Monumenti della pittura antica, Ostia, I*), Rome, 1961.

Ferrua, Antonio, *Le pitture della nuova catacomba di via Latina*, Vatican City, 1960.

Frova, Antonio, *Pittura romana in Bulgaria*, Rome, 1943.

Gabra, Sami, and Drioton, E., *Peintures à fresques et scènes peintes à Hermoupolis Ouest*, Cairo, 1954.

Gabriel, Mabel McAfee, *Masters of Campanian Painting*, New York, 1952.

Helbig, Wolfgang, *Die Wandgemälde der vom Vesuv verschütteten Städte Campaniens*, Leipzig, 1868.

Herbig, Reinhard, "Neue Beobachtungen am Fries der Mysterienvilla in Pompeji," in *Deutsche Beiträge zur Altertumswissenschaft*, X, 1958.

Hermann, Paul, Herbig, R., and Bruckmann, F., *Denkmäler der Malerei des Altertums*, Munich, 1906–.

Ippel, Albert, *Der dritte pompejanische Stil*, Berlin, 1910.

Kempf, T. K., "Konstantinische Deckenmalereien aus dem Trierer Dom," in *Trierer Zeitschrift*, XIX, 1950.

Krahmer, W., "Das Kentaurenbild des Zeuxis," in *16 Berliner Winckelmannsprogramm*, Berlin, 1950.

Kraiker, Wilhelm, *Die Malerei der Griechen*, Stuttgart, 1956.

Lehmann, Phyllis (Williams), *Roman Wall Paintings from Boscoreale in the Metropolitan Museum of Art*, Cambridge, Mass., 1953.

Lepik Kopaczynska, W., *Die antike Malerei*, Berlin, 1963.

————, *Appelles, der berühmteste Maler der Antike*, Berlin, 1962.

Lippold, Georg, *Antike Gemäldekopien*, Munich, 1951.

Loewy, Emmanuel, *Polygnot, ein Buch von griechischer Malerei*, Vienna, 1929.

Maiuri, Amedeo, *Le pitture della Casa di M. Fabius Amandio, del Sacerdos Amandius e di P. Cornelius Teges* (*Monumenti della pittura antica, Pompei, II*), Rome, 1938.

————, *Roman Painting*, Geneva, 1953.

————, *La Villa dei Misteri*, Rome, 1947.

Mansuelli Guido A., *Ricerche sulla pittura ellenistica*, Bologna, 1950.

Marconi, Pirro, *La pittura dei Romani*, Rome, 1929.

Mau, August, *Geschichte der dekorativen Wandmalerei in Pompei*, Leipzig, 1882.

————, *Pompeji in Leben und Kunst*, 2d ed., Leipzig, 1908.

Méautis, Georges, *Chefs-d'œuvre de la peinture grecque*, Paris, 1939.

Miatev, Krsto, *La peinture décorative de la nécropole de Serdica*, Sofia, 1925.

Napoli, Mario, *Pittura antica in Italia*, Bergamo, 1960.

Neutsch, Bernhard, *Der Maler Nikias von Athen*, Bern-Leipzig, 1939.

Niccolini, Fausto, *Le case e i monumenti di Pompei, disegnati e descritti*, Naples, 1854–1896.

Nogara, Bartolomeo, *Antichi affreschi del Vaticano e del Laterano*, Milan, 1907.

Parlasca, Klaus, *Römische Wandmalereien in Augsburg*, Kallmünz, 1956.

Peters, W. J. T., *Landscape in Romano-Campanian Painting*, Assen, 1963.

Pfuhl, Ernst, *Malerei und Zeichnung der Griechen*, Munich, 1923. English trans. by John D. Beazley, *Masterpieces of Greek Drawing and Painting*, New York, 1955.

Presuhn, Emil, *Die pompejianischen Wanddekorationen*. Leipzig, 1882.

Ragghianti, Carlo L., *Pittori di Pompei*, Milan, 1963.

Reinach, Adolphe J. *Recueil Millet*, Paris, 1921.

Reinach, Salomon, *Répertoire des peintures grecques et romaines*, Paris, 1922.

Richter, Gisela M. A., *Greek Painting: The Development of Pictorial Representation from Archaic to Graeco-Roman Times*, New York, 1944.

Rizzo, Giulio E., *La pittura ellenistico-romana*, Milan, 1929.

————, *Le pitture dell'Aula isiaca di Caligola* (*Monumenti della pittura antica, Roma, II*), Rome, 1936.

————, *Le pitture della Casa dei Grifi* (*Monumenti della pittura antica, Roma, I*), Rome, 1936.

————, *Le pitture della Casa di Livia* (*Monumenti della pittura antica, Roma, III*), Rome, 1937.

————, *Ritratti di età ellenistica* (*Monumenti della pittura antica, Centuripe, I*), Rome, 1940.

Robertson, Martin, *Greek Painting*, Geneva, 1959.

Rodenwaldt, Gerhardt, *Die Komposition der pompejanischen Wandgemälde*, Berlin, 1909.

Rumpf, Andreas, *Handbuch der Archäologie*, VI, 4: *Malerei und Zeichnung*, 1953.

Schefold, Karl, *Pompejanische Malerei*, Basel, 1952.

————, *Die Wände Pompejis: Topographisches Verzeichnis der Bildmotive*, Berlin, 1957.

Schiavi, Elena, *Il sale della terra*, Milan, 1961.

Schweitzer, Bernhard, *Vom Sinn der Perspective*, Tübingen, 1953.

Simon, Erika, *Die Fürstenbilder von Boscoreale: Ein Beitrag zur hellenistischen Wandmalerei*, Baden-Baden, 1958.

Spinazzola, Vittorio, *Le arti decorative a Pompei*, Milan, 1928.

Swindler, Mary H., *Ancient Painting*, New Haven, 1929.

White, John, *Birth and Rebirth of Pictorial Space*, London, 1957.

————, *Perspective in Ancient Drawing and Painting*, London, 1956.

Wilpert, Joseph, *Die Malereien der Katakomben Roms*, Freiburg-Rome, 1903.

————, *Die römischen Mosaiken und Malereien der kirchlichen Bauten vom IV bis XIII Jahrh.*, Freiburg, 1917.

Wirth, Fritz, *Römische Wandmalerei vom Untergang Pompejis bis aus Ende des dritten Jahrh.*, Berlin, 1934.

Wit, Johannes de, *Spätrömische Bildnismalerei, Stilkritische Untersuchungen zur Wandmalerei der Katakomben und verwandter Monumenten*, Berlin, 1938.

Zahn, W., *Die schönsten Ornamente und merkwürdigsten Gemälde aus Pompeji, Herculanum und Stabiae*, Berlin, 1828–1852.

Zuntz, G. G., *On the Dionysiac Fresco in the Villa dei Misteri at Pompei*, London, 1965.

GREEK AND ROMAN MOSAICS

Aurigemma, Salvatore, *L'Italia in Africa, Tripolitania, I, 1: I mosaici*, Rome, 1960.

————, *I mosaici di Zliten* (*Africa Italiana, Monografie 2*), Rome, 1926.

Avi-Yonah, Michael, *Israel: Ancient Mosaics* (UNESCO), Greenwich, Conn., 1960.

———, *The Madaba Mosaic Map*, Jerusalem, Israel, 1954.

———, "Mosaic Pavements in Palestine," in *The Quarterly of the Department of Antiquities in Palestine*, II–III, 1934.

Balil, Alberto, *Consideraciones sobre el mosaico hispano-romano*, Guimaraes 1958.

Becatti, Giovanni, *Scavi di Ostia*, IV: *Mosaici e pavimenti marmorei*, Rome, 1961.

Berchem, Marguerite van, and Clouzot, Étienne, *Mosaïques chrétiennes du IVe au Xe siècle*, Geneva, 1924.

Blake, Marion E., "Mosaics of the Late Empire in Rome and Vicinity," in *Memoirs of the American Academy in Rome*, XVII, 1940.

———, "The Pavements of the Roman Buildings of the Republic and Early Empire," in *Memoirs of the American Academy in Rome*, VIII, 1930.

———, "Roman Mosaics of the Second Century in Italy," in *Memoirs of the American Academy in Rome*, XIII, 1936.

Blanchet, Andrien, *La mosaïque*, Paris, 1928.

Brett, Gerard, "The Mosaic," in *The Great Palace of the Byzantine Emperors*, London, 1947.

Brown, Blanche R., *Ptolemaic Painting and Mosaic and the Alexandrian Style*, Cambridge, Mass., 1957.

Brusin, Giovanni, "Il mosaico antico nel Veneto," in *Arte Veneta*, IV, 1950.

———, and Zovatto, P. L., *Monumenti paleocristiani di Aquileia e Grado*, Udine, 1957.

Boulard, L., "Peintures murales et mosaïques de Délos," in *Monuments Piot*, XIV, 1908.

Caputo, G., and Driss, A., *Tunisia: Ancient Mosaics* (UNESCO), Greenwich, Conn., 1962.

Carandini, Andrea, "Ricerche sullo stile e la cronologia dei mosaici della villa di Piazza Armerina," in *Studi Miscellanei*, no. 7, Rome, 1964.

Cecchelli, Carlo, *I mosaici di Santa Maria Maggiore*, Rome, 1956.

———, "Le origini del mosaico parietale cristiano," in *Architettura e Arti Decorative*, II, 1922–1923.

Chéhab, Maurice, "Mosaïques du Liban,'" in *Bulletin du Musée de Liban*, XIV–XV, 1958–1959.

Dohrn, Tobias, "Crustae," in *Römische Mitteilungen des Deutschen Archäologischen Instituts*, 1965.

Espérandieu, Émile, *Les mosaïques romaines de Nîmes*, Nîmes, 1935.

Fabia, Phillippe, *Mosaïques romaines du Musée de Lyon*, Lyons, 1923.

———, *Recherches sur les mosaïques romaines de Lyon*, Lyons, 1924.

Fasiolo, Onorio, *I mosaici d'Aquileia*, Rome, 1915.

Foucher, Louis, *Inventaire des mosaïques: Sousse*, Tunis, 1960.

———, *Navires et barques figurées sur des mosaïque découvertes à Sousse*, Tunis, 1957.

Franciscis, Alfonso. de, *Antichi mosaici al Museo di Napoli*, Cava dei Tirreni, 1962.

Fremersdorf, Fritz, *Das Dionysosmosaik im römischen Palast am Dom in Köln*, Cologne, 1956.

Gentili, Gino V., *La villa erculia di Piazza Armerina*, Milan, 1959.

Gioseffi, Decio, "La terminologia dei sistemi di pavimentazione marmorea e una pagina della 'Naturalis Historia'," in *Rendiconti dell'Accademia dei Lincei*, 1955.

Gonzenbach, Victorine von, *Die römischen Mosaiken der Schweitz*, Basel, 1961.

Gullini, Giorgio, *I mosaici di Palestrina*, Rome, 1955.

Hinks, Roger P., *Catalogue of the Greek, Etruscan and Roman Paintings and Mosaics in the British Museum*, London, 1933.

Inventaire des mosaïques de la Gaule et de l'Afrique, I: A. Blanchet, *Gaule romaine*, Paris, 1909; II: P. Gauckler, *Afrique proconsulaire* (*Tunisie*), Paris, 1910, and *Supplément* by A. Merlin; III: F. G. de Pachtère, *Afrique proconsulaire, Numidie, Maurétanie* (*Algérie*), Paris, 1911; *Atlas*, 1922–1925.

Ivanov, Teofil, *Une mosaïque romaine de Ulpia Oescus*, Sofia, 1954.

Kähler, Heinz, *Die Stiftermosaiken in der Konstantinischen Südkirche von Aquileia*, Cologne, 1962.

Lassus, Jean, *Réflexions sur la technique de la mosaïque*, Algiers, 1957.

Lavin, Irving, "The Hunting Mosaics of Antioch and their Sources," in *Dumbarton Oaks Papers*, XVII, 1963.

Levi, Doro, *Antioch Mosaic Pavements*, Princeton, 1947.

Moreau, Jacques, *Die Trierer Kornmarktmosaik*, Cologne, 1960.

Morey, Charles R., *The Mosaics of Antioch*, New York, 1938.

Morgan, Thomas, *Romano-British Mosaic Pavements*, London, 1886.

Nogara, Bartolomeo, *I mosaici antichi conservati nei Palazzi Pontifici del Vaticano e del Laterano*, Milan, 1910.

Pace, Biagio, *I mosaici di Piazza Armerina*, Rome, 1955.

Parlasca, Klaus, *Die römischen Mosaiken in Deutschland*, Berlin, 1959.

Perler, Othmar, *Die Mosaiken der Juliergruft in Vatikan*, Fribourg, 1953.

Pernice, Erich, *Die hellenistische Kunst in Pompeji*, VI: *Pavimente und figürliche Mosaiken*, Berlin, 1938.

Rice, David Talbot (ed.), *The Great Palace of the Byzantine Emperor: Second Report*, Edinburgh, 1958.

Robertson, C. M., "Greek Mosaics," in *Journal of Hellenic Studies*, 1965.

Robinson, David M., *Excavations at Olynthus: Mosaics, Vases and Lamps*, V, Baltimore, 1933.

Roncewski, Konstantin, *Gewölbeschmuck im römischen Altertum*, Berlin, 1903.

Solomonson, J. W., *La mosaïque aux chevaux de l'antiquarium de Carthage*, The Hague, 1965.

———, *Mosaïques romaines de Tunisie*, Brussels, 1964.

Stern, Henri, "Mosaïque de Hellin (Albacete-Spagna)," in *Monuments Piot*, LIV, 1965.

———, *Recueil général des mosaïques de la Gaule*, I: *Gaule Belgique* (*Gallia: fouilles et monuments archéologiques en France métropolitaine, Supplément* 10), Paris, 1957–1963.

Thouvenot, Raymond, "L'art provincial en Maurétanie tingitane: Les mosaïques," in *Mélanges d'archéologie et d'histoire*, LIII, 1936.

GREEK AND ITALIC METALWORK

Adriani, Achille, *Divagazioni intorno a una coppa paesistica del Museo di Alessandria*, (*Documenti e Ricerche di arte alessandrina*, III–IV), Rome, 1959.

Hoffmann, Herbert, *Griechische Kleinkunst*, Hamburg, 1963.

Jantzen, Ulf, "Bronzewerkstätten in Grossgriechenland und Sizilien," in *Jahrbuch des Deutschen Archäologischen Instituts, Ergänzungsheft* XIII, Berlin, 1937.

———, *Griechische Greifenkessel*, Berlin, 1955.

———, "Griechische Griffphialen," in *114 Berliner Winckelmannsprogramm*, Berlin, 1958.

Kunze, Emil, "Archaische Schildbänder," in *Olympische Forschungen*, II, 1950.

———, *Kretische Bronzereliefs*, Stuttgart, 1931.

Kuthmann, Harald, *Untersuchungen zur Toreutik des zweiten und ersten Jahrhunderts v. Chr.*, Kallmünz, 1959.

Lamb, Winifred, *Greek and Roman Bronzes*, London, 1929.

Maryon, Herbert, "Metal Working in the Ancient World," in *American Journal of Archaeology*, LIII, 1949.

Neugebauer, Karl A., *Bronzegerät des Altertums*, Bielefeld-Leipzig, 1927.

Pernice, Erich, *Die hellenistische Kunst in Pompeji*, IV: *Gefässe und Geräte aus Bronze*, Berlin-Leipzig, 1925.

Richter, Gisela, M. A., "Ancient Plaster Casts of Greek Metalware," in *American Journal of Archaeology*, LXII, 1958.

Schreiber, Theodor, *Die Alexandrinische Toreutik*, Leipzig, 1894.

Schröder, Bruno, "Griechische Bronzeeimer," in *17 Berliner Winckelmannsprogramm*, Berlin, 1914.

Segall, Berta, "Tradition und Neuschöpfung in der frühalexandrinischen Kleinkunst," in *119–120 Berliner Winckelmannsprogramm*, Berlin, 1966.

Strong, D. E., *Greek and Roman Gold and Silver Plate*, London, 1966.

Svoboda, Bedřich, and Končev (Zoncev), D., *Neue Denkmäler antiker Toreutik*, Prague, 1956.

Thompson, Dorothy Burr, "Mater Caelaturae: Impressions from Ancient Metalwork," in *Hesperia*, VIII, 1939.

Züchner, Wolfgang, "Griechische Klappspiegel," in *Jahrbuch des Deutschen Archäologischen Instituts, Ergänzungsheft* XIV, 1942.

———, "Von Toreuten und Töpfern," in *Jahrbuch des Deutschen Archäologischen Instituts*, LXV–LXVI, 1950–1951.

GREEK AND ITALIC
GOLD AND SILVERWORK

Adriani, Achille, *Le gobelet en argent des amours vendangeurs du Musée d'Alexandrie* (*Societé Royale d'Archéologie d'Alexandrie*, I), 1939.

Alexander, Christine, *Metropolitan Museum of Art: Greek and Etruscan Jewelry*, New York, 1940.

Amandry, Pierre, *Collection H. Stathatos: Bijoux antiques*, Strasbourg, 1953.

Babelon, Ernest, *Trésor de Berthouville près Bernay*, Paris, 1916.

Bartoccini, Renato, "La tomba degli ori di Canosa," in *Japigia*, VI, 1935.

Battke, Heinz, *Geschichte des Ringes*, Baden-Baden, 1953.

Becatti, Giovanni, *Oreficerie antiche dalle minoiche alle barbariche*, Rome, 1955.

Bendinelli, Goffredo, *Il tesoro di Marengo*, Turin, 1937.

Breglia, Laura, *Catalogo delle oreficerie del Museo Nazionale di Napoli*, Rome, 1941.

———, "Le oreficerie del Museo di Taranto," in *Japigia*, X, 1939.

Bruns, Gerda, *Schatzkammer der Antike: Berliner Museum*, Berlin, 1946.

Carducci, Carlo, *Ori e argenti dell'Italia antica*, Milan, 1962.

Coche de la Ferté, Étienne, *Les bijoux antiques*, Paris, 1956.

Končev (Zoncev), D., and Svoboda, Bedřich, *Der Goldschatz von Panaguriste*, Berlin, 1959.

Drexel, Friedrich, *Alexandrinische Silbergefässe der Kaiserzeit*, Bonn, 1905.

Filow, Bogdan D., *Die archaische Nekropole von Trebenischte am Ocrida-See*, Berlin-Leipzig, 1927.

———, *Die Grabhügelnekropole bei Duvanlij in Südbulgarien*, Sofia, 1934.

Hadaczek, Carl, *Der Ohrschmuck der Griechen und Etrusker*, Vienna, 1903.

Héron de Villefosse, Antoine, "Le trésor de Boscoreale," in *Monuments Piot*, V, Paris, 1899.

Higgins, Reynold A., *Greek and Roman Jewellery*, London, 1961.

———, *Jewellery from Classical Lands*, London, 1965.

Hoffman, Herbert, and Davidson, Patricia F., *Greek Gold Jewellery from the Age of Alexander*, Mainz, 1965.

Ippel, Albert, *Der Bronzefund von Galiub: Modelle eines hellenistischen Goldschmieds*, Berlin, 1922.

———, "Guss und Treibarbeit in Silber," in *97 Berliner Winckelmannsprogramm*, Berlin-Leipzig, 1937.

Joffroy, René, "Le trésor de Vix," in *Monuments Piot*, LXVIII, 1954.

Kurz, O., in J. Hackin, *Nouvelles recherches archéologiques à Begram*, Paris, 1954.

Lopez Cuevillas, F., *Las joyas castrenas*, Madrid, 1951.

Maiuri, Amadeo, *La Casa del Menandro e il suo tesoro di argenteria*, Rome, 1933.

Marshall, Frederick H., *Catalogue of the Finger Rings (Greek, Etruscan and Roman): British Museum*, London, 1907.

———, *Catalogue of the Jewellery (Greek, Etruscan and Roman): British Museum*, London, 1911.

Ohly, Dieter, *Griechische Goldbleche des 8 Jahrhunderts v. Chr.*, Berlin, 1953.

Ori e argenti dell'Emilia antica (catalogue), Bologna, 1958.

Mélida y Alinari, José R., *Tesoro de Aliseda*, Madrid, 1921.

Pernice, Erich, and Winter, Franz, *Hildesheimer Silberfund*, Berlin, 1901.

Pollak, Ludwig, *Klassisch-antike Goldschmiedarbeiten im Besitze sr. Ex. A. J. von Nelidow*, Leipzig, 1903.

Reichel, W., *Griechisches Goldrelief*, Berlin, 1943.

Reinach, Salomon, *Antiquités du Bosphore Cimmerien*, Paris, 1892.

Richter, Gisela M. A., "Greek Fifth-Century Silverware and Later Imitations," in *American Journal of Archaeology*, LIV, 1950.

———, "A Greek Silver Phiale in the Metropolitan Museum," in *American Journal of Archaeology*, XLV, 1941.

Ridder, André de, *Catalogue sommaire des bijoux antiques du Musée National du Louvre*, Paris, 1924.

———, *Collection de Clerq, VII: Le bijoux et les pierres gravées*, Paris, 1911.

Rosenberg, Marc, *Geschichte der Goldschmiedkunst auf technischer Grundlage*, Frankfort, 1910–1925.

Rostovtzeff, Michael, *Iranians and Greeks in South Russia*, Oxford, 1922.

Rubensohn, Otto, *Hellenistisches Silbergerät in antiken Gipsabgüssen*, Berlin, 1911.

Ruxerowna, M., *History of the Greek Necklace*, Poznan, 1938.

San Valero Aparisi, J., *El tesoro preimperial de plata de Drieves (Guadalajara)*, Madrid, 1945.

Sandars, H., *Joyas ibero-romanas halladas en Mogón, Villacarillo*, Jaen, 1917.

Schkorpil, Karl, *Die archaische Nekropole von Trebenischte*, Berlin, 1927.

Segall, Berta, *Museum Benaki: Katalog der Goldschmiedarbeiten*, Athens, 1938.

———, "Two Hellenistic Gold Medallions from Thessaly," in *Record of the Art Museum, Princeton University*, IV, no. 2, 1945.

Siviero, Rodolfo, *Gli ori e le ambre del Museo Nazionale di Napoli*, Florence, 1958.

Sutherland, Carol H., *Gold: Its Beauty, Power and Allure*, London, 1959.

Walters, Henry B., *Catalogue of Silver Plate, Greek, Etruscan and Roman: British Museum*, London, 1921.

Wuilleumier, Pierre, *Le trésor de Tarente*, Paris, 1930.

Zahn, Robert, *Ausstellung von Schmuckarbeiten in Edelmetall aus den Staatlichen Museen zu Berlin*, Berlin, 1935.

———, *Galerie Bachstitz*, II, Berlin, 1921.

GEMS

Beazley, John D., *Lewes House Collection of Ancient Gems*, Oxford, 1920.

Biesantz, Hagen, *Rätsel Portlandvase*, Mainz, 1965.

Boardman, John, *Island Gems — A Study of Greek Seals in the Geometric and Early Archaic Periods*, London, 1963.

Furtwängler, Adolf, *Die antiken Gemmen*, I–III, Leipzig-Berlin, 1900.

Haynes, D. E. L., *The Portland Vase*, London, 1964.

Lippold, Georg, *Gemmen und Kameen des Altertums und der Neuzeit*, Berlin, 1922.

Richter, Gisela M. A., *Catalogue of Engraved Gems, Greek, Etruscan and Roman, in the Metropolitan Museum of Art*, Rome, 1956.

Sena Chiesa, Gemma, *Gemme del Museo Nazionale di Aquileia*, Padua, 1966.

Strong, D. E., *Catalogue of the Carved Amber in the British Museum*, London, 1966.

Vermeule, Cornelius C., *Greek and Roman Gems: Catalogue, Museum of Fine Arts, Boston*, Boston, 1966.

Walters, Henry B., *Catalogue of the Engraved Gems and Cameos, Greek, Etruscan and Roman: British Museum*, London, 1926.

ETRUSCAN AND ITALIAN ART

Adriani, Achille, *Cataloghi illustrati del Museo Campano: Sculture in tufo*, Alexandria, 1939.

Åkerström, Åke, *Der geometrische Stil Italiens*, Uppsala, 1943.

_____, *Studien über die etruskische Gräber*, Uppsala, 1934.

Andrén, Arvid, *Architectural Terracottas from Etrusco-Italic Temples*, Lund-Leipzig, 1939–1940.

Anti, Carlo, "Il problema dell'arte italica," in *Studi Etruschi*, IV, 1930.

Banti, Luisa, *Luni*, Florence, 1937.

_____, *Il mondo degli Etruschi*, Rome, 1960.

Bartoccini, Renato, *La tomba delle Olimpiadi*, Rome, 1958.

Beazley, John D., *Etruscan Vase Painting*, Oxford, 1947.

Becatti, Giovanni, and Magi, Filippo, *Le pitture delle Tombe degli Auguri o del Pulcinella (Monumenti della Pittura Antica)*, Rome, 1956.

Bernabò-Brea, Luigi, *Museen und Kunstdenkmäler in Sizilien*, Munich, 1959.

_____, "I rilievi tarantini in pietra tenera," in *Rivista dell'Istituto di Archeologia e Storia dell'Arte*, N.S. I, 1952.

Bianchi-Bandinelli, Ranuccio, "Clusium," in *Monumenti Antichi dei Lincei*, XXX, 1925.

_____, *Le pitture delle tombe arcaiche di Chiusi (Monumenti della pittura antica)*, Rome, 1939.

_____, *Sovana*, Florence, 1929.

_____, *Storicità dell'arte classica*, 2d ed., Florence, 1950.

_____, *Zum Problem des "Illusionismus" und der Originalität in der etruskischen Kunst*, Rome, 1933.

_____, and Biasutti, R., *La Val d'Ambra e la Val di Chiana*, Florence, 1927.

Block, Raymond, *Etruscan Art*, Greenwich, Conn.-New York, 1959.

_____, *Gli Etruschi*, Milan, 1955.

Boëthius, Axel, and Others, *Etruscan Culture: Land and People*, New York-Malmo, 1962.

Bonghi Iovino, M., *Capua preromana: terrecotte votive*, Florence, 1965.

Brown, William L., *The Etruscan Lion*, Oxford, 1960.

Brunn, Heinrich von, and Körte, Gustavo, *I rilievi delle urne etrusche*, 3 vols., Rome, 1870–1916.

Caputo, Giacomo, *Guida alla scultura di Luni*, Florence, 1965.

Consortini, Luigi, *Volterra nell'antichità*, Volterra, 1940.

Cristofani, Mauro, *La tomba delle iscrizioni a Cerveteri*, Florence, 1965.

Curtis, Charles D., "The Barberini Tomb," in *Memoirs of the American Academy in Rome*, V, 1921.

_____, "The Bernardini Tomb," in *Memoirs of the American Academy in Rome*, III, 1919.

Della Seta, Alessandro, *Guida del Museo di Villa Giulia*, Rome, 1918.

_____, *Italia antica*, Bergamo, 1928.

Demus Quatember, M., *Etruskische Grabarchitektur*, Baden-Baden, 1958.

Dennis, George, *The Cities and Cemeteries of Etruria*, London, 1883.

Devoto, Giacomo, *Gli antichi Italici*, Florence, 1951.

Dohrn, Tobias, "Grundzüge Etruskische Kunst," *Deutsche Beiträge zur Altertumswissenschaft*, VIII, Baden-Baden, 1958.

_____, *Die schwarzfigurige etruskische Vasen aus der zweiten Hälfte des sechsten Jahrhunderts*, 1937.

Ducati, Pericle, *Etruria Antica*, Florence, 1925.

_____, *Italia antica*, Milan, 1936.

_____, "Le pietre funerarie felsinee," in *Monumenti Antichi dei Lincei*, XX, 1911.

_____, *Le pitture delle Tombe delle Leonesse e dei Vasi Dipinti (Monumenti della pittura antica)*, Rome, 1937.

_____, *La scultura etrusca*, Novara, 1941.

_____, *Storia dell'arte etrusca*, Florence, 1927.

Dunbabin, Thomas J., *The Western Greeks*, Oxford, 1948.

Durm, Josef, *Die Baukunst der Etrusker und der Römer*, 3d ed., Leipzig, 1910.

Falchi, Isidoro, *Vetulonia e la sua necropoli antichissima*, Florence, 1891.

Frova, Antonio, *L'arte etrusca*, Milan, 1957.

Gerhard, E., Körte, G., and Klugman, A., *Etruskische Spiegel*, Berlin, 5 vols., 1840–1897.

Gerkan, Armin, von, and Messerschmidt, Franz, "Das Grab der Volumnier bei Perugia," in *Römische Mitteilungen des Deutschen Archäologischen Instituts*, LXII, 1942.

Gervasio, Michele, *Bronzi arcaici e ceramica geometrica nel Museo di Bari*, Bari, 1921.

Giglioli, Giulio Q., *L'arte etrusca*, Milan, 1935.

Goldscheider, Ludwig, *Etruscan Sculpture*, London, 1941.

Hampe, Roland, and Simon, Erika, *Griechische Sagen in der frühen etruskischen Kunst*, Mainz, 1964.

Hanfmann, George M. A., *Altetruskische Plastik*, Würzburg, 1936.

Hausenstein, Wilhelm, *Die Bildnerei der Etrusker: Auswahl und Nachwort*, Munich, 1922.

Haynes, Sybille, *Etruscan Bronze Utensils*, London, 1965.

_____, "Zwei archaisch-etruskische Bildwerke aus dem Isis-Grab von Vulci," in *Antike Plastik*, IV, 1965.

Herbig, Reinhard, *Die jüngeretruskischen Steinsarkophage*, Berlin, 1952.

Holland, L. A., *The Faliscans in Prehistoric Times*, Rome, 1925.

Huls, Yvette, *Ivoires d'Etrurie*, Brussels-Rome, 1957.

Hus, Alain, *Recherches sur la statuaire en pierre étrusque archaïque, (Bibliothèque des Écoles françaises d'Athènes et de Rome, vol. 198)*, Paris, 1961.

Klumbach, Hans, *Tarentiner Grabkunst*, Reutlinger, 1937.

Koch, Herbert, *Dachterrakotten aus Kampanien*, Berlin, 1912.

Langlotz, Ernst, and Hirmer, Max, *Ancient Greek Sculpture of South Italy and Sicily*, New York, 1965.

Laviosa, Clelia, *Scultura tardo-etrusca di Volterra*, Florence, 1965.

Leisiger, Hermann, *Malerei der Etrusker*, Zurich-Stuttgart, 1953.

Levi, Alda, *Le terracotte figurate del Museo Nazionale di Napoli*, Florence, 1916.

Levi, Doro, "La necropoli etrusca dell'Accesa nel territorio di Massa Marittima," in *Monumenti Antichi dei Lincei*, XXXV, 1933.

————, "La tomba della Pellegrina a Chiusi," in *Rivista dell'Istituto di Archeologia e Storia dell'Arte*, IV, 1932–1933.

Lukomski, Georgii K., *Art étrusque*, Paris, 1930.

Magi, Filippo, "Stele e cippi fiesolani," in *Studi Etruschi*, VI–VIII, 1932–1934.

Mansuelli, Guido A., *Etrurien und die Anfänge Roms*, Baden-Baden, 1963.

————, "Gli specchi figurati etruschi," in *Studi Etruschi*, XIX–XX, 1946–1949.

Marinis, Simonetta de, *La tipologia del banchetto nell'arte etrusca arcaica*, Studia Archaeologica, I, Rome, 1961.

Martha, Jules, *L'art étrusque*, Paris, 1889.

Marzullo, Antonio, *Tombe dipinte scoperte nel territorio pestano*, Salerno, 1935.

Mayer, Maximilian, *Apulien*, Leipzig, 1914.

Messerschmidt, Franz, *Beiträge zur Chronologie der Etruskische Wandmalerei*, I: *Die archaische Zeit*, Rome, 1928.

————, "Probleme der etruskische Malerei der Hellenismus," in *Jahrbuch des Deutschen Archäologischen Instituts*, XLV, 1930.

————, and Gerkan, Armin von, *Die Nekropole von Vulci*, Berlin, 1930.

Minto, Antonio, *Marsigliana d'Albegna*, Florence, 1921.

————, *Populonia*, Florence, 1943.

————, *Populonia: la necropoli arcaica*, Florence, 1921.

————, "Saturnia, etrusca e romana," in *Monumenti Antichi dei Lincei*, XXX, 1925.

Montelius, Oscar, *La civilisation primitive en Italie depuis l'introduction des métaux*, Stockholm, I–II, 1896–1904.

Moretti, Giuseppe, *Il guerriero di Capestrano*, Rome, 1936.

Moretti, Mario, *I nuovi monumenti della pittura etrusca*, Milan, 1966.

Mostra dell'Etruria Padana e della città di Spina (catalogue), Bologna, 1961.

Mülenstein, H., *Die Kunst der Etrusker: Die Ursprünge*, Berlin, 1929.

Müller, C. O., and Deecke, W., *Die Etrusker*, Stuttgart, 1877.

Neppi Modona, Aldo, *Cortona etrusca e romana*, Florence, 1925.

Neutsch, Bernhard, "Tarentinische und lukanische Vorstufen zu den Kopfkapitellen am Italischen Forumstempel von Paestum," in *Römische Mitteilungen des Deutschen Archäologischen Instituts*, 1965.

Nogara, Bartolomeo, *Gli Etruschi e la loro civiltà*, Milan, 1934.

Orlandini, Piero, *Arte indigena e colonizzazione greca in Sicilia*, Palermo, 1964.

Pace, Biagio, *Arte e civiltà della Sicilia antica*, Milan, I–III, 1935–1946.

Pallottino, Massimo, *Etruscan Painting*, Geneva, 1953.

————, *Gli Etruschi*, Rome, 1940.

————, *Etruscologia*, Milan, 1950.

————, *Mostra dell'arte e della civiltà etrusca*, Milan, 1955.

————, *La Scuola di Vulca*, Rome, 1945.

————, "Tarquinia," in *Monumenti Antichi dei Lincei*, XXXV, 1937.

————, and Hürliman, M., *The Art of the Etruscans*, New York, 1955.

Paoletti, Anna, *Studi su Perugia etrusca*, Perugia, 1923.

Pareti, Luigi, *La tomba Regolini-Galassi del Museo Gregoriano Etrusco e la civiltà dell'Italia centrale nel VII sec. a. C.*, Vatican City, 1947.

————, Griffo, P., and Matt, L. von, *Ancient Sicily*, Genoa, 1959.

Paribeni, Enrico, "I rilievi chiusini arcaici," in *Studi Etruschi*, XII–XIII, 1938–1939.

Patroni, Giovanni, *Architettura preistorica generale ed etrusca: Architettura etrusca*, Bergamo, 1941.

Perali, Pericle, *Orvieto etrusca*, Rome, 1928.

Polacco, Luigi, *Tuscanicae dispositiones*, Padua, 1952.

Poulsen, Frederik, *Etruscan Tomb Paintings: Their Subjects and Significance* (English trans. by Ingeborg Andersen, Oxford, 1922.

————, *Den Etruskische Samling: Ny Carlsberg Glyptothek*, Copenhagen, 1966.

Puglisi, Salvatore, *Studi e ricerche su Orvieto etrusca*, Catania, 1934.

Randall-MacIver, David, *Villanovans and Early Etruscans*, Oxford, 1924.

Richter, Gisela M. A., *Ancient Italy*, Ann Arbor, 1955.

Riis, Poul J., *An Introduction to Etruscan Art*, Copenhagen, 1953.

————, *Tyrrhenikà*, Copenhagen, 1941.

Romanelli, Pietro, *Le pitture della Tomba della Caccia e della Pesca* (*Monumenti della pittura antica*), Rome, 1938.

Roncalli, F., *Le lastre dipinte da Cerveteri*, Florence, 1965.

Rumpf, Andreas, *Die etruskischen Skulpturen: Staatliche Museen zu Berlin*, Berlin, 1928.

————, *Die Wandmalereien in Veji*, Leipzig, 1915.

Ruyt, Franz de, *Charun démon étrusque de la mort*, Brussels, 1934.

Sestieri, Pellegrino C., "Tombe dipinte di Paestum," in *Rivista dell'Istituto di Archeologia e Storia dell'Arte*, 1956–1957.

Stryk, F. von, *Studien über die etruskische Kammergräber*, Dorpat, 1910.

Sundwall, Johannes, *Die älteren italischen Fibeln*, Berlin, 1943.

Thimme, Jürgen, "Chiusinische Aschenkisten und Sarkophage der hellenistischen Zeit," in *Studi Etruschi*, XXIII—XXV, 1954–1957.

Tiné Bertocchi, Fernanda, *La pittura funeraria Apula* (*Monumenti Antichi della Magna Grecia*, I), Naples, 1964.

Van Buren, Elizabeth, D., *Figurative Terracotta Revetments in Etruria and Latium*, London, 1921.

Ward-Perkins, John B., *Veii: the Historical Topography of the Ancient City* (*Papers of the British School at Rome*, XXXIX, N.S. XVI), London, 1961.

Weege, Fritz, *Etruskische Malerei*, Halle, 1921.

————, "Oskische Grabmalerei," in *Jahrbuch des Deutschen Archäologischen Instituts*, XXIV, 1909.

Zanotti Bianco, Umberto, and Matt, Leonard von, *Magna Graecia*, trans. by H. Hoffman, New York, 1962.

HANDBOOKS AND GENERAL WORKS ON ROMAN ART

Becatti, Giovanni, *Arte Romana*, Milan, 1961.

Brilliant, Richard, *Gesture and Rank in Roman Art* (*Memoirs of the Connecticut Academy*, XIV), New Haven, 1963.

Byvanck, A. W., *De Kunst der Oudheid*, V, Leiden, 1965.

————, *Les origines du Bas Empire*, Leiden, 1964.

Della Seta, Alessandro, *Italia Antica*, 2d ed., Bergamo, 1928.

————, *Monumenti dell'antichità classica*, II: *Italia*, 2d ed., Naples, 1933.

Ducati, Pericle, *L'arte in Roma dalle origini al sec. VIII*, Bologna, 1938.

Essen, Carel C. van, *De Kunst van het oude Rome*, The Hague, 1954.

————, *Précis d'histoire de l'art antique en Italie*, (Collection Latomus, XLII), Brussels, 1960.

Frova, Antonio, *L'arte di Roma e del mondo romano*, Turin, 1961.

Garcia y Bellido, Antonio, *Arte Romana*, Madrid, 1957.

Hanfmann, George M. A., *Roman Art*, Greenwich, Conn., 1964.

Kähler, Heinz, *Rom und sein Imperium (Kunst der Welt)*, Baden-Baden, 1962.

———, *Rom und seine Welt*, 2 vols., Munich, 1958–1960.

Koch, Herbert, *Römische Kunst*, Breslau, 1925; 2d ed., Weimar, 1949.

Pallottino, Massimo, *Arte figurativa e ornamentale*, Rome, 1940.

Pijoán, José, *Summa Artis*, V: *El arte romano hasta la muerte de Diocleziano*, Madrid, 1935.

Rodenwaldt, Gerhart, *Kunst der Antike (Propyläen Kunstgeschichte*, III), 2d ed., Berlin, 1927.

Strong, Eugenie S., *Art in Ancient Rome*, 2 vols., New York, 1928.

Technau, Werner, *Die Kunst der Römer (Geschichte der Kunst des Altertums*, II), Berlin, 1940.

Toynbee, Jocelyn M. C., *The Art of the Romans*, London, 1965.

Wheeler, Sir Mortimer, *Roman Art and Architecture*, London, 1964.

ROMAN ART: SOURCES

Becatti, Giovanni, *Arte e gusto negli scrittori latini*, Florence, 1951.

Choisy, August, *Vitruvius*, 4 vols., Paris, 1909.

Ferri, Silvio, *Plinio il Vecchio, storia delle arti antiche*, Rome, 1946.

———, *Vitruvio*, Roma, 1960.

Jücker, Hans, *Vom Verhältnis der Römer zur bildenden Kunst der Griechen*, Bamberg, 1950.

Pliny the Elder, *Natural History*, English trans. by H. Rackham (Loeb Classical Library), 10 vols., Cambridge, Mass., 1938–1962.

Vitruvius, Pollio, *On Architecture*, English trans. by F. Granger (Loeb Classical Library), 2 vols., 1931–1934.

ROMAN ARCHITECTURE

Altmann, Walter, *Die italische Rundbauten*, Berlin, 1906

Anderson, William James, Spiers, R. Phené, and Ashby, Thomas, *The Architecture of Ancient Rome: An Account of Its Historic Development*, rev. ed., London 1927.

Benoit, François, *L'architecture: Antiquité*, Paris, 1911.

Bertoldi, Maria E., "Ricerche sulla decorazione architettonica del Foro di Traiano," in *Studi Miscellanei*, 3, Rome, 1962.

Blake, Marion E., *Ancient Roman Construction in Italy from the Prehistoric Period to Augustus*, Washington, 1947; *Roman Construction in Italy from Tiberius through the Flavians*, Washington, 1959.

Boëthius, Axel, *The Golden House of Nero*, Ann Arbor, 1960.

———, *Roman and Greek Town Architecture*, Gothenburg, 1948.

Brown, Frank E., *Roman Architecture*, New York, 1961.

Bulić, Frane, *Kaiser Diokletians Palast in Split*, Zagreb, 1929.

Choisy, August, *L'art de bâtir chez les Romains*, Paris, 1873.

Cozzo, Giuseppe, *Ingegneria romana*, Rome, 1928.

Crema, Luigi, "Architettura romana," *Enciclopedia Classica*, ser. III, vol. XII, Turin, 1959.

———, *Manuale di storia dell'architettura antica*, Milan, 1962.

Durm, Josef, *Die Baukunst der Etrusker und Römer*, 2d ed., Stuttgart, 1905.

Dyggve, Ejnar, *Aula Sacra — Aula Sanctum*, Copenhagen, 1959.

———, *Ravennatum Palatium Sacrum*, Copenhagen, 1941.

Frank, Tenny, *Roman Buildings of the Republic*, (Papers and Monographs of the American Academy in Rome III), Rome, 1924.

Giovannoni, Gustavo, *La tecnica della costruzione presso i Romani*, Rome, 1925.

Hassel, F. J., *Der Trajansbogen in Benevent*, Mainz, 1966.

Kähler, Heinz, *Hadrian und seine Villa bei Tivoli*, Berlin, 1950.

Lezine, Alexandre, *Architecture romaine d'Afrique*, Paris, 1961.

Lugli, Giuseppe, *La tecnica edilizia romana*, Rome, 1957.

Mac Donald, William L., *The Architecture of the Roman Empire*, London, 1965.

Mercklin, Eugen von, *Antike Figuralkapitelle*, Berlin, 1962.

Noack, Ferdinand, *Die Baukunst des Altertums*, Berlin, 1910.

Rivoira, Giovanni T., *Architettura romana: Costruzione e statica nell'età imperiale*, Milan, 1921. English trans. by G. McN. Rushforth, *Roman Architecture and Its Principles of Construction Under the Empire*, New York, 1930.

Robertson, Donald S., *A Handbook of Greek and Roman Architecture*, 2d ed., Cambridge, 1954.

Shoe, Lucy T., "Etruscan and Republican Roman Mouldings," in *Memoirs of the American Academy in Rome*, XXVII, 1965.

Swoboda, Karl M., *Römische und romanische Paläste*, Vienna, 1924.

Tamm, Birgitta, *Auditorium and Palatium*, Stockholm, 1963.

Töbelmann, Fritz, *Römische Gebälke*, Heidelberg, 1923.

Ward-Perkins, John B., *Constantine and the Origin of the Christian Basilica*, (Papers of the British School at Rome, 22), London, 1954.

Wataghin Cantino, G., *La domus augustana: personalità e problemi della architettura flavia*, Turin, 1965.

Wegner, Max, *Schmuckbasen des antiken Rom*, Münster, 1965.

Wheeler, Sir Mortimer, *Roman Art and Architecture*, London, 1964.

Winter, Franz, *Griechische und Römische Baukunst*, Leipzig, 1926.

Temples

Cagiano de Azevedo, M., "I Capitolia dell'Impero Romano," in *Memorie della Pontificia Accademia*, ser. III, 1940.

Delbrück, Richard, *Die drei Tempel am Forum Holitorium*, Rome, 1903.

———, *Hellenistische Bauten in Latium*, I–II, Strasbourg, 1907–1912.

Gullini, Giorgio, and Fasolo, Furio, *Il santuario della Fortuna Primigenia a Palestrina*, Rome, 1953.

Lewis, M. J. J., *Temples in Roman Britain*, Cambridge, 1965.

Theaters

Bieber, Margarete, *The History of the Greek and Roman Theater*, Princeton, rev. ed., 1961.

Hanson, J. A., *Roman Theater-Temples*, Princeton, 1959.

Neppi Modona, Aldo, *Gli edifici teatrali greci e romani*, Florence, 1961.

Staccioli, Romolo A., and Tognelli, J., *Le Terme e il teatro di Caracalla*, Rome, 1965.

Traversari, Gustavo, *Gli spettacoli in acqua nel teatro tardoantico*, Rome, 1959.

Baths

Angelis D'Ossat, Guglielmo de, *Tecnica costruttiva e impianti delle terme*, Rome, 1943.

Krencker, Daniel, and Krüger, E., *Die Trierer Kaiserthermen*, Berlin, 1951.

Triumphal arches

Kähler, Heinz, "Triumph und Ehrenbogen," in Pauly-Wissowa, *Real-Encyklopädie der Altertumswissenschaft*, VII, 1939.

Mansuelli, Guido A., "El arco honorifico en el dessarrollo de la arquitectura romana," in *Archivo Español de Arqueologia*, XXVII, 1954.

Aqueducts

Van Deman, Esther Boise, *The Building of the Roman Aqueducts*, Washington, 1934.

Walls

Collingwood, B., *Handbook to the Roman Wall*, Newcastle, 1966.

Säflund, Gösta, *Le mura di Roma repubblicana*, Lund, 1932.

Villas

Aurigemma, Salvatore, *Villa Adriana*, Rome, 1961.

Drerup, Heinrich, "Die römische Villa," in *Marburger Winckelmannsprogramm*, Marburg, 1959.

Mansuelli, Guido A., *Le ville del mondo romano*, Milan, 1958.

Thomas, Edit B., *Römische Villen in Pannonien*, Budapest, 1964.

Gardens

Grimal, Pierre, *Les jardins romains à la fin de la république et aux deux premiers siècles de l'Empire*, Paris, 1943.

ROMAN SCULPTURE : GENERAL WORKS

Arias, Paolo E., *La scultura romana*, 2d ed., Messina, 1943.

Blümel, Carl, *Römische Skulpturen: Antiken Sammlung*, Berlin, 1963.

Courbaud, Edmond, *Le bas-relief romain à représentations historiques*, Paris, 1899.

Firatli, N., and Robert, L., *Les stèles funeraires de Bysance gréco-romaine*, Paris, 1964.

Hamberg, Per G., *Studies in Roman Imperial Art*, Uppsala, 1945.

Kaschnitz-Weinberg, Guido, *Das Schöpferische in der römischen Kunst*, ed. by H. von Heintze, Hamburg, 1961.

Oehler, Hans, *Untersuchungen zu den männlichen römischen Mantelstatuen: Der Schulterbauschtypus*, Berlin, 1961.

Strong, Eugenie S., *Roman Sculpture from Augustus to Constantine*, London, 1907.

Will, Ernest, *Le relief cultuel gréco-romain*, Paris, 1956.

PORTRAITS

Bartels, Heiner, *Studien zum Frauenporträt der Augusteischen Zeit*, 1963.

Bernoulli, Johann J., *Römische Ikonographie*, Stuttgart, 1882–1894.

Bethe, Erich, *Ahnenbild und Familiengeschichte bei Römern und Griechen*, Munich, 1935.

Bianchi-Bandinelli, Ranuccio, "Sulla formazione del ritratto romano," in *Società*, 1957. Reprinted in R. Bianchi-Bandinelli, *Archeologia e Cultura*, Milan, 1961.

Blümel, Carl, *Römische Bildnisse: Katalog der Sammlung antiken Skulpturen*, Berlin, 1933.

Boehringer, Erich, *Der Caesar von Acireale*, Stuttgart, 1933.

Bolten, J., *Die Imago Clipeata*, Paderborn, 1937.

Bonacasa, Nicola, *Ritratti greci e romani della Sicilia*, Palermo, 1964.

Bovini, Giuseppe, "Gallieno, la sua iconografia e i riflessi delle vicende storiche e culturali del tempo," in *Atti della Reale Accademia d'Italia, Memorie*, series VII, II, 1, Rome, 1941.

———, "Osservazioni sulla ritrattistica romana da Treboniano Gallo a Probo," in *Monumenti antichi dei Lincei*, XXXIX, 1943.

Brendel, Otto, *Römische Ikonographie des Kaisers Augustus*, Berlin, 1933.

Budde, Ludwig, "Imago clipeata des Kaisers Trajan in Ankara," in *Antike Plastik*, IV, 11, 1965.

———, *Jugendbildnisse des Caracalla und Geta*, Münster, 1951.

Buscholz, K., *Die Bildnisse der Kaiserinnen der Severischen Zeit, nach ihren Frisuren (193–235)*, Berlin, 1963.

Calza, Raissa, *Scavi di Ostia, V: Ritratti greci e romani fino al 160 circa d. C.*, Rome, 1964.

Curtius, Ludwig, "Ikonographische Beiträge zum Porträt der römischen Republik und der Julisch-Claudischen Familie," in *Römische Mitteilungen des Deutschen Archäologischen Instituts*, 1932, 1933, 1935, 1939.

Daltrop, Georg, *Die Stadtrömischen männlichen Privatbildnisse Trajanischer und Hadrianischer Zeit*, Münster, 1958.

Delbrück, Richard, *Antike Porträts*, Bonn, 1912.

———, *Die Münzbildnisse von Maximinus bis Carinus*, Berlin, 1940.

———, *Spätantike Kaiserporträts*, Berlin-Leipzig, 1933.

Fabbrini, Laura, "Il ritratto giovanile di Tiberio," in *Römische Mitteilungen des Deutschen Archäologischen Instituts*, 1964.

Felletti-Maj, Bianca M., *Iconografia imperiale da Severo Alessandro a Carino (222–285)*, Rome, 1958.

———, *I ritratti del Museo Nazionale Romano*, Rome, 1953.

Franciscis, Alfonso de, *Il ritratto romano a Pompei*, Naples, 1951.

Franke, P. B., *Römische Kaiserporträts in Münzbild*, Munich, 1961.

Giuliano, Antonio, *Catalogo dei ritratti romani del Museo Profano Lateranense*, Vatican City, 1957.

Goldscheider, Ludwig, *Roman Portraits*, London, 1945.

Gross, Walter H., *Bildnisse Traians*, Berlin, 1940.

Gross, Walter H. *Iulia Augusta*, Göttingen, 1962.

Hanfmann, George M. A., *Observations on Roman Portraiture*, Brussels, 1953.

Harrison, Evelyn B., *The Athenian Agora*, I: *Portrait Sculpture*, Princeton, 1953.

Hekler, Antal, *Die Bildnisse der Griechen und Römer*, Stuttgart, 1912.

Heintze, Helga von, *Römische Porträtsplastik*, Stuttgart, 1961.

———, "Studien zu den Porträts des 3 Jahrhunderts n. Chr.," in *Römische Mitteilungen des Deutschen Archäologischen Instituts*, 1955, 1956, 1957, 1959.

418

Hinks, Roger P., *Greek and Roman Portrait-Sculpture of the British Museum*, London, 1935.

Inan, Jale, *Römische Porträts aus Gebiet von Antakya*, Ankara, 1965.

————, and Rosenbaum, E., *Roman and Early Byzantine Portrait Sculpture in Asia Minor*, London, 1966.

Jucker, Haus, *Retratos romanos procedentes de las murallas de Barcelona*, Barcelona, 1963.

————, *Das Bildnis im Blätterkelch*, Olten 1961.

Kallipolitis, Vassili, "Portrait grec en bronze de l'epoque de Gallien,'" in *Monuments Piot*, LIV, 1965.

Kaschnitz Weinberg, Guido, *Römische Bildnisse (Ausgewählte Schriften, II)*, Berlin, 1965.

L'Orange, Hans P., *Apotheosis in Ancient Portraiture*, Oslo, 1947.

————, *Studien zur Geschichte des spätantiken Porträts*, Oslo, 1933.

Michalowski, Kazimierz, *Les portraits héllenistiques et romains*, (*École française d'Athène, Exploration archéologique de Délos*, fasc. 13), Paris, 1932.

Monaco, Giorgio, "L'iconografia imperiale nell'Ara Pacis," in *Bollettino Comunale*, Rome, 1934.

Montini, Italo, *Il ritratto di Augusto*, Rome, 1938.

Paribeni, Roberto, *Il ritratto nell'arte antica*, Milan, 1934.

Parlasca, Klaus, *Mumienporträts und verwandte Denkmäler*, Wiesbaden, 1966.

Pietrangeli, Carlo, *La famiglia di Augusto*, Rome, 1938.

Polacco, Luigi, *Il volto di Tiberio*, Padua, 1955.

Poulsen, Frederik, *Greek and Roman Portraits in English Country Houses*, Oxford, 1923.

————, *Probleme der römischen Ikonographie*, Copenhagen, 1937.

————, *Römische Privatporträts und Prinzenbildnisse*, Copenhagen, 1939.

Poulsen, Vagn, *Les Portraits romains, I: République et dynastie julienne* (*Publications de la Glyptothèque Ny Carlsberg*, no. 7), Copenhagen, 1962.

Richter, Gisela M. A., *The Metropolitan Museum of Art: Roman Portraits*, New York, 1941.

Rodenwaldt, Gerhart, "Griechische Porträts aus dem Ausgang der Antike, in *76 Berliner Winckelmannsprogramm*, Berlin, 1919.

Schmidt, Eduard, "Römerbildnisse vom Ausgang der Republik," in *103 Berliner Winckelmannsprogramm*, Berlin, 1944.

Schweitzer, Bernhard, *Die Bildniskunst der römischen Republik*, Leipzig, 1948.

Stuart, Meriwether, *The Portraiture of Claudius*, New York, 1938.

Traversari, Gustavo, *Statue iconiche femminili cirenaiche*, Rome, 1960.

Vermeule, Cornelius C., "Egyptian Contribution to Late Roman Imperial Portraiture," in *Journal of the American Research Center in Egypt*, I, 1962.

Wegner, Max, *Hadrian, Plotina, Marciana, Matidia, Sabina*, Berlin, 1957.

————, *Die Herrscherbildnisse in antoninischer Zeit*, Berlin, 1939.

West, Robert, *Römische Porträtplastik*, I–II, Munich, 1933–1941.

Zadoks, Annie N. (Josephus Jitta), *Ancestral Portraits in Rome and the Art of the Last Century of the Republic*, Amsterdam, 1932.

SCULPTURE OF THE REPUBLICAN PERIOD

Bianchi-Bandinelli, Ranuccio, *Una terracotta dei Musei di Berlino e alcuni elementi formativi dello stile romano*, Milan, 1933.

Carettoni, Gianfilippo, "Il fregio figurato della Basilica Emilia," in *Rivista dell'Istituto di Archeologia e Storia dell'Arte*, new series X, 1961.

Essen, Carel C. van, "Chronologie van de Romeinsche Sculpturtijdens de Republik," in *Mededeelingen van het Nederlandsch Historisch Institut te Rome*, VII, 1928.

Goethert, Friedrich W., *Zur Kunst der römischen Republik*, Berlin, 1931.

Poulsen, Frederik, "Die Römer republikanischer Zeit und ihre Stellung zur Kunst," in *Die Antike*, XIII, 1937.

Vessberg, Olof, *Studien zur Kunstgeschichte der römischen Republik*, Lund, 1941.

Zinserling, Gerhard, "Das sogenannte Esquilinische Wandgemälde im Konservatorenpalast: Datierung und Deutung," in *Eirene*, I, 1960.

SCULPTURE OF THE AUGUSTAN AND JULIO-CLAUDIAN PERIOD

Charbonneaux, Jean, *L'art au siècle d'Auguste*, Paris, 1948.

Goethert, Friedrich W., "Studien zur Kopienforschung I: Die Stil und Trachtgeschichtliche Entwicklung der Togastatuen in den beiden ersten Jahrhunderten der Kaiserzeit," in *Römische Mitteilungen des Deutschen Archäologischen Instituts*, 1939.

Gross, Walter, *Zur Augustusstatue von Prima Porta*, Göttingen, 1959.

Jacopi, Giulio, *L'antro di Tiberio e il Museo di Sperlonga*, Rome, 1965.

Kähler, Heinz, *Die Augustusstatue von Prima Porta*, Berlin, 1959.

Kraus, Theodor, *Die Ranken der Ara Pacis*, Berlin, 1953.

Moretti, Giuseppe, *L'Ara Pacis Augustae*, Rome, 1948.

Mustilli, Domenico, "L'arte augustea," in *Augustus*, Rome, 1938.

Poinssot, Louis, *L'autel de la gens Augusta à Carthage*, Paris, 1929.

Poulsen, Vagn, "Claudische Prinzen," in *Deutsche Beiträge zur Altertumswissenschaft*, 14, Baden-Baden, 1960.

Rizzo, Giulio E., "La base di Augusto," in *Bollettino Comunale*, Rome, 1932.

Rodenwaldt, Gerhart, *Kunst um Augustus*, Berlin, 1942.

Säflund, Gösta, *Fynden in Tiberinsgrotten*, Stockholm, 1966.

Simon, Erika, *Der Augustus von Prima Porta*, Bremen, 1959.

Strocka, Volker M., "Die Brunnenreliefs Grimani," in *Antike Plastik*, IV, 10, 1965.

Toynbee, Jocelyn M. C., "Ara Pacis Reconsidered and Historical Art in Roman Italy," in *Proceedings of the British Academy*, 39, London, 1953.

SCULPTURE OF THE FLAVIAN PERIOD

Blanckenhagen, Peter H. von, "Elemente der römischen Kunst am Beispiel des flavischen Stils," in H. Berve, *Das neue Bild der Antike*, Leipzig, 1942.

————, *Flavische Architektur und ihre Dekoration untersucht am Nervaforum*, Berlin, 1940.

Lehmann-Hartleben, Karl, "L'arco di Tito," in *Bollettino Comunale*, Rome, 1934.

Magi, Filippo, *I rilievi flavi del Palazzo della Cancelleria*, Rome, 1945.

Toynbee, Jocelyn M. C., *The Flavian Reliefs from the Palazzo della Cancelleria in Rome*, London-Oxford, 1957.

SCULPTURE OF THE TRAJANIC PERIOD

Becatti, Giovanni, *La colonna coclide istoriata*, Rome, 1960.

Bertoldi, Maria E., "Ricerche sulla decorazione architettonica del Foro Traiano," in *Studi Miscellanei*, no. 3, Rome, 1962.

Bianchi-Bandinelli, Ranuccio, "Il maestro delle imprese di Traiano," in *Le Arti*, 1939. Reprinted in R. Bianchi-Bandinelli, *Storicità dell'arte classica*, Florence, 1950.

Goethert, Friedrich W., "Traianische Friese," in *Jahrbuch des Deutschen Archäologischen Instituts*, 1936.

Hamberg, Per G., *Studies in Roman Imperial Art*, Uppsala, 1945.

Hassel, Franz J., *Der Trajansbogen in Benevent*, Mainz, 1966.

Lehmann-Hartleben, Karl, *Die Traianssäule*, Berlin, 1926.

Pallottino, Massimo, *Il grande fregio di Traiano*, Rome, 1933.

Smallwood, E. M., *Documents Illustrating the Principates of Nerva, Trajan and Hadrian*, Cambridge, 1966.

Snijder, Geerto A., "Der Trajansbogen in Benevent: Bemerkungen zur Trajanischen und Hadrianischen Skulptur," in *Jahrbuch des Deutschen Archäologischen Instituts*, 1926.

Strack, Paul, *Untersuchungen zur römischen Reichsprägung des zweiten Jahrhunderts*, I: *Trajan*, Stuttgart, 1931.

Stucchi, Sandro, "Contributo alla conoscenza della topografia, dell'arte e della storia della Colonna Traiana" in *Atti dell'Accademia di Udine*, 1957–1960, VII, vol. I, Udine, 1960.

SCULPTURE OF THE HADRIANIC PERIOD

Clairmont, Christophe W., *Die Bildnisse des Antinous*, Neuchâtel, 1966.

Graindor, Paul, *Athènes sous Hadrien*, Cairo, 1932.

Holm, E., *Das Bildnis des Antinous*, Leipzig, 1933.

Marconi, Pirro, "Antinoo: Saggio sull'arte adrianea," in *Monumenti antichi dei Lincei*, XXIX, 1923.

Toynbee, Jocelyn M. C., *The Hadrianic School: A Chapter in the History of Greek Art*, Cambridge, Eng., 1934.

SCULPTURE OF THE ANTONINE PERIOD

Becatti, Giovanni, *La colonna coclide istoriata*, Rome, 1960.

Budde, Ludwig, *Die Entstehung des antiken Repräsentationsbildes*, Berlin, 1957.

Caprino, Catia, and Others, *La Colonna di Marco Aurelio illustrata a cura del Comune di Roma*, Rome, 1955.

Hamberg, Per G., *Studies in Roman Imperial Art*, Uppsala, 1945.

Rodenwaldt, Gerhart, "Über den Stilwandel in der antoninischen Kunst," in *Abhandlungen der Preussischen Akademie der Wissenschaften*, 1935.

Wegner, Max, "Bemerkungen zu den Ehrendenkmälern des Marcus Aurelius," in *Jahrbuch des Deutschen Archäologischen Instituts, Archäologische Anzeiger*, LIII, 1938.

———, "Die kunstgeschichtliche Stellung der Marcussäule," in *Jahrbuch des Deutschen Archäologischen Instituts*, 1931.

Zwikker, W., *Studien zur Markussäule*, Amsterdam, 1941.

SCULPTURE OF THE SEVERAN PERIOD

Bianchi-Bandinelli, R., Caputo, G., and Vergara Caffarelli, E., *Leptis Magna*, Rome, 1963.

Budde, Ludwig, *Severische Relief im Palazzo Sacchetti*, Berlin, 1955.

Franchi, Luisa, "Ricerche sull'arte di età severiana in Roma," in *Studi Miscellanei*, no. 4, Rome, 1964.

Pallottino, Massimo, *L'arco degli Argentari*, Rome, 1946.

Squarciapino, Maria, *La Scuola di Afrodisia*, Rome, 1943.

Ward-Perkins, John, "The Art of the Severan Age," in *Proceedings of the British Academy*, 1951.

SCULPTURE OF THE LATE EMPIRE

Becatti Giovanni, *La colonna coclide istoriata*, Rome, 1960.

Berenson, Bernard, *L'arco di Costantino*, Florence, 1952.

Bettini, Sergio, *L'arte alla fine del mondo antico*, Padua, 1948.

Bianchi-Bandinelli, Ranuccio, "La crisi artistica della fine del mondo antico," in *Società*, VII, 1952. Reprinted in R. Bianchi-Bandinelli, *Archeologia e cultura*, Milan, 1961.

———, "Il problema della scultura romana del III–IV secolo," in *Acme*, 1952. Reprinted in R. Bianchi-Bandinelli, *Archeologia e cultura*, Milan, 1961.

Bonicatti, Maurizio, *Studi di storia dell'arte sulla Tarda Antichità e sull'Alto Medioevo*, Rome, 1963.

Bruns, Gerda, *Der Obelisk und seine Basis auf dem Hippodrom zu Konstantinopel*, (*Istanbuler Forschungen*, VII), Istanbul, 1935.

Cagiano da Azevedo, Michelangelo, "I cosiddetti Tetrarchi di Venezia," in *Commentari*, 1962.

Delbrück, Richard, *Antike Porphyrwerke*, Berlin-Leipzig, 1932.

———, *Spätantike Kaiserporträte vom Konstantinus Magnus bis zum Ende des Westreiches*, Berlin, 1926.

Ferri, Silvio, "Plotino e l'arte del III secolo," in *La Critica d'Arte*, 1936.

Giglioli, Giulio Q., *La Colonna di Arcadio*, Naples, 1952.

Giuliano, Antonio, *L'arco di Costantino*, Milan, 1955.

Grabar, André, "Plotin et les origines de l'esthétique médiévale," in *Cahiers Archéologiques*, I, 1945.

Gullini, Giorgio, *Maestri e botteghe in Roma da Gallieno alla Tetrarchia*, Turin, 1960.

Kähler, Heinz, "Zwei Sockel eines Triumphbogens im Boboligarten zu Florenz," in *96 Berliner Winckelmannsprogramm*, Berlin, 1936.

———, *Das Fünfsäulendenkmal für die Tetrarchen auf dem Forum Romanum*, Cologne, 1964.

Kinch, K.-F., *L'arc de triomphe de Salonique*, Paris, 1890.

Koch, H., "Spätantike Kunst," in *Probleme der Spätantike*, Stuttgart, 1930.

Kollwitz, Johannes, *Oströmische Plastik der theodosianischen Zeit*, Berlin, 1941.

Lietzmann, Hans, "Das Problem der Spätantike," in *Sitzungsberichte der Preussischen Akademie der Wissenschaften*, 1927.

L'Orange, Hans P., "Ein Tetrarchisches Ehrendenkmal auf dem Forum Romanum," in *Römische Mitteilungen des Deutschen Archäologischen Instituts*, LIII, 1938.

———, and Gerkan, Armin von, *Spätantiker Bildschmuck des Konstantinsbogens*, Berlin, 1936.

Ragona, Antonino, *I Tetrarchi dei gruppi porfirei di San Marco a Venezia*, Caltagirone, 1963.

Rodenwaldt, Gerhart, "Römische Reliefs: Vorstufen zur Spätantike," in *Jahrbuch des Deutschen Archäologischen Instituts*, 1940.

———, "Zur Kunstgeschichte der Jahre 220 bis 270," in *Jahrbuch des Deutschen Archäologischen Instituts*, 1936.

Rumpf, Andreas, *Stilphasen der spätantiken Kunst: ein Versuch*, Cologne, 1957.

Schweitzer, Bernhard, *Die spätantiken Grundlagen der mittelalterlichen Kunst*, Leipzig, 1949.

Sieveking, Johannes, "Zu den beiden Triumphbogensockeln im Boboligarten," in *Römische Mitteilungen des Deutschen Archäologischen Instituts*, LII, 1937.

SARCOPHAGI

Altmann, Walter, *Architektur und Ornamentik der antiken Sarkophage*, Berlin, 1902.

Andreae, Bernard, *Motivgeschichtliche Untersuchungen zu den römischen Schlachtsarkophagen*, Berlin, 1956.

————, "Studien zur römischen Grabkunst," in *Römische Mitteilungen des Deutschen Archäologischen Instituts, Ergänzungsheft* IX, 1964.

Bartoccini, Renato, "Il sarcofago di Velletri," in *Rivista dell'Istituto di Archeologia e Storia dell'Arte*, VII, 1958.

Bianchi-Bandinelli, Ranuccio, "Sarcofago di Acilia con la designazione di Gordiano III," in *Bollettino d'Arte*, 1954. Reprinted in R. Bianchi-Bandinelli, *Archeologia e cultura*, Milan, 1961.

Bovini, Giuseppe, *I sarcofagi paleocristiani*, Vatican City, 1949.

————, *I sarcofagi paleocristiani della Spagna*, Vatican City, 1954.

Cumont, Franz, *Recherches sur le symbolisme funéraire des Romains*, Paris, 1942.

Ferrari, Gloria, *Il commercio dei sarcofagi asiatici*, Rome, 1966.

Gerke, Friedrich, *Die Christliche Sarkophagen der vorkonstantinischer Zeit*, Berlin, 1940.

Giuliano, Antonio, *Il commercio dei sarcofagi attici* (*Studia Archaeologica*, IV), Rome, 1962.

Gütschow, Margarete, "Das Museum der Praetextat Katakomben," in *Memorie della Pontificia Accademia*, IV, 1938.

Hanfmann, George M. A., *The Season Sarcophagus in Dumbarton Oaks*, Cambridge, Mass., 1951.

Himmelmann-Wildschütz, Nikolaus, "Sarkophag eines gallienischen Konsuls," in *Festschrift für F. Matz*, Mainz, 1962.

Lücken, Gottfried von, "Zu römischen Hochzeitsarkophagen," in *Das Altertum*, II, 1956.

Marrou, Henri I., *Mousikòs Anér: Étude sur les scènes de la vie intellectuelle figurant sur les monuments funéraires romains*, Grenoble, 1938; 2d ed., 1964.

Matz, Friedrich, "Ein römisches Meisterwerk," in *Jahrbuch des Deutschen Archäologischen Instituts, Ergänzungsheft* XIX, 1958.

Olsen, Erling C., and Lehmann-Hartleben, Karl L. H., *Dionysiac Sarcophagi in Baltimore*, New York, 1942.

Pesce, Gennaro, *Sarcofagi romani in Sardegna*, Rome, 1957.

Pietrogrande, Antonluigi, "Sarcofago policromo," in *Bollettino Comunale*, LX, Rome, 1933.

Reschke, Eberhard, *Römische Sarkophagkunst zwischen Gallienus und Constantin der Grosser*, Berlin, 1966.

Robert, Karl, Rodenwaldt, Gerhart, and Rumpf, Andreas, *Die antiken Sarkophagreliefs*, Berlin, 1890–.

Rodenwaldt, Gerhart, "Der Klinensarkophag von San Lorenzo," in *Jahrbuch des Deutschen Archäologischen Instituts*, XLV, 1930.

————, "Römische Löwen," in *La Critica d'Arte*, V, 1936.

————, *Der Sarkophag Caffarelli*, Berlin, 1925.

————, "Säulensarkophage," in *Römische Mitteilungen des Deutschen Archäologischen Instituts*, 1923.

————, "Eine spätantike Kunstströmung in Rom," in *Römische Mitteilungen des Deutschen Archäologischen Instituts*, 1921–1922.

Schönebeck, H. von, "Die christliche Sarkophagplastik," in *Römische Mitteilungen des Deutschen Archäologischen Instituts*, LI, 1936.

Sichtermann, Hellmut, *Späte Endymion-Sarkophage*, Baden-Baden, 1966.

Stommel, Eduard, *Beiträge zur Ikonographie der Konstantinischer Sarkophagplastik*, Bonn, 1954.

Toynbee, Jocelyn M. C., *The Hadrianic School: A Chapter in the History of Greek Art*, Cambridge, 1934.

Traversari, Gustavo, *Classico e barocco nei rilievi dei sarcofagi romani*, Padua, 1965.

Turcan, Robert, *Les sarcophages romaines à représentations Dionysiaques*, Paris, 1966.

Tusa, Vincenzo, *I sarcofagi romani in Sicilia*, Palermo, 1957.

Uggeri, Giovanni, "Il sarcofago del Coemeterium cis Callisti ad viam Ardeatinam," in *Studi Miscellanei*, no. 11, Rome, 1966.

Vaccaro Melucco, A., "Sarcofagi romani di caccia al leone," in *Studi Miscellanei*, no. 11, Rome, 1966.

Wegner, Max, *Die Musensarkophage*, Berlin, 1966.

Wiegartz, Hans, *Kleinasiatische Säulensarkophage*, Berlin, 1965.

Wilpert, Joseph, *I sarcofagi cristiani antichi*, Rome, 1929–1936.

DECORATIVE WORKS

Altmann, Walter, *Die römische Grabaltäre der Kaiserzeit*, Berlin, 1905.

Gusman, Pierre, *L'art décoratif de Rome*, I–II, Paris, 1912.

Hermann, Werner, *Römische Götteraltäre*, Kallmünz, 1961.

Pernice, Erich A., and Behncke, Wilhelm, "Das Kunstgewerbe im Altertum," in Lehnert, G. H., *Geschichte des Kunstgewerbes*, Berlin, 1907.

Richter, Gisela M. A., *Ancient Furniture: A History of Greek, Etruscan and Roman Furniture*, Oxford, 1926; 2d ed., London, 1966.

Spinazzola, Vittorio, *Le arti decorative in Pompei e nel Museo Nazionale di Napoli*, Milan, 1928.

ROMAN TERRACOTTAS

Deonna, Waldemar, *Les statues de terre cuite dans l'antiquité: Sicile, Grand Grèce, Etrurie et Rome*, Paris, 1908.

Hafner, German, "Frauen- und Mädchenbilder aus Terrakotta im Museo Gregoriano Etrusco," in *Römische Mitteilungen des Deutschen Archäologischen Instituts*, 1965.

La Baume, Peter, *Römische Kunstgewerbe*, Brunswick, 1964.

Rohden, Hermann von, *Die Terrakotten von Pompeji*, Stuttgart, 1880.

————, and Winnefeld, Hermann, *Architektonische römische Tonreliefs von der Kaiserzeit*, Berlin, 1911.

GOLDWORK AND SILVERWORK

Arias, Paolo E., "Il piatto argenteo di Cesena," in *Annuario della Scuola Archeologica Italiana di Atene*, XXIV–XXV, new series VIII–X, 1946–1948.

Beckwith, John, *The Basilewski Situla*, London, 1963.

Bendinelli, Goffredo, *Il tesoro di argenteria di Marengo*, Turin, 1937.

Carandini, Andrea, "La secchia Doria: Una 'storia di Achille' tardo antica," in *Studi Miscellanei*, no. 9, Rome, 1965.

Curle, Alexander O., *The Mildenhall Treasure*, London, 1955.

————, *The Treasure of Traprain: A Scottish Hoard of Roman Silver Plate*, Glasgow, 1923.

Dalton, Ormonde M., *The Treasure of the Oxus with other Examples of Early Oriental Metalwork*, London, 1926.

Dodd, Erica C., *Byzantine Silver Stamps*, Washington, 1961.

421

Dohrn, Tobias, "Spätantikes Silber aus Britannien," in *Mitteilungen des Deutschen Archäologischen Instituts*, II, 1949.

Laur-Belart, Rudolf, *Der spätrömische Silberschatz von Kaiseraugst: Katalog des Römermuseums in Augst (Switzerland)*, Augst, 1963.

Levi, Alda, *La pateva d'argento di Parabiago*, Rome, 1935.

Matzulewitsch, Leonid A., *Byzantinische Antike: Studien auf Grund der Silbergefässe der Ermitage*, Berlin-Leipzig, 1929.

The Mildenhall Treasure: A Provisional Handbook, London, 1947.

Odobescu, Alexandru, *Le trésor de Petrossa: Étude sur l'orfèvrerie antique*, Paris, 1889–1900.

Walters, Henry B., *Catalogue of Silver Plate in the British Museum*, London, 1921.

ROMAN GLASS

Berger, Ludwig, *Römische Gläser aus Vindonissa (Veröffentlichungen der Gesellschaft pro Vindonissa*, 4), Basel, 1960.

Coarelli, Filippo, "Alcuni vetri dipinti scoperti nella Germania indipendente e sul commercio alessandrino nei primi due secoli dell'impero," in *Archeologia Classica*, XV, I, 1963.

Eisen, Gustavus A., and Kouchakji, Fahim, *Glass: its Origin, History, Chronology, Technic and Classification to the Sixteenth Century*, I–II, New York, 1927.

Fremersdorf, Fritz, *Figürliche geschliffene Gläser einer Kölner Werkstatt des 3 Jahrhunderts (Römisch-Germanische Forschungen*, 19), Berlin, 1951.

―――, *Römisches Buntglas in Köln*, Cologne, 1958.

Harden, Donald B., *Roman Glass from Karanis*, Ann Arbor, 1936.

Honey, William B., *Glass*, London, 1946.

Isings, Clasina, *Roman Glass from Dated Finds*, Groningen, 1957.

Kisa, Anton C., *Das Glas im Altertume*, I–III, Leipzig, 1908.

Morin, Jean, *La verrerie en Gaule sous l'empire romain*, Paris, 1913.

Neuberg, Frederic, *Antikes Glas*, Darmstadt, 1962. English trans. by M. Bullock and A. Jaffa, *Ancient Glass*, Toronto, 1962.

Neuburg, Frederic, *Glass in Antiquity*, London, 1949.

Sangiorgi, Giorgio, *Collezione di vetri antichi*, Milan-Rome, 1914.

Simon, Erika, *Die Portlandvase*, Mainz, 1957.

IVORIES OF THE IMPERIAL AND LATE ANTIQUE PERIODS

Belloni, Gianguido, *Avori tardo-classici e alto-medioevali*, Milan, 1958.

Delbrück, Richard, *Die Consulardiptychen und verwandete Denkmäler*, Berlin, 1929.

Kanzler, Rodolfo, *Gli avori dei Musei profano e sacro della Biblioteca Vaticana*, Rome, 1903.

Kollwitz, Johannes, *Die Lipsanothek von Brescia*, Berlin, 1933.

Volbach, Wolfgang F., *Elfenbeinarbeiten der spätantike und des frühen Mittelalters*, Mainz, 1952.

GEMS OF THE IMPERIAL AND LATE ANTIQUE PERIODS

Alföldi, Andreas, "Der grosse römische Kameo der Trierer Stadtbibliothek," in *Trierer Zeitschrift*, XIX, 1950.

Babelon, Ernest, *Catalogue des cammées antiques et modernes de la Bibliothèque Nationale*, Paris, 1897.

Bruns, Gerda, *Staatskameen des Altertums und der Neuzeit*, Berlin, 1948.

Coche de la Ferté, Étienne, *Le Camée Rothschild: Un chef d'oeuvre du IVe siècle ap. J. C.*, Paris, 1957.

Eichler, Fritz, *Die Kameen im Kunsthistorischen Museum*, Vienna, 1927.

PROVINCIAL ROMAN ART

Almagro-Basch, Martín, and Garcia y Bellido, Antonio, *Ars Hispaniae*, I, Madrid, 1946.

Arte e civiltà romana nell'Italia settentrionale dalla repubblica alla tetrarchia, Bologna, I–II, 1964–1965.

Babelon, E., Cagnat, R., and Reinach, S., *Atlas archéologique de la Tunisie*, Paris, 1892–1913.

Bartoccini, Renato, "L'arco quadrifronte dei Severi a Leptis," in *Africa Italiana*, 1931.

Blanchet, Adrien, *Étude sur la décoration des édifices de la Gaule romaine*, Paris, 1913.

Braemer, François, *Les stèles funeraires à personnages de Bordeaux, I–III siècles*, Paris, 1959.

Buber, Paul, *Die griechisch-äegyptischen Mumienbildnisse der Sammlung Graf*, Vienna, 1922.

Camón Aznar, José, *Las artes y los pueblos de la España primitiva*, Madrid, 1954.

Caputo, Giacomo, *Il teatro di Sabratha e l'architettura teatrale Africana*, Rome, 1959.

Chenet, Georges, *La céramique gallo-romaine d'Argonne du IVe siècle et le terre sigillé decorée a la molette*, Mâcon, 1941.

―――, and Gaudron, Guy, *La céramique sigilée d'Argonnes des II et III siècles*, Paris, 1955.

Coche de la Ferté, Étienne, *Les portraits romano-égyptiens du Louvre*, Paris, 1952.

Collingwood, Robin G., *The Archaeology of Roman Britain*, London, 1930.

Cončev (Zoncev), D., *Monuments de la sculpture romaine en Bulgarie méridionale (Collection Latomus, XXXIX)*, Brussels, 1959.

Déchelette, Joseph, *Les vases céramiques ornées de la Gaule romaine (Narbonnaise, Aquitaine, et Lyonnaise)*, 2 vols., Paris, 1904.

Deonna, Waldemar, *L'art romain en Suisse*, Geneva, 1942.

Dimitrov, Dimitar, *Die Grabstelen römischer Zeit in Nordbulgarien*, Sofia, 1942.

Drack, Walter, *Die römische Wandmalerei der Schweiz*, Basel, 1950.

Dragendorf, Hans, and Krüger, E., *Das Grabmal von Igel*, Trier, 1924.

Du Mesnil du Buisson, Robert, Comte, *Les peintures de la Synagogue de Doura-Europos*, Rome, 1939.

Edgar, Campbell, C., *Greco-Egyptian Coffins, Masks and Portraits: Catalogue général des antiquités égyptiennes du Musée du Caire*, XXVI, Cairo, 1905.

Eggers, Hans J., *Der römische Import im freien Germanien*, Hamburg, 1951.

Espérandieu, Émile, *Recueil général des bas-reliefs, statues et bustes de la Gaule romaine*, I–XI, Paris, 1907–1938; XII–XIII, ed. by R. Lantier, Paris, 1947–1949.

―――, *Recueil général des bas-reliefs, statues et bustes de la Germanie romaine*, Paris, 1931.

Eydoux, Henri P., *Monuments et trésors de la Gaule: Les récentes découvertes archéologiques*, Paris, 1958.

Felletti-Maj, Bianca M., *Siria, Palestina e Arabia settentrionale nel periodo romano*, Rome, 1950.

Ferri, Silvio, *Arte romana sul Danubio*, Milan, 1933.

―――, *Arte romana sul Reno*, Milan, 1931.

Filov, Bogdan D., *L'art antique en Bulgarie*, Sofia, 1925.

Florescu, Florea B., *Monumentul de la Adamklissi Tropaeum Traiani*, Bucharest, 1959; 2d ed., 1961.

Frova, Antonio, *Pittura romana in Bulgaria*, Rome, 1943.

Gabra, Sami, and Drioton, Étienne, *Peintures à fresques et scènes peintes à Hermoupolis Ouest*, Cairo, 1954.

Garcia y Bellido, Antonio, *Esculturas romanas de España y Portugal*, Madrid, 1949.

Giuliano, Antonio, *La cultura artistica della provincia Grecia*, Rome, 1965.

Graindor, Paul, *Terres cuites de l'Égypte gréco-romain*, Antwerp, 1939.

Grenier, Albert, *Habitations gauloises et villas latines dans la cité des Médiomatrices*, Paris, 1906.

Gsell, Stéphane, *Atlas archéologique de l'Algérie*, Algiers-Paris, 1902–1911.

Hahl, Lothar, *Zur Stilentwicklung der provinzialrömischen Plastik in Germanien und Gallien*, Darmstadt, 1937.

Hart, J. J., *Sculptures Gaulois*, Paris, 1966.

Hermet, Frédéric, *La Graufesenque*, I–II, Paris, 1934.

Hettner, Felix, *Die römische Steindenkmäler des Provinzialmuseums zu Trier*, Trier, 1893.

Ingholt, Harald, *Studien over Palmyrensk Skulptur*, Copenhagen, 1928.

Jenny, Wilhelm A. Ritter von, *Keltische Metallarbeiten aus heidnischer und christlicher Zeit*, Berlin, 1935.

Kähler, Heinz, *Die römische Kapitelle im Rheingebiete* (*Römische Germanische Forschungen*, 13), Berlin, 1939.

Lantier, Raymond, *Bas-reliefs de la Gaule romaine*, Paris, 1965.

Leschi, Louis, *Algérie antique*, Paris, 1952.

Lewis, M. J. T., *Temples in Roman Britain*, Cambridge, 1965.

Lezine, Alexandre, *Architecture romaine d'Afrique*, Paris, 1964.

Liversidge, Joan, *Furniture in Roman Britain*, London, 1955.

Luickenheld, E., *Les stèles funéraires en forme de maison chez les Médiomatrices et en Gaule*, Paris, 1927.

Lyons, Islay, and Ingholt, Harald, *Gandharan Art in Pakistan*, New York, 1957.

Mariën, Marcel E., *La sculpture à l'époque romaine en Belgique*, Brussels, 1945.

Melida y Alinari, José R., *Monumentos romanos de España*, Madrid, 1925.

Meunier, M., *La villa Belgo-romaine de "Fin de ville,"* Brussels, 1964.

Miatev, Krsto, *La peinture décorative de la nécropole de Serdica*, Sofia, 1925.

Morey, Charles R., *Excavations at Sardis: Roman and Christian Sculpture, The Sarcophagus of Claudia Antonia Sabina and the Asiatic Sarcophagi*, Leiden, 1926.

Noll, Rudolf, *Kunst der Römerzeit in Oesterreich*, Salzburg, 1949.

Panaitescu, Emil, *Monumenti della civiltà romana nella Mesia* (*Studi Romani del mondo*, II), 1935.

Parlasca, Klaus, *Römische Wandmalerei in Augsburg*, Kallmünz, 1956.

Pericot Garcia, Luis, *Historia de España*, Barcelona, 1934.

Pobé, M., and Roubier, J., *The Art of Roman Gaul*, Paris, 1961.

Poulsen, Frederik, *De Palmyrenske Skulpturer*, Lund, 1921.

————, *Sculptures antiques des musées de province espagnoles*, Copenhagen, 1933.

Quilling, Friedrich, *Die Nerosäule*, Leipzig, 1919.

Le rayonnement des civilizations grecque et romaine sur les cultures péripheriques (*VIII Congrès International d'Archéologie Classique, Paris, 1963*), Paris, 1965.

Richmond, Ian Archibald, *Roman Britain*, London, 1947.

Rostovtzev, Michael, *L'art grec iranien*, Paris, 1933.

Schober, Arnold, *Die Grabsteine von Noricum und Pannonien*, Vienna, 1923.

————, *Die Römerzeit in Oesterreich*, Vienna, 1955.

Schoppa, Helmut, *Die Kunst der Römerzeit in Gallien, Germanien und Britannien*, Munich, 1957.

Squarciapino, Maria, *La scuola di Afrodisia*, Rome, 1943.

Taracena Aguirre, Blas, and Hughet, P. B., *Ars Hispaniae*, II, Madrid, 1947.

Toynbee, Jocelyn M. C., *Art in Britain under the Romans*, Oxford, 1964.

————, *Art in Roman Britain*, London, 1962.

Wacher, Jolm S., *The Civitas Capitals of Roman Britain*, Leicester, 1966.

West, Louis C., *Roman Gaul: The Objects of Trade*, Oxford, 1935.

Wheeler, Sir Mortimer, *Rome beyond the Imperial Frontier*, Harmondsworth, 1954.

Will, Ernest, *La sculpture romaine au Musée lapidaire de Vienne*, Vienne, 1952.

Wuilleumier, Pierre, and Audin, A., *Les médaillons d'applique gallo-romains de la vallée du Rhone*, Paris, 1952.

PHOTOGRAPHIC CREDITS

The author wishes to thank all those who have helped him in collecting the illustrations for this book and in particular the German Archaeological Institute of Rome, the German Archaeological Institute of Athens, the Soprintendenze alle Antichità of Florence, Rome, Ostia, and Naples, the Gabinetto Fotografico Nazionale of Rome, the Encyclopedia of World Art, the Enciclopedia dell'Arte Antica, the museums of Munich, Berlin, and Athens, the Agora Museum in Athens, the Louvre, the British Museum, the Museum of Fine Arts, Boston, and the Metropolitan Museum of Art, New York. Photographs have been supplied by the museums or collections owning the works of art, except in the following cases:

Adriani, Alexandria (256), Agora Excavations, Athens (176, 187, 192); Alinari, Rome (27, 50, 54, 56, 102, 122, 123, 127, 128, 132, 133, 136, 160, 166, 171, 189, 190, 193, 205, 209, 219, 229, 230, 235, 241, 242, 244, 247, 253, 255, 260, 269, 271, 274, 284, 290, 291, 292, 298, 311, 312, 333, 363, 366, 367, 368); Anderson, Rome (322); Assessorato Turismo-Spettacolo, Palermo (212); Bertoni (28, 63, 142, 144, 173); Bittoli, Volterra (265, 266, 267); M. Bovis (380); British School, Athens (2); J. Cignovic, Rome (372); Deutsches Archaeologisches Institut, Athens (3, 7, 9, 16, 19, 29, 40, 41, 42, 61, 66, 109, 110, 186, 188); Deutsches Archaeologisches Institut, Rome (14, 17, 47, 48, 49, 143, 181, 262, 287, 302, 303, 304, 305, 306, 307, 308, 309, 316, 317, 337, 338, 339, 340, 341, 342, 343, 344, 346, 347, 348, 349, 351, 353, 354, 355, 356, 357, 358, 361, 362, 370, 373, 374, 377, 379); E. W. A. (15, 53, 62, 72, 86, 213, 214, 225, 285, 375, 382); Fotofast, Bologna (74); G. Franceschi, Châlons-sur-Marne (92); Alison Frantz, Athens (65); Gabinetto Fotografico Nazionale, Rome (55, 57, 58, 94, 95, 112, 113, 116, 117, 137, 138, 139, 140, 141, 161, 179, 191, 194, 204, 221, 228, 233, 243, 248, 275, 283, 296, 297, 310, 314, 315, 318, 319, 320, 321); Giraudon, Paris (35, 60, 120, 175, 177, 178, 249, 254, 257, 261, 278, 288); Giuliano, Osimo (277); Urs Graf, Basel (359); Hege, Karlsruhe (124, 125, 126, 156, 163); Hirmer, Munich (1, 4, 20, 21, 23, 24, 25, 44, 46, 69, 71, 73, 77, 79, 80, 81, 82, 84, 85, 88, 89, 90, 107, 118, 168, 381); Foto-Marburg, Marburg/Lahn (252); MAS, Barcelona (224); Mercurio, Milan (217); Palmarocchi, Chieti (195); M. Perotti, Milan (216); Pozzi Bellini (105, 206, 207, 272); Ezio Quiresi, Cremona (135); E. Richter, Rome (295); O. Savio, Rome (45, 101, 121, 182, 196, 220, 232, 236, 301, 323, 324, 325, 345); Scala, Florence (78, 98, 99, 259, 264, 268, 270, 273); Scuola Archeologica Italiana, Athens (31, 33, 103); Soprintendenza alle Antichità della Calabria, Reggio Calabria (134): Soprintendenza alle Antichità della Cirenaica (119); Soprintendenza alle Antichità dell'Etruria Meridionale, Rome (172, 210); Soprintendenza alle Antichità di Firenze, Florence (11, 100); Soprintendenza alle Antichità del Lazio, Rome (158); Soprintendenza alle Antichità di Napoli, Naples (115); Soprintendenza alle Antichità di Siracusa, Syracuse (32, 103); Soprintendenza Foro Romano e Palatino, Rome (282); Soprintendenza Scavi di Ostia, Rome (222, 281, 293); Tombazi (64); A. Villani, Bologna (147); The Warburg Institute, London (334, 335); G. Wehrheim, Munich (5); D. Widmer, Basel (198).

INDEX

NOTE: Page references are in roman type; figure numbers are in *italic type*, with colorplates specifically indicated.

429

Delphi (cont'd)
  charioteer, *118 (color)*, 131
  Cleobis and Biton, *44*
    by Lysippos, 219, 220
    monument dedicated by Polyzalus of
      Gela, *118 (color)*, 131
    monumental ex-voto by Onatas and
      Kalynthos, 136
    by Myron, 142
    by Phidias, 168
    quadriga of Cleosthenes, 137
    reliefs, 103
    Sphinx, *64*, 78–80
Demaratos, 114
Demeter
  on acrolith, 276, 277
  on relief, 180
  statues of
    from Cnidus, *201*, 223
    Demeter Malaina ("Black Demeter"),
      136
    by Eukleides, 276
    by Praxiteles, 204–5
    Roman copy of, 132
Demetrios, 275
Demetrios of Alexandria, 290
Demetrios of Alopeke, 220
Demetrius, King, 230
Demetrius of Phaleron, 226
Demetrius Poliorcetes, King, 226
  portrait of, 261
Democracy, personification of, 216
Democritus, 190
Demos
  painting of, 216
  statue of, 215
Demosthenes, statue by Polyeuktos of,
  227, 256–58
Dermis, statue of, 56
Descriptio Orbis, 310
Desenzan, villa at, 372
Despoina, on acrolith, 276
Dexamenos of Chios, gem engraved by, *165*
Dexileos, funerary stele of, 226
Diadoumenus, *145*, 164, 168
Dialogues (Lucian), 131
Diana
  antefix from Scasato temple of, 285
  painting of, 298
  sanctuary of, painting in, 319
  See also Artemis
Didyma, Temple of Apollo at, 84
Didymeion of Miletus, 252
Dike (Justice), on *Cypselus Chest*, 103
Dindia Macolinia, 246
Diocletian, 369
  architecture under, 372
  Edict of Prices by, 308
  Mausoleum of, 376
  statue of, 372
Diodorus Siculus, 43, 44
Diogenes Laertius, 137
Diognetus, 307
Dione, on pediment, *151*, 176
Dionysiac rites, 61
Dionysiades, 266
Dionysios (*anthropographos*), 300
Dionysios (second-century sculptor), 277
  statue of Gaius Ofellius Ferus by, 292
Dionysios of Argos, 137
Dionysios of Colophon, 190
Dionysus, 198, 253
  on frieze, 198
  in Hellenistic art, 250
  on metope, 71
  in Mycenaean culture, 10
  paintings of, 228, 230
  on pediments, *150*, 285
  on pottery, 91–92, 94, 99, 232
  on sarcophagi, 339, 356
  statues of
    by Alkamenes, 182
    Antinous as, 337
    by Bryaxis, 215
    by Eukleides, 276
    by Lysippos, 220
    on monument of Thrasyllus, 276
    by Myron, 142
    by Praxiteles, 205–6
    by Skopas, 208

at Tanagra, 131
  Theater of, 199, 256
Dioscuri, 250
  on coins, 293
  on metope, 69
  on pottery, 94
  sanctuary of, painting in, 148
  statue at Delphi of, 197
Dioscurides, *Gemma Augustea* by, 312
Dipoinos, 78
Dipylon, 14
  ivory statuette from, *9*
Dipylon head, *43*, 53–55
Dipylon Painter, 14–15, 24
  funerary amphora by, *4*
Dipylon tombs, ivory statuette from, *9*, 18
Dirce, sculpture of, 271
Discobolus (Discus Thrower), 142
  Roman copy of, *121*
Discus Thrower, *see Discobolus*
Dobrudja, Monument at Adam-Klissi in,
  312, 334
Dodecanese, proto-Geometric pottery of, 14
Doidalsas of Bithynia, Aphrodite by, *232*,
  233, 259
D'Olanda, Francesco, 317
Domitian, Emperor
  architecture under, 325, 334
  portrait of, *293*, *300*, 322, 324
Domitilla, catacomb of, 342
Domna, Julia, 357, 362
  on Arch of Septimius Severus, *348*, 360
  portrait of, *352*
Domus Aurea (Golden House), 317–18, 372
  artifical lake of, 325
Domus Flavia, 325
Dontas, 78
Dorotheos, 182
Dorykleidas, 78
Doryphorus, 128, *143*, *144 (color)*, 162–64
Douris, 122, 124, 261
Droop (Antidoros) cup, 93
Dromeus of Stynphalion, 137
Dresden Artemis, 204, 213
Dresden Zeus, 180
Dreros, statuettes from, 49
Duilius, Gaius, column commemorating, 289
Dura Europos, painting of, 347–48
Durostorum, tomb painting at Silistra in,
  380–81
Dying Gaul, statue from Pergamon of, 265

Egypt
  Imperial quarries in, 369
  influence of, 9–10
    on Daedalic art, 44
    on Rome, 301, 337–38
  Ionian influence on, 108
  sculpture of
    obelisk, 309
    statue of Hadrian, 337
  Roman influence on painting in, 348
  See also Alexandria
Eileithyia, statue by Eukleides of, 276
Eirene, statue of, *174*
Ekphantos, 26
Elatea, sculpture of Athena from, 278
Elche
  Iberian style vase from, *225 (color)*, 248
  so-called *Dama de*, *224*, 248
Electra
  on pottery, 236
  statue by Menelaos of, 301
Eleusis
  amphora by Polyphemus Painter from,
    19, 29
  sculpture of
    Isocrates, 215
    relief, 180
Eleutherna, sculpture of, 49
Elis, Aphrodite from, 178
Enceladus, on pediment, 64
Endoios, 86
Endymion, 250
  mosaics of, 374
  on sarcophagi, 364
Enneapylon, 11
Ennrus, 287
Eos, on pottery, 122, 244
Epaminondas, 230

Ephesus
  architecture of, 82
    agora, 254
    Artemision, 56, 59, 84, 199, *202*, 223,
      224, 252
    Temple of Hadrian, 348
    theater, 253
  gold work of, 36
  influence on Crete of, 39
  sculpture of
    Amazon by Phidias, 178
    Amazon by Polykleitos, 164
    Artemis, 86
    fifth-century A.D., 389
    Ionic head, *67*, 84
    monument to Lucius Verus, *331*, 346
Epicharinus, statue of, 128
Epicurus, 230
Epidaurus, architecture of
  Temple of Artemis, 198
  Temple of Asclepius, 198, 210–13,
    214–15
  theater, 199
  tholos, 198
Epiktetos, 99
  kylixes by, *85*, 100
Epione, akroterion of, *188*, 213
Epistemon, 86
Erechtheion, 11, 14, 185–86
Erechtheion Caryatids, 182
  copies of
    in Forum of Augustus, 310
    at Hadrian's Villa, *319*
Erechtheus, 11
Eretria, Athena Polias from, 86
Eretria Painter, 190, 194
Erginos, 194
Ergoteles, 88
Ergotimos, François vase by, *78 (color)*,
  90–92
Erichthonius, on relief, 182
Erinys, on metope, 68
Eris, painting of, 148
Eros, 198, 250, 251
  Centuripae terracottas of, 282
  mosaics of, 374
  paintings of, 193
  on pottery, 146, 234
  on reliefs, 278
  statues of
    by Lysippos, *194*, 219
    by Praxiteles, 204, 219
    by Skopas, 210
Erostratus, 199
Erymanthian boar, on metope, *57*, 70
Eryphile, on pottery, 146
Esquiline, 310
  base from, *161*
  Basilica of Junius Bassus on, 382, *382
    (color)*
  frieze on, 301, 306
  paintings from *Odyssey* in house on, 300
  paintings from tomb on, *270 (color)*,
    290–92
  Villa Palombara on, bust of Commodus
    from, *345*
Etruria
  architecture of, 74–78
  described, in seventh century, 39
  gold work of, 39–42, 96
  Greece and, 20
  monument to Lucumonic cities of, 316–17
  pottery of, 89, 110–11
    alabaster urns, *265–67*, 285
    bucchero ware, 42, 113–14
    "canopic" vases, *28 (color)*, 42
    fourth-century B.C., 241–43
    Geometric, 20, 21
    influence of Classical style on, 196
    Ionian influence on, 112–13
    Italiot, 236
    Italo-Corinthian, 42
  sarcophagi of, 243–44, 286
  sculpture of, 56
    Daedalic, 56
    Hellenistic period, *263*, *264 (color)*, 282–
      85
    influence of Classical style on, 196
    Severe style, *142 (color)*, 160
  tomb painting of, 239

Helen (cont'd)
  on pottery, 15, 25, 124
  on relief, 278
Helena (mother of Constantine)
  Baths of, 376
  statues of, 182, 375
Helena (painter), 275
Helicon, Mount, statues of Muses on, 200
Heliogabalus, 307
  portraits of, 362
Helius, 280
  on metope, 262
  on shield of Athena Parthenos, 177
  statues of
    Colossus of Rhodes, 262
    Constantine as, 378
    by Lysippos, 220
Hellas, personification of, 216
Hellenistic Ruler, statue of, 292
Hemeresios, 228
Hemeroscopeion, Phocaeans in, 118
Hephaestus, 177
  on altar, 205
  on pottery, 90
  statue by Alkamenes of, 182, 278
Hephaesteion
  frieze of, 74, 182
  metopes of, 182
  paintings in, 148
  statues of Athena and Hephaestus in, 182, 278
Hera, 47, 275
  on candelabrum, 260
  on metope, 141, 156
  in Mycenaean culture, 10
  on pediment, 62
  sanctuary at Samos of, 82
  statues of, 182
    at Argos, 164
    in Paestum, 111
    at Samos, 35, 48, 82
Heracles, 15, 214, 280
  on Cypselus Chest, 103
  on frieze, 72
  on metopes, 54, 55, 57, 68, 70, 112, 139, 144, 145-46, 182
  paintings of, 193, 228, 230, 267, 268
  on pediments, 62, 208
  on pottery, 20, 21, 30 34, 37, 94, 98, 101, 102, 105, 111, 112, 124, 190, 232, 235, 236
  on relief, 180
  statues of
    by Glykon, 220, 365
    in Hellenistic age, 272
    by Lysippos, 195, 219-20, 288
    by Myron, 142
    by Polykleitos, 164
    by Skopas, 208
    at Veii, 76
  See also Hercules
Heracles Epitrapezius, 220
Heraion
  at Olympia, 56, 57, 103, 205
  of Samos, 56, 59, 82, 252
  of Sele
    temple at, 95, 111, 114
    Treasury of, 55, 57, 66, 68, 70, 114
Herakleitos, 268
Hercules
  on Arch of Galerius, 372
  mosaics of, 374
  sanctuary in Ostia of, relief in, 281
  statues of
    Commodus as, 356
    Roman, 302
    by Vulca, 78
  Temple in Rome of, 290
Herculaneum
  painting from, 247, 268
  sculpture of, 313
    bronze herm of Doryphorus, 162
    bronze herm of Ephesus Amazon, 178
Hermaphroditus, in Hellenistic art, 250
Hermes, 250, 280
  on altar, 179, 205
  on candelabrum, 275
  on pottery, 108, 194
  on reliefs, 152, 180
  statues of, 223

Hermes Propylaios, 182, 248, 278
  at Lysimachia, 164
  by Praxiteles, 200, 205-6
  at Tanagra, 131
  at Veii, 62 (color), 76
Hermaios Painter, 100
Hermione, 182
Hermogenes, 72, 93, 252
Hero, 250
Herodas, 251, 256
Herodotus, 84
Heroön of Gjölbaschi, burial enclosure of, 188
Hesiod, statue of, 137
Hesion, mosaics of, 374
Hesion Painter, 243
Hesperides, garden of the, on pottery, 232
Hestia
  on altar, 179, 205
  on pediment, 151
  statues of
    by Kephisodotos the Elder, 256
    by Skopas, 208
Hierapydna, statue of Hadrian at, 337
Hieron (painter), 298
Hieron (potter), 124, 131
Hieron of Syracuse, paintings of Roman campaigns against, 289
Hierothesion, in Commagene, 280
Himera, temple in, 155
Himerius, 193
Himeros, 250
  statue of, 210
Hippodamia, 250
Hippodamos of Miletus, 161, 199
Hippodrome in Constantinople, 385
  Sphendone of, 378
Hippolytus, portrait of, 214
Hipponattes, portrait of, 78
Hipponium, pediments in, 61
Hirschfeld series of kraters, 15
Hirtius, Aulus, tomb of, 324
Hischylos, 100
  kylix by, 85
Historia Augusta, 365
Hoby, cups from, 313
Homer, 179, 387
  Apotheosis of, on relief, 264
  portrait of, 255, 274
  statue of, 137
Homeric cup of Nestor, 268
Honor, personification of, 331
Honorius, 386
  arch dedicated to, 382
  on Column of Arcadius, 387
Horace, Ars Poetica by, 308
Horai, on panel by Damophon, 277
Horatius Cocles, statue of, 264
Horti Liciniani, nymphaeum of, 376
Horti Luculliani, 298
Horti Maiani, portrait of Nero in, 319
Horti Sallustiani, 298
House of Amor and Psyche, 373
House of Augustus, painting in, 231
House of Livia, mural in, 274, 301
House of the Faun
  mosaic from, 275
  painting from, 207 (color), 229-30
House of the Griffins, mural in, 300
House of the Nymphaeum, paintings in, 379-80
House of the Tragic Poet, painting in, 205, 228
House of the Vettii, painting in, 273 (color)
Hunt Painter, kylix by, 87, 104
Hyacinth, painting of, 228
Hydra of Lerna, on pediment, 62
Hygieia, 198
  on ivory diptychs, 388
  paintings of, 228
  statues of
    by Bryaxis, 215
    by Skopas, 208
Hylas
  on marble wall panel, 382
  painting of, 317
Hymn to Apollo Pythius, 47
Hypnos (Sleep)
  on Cypselus Chest, 103
  on pottery, 194

Iaia of Cizicos, 300
Ialysos, painting of, 228, 230
Ialysus, hydria by Hunt Painter from, 104
Iberia
  architecture under Trajan of, 334
  Greek influence in, 117-18
  Hellenistic period in, 280-82
  painting under Hadrian in, 342
  pottery of, 248
    vase, 225 (color)
  sculpture of
    Dama de Elche, 224, 248
    Gran Dama, 223, 248
  Severe style in, 160
  See also specific cities
Icarus Painter, 146
Iktinos, 185, 198, 327
  Temple of Apollo at Bassae by, 74, 184
Iliad
  Catalogue of Ships in, 10
  paintings of scenes from, 300, 319
Iliupersis
  on metopes, 69, 70
  on Pompeian helmets, 319
  on pottery, 244
Iliupersis Painter, 235
Imperial Palace in Constantinople, 387
  mosaics of, 389
Io, painting of, 228
Iole, on pottery, 34
Iolaus, on pediment, 62
Ionia
  fourth-century B. C. painting of, 231
  influence on Etruria of, 112-13
  Severe style sculpture of, 153
  sixth-century B. C. pottery of, 90, 105-6
Iphigenia
  painting of, 205, 228
  on pottery, 285
  statue from Pergamon of, 265
Ireland, Christian art of, 389-90
Iris
  akroterion of, 213
  on metopes, 68, 176
Ischia, krater from, 14, 22
Isignos, 264
Isis, 337
  images of, 275
  portraits of priests of, 303
Isis Tomb in Vulci, statuette from, 56
Isocrates, statue of, 215
Issus, painting of battle of, see Alexander the Great
Istacidi, mausoleum at Pompeii of, 315
Italy
  pottery of
    Fikellura ware, 105
    Geometric, 19-24
    Roman conquest of, 287
  sculpture of, 350
  See also Etruria; Magna Graecia; Rome
Itys, statue of, 182
Ixion Painter, 236

Jaén, bronze satyr from, 282
Jason, on pottery, 122
Jena Painter, 232
Jerusalem
  conquest of, on Arch of Titus, 298, 323-24
  mosaics in, 374
Jesus Christ, see Christ
Jocasta, statue by Silanion of, 222
Jonah, on sarcophagi, 367
Joy (Apolausis), personification of, 374
Juba II, 315
Jugurtha, on coin, 305
Julian the Apostate, 388
Julii family
  coat of arms of, 293
  Mausoleum at Saint-Rémy-en-Provence of, 287, 314-15
Julius II, Pope
  Apollo Belvedere placed in Vatican by, 190
Junius, Publius, statue of, 246
Junius Bassus, sarcophagus of, 381, 382
Jupiter
  on Arch of Galerius, 372
  column in Mainz dedicated to, 320

435

438

Troilus
   painting of, *98 (color)*, 114
   on pediment, 62
   on pottery, 89, 90, 120
Trojan horse, on pottery, *16*
Trojan War, on pottery, 98
Troy, metope from Temple of Athena at, 262
Tuchulcha, 243
   painting of, 285
Turms, statue of, *62 (color)*
Turpilius, 307
Tyche, 275
   in Hellenistic culture, 250
   statues of
      in Constantinople, 378
      by Eutychides, *234*, 261
Typhon, on pottery, 33
Tyrannicides (Harmodius and Aristogiton), statues of, 88, *113*, 128–29, 156

Ulysses
   mosaic of, 374
   See also Odysseus
Umbria, 114
Urartu, bronze appliqués from, 39

Vaison, statue of Hadrian at, 337
Vale of Tempe, 339
Valencia, fourth-century B. C. pottery of, 248
Valens, arch dedicated to, 383
Valentinian II, statue from Aphrodisia of, 386
Valentinianus, 307
Valentianius, Gratianus, arches dedicated to, 382
Valerii, tomb of, *322*, 341
Vanth, painting of, 243
Varro, 142, 162, 301
Vasari, 231
Vatican G 57 vases, *83*
Veii
   painting of Campana Tomb at, 42
   sculpture of, 116
      head of boy, *172*, 196
      terracotta Hermes, *62 (color)*, 76
   Roman capture of, 241, 246
   Severe style in, 160
   temples in, 76
Velabrum, Arch of Janus Quadrifrons in, 369
Velcha family, painting of lady of, 243
Venus
   painting of, 380
   relief of, 315
   statues of
      Empress Sabina as Venus Genetrix, 337
      Venus de Milo, *229*, 258–59
      Venus Genetrix by Arkesilaos, 302
   Temples of
      at Baalbek, 348
      Temple of Venus Genetrix in Rome, Caesar's gem collection in, 298
      Temple of Venus and Rome, 340, 376, 380
   theater dedicated to Venus Victrix, 296
   See also Aphrodite
Venus de Milo, *229*, 258–59
Venus Genetrix
   statues of
      by Arkesilaos, 302
      Empress Sabina as, 337
   Temple in Rome of, Caesar's gem collection in, 298
Venus Victrix, theater dedicated to, 296
Verdolay, fourth-century B. C. pottery of, 248
Verona, siege of, on Arch of Constantine, 378

Verres, Caius, 298
Versailles Artemis, 215
Vertumnus, Antinous as statue of, 337
Verus, Lucius
   monument at Ephesus to, *331*, *332*, 346
   portrait of, 346
Vespasian, 298
   portraits of, *299*, *300*, 321
Vesta, Temple in Rome of, on coin, 305
Vetralla, Geometric pottery of, 21
Vetulonia
   gold work of, 42
   personification of, 317
Via Aemilia, viaducts of, on coin, 305
Via Appia, Circus on, 376
Via dei Cerchi, painting from house on, 365
Via della Lungara, cinerary urn from tomb of the Platorinii on, *295*
Via Labicana, statue of Augustus from, 313
Via Latina
   tomb of the Pancratii on, 341
   tomb of the Valerii on, *322*, 341
Via Praenestina
   relief on slabs from, 306
   Tor' de' Schiavi on, 376
Via Sacra
   arches on, 289
      of Titus, *298*, 323–24
   pearl dealers on, 298
Via Trajana, 331
Vibenna, painting of, 243
Vico, Enea, view of Rome by, *336*
Vicomagistri, procession of on frieze, *289*, 317
Victor, Aurelius, 307
Victory
   on coins, 293
   on Column of Marcus Aurelius, 351, 353
   on Column of Trajan, 327, 331
   in Constantinople, 378
   on cup from Boscoreale, 312
   paintings of, 347, 380
   relief of, 324
   on sarcophagi, 339
   at Temple of Sulis-Minerva, 350
   See also Nike
Vicus Sandalarius, 313
Vienne, Romanization of, 314
Vignanello, 96
Villa Albani, statue of Kore in, 182
Villa Borghese, mosaic in, 374
Villa Giulia, Ficoroni cist in, *221*, 244–46
Villa Giulia Painter, 146
Villa of Hadrian, *see* Hadrian's Villa
Villa of Livia
   painting from, *285 (color)*, 313
   statue of Augustus from, *286*, 313
Villa of the Mysteries, frieze of, *272 (color)*
Villa Palombara, bust of Commodus from, *345*
Villa Publica, on coin, 305
Villard series of kraters, 15
Vin lex, Novius, 220
Vindobona, funerary steles in, 350
Virgin Mary, painting of, *366*, 367
Virtus, personification of, 216
Vitelliani, entry into Rome of, on Column of Trajan, 331
Vitruvius, 24, 72
   on architecture, 76, 252, 295
   on mural decoration, 300, 301
Vix, krater from tomb at, *92*, 108–10
Volcacius, portrait of, *330*
Volterra, pottery of
   alabaster urns, *265–67*, 285
   fourth-century B. C., 241–42
   stele of Aule Tite at, 115
Vroulia *kylix*, 106

Vulca, 78
Vulci
   painting of François Tomb at, 243
   personification of, 317
   pottery of
      amphora by Berlin Painter, *108*
      amphora by Kleophrades Painter, *107 (color)*
      Geometric, 21
      "Pontic," 112
      red-figure, 241
      seventh-century B. C., *25*
   sarcophagi from, *218*, 243–44
   sculpture of
      cast figurines, 114
      from Isis Tomb, 56
      sepulchral *cippi*, 112
      stone centaur, *45*
Vulneratus deficiens, 183

West Slope ware, 234, 238
Westmacott Athlete, 164
Winged Nike of Samothrace, *235*, 263
Workshop of Athens 810, 18
Workshop of Athens 894, 17

Xanthos
   funerary monument at, 186–87, 188
   sculpture of *peplophoroi* of, 153
Xenocles of Mainalos, statue of, 162
Xenoclos, 93
Xenokrates, 261
Xenophantos, 234
Xerxes, 88, 128

Yugoslavia, necropolis of Trebenischte in, 110

Zenodorus, statue of Nero by, 319
Zenon, Flavius, 346
Zephyr Painter, 147
Zethus
   relief of, 341
   sculpture of, 271
Zeus
   Altar to Athena Nikephoroi and, *245*, *246*, 264, 266–70
   on candelabrum, *260*
   in Mycenaean culture, 10
   mythical grotto of, 38
   paintings of, 193, 230
   on table by Damophon, 277
   on pediments, 61, 62, 176
   on pottery, 236
   statue of, 144
      by Bryaxis 215, 216
      from Cape Artemision, *114*, 129, 137, 156
      at Delphi, 197
      Dresden Zeus, 180
      from Falerii, 196
      by Leochares, 215
      by Lysippos, 220
      at Olympia, 170, 179–80, 276, 278
      in Olympieion at Athens, 339
      in Paestum, *94*, 111
      Zeus Hypatos in Sparta, 108
      Zeus Ithomatas, 137
      Zeus Meilidios at Argos, 164
      Zeus Oromazdes, 280
   Temple of, at Olympia, 69–70, *123–28*, 144–46, 179, 182, 186
Zeus Olympios, Temple in Athens of, 252, 339
Zeus Theos, Temple in Dura Europos of, painting in, 347–48
Zeuxis, 193, 198
   copies of, 319